W9-BVD-694

Economic Demography
Volume I

The International Library of Critical Writings in Economics

Series Editor: Mark Blaug

Professor Emeritus, University of London
Professor Emeritus, University of Buckingham
Visiting Professor, University of Exeter

This series is an essential reference source for students, researchers and lecturers in economics. It presents by theme an authoritative selection of the most important articles across the entire spectrum of economics. Each volume has been prepared by a leading specialist who has written an authoritative introduction to the literature included.

A full list of published and future titles in this series is printed at the end of this volume.

Wherever possible, the articles in these volumes have been reproduced as originally published using facsimile reproduction, inclusive of footnotes and pagination to facilitate ease of reference.

For a list of all Edward Elgar published titles visit our site on the World Wide Web at
http://www.e-elgar.co.uk

Economic Demography Volume I

Edited by

T. Paul Schultz

Malcolm K. Brachman Professor of Economics
Yale University, USA

THE INTERNATIONAL LIBRARY OF CRITICAL WRITINGS IN ECONOMICS

An Elgar Reference Collection
Cheltenham, UK • Northampton, MA, USA

Published by
Edward Elgar Publishing Limited
8 Lansdown Place
Cheltenham
Glos GL50 2HU
UK

Edward Elgar Publishing, Inc.
6 Market Street
Northampton
Massachusetts 01060
USA

A catalogue record for this book is available from the British Library.

Library of Congress Cataloguing in Publication Data

Economic demography / edited by T. Paul Schultz.
  (The international library of critical writings in economics : 86) (Elgar reference collection)
    Includes bibliographical references.
    1. Demography — Economic aspects. I. Schultz, T. Paul. II. Series. III. Series: Elgar reference collection.
HB849.41.E25 1998
304.6—dc21

97–38476
CIP

3 2280 00609 0781

Printed and bound in Great Britain by Bookcraft (Bath) Limited.

ISBN 1 85898 517 X (2 volume set)

Contents

Acknowledgements

The editor and publishers wish to thank the authors and the following publishers who have kindly given permission for the use of copyright material.

American Economic Association for article: H. Elizabeth Peters (1986), 'Marriage and Divorce: Informational Constraints and Private Contracting', *American Economic Review*, **76** (3), June, 437–54.

Blackwell Publishers Ltd for article: Gary S. Becker (1965), 'A Theory of the Allocation of Time', *Economic Journal*, **LXXV**, September, 493–517.

Econometric Society for article: Zvi Griliches (1977), 'Estimating the Returns to Schooling: Some Econometric Problems', *Econometrica*, **45** (1), January, 1–22.

International Economic Review for article: Marjorie B. McElroy and Mary Jean Horney (1981), 'Nash-Bargained Household Decisions: Toward a Generalization of the Theory of Demand', *International Economic Review*, **22** (2), June, 333–49.

Johns Hopkins University Press for excerpts: Inderjit Singh, Lyn Squire and John Strauss (1986), 'The Basic Model: Theory, Empirical Results, and Policy Conclusions', in Inderjit Singh, Lyn Squire and John Strauss (eds), *Agricultural Household Models: Extensions, Applications, and Policy*, Chapter 1, 17–47; Inderjit Singh, Lyn Squire and John Strauss (1986), 'Methodological Issues', in Inderjit Singh, Lyn Squire and John Strauss (eds), *Agricultural Household Models: Extensions, Applications, and Policy*, Chapter 2, 48–70; John Strauss (1986), 'Appendix: The Theory and Comparative Statics of Agricultural Household Models: A General Approach', in Inderjit Singh, Lyn Squire and John Strauss (eds), *Agricultural Household Models: Extensions, Applications, and Policy*, 71–91.

MIT Press Journals for article: Joshua D. Angrist and Alan B. Krueger (1991), 'Does Compulsory School Attendance Affect Schooling and Earnings?', *Quarterly Journal of Economics*, **CVI** (4), November, 979–1014.

National Bureau of Economic Research, Inc. for excerpt: Jacob Mincer (1974), 'Individual Acquisition of Earning Power', in *Schooling, Experience, and Earnings*, Chapter 1, 7–23 and references.

The Nobel Foundation and American Economic Association for article: Robert W. Fogel (1994), 'Economic Growth, Population Theory, and Physiology: The Bearing of Long-Term Processes on the Making of Economic Policy', *American Economic Review*, **84** (3), June, 369–95.

University of Chicago Press for articles and excerpt: Finis Welch (1970), 'Education in Production', *Journal of Political Economy*, **78** (1), January/February, 35–59; Reuben Gronau (1977), Leisure, Home Production, and Work – The Theory of the Allocation of Time Revisited', *Journal of Political Economy*, **85** (6), December, 1099–1123; Mark R. Rosenzweig and T. Paul Schultz (1983), 'Estimating a Household Production Function: Heterogeneity, the Demand for Health Inputs, and Their Effects on Birth Weight', *Journal of Political Economy*, **91** (5), October, 723–46; John Strauss (1986), 'Does Better Nutrition Raise Farm Productivity?', *Journal of Political Economy*, **94** (2), April, 297–320; David Lam and Robert F. Schoeni (1993), 'Effects of Family Background on Earnings and Returns to Schooling: Evidence from Brazil', *Journal of Political Economy*, **101** (4), August, 710–40; Martin Browning, François Bourguignon, Pierre-André Chiappori and Valérie Lechene (1994), 'Income and Outcomes: A Structural Model of Intrahousehold Allocation', *Journal of Political Economy*, **102** (6), December, 1067–96; Samuel H. Preston (1980), 'Causes and Consequences of Mortality Declines in Less Developed Countries during the Twentieth Century', with Comments by J.D. Durand, Victor R. Fuchs and Richard W. Parks, in Richard A. Easterlin (ed.), *Population and Economic Change in Developing Countries*, Chapter 5, 289–360.

University of Wisconsin Press for articles: T. Paul Schultz (1990), 'Testing the Neoclassical Model of Family Labor Supply and Fertility', *Journal of Human Resources*, **XXV** (4), Fall, 599–634; Duncan Thomas (1994), 'Like Father, Like Son; Like Mother, Like Daughter: Parental Resources and Child Height', *Journal of Human Resources*, **XXIX** (4), Fall, 950–88.

Every effort has been made to trace all the copyright holders but if any have been inadvertently overlooked the publishers will be pleased to make the necessary arrangement at the first opportunity.

In addition, the publishers wish to thank the Library of the London School of Economics and Political Science, the Marshall Library of Economics, Cambridge University and B & N Microfilm, London, for their assistance in obtaining these articles.

Introduction

T. Paul Schultz

These readings trace some of the ideas that have helped to adapt economic theory and methods to analyse the determinants and consequences of demographic behaviour, and relate these behaviours to investments in human capital that account for much of modern economic growth. Traditionally, demography encompassed basic population processes such as fertility, mortality and migration, of which only migration was thought to be determined by economic considerations. In order to describe the decision-making unit most relevant to these demographic outcomes, economists needed a theory of what constitutes a household or family and why these groups occur and dissolve over the lifetime of an individual. Less demographic and more economic is the study of production and consumption activities in which individuals and households engage, but previous economic studies of consumption had to be rethought because they took as given the demographic composition of the household. The intertemporal problems associated with lifetime allocations of production and consumption open up broad issues of saving, risk-coping strategies and intergenerational transfer, each of which provides a realm for theorizing and empirical analysis at both the micro and macro level.

Much of modern economic demography is none the less an extension of labour, consumption and production microeconomics applied to individuals and the elusive combination called families which are particularly fragile today. But there is a difference in orientation between economic demography and labour or consumption economics that is reflected in what factors are taken as given (exogenous) and what factors are partially determined (endogenously) within the extended economic framework of family life cycle-constrained choices. This distinction between exogenous and endogenous variables becomes important in microeconometric analysis which has been a key factor in guiding the evolution of the field as it has in labour economics. The increased range of statistical methods designed for micro data, the reduction in cost of computing and the multiplication of random sample surveys of households (as well as Population Censuses) have together created vast new opportunities for integrated studies of economic and demographic behaviour that were unimaginable before the 1970s. Intercountry comparisons of microestimations of parallel models have only begun to examine cross-cultural uniformities in behavioural responses which social scientists should expect to find if their models are reasonably specified. These readings are about equally drawn from studies of high-income industrially advanced countries and low-income developing countries. Volume II, Part V is devoted to historical studies.

The first section of readings (Volume I, Part I) draws from the voluminous empirical literature estimating wage functions. The wage function is a key building block for economic demography, because it provides the explanation for how human capital formation affects human productivity and thus contributes to modern economic growth. At the same time, the process that endogenously determined wages, generates the key shadow prices of time for individuals that determine many economic–demographic outcomes or households' demands, including labour supply or, more broadly, time allocation, marriage and fertility, migration, and intergenerational investments and transfers. I start with the initial human capital framework for the earnings function proposed by Mincer (1974), and include Welch's (1970) consideration of why education affects the productivity of workers and Griliches' (1977) summary of the first two decades of statistical research on estimating the returns to schooling. The final, more recent, readings illustrate first the use of instrumental variable estimation methods (exploiting demography and regional variation in regulations) for dealing with the problems of family endogeneity of schooling in the wage function in the US (Angrist and Krueger, 1991), and then how controls for parent education can provide minimum values for returns to schooling from wage function estimates in a highly stratified low-income country, Brazil (Lam and Schoeni, 1993).

Part II of the first volume provides different perspectives on the second most notable source of human capital accumulation in modern times: health and longevity. Preston (1980) surveys the form of the mortality decline and provides ideas for analysing these changes. Rosenzweig and Schultz (1983) indicate the problems of estimating health production technology in the family when humans are heterogeneous and they know more about their health than do statistical researchers. Strauss (1986) formulates the problem of estimating the productive pay-off from improved nutrition at the family level in a low-income country, whereas Fogel (1994) raises similar questions at the historical level using micro and aggregate data.

Part III traces the evolution of the household production model of Becker (1965) that first viewed the household as a producer of basic commodities that were the ultimate source of consumers' utility in the unified household. Gronau (1977) simplifies Becker's model and highlights the separation of production decisions from consumption decisions, which then subsequently become the basis for the agricultural household models (Singh et al., 1986) which are widely used to analyse economic and demographic behaviour in low-income countries.

But the idea that the household is a unified decision-making entity is not entirely satisfactory, for clearly individuals who combine into households retain their own interests and priorities, and sometimes even their own physical resources, although they may temporarily team up to benefit from specialization and reproduction. The cooperative Nash-bargained model of McElroy and Horney (1981) (Part IV) provides an alternative approach to Becker's for the study of household demand behaviour, which has gradually changed how economists analyse marriage and intrahousehold resource allocations (Peters, 1986; Schultz, 1990; Thomas, 1994). Non-cooperative allocation rules can nonetheless be Pareto optimal, and allow for an even wider range of outcomes and still be empirically distinguishable from the unified household model of Becker (Browning et al., 1994).

Part I of Volume II introduces models that treat fertility and female labour supply as joint decisions (Rosenzweig and Wolpin, 1980) and fertility with heterogeneous fecundity (Rosenzweig and Schultz, 1985). The chapter from Goldin's (1990) book on American women describes in rich detail the evolving commitments to the labour force of a sequence of female birth cohorts. In Part II models analyse additional related family outcomes: time allocation, schooling investments and fertility across Indian districts (Rosenzweig and Evenson, 1977), and then the fertility and schooling of children, using the innovation of twins to test for substitution of quality and quantity (Rosenzweig and Wolpin, 1980). The paper by

Becker and Tomes (1976) also explores the quality–quantity trade-off for parents, whereas the later study of US twins by Behrman et al. (1994) considers an even richer set of alternatives, including the matching of marriage partners.

Part III explores gender differences in productivity, in search of a better understanding of their determinants and consequences. The study of rural India by Rosenzweig and Schultz (1982) documents the large excess of female to male child mortality in that diverse country, and accounts for part of this pattern in terms of the relative productivity of female and male agricultural workers. Schultz (1993) surveys the world patterns in gender differences in education and health and their convergence in this century, and asks whether differences in schooling by sex can be understood in terms of lower wage returns to female than male schooling. The excerpts from Fuchs' (1988) book provide another perspective on the persistence of gender inequalities in productivity in the United States.

Part IV illustrates how changes in the relative size of a cohort influence its relative wages, as illustrated by the baby boom cohort that reached the US labour market in the 1970s (Welch, 1979). The subsequent increase in wage differentials by education and experience during the 1980s is less readily explained by cohort size (labour supply) effects (Murphy and Welch, 1992). Griliches' (1969) exploration of the complementarity of physical capital and skilled labour is included to indicate one direction in which labour economists are searching for an explanation to the current widening of wage differentials between skilled and unskilled labour. Eventually this increase in earnings inequality may be explained by the demand factors in conjunction with the demographic supplies.

Economic–demographic interactions before the 20th century are the focus of Part V. Boserup (1987) proposes the idea that population growth induces agricultural technological change which may facilitate economic development. Lee (1980) summarizes the evidence of the pre-industrial Malthusian equilibrium between population and productive possibilities in Europe over the long term, whereas the study of Sweden from 1750 to 1860 (Eckstein et al., 1985) analyses, using vector auto regression methods, the short-run fluctuations in the weather, crops, death rates, birth rates and wages. The last paper in this section considers the transition from high to low infant death and birth rates in Sweden from 1860 to 1910 across provinces (Schultz, 1985).

The effects of population growth on economic development has been a major policy issue since the 1950s, when the magnitude of the acceleration in population growth in the low-income countries was first appreciated. Part VI includes an excerpt from a recent National Academy of Sciences report (1986) and a survey by Kelley (1988) which offer alternative points of view on this neo-Malthusian problem. An intercountry study of the determinants of birth rates, death rates and population growth rates offers an empirical assessment of some of the implications of the models of fertility and mortality introduced earlier (Schultz, 1994).

The last section, Part VII, starts with Modigliani's (1986) restatement of his life cycle savings hypothesis that includes evidence from recent studies. Auerbach et al. (1992) introduce their ideas of 'generational accounting' which have important implications for fiscal policies when the age composition of a population is changing and governments assume responsibility for old age pensions. Finally, a paper by Rosenzweig and Stark (1989) offers an interpretation of marriage practices in India as a means by which families can cope with the special covariance of risks due to weather in semi-arid agriculture. Each of these papers is related to a substantial literature that extends and explores different aspects of these connections between generations and changing age compositions of populations. A growing awareness today of the dislocating consequences of the rapid ageing of the world's population is beginning to displace the attention accorded the threat of rapid population growth in the last 50 years. With further declines in fertility possible in many populations, and continuing growth in longevity likely in most parts of the world, the social and economic problems of ageing are likely to become the central theme in economic demography in the next century.

Part I
Estimation of Wage Functions and Returns to Human Capital

1

Individual Acquisition of Earning Power

Investments in people are time consuming. Each additional period of schooling or job training postpones the time of the individual's receipt of earnings and reduces the span of his working life, if he retires at a fixed age. The deferral of earnings and the possible reduction of earning life are costly. These time costs plus direct money outlays make up the total cost of investment. Because of these costs investment is not undertaken unless it raises the level of the deferred income stream. Hence, at the time it is undertaken, the present value of real earnings streams with and without investment are equal only at a positive discount rate. This rate is the internal rate of return on the investment.

For simplicity the rate of return is often treated as a parameter for the individual. This amounts to assuming that a change in an individual's investment does not change his marginal (hence average) rate of return. Another empirically convenient assumption is that all investment costs are time costs. This assumption is more realistic in such forms of human capital investments as on-the-job training, but less so in others, such as schooling, migration, or investments in health. In calculating schooling costs, an equivalent assumption is that students' direct private costs are exactly offset by their part-

8   THEORETICAL ANALYSIS

time earnings during the year.[1] Like the preceding one, this assumption is not essential. Detailed information on direct costs can be incorporated into the model to yield a more precise empirical analysis. We forego precision, in order to gain in the simplicity of exposition and analysis.

The first step is to analyze the effects of investments in schooling. This is done by assuming that no further human capital investments are undertaken after completion of schooling and also, at this stage, that the flow of individual earnings is constant throughout the working life. For this the cessation of net investment is a necessary, but not sufficient, condition. Also excluded are economywide changes affecting individual productivity and earnings during the life cycle.

Since changes in earnings are produced by *net* investments in human capital stock, the net concept is used in most of the analysis. In this section, zero depreciation is, in effect, assumed during the school years and zero net investment during the working life. These assumptions are amended in later sections and in empirical interpretations.

In specifying the lengths of earning lives it is first assumed that each additional year of schooling reduces earning life by exactly one year. An alternative, and mathematically simpler, formulation is one in which the span of earning life remains the same in all cases, with more educated people retiring at correspondingly later ages. Empirically, this assumption is more nearly the correct one.[2]

---

1. This assumption was defended and used by Hanoch (1967, pp. 317–320).

2. More educated men retire later. The length of working life is roughly constant. Only after high school does an additional year of schooling reduce earning life somewhat (by less than half a year).

The following table contains estimates of the average "retirement" age and length of working life of men classified by level of schooling. It is based on a March 1970 BLS labor force survey (1970b, Table E, p. A-11). Very similar estimates are produced from data in years before 1970.

Years of Schooling	Estimated Average Retirement Age	Estimated Length of Working Life
8	65	47
9–11	66	47
12	67	47
13–15	67	45
16	68	45
17 or more	70	45

(note continued)

When earning life is long, the alternative formulations cannot make much of a difference. What matters is the deferral of earnings: The cost of currently postponing earnings by one year is much more significant than the present cost of reducing earnings by one year, four or five decades hence. An infinite earning life can, of course, be viewed as a special case of the equal-span assumption. The advantage of the latter formulation is both its greater tractability and its flexibility in empirical interpretation.

1.1 THE SCHOOLING MODEL

In calculating the effects of schooling on earnings, it is first assumed that postponement of earnings due to lengthier schooling is tantamount to a reduction of the earning span.

Let

n = length of working life plus length of schooling
    = length of working life for persons without schooling
Y_s = annual earnings of an individual with s years of schooling
V_s = present value of an individual's lifetime earnings at start of schooling
r = discount rate
t = 0, 1, 2, . . . , n time, in years
d = difference in the amount of schooling, in years
e = base of natural logarithms

Then

$$V_s = Y_s \sum_{t=s+1}^{n} \left(\frac{1}{1+r}\right)^t,$$

(*Note 2 concluded*)

Estimates of retirement age are obtained by adding to age 45 the product of participation rates and years beyond the age of 45. The length of working life is the sum of products of participation rates and age intervals.

     Estimates of lengths of working life in eight broad occupational groups, based on 1930–50 Census data, suggested larger differences in the earning spans among occupations. Note, however, that because of occupational mobility, length of stay in an occupational class, even when that is broadly defined, is not coextensive with length of stay in the labor force. Compare Mincer (1958, p. 284, n. 12).

     The finding that the length of earning life of more educated men is the same as that of the less educated is not inconsistent with the observed positive relation between schooling and labor force participation at the middle and older ages (Bowen and Finnegan, 1969): A negative relation holds when the more educated are still at school.

10   THEORETICAL ANALYSIS

when the discounting process is discrete. And, more conveniently, when the process is continuous:

$$V_s = Y_s \int_s^n e^{-rt}dt = \frac{Y_s(e^{-rs} - e^{-rn})}{r}.$$

Similarly, the present value of lifetime earnings of an individual who engages in $s - d$ years of schooling is:

$$V_{s-d} = \frac{Y_{s-d}}{r}(e^{-r(s-d)} - e^{-rn}).$$

The ratio, $k_{s,s-d}$, of annual earnings after s years to earnings after $s - d$ years of schooling is found by letting $V_s = V_{s-d}$:

$$k_{s,s-d} = \frac{Y_s}{Y_{s-d}} = \frac{e^{-r(s-d)} - e^{-rn}}{e^{-rs} - e^{-rn}} = \frac{e^{r(n+d-s)} - 1}{e^{r(n-s)} - 1}. \tag{1.1}$$

It is easily seen that $k_{s,s-d}$ is (1) larger than unity, (2) a positive function of r, (3) a negative function of n. In other words, (1) people with more schooling command higher annual pay; (2) the difference between earnings of individuals due to the difference in investment of d years of schooling is larger the higher the rate of return on schooling; (3) the difference is larger the shorter the general span of working life, since the costs of schooling must be recouped over a *relatively* shorter period.

These conclusions are quite obvious. Less obvious is the finding that $k_{s,s-d}$ is a positive function of s (d fixed); that is, relative income differences between, for example, persons with 10 years and 8 years of schooling are larger than those between individuals with 4 and 2 years of schooling, respectively. However, since the change in $k_{s,s-d}$ with a change in s and n is negligible [3] when n is large, it can be, for all practical purposes, treated as a constant, k.

The conclusion that k is constant holds exactly when spans of

---

3. $\dfrac{\partial k}{\partial s} = \dfrac{r[e^{r(n+d-s)} - e^{r(n-s)}]}{[e^{r(n-s)} - 1]^2} > 0; \dfrac{\partial k}{\partial s} \to 0$, when $n \to \infty$;

$\dfrac{\partial k}{\partial n} = \dfrac{r[e^{r(n-s)} - e^{r(n+d-s)}]}{[e^{r(n-s)} - 1]^2} > 0; \dfrac{\partial k}{\partial n} \to 0$, when $n \to \infty$.

Both partial derivatives are numerically very small when r and n are in a wide neighborhood of 0.10 and 40, respectively.

INDIVIDUAL ACQUISITION OF EARNING POWER   11

earning life are assumed fixed, regardless of schooling. Redefine *n* as the fixed span of earning life.

Then

$$V_s = Y_s \int_s^{n+s} e^{-rt}dt = \frac{Y_s}{r} e^{-rs}(1 - e^{-rn});$$

$$V_{s-d} = Y_{s-d} \int_{s-d}^{n+s-d} e^{-rt}dt = \frac{Y_{s-d}}{r} (1 - e^{-rn})e^{-r(s-d)};$$

and solving for $k_{s,s-d}$ from the equalization of present values, we get:

$$k_{s,s-d} = \frac{Y_s}{Y_{s-d}} = \frac{e^{-r(s-d)}}{e^{-rs}} = e^{rd}. \tag{1.2}$$

Here, in contrast to (1.1) the earnings ratio, *k*, of incomes differing by *d* years of schooling does not at all depend on the level of schooling (*s*) nor, more interestingly, on the length of earning life (*n*), when that is finite, even if short.

Now, define $k_{s,0} = Y_s/Y_0 = k_s$. By (1.2), $k_s = e^{rs}$. In logarithms the formula becomes:

$$\ln Y_s = \ln Y_0 + rs. \tag{1.3}$$

Equation (1.3) exhibits the basic conclusion that percentage increments in earnings are strictly proportional to the absolute differences in the time spent at school, with the rate of return as the coefficient of proportionality. More precisely, equation (1.3) shows the logarithm of earnings to be a strict linear function of time spent at school.

1.2 POST-SCHOOL INVESTMENTS: INDIVIDUAL EARNINGS PROFILES

The "schooling model" represented by equation (1.3) is the most primitive form of a human capital earnings function: Y_s in (1.3) is the level of earnings of persons who do not invest in human capital beyond *s* years of schooling. Since most individuals continue to develop their skills and earning capacity after completion of schooling, Y_s cannot be directly observed. Instead, an "earnings profile" is observed: the variation of earnings with age during the working life.

12   THEORETICAL ANALYSIS

We proceed to a human capital analysis of the earnings profile, at first ignoring depreciation phenomena.

After entering the labor force in year j, the worker devotes resources C_j mainly in furthering his job skills and acquiring job-related information, whether in the form of direct dollar outlays or opportunity costs of time devoted to these purposes, on or off the job. His "net" earnings Y_j in year j are obtained, therefore, by deducting C_j dollars from his "gross" earnings or "earnings capacity" E_j, which he would earn if he did not continue to invest in himself.[4]

Accordingly, earnings during the first year of work experience, $j = 0$, are $Y_0 = Y_s - C_0$, where Y_s $(= E_s)$ is the initial earning capacity after completion of s years of schooling.

If investment ceased subsequently, earnings in the next year (and afterward) would be: $Y_1 = Y_s + r_0 C_0$. However, if investment in that year is C_1, then $Y_1 = Y_s + r_0 C_0 - C_1$. More generally, net earnings in year j are:

$$Y_j = Y_s + \sum_{t=0}^{j-1} r_t C_t - C_j = E_j - C_j. \qquad (1.4)$$

The generality of expression (1.4) is evident, since the start of index t is essentially arbitrary. In Becker's original statement of the accounting equation (1.4), Y_0 replaces Y_s; and in instalments C_t, schooling and post-school investments are not distinguished. In fact, the expression for Y_s, the schooling model, is a special case of (1.4), in which investments are restricted to time costs of schooling and rates of return are the same in all periods. Then, with $C_t = E_t$:

$$E_s = Y_0 + r \sum_{t=1}^{s} E_{t-1} = Y_0(1 + r)^s, \qquad (1.5)$$

which is a discrete approximation of (1.3).

Using equation (1.4) we can proceed to the analysis of variation of earnings over the working life.[5] On the assumption that working

---

4. Note that observed earnings, as they are usually reported, would equal "net" earnings if C_j consisted of opportunity costs only. However, direct costs are included in reported earnings. Thus observed earnings overstate "net" earnings, but since direct costs are much smaller than opportunity costs, observed earnings more closely approximate Y_j than E_j.

5. At this point we are abstracting from variations in hours or weeks of labor supplied over the life cycle. Some consideration is given to this factor later.

INDIVIDUAL ACQUISITION OF EARNING POWER   13

life starts in the period following the completion of schooling, equation (1.4) points to post-school investments C_j as the variable which traces out the individual "age profile" of earnings. The initial earning capacity Y_s acquired in years of schooling s is taken as constant for a given individual, though it may vary among individuals. Y_s is not readily observed, since most or all individuals are assumed to engage in post-school investment of one form or another.

The variation of earnings with experience is best observed by considering the annual increment of earnings in (1.4):

$$\Delta Y_j = Y_{j+1} - Y_j = r_j C_j - (C_{j+1} - C_j). \tag{1.6}$$

According to (1.6), earnings grow with experience so long as net investment (C_j) is positive and its annual instalments either diminish $[(C_{j+1} - C_j) < 0]$ or increase at a rate lower than the rate of return:

$$\text{for } \Delta Y_j > 0, \frac{C_{j+1} - C_j}{C_j} < r_j.$$

Note that if investments increase sharply (at a faster rate than r), net earnings will decline, presumably temporarily. However, gross earnings always increase, so long as investment is positive, since

$$\Delta E_j = r_j C_j. \tag{1.7}$$

If both r_j and investment are the same in all periods ($C_j = C_{j+1}$; $r_j = r$), net and gross earnings grow linearly. Henceforth we shall assume that all $r_j = r$.

While constant or linearly increasing investment C_j is conceivable for some stages of individual work experience, these assumptions cannot be expected to hold over any long periods of the working life. Such assumptions are inconsistent with the theory of optimal allocation of investment in human capital over the life cycle. Rational allocation requires that most of the investment be undertaken at younger ages. Thus schooling, a largely full-time activity, precedes job-training, a largely part-time activity, and the latter diminishes with age, terminating years before retirement.

According to Becker (1964 and 1967) this tendency is due to the following incentives for shifting from learning to earning activities as soon as possible: (1) With finite lifetimes, later investments produce returns over a shorter period; so total benefits are smaller. (2) To the extent that investments in human capital are profitable, their

14   THEORETICAL ANALYSIS

postponement reduces the present value of net gains. (3) A person's time is an important input in his investment, but the consequence of human capital accumulation is an increase in the value of his time; thus investments at later periods are more costly, because forgone earnings (per hour) increase. However, these incentives would be overridden in the special or temporary cases where productivity in learning grows as fast or faster than productivity in earning.

Should we then not expect an early and quick accumulation of all the desired human capital even before individuals begin their working life? The answer of human capital theory to this question is twofold: Investments are spread out over time because the marginal cost curve of producing them is upward sloping within each period. They decline over time both because marginal benefits decline and because the marginal cost curve shifts upward.

Specifically, the argument (Ben-Porath, 1967; Becker, 1967) visualizes individuals as firms which produce additions (Q) to their own human capital stock (H) by combining their human capital with their own time (T) and with other market resources (R) in a production function:

$$Q = f(H, T, R).$$

Attempts to increase investments Q within a given period run into diminishing returns: Costs rise with the speed of production. Thus the marginal cost curve in Figure 1.1 is upward sloping.

The marginal revenue obtained by adding a unit of investment to the capital stock is the discounted flow of future increases in earning power. For reasons indicated, the benefits of later investments decline. The MR curve slides downward with increasing age, tracing out a declining pattern of investment over the life cycle.

The decline is reinforced if the MC curve shifts to the left with advancing age. As already mentioned, this is not a logical necessity: MC would remain fixed if earning and learning powers increased at the same rate. A recent attempt by Ben-Porath (1970) to test for such "neutrality" empirically suggests that investments decline over earning life faster than would be predicted by the mere downward slide of MR on a fixed MC curve in Figure 1.1. By implication, marginal costs rise over the life cycle.

Investments, however, need not decline throughout the life cycle. Ben-Porath (1967) has shown that the optimization process

INDIVIDUAL ACQUISITION OF EARNING POWER   15

FIGURE 1.1
PRODUCTION OF HUMAN CAPITAL

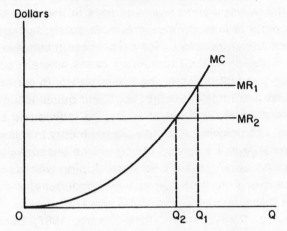

may lead to an increase in investment during the early stages because of "corner solutions": The initial stock (H_0) may be so small that even an input of all the available time, other resources not being highly substitutable, produces less than the optimal amount of output. As the stock increases, investment output will increase for a while until an optimum is reached with an input of less than the total available time. At this point investments and the time devoted to them begin to decline. The initial period of complete specialization in the production of human capital is devoted to full-time schooling. It is identified by the absence of earnings, a condition which may end before the completion of schooling.

The optimization process described above applies explicitly (Ben-Porath, 1967) to gross investments in human capital. Note, however, that the predicted decline in gross investment applies a fortiori to net investment if depreciation is constant or increases with age.

Two major conclusions can be drawn from the Ben-Porath analysis:

1. The higher the marginal revenue curve and the lower the marginal cost curve (cf. Figure 1.1), the larger the investment in human capital in any given period. Marginal revenue is higher the lower the discount rate and the depreciation rate, and the longer the expected length of working life. Marginal cost is lower, the greater the learning

16   THEORETICAL ANALYSIS

ability of the individual. Since the nature and conditions of individuals which these factors describe change rather slowly, the size of single-period investments is likely to be an index of lifetime investments. Longer schooling is likely to be followed by greater post-school investment, and generally, the serial correlation of instalments of investment is likely to be positive.

2. While the preceding inference is significant for a distributional analysis, the major implication of Ben-Porath's optimization analysis for the individual investment profile is that investment costs can be expected to decline after the schooling stage. As a result, both gross and net earnings slope upward during the positive net investment period. Moreover, the age profile of gross earnings is concave from below. From (1.7), we have the second difference:

$$\Delta^2 E_j = r\Delta C_j < 0, \tag{1.8}$$

since $\Delta C_j < 0$. Net earnings need not be concave throughout. The profile is concave if the decline of investments (C_j) is a nonincreasing function of j, i.e., if

$$\Delta^2 Y_j = r\Delta C_j - \Delta^2 C_j < 0. \tag{1.9}$$

If investments decline at a strongly increasing rate for a while, so that the inequality sign is reversed, age profiles may rise at an accelerating rate for a while; but eventually they become concave as net investment terminates.

The profile of net earnings has a steeper slope than gross earnings, since $\Delta Y_j = \Delta E_j - \Delta C_j$, and $\Delta C_j < 0$. The peak of both gross and net earnings is reached when positive net investments equal zero.[6]

Figure 1.2 indicates the shape of gross earnings E_j and net earnings Y_j during the post-school investment period OP. Of particular interest are the initial earnings capacity Y_s and peak earnings Y_p. The former, Y_s, is the earnings concept used in the schooling model. Its estimate is particularly useful for the empirical analyses in this study. Estimates of Y_s and of Y_p would make possible quick and simple methods of estimating rates of return and amounts of investment costs.

During the early years of experience, earnings of continuing in-

---

6. I abstract from depreciation and from changing hours of work.

INDIVIDUAL ACQUISITION OF EARNING POWER   17

FIGURE 1.2
EARNINGS PROFILES

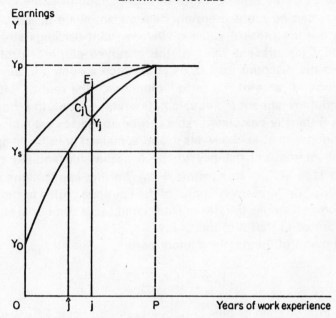

vestors are smaller than the Y_s earnings that can be obtained after s years of schooling without further investments. But earnings of investors continue to grow and, before long, exceed Y_s. In Figure 1.2, $\hat{j}$ is the overtaking year of experience. Knowledge of $\hat{j}$ permits one to read off the value Y_s from the profile of observed earnings Y_j. It turns out that $\hat{j}$ is an early stage of experience, and its upper limit can be estimated from equation (1.4):

$$Y_j = Y_s + r \sum_{t=0}^{j-1} C_t - C_j = Y_s, \quad \text{when} \quad r \sum_{t=0}^{j-1} C_t = C_j.$$

If instalments C_t from $t = 0$ to $t = \hat{j}$ are equal, then $r\hat{j}C_j = C_j$; so $\hat{j} = 1/r$. If C_t declines, $\hat{j}$ is reached sooner; therefore, assume C_t is not increasing. Then,

$$\hat{j} \leqslant \frac{1}{r}. \tag{1.10}$$

To illustrate, if r exceeds 10 per cent, it takes less than a decade for the trained person to overtake the untrained one, if both start their working life with the same initial earning capacity.

18   THEORETICAL ANALYSIS

Even for the rough estimate of Y_s by (1.10) it is necessary to know the value of r_p, the rate of return to post-school investment. If r_p is known, Y_s can be more precisely determined, since at the start of working life the present value of the constant earnings stream Y_s must equal the present value of the observed earnings profile Y_j, with r_p as the discount rate. If, as is perforce assumed in empirical calculations of rates of return to "education," the rate of return to post-school investment (r_p) equals r_s, the rate of return to schooling, the conventionally calculated rates can be applied to estimate Y_s. In turn, estimates of Y_s at two levels s_1 and s_2 make it possible to apply a check of internal consistency to the hypothesized equality $r_s = r_p$, since, by (1.3) $\ln Y_{s2} - \ln Y_{s1} = r_s(s_2 - s_1)$. Further applications of the "overtaking" or "crossover" point of the earnings profile to short-cut estimation of changes in rates of return and to distributional analysis are elaborated in Part II of this study.

At the end of the net investment period,

$$Y_p = Y_s + r_p \sum_{t=0}^{p} C_t. \tag{1.11}$$

The total volume of post-school investment costs $\sum_{t=0}^{p} C_t$ can be estimated, once r_p, hence Y_s, are known,[7] since

$$\sum_{t=0}^{p} C_t = \frac{Y_{p'} - Y_s}{r_p}. \tag{1.12}$$

Similarly, the costs of rising from schooling level s_1 to level s_2 are:

$$\sum_{s_1}^{s_2} C_s = \frac{Y_{s2} - Y_{s1}}{r_s}. \tag{1.13}$$

The above analysis of dollar profiles of earnings is easily translated into an analysis of logarithmic earnings profiles. This is not only useful but necessary, for two reasons: (1) Relative (percentage) variation in earnings is of major interest in the study of income inequality; and (2) for empirical analysis, post-school investments must be expressed in the same "time" units as schooling. Indeed, the conversion of investment costs into time-equivalent values trans-

---

7. In Figure 1.2, total post-school investment costs are given by the area $Y_0 Y_s Y_p$.

INDIVIDUAL ACQUISITION OF EARNING POWER   19

forms the earnings equation (1.4) into its logarithmic version. This is accomplished by the following device: [8]

Let k_j be the ratio of investment costs C_j to gross earnings E_j in period j. This ratio can be viewed as the fraction of time (or "time-equivalent," if investment costs include direct outlays as well as time costs) the worker devotes to the improvement of his earning power. His net earnings in year j are, therefore, smaller by this fraction than they would be if he did not invest during year j:

$$C_j = k_j E_j,$$

and

$$E_j = E_{j-1} + rC_{j-1} = E_{j-1}(1 + rk_{j-1}).$$

By recursion, therefore:

$$E_j = E_0 \prod_{t=0}^{j-1} (1 + r_t k_t).$$

Assuming $k \leqslant 1$ and r relatively small, this is approximately:

$$\ln E_j = \ln E_0 + \sum_{t=0}^{j-1} r_t k_t; \tag{1.14}$$

and since $Y_j = E_j(1 - k_j)$, we get

$$\ln Y_j = \ln E_0 + \sum_{t=0}^{j-1} r_t k_t + \ln (1 - k_j). \tag{1.15}$$

The assumption that $k_j = 1$ during the school years shows (1.15) to be an expansion of the schooling model:

$$\ln Y_j = \ln E_0 + r_s s + r_p \sum_{t=0}^{j-1} k_t + \ln (1 - k_j). \tag{1.16}$$

The assumption that r_j is the same for all post-school investments simplifies matters. Let

$$K_j = \sum_{t=0}^{j-1} k_t,$$

the cumulative amount of "time" expended in post-school investments before year j. Then

$$\ln E_j = \ln E_0 + r_s s + r_p K_j = \ln Y_s + r_p K_j. \tag{1.17}$$

---

8. This device was applied by Becker and Chiswick (1966) to schooling investment. Here it is extended to cover post-school investments.

20   THEORETICAL ANALYSIS

If $r_s = r_p$, we have, denoting $h_j = (s + K_j)$, the simplest generalization of the schooling model:

$$\ln E_j = \ln E_0 + rh_j. \tag{1.18}$$

When the investment period is completed, K_p is total "time" devoted to post-school investment. It can be calculated from (1.17), if r_p is known:

$$K_p = \frac{\ln Y_p - \ln Y_s}{r_p}. \tag{1.19}$$

The earnings profiles under these assumptions provide information on the number of "years" of post-school "training," a statistic that is impossible to obtain in surveys of workers or firms, and one that is bound to be greatly underestimated if it is based on reported apprenticeship periods or other formal training programs in firms.[9]

The shape of the log-earnings profile is upward sloping so long as $k_j > 0$. Its rate of growth and concavity are given by the first and second derivative of (1.15) with the same conclusions as in the dollar profiles, with k_j replacing C_j.

Note that the decline in k_j with experience follows a fortiori from the assumption of declining dollar values of post-school investments, and that consequently concavity in the logarithmic profile is to be expected more frequently, that is, even when the dollar profile is linear or S-shaped.

In the foregoing analysis it was assumed that (1) net investment is never negative, that is, the formulation abstracts from depreciation phenomena; and (2) changes in earnings over the life cycle represent changes in earning capacity rather than changes in hours of work supplied to the labor market (including the hours spent in on-the-job training).

The first assumption is not seriously misleading in the life-cycle context if the second is maintained: As Chart 4.4 in Part II shows, "full-time" earnings or wage rates reach a peak and remain on a plateau until men reach an age near retirement. On average (the data are mean earnings classified by years of education), net investment may be viewed as non-negative through most of the working life. Still, the finiteness of life, the increasing incidence of illness at older

---

9. Cf. discussion in Mincer (1962). Of course K_p includes forms of investment other than post-school training. Information and job mobility are examples.

INDIVIDUAL ACQUISITION OF EARNING POWER 21

ages, and the secular progress of knowledge, which makes older education and skill vintages obsolescent, are compelling facts suggesting that as age advances, effects of depreciation eventually begin to outstrip gross investment.

To accommodate these phenomena the formulation is amended by positing a rate δ_t at which the human capital stock H_t depreciates in time period t. Then

$$E_t = E_{t-1} + rC^*_{t-1} - \delta_{t-1}E_{t-1}, \tag{1.20}$$

where C^*_t denotes gross investment, as C_t denoted net investment. Letting the gross investment ratio $k^*_t = C^*_t/E_t$, we get:

$$\frac{E_t}{E_{t-1}} = 1 + rk^*_{t-1} - \delta_{t-1} = 1 + rk_{t-1};$$

thus $k_t = [k^*_t - (\delta_t/r)]$, and

$$\ln E_t = \ln E_{t-1} + \ln (1 + rk^*_{t-1} - \delta_{t-1})$$

by recursion, and assuming $(rk^*_t - \delta_t)$ is small, we have:

$$\ln E_t = \ln E_0 + \sum_{j=0}^{t-1} (rk^*_j - \delta_j), \tag{1.21}$$

and

$$\ln Y_t = \ln E_t + \ln (1 - k^*_t) \tag{1.22}$$

as an amendment to (1.14). It is clear that the peak of earning capacity E_t is reached when $k_t = 0$, i.e., when $k^*_t = \delta_t/r$; call it $k^*(E \text{ max})$. It is also clear that observed wage rates reach a peak some time thereafter, since from (1.22):

$$\ln Y_t = \ln Y_{t-1} + \ln (1 + rk^*_{t-1} - \delta_{t-1}) + \ln (1 - k^*_t) - \ln (1 - k^*_{t-1}) = 0 \tag{1.23}$$

only when $rk^*_{t-1} < \delta_{t-1}$, i.e., when net investment is negative. It can be shown [10] that if δ is fixed and if the gross investment ratio k^*_t declines

---

10. From (1.23) Y_t reaches a maximum when, approximately

$$rk^*_{t-1} - \delta = k^*_t - k^*_{t-1}.$$

Then

$$r[k^*_{t-1} - k^*(E \text{ max})] = k^*_t - k^*_{t-1}$$

and

$$\hat{t} = \frac{k^*(E \text{ max}) - k^*_{t-1}}{k^*_{t-1} - k^*_t} = \frac{1}{r}.$$

linearly over time, the (unobservable) peak of earning capacity precedes the (observed) peak of wage rates by $\hat{t} = 1/r$, that is, by about a decade or even earlier if the rate of decline of k_t^* diminishes over the life cycle. Note, also, that while the net investment period terminates before peak earnings (wage rates) are observed, the gross investment period continues beyond it.

In a few recent human capital analyses in which depreciation is taken into account, the rate is assumed to be fixed purely for mathematical convenience.[11] Yet, the depreciation rate on human capital is likely to be related to age, experience, and size and vintage of stock. If descriptions in developmental psychology can serve as a guide, the life-cycle pattern of δ_t after the individual matures is plausibly described as flat and very low, beginning to rise in the fifties.[12]

To the extent that hours of work vary over the life cycle, the profile of annual earnings is affected. Under conditions of certainty, for example, individual wealth can be considered fixed, while the cost of time grows with experience until peak earning capacity is reached. If so, the growth and decline of earning capacity is likely to induce a corresponding pattern of hours of work supplied to the market. Hence, the growth of observed *annual* earnings leads to overestimates of investments in human capital or of rates of return. Hours of

---

11. Cf. Johnson (1970), Rosen (1974), and Koeune (1972).

12. Health statistics show the proportions of workers with some limitations of work activities during the year to be rising slowly to 13 per cent of those in the 45–54 age range, and accelerating to 55 per cent at age 75. However, in a survey of the psychological literature, Birren (1968, pp. 180–181) states: "Except for individuals with cumulative injuries or problems of health, worker performance up to age 60 should be little influenced by *physiological* changes in aging." In discussing age changes in *learning capacity*, the same author states: "There has been a general tendency since the work of E. L. Thorndike in the 1920's to advance continually the age at which subjects in learning research are regarded as aged. At the present time there is little evidence to suggest that there is an intrinsic age difference in learning capacity over the employed years, i.e. up to age 60."

Psychologists note, of course, that it is difficult empirically to isolate *intrinsic* age patterns in productivity, that is, changes that are not affected by the individual's adaptation, such as health care and training—gross investment, in our terminology. Hence, their observations of time changes in "productive capacity" often show systematic differences when individuals are stratified by education, social background, ability measures, and so forth. [See Mincer (1957, Chap. 1, n. 1).] To the extent that these patterns reflect differential patterns of "adaptation," the analysis of human capital investment behavior is likely to contribute to an understanding of these findings, rather than conversely.

INDIVIDUAL ACQUISITION OF EARNING POWER   23

work may peak before observed wage rates because, as noted above (cf. note 10), capacity wage rates decline before observed wage rates do, given human capital depreciation.[13]

Variation in hours (weeks) worked is taken account of in the empirical analyses. The analysis of the relation between hours of work and human capital investments is not theoretically integrated into the present model. Though the problem is discussed in several places below, its fuller development is relegated to a future study.

---

13. Recent analyses of optimal allocation of consumption and work over the life cycle by Becker and Ghez (1967 and 1972) suggest that hours of work are likely to peak before earning capacity, a fortiori before observed wage rates decline.

References

Becker, G. S. *Human Capital*. New York: NBER, 1964.
———. "Human Capital and the Personal Distribution of Income." *W. S. Woytinsky Lecture No. 1*. Ann Arbor: University of Michigan, 1967.
Becker, G. S., and Chiswick, B. R. "Education and the Distribution of Earnings." *American Economic Review*, May 1966.
Becker, G. S. and Ghez, G. "The Allocation of Time and Goods Over the Life Cycle." Processed. New York: NBER, 1972.
Ben-Porath, Y. "The Production of Human Capital and the Life-Cycle of Earnings." *Journal of Political Economy*, August 1967.
———. "The Production of Human Capital Over Time." In *Education, Income and Human Capital*. Studies in Income and Wealth 35. New York: NBER, 1970.
Birren, J. E. "Psychological Aspects of Aging." In *International Encyclopedia of the Social Sciences*, Vol. 1, 1968.
Bowen, W., and Finegan, T. *The Economics of Labor Force Participation*. Princeton, N.J.: Princeton University Press, 1969.
Hanoch, G. "An Economic Analysis of Earnings and Schooling." *Journal of Human Resources*, Summer, 1967.
Johnson, T. "Returns from Investment in Schooling and On-the-Job Training." Ph.D. dissertation. North Carolina State University at Raleigh, 1969.
Koeune, J. C. "The Obsolescence of Human Capital." Ph.D. dissertation. Columbia University, 1972.
Mincer, J. "A Study of Personal Income Distribution." Ph.D. dissertation. Columbia University, 1957.
———. "Investments in Human Capital and Personal Income Distribution." *Journal of Political Economy*, August 1958.
———. "Labor Force Participation of Married Women." In *Aspects of Labor Economics*. Universities–National Bureau Conference 14. Princeton, N.J.: Princeton for NBER, 1962 (1962a).
———. "On-the-Job Training: Costs, Returns and Some Implications." *Journal of Political Economy*, Supplement, October 1962 (1962b).
Rosen, S. "Measuring the Obsolescence of Knowledge." In F. T. Juster, ed *Education, Income and Human Behavior*. Carnegie Commission on Higher Education, New York: McGraw-Hill, 1974.

[2]

Education in Production

F. Welch

Southern Methodist University and National Bureau of Economic Research

There have been several studies of the demand for education as an investment good[1] which generally take input and product prices as given and concentrate on computing (internal) rates of return to investment in schooling. Although these estimates usually indicate returns that are high by most standards, there is considerable variation, both through time and space, which points to the need for a clearer understanding of the underlying factors affecting profitability of investment in people. For such an analysis, education must be viewed not only as an investment but also as a factor of production.

In this paper, I consider the question: Why has the incentive been maintained for a relative expansion in the supply of skilled labor in the United States? Three alternative explanations are considered, and one is pursued with an empirical analysis of factors determining relative wages among skill classes in agriculture. As we would expect for any factor of production, the evidence suggests that the return to education is affected by factor ratios, but ratios do not tell the whole story. In agriculture, much of the "leverage" distinguishing college graduates from less schooled persons has its roots in technical change as reflected in the level of research activity. Thus the incentive for acquiring a college education is based on dynamical considerations of changing technology; and if technology becomes stagnant, this incentive is reduced and may disappear.

Convincing evidence of the maintained incentive for acquiring schooling is found in Gary Becker's (1964) estimates of private rates of return which are reproduced in table 1. When these rates of return are compared to the

This research is supported by a grant from the Rockefeller Foundation for a series of studies on production functions and income distributions. I am indebted to many people for their comments on earlier versions of this paper. Bob Evenson, Lee Lillard, and Bob Tinney commented on all aspects of the paper. I also received valuable comments from Zvi Griliches, Marvin Kosters, and T. W. Schultz.

[1] See, for example, Gary S. Becker's estimates for college graduates (1960) and for high school graduates (1964).

TABLE 1

PRIVATE RATES OF RETURN FROM COLLEGE AND HIGH SCHOOL EDUCATION FOR
SELECTED YEARS SINCE 1939
(%)

Year of Cohort	College Graduates (1)	High School Graduates (2)
1939	14.5	16
1949	13+	20
1956	12.4	25
1958	14.8	28
1959⎱ 1961⎰	Slightly higher than in 1958	

SOURCE.—Gary Becker 1964, table 14.

accompanying rise in average educational levels (table 2), the paradox of
education as a factor of production becomes clear: *With the phenomenal
rise in average education, why have rates of return failed to decline?* As
table 2 shows, in 1940 about one adult in four had a high school education;
by 1950, one in three had that much schooling; and the corresponding
figure for 1960 is two in five. Thus, during two decades, the proportion of
high school graduates increased by two-thirds, and the rate of return to a
high school education increased by three-fourths (from 16 to 28 percent).
During that same period, the proportion of college graduates also increased by two-thirds, and the rate of return to a college education failed
to fall. It is obvious that changes have occurred to prevent the decline in
returns to acquiring education that would normally accompany a rise
in average educational levels. Presumably, these changes have resulted in
growth in demand for the investment good, education, sufficient to absorb
the increased supply with constant or rising returns. When the value of the
services provided by education is determined in production, growth in
demand for the investment good must be accompanied by growth in
demand for the factor of production relative to supply cost.

TABLE 2

SCHOOLING OF THE POPULATION, 25 YEARS OLD AND OVER (1940–60)

Amount of Schooling	1940 (%)	1950 (%)	1960 (%)
Less than 8 years of school completed	31.8	26.7	22.1
4 years of high school or more	24.1	33.4	40.1
Completed college	4.6	6.0	7.7

SOURCE.—U.S. Bureau of the Census, *Statistical Abstract of the United States: 1966.* 87th ed. (Washington: Government Printing Office, 1966), table 154.

The most creditable explanations of growth in the demand for education can be grouped as follows:

1. *Growth industries.*—The pattern of growth in the value of industrial output may have been such that the most rapidly expanding industries are the most skill intensive. The important considerations are the income and demand elasticities for the industries' products together with rates of income growth and differential rates of technical change.

If the impetus for expansion of an industry comes through expanding product demand, then income elasticities are important. As incomes rise, the composition of consumption changes; and if income elasticities of demand are positively related to the share of skilled labor among industries, the demand for skilled labor will rise relative to the demand for other forms of labor.

If the impetus for expansion comes from reduced costs of production, then demand elasticities are clearly relevant. Holding constant the level of technology in other industries, suppose that neutral technical change shifts the cost curves of all firms in an industry downward as a result of an equiproportionate increase in the marginal productivity of all factors. This change will result in an increased demand for factors used by the industry only if the resultant decline in product price is accompanied by a rise in total revenue, that is, if the demand for the industry's product is price elastic. Growth in total revenue is necessary for growth in the demand for factors used by an industry.[2] If growth rates in total revenue resulting from differential rates of neutral technical change are positively related among industries to the share of skilled labor, changing technology will increase the demand for skilled relative to unskilled labor.

The changing composition of industrial activity may have been an important source of growth in the demand for education, particularly in light of the expansion of the skill-intensive industries associated with government expenditures for defense, space exploration, research, and so forth.

2. *Non-neutrality in production.*—The changing composition of production may have increased the demand for education. There are two possibilities here:

a) Physical inputs other than labor may be relatively enhancing to the productivity of skilled labor. As the quantity and the quality

[2] The rate of growth in total revenue resulting from neutral technical change is simply the rate of technical changes times the elasticity of total revenue with respect to technical change. Since a 1 percent increase in the marginal productivity of all factors results in (approximately) a 1 percent fall in product price, the elasticity of total revenue with respect to neutral technical change is the elasticity of total revenue with respect to product price (one plus the price elasticity of demand) with opposite sign. Combining the two "growth effects," the rate of change in an industry's total revenue (holding constant the quantity of factors used) is $i\xi + \dot{r}(|\eta| - 1)$, where i is the percentage growth rate in income; ξ, the income elasticity of demand; $\dot{r}$, the percentage rate of change in neutral factor productivity in this relative to the average of other industries; and η is the price elasticity of demand for the industry's product.

of nonlabor inputs have increased through time, this growth may have tended to increase the productivity of more, relative to less, skilled labor.

b) Technical change may not be neutral between skill classes. It may be that increments in technology result in increments in the relative productivity of labor that are positively related to skill level.

Although the distinction between (*a*) and (*b*) disappears if we view the rise in the quality of nonlabor inputs as the embodiment of technical change, there is another sense in which technical change may be non-neutral between skills. Nelson and Phelps (1966) have argued that at any point in time the level of available technology differs from the level of embodied or used technology, the difference being the "technology gap." They also argue that one dimension of education is the ability to adjust to changing conditions and that another dimension may be the ability to innovate. As such, the productivity of education would be positively related to the rate of change in useful technology (the ability to change) and to the size of the technological gap (room for innovation). In this case, if the rate of utilization of technology is accelerating or if the technology gap is growing, the return to education will rise relative to that of other inputs.

3. *Changing "quality" of schooling.*—Other things being equal, if the rate of skill assimilation (learning) per unit of resource commitment rises, the return to education will rise, relative to the cost.

From a social point of view, an increase in learning per unit of resource commitment corresponds to technical change in industries producing "learning."

From a private point of view, this change may refer to an increase in the commitment of resources whose costs are not borne privately relative to those that are. An increase in quality of schooling is an obvious example. In public schools, the most important private cost is the opportunity cost of school attendance. An increase in quality of schooling—either technical change in the production of schooling or an increase in the commitment of resources supplied by school systems—will result in increased learning per unit of student time in attendance and will increase the private return to school attendance.

While there may be numerous other explanations, I think that these represent the most fruitful avenues for research. The first refers to the changing composition of industrial activity and requires an analysis, industry by industry, of changes in skill requirements. The second refers to the physical production process and within it to the interrelationships between all productive factors including "technology" and is pursued in the final sections of this paper. Finally, there is quality of schooling. To date, we have been unable to say much about factors determining quality. Although we know something about factors determining test scores (production functions?), we have been unable to bridge the gap between test scores and the value of education.[3]

It should be noted that fully neutral technical growth which proceeds at the same rate in all industries is not included, although it is an explanation which has been put forward.[4] In his benchmark analysis, *Human Capital*, Becker (1964) indicated that fully neutral technical growth which is uniform in all industries, including those producing human capital, is capable of providing an incentive for expanding the relative supply of skilled labor. His argument is:

> If progress were uniform in all industries and neutral with respect to all factors, and if there were constant costs, initially all wages would rise by the same proportion and the prices of all goods including the output of industries supplying the investment in human capital would be unchanged. Since wage ratios would be unchanged, firms would have no incentive initially to alter their factor proportions. Wage differences, on the other hand, would rise at the same rate as wages and since investment costs would be unchanged, there would be an incentive to invest more in human capital and thus to increase the relative supply of skilled persons [p. 53].

There is no reason to doubt the validity of this argument. It is sufficient that *all* of Becker's "leverage" stems from the assumed technical growth in education-producing industries. Consider a situation in which neutral technical growth occurs in all industries *except* those producing education. In other industries, the return to all factors will rise as a result of the increased productivity. Thus, the return to education will have increased. Since the presumed growth is neutral, the increase in return will be proportional to that of other factors. But it is important that increased returns cannot be considered as providing an incentive to expand the supply of skilled labor unless it can be demonstrated that costs have not risen in proportion to returns. In this case, if education-producing industries are competitive purchasers of the inputs they use in the sense that the input supply functions facing the industry are perfectly elastic, costs will rise in proportion to returns, leaving the profitability of educational investments

---

[3] In particular see Thomas (1962) and Coleman (1966).

[4] See, in particular, Ruth Klinov-Malul (1966), where she states: "Suppose per capita income increases by K percent annually, in such a way that every earner gets an additional K percent of income each year. This in itself would make additional education more profitable, since absolute differentials will increase" (p. 7). This change is sufficient for an increased demand for education only if costs do not rise in proportion to returns, that is, if there is technical change in producing education.

unaffected.[5] Education-producing industries will find that input prices will rise in response to improved alternatives in other industries, and, since productivity has not increased in the education industries, costs will rise in proportion to factor prices.

The primary purpose of this paper is to speculate about the nature of education when it is viewed as a factor of production. In doing so it seems natural to concentrate on factors determining marginal productivity or relative wages between schooling classes. Evidence provided by Zvi Griliches (1968) and reproduced in table 3 shows that the time path of relative wages has been similar to Becker's estimates for the path of rates of return. For college graduates, relative wages have shown no downward tendency, and for high school graduates there is an apparent upward tendency, although it is less marked than seems true of rates of return.

In shifting the focus to relative wages we lose little information about factors affecting the profitability of educational investments since rates of return are likely to be dominated by relative wages, as is demonstrated in the agreement in their time paths. In fact, this association can easily be seen by simple manipulation of the internal rate formula.[6] For private rates

TABLE 3

RATIOS OF MEAN INCOMES FOR U.S. MALES BY SCHOOLING CATEGORIES, 1939–66

Selected Year	High School Graduates to Elementary School Graduates		College Graduates to High School Graduates	
1939	1.40*	. . .	1.57†	. . .
1949	1.41	1.34‡	1.63	. . .
1958	. . .	1.48	1.65	. . .
1959	. . .	1.30	. . .	1.51§
1963	. . .	1.49	. . .	1.45
1966	. . .	1.56	. . .	1.52

SOURCE.—Griliches (1968).
* Elementary: 7–8 years.
† College: 4+ years.
‡ Elementary: 8 years.
§ College: 4 years.

[5] "Profitability" refers to the rate of return on the investment. If there are capital market imperfections, as is commonly asserted, since education is internally financed by the family, then this change could actually reduce the incentive to invest in schooling. This, because the cost of schooling would have increased. Of course, the family's earned income would also have increased.

[6] Let

$$\sum_{t=1}^{L} R_t (1 + r)^{-t} = 0 \qquad (1)$$

define the internal rate of return, r, where R_t refers to net benefits in period t, and L

of return, the most important factors are: (1) the relative wage, (2) the shape of the age-income profile, and (3) either quality of schooling or, what amounts to the same thing, the state of educational technology.

In the remainder of the paper, I concentrate on factors determining the

---

is the life of the investment. For an investment in schooling, net benefits correspond to cost incurred in school and afterward to differences between the wage of schooled and unschooled labor.

Suppose that, in order to acquire a given skill, it is necessary to attend school for e years; that without the skill, a laborer earns W_{ut} in period t; and, W_{st} with the skill. For this skill, the internal rate of return is given by

$$\sum_{t=1}^{e} W_{ut}(1 + r)^{-t} = \sum_{t=e+1}^{L} (W_{st} - W_{ut})(1 + r)^{-t}. \tag{2}$$

Notice that direct cost of schooling is ignored. When considering private rates of return to public elementary and secondary schooling, direct cost is often trivial in comparison to the student's opportunity cost, and, even for college, private cost is dominated by opportunity cost. For example, Becker (1964, pp. 74–75) estimates that in 1939 about 74 percent of the private cost of college students was foregone income and the remaining 26 percent was direct cost. And, in any case, I am concerned with partial effects of the variables in equation (2) on the internal rate of return, and it is obvious that, *ceteris paribus*, an increase in direct cost will reduce the rate of return. There is an element of ambiguity here since skilled labor accounts for a fairly large share of direct cost. Thus, in considering the effects of an increase in the relative wage of skilled labor, this increase will cause both costs and returns to rise. Excluding direct cost from the analysis amounts to the assumption that the effect on the return to education of a change in the wage of skilled labor swamps the effect on cost.

In equation (2), factor W_{ut} to the left of each term and divide the equation by W_u'. We have then

$$\sum_{t=1}^{e} \frac{W_{ut}}{W_u'} (1 + r)^{-t} = \sum_{t=e+1}^{L} \frac{W_{ut}}{W_u'} \left(\frac{W_{st}}{W_{ut}} - 1\right)(1 + r)^{-t}. \tag{3}$$

Assume that

$$W_u' = \sum_{t=1}^{L} W_{ut},$$

that is, W_u' is equal to the total undiscounted lifetime earnings of an unskilled laborer. Then $W_{ut}/W_u' = p_t$ is the proportion of the unskilled laborer's lifetime earnings realized in year t. The set of p's (p_t; $t = 1, \ldots, L$) can be considered as a distribution function which implies the shape of the lifetime age-earning profile for unskilled labor.

Since the first-order conditions for cost minimization require that marginal physical productivities of factors be proportionate to marginal factor costs, by assuming competitive markets in which factor prices are marginal factor costs and assuming cost minimization, we have the implication that W_{st}/W_{ut} is the marginal rate of substitution, MRS_t, of unskilled for skilled laborers in period t.

Substituting p_t and MRS_t into equation (3) gives

$$\sum_{t=1}^{e} p_t(1 + r)^{-t} = \sum_{t=e+1}^{L} p_t(MRS_t - 1)(1 + r)^{-t}. \tag{4}$$

Thus, the internal rate of return to schooling can be viewed as a function dominated by three classes of variables: first, the marginal rates of substitution (through time) between laborers with differing skills; second, the "shape" of the age-income profile; and third, the state of the "arts" in the production of skill. Restated, $r = r[MRS(t), p(t), e/L]$.

productive value of education in a single industry. The changing composition of demand between industries and changes in the quality of schooling are left for another day.

The Productive Value of Education

Standard competitive theory, in its assumption of perfect information, rules out allocative ability as a source of the return to a factor. With complete information, there is no room for the concept of a superior alternative since in equilibrium all alternatives are equally good at the margin. That is, the perfect information assumption implies that the return to a factor is proportional to its marginal contribution to *physical* product. But, for education and some other intangibles, it is not clear that the direct contribution to physical production accounts for the total contribution to revenue. There have been attempts to modify the competitive model to allow for "entrepreneural capacity," but the return to this ability is almost always computed as a residual, total revenue less the cost of other things, which does not facilitate marginal analysis. Yet, firms clearly make marginal decisions vis-à-vis allocative abilities. They sometimes hire new "managers" and invest both in market and production information. As an alternative to computing marginal factor revenue as being proportional to marginal physical product in which all other things are held *constant*, I explore the implications of variations of an input (education) whose function, in part, is to *vary* the use of other inputs.

It seems plausible that the productive value of education has its roots in two distinct phenomena. Increased education simply may permit a worker to accomplish more with the resources at hand. This "worker effect" is the marginal product of education as marginal product is normally defined, that is, it is the increased output per unit change in education holding other factor quantities constant. On the other hand, increased education may enhance a worker's ability to acquire and decode information about costs and productive characteristics of other inputs. As such, a change in education results in a change in other inputs including, perhaps, the use of some "new" factors that otherwise would not be used. The return to education is therefore considered as consisting of two effects: a "worker effect" and an "allocative effect."

In recent years, we have stressed the importance of education as a factor of production and have included it, often as an adjustment for quality of labor, as a variable in estimates of production functions. Consider three "production functions" to distinguish the role of education in each: (1) the engineering production function of a single commodity; (2) a production function of gross sales; and (3) a production function of value added by some subset of factors supplied by the firm or industry, the other inputs being "purchased." As I show, when the marginal product of education is treated as a partial derivative, the composition of the bundle of "other things" held constant is crucial.

In each case, production is assumed to be technically efficient in the sense that for given inputs, physical output is maximized.

For the engineering function, we have

$$Q = q(X, E),$$

where Q, physical output, is a function of education, E, and other inputs, X. In this case, the marginal product of education is $\partial q/\partial E$ and refers only to the worker effect. As noted earlier, it refers to the ability to accomplish more (physical output), given the resources at hand. By including education or "knowledge" as an explicit factor of production, the concept of technical efficiency becomes something of a tautology. *Production is technically efficient if producers do not knowingly waste resources.* If they waste resources but are ignorant of doing so, the loss is attributed to a lack of knowledge. Presumably, the worker effect is related to the complexity of the physical production process. In the engineering function there is no room for allocative ability, since questions of allocation do not arise. In the remaining functions, education is excluded as an explicit factor. To include it would only reiterate the worker effect which is obvious in the engineering function.

Now consider gross sales for firms producing more than one product. With two commodities, we have,

$$Q = p_1 q_1(x_1) + p_2 q_2(x_2),$$

where p_1 and p_2 refer to the prices (assumed exogenous to the producer) of the respective commodities, q_1 and q_2. Both commodities are assumed to be functions of the input vector, X. The quantity of X used in producing q_1 is denoted by x_1 and similarly for x_2. In this case, assume that X is given, but that its allocation among competing uses x_1 and x_2 is not. Here, technical efficiency refers to being on the product transformation frontier, that is, of maximizing q_1, given q_2 and X, and does not correspond to maximization of sales, Q, given X. To maximize Q, we have

$$\frac{\partial Q}{\partial x_1} = p_1 \frac{\partial q_1}{\partial x_1} - p_2 \frac{\partial q_2}{\partial x_2} = 0$$

as the first-order condition. Maximization of sales requires technical efficiency and that the marginal value product of X be equated between its competing uses. Suppose that productive capacities of some factors are not equally understood by all who use them so that Q, given X, is not necessarily maximized. Suppose further that the allocation of X among its alternatives is a function of education, that is, $x_1 = x_1(E)$. In this case, the marginal product of education,

$$\frac{\partial Q}{\partial E} = \left(p_1 \frac{\partial q_1}{\partial x_1} - p_2 \frac{\partial q_2}{\partial x_2} \right) \frac{dx_1}{dE}$$

is positive if education enhances allocative ability. Thus when education is treated as a factor in functions producing gross sales, if the allocation of inputs among alternatives is not an explicit part of the function, we have the inference that the marginal product of education includes gains in allocative efficiency as well as the worker effect.

In considering value added, assume that there is only one product. Nothing is gained by multiple products since the question of allocation between competing uses is obvious in the previous example. Value added is expressed as $Q = pq(X, Z) - p_x X$, where p refers to commodity price and q, physical product, is a function of purchased inputs, X, and inputs supplied by the firm or industry, Z. The price of X is p_x, and both p_x and p are assumed exogenous to the producer. Here, maximization of Q with respect to X gives $\partial Q/\partial X = p(\partial q/\partial x) - p_x = 0$, which is the marginal productivity theory, that is, in equilibrium the value of the marginal product of X should equal its price. When Q is maximized with respect to X, we have the inference that value added is a function of Z only. But, again assume that producers are not equally adept at assessing productivity and that the quantity of X purchased is a function of education. In this case, the marginal product of education,

$$\frac{\partial Q}{\partial E} = \left(p \frac{\partial q}{\partial x} - p_x \right) \frac{dX}{dE}.$$

Here, the question of the *ceteris paribus* bundle is obvious. If a production function of value added is estimated and X is introduced as an explanatory variable, a positive marginal product denotes underutilization (at the mean) and vice versa for a negative marginal product. Alternatively, X can be excluded as an explicit variable and education included, in which case the marginal product of education reflects comovement between X and E with any resulting allocative gains or losses. Thus, if a value-added function, based on multiple products, is estimated which specifies the quantity of supplied inputs, Z, but does not specify allocation among competing uses, and if purchased inputs are omitted, the marginal product of education will contain three elements. First is the worker effect, then there is the question of selecting the quantity of other inputs, and finally the allocation of these inputs among their alternatives.

These effects can be combined by considering a value-added production function in which there are two products produced, q_1 and q_2, and each is a function of three inputs: education, E; other inputs supplied by the firm, Z; and purchased inputs, X. The respective commodity prices are p_1 and

EDUCATION IN PRODUCTION   45

p_2, and p_x is the price of X. We have value added by education and other supplied inputs,

$$Q = p_1 q_1(x_1, z_1, E_1) + p_2 q_2(x_2, z_2, E_2) - p_x X.$$

Where $E = E_1 + E_2, Z^0 = z_1 + z_2, X = x_1 + x_2$; and

$$1 = \frac{dE_1}{dE} + \frac{dE_2}{dE}, \qquad 0 = \frac{dz_1}{dE} + \frac{dz_2}{dE}, \quad \text{and} \quad \frac{dX}{dE} = \frac{dx_1}{dE} + \frac{dx_2}{dE}.$$

If value added is taken as a function of the total quantities of education and supplied inputs, $Q = f(E, Z^0)$, the marginal product of education,

$$\frac{\partial f}{\partial E} = p_2 \frac{\partial q_2}{\partial E} + \left(p_1 \frac{\partial q_1}{\partial E} - p_2 \frac{\partial q_2}{\partial E} \right) \frac{dE_1}{dE} + \left(p_1 \frac{\partial q_1}{\partial z} - p_2 \frac{\partial q_2}{\partial z} \right) \frac{dz_1}{dE}$$

$$+ \left(p_1 \frac{\partial q_1}{\partial x} - p_2 \frac{\partial q_2}{\partial x} \right) \frac{dx_1}{dE} + \left(p_2 \frac{\partial q_2}{\partial x} - p_x \right) \frac{dE}{dE}.$$

Where the first term is the "own" value of the marginal product of education, the worker effect, the next three terms refer to the gains from allocating the respective factors, education, supplied inputs, and purchased inputs, efficiently between competing uses, and the last term refers to the allocative gain from selecting the "right" quantity of purchased inputs, X. If this were a production function of sales, dX/dE would equal zero and the effects of selecting the input bundle would be lost.

Since returns to education include allocative ability, estimates of the productive value of education should include a provision for these returns. This can be done explicitly by the use of total derivatives or implicitly through profit or value-added functions.[7] Production functions of gross revenue include the worker effect and the effect of allocating factors between competing uses but exclude the effect of selecting the "right" quantities of other inputs. Engineering production functions reveal only the worker effect.

Perhaps this helps reconcile the inconsistency between the esimates of Griliches (1964) and Kislev (1965) of the productive value of education in agriculture. Using similar data, both estimated an agricultural production function of gross revenue for 1959. At the state level of aggregation, Griliches found schooling to be an important source of productivity, whereas Kislev, working with county data, found little or no return to schooling. The level of aggregation may be the key to understanding the difference in their estimates. While both used gross revenue as their measure of output and therefore permit education to capture the gains from allocating resources between competing uses, it is clear that agriculture at the state level is much more diversified, vis-à-vis product, than at the county

[7] Value-added functions become profit functions in the extreme as all inputs are treated as purchased (variable).

level. Thus the state aggregate permits more "room" for allocative ability than does the county. It is also clear that to the extent that education affects the choice of which inputs to use, both Griliches and Kislev understated the productive value of education because both held other input quantities (including purchased inputs) constant in estimating marginal productivity.

This also helps interpret a peculiar result of an earlier attempt of my own (Welch 1966) to analyze the determinants of the value of schooling in U.S. agriculture. The dependent variable in my analysis, the return to eight years of schooling, was assumed to be the value of the marginal product (as a partial derivative) of schooling in agriculture. Clearly, when the return to schooling is estimated from wages, it includes gains to allocative ability. The coefficient estimates indicated that the share of labor in agriculture is about three-fourths of total output and the share of nonlabor inputs is one-fourth; factor shares more relevant to value-added than to gross sales.[8]

The first clear-cut distinction between worker and allocative effects is provided by Chaudhri (1968). In trying to assess the impact of education on Indian agriculture, he estimates an aggregate production function (at the state level) of gross revenue. Although statistical problems of few observations and large error-variance in coefficients preclude strong statements, Chaudhri fails to demonstrate that education is an important source of productivity. He argues (partly in error) that, in his estimated function, marginal product of education refers to the worker effect alone, and to capture the allocative effect he provides evidence showing in case after case that the composition of the "other" input bundle varies with the incidence of secondary schooling in the farm labor force. His conclusions reinforce the Nelson and Phelps (1966) contention that education enhances innovative ability as he demonstrates that the use of modern, as opposed to conventional, inputs is positively related to education. In this context, innovative ability is one dimension of allocative ability.

The Case of Agriculture

The empirical analysis of factors determining the productivity of schooling is restricted to agriculture in the United States. There are two good reasons for doing so. First, the data are fairly accessible. The effort of others, particularly Griliches in his work on the sources of measured productivity growth (1963a, and 1963b, 1964) shows many relevant considerations; also the work of Evenson (1967, 1968) refines some aspects of the original

[8] I failed to recognize the significance of this result, and although I referred to the underlying production process as one of value added, the measure of nonlabor inputs included purchased inputs.

Griliches measures. The ability to build on this kind of empirical foundation does not exist outside of agriculture. The second reason is that U.S.
agriculture is highly dynamic technically. The well-known concept of the
farmer on the treadmill places peculiar emphasis upon innovative effort. A
rapid rate of "technical change" together with an inelastic aggregate
product demand implies that there is continual pressure on some factors,
particularly labor, to leave agriculture, and the ability to stay current with
respect to productive techniques determines whether a firm will exist in the
long run. While these factors favor the selection of agriculture, there is
one shortcoming.

Agriculture is probably atypical inasmuch as a larger share of the
productive value of education may refer to allocative ability than in
most industries. Farming usually includes a diversified set of activities
for which allocative decisions are made continuously as part of the normal
routine. In other industries, the jobs of a large portion of the work force
do not involve decisions for which prices are relevant. Too, in most
industries jobs performed by persons with different education are more
sharply differentiated than in agriculture, and, in these cases, the physical
productivity of education is more easily understood. In agriculture, differences in job complexity associated with differences in education are less
noticeable, and the product of education is more likely to be associated with
allocative efficiency. Does education enable one to pick more grapes or do
a better job of driving a tractor? Even if it does, these "worker" effects are
probably small when compared with the considerable differences revealed
in income. Allocative ability plays a key role in determining education's
productivity in agriculture and is most relevant in a dynamic setting.

The relevance of dynamical factors is stressed by Schultz (1964) when
he suggests that, in economies in which agricutural production is accomplished almost solely by the use of "traditional" factors, there is reason
to believe that factors are more efficiently allocated than in "modern"
agricultural economies. Schultz's interpretation is that traditional agriculture is close to an economic equilibrium in adjusting to relatively stationary
techniques. Because of this, judgments about factors are based upon
extensive observation; the stationary technology guarantees ample time
to explore the potential of factors being used.

In contrast, in a technically dynamic agriculture, a factor may be
obsolete before its productivity can be fully explored! Herein, I think,
lies the explanation of education's productivity. If educated persons are
more adept at critically evaluating new and reportedly improved input
varieties, if they can distinguish more quickly between the systematic
and random elements of productivity responses, then in a dynamical context educated persons will be more productive. Furthermore, the *extent*
of the productivity differentials between skill levels will be directly related
to the rate of flow of new inputs into agriculture.

In the empirical analysis that follows, I concentrate on determinants of relative wages among three skill classes: college graduates, high school graduates, and persons with one to four years of schooling (functional illiterates). As is described in the Appendix, laborers in intermediate classes are treated as linear combinations of persons in these three classes. For example, a person with eight years of schooling is "counted" as 0.46 of a person with one to four years of schooling, 0.53 of a high school graduate, and so on for the schooling classes: 0, 5–7, 9–11, and 13–15 years. Wages refer to males 45–54 years old, and the associated number of persons in each skill class refers to a white male, 45–54 years old, equivalent wage earner. It is assumed that a laborer's wage is his marginal product from an underlying production process of value added by labor and inputs supplied by farms. Nonlabor inputs include a measure of the flow of services from land, machinery, and livestock inventories. Purchased inputs are excluded.

The measure that I use for the rate of flow of new inputs is a weighted average of expenditures per farm for research over the past nine years. As a measure of the availability of information about new inputs, I include an average over the past four years of the number of days spent (per farm) on farms by state and federal extension staff.

The unit of observation is the "state" of which there are forty-nine. The thirty-nine "states" used by Griliches (1964) are included together with a breakdown of ten Southern states[9] into white and nonwhite. The white-nonwhite specification is in recognition of the segregation of the Federal Extension Service prior to 1962. While factor ratios and research are treated as the same level in the white and nonwhite sector of each of the ten states, the extension variable refers to days spent on white and nonwhite farms, respectively.[10]

Table 4 provides estimates of factors affecting relative wages in agriculture. Although coefficients on inputs are reported separately, the equations are estimated using factor ratios so that the sum of the coefficients on the inputs is constrained to equal zero. All variables except research and extension are in logarithms.

In Table 4, regression equations (1) and (2) raise as many questions as they answer. Notice that in each equation the coefficient estimates indicate that the relative productivity of a college graduate is increased by increasing the number of college graduates, although not "significantly" so. There is another peculiarity of these two equations. In equation (1) an increase in the number of functional illiterates *reduces* the wage of high school relative to college graduates. In equation (2) an increase in

---

[9] The states are Alabama, Arkansas, Georgia, Louisiana, Mississippi, North Carolina, South Carolina, Tennessee, Texas, and Virginia.

[10] For an enlightening discussion of the segregation of the Federal Extension Service, see U.S. Commission on Civil Rights (1965).

TABLE 4

ESTIMATES OF FACTORS AFFECTING THE PRODUCTIVITY OF MORE RELATIVE TO LESS
SCHOOLED PERSONS IN U.S. AGRICULTURE, 1959

INDEPENDENT VARIABLES	DEPENDENT VARIABLES			
	W_{16+}/W_{12} (1)	W_{16+}/W_{1-4} (2)	W_{12}/W_{1-4} (3)	(4)
1. Functional illiterates	.054	.442	.388	.359
	(.037)	(.048)	(.039)	(.038)
2. High school graduates	.034	−.426	−.460	−.359
	(.084)	(.109)	(.089)	(.038)
3. College graduates	.048	.062	.014	...
	(.064)	(.083)	(.068)	
4. Nonlabor inputs	−.136	−.078	.058	...
	(.034)	(.045)	(.036)	
5. Research expenditures ($00) per farm	.056	.179	.123	...
	(.094)	(.122)	(.100)	
6. Day per farm by extension personnel	−.130	−.136	−.006	...
	(.078)	(.101)	(.082)	
7. Nonwhite	.138	−.122	−.260	−.281
	(.043)	(.056)	(.045)	(.045)
8. Intercept	1.742	2.008	.266	.744
R^2	.578	.737	.722	.671
Residual sum of squares (degrees of freedom)	.436	.737	.486	.574
	(42)	(42)	(42)	(46)

NOTE.—Subscripts indicate years of school completed. Standard errors of the coefficient estimates are in parentheses. Variables other than research, extension, and nonwhite (a dummy variable) are in logarithms.

Definitions of Variables:

1. *Wages.*—Wages refer to total income in 1959, for males with income, age 45–54 years. The estimation procedure is discussed in the Appendix.

2. *Number of persons.*—The number of persons in each schooling class is estimated in terms of age constant, white, male equivalent earners. The estimation procedure and the procedure for reducing the schooling distribution to three classes is described in the Appendix. The procedure described there results in estimates of number of persons in the rural farm population, not in the farm labor force per se. To adjust for this overstatement of numbers of persons, the number in each schooling class was multiplied by the ratio, R, for each state. Where R = number of employed male farmers, farm managers, farm laborers, and foremen in 1960 divided by the number of rural farm males employed in 1960 (*1960 Census of Population*, tables[s] 121). The national average for this ratio is .965.

3. *Nonlabor inputs supplied by farms.*—A linear aggregate of the estimated flow of services from land and buildings, machinery, and livestock inventories. The measure includes:

a) 3 percent of the value of farm land and buildings. The land and buildings variable is taken from Griliches (1964). His series adjusts for differences in quality of crop, irrigation, pasture land, and so forth, using relative prices for 1940. A uniform price index adjustment was used by Griliches to express values in 1949 dollars, and I multiplied his values by 1.69 (the ratio of the 1959–1949 price indexes for farm real estate) so that value is in 1959 dollars. The 3 percent refers to an assumed 8 percent competitive rate of return (à la Griliches) and an assumed 5 percent rate of appreciation in farm real estate values.

b) 15 percent of the value of machinery on farms. A measure of the value of machinery on farms is constructed using price indexes supplied by Kislev (1965) and *Census of Agriculture* estimates of the stock of machines on farms. The 0.15 refers to an assumed average machine life of ten years and an 8 percent rate of interest.

c) 8 percent of the value of the livestock inventory: *U.S. Census of Agriculture*, 1959 estimates.

4. *Research per farm.*—A weighted average of total research expenditures over the past nine years divided by *Census of Agriculture* number of farms. Research expenditures refer to all federal and state expenditures (including farm management research). These data are provided by Evenson (1968). The annual weights are: .04, .08, .12, .16, .20, .16, .12, .08, and .04 for the years 1959 to 1951, respectively.

5. *Days per farm by extension personnel:* A weighted average over four years of the total days spent by extension personnel in eight selected activities divided by *Census of Agriculture* number of farms. The included activities are: crops, livestock, marketing, soils, planning and management, land, buildings and machinery, and forestry. These data are obtained from unpublished reports of the Federal Extension Service. The annual weights are: 1/3, 1/3, 1/6, 1/6 for the years 1959 to 1956, respectively. For the Southern states, days per farm is computed from separate statistics for the Negro and white extension services, and number of farms similarly refers to Negro and white farm operators.

In the Southern states, the number of persons in a schooling class refers to the number of whites plus the product of the number of nonwhites and the relative wage of nonwhites. This number is interpreted as "white" equivalent laborers.

the number of high school graduates *increases* the wage of functional illiterates relative to college graduates. That is, high school graduates enhance the relative productivity of functional illiterates, but functional illiterates detract from the relative productivity of high school graduates. Strictly speaking, these results are not necessarily contradictory because the coefficients refer to the elasticity of the relative wage of two factors with respect to a third and are not transitive. Nevertheless, this result is contrary to the usual interpretation of factor substitutability and questions the form in which equations (1) and (2) are specified.

Before discarding these two equations, consider the remaining results. In each case, nonlabor inputs supplied by farms detract from the *relative* productivity of college graduates. Too, the evidence is that research activity, the rate of flow of new inputs, enhances the relative productivity of college graduates and that extension activity, the flow of information about new inputs, detracts from the relative productivity of college graduates. This is as it should be. If education enhances the ability of a producer to decode information about the productive characteristics of new inputs, then the more rapid the rate of flow of new inputs, the greater will be the productivity differential associated with additional education. Further, if the advantages associated with added education refer to a differential ability to acquire and decode information, then an activity of disseminating information (extension) can short-circuit the gains to education. In a sense, the Extension Service may serve the purpose of overcoming the disadvantages associated with insufficient schooling. Unfortunately, the effect of extension seems more apparent than real, inasmuch as in considering a (hopefully) superior specification of equations (1) and (2), the effect of extension disappears.

Regression equations (3) and (4) provide the most valuable information of table 4. In fact, equation (3) is implied by equations (1) and (2) and can be calculated simply as equation (2) less (1). Nevertheless, when (3) is compared with (4), the evidence is that the wage of high school graduates relative to functional illiterates depends neither upon the number of college graduates, the quantity of nonlabor inputs, research, nor upon extension activities. Equation (4) is estimated with the constraint that the coefficient on each of these four variables is zero. Deleting these variables reduces R^2 by only .051 (from .722 to .671), indicating that the partial R^2 of these four variables with the relative wage is .16. In testing for the joint significance of these variables, the computed $F_{(4, 42)}$ statistic is 1.90, whereas the associated critical value of F at a confidence level of .05 is 2.59.[11] I therefore accept the hypothesis that the marginal rate of substitution (assumed equal to the relative wage) of functional illiterates for high

---

[11] The test that a subset of coefficient in a regression equation is equal to zero is given in Graybill (1961, pp. 133–40).

EDUCATION IN PRODUCTION 51

school graduates is a function of the ratio of high school graduates to functional illiterates only. Under this hypothesis the coefficient on the factor ratio, .359, can be interpreted as an estimate of a special kind of elasticity of substitution. It is not the partial elasticity in its most general form, but it is the elasticity of the factor ratio with respect to the marginal rate of substitution. The point estimate of the elasticity of substitution is 2.8 (the reciprocal of .359). The evidence here is that the elasticity of substitution between these classes is significantly different from unity so that the commonly used Cobb-Douglas and linear forms for combining inputs seem inappropriate.

Solow (1956), à la the Leontief separability theorem, has pointed out that, if the marginal rate of substitution between two inputs is independent of other inputs, production can be considered as a multistage process in which the two are first combined into an intermediate good which is then combined with other inputs to form the final product. The evidence here is that functional illiterates and high school graduates can be aggregated into an intermediate good. Call it "conventional labor" in contrast to the "modern" skills acquired in college. If the production process is viewed as a nested C-E-S function of the form suggested by Mundlak and Razin (1967) and if high school graduates and functional illiterates belong in the same subaggregate, then equation (4) is correctly specified, and equations (1) and (2) are not.

TABLE 5

ESTIMATES OF FACTORS DETERMINING THE PRODUCTIVITY OF COLLEGE GRADUATES RELATIVE TO LABORERS WITH CONVENTIONAL SKILL, AN AGGREGATE OF FUNCTIONAL ILLITERATES AND HIGH SCHOOL GRADUATES, IN U.S. AGRICULTURE, 1959

INDEPENDENT VARIABLES	DEPENDENT VARIABLES, THE RELATIVE WAGE		
	(1)	(2)	(3)
1. The aggregate of functional illiterates and high school graduates . . .	.699	.699	.711
	(.062)	(.061)	(.081)
2. College graduates . . .	−.377	−.377	−.711
	(.084)	(.084)	(.081)
3. Nonlabor inputs	−.322	−.322	. . .
	(.056)	(.055)	
4. Research expenditures ($00)/farm	.485	.482	.663
	(.163)	(.150)	(.194)
5. Days per farm by extension personnel.	−.009	. . .	. . .
	(.148)		
6. Nonwhite	−.637	−.637	−.540
	(.084)	(.079)	
7. Intercept	1.167	1.157	−2.314
R^2	.803	.803	.648

NOTE.—Standard errors are in parentheses. Inputs and wages are in logarithms. The equations are estimated subject to the constraint that the coefficients on inputs (excluding research and extension) sum to zero. For definitions of variables, see the notes to table 4.

Table 5 provides estimates of regressions when high school graduates and persons with one to four years of schooling are aggregated using the C-E-S form into conventional labor, CL, and the wage is estimated as the average cost of CL. The aggregate is:

$$CL = (\delta N_{12}^{-\beta} + (1 - \delta)N_{1-4}^{-\beta})^{-1/\beta}$$

$$1 + \beta = .359$$

$$\log_e\left(\frac{\delta}{1 - \delta}\right) = .744,$$

where N_{12} and N_{1-4} indicate the numbers, respectively, of high school graduates and functional illiterates. The wage of the aggregate is computed as

$$W_{CL} = \frac{W_{12}N_{12} + W_{1-4}N_{1-4}}{CL}.$$

These results appear superior to those provided in equations (1) and (2) of table 4. The major change in specification is the form of the labor variables, and coefficients on labor inputs have much smaller standard errors relative to the estimated coefficients than in the earlier equations.

If the average cost of the combined high school graduates and functional illiterates is considered as the marginal product from an underlying production process, then the relations between the wages (marginal products) of high school graduates and functional illiterates are given as:

$$W_{12} = W_{CL}\frac{\partial CL}{\partial N_{12}}$$

and

$$W_{1-4} = W_{CL}\frac{\partial CL}{\partial N_{1-4}}.$$

From this it follows that equations (1) and (2) of table 4 should be:

$$\frac{W_{16+}}{W_{12}} = \frac{W_{16+}}{W_{CL}}\delta\left(\frac{N_{12}}{CL}\right)^{1+\beta}$$

and

$$\frac{W_{16}}{W_{1-4}} = \frac{W_{16+}}{W_{CL}}(1 - \delta)\left(\frac{N_{1-4}}{CL}\right)^{1+\beta}.$$

Since the function W_{16+}/W_{CL} is estimated in table 5 and $(1 + \beta)$ and δ are estimated in equation (4) of table 4, estimates of these relative wage equations are easily derived. Too, when viewed this way, the misspecification of equations (1) and (2) of table 4, is obvious. The variable, conventional labor, is simply left out.

Thus, table 5 together with equation (4), of table 4, provides an internally consistent set of estimates of factors determing relative wages in agriculture.

In table 5, equation (1) indicates that extension activities are not important in determining relative wages, and equation (2) presents the regression estimates when this factor is deleted. It represents my "best" estimate of the equation. The third column also excludes nonlabor inputs to provide an estimate of the long-run (since other factors are left free to vary) elasticity of substitution between college graduates and conventional labor. That estimate is 1.41 (the reciprocal of .711).

One important by-product of these estimates is that the marginal rate of substitution between college graduates and other labor appears to be *significantly* related to the quantity of nonlabor inputs. As such, it does not appear that all forms of labor can be aggregated into a single input.

From regression equation (2) of table 5, the coefficient on research can best be interpreted by asking the question: What would happen to the relative wage of college graduates if the research variable were to become zero? At the sample's geometric mean, the wage of college graduates relative to high school graduates is 1.62, and relative to functional illiterates it is 1.75. The sample mean value of research expenditures per farm is $26.74. If this value were to fall to zero, the estimate here is that the relative wage in each case would fall by about 14 percent or to 1.39 and 1.50, respectively. Thus, about one-third of the productivity differential between college graduates and either high school graduates or functional illiterates is directly attributable to research. In fact, this is probably an understatement of the impact of research. If production were to become technically static, eventually the productive characteristics of all inputs would become fairly well understood. This common information would be passed by word of mouth from one generation of farmers to the next, and under such conditions it is difficult to understand how education could enhance allocative efficiency. In a dynamic setting discretionary abilities may be the key to allocative efficiency. In a static setting these abilities seem unimportant.

That the partial effect of nonlabor inputs supplied by farms is negative (with respect to the relative wage of college graduates) is consistent with many explanations that cannot be distinguished with these data.[12] It is likely that the productive characteristics of land, buildings, machinery,

---

[12] One possibility is that, given existing factor and product prices and the quantities of labor inputs, there will exist a corresponding combination of nonlabor inputs that is optimal. Call that combination K^*. If we assume that the farm enters the production period with K of these inputs (K denotes the inputs supplied by the farm), then $K^* - K$ remain to be purchased. If more educated persons possess superior allocative ability, the gains to this ability will be positively related to the "room" for selecting inputs, that is, to $K^* - K$, and will therefore be negatively related to K. This, of course, is true only if K^* is independent of K, which seems unlikely, and if the "superior" allocative ability is superior only in the short run. Otherwise, this ability would be reflected in the previous selection of K.

and livestock (the supplied inputs) are more commonly understood than are the characteristics of the purchased inputs, seeds, commercial fertilizers, pesticides, and so forth. If true, we would expect farmers who are adept at assessing the productivity of modern inputs to rely more heavily on them, that is, to allocate a larger share of their input bundles to modern inputs than would farmers less certain of the capacities of modern inputs; and if this is true, a plausible explanation of the negative effect of supplied inputs is that, for college graduates, the productivity gains associated with increments in supplied inputs are less than proportionate to relative wages. Recall that, at the sample mean, the relative wage of college to high school graduates is 1.62. For supplied inputs to be neutral between high school and college graduates, the rate of increase in productivity of college graduates from increments in supplied inputs would have to be 1.62 times the corresponding rate for high school graduates. The evidence here is that, while it is possible that an increment in supplied inputs increases the productivity of college graduates by more in absolute terms than for less schooled persons, the ratio of the absolute increments is less than the prevailing relative wages. College graduates presumably get the added leverage (that results in relative wages being what they are) through the use of other inputs.

Since the effects of extension activities appear neutral, that is, they do not seem to alter relative wages, a question arises as to whether the nonwhite "states" should be included in the analysis. This is because extension is the only variable other than the dummy for the "level effect" distinguishing the Southern white and nonwhite observations. To "test" for the sensitivity of the coefficient estimates to the nonwhite observations, the regressions presented in tables 4 and 5 are estimated for the thirty-nine white "states" and are provided in the Appendix in tables 7 and 8. There is marked agreement in the two sets of estimates.

Summary and Conclusions

One of the most important phenomena of our time is that rates of return to investments in schooling have failed to decline under the pressure of rapidly rising average educational levels. Viewing education as a factor of production, for "other things" equal, we would expect returns to decline as the quantity of education rises; so the obvious implication is that "other things" have *not* been equal. This is an analysis of underlying changes that may have resulted in the maintained incentive for investing in education.

Three broad classes of changes which may explain the phenomenon are considered. Roughly, they include the changing composition of industrial activity, non-neutralities in production, and rising quality of schooling. I then focus upon the second: non-neutralities in production.

First, the role of education in production is stressed, showing that, while it can be considered as any other factor in the sense that it may directly contribute to physical product, the effects of allocating other factors must also be recognized. If education enhances allocative ability in the sense of selecting the appropriate input bundles and of efficiently distributing inputs between competing uses, the return to this ability is part of the return to education. The empirical analysis refers to determinants of relative wages in agriculture.

The evidence is that, while factor ratios are important, much of the "leverage" associated with added schooling is drawn from the dynamical implications of changing technology. But this appears to hold only for skills that result from college. Relative wages for persons who have not attended college are determined by labor ratios only.

Thus the empirical evidence says nothing about the stability of the relative wage of high school graduates. One possibility is that production processes have simply become more complicated through time and require increasing skill. This phenomenon cannot be captured in a cross-sectional analysis of the type presented here. On the other hand, the information presented here is important in explaining the growth in demand for college graduates. Consider the effects of research. Research expenditures per farm were \$4.30 in 1940 and \$28.40 in 1959.[13] Based on coefficient estimates in table 5, if research were to fall from \$28.40 to \$4.30, holding factor ratios constant, the relative wage of college to high school graduates would fall from 1.62 to 1.43, indicating that about one-third of the wage differential would disappear. Too, purchased inputs have become relatively more important. In 1939, inputs purchased from other industries accounted for 38 percent of agricultural output, and by 1959 the share had increased to 48 percent.[14] This trend should have increased the role of the innovator-allocator.

Appendix

The *Census of Population* provides data for persons with 0, 1–4, 5–7, 8, 9–11, 12, 13–15, and 16 or more years of school completed. In this Appendix, I describe the computation technique used to derive wages representative of each schooling class in each state and, correspondingly, the "number" of persons in each class.

Wages.—The wage variable refers to total income for persons in the rural farm population in 1959. Although data for earnings which exclude transfers and income from property not managed directly are preferable, they are not available. The U.S. Census (1963) provides for each state the joint income-schooling (tables 138), age-income (tables 134), and age-schooling (tables 103)

[13] Constant 1959 dollars (Evenson 1968).

[14] Agricultural output excludes the intermediate goods, feed and livestock (Welch 1969b).

distributions for males 25 years old and over. These three distributions are used to compute the cross-products matrix required for a regression of the logarithm of income on two classes of dummy variables, the eight schooling classes and six age classes (25–34, 35–44, 45–54, 55–64, 65–74, and 75 and over). Income estimates are interval midpoints for the $1,000 intervals from $0 to $7,000; for the interval $7,000–$9,999, $8,200 is used, and for the open-ended interval $10,000 and over, the mean is estimated from a Pareto distribution. With this cross-products matrix, the regression coefficients are computed using the standard linear regression formula. For each schooling class, the antilog of the predicted log of income for persons 45–54 years old is multiplied by the ratio of the arithmetic to the geometric mean of income for the class. This is so that estimates refer to mean rather than geometric mean values of income. In the joint age-schooling distributions, it is not possible to identify persons without income so that all persons, with and without income, are included in the income predictions. To correct for this error, a regression equation is estimated in which the dependent variable is the proportion of persons in an age or schooling class with income in 1959 and the independent variables are the same age and schooling "dummies." With the estimate of this equation, the probability of having income is computed for each schooling class (conditional on age = 45–54), and that probability is divided into the income estimate. The resulting wage is interpreted as the wage representative of a schooling class for males 45–54 years old with income in 1959.

Number of persons.—The number of persons in each schooling class is computed in terms of male, 45–54 years old, earning units. This number is calculated as the total income of all persons in a schooling class including females 25 years old and over and young persons ages 14–24, divided by the wage representative of the class. The estimates of total income are derived for persons 25 and over from census tables 138 and for persons 14–24, from census tables 134. The income estimates for the closed intervals are the same as those used in the estimation of wages, but for the open-ended intervals, means are estimated using separate approximations to Pareto distributions.

TABLE 6

ESTIMATED LINEAR RELATIONSHIPS AMONG WAGE RATES (ANNUAL INCOMES) OF THE EIGHT SCHOOLING CLASSES FOR THE UNITED STATES, 1959

WAGE RATES TAKEN AS INDEPENDENT VARIABLES	WAGE RATES TAKEN AS DEPENDENT VARIABLES, THEIR COEFFICIENTS AND STANDARD ERRORS				
	W_0	W_{5-7}	W_8	W_{9-11}	W_{13-15}
Regression no.	1c.	2c.	3c.	4c.	5c.
W_{1-4}	1.147	.633	.456	.210	−.084
	(.082)	(.034)	(.045)	(.026)	(.069)
W_{12}	−.170	.322	.529	.758	.588
	(.050)	(.021)	(.027)	(.016)	(.130)
W_{16+}	. . .	. . .	. . .	. . .	.431
					(.075)
R^2	.991	.984	.980	.995	.981

SOURCE.—The basic data are derived as described in the above, except in this case wages refer to the total population instead of rural farm only. There are 58 observations including the 48 states of the conterminous United States with a separation of 10 Southern states into 10 white and 10 nonwhite states.
NOTE.—Subscripts on the wage variables indicate years of school completed.

TABLE 7

ESTIMATES OF FACTORS AFFECTING THE PRODUCTIVITY OF MORE RELATIVE TO LESS
SCHOOLED PERSONS IN U.S. AGRICULTURE, 1959; 39 "STATES" ONLY

INDEPENDENT VARIABLES	DEPENDENT VARIABLES			
	W_{16+}/W_{12} (1)	W_{16+}/W_{1-4} (2)	W_{12}/W_{1-4} (3)	(4)
1. Functional illiterates	.065	.456	.391	.362
	(.033)	(.038)	(.040)	(.039)
2. High school graduates . . .	.008	−.471	−.479	−.362
	(.082)	(.098)	(.101)	(.039)
3. College graduates	.081	.107	.026	. . .
	(.064)	(.094)	(.077)	
4. Nonlabor inputs	−.154	−.092	.062	. . .
	(.033)	(.040)	(.041)	
5. Research expenditures ($00)/farm	.045	.170	.125	. . .
	(.090)	(.107)	(.110)	
6. Days per farm by extension personnel.	−.166	−.173	−.007	. . .
	(.072)	(.086)	(.088)	
7. Intercept	1.992	2.250	0.258	0.745
R^2	.517	.844	.760	.701
Residual sum of squares (degrees of freedom)	.264	.369	.389	.482
	(33)	(33)	(33)	(37)

NOTE.—Subscripts indicate years of school completed. Standard errors of the coefficient estimates are in parentheses. For notes, see table 4.

TABLE 8

ESTIMATES OF FACTORS DETERMINING THE PRODUCTIVITY OF COLLEGE GRADUATES
RELATIVE TO LABORERS WITH CONVENTIONAL SKILL IN U.S. AGRICULTURE, 1959;
39 "STATES" ONLY

INDEPENDENT VARIABLES	DEPENDENT VARIABLES, THE RELATIVE WAGE		
	(1)	(2)	(3)
1. The aggregate of functional illiterates and high school graduates . . .	.743	.741	.756
	(.055)	(.056)	(.078)
2. College graduates . . .	−.420	−.423	−.756
	(.079)	(.078)	(.078)
3. Nonlabor inputs	−.323	−.318	. . .
	(.055)	(.053)	
4. Research expenditures ($00)/farm	.557	.535	.720
	(.138)	(.135)	(.184)
5. Days per farm by extension personnel . .	−.052	. . .	. . .
	(.138)		
6. Intercept	1.173	1.102	−2.334
R^2	.865	.864	.724

NOTE.—Standard errors are in parentheses. For notes, see table 4.

Following the derivation of the stadardized schooling distribution for each state, the number of schooling classes is reduced from the eight census classes to three: 1–4 years, 12, and 4 or more years of college following a procedure described in Welch (1969*a*). The procedure is used in recognition of the fact that 99+ percent of the total wage variation between states and across schooling classes for the five classes, 0, 5–7, 8, 9–11, and 13–15 years of schooling is reflected in the variance of the three remaining classes, 1–4, 12, and 16+ years. Table 6 summarizes results for regressions of wages for the five excluded classes on the remaining three. Let the coefficient falling on the *i*th row and the *j*th column of table 6 be a_{ij}, and let N_i represent the age-adjusted number of persons in each schooling class. Then

$$N_i^* = N_i + \sum_{j=1}^{5} N_j a_{ij}$$

($i = 1$–4, 12, and 16+) defines the estimated number of persons for each of the three classes.

References

Becker, Gary S. "Underinvestment in College Education?" *A.E.R.* (May 1960).

——. *Human Capital.* New York: Nat. Bur. Econ. Res., 1964.

Chaudhri, D. P. "Education and Agricultural Productivity in India." Ph.D. dissertation, Univ. Delhi, 1968.

Coleman James S., et al. *Equality of Educational Opportunity.* Washington: U.S. Office of Education, 1966.

Evenson, Robert. "The Contribution of Agricultural Research to Production." *J. Farm Econ.* (December 1967)

——. "The Contribution of Agricultural Research and Extension to Agricultural Production." Ph.D. dissertation, Univ. Chicago, 1968.

Graybill, Franklin A. *An Introduction to Linear Statistical Models.* Vol. 1. New York: McGraw-Hill, 1961.

Griliches, Zvi. "Estimates of the Aggregate Agricultural Production Function from Cross-sectional Data." *J. Farm Econ.*, vol. 45 (May 1963). (*a*)

——. "The Sources of Measured Productivity Growth: U.S. Agriculture, 1940–1960." *J.P.E.* 71 (August 1963): 331–46. (*b*)

——. "Research Expenditures, Education, and the Aggregate Agricultural Production Function." *A.E.R.* 54 (December 1964): 961–74.

——. "Notes on the Role of Education in Production Functions and Growth Accounting." Unpublished paper, 1968.

Kislev, Voav. "Estimating a Production Function from U.S. Census of Agriculture Data." Ph.D. dissertation, Univ. Chicago, 1965.

Klivov-Malul, Ruth. *The Profitability of Investment in Education in Israel.* Jerusalem: Maurice Falk Inst. Econ. Res. Israel, April 1966.

Mundlak, Y., and Razin, A. "On Multistage Production Functions, the Theory of Aggregation and Technical Change." CMSBE report no. 6716, Chicago, 1967.

Nelson, R. R., and Phelps, E. S. "Investment in Humans, Technological Diffusion, and Economic Growth." *A.E.R.* (May 1966), pp. 69–75.

Schultz, T. W. *Transforming Traditional Agriculture.* New Haven, Conn.: Yale Univ. Press, 1964.

Solow, R. M. "The Production Function and the Theory of Capital." *Rev. Econ. Studies*, vol. 2 (1956).

Thomas, J. Allan. "Efficiency in Education: A Study of Mean Test Scores in a Sample of Senior High Schools." Ph.D. dissertation, Stanford Univ., 1962.

U.S. Bureau of the Census. *U.S. Census of Population: 1960.* Washington: Government Printing Office, 1963.

U.S. Commission on Civil Rights. "Equal Opportunity in Farm Programs." A report of the U.S. Commission on Civil Rights, 1965.

Welch, Finis. "Measurement of the Quality of Schooling." *A.E.R.* 56 (May 1966):379–92.

————. "Linear Synthesis of Skill Distributions." *J. Human Resources* (Summer 1969). (*a*)

————. "Some Aspects of Structural Change and the Distributional Effects of Technical Change and Farm Programs in Agriculture." Unpublished paper, 1969. (*b*)

[3]

ECONOMETRICA

Volume 45   January, 1977   Number 1

ESTIMATING THE RETURNS TO SCHOOLING: SOME ECONOMETRIC PROBLEMS[1]

By Zvi Griliches

This paper surveys various econometric issues that arise in estimating a relation between the logarithm of earnings, schooling, and other variables and focuses on the problem of "ability" as a left-out variable and the various solutions to it. It points out that in optimizing models the "ability bias" need not be positive and shows, using recent analyses of NLS data, that when schooling is treated symmetrically, allowing it too to be subject to errors of measurement and correlated to the disturbance in the earnings function, the usual conclusion of a significantly positive "ability bias" in the estimated schooling coefficients is not only not supported but possibly even reversed.

1. INTRODUCTION

MUCH OF RECENT APPLIED WORK in the economics of education has concentrated on estimating a version of the following equation:

$$(1.1) \qquad y_i = \ln Y_i = \alpha + \beta S_i + X_i \delta + u_i$$

where Y is a measure of income, earnings, or wage rates, S is a measure of schooling, usually in units of years or grades completed, X is a set of other variables assumed to affect earnings, u is a disturbance, representing the other not explicitly measured forces affecting earnings, assumed to be distributed independently of the X's and possibly of S, and i is an index identifying a particular individual in the sample.

Having written down such an equation, which goes under the name of earnings or income-generating function, one can ask immediately a long list of questions about it, questions that can serve as an outline for a text in applied econometrics (though the order in which they are asked might be different):

(i) What is income?

(ii) What is schooling?

(iii) Why should the equation have this particular functional form?

(iv) What other variables should be included in the equation (among the X's)?

(v) Why should there be a relation like that in the first place? In other words: (a) What interpretation can be given to such an equation? (b) What interpretation can be given to the estimated β coefficient? (c) Can one expect it to be "stable" across different samples and time periods?

(vi) Given answers to the previous questions, how should it be best estimated?

(vii) Who cares?

[1] Presidential Address, Third World Congress of the Econometric Society, Toronto, August 22, 1975. I am indebted to the National Institute of Education and the National Science Foundation for financial support of the work on which this paper is based, to Bronwyn Hall and Stephen Messner for research assistance, to Gary Chamberlain, Richard Freeman, and Sherwin Rosen for many discussions on this and related topics, and to Arthur Goldberger, Jerry Hausman, Christopher Jencks, and Paul Taubman for comments on an earlier version. All remaining errors are my own.

2   ZVI GRILICHES

Obviously, I don't intend to, nor am I able to, answer all these questions today. There is also no clear natural order among them. Instead, I'll indulge in a bit of autobiography (question (vii)), skip lightly over the first three questions and the one really hard one on this list (question (v)), concentrating on the more purely "econometric" questions of specification (question (iv)) and estimation (question (vi)), especially on what is to be done if one believes that an important variable has been left out from the equation, and present several empirical examples of such estimates, based on samples from the National Longitudinal Survey of young males in the United States.

2. BACKGROUND

My first published paper [18], building on the work of Theil [46], dealt with the consequences of leaving out a relevant variable from the equation one was estimating. Three years later [19], building on the work of Schultz and Becker, I produced one of the first estimates of the contribution of schooling to the growth of total factor productivity (in agriculture), using income-by-schooling weights to construct an appropriate quality-of-labor index. Almost immediately the possible issue of bias in using such weights arose to haunt these and subsequent estimates of sources of growth. While continuing to produce various estimates of the contribution of schooling to economic growth (cf. Jorgenson and Griliches [34]), I tried to validate them by including a schooling variable when estimating production function in agriculture [20, 21] and in manufacturing [22], and check them against possible biases by estimating earnings functions including various ability measures [11, 23, and 27]. It is this last set of studies that I want to discuss with you today, using language and concepts that date back to my first paper on specification bias.

Before doing that, it is worth noting, however, that much of the work on earnings functions by others was rather differently motivated. A major line of work, going back to Miller [36], Houthakker [30], and Mincer [37], put the emphasis on estimating the average rate of return to individuals from additional schooling. Another, but related, line of work, going back at least to Friedman and Kuznets [16], culminating in Hanoch [28] and since then spreading into a vast river of econometric studies threatening to engulf us all, uses the framework of the earnings function to ask questions about discrimination, attributing "unexplained" group differences in earnings to discrimination or other named but not directly measured interferences with the market.

I am making these distinctions to point out that the issue of specification bias is much more serious for the last type of studies. In the context of my original work, left-out variables would not affect the estimate of the potential contribution of schooling to economic growth if (i) they were uncorrelated with schooling or if (ii) the relationship between them and schooling persisted into the forecast period. Even if (i) or (ii) did not hold exactly, the consequence of that for my estimate of β would be relatively minor. But studies which identify the "residual" with something particular such as discrimination, are much more dependent on the original equation having accounted for "*everything* else".

3. EARNINGS AND SCHOOLING

Before one can discuss the appropriate empirical counterparts to be used in estimating such an equation, one has to say something about its interpretation. It is simplest to think of it as a kind of "hedonic" equation for labor. At any one time there are a number of different types of labor in the market, differing in their productivity but otherwise reasonably easily substitutable for one another. Market transactions and competition among employers and employees will establish relative prices proportional to the different marginal productivities of different types of labor. There are well known difficulties with this view (cf. Lucas [35] and Rosen [43]), and I'll come back to discuss some of them below. But it is the only interpretation that makes a modicum of sense.

Having accepted such an interpretation, we shall want a measure of earnings that comes closest to some transaction price for a well defined quantity of labor and a measure of schooling that corresponds to the qualities that employers are willing to pay for. The first will lead us to use wage rates per hour or week, when available. Using annual earnings, or income per year, will confound market transactions with issues of labor-leisure choice and the more transitory effects of unemployment. The second desideratum, having an "output" measure of schooling, is almost impossible to attain and we shall have to settle for much less than that.

The actual situation on measures of earnings or wages is much more complicated than is outlined above. Each job and each person are multidimensional. Jobs differ in their fringe benefits, in their conditions of work, and in their opportunities for training and advancement. The on-the-job training issue has been the focus of Mincer's [38 and 39] work and I shall not pursue it further here, except to note that unless one has a whole life history of the wages of an individual, it is best to have data on people who have been full-time in the labor market for a decade or so, i.e., in Mincer's terms, one wants to have observations in the neighborhood of the "overtaking" point. Otherwise, one has to be rather careful in defining and measuring a relevant "experience" variable.

Since one views schooling and other forms of training as production processes for human capital, one would like to have independent output measures of such processes. But nobody believes that we can get close to it by having an elaborate examination and summarizing the results by one final grand test score. We are stuck therefore, with input measures of schooling, measures of the time spent in institutions that are called "educational". We should keep this discrepancy between desires and reality in mind when we come later on to interpret the results of our analyses.

The simplest model that summarizes such considerations can be written as follows:

(3.1) $Y = p_h H e^u$,

(3.2) $H = e^{\beta S} \cdot e^v$,

(3.3) $y = \ln Y = \ln p_h + \beta S + u + v$,

4 ZVI GRILICHES

where p_h is the market rental price of a unit of human capital which may vary over time and space, H is the implied unobserved quantity of human capital, while u stands for other, preferably random influences on wages. Equation (3.2) is an implicit production function for human capital with time spent in school (S) as the major input and other human capital augmenting influences such as differences in the quality of schooling, or differences in the efficiency (ability) with which the time in school was spent by different individuals, represented by the v variable. Most of the issues of "ability bias" and simultaneity can be discussed in terms of the content of the u and v variables and the relationship of S to them.[2]

Before we turn to that, however, note that the functional form of (3.2) implies increasing returns to S. As such, it only makes sense if the costs of S, both direct and in terms of income foregone, rise at least as fast or faster than the return from it. In fact, the functional form can be interpreted as arising from a cost function whose only components are the rising interest costs of foregone income (cf. Mincer [39, p. 19]). If foregone income is the only cost of an additional year of schooling, and if the increment in log income due to this additional year of schooling (β) were constant in perpetuity, then $\beta \simeq (\partial Y/\partial S)/Y$ has the interpretation of the "rate of return to the investment in schooling". Whether such a formulation is adequate to the problem has been a source of much debate and of many attempts at improvement (cf. Ben-Porath [5], Rosen [42], and Wallace and Ihnen [47], among others). I'll come back to this issue briefly below, but for our purposes this simple interpretation will suffice for now. In any case, the empirical evidence for the semi-log form is reasonably strong (see Heckman and Polachek [29]).[3] We turn, therefore, to the consideration of the estimation problems raised by equation (1.1) or (3.3), specifically the content of the X's and the relationship of u to S.

4. ABILITY AS A LEFT-OUT VARIABLE

Let us assume, provisionally, that the true equation to be estimated is:

(4.1) $y = \alpha + \beta S + \gamma A + u$

where A is a measure of "ability" which we have ignored in our estimation procedure. Then, as is well known,

(4.2) $Eb_{ys} = \beta + \gamma b_{AS} = \beta + \gamma \operatorname{cov}(AS)/\operatorname{var} S,$

which leads to the conclusion that the simple least squares coefficient of $\ln Y$ on S is biased upward (relative to β). This is based on the following assumptions: (i) that "ability" has an independent positive effect on earnings ($\gamma > 0$) above and beyond its effect on the amount of schooling (correctly measured) accumulated; (ii) that the relationship in the sample between the excluded ability and included schooling variables is positive ($b_{AS} > 0$); and (iii) that this is the *only* variable that has been left out *and* that all the other usual least squares assumptions hold.

---

[2] I shall ignore the possible variations in p_h in what follows below.
[3] In our data there is almost no improvement in fit when the schooling variable is divided into six categories and separate dummy variables are substituted for the continuous measure.

RETURNS TO SCHOOLING   5

The simplest way of dealing with this problem is to find a measure of "ability" and include it in such an equation. If one is willing to accept IQ, AFQT, or similar test score measures developed by psychologists as being relevant to our "ability" concept, one can (with quite a bit of effort) find samples of individuals for whom such test scores are available, estimate the correct equation, and infer the magnitude of the bias that would occur if the particular variable were left out from the equation. Much of recent work, to which I have also contributed [11, 23, and 27], has concentrated on producing estimates of the percentage "ability bias" in b_{ys}, based on estimates of $\gamma b_{AS}/\beta$.[4]

I have the feeling now that much of this work, including my own, was somewhat misdirected. There is no good reason to expect the "relative ability bias" to be constant across different samples or to generalize easily from one study to another and to the population at large. Even if γ is a constant, the magnitude of the relative bias will depend on β and b_{AS}. The estimated β will differ across studies, depending, for example, on the parameterization of the equation. If, as has become rather common following Mincer's work, β is estimated holding "experience" constant, it will tend to be higher than in studies that hold the age of the observed individuals constant. Since most measures of experience equal or are close to age minus schooling, their use will increase the schooling coefficient by an amount equal to the age coefficient, leaving everything else largely unchanged, including the estimated γb_{AS}. Thus, while the absolute bias may be the same, the relative bias will be smaller in "experience" based equations. Also, one may expect β itself to differ somewhat across age and other groupings. More importantly, the bias depends crucially on b_{AS}, the relationship of the left-out ability variable to the included schooling variable, which may differ greatly across time and across different samples. Selection rules as to who goes to college (for example) have changed significantly over time (see [45]). The relationship of ability to schooling within families (when we look into the behavior of brothers or twins) may differ significantly from that between families. And finally, different samples may be selected differently, cutting off significant portions of the variance of schooling, changing thereby b_{AS} and the implied estimate of the "ability bias."

An example of such dependence of the estimate of the "ability bias" on the parameterization of the equation is illustrated in Table I, which reports several estimates of the earnings function based on 1969 wage rates (per hour) of not-enrolled young men with valid IQ scores ($N = 1362$).[5] Two sets of estimates are presented, one using the age of the respondent (in 1969) as an independent variable and the other using a nonlinear measure of work experience, based on independent data on weeks worked since end of school or age 14, whichever is later. The latter measure ($XBT = \exp - 0.1 \times EXPERIENCE$ 69) is constructed along the lines suggested by Mincer [39] and its use improves significantly the fit of the equation without changing the estimated "ability bias" by much.[6] It is about

---

[4] This work has been recently surveyed by myself [26] and by Welch [48] among others.
[5] See the Appendix for more details on this data set.
[6] Using a cubic in experience gives about the same results.

6   ZVI GRILICHES

.008 in the age-held-constant equation and about .006 in the experience-held-constant version. But the implied estimates of the *relative* (percentage) ability bias differ by a factor of four! The point here is not that the last estimate is necessarily the correct one, but rather that one's estimate of the "percentage bias" is model-dependent and hence not easily generalizable across different data sets and formulations.

TABLE I

ALTERNATIVE EARNINGS FUNCTION ESTIMATES
NOT-ENROLLED YOUNG MEN FROM THE NATIONAL LONGITUDINAL SURVEY
DEPENDENT VARIABLE: $LW69$[a] ($N = 1362$)

| Equation Number | Coefficient of: (and Standard error) | | | | R^2 |
	$S69$[b]	IQ	AGE	XBT[c]	SEE
1	.022 (.005)		.048 (.003)		.288 .337
2	.014 (.005)	.0023 (.0007)	.049 (.003)		.294 .336
4	.065 (.005)			−.85 (.05)	.309 .332
5	.059 (.005)	.0019 (.0007)		−.86 (.05)	.313 .331

[a] $LW69$ = log of wage rate per hour on current or last job in 1969.
[b] $S69$ = schooling completed, in years.
[c] $XBT = e^{-.1EXP69}$, $EXP69$ = work experience since left school or since age 14, in years. The effect of an additional year of experience is .062, at the mean of the sample, falling from .078 after one year of experience to .032 after 10 years of experience.

5. ABILITY AS AN UNOBSERVABLE

"The difference of natural talents in different men is, in reality much less than we are aware of; and the very different genius which appears to distinguish men of different professions, when grown up to maturity, is not upon many occasions so much the cause, as the effect of the division of labor." Adam Smith, *The Wealth of Nations*.

Because of the variability of the various econometric results and the lack of agreement on the role of "ability" in such an equation and on how it should be measured, the debate has see-sawed between those (such as myself) who explain high estimates of "ability bias" as due to the interrelationship of "ability" with other left-out variables such as the quality of schooling, and those who explain low estimates of ability bias (such as Cardell and Hopkins [8]) as the result of the use of erroneous measures of ability. I shall come back to the first point of view below, after we consider the definition, measurement, and role of "ability" in somewhat greater detail.

Two polar views are possible. "Ability" is IQ, or something close to it, and the only problem is that our measures of it are subject to possibly large (test-retest) errors. If we had data on more than one test or on some other relevant instrumental variables, this would be a simple garden-variety "errors-in-the-variables" problem, to be solved by standard econometric techniques. The alternative view is that "ability", in the sense of being able to earn higher wages, other things equal, has little to do with IQ. It is "the thing with feathers" (cf. Emily Dickinson and Woody Allen [1]). It is an unobserved latent variable that both drives people to get relatively more schooling and earn more income, given schooling, and perhaps also enables and motivates people to score better on various tests. Basically, it is a hypothesis about the cause of and a re-interpretation of the correlation among the residuals from individual income, schooling, test scores, and other equations. As such, it is only loosely related to "ability" as it is commonly understood by psychologists.[7] It could just as well be "energy" or "motivation". To the extent, however, that test scores are admitted as "indicators" of such an unobservable, one can stake out some middle ground between these two extreme views.

Thinking this way leads one fast into simultaneous equations with errors of measurement models, a topic surveyed recently by Goldberger [17] and myself [24]. In such models the problem of identification is quite acute and requires a more careful and explicit specification of the way one assumes the data to have been generated. In particular, if one can assume that different observations, across equations or across individuals, share the same values of the unobservable variable, this will provide a source of "replication" and a way of identifying some of the parameters of the model. Such considerations explain the recent interest in data on siblings or twins (cf. Chamberlain and Griliches [11], Olneck [40], and Taubman [44]), since one would expect them to share some common components of the unobservable ability variable. Hence also the name of "variance-components" that keeps reappearing in such models.

At this point it is worthwhile to outline a more complete model of the whole process. It is not the most general model possible but it formalizes some of the arguments made in the literature and should suffice for the interpretation of the empirical examples to be discussed below.[8] We shall assume that:

$$(5.1) \quad \ln Y = y_1 = \alpha_1 + \beta_1 S + \gamma_1 A + u_1,$$

$$(5.2) \quad LT = y_2 = \alpha_2 + \beta_2 SB + \gamma_2 A + u_2,$$

$$(5.3) \quad S = y_3 = \alpha_3 + \beta_3 SB + \delta_3 B + \gamma_3 A + u_3,$$

$$(5.4) \quad SB = y_4 = \alpha_4 + \delta_4 B + \gamma_4 A + u_4,$$

$$(5.5) \quad T = y_5 = \alpha_5 + \gamma_5 A + u_5,$$

$$(5.6) \quad A_{ij} = \delta_5 B + f_i + g_{ij}.$$

---

[7] Becker's [2, p. 18] definition of "ability" as "earnings received when the investment in Human Capital is held constant" is close to this second polar view. Unfortunately, it is not operational since actual human capital accumulated and the ex-ante marginal rate of return to it are both unobservable. In our context it is easiest to identify Becker's view with the proposition that β differs across individuals.

[8] This model is an adaptation of the one outlined in Griliches and Mason [27]. See also Chamberlain [10].

8   ZVI GRILICHES

This model contains alternative test and schooling equations, depending on the exact dating of the tests. Thus LT stands for "late test" which is itself a function of the schooling already achieved at the time of the test. Such a distinction between early (T) and late (LT) tests introduces also two schooling variables into the model and forces us to specify two separate schooling equations, one for current or expected schooling (S) and the other for early, before late test, schooling (SB). The unobservable ability variable (A) is interpreted as a measure of "initial human capital",[9] consisting of measured family effects ($\delta_5 B$), unmeasured family effects (f), and individual (g) random components.

In general, one would expect a positive correlation between B and f, but the model can be reparameterized so that f is defined net of B.[10] Note that the measured family background variables (B) are assumed to affect income only via schooling or the ability variables. This is an identifying restriction which may be testable if the model is overidentified enough.

I have said nothing yet about the source of the schooling equations ((5.3) and (5.4)). Together, they make completed schooling depend on social and regional background variables, the unobserved ability measure, and a random component. The important point here is that these equations formalize the argument for an "ability bias" in the least squares estimates of β_1 (given that γ_1, γ_3, and $\gamma_4 > 0$). Ideally, we would like to derive such equations from the optimizing behavior of individuals and I shall come back to this point, even if only briefly, below.

The estimation of such models depends crucially on what is assumed about the distribution of the left-out variable A and all the other disturbances (the u's). Assuming that A is the *only* left-out variable common to more than one equation and that the u's are distributed independently of A *and* of each other results in the most overidentified and simplest to interpret version of the model. In this model u_2 and u_5 are independent "nontransmitted" errors of measurement in the respective tests and the only source of bias in the least squares estimates of the schooling coefficient is due to the dependence of S on A. Some of these assumptions could be relaxed to allow for a dependence of S on u_5 (or a correlation between u_3 and u_5) which could be interpreted as "test-wiseness", something that makes one do better both on tests and in school but does not lead to additional income beyond its effects on schooling. It is possible, also, to test for the presence of more than one common factor in such models.[11]

If test scores are available, the simplest way of estimating equation (5.1) is to substitute one of them for the unobserved ability variable and use the background variables and the other test scores (if more than one is available) as instruments.

---

[9] This version can be reconciled with the one outlined in Section 2 by assuming that schooling augments an initial human capital measure: $H(t) = H(0) e^{\beta S(t)} e^{v(t)}$, that test scores are proportional to the logarithm of $H(t)$: $e^{T(t)} = CH(t)^\gamma e^{z(t)}$, and by defining $A = \ln H(0)$. If ability were also to affect the rate at which human capital is accumulated per time unit spent in school, it would introduce additional interaction terms between A and S in the income equation.

[10] Given our data we cannot really get into the question of whether A is largely genetic or due to common environments. With data on twins or other relatives of different degrees, such a model could be extended to encompass this question also (cf. Behrman and Taubman [4]).

[11] Such extensions are explored in Chamberlain and Griliches [12].

Depending on which test score is available we get either

(5.1a) $y_1 = \alpha_1 + \beta_1 y_3 + (\gamma_1/\gamma_5)y_5 + u_1 - (\gamma_1/\gamma_5)u_5$ or

(5.1b) $y_1 = \alpha_1 + \beta_1 y_3 + (\gamma_1/\gamma_3)y_2 - (\gamma_1/\gamma_3)\beta_2 y_4 + u_1 - (\gamma_1/\gamma_3)u_3$

and use instrumental variables to estimate the coefficients of the endogeneous early (y_5) or late (y_2) tests variables. This is not fully efficient, but should give one consistent and reasonable estimates of the parameters of interest.[12]

An example of such an approach is given in Table II, which uses the logarithm of the median income of the expected occupation at age 30 (*EXLOMY*) as its dependent variable and expected schooling (*ES*) as the major independent variable. It is based on a sample of all young men with valid IQ scores, including those still enrolled in school in 1969 ($N = 3025$).[13] In this sample, and for these variables, including a measure of ability into the earnings equation reduces the estimated coefficient of schooling by about .003 to .009, depending on the measure of ability used. Allowing for measurement errors in the reported test scores increases their coefficients substantially, reduces the estimated schooling coefficients somewhat more, by another .007 or so, but doesn't change the major conclusions. The overall direct contribution of "ability" as measured by test scores to the explanation of the variance of individual expected earnings is quite small, on the order .01 (the adjustment for measurement error doesn't change this estimate; the increase in the estimated coefficient of ability is almost exactly offset by lowering the estimate of its "true" variance).[14]

The rather large swings exhibited by the "ability" coefficients when errors in measurement are allowed for imply that these measures are quite unreliable. Among the two tests scores available to us, IQ comes off a bit better, with an implied reliability of 0.7 as against only 0.5 for the KWW measure. That is, about 30 per cent of the observed variance of IQ is estimated to be in "error", at least as far as its impact on expected earnings is concerned. Given the unreliability of these measures it becomes important and interesting to impose more prior structure on our model and utilize the additional information that might be available in data on siblings. To the extent that siblings share some of the unobservables, they can effectively serve as "instruments" for each other.

The workings of a siblings model have been described in some detail in Chamberlain and Griliches [11] and Griliches [24]. I will not recapitulate it here except to note that the basic idea of that model is to take advantage of the somewhat different information contained in the between-families and the within-families variance-covariance matrices of all of the endogeneous variables.

---

[12] More efficient complete model methods are outlined in Chamberlain [9], Joreskog and Goldberger [31], and Joreskog and Van Thillo [33].

[13] The advantages and disadvantages of using such expected variables are discussed in the Appendix. The advantages briefly are: The data (i) are conceptually closer to the "overtaking" point; (ii) more relevant to models which postulate ex-ante optimizing; (iii) allow us to analyze a much larger sample, especially of brothers where the sample size is quite important to us.

[14] Note that the overall results are very similar to those in Table I using "actual" instead of "expected" data, holding experience constant.

10 ZVI GRILICHES

TABLE II

ESTIMATES OF EARNINGS FUNCTION COEFFICIENTS FROM THE
NLS YOUNG MEN SURVEY

DEPENDENT VARIABLE: $EXLOMY^a$ ($N = 3025$)

Estimation Method and Equation Number	Coefficient of[f,j]				R^2	SEE^i
	$EXSC^b$	KWW^d	IQ^e	$S66^c$		
a. OLS	.068 (.003)				.182	.349
b. OLS	.065 (.003)	.0057 (.0010)		−.010 (.006)	.191	.348
c. OLS	.059 (.003)		.0028 (.0005)		.192	.347
d. TSLS:[g] KWW endog.	.057 (.004)	.0177 (.0022)		−.026 (.006)	n.a.[h]	.356
e. TSLS:[g] IQ endog.	.052 (.004)		.0051 (.0009)		n.a.[h]	.356

[a] $EXLOMY$ = logarithm of median earnings of the expected occupation at age 30.
[b] $EXSC$ = expected total schooling.
[c] $S66$ = actual schooling in 1966.
[d] KWW = score on a test of the "knowledge of the world of work" (administered in 1966).
[e] IQ = score in high school.
[f] Other variables in the equation: age and dummy variables ($DATELOMY$ and $DATE$ 66) for dating the expectational variables.
[g] Additional instruments used in TSLS estimation: mother's education (MED), father's occupation when R 14 ($FOMY$14), home culture index ($CULTURE$), $SIBLINGS$, $RACE$, $REGION$, and IQ in the equation in which KWW appears and KWW in the equations when IQ appears.
[h] n.a. = not applicable.
[i] SEE = standard error of estimate (estimated standard deviation of the residuals).
[j] Numbers in parentheses are the estimated standard errors of the respective coefficients.

Table III presents maximum likelihood estimates of the sibling version of the model outlined in equations (5.1) and (5.6), assuming that the u's are all independent of each other.[15] "A" is interpreted to be a normal "ability" variable, affected by the two test measures and affecting the two schooling levels and possibly also the expected income measure. It is composed of a measured family

TABLE III

NLS BROTHERS: ESTIMATES OF EXPECTED
EARNINGS AND SCHOOLING MODEL ($N = 580$)[a]

Equation and Dependent Variable	Coefficients of			
	$EXSC$	$S66$	A	$\hat{\sigma}_u$
1 $y_1 = EXLOMY$	.057		.034	.363
2 $y_2 = KWW$		.651	2.19	5.64
3 $y_3 = EXSC$		.368	.681	1.59
4 $y_4 = S66$			.322	.903
5 $y_5 = IQ$			6.88	9.10

[a] $\tau = \sigma_g^2/\sigma_f^2$, $\hat{\tau} = .72$, $\sigma_g^2/\sigma_A^2 = .21$.

[15] I am indebted to Gary Chamberlain for computing these estimates. See Chamberlain and Griliches [12] for more details and alternative versions. The computations were made using an amended version of the Joreskog, et al. [32] ACOVSM program. Since we partialed out first the age and "dates" variables, the resulting estimates are not fully efficient.

background component $B\delta_5$, an unmeasured family component f_i, and an individual independently distributed component $g_{ij} (A_{ij} = B\delta_5 + f_i + g_{ij})$.

All equations contain also the age, region of origin south, and dates variables. Background variables (father's occupation, mother's education, number of siblings, race, and "culture") enter in an unconstrained fashion in the schooling equation and are constrained to have proportionally the same coefficients in the ability variable with the constraint effective across the two test scores and the expected income equations. The simple least squares estimates of $b_{y_1 y_3}$ holding age and dates constant is .075. It is .069 when estimated solely from the "within" brothers variance components (Σ). The comparable least squares estimates holding IQ constant ($b_{y_1 y_3 \cdot y_5}$) is .066, with the coefficient by IQ ($b_{y_1 y_5 \cdot y_3}$) estimated at .0024. The estimated asymptotic standard errors are about .008 for β_1 and .02 for γ_1.

On the whole, the results are very similar to the earlier ones (given in Table II). By allowing for errors in the test scores and by using the fact that we have two test scores *and* information on the family structure of the observations, we reduce the estimated coefficient of schooling by an additional .009 beyond the simple least squares estimates which already include an ability variable, while doubling the estimated *IQ* coefficient (from .0024 to .0049 (= .034/6.88)). The relatively small movement in the schooling coefficient is connected to the rather small direct role of the ability variable in the expected income equation. It accounts for only about three per cent of the estimated total disturbance variance in that equation. About 79 per cent of the total variance of the ability variable is due to common family components, both measured and unmeasured. This is higher than would be predicted by a purely-genetic-no-environment-effects model for brothers (.5 to .6). About 62 per cent of the estimated variance of these common family effects are associated with the measured background variables (father's occupation, mother's education, number of siblings, "culture" index, and race). The variance of the expected schooling variable can be apportioned as follows (after solving out the $S66$ equation): due to unmeasured "ability" components: 23 per cent (joint among brothers 13 per cent, individual 9 per cent); due to common measured family background (both direct and indirect via ability): 26 per cent; due to other individual effects uncorrelated with either "ability" or measured "background": 50 per cent. A similar decomposition can be computed for the IQ and KWW variables, indicating that the "pure" error components account for 34 and 62 per cent, respectively, of the observed variances of these variables.[16]

Since the estimated model is significantly over identified, one could relax some of the imposed independence assumptions and test several additional interesting hypotheses. But that would take us too far afield.[17] On the other hand, before we accept the above results as final there are at least two more arguments worth considering.

[16] All of these decompositions are net of the age and dates variables.

[17] See Chamberlain and Griliches [12] for such additional tests and an extension to the two-left-out-factors case. Adding another factor improves the fit significantly, reduces the implied error variance of IQ to 23 per cent and raises the schooling coefficient to .064.

12   ZVI GRILICHES

6. ON OVER DOING IT: A DIGRESSION[18]

Most of the discussion above has been asymmetric. It has focused on thinking about potential *upward* biases in the estimated β and trying to guard against them by adding "ability" or other types of variables (such as "background") to the original earnings function. But excessive zeal can eaily result in serious downward biases in our estimated $\hat{\beta}$'s. This is particularly true if, as is most often the case, our measures of schooling (S) are far from perfect, and especially if they too are subject to random errors of measurement.

One doesn't usually think that such a well defined variable as "years of school completed" could be subject to much recording or recall error. But in cross-sectional household interview data all of the variables are subject to some error. Even if the errors are small, their effect will be magnified as more variables are added to the equation in an attempt to control for "other possible sources of bias". We may kill the patient in our attempts to cure what may have been a rather minor desease originally.[19]

A small but not unrealistic numerical example may be of help here. Let the true equation be

$$y = .1S^* + .01A + u$$

where S^* is "true" unobserved level of schooling. The observed level of schooling is $S = S^* + e$, with e random and independent of S^*, and $\lambda = \sigma_e^2/\sigma_S^2 = .1$. That is, we are assuming that ten per cent of the observed variance of schooling is due to random measurement error, a figure that is of the right order of magnitude (cf. Bishop [6]). For simplicity we shall assume that A is measured without error. Let $\sigma_S = 3$, $\sigma_A = 15$, and $r_{AS} = .5$. Then, the simple least squares coefficient of schooling, ignoring A, equals

$$Eb_{ys} = \beta - \lambda\beta + \gamma b_{AS}$$
$$= .1 - .1 \times .1 + .01 \times 2.5 = .115$$

while including A in the equation leads to

$$Eb_{ys \cdot A} = \beta - \lambda\beta/(1 - r_{AS}^2)$$
$$= .1 - .1 \times .1/.75 = .087,$$

raising the downward bias due to errors of measurement by one-third. Now consider adding some more background variables (B) to the equation which really do not belong in it explicitly, affecting income only via schooling. Such variables, together with ability, may be correlated with schooling on the order of .7 or an

---

[18] This section can be thought of as a restatement of the point originally made by Friedman [**15**, pp. 85–89] in his "Digression on the Use of Partial Correlation Coefficients in Consumption Research" in the *Theory of the Consumption Function*. I am indebted to Gary Chamberlain for reminding me of this passage.

[19] This point has also been recently made by Bishop [**6**] and Welch [**48**]. It is worth restating, however.

Economic Demography I

$R^2_{S \cdot AB} = .5$. This would imply

$$Eb_{yS \cdot AB} = \beta - \lambda\beta/(1 - R^2_{S \cdot AB})$$
$$= .1 - .1 \times .1/.5 = .080,$$

or a doubling of the downward bias due to the originally rather small errors in the measurement of schooling. As more variables are added in, or as the range of schooling is restricted by considering only the within-family, between-brothers, or between-twins variance of schooling, the implied $R^2_{S \cdot AB...x}$ rises towards $1 - \lambda$ while the estimated schooling coefficient goes to zero. Clearly, the more variables we put into the equation which are related to the systematic components of schooling, and the better we "protect" ourselves against various possible biases, the worse we make the errors of measurement problem.

It is a sad fact that in doing empirical work we must continuously search for the passage between the Scylla of biased inferences due to left-out and confounded influences and the Charybdis of overzealously purging our data of most of their identifying variance, being left largely with noise and error in our hands. In a sense, we run into a kind of uncertainty principle: The amount of information contained in any one specific data set is finite and, therefore, as we keep asking finer and finer questions, our answers become more and more uncertain.[20]

7. THE ENDOGENEITY OF SCHOOLING[21]

There are (at least) two problems with simple least squares estimates of earnings functions. The first, and the one we have been discussing at length above, is the "ability" problem. That problem can be solved by either getting hold of a good ability measure or by estimating its effect in some errors-in-variables context. As serious, or perhaps even more so, is the second problem: Schooling is the result, at least in part, of optimizing behavior by individuals and their families. This behavior is based on some *anticipated* earnings function. To the extent that the "errors" (from the point of view of us as observers) in the ex-post and ex-ante earnings functions are correlated, they will be "transmitted" to the schooling equation and induce an additional correlation between schooling and these disturbances. This again suggests the use of simultaneous equations methods in estimating the coefficient of schooling in such equations.

Whether the second problem is really serious depends on one's view as to how close individuals are to guessing their own and the economy's future and to what extent their actions can be interpreted as optimizing. I would think that it is not as serious as it appears at first sight because of (i) the large influence of random, and probably unanticipated, events on the actual earnings experience of an individual and (ii) the large influence of parents, the state, teachers, and classmates on the actual level of schooling achieved by an individual, only part of which can be interpreted as the result of his own ex-ante optimizing behavior.

[20] For a vivid exposition of the uncertainty principle, see Bronowski [7, Chapter 11].

[21] This section parallels the discussion in Mincer [39, pp. 137–140] and the appendix to the second edition of Becker's [3] book. I am also indebted to Sherwin Rosen for many discussions of this topic.

14   ZVI GRILICHES

It is hard to be more precise about this, beyond such brief generalities. To do more one has to set up an explicit model of individual optimal behavior *and* embed it in a *general equilibrium* solution for the economy as a whole. The first task has been the focus of much recent work in human capital theory initiated by Ben-Porath's [5] seminal paper. By and large, it hasn't led to any econometrically tractable results. To get simple closed-form solutions for the optimal schooling levels and on-the-job training trajectories requires extremely strong assumptions about functional forms and individual behavior.

I shall borrow from Rosen [42] a very simple model to illustrate the various problems that arise in this context. Assume that the individual is trying to maximize his wealth (W) at "birth" (i.e., before deciding on schooling):

$$(7.1) \qquad W(S) = \int_{s}^{\infty} y(S, A, u) \, e^{-r(S+t)} \, dt$$

where $Y = y(S, A, u)$ is the anticipated earnings function which depends on schooling, ability, and other factors (u) unknown to us, but not to the chooser. The interest rate by which the individual discounts the future is r and t is the post-schooling time (experience) index. Note the strong assumptions: infinite life, no post-school investments or age effects, a constant rate of interest, earnings foregone as the only cost of schooling, and no subsidies or taxes. For this simplified model it can be shown (cf. Rosen [42]) that the marginal conditions are given by

$$(7.2) \qquad \frac{\partial Y}{\partial S} \Big/ r = y(S \dots)$$

which says that the present value of the marginal increment (in perpetuity) in income due to a change in schooling should equal foregone income per unit of time spent on schooling. The optimal individual level of S, say S^*, is the solution of this equation. If the y function has the form we have assumed earlier,

$$(7.3) \qquad Y = e^{\beta S + \gamma A + u},$$

then

$$(7.4) \qquad \frac{\partial Y}{\partial S} = \beta y(S \dots) = r y(S \dots), \quad \text{and} \quad \beta_i = r,$$

which gives us the interpretation of β as "the" rate of return but unfortunately produces no S^*. This is the case where the "demand" and "supply" functions are perfectly parallel, and either S^* is at its upper limit or at zero, or it is undefined. For a nontrivial solution we need either diminishing returns in the human capital accumulation function or increasing borrowing costs.

A simple extension of the above model will get us part of the way. Assume that some of the costs of schooling are subsidized by somebody (parents or the state) by the amount TR. Then (7.4) becomes

$$(7.5) \qquad \beta Y = r(Y - TR).$$

Substituting (7.3) for Y, taking logarithms, and solving for S gives

(7.6) $S^* = \dfrac{1}{\beta}\left[-\log\dfrac{r-\beta}{r} + \log TR - \gamma A\right].$

Note that in this formulation "ability" only affects the amount of initial human capital and, hence, the correlation between such ability and the optimal amount of schooling is *negative*! To get a positive effect of ability on schooling we have to allow it to interact with β, more able people accumulating more human capital per unit of schooling or, alternatively, let it lower the cost of schooling to the more able. The latter version would allow the more able to have more leisure or forego less income per unit of time in school or (more relevantly) per grade completed. If the real costs of schooling per unit of time are lower by the amount δA, then

(7.7) $\beta Y = r(Y - TR - \delta A)$

and

(7.8) $S^* = \dfrac{1}{\beta}\left[-\log\dfrac{r-\beta}{r} + \log(TR + \delta A) - \gamma A\right]$

with a possible positive net effect of A on S^*. Note that such an effect need not translate itself into a correlation with the disturbances in the earnings function. It makes schooling "cheaper" for the more able, but it doesn't lead employers to pay more for it given the achieved level of schooling.

This discussion also points out the possibility of a negative relationship between optimized schooling and the disturbance in the actual or expected income equation. Let us distinguish between expected income, foregone income, and "permanent" income, the piece that is joint to both concepts, and add another unmeasured individual income generating factor, μ_i, unrelated to the usual ability measure A (for example, "motivation" or "energy"). We can write "expected income" as

$EY = Y_p \cdot e^u$

where u's are the anticipated future differences in income that are unrelated to current income foregone, "net foregone income" as

$FY = Y_p \cdot e^t - TR - \delta A$

where t's are current transitory fluctuations which will not be transmitted into the future, and "permanent income" as

$Y_p = e^{\beta S + \delta A + \mu}.$

Then (7.8) can be rewritten as

(7.9) $S^* = \dfrac{1}{\beta}[\log(TR + \delta A) - \gamma A - \mu_i - \log\dfrac{1}{r}(re^{t_i} - \beta e^{u_i})].$

16   ZVI GRILICHES

This messy expression is not intended to provide a realistic schooling decision estimating equation but only to illustrate the possiblity that schooling and the disturbance in the earnings function may be negatively correlated, leading to a *downward* bias in the usual least squares estimates of the schooling coefficient and implying that the schooling variable, too, should be treated as endogenous and its coefficient estimated using simultaneous equations methods.

Such estimates are presented in Table IV for different subsamples of the NLS young men.[22] In addition to the ability variables, the schooling variables and associate variables such as experience are now considered endogenous. The estimates which use the late test scores (*KWW*) in the equation use the early test score (*IQ*) and family background variables as instruments for all three right-hand side endogenous variables (*EXSC, KWW,* and *S*66). The versions containing *IQ* use *KWW* as an instrument, instead. The latter is only legitimate if early schooling is assumed not to affect the later test. The results presented in Table IV, while not very precise, are quite surprising. They indicate that the original simple least squares estimates of the schooling coefficient may have *seriously under-estimated* rather than over-estimated it. Note also the drop in size and significance of the ability coefficients relative to the estimates presented in Table II. This is consistent with the view that they were "robbing" the schooling coefficient earlier. While the estimated coefficients of *S*66 are not very precise, they have the right sign in the

TABLE IV

EARNINGS FUNCTION COEFFICIENTS:
TSLS ESTIMATES WITH SCHOOLING ENDOGENEOUS
DIFFERENT NLS SAMPLES[a]

Coefficient of	Expected Variables Dependent Variable: *EXLOMY*			"Actual" Variables Not enrolled Dependent Variable: *LW*69
	N = 4601	*N* = 3025 a	b	*N* = 1362
EXSC	.098	.097	.085	.096
(*S*69 for cols. 4 and 5)	(.011)	(.022)	(.009)	(.017)
KWW	.012	.011		
	(.002)	(.003)		
S66	−.071	−.059		
	(.014)	(.046)		
IQ			.0020	−.006
			(.0011)	(.023)
SEE	.368	.356	.352	.339

[a]See notes to Tables I and II. Equations reported in Columns 1, 2, and 3 also contain age and dates variables. The equation in Column 4 contains, in addition, *XBT* (which is also treated as endogenous), *RNS, SMSA,* and *BRNS.* Excluded instrumental variables in columns 2, 3, and 5 are the same as in Table II. Estimates in Column 1 use *also* a dummy variable for observations with missing *IQ* scores and interactions of all other instrumental variables with this variable.

[22] The brothers discussed in Table III are a subsample of the second set and, hence, are not discussed explicitly here. It is not obvious how to superimpose the endogeneity of schooling onto a family structure. A two-factor model would allow for a differential dependence between schooling and the disturbance in the income equation. Such a model yields .064 as its estimate of β_1. See Chamberlain and Griliches [12] for more details on this.

expected earnings and schooling equations, and indicate a positive effect of early schooling on late tests ($\beta_2 > 0$). In short, treating schooling and ability symmetrically turns most of our original conclusions around.

8. COMMENTS AND CONCLUSIONS

We have had only time to discuss a few problems raised by such estimates. We have, for example, devoted almost no attention to what is currently a major empirical gap in such models: the lack of explicit measures of on-the-job training and the use of "experience" as a kind of trend or "residual" measure to approximate them. We need a more direct attack on this problem and more specific measures of the phenomenon itself. Here and more generally, advantage should be taken of the time series nature of the various survey panels that have become available. All of the studies mentioned, including my own, have yet to approach such data from a truly dynamic point of view. Looking at the process of investment in human capital in greater detail should teach us more about the real world and help us to develop better "complete" models.

As we move in that direction, we shall soon wish to abandon the monolithic concept of schooling and of one human capital and start looking for different decisions and different pay-offs at different levels and for different types of schooling. Unfortunately, as we do that, our samples will start shrinking again and the quality of our inferences will deteriorate. Here too, models which postulate common unobservables appearing in different equations may help us to impose more structure on the data and reduce the information loss that occurs when we are tempted to slice our data sets thinner and thinner.

In addition, we still have a serious conceptual problem left. All such models take the $y(S, A \ldots)$ function as given. Since it reflects peoples' estimates of future market opportunities it should be similar across individuals, errors of forecast aside. To the extent, however, that the β's differ across individuals, we will have errors due to the mismeasurement of actual human capital accumulation by the observed years of schooling.[23] But the correct β at the macro-level will be still the slope of the current market opportunities locus, and not the ex-ante β's of particular individuals. Unfortunately, we have almost no workable theory of how such a locus is actually determined (cf. Rosen [42 and 43] for the difficulties we get into when we ask such questions). An interpretation that makes some sense argues that because different levels of human capital can be produced in the long-run with a relatively high supply elasticity according to the production function (7.3), even if the different types of human capital are not perfectly substitutable on the demand side, the resulting loci of ex-post intersections of demand and supply schedules will lie roughly along the long-run supply schedule. In the shorter-run, given the long leads and lags in the production and utilization of human skills, one should expect that particular groups will deviate from such a schedule according to

---

[23] If "ability" is interpreted as implying different ex-ante β's, then there should be an interaction between the schooling and ability measures in the earnings equation. We have not been able to detect such interactions in our data.

18　　　　　　　　　　ZVI GRILICHES

their shorter-run supply and demand elasticities.[24] In any case, there is no good reason to expect that such loci will remain constant over time. To go beyond such crude "hedonic" functions will require more explicit theories of the demand and supply structure for human skills.

In the mean time we may wish to summarize what we have learned from this particular excursion. Two theoretical points are worth reiterating: (i) In optimizing models there is no good a priori reason to expect the "ability bias" (or the direct coefficient of a measure of ability in the earnings function) to be positive. Thus, it shouldn't be too surprising if it turns out to be small or negative. (ii) An asymmetrical attempt to protect oneself against possible biases by putting more variables into the equation or by looking only within finer and finer data cuts, can make matters worse, by exacerbating other biases already present in the data. The empirical evidence examined here also points in the same direction: (i) Treating the problem asymmetrically and including direct measures of "ability" in the earnings function indicates a relatively small direct contribution of "ability" to the explanation of the observed dispersion in expected and actual earnings. The implied upward bias in the estimated schooling coefficient is about .01. (ii) Allowing for errors in measurement in such ability measures does little to change these conclusions except increase the estimated bias by another .005 or so. But (iii) when schooling is treated symmetrically with ability measures, allowing it, too, to be subject to errors of measurement and to be correlated to the disturbance in the earnings function, the conclusions are reversed. The implied net bias is either nil or negative. In addition, (iv) a more detailed examination of data on brothers indicates that if we identify "ability" with the thing that is measured (albeit imperfectly) by test scores, and if we accept the underlying genetic model which postulates that such a variable has a family components of variance structure, then the "unobservable" that fits these requirements seems to have little to do with earnings beyond its indirect effect via schooling.

In a sense, we have circled around our problem and data. We started looking for biases and at first found little. We kept on looking for more and leaned over more until we suddenly found ourseves on the other side of the original question. The whole process of such a research venture is perhaps best described by the following conversation between Pooh and Rabbit:

> "How would it be," said Pooh slowly, "if, as soon as we're out of sight of this Pit, we try to find it again?"
> "What's the good of that?" said Rabbit.
> "Well," said Pooh, "we keep looking for Home and not finding it, so I thought that if we looked for this Pit, we'd be sure not to find it, which would be a Good Thing, because then we might find something that we weren't looking for, which might be just what we were looking for, really."
> "I don't see much sense in that," said Rabbit.
> "No," said Pooh humbly, "there isn't. But there was going to be when I began it. It's just that something happened to it on the way."
>
> A. A. Milne, *The House at Pooh Corner*

Harvard University

[24] Cf. Freeman [13 and 14] for work along such lines.

APPENDIX

THE DATA BASE

The examples in the text are based on several subsamples from the National Longitudinal Survey of Young Men. In this survey, a random sample of about 5,000 young men was interviewed in 1966, followed up annually through 1971, and bi-annually thereafter.[25] At the moment only the 1966 through 1970 surveys are publicly available. Besides the usual economic and demographic variables, a test of the "knowledge of the world of work" was administered at the time of the initial interview (1966) and IQ-type test scores were collected from the high-schools of the respondents. I shall interpret the first test (KWW) as a test of "late" ability and the second (IQ) as a test of "early" ability. Unfortunately, the latter tests are unavailable for about a third of the sample, including all those who did not continue school beyond the ninth grade.

To save on sampling costs the Census Bureau based this sample and the parallel samples on the older men, mature women, and young women on one larger sample of households. Thus, there is some overlap of family members in the various surveys. In particular we have succeeded in identifying over 1,000 brothers, a subset of which is used in the analysis reported in the text.

From our point of view, the basic difficulty with this sample is the extreme youth of the members. As of 1969 close to half of the total sample was still in school. Moreover, those who were out of school and working were only about 22 years old, on average, and had only an average of four years of work experience (see Table V for details). Hence, it is hard to interpret their current status as being a good indication of their ultimate success in life. However, in addition to current status, the respondents were also asked about their expected total educational attainment and their expected ("desired" at age 30) occupation.[26] I have scaled (valued) their (three-digit) occupational expectations, by the median earnings of all United States males in 1959 in these occupations, converting it thereby into an "expected" income concept. Taking logarithms gives the major dependent variable ($EXLOMY$) used above.

The use of such "expected" variables has several advantages and disadvantages:

    (i) It allows us to deal with expected income and schooling as of around the "overtaking" point and to ignore the difficulties created by the youthfulness of our cohort and the lack of explicit on-the-job training measures.

    (ii) It comes close to dealing with the ex-ante optimizing behavior of individuals, as discussed in the Becker [2] or Rosen [42] models, uncontaminated by the ex-post encounter with reality.

    (iii) Most importantly, it allows us to analyze almost the entire sample of individuals and to triple the available sample of brothers, avoiding also thereby the self-selection problem that would be posed by an analysis of only those who recently decided to stop their schooling.

The disadvantages are obvious:

    (i) We are dealing with expectations and not "reality".

    (ii) The use of occupational expectations as a proxy for income expectations ignores the expected returns to schooling and ability within occupations and the imposition of a uniform median income scale on the occupational expectations does not allow for differences in individual expectations about the differential future of various occupations.

    (iii) The causality from schooling to earnings is much less clear for expectational variables.

Nevertheless, I believe that the expectational data are of intrinsic interest and that the advantages enumerated above outweigh the disadvantages. In any case, one gets rather similar results when "real" data for the "not-enrolled in 1969" subsample are used (see Tables I and IV).

[25] See Griliches [26] and Parnes, et al. [41] for more details on these data. They are based on a national sample of the civilian non-institutional population of males who were 14 to 24 years old in 1966. Blacks were over-sampled in a 3 to 1 ratio. The original sample consisted of 5,225 individuals, of whom 3,734 were white. By 1969 about 23 per cent of the original sample was lost, 13 per cent of it only temporarily (to the army).

[26] These are answers to questions "As things now stand, how much more education do you think you will actually get?" and "What kind of work would you like to be doing when you are 30 years old?" The first question was asked in every survey, the second only in 1966 and 1969. The latest available answers were taken and dummy variables were added for those observations which did not originate from the 1969 survey ($DATELOMY$ and $DATE$ 66, identified collectively as $DATES$).

20   ZVI GRILICHES

TABLE V
DIFFERENT SUBSAMPLES OF YOUNG MEN FROM THE
NATIONAL LONGITUDINAL SURVEY
MEANS AND STANDARD DEVIATIONS[a]

Variable	All	All Valid IQ Scores	Brothers (pairs) Total	Within	Not Enrolled in 1969 All	With Valid IQ Scores
N	4601	3025	580		2026	1362
AGE 69	21.2	21.5	20.3		22.2	22.3
	3.2	3.0	2.3	1.4	3.2	3.2
EXSC[b]	13.8	14.4	14.8		12.7	13.4
	3.0	2.4	2.3	1.1	2.8	2.3
S69[c]					11.6	12.5
					2.4	1.9
S66[d]	10.7	11.5	11.3		10.8	11.6
	2.4	1.9	1.7	1.1	2.4	2.0
EXLOMY[e]	8.61	8.65	8.67		8.53	8.58
	.403	.386	.404	.270	.389	.366
LW69[f]					5.60	5.68
					.426	.398
KWW[g]	33.3	35.5	34.9		33.0	35.1
	8.6	7.6	7.7	4.5	9.0	7.9
IQ[h]		101.2	102.8			97.7
		15.9	15.9	7.5		15.3
FOMY14[i]	5120	5372	5418		4826	5095
	1951	1960	2179		1779	1777
BLACK	.27	.17	.20		.28	.19
CULTURE[j]	2.2	2.4	2.5		2.0	2.3
	.97	.80	.76		1.0	.9
SIBLINGS	3.3	2.9	3.6		3.6	3.1
	2.6	2.3	2.1		2.7	2.4
EXP69[k]					4.0	3.7
					3.1	2.8
XBT[l]					.70	.72
					.27	.18
SMSA[m]			.67		.61	.65
ROS[n] or RNS[o]	.34	.33	.32		.41	.33

[a] The lower number in a pair of numbers is the standard deviation.
[b] EXSC = Expected total schooling to be completed eventually, in years.
[c] S69 = Schooling completed in 1969, in years.
[d] S66 = Schooling completed in 1966, in years.
[e] EXLOMY = Logarithm of the 1959 median earnings (in dollars) of all males in the occupation expected (desired) at age 30.
[f] LW69 = Logarithm of hourly earnings (in cents) on the current or last job in 1969.
[g] KWW = Score on the "knowledge of the world of work" test, administered in 1966.
[h] IQ = Score on IQ-type tests, collected from the high school last attended by the respondent.
[i] FOMY14 = Occupation of father or head of household when respondent was 14, scaled by the median earnings of all United States males in this occupation in 1959.
[j] CULTURE = Index based on the availability of newspapers, magazines, and library cards in the respondents home.
[k] EXP69 = Post-school work experience. Estimated on the basis of the work record (in weeks) since 1966 and the date of first job after school and the date stopped school. Truncated at age 14, if respondent started working earlier. In years.
[l] $XBT = e^{-0.1 \times EXP69}$
[m] SMSA = Respondent in SMSA in 1969.
[n] ROS = Respondent in South when 14, columns 1–3.
[o] RNS = Respondent in South now (1969), columns 6–7.

We discuss the results for five subsamples: three subsamples based on expectational variables and two "not-enrolled in 1969" subsamples based on realized data on wage rates and schooling. The first sample is the largest; it contains almost all of the original sample ($N = 4601$). The main problem with this sample is that over 30 per cent of the respondents are missing IQ scores. The second sample is limited only to those having IQ scores ($N = 3025$). The third sample is a subsample of 290 pairs of brothers from sample two ($N = 580$). The fourth sample is a sample of all not enrolled young men in 1969 with valid wage and work experience data. It is a subsample of the first sample with $N = 2062$. The last sample is a subsample of the fourth sample, restricted to those respondents with valid IQ scores ($N = 1362$). Table V gives the means and standard deviations for the major variables in these samples and the definitions of these variables.

REFERENCES

[1] ALLEN, W.: *Without Feathers.* New York: Warner Books, 1975.

[2] BECKER, G. S.: "Human Capital and the Personal Distribution of Income," Woytinski Lecture No. 1. Ann Arbor: University of Michigan Press, 1967.

[3] ———: *Human Capital.* New York: NBER, 2nd edition, 1975.

[4] BEHRMAN, J. R., AND P. TAUBMAN: "Nature and Nature in the Determination of Earnings and Occupational Status," University of Pennsylvania, unpublished, 1975.

[5] BEN-PORATH, Y.: "The Production of Human Capital and the Life Cycle of Earnings," *Journal of Political Economy,* 75 (1967), 352–365.

[6] BISHOP, J. H.: "Biases in Measurement of the Productivity Benefits of Human Capital Investments," Institute for Research on Poverty, Discussion Paper No. 323-74, Madison, Wisconsin, 1974.

[7] BRONOWSKI, J.: *The Ascent of Man.* Boston: Little, Brown, 1974.

[8] CARDELL, N. S., AND M. HOPKINS: "The Influence of IQ on Income and on the Relationship Between Education and Income," Harvard University, unpublished, 1974.

[9] CHAMBERLAIN, G.: "Education, Income and Ability Revisited," Harvard Institute of Economics Research Discussion Paper No. 302, forthcoming in *Journal of Econometrics.*

[10] ———: "Unobservables in Econometric Models," unpublished Ph.D. dissertation, Harvard University, Cambridge, Ma., 1975.

[11] CHAMBERLAIN, G., AND Z. GRILICHES: "Unobservables with a Variance-Components Structure: Ability, Schooling and the Economic Success of Brothers," *International Economic Review,* 16 (1975), 422–449.

[12] ———: "More on Brothers," Harvard Institute of Economic Research Discussion Paper No. 469, Cambridge, Ma., 1976.

[13] FREEMAN, R. B.: *The Labor Market for College-Trained Manpower.* Cambridge, Ma.: Harvard University Press, 1971.

[14] ———: "The Declining Economic Value of Higher Education and the American Social System," Harvard Institute of Economic Research Discussion Paper No. 421, Cambridge, Ma., 1975.

[15] FRIEDMAN, M.: *A Theory of the Consumption Function.* Princeton, N.J.: NBER and Princeton University Press, 1975.

[16] FRIEDMAN, M., AND S. KUZNETS: *Income from Independent Professional Practice.* New York: NBER, 1945.

[17] GOLDBERGER, A. S.: "Unobservable Variables in Econometrics," in *Frontiers in Econometrics,* ed. by P. Zarembka. New York: Academic Press, 1974.

[18] GRILICHES, Z.: "Specification Bias in Estimates of Production Functions," *Journal of Farm Economics,* 39 (1957), 8–20.

[19] ———: "Measuring Inputs in Agriculture: A Critical Survey," *Journal of Farm Economics,* Proceedings issue, 42 (1960), 1411–1427.

[20] ———: "The Sources of Measured Productivity Growth: U.S. Agriculture, 1940–1960," *Journal of Political Economy,* 71 (1963), 331–346.

[21] ———: "Research Expenditures, Education, and the Aggregate Agricultural Production Function," *American Economic Review,* 54 (1964), 961–974.

[22] ———: "Production Functions in Manufacturing: Some Preliminary Results," in *The Theory and Empirical Analysis of Production,* ed. by M. Brown. Studies in Income and Wealth, Vol. 31. New York: Columbia for NBER, 1967.

[23] ———: "Notes on the Role of Education in Production Functions and Growth Accounting," in *Education and Income,* ed. by Lee Hansen. Studies in Income and Wealth, Vol. 35. New York: National Bureau of Economic Research, 1970.

[24] ———: "Errors in Variables and Other Unobservables," *Econometrica,* 42 (1974), 971–998.

[25] ———: "The Changing Economics of Education," Harvard Institute of Economic Research Discussion Paper No. 426, Cambridge, Ma., 1975.

22 ZVI GRILICHES

[26] ———: "Wages of Very Young Men," *Journal of Political Economy*, 84 (1976), Part 2, 569–586.

[27] GRILICHES, Z., AND W. MASON: "Education, Income and Ability," *Journal of Political Economy*, 80 (1972), Part 2, 74–103; and in *Structural Equation Models in the Social Sciences*, ed. by O. D. Duncan and A. S. Goldberger. New York: Seminar Press, 1973.

[28] HANOCH G.: "An Economic Analysis of Earnings and Schooling," *Journal of Human Resources*, 2 (1967), 310–329.

[29] HECKMAN, J., AND S. POLACHEK: "Empirical Evidence on the Functional Form of the Earnings-Schooling Relationship," *Journal of the American Statistical Association*, 69 (1974), 350–354.

[30] HOUTHAKKER, H. S.: "Education and Income," *Review of Economics and Statistics*, 41 (1959), 24–28.

[31] JORESKOG, K. G., AND A. S. GOLDBERGER: "Estimation of a Model with Multiple Indicators and Multiple Causes of a Single Latent Variable," *Journal of the American Statistical Association*, 70 (1975), 631–639.

[32] JORESKOG, K. G., G. T. GRUVAEUS, AND M. V. THILLO: "ACOVSM: A General Computer Program for Analysis of Covariance Structures," Research Bulletin RB-71-1, Princeton Educational Testing Service, 1971.

[33] JORESKOG, K. G., AND M. V. THILLO: "Lisrel: A General Computer Program for Estimating a Linear Structural Equations System Involving Multiple Indicators of Unmeasured Variables," Research Bulletin RB-72-56, Princeton Educational Testing Service, 1972.

[34] JORGENSON, D., AND Z. GRILICHES: "The Explanation of Productivity Change," *Review of Economic Studies*, 34 (1967), 249–283.

[35] LUCAS, R. E. B.: "Hedonic Price Functions," *Economic Inquiry*, 13 (1975), 157–178.

[36] MILLER, H. P.: "Annual and Lifetime Income in Relation to Education," *American Economic Review*, 50 (1960), 962–986.

[37] MINCER, J.: "Investment in Human Capital and Personal Income Distribution," *Journal of Political Economy*, 66 (1958), 281–302.

[38] ———: "On-the-Job Training: Costs, Returns and Some Implications," *Journal of Political Economy*, 70 (1962), Part 2, 50–79.

[39] ———: *Schooling, Experience, and Earnings*. New York: NBER, 1974.

[40] OLNECK, M.: "Bias in the Income-Schooling Relationship: Some Results from the Kalamazoo Brothers Study," presented at the Third World Congress of the Econometric Society at Toronto. Madison, Wisconsin, unpublished, 1975.

[41] PARNES, H. S., et al.: *Career Thresholds*, Vols. 1–4. Columbus, Ohio: Center for Human Resource Research, Ohio State University, 1970–1973.

[42] ROSEN, S.: "Income Generating Functions and Capital Accumulation," Harvard Institute of Economic Research, Discussion Paper No. 306, Cambridge, Ma., 1973.

[43] ———: "Hedonic Prices and Implicit Markets," *Journal of Political Economy*, 82 (1974), 34–55.

[44] TAUBMAN, P.: "The Determinants of Earnings: Genetic, Family and other Environments: A Study of White Male Twins," University of Pennsylvania, mimeograph, 1975.

[45] TAUBMAN, P., AND T. WALES: *Mental Ability and Higher Educational Attainment in the Twentieth Century*. Berkeley, California: NBER and Carnegie Commission on Higher Education, 1972.

[46] THEIL, H.: "Specification Errors and the Estimation of Economic Relationships," *Revue de L'Institut International de Statistique*, 25 (1957), 41–51.

[47] WALLACE, T. D., AND L. A. IHNEN: "Full Time Schooling in Life-Cycle Models of Human Capital Accumulation," *Journal of Political Economy*, 83 (1975), 137–156.

[48] WELCH, F.: "Human Capital Theory: Education, Discrimination, and Life-Cycles," *American Economic Review*, 65 (1975), 63–73.

[4]

THE
QUARTERLY JOURNAL
OF ECONOMICS

Vol. CVI   November 1991   Issue 4

DOES COMPULSORY SCHOOL ATTENDANCE AFFECT SCHOOLING AND EARNINGS?*

JOSHUA D. ANGRIST AND ALAN B. KRUEGER

We establish that season of birth is related to educational attainment because of school start age policy and compulsory school attendance laws. Individuals born in the beginning of the year start school at an older age, and can therefore drop out after completing less schooling than individuals born near the end of the year. Roughly 25 percent of potential dropouts remain in school because of compulsory schooling laws. We estimate the impact of compulsory schooling on earnings by using quarter of birth as an instrument for education. The instrumental variables estimate of the return to education is close to the ordinary least squares estimate, suggesting that there is little bias in conventional estimates.

Every developed country in the world has a compulsory schooling requirement, yet little is known about the effect these laws have on educational attainment and earnings.[1] This paper exploits an unusual natural experiment to estimate the impact of compulsory schooling laws in the United States. The experiment stems from the fact that children born in different months of the year start school at different ages, while compulsory schooling laws generally require students to remain in school until their sixteenth or seventeenth birthday. In effect, the interaction of school-entry requirements and compulsory schooling laws compel students born

*We thank Michael Boozer and Lisa Krueger for outstanding research assistance. Financial support was provided by the Princeton Industrial Relations Section, an NBER Olin Fellowship in Economics, and the National Science Foundation (SES-9012149). We are also grateful to Lawrence Katz, John Pencavel, an anonymous referee, and many seminar participants for helpful comments. The data and computer programs used in the preparation of this paper are available on request.

1. See OECD [1983] for a comparison of compulsory schooling laws in different countries.

in certain months to attend school longer than students born in other months. Because one's birthday is unlikely to be correlated with personal attributes other than age at school entry, season of birth generates exogenous variation in education that can be used to estimate the impact of compulsory schooling on education and earnings.

In the next section we present an analysis of data from three decennial Censuses that establishes that season of birth is indeed related to educational attainment. Remarkably, in virtually all of the birth cohorts that we have examined, children born in the first quarter of the year have a slightly *lower* average level of education than children born later in the year. School districts typically require a student to have turned age six by January 1 of the year in which he or she enters school (see HEW [1959]). Therefore, students born earlier in the year enter school at an older age and attain the legal dropout age at an earlier point in their educational careers than students born later in the year. If the fraction of students who want to drop out prior to the legal dropout age is independent of season of birth, then the observed seasonal pattern in education is consistent with the view that compulsory schooling constrains some students born later in the year to stay in school longer.

Two additional pieces of evidence link the seasonal pattern in education to the combined effect of age at school entry and compulsory schooling laws. First, the seasonal pattern in education is *not* evident in college graduation rates, nor is it evident in graduate school completion rates. Because compulsory schooling laws do not compel individuals to attend school beyond high school, this evidence supports our hypothesis that the relationship between years of schooling and date of birth is entirely due to compulsory schooling laws. Second, in comparing enrollment rates of fifteen- and sixteen-year olds in states that have an age sixteen schooling requirement with enrollment rates in states that have an age seventeen schooling requirement, we find a greater decline in the enrollment of sixteen-year olds in states that permit sixteen-year olds to leave school than in states that compel sixteen-year olds to attend school.

The variety of evidence presented in Section I establishes that compulsory schooling laws increase educational attainment for those covered by the laws. In Section II we consider whether students who attend school longer because of compulsory schooling receive higher earnings as a result of their increased schooling.

Two-stage least squares (TSLS) estimates are used in which the source of identification is variation in education that results solely from differences in season of birth—which, in turn, results from the effect of compulsory schooling laws. The results suggest that men who are forced to attend school by compulsory schooling laws earn higher wages as a result of their increased schooling. The estimated monetary return to an additional year of schooling for those who are compelled to attend school by compulsory schooling laws is about 7.5 percent, which is hardly different from the ordinary-least-squares (OLS) estimate of the return to education for all male workers.

To check further whether the estimated schooling-earnings relationship is truly a result of compulsory schooling, we explore the relationship between earnings and season of birth for the subsample of college graduates. Because these individuals were not constrained by compulsory schooling requirements, they form a natural control group to test whether season of birth affects earnings for reasons other than compulsory schooling. The results of this exploration suggest that there is no relationship between earnings and season of birth for men who are not constrained by compulsory schooling. This strengthens our interpretation that the TSLS estimate of the return to education reflects the effect of compulsory school attendance.

Our findings have important implications for the literature on omitted variables bias in estimates of the return to education (see Griliches [1977] and Willis [1986] for surveys). Economists have devoted a great deal of attention to correcting for bias in the return to education due to omitted ability and other factors that are positively correlated with both education and earnings. This type of a bias would occur, for example, in Spence's [1973] signaling model, where workers with high innate ability are assumed to find school less difficult and to obtain more schooling to signal their high ability. In contrast to this prediction, estimates based on season of birth indicate that, if anything, conventional OLS estimates are biased slightly downward.

I. SEASON OF BIRTH, COMPULSORY SCHOOLING, AND YEARS OF EDUCATION

If the fraction of students who desire to leave school before they reach the legal dropout age is constant across birthdays, a student's birthday should be expected to influence his or her ultimate educational attainment.[2] This relationship would be expected because, in the absence of rolling admissions to school, students born in different months of the year start school at different ages. This fact, in conjunction with compulsory schooling laws, which require students to attend school until they reach a specified birthday, produces a correlation between date of birth and years of schooling.[3]

Students who are born early in the calendar year are typically older when they enter school than children born late in the year. For example, our tabulation of the 1960 Census (the earliest census that contains quarter of birth), shows that, on average, boys born in the first quarter of the year enter first grade when they are 6.45 years old, whereas boys born in the fourth quarter of the year enter first grade when they are 6.07 years old.[4] This pattern arises because most school districts do not admit students to first grade unless they will attain age six by January 1 of the academic year in which they enter school. Consequently, students who were born in the beginning of the year are older when they start school than students who were born near the end of the year. Because children born in the first quarter of the year enter school at an older age, they attain the legal dropout age after having attended school for a shorter period of time than those born near the end of the year. Hence, if a fixed fraction of students is constrained by the compulsory attendance law, those born in the beginning of the year will have less schooling, on average, than those born near the end of the year.

Figures I, II, and III document the relationship between education and season of birth for men born 1930–1959. Each figure depicts the average years of completed schooling by quarter and

---

2. Beginning with Huntington [1938], researchers in many fields have investigated the effect of season of birth on a variety of biological and behavioral variables, ranging from fertility to schizophrenia. We consider the impact of other possible season of birth effects below.

3. Angrist and Krueger [1990] formally model the link between age at school entry and compulsory schooling. A testable implication of this model is that age at school entry should be linearly related to years of education. Data on men born 1946 to 1952 are generally consistent with this prediction.

4. Figures in the text are for normal boys born in 1952. The average entry age to first grade for those born in the second quarter is 6.28, and the average age of first graders born in the third quarter is 6.08. Other years show a similar pattern (see Angrist and Krueger [1990]). These averages are affected by holding back or advancing students beyond the normal start age, and by differences in start age policy across schools. Nonetheless, the results show that students born in the beginning of the year tend to enter school at an older age than those born near the end of the year.

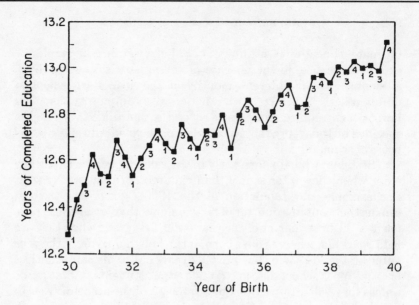

FIGURE I
Years of Education and Season of Birth
1980 Census
Note. Quarter of birth is listed below each observation.

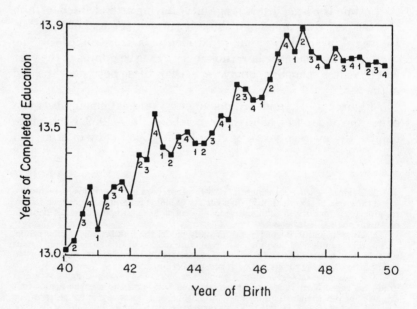

FIGURE II
Years of Education and Season of Birth
1980 Census
Note. Quarter of birth is listed below each observation.

984   QUARTERLY JOURNAL OF ECONOMICS

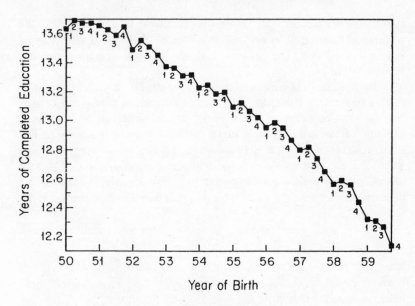

FIGURE III
Years of Education and Season of Birth
1980 Census
Note. Quarter of birth is listed below each observation.

year of birth, based on the sample of men in the 1980 Census, 5
percent Public Use Sample. (The data set used in the figures is
described in greater detail in Appendix 1.) The graphs show a
generally increasing trend in average education for cohorts born in
the 1930s and 1940s. For men born in the late 1950s, average
education is trending down, in part because by 1980 the younger
men in the cohort had not completed all of their schooling, and in
part because college attendance fell in the aftermath of the
Vietnam War.

A close examination of the plots indicates that there is a small
but persistent pattern in the average number of years of completed
education by quarter of birth. Average education is generally
higher for individuals born near the end of the year than for
individuals born early in the year. Furthermore, men born in the
fourth quarter of the year tend to have even more education than
men born in the beginning of the *following* year. The third quarter
births also often have a higher average number of years of
education than the following year's first quarter births. Moreover,

this seasonal pattern in years of education is exhibited by the cohorts of men that experienced a secular decline in educational levels, as well as by the cohorts that experienced a secular increase in educational levels.

To further examine the seasonal pattern in education, it is useful to remove the trend in years of education across cohorts. A flexible way to detrend the series is by subtracting off a moving average of the surrounding birth cohort's average education. For each quarter we define a two-period, two-sided moving average, $MA(+2,-2)$, as the average education of men born in the two preceding and two succeeding quarters.[5] Specifically, for the cohort of men born in year c and quarter j, the $MA(+2,-2)$, denoted MA_{cj}, is

$$MA_{cj} = (E_{-2} + E_{-1} + E_{+1} + E_{+2})/4,$$

where E_q is the average years of education attained by the cohort born q quarters before or after cohort c,j. The "detrended" education series is simply $E_{cj} - MA_{cj}$.

The relationship between season of birth and years of education for the detrended education series is depicted in Figure IV for each ten-year-age group. The figures clearly show that season of birth is related to years of completed education. For example, in 27 of the 29 birth years, the average education of men born in the first quarter of the year (January–March) is less than that predicted by the surrounding quarters based on the $MA(+2,-2)$.

To quantify the effect of season of birth on a variety of educational outcome variables, we estimated regressions of the form,

$$(E_{icj} - MA_{cj}) = \alpha + \sum_{j}^{3} \beta_j Q_{icj} + \epsilon_{icj}$$

$$\text{for } i = 1, \ldots, N_c; \quad c = 1, \ldots, 10; \quad j = 1,2,3,$$

where E_{icj} is the educational outcome variable for individual i in cohort c (i.e., years of education, graduated high school, graduated college, or years of post-high school education), MA_{cj} is the $MA(+2,-2)$ trend for the education variable, and Q_{icj} is a dummy

5. We note that none of our conclusions is qualitatively changed when we use a linear age trend (with age measured to the quarter of the year), a quadratic age trend, or unrestricted year-of-birth dummies.

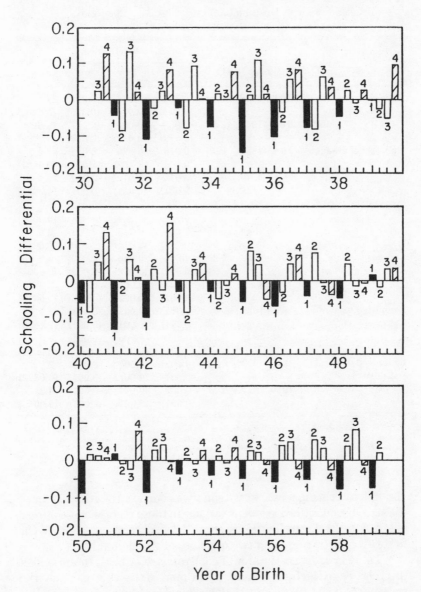

FIGURE IV
Season of Birth and Years of Schooling
Deviations from $MA(+2,-2)$

THE EFFECTS OF COMPULSORY SCHOOL ATTENDANCE   987

TABLE I
THE EFFECT OF QUARTER OF BIRTH ON VARIOUS EDUCATIONAL
OUTCOME VARIABLES

Outcome variable	Birth cohort	Mean	Quarter-of-birth effect[a]			F-test[b] [P-value]
			I	II	III	
Total years of education	1930–1939	12.79	−0.124 (0.017)	−0.086 (0.017)	−0.015 (0.016)	24.9 [0.0001]
	1940–1949	13.56	−0.085 (0.012)	−0.035 (0.012)	−0.017 (0.011)	18.6 [0.0001]
High school graduate	1930–1939	0.77	−0.019 (0.002)	−0.020 (0.002)	−0.004 (0.002)	46.4 [0.0001]
	1940–1949	0.86	−0.015 (0.001)	−0.012 (0.001)	−0.002 (0.001)	54.4 [0.0001]
Years of educ. for high school graduates	1930–1939	13.99	−0.004 (0.014)	0.051 (0.014)	0.012 (0.014)	5.9 [0.0006]
	1940–1949	14.28	0.005 (0.011)	0.043 (0.011)	−0.003 (0.010)	7.8 [0.0017]
College graduate	1930–1939	0.24	−0.005 (0.002)	0.003 (0.002)	0.002 (0.002)	5.0 [0.0021]
	1940–1949	0.30	−0.003 (0.002)	0.004 (0.002)	0.000 (0.002)	5.0 [0.0018]
Completed master's degree	1930–1939	0.09	−0.001 (0.001)	0.002 (0.001)	−0.001 (0.001)	1.7 [0.1599]
	1940–1949	0.11	0.000 (0.001)	0.004 (0.001)	0.001 (0.001)	3.9 [0.0091]
Completed doctoral degree	1930–1939	0.03	0.002 (0.001)	0.003 (0.001)	0.000 (0.001)	2.9 [0.0332]
	1940–1949	0.04	−0.002 (0.001)	0.001 (0.001)	−0.001 (0.001)	4.3 [0.0050]

a. Standard errors are in parentheses. An $MA(+2, -2)$ trend term was subtracted from each dependent variable. The data set contains men from the 1980 Census, 5 percent Public Use Sample. Sample size is 312,718 for 1930–1939 cohort and is 457,181 for 1940–1949 cohort.
b. F-statistic is for a test of the hypothesis that the quarter-of-birth dummies jointly have no effect.

variable indicating whether person i was born in the jth quarter of the year. Because the dependent variable in these regressions is purged of $MA(+2,-2)$ effects, it is necessary to delete observations born in the first two quarters and last two quarters of the sample.

Table I reports estimates of each quarter of birth (main) effect (β_j) relative to the fourth quarter, for men in the 1980 Census who were born in the 1930s and 1940s.[6] The F-tests reported in the last

---

6. We focus on men born in the 1930s and 1940s because many individuals in the 1950s birth cohorts had not yet completed their education by 1980.

column of the table indicate that, after removing trend, the small within-year-of-birth differences in average years of education are highly statistically significant. For both cohorts the average number of completed years of schooling is about one tenth of a year lower for men born in the first quarter of the year than for men born in the last quarter of the year. Similarly, the table shows that, for the 1930s cohort, men born in the first quarter of the year are 1.9 percentage points less likely to graduate from high school than men born in the last quarter of the year.[7] For the 1940s cohort the gap in the high school graduation rate between first and fourth quarter births is 1.5 percentage points. Because the high school dropout rate is 23 percent for men born in the 1930s and 14 percent for men born in the 1940s, first quarter births are roughly 10 percent more likely to drop out of high school than fourth quarter births.

The seasonal differences in years of education and in high school graduation rates are smaller for men born in the 1940s than for men born in the 1930s, but the quarter-of-birth effects are still statistically significant. As discussed below, one explanation for the attenuation of the seasonal pattern in education over time is that compulsory attendance laws are less likely to be a binding constraint on more recent cohorts.

The evidence that children born in the first quarter of the year tend to enter school at a slightly older age than other children, and that children born in the first quarter of the year also tend to obtain less education, is at least superficially consistent with the simple age at entry/compulsory schooling model.

To further explore whether the differences in education by season of birth are caused by compulsory schooling laws, the bottom part of Table I estimates the same set of equations for measures of post-secondary educational achievement. This sample provides a test of whether season of birth influences education even for those who are not constrained by compulsory schooling laws (because compulsory schooling laws exempt students who have graduated from high school). Consequently, if compulsory schooling is responsible for the seasonal pattern in education, one would not expect to find such a pattern for individuals who have some post-secondary education.

The seasonal pattern in years of education is much less

7. Notice that because the quarter-of-birth dummies are mutually exclusive, the linear probability model is appropriate in this situation.

pronounced and quite different for the subsample of individuals who have at least a high school education. In this sample, second quarter births tend to have higher average education, while those born in other quarters have about equal levels of education. The difference in average years of education between first and fourth quarter births is statistically insignificant for high school graduates. On the other hand, first quarter births are slightly less likely to graduate from college, and the gap is statistically significant. In view of the enormous sample sizes (in excess of 300,000 observations), however, the F-tests are close to classical critical values for the null hypothesis that season of birth is unrelated to post-high school educational outcomes.

Table I also shows the effect of quarter of birth on the proportion of men who have a master's degree and on the proportion of men who have a doctoral degree.[8] These results show no discernible pattern in educational achievement by season of birth. Because individuals with higher degrees did not discontinue their education as soon as they were legally permitted, these findings provide further support for the view that compulsory schooling is responsible for the seasonal pattern in education. Moreover, because season of birth is correlated with age at school entry, the lack of a seasonal pattern in postsecondary education suggests that differences in school entry age alone do not have a significant effect on educational attainment. In the absence of compulsory schooling, therefore, we would not expect to find differences in education by season of birth.

A. *Direct Evidence on the Effect of Compulsory Schooling Laws*

For the combined effects of compulsory schooling and school start age to adequately explain the seasonal pattern in education, it must be the case that compulsory attendance laws effectively force some students to stay in school longer than they desire. Table II provides evidence that compulsory schooling laws are effective in compelling a small proportion of students to remain in school until they attain the legal dropout age. This evidence makes use of the fact that some states allow students to drop out of school upon attaining their sixteenth birthday, while others compel students to

8. For purposes of Table I we assumed that individuals with a college degree completed sixteen or more years of education, individuals with a master's degree completed eighteen or more years of education, and individuals with a doctoral degree completed twenty or more years of education.

990   *QUARTERLY JOURNAL OF ECONOMICS*

TABLE II

PERCENTAGE OF AGE GROUP ENROLLED IN SCHOOL BY BIRTHDAY AND LEGAL
DROPOUT AGE[a]

| Date of birth | Type of state law[b] | | |
	School-leaving age: 16 (1)	School-leaving age: 17 or 18 (2)	Column (1) − (2)
	Percent enrolled April 1, 1960		
1. Jan 1–Mar 31, 1944	87.6	91.0	−3.4
(age 16)	(0.6)	(0.9)	(1.1)
2. Apr 1–Dec 31, 1944	92.1	91.6	0.5
(age 15)	(0.3)	(0.5)	(0.6)
3. Within-state diff.	−4.5	−0.6	−4.0
(row 1 − row 2)	(0.7)	(1.0)	(1.2)
	Percent enrolled April 1, 1970		
4. Jan 1–Mar 31, 1954	94.2	95.8	−1.6
(age 16)	(0.3)	(0.5)	(0.6)
5. Apr 1–Dec 31, 1954	96.1	95.7	0.4
(age 15)	(0.1)	(0.3)	(0.3)
6. Within-state diff.	−1.9	0.1	−2.0
(row 1 − row 2)	(0.3)	(0.6)	(0.6)
	Percent enrolled April 1, 1980		
7. Jan 1–Mar 31, 1964	95.0	96.2	−1.2
(age 16)	(0.1)	(0.2)	(0.2)
8. Apr 1–Dec 31, 1964	97.0	97.7	−0.7
(age 15)	(0.1)	(0.1)	(0.1)
9. Within-state diff.	−2.0	−1.5	0.5
(row 1 − row 2)	(0.1)	(0.2)	(0.3)

a. Standard errors are in parentheses.
b. Data set used to compute rows 1–3 is the 1960 Census, 1 percent Public Use Sample; data set used to compute rows 4–6 is 1970 Census, 1 percent State Public Use Sample (15 percent form); data set used to compute rows 7–9 is the 1980 Census, 5 percent Public Use Sample. Each sample contains both boys and girls. Sample sizes are 4,153 for row 1; 12,512 for row 2; 7,758 for row 4; 24,636 for row 5; 42,740 for row 7; and 131,020 for row 8.

attend school until their seventeenth or eighteenth birthday.[9] A summary of the compulsory schooling requirement in effect in each state in 1960, 1970, and 1980 is provided in Appendix 2.

The first three rows of Table II focus on individuals who were

9. There are three exceptions: Mississippi and South Carolina eliminated their compulsory schooling laws in response to *Brown v. Board of Education* in 1954. South Carolina reenacted compulsory schooling in 1967, and Mississippi in 1983. In 1960 Maine had an age fifteen compulsory schooling law. Ehrenberg and Marcus [1982] and Edwards [1978] also provide evidence on the impact of compulsory schooling legislation on school enrollment.

THE EFFECTS OF COMPULSORY SCHOOL ATTENDANCE   991

born in 1944 using data from the 1960 Census.[10] Students who were born between January and March of 1944 were age sixteen when the 1960 Census was conducted (Census Day is April 1), while those who were born between April and December of 1944 were not yet age sixteen. Consequently, students born in January–March were able to drop out of school in the states that had an age sixteen compulsory attendance law, but were not able to legally drop out of school in states that had an age seventeen or age eighteen compulsory attendance law. On the other hand, students born in April–December of 1944 were not able to legally withdraw from school under either regime.

This institutional framework allows for a difference-in-differences analysis. The figures in columns (1) and (2) of Table II are the percentage of students enrolled in school on April 1, broken down by the compulsory schooling age in the state and by the age of the student. The results for 1960 are striking. In states where sixteen-year olds are permitted to drop out of school, the percent of students enrolled is 4.5 points lower for students who have turned age sixteen than for those who are almost age sixteen (see row 3). In contrast, there is only a statistically insignificant 0.6 percentage point decline in the enrollment rate between age fifteen and sixteen in states where students must wait until age seventeen or eighteen to drop out.

Column 3 of Table II reports the difference in the enrollment rate for children of a given age between states with different compulsory schooling laws. For example, sixteen year olds are 3.4 percent less likely to be enrolled in states with a school-leaving age of sixteen, whereas fifteen year olds have a similar enrollment rate in both sets of states. The contrast between the within-state and within-age-group comparisons is a difference-in-differences estimator of the effect of compulsory school attendance that controls for both additive age and state effects. For the 1944 cohort the difference-in-differences estimate indicates that compulsory school attendance laws increased the enrollment rate by four percentage points in states with an age seventeen or age eighteen minimum schooling requirement.

Rows 4–6 of Table II report the corresponding statistics for individuals born in 1954 using data from the 1970 Census, and

---

10. The sample underlying this table includes both boys and girls. Wisconsin and Texas require students to complete the school term in which they reach the legal dropout age, and therefore were dropped from the sample. In addition, school districts in metropolitan sections of New York were excluded from the sample because they are allowed to alter the compulsory schooling requirement.

rows 7–9 report the corresponding statistics for individuals born in 1964 using data from the 1980 Census. These results lead to a similar conclusion: the dropout rate is increased for students when they become legally eligible to leave school. The difference-in-differences estimates of the enrollment effect of compulsory schooling for the 1954 and 1964 cohorts are 2 and 0.5 percentage points. A significant number of students leave school around the time of their birthday, although the effect of compulsory attendance laws is smaller in 1970 than in 1960, and smaller still in 1980 than in 1970.

Although the fraction of students kept in school by compulsory education laws may seem small relative to the total population of students, the estimate represents a nontrivial fraction of the pool of students who eventually drop out of high school. In 1960 about 12 percent of sixteen-year-old students had dropped out of school in states where they were permitted to do so. Therefore, our estimates imply that in 1960 compulsory attendance laws kept approximately one third of potential dropouts in school. By 1980 only 5 percent of sixteen-year olds had dropped out of school, so our estimates imply that compulsory schooling laws kept roughly 10 percent of potential dropouts in school in that year.

The waning effect of compulsory schooling may result from an increase in desired levels of education for more recent cohorts, which makes compulsory schooling less of a constraint, or from increasingly lax enforcement of compulsory schooling laws. In either case the declining effect of compulsory schooling laws is consistent with the smaller seasonal pattern in education for recent cohorts.

B. Why Do Compulsory Schooling Laws Work?

The evidence presented so far suggests that compulsory schooling laws are effective at increasing the enrollment and education of at least some students. What explains the efficacy of this legislation? Although we'do not have any direct evidence on why compulsory schooling laws are effective, in principle, there are two main enforcement mechanisms for the laws.[11] First, the Fair Labor Standards Act prohibits the employment of children under age fourteen, and every state in the United States has a child labor

---

11. This subsection draws heavily from information presented in Kotin and Aikman [1980], to which the reader is referred for further information on the enforcement and requirements of state compulsory schooling laws.

THE EFFECTS OF COMPULSORY SCHOOL ATTENDANCE   993

law that further restricts employment of youths. In most states children are prohibited from working during school hours unless they have reached the compulsory schooling age in that state. Moreover, in all states young workers must obtain a work certificate (or work permit) to be eligible for employment. These work certificates are often administered and granted by the schools themselves, which provides an opportunity to monitor whether students below the compulsory school age are seeking employment. Consequently, child labor laws restrict or prohibit children of compulsory school age from participating in the work force, the principal alternative to attending school.

Second, compulsory school attendance laws provide for direct enforcement and policing of school attendance. Every state compulsory schooling law provides for truant officers to administer the law, and for other enforcement mechanisms. Truant officers typically have broad powers, such as the right to take children into custody without a warrant. However, the principal responsibility for school attendance rests with the child's parents. A parent who fails to send his or her child to school could face criminal penalties, such as misdemeanor-level fines or imprisonment.

Although we have outlined the ways in which compulsory schooling laws are enforced, it should also be noted that there are several exemptions to compulsory schooling laws in many states. As mentioned previously, students are exempt from compulsory school attendance if they have a high school or equivalent degree. Furthermore, in many states children are exempt from the schooling requirement if they suffer from certain physical, mental, or emotional disabilities; if they live far from a school; or if they are disruptive to other students. Additionally, all states are constitutionally bound to allow students to attend private schools in lieu of public schools, and 26 states permit "home schooling" as an alternative to public schools.

Finally, we note that compulsory schooling laws are believed to effectively increase schooling in other countries as well (see OECD [1983]). Moreover, the fact that age at school entry is correlated with educational attainment because of compulsory schooling is well-known in countries where the impact of compulsory schooling laws is more prominent. For example, a federal government document from Australia contains the following caution: "There are differences between states in the ages of students at similar levels of schooling. This is largely due to the time students may commence school [which differs by as much as one year across states]. Such factors should be borne in mind when utilizing school leaver data" [Department of Employment, Education, and Training, 1987].

II. ESTIMATING THE RETURN TO EDUCATION

Do the small differences in education for men born in different months of the year translate into differences in earnings? This question is first addressed in Figure V, which presents a graph of the mean log weekly wage of men age 30–49 (born 1930–1949), by quarter of birth. The data used to create the figure are drawn from the 1980 Census, and are described in detail in Appendix 1.

Two important features of the data can be observed in Figure V. First, men born in the first quarter of the year—who, on average, have lower education—also tend to earn slightly less per week than men born in surrounding months. Second, the age-earnings profile is positively sloped for men between ages 30 and 39 (born 1940–1949), but fairly flat for men between ages 40 and 49

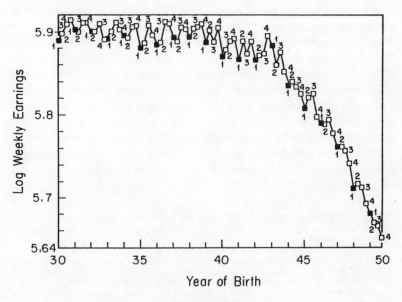

FIGURE V
Mean Log Weekly Wage, by Quarter of Birth
All Men Born 1930–1949; 1980 Census

(born 1930–1939).[12] The latter observation is important because quarter of birth is naturally correlated with age: men born in the beginning of the year are older than those born at the end of the year, and will have higher earnings if they are on the upward sloping portion of the age-earnings profile. Therefore, we mainly focus on 40–49 year-old men, whose wages are hardly related to age. Analyzing this sample enables us to avoid the effects of life-cycle changes in earnings that are correlated with quarter of birth.

In Table III we use the seasonal pattern in education to calculate the rate of return to a year of education based on an application of Wald's [1940] method of fitting straight lines. This estimator simply computes the return to education as the ratio of the difference in earnings by quarter of birth to the difference in years of education by quarter of birth. We present estimates that compare earnings and education between men born in the first quarter of the year and men born in the last three quarters of the year.[13] This comparison is selected because the first quarter showed the largest blip in education in Figure IV. Panel A of Table III provides estimates for the sample of 40–49 year-old men (born 1920–1929) in the 1970 Census, and Panel 4B provides estimates for 40–49 year-old men (born 1930–1939) in the 1980 Census.[14]

The results of the Wald estimates are very similar to typical OLS estimates of the return to education for this population. In 1970, for example, men born in the first quarter of the year earned a 0.7 percent lower weekly wage and had completed 0.126 fewer years of education than men born in the last three quarters of the year. The ratio of these two numbers, 0.072, is a consistent estimate of the return to education provided that season of birth is uncorrelated with earnings determinants other than education. Intuitively, the Wald estimator is likely to provide a consistent

12. Longitudinal estimates of the age-earnings profile, which follow the same cohorts over time, also typically show a relatively flat relationship between age and earnings for 40–49 year-old men.

13. The Wald estimate is a special case of instrumental variables [Durbin, 1954]. In this case the Wald estimate is equivalent to instrumental variables where a dummy variable indicating whether an individual is born in the first quarter of the year is used as an instrument for education, and there are no covariates.

14. Elsewhere, we have shown that World War II veteran status is related to quarter of birth for men born between 1925 and 1928. This is not an issue for men born after 1930, however, because they were not covered by the World War II draft. Furthermore, the veterans' earnings premium for men born 1925–1928 is negative but very close to zero (see Angrist and Krueger [1989]).

TABLE III
PANEL A: WALD ESTIMATES FOR 1970 CENSUS—MEN BORN 1920–1929[a]

	(1) Born in 1st quarter of year	(2) Born in 2nd, 3rd, or 4th quarter of year	(3) Difference (std. error) (1) − (2)
ln (wkly. wage)	5.1484	5.1574	−0.00898 (0.00301)
Education	11.3996	11.5252	−0.1256 (0.0155)
Wald est. of return to education			0.0715 (0.0219)
OLS return to education[b]			0.0801 (0.0004)

Panel B: Wald Estimates for 1980 Census—Men Born 1930–1939

	(1) Born in 1st quarter of year	(2) Born in 2nd, 3rd, or 4th quarter of year	(3) Difference (std. error) (1) − (2)
ln (wkly. wage)	5.8916	5.9027	−0.01110 (0.00274)
Education	12.6881	12.7969	−0.1088 (0.0132)
Wald est. of return to education			0.1020 (0.0239)
OLS return to education			0.0709 (0.0003)

a. The sample size is 247,199 in Panel A, and 327,509 in Panel B. Each sample consists of males born in the United States who had positive earnings in the year preceding the survey. The 1980 Census sample is drawn from the 5 percent sample, and the 1970 Census sample is from the State, County, and Neighborhoods 1 percent samples.

b. The OLS return to education was estimated from a bivariate regression of log weekly earnings on years of education.

estimate in this case because unobserved earnings determinants (e.g., ability) are likely to be uniformly distributed across people born on different dates of the year.[15]

The last row of each panel in Table III provides the OLS

15. We note that our procedure will slightly understate the return to education because first-quarter births, whose birthdays occur midterm, are more likely to attend some schooling beyond their last year completed. Consequently, the difference in years of school attended between first and later quarters of birth is less than the difference in years of school completed. Since the difference in completed education rather than the difference in years of school attended appears in the denominator of the Wald estimator, our estimate is biased downward. In practice, however, this is a small bias because the difference in completion rates is small.

estimate of the return to education. The OLS estimate is the coefficient on education from a bivariate regression of the log weekly wage on years of education. The Wald estimate of the return to education (0.072) is slightly less than the OLS estimate (0.080) for middle-aged men in the 1970 Census, but the difference between the two estimates is not statistically significant.

Panel B of Table III presents the corresponding set of estimates for 40–49 year-old men (born 1930–1939) using the 1980 Census. For this sample the Wald estimate of the return to education, 0.102, is greater than the estimate from an OLS regression. But again, the difference between the Wald and OLS estimates of the return to education is not statistically significant.

We have also computed Wald estimates of the return to education for 30–39 year-old men using the 1970 and 1980 Censuses. In contrast to the estimates for 40–49 year-old men, estimates for younger men yield a trivial and statistically insignificant return to education. However, unless the effect of age on earnings is taken into account, simple Wald estimates for men this age will be biased downward because they are on the upward sloping portion of the age-earnings profile.

A. TSLS Estimates

To improve efficiency of the estimates and control for age-related trends in earnings, we estimated the following TSLS model:

$$(1) \qquad E_i = X_i\pi + \Sigma_c Y_{ic}\delta_c + \Sigma_c\Sigma_j Y_{ic}Q_{ij}\theta_{jc} + \epsilon_i$$

$$(2) \qquad \ln W_i = X_i\beta + \Sigma_c Y_{ic}\xi_c + \rho E_i + \mu_i,$$

where E_i is the education of the ith individual, X_i is a vector of covariates, Q_{ij} is a dummy variable indicating whether the individual was born in quarter j ($j = 1,2,3$), and Y_{ic} is a dummy variable indicating whether the individual was born in year c ($c = 1, \ldots, 10$), and W_i is the weekly wage. The coefficient ρ is the return to education. If the residual in the wage equation, μ, is correlated with years of education due to, say, omitted variables, OLS estimates of the return to education will be biased.

The excluded instruments from the wage equation in the TSLS estimates are three quarter-of-birth dummies interacted with nine year-of-birth dummies. Because year-of-birth dummies are also included in the wage equations, the effect of education is identified by variation in education across quarters of birth within each birth year.[16] Quarter of birth (Q_j) is a legitimate instrument if it is uncorrelated with μ and correlated with education.

Tables IV, V, and VI present a series of TSLS estimates of equation (2) for the 1920–1929 cohort, 1930–1939 cohort, and 1940–1949 cohort, respectively. For comparison, the OLS and TSLS estimates of each specification are presented. For example, column (1) of Table IV shows that the OLS estimate of the return to education for 40–49 year-old men in the 1970 Census is 0.080 (with a t-ratio of 200.5), holding year-of-birth effects constant. Column (2) shows that when the same model is estimated by TSLS using quarter-of-birth dummies as instruments for years of education, the return to education is 0.077 (with a t-ratio of 5.1). In columns (3) and (4) we add a quadratic age term to the OLS and TSLS equations. This variable, which is measured up to the quarter of a year, is included to control for within-year-of-birth age effects on earnings.

The remaining columns repeat the first four columns, but also include race dummies, a dummy for residence in an SMSA, a marital status dummy, and eight region-of-residence dummies. Regardless of the set of included regressors, the TSLS and OLS estimates of the return to education for this sample are close in magnitude, and the difference between them is never statistically significant.[17]

In Table V we present estimates of the same set of models using 40–49 year-old men from the 1980 Census. Again, the similarity between the various OLS and TSLS estimates of the return to education is striking. For example, comparing the OLS and TSLS models in columns (7) and (8)—which include quadratic age and several covariates—the OLS estimate of the return to education is 0.063 (with a t-ratio of 210.7), and the TSLS estimate of the return to education is 0.060 (with a t-ratio of 2).

Table VI presents estimates for 30–39-year-old men (born 1940–1949) using data from the 1980 Census. This sample has a

---

16. The TSLS estimates differ from the Wald estimates in two important respects. First, the TSLS estimates include covariates. Second, the TSLS models are identified by the variation in education across each quarter of birth in each year, whereas the Wald estimate is identified by the overall difference in education between the first quarter and the rest of the year.

17. Because the OLS estimates of the return to education are extremely precise with these large samples, the standard error of the TSLS estimates is approximately equal to the standard error of the difference between the OLS and TSLS estimates. The TSLS standard error can thus be used to perform an approximate Hausman [1978] specification test.

THE EFFECTS OF COMPULSORY SCHOOL ATTENDANCE   999

TABLE IV

OLS AND TSLS ESTIMATES OF THE RETURN TO EDUCATION FOR MEN BORN 1920–1929: 1970 CENSUS[a]

Independent variable	(1) OLS	(2) TSLS	(3) OLS	(4) TSLS	(5) OLS	(6) TSLS	(7) OLS	(8) TSLS
Years of education	0.0802 (0.0004)	0.0769 (0.0150)	0.0802 (0.0004)	0.1310 (0.0334)	0.0701 (0.0004)	0.0669 (0.0151)	0.0701 (0.0004)	0.1007 (0.0334)
Race (1 = black)	—	—	—	—	0.2980 (0.0043)	-0.3055 (0.0353)	-0.2980 (0.0043)	-0.2271 (0.0776)
SMSA (1 = center city)	—	—	—	—	0.1343 (0.0026)	0.1362 (0.0092)	0.1343 (0.0026)	0.1163 (0.0198)
Married (1 = married)	—	—	—	—	0.2928 (0.0037)	0.2941 (0.0072)	0.2928 (0.0037)	0.2804 (0.0141)
9 Year-of-birth dummies	Yes	Yes	Yes	Yes	Yes	Yes	Yes	Yes
8 Region of residence dummies	No	No	No	No	Yes	Yes	Yes	Yes
Age	—	—	0.1446 (0.0676)	0.1409 (0.0704)	—	—	0.1162 (0.0652)	0.1170 (0.0662)
Age-squared	—	—	-0.0015 (0.0007)	-0.0014 (0.0008)	—	—	-0.0013 (0.0007)	-0.0012 (0.0007)
χ^2 [dof]	—	36.0 [29]	—	25.6 [27]	—	34.2 [29]	—	28.8 [27]

a. Standard errors are in parentheses. Sample size is 247,199. Instruments are a full set of quarter-of-birth times year-of-birth interactions. The sample consists of males born in the United States. The sample is drawn from the State, County, and Neighborhoods 1 percent samples of the 1970 Census (15 percent form). The dependent variable is the log of weekly earnings. Age and age-squared are measured in quarters of years. Each equation also includes an intercept.

TABLE V

OLS AND TSLS ESTIMATES OF THE RETURN TO EDUCATION FOR MEN BORN 1930–1939: 1980 CENSUS[a]

Independent variable	(1) OLS	(2) TSLS	(3) OLS	(4) TSLS	(5) OLS	(6) TSLS	(7) OLS	(8) TSLS
Years of education	0.0711	0.0891	0.0711	0.0760	0.0632	0.0806	6.0632	0.0600
	(0.0003)	(0.0161)	(0.0003)	(0.0290)	(0.0003)	(0.0164)	(0.0003)	(0.0299)
Race (1 = black)	—	—	—	—	-0.2575	-0.2302	-0.2575	-0.2626
					(0.0040)	(0.0261)	(0.0040)	(0.0458)
SMSA (1 = center city)	—	—	—	—	0.1763	0.1581	0.1763	0.1797
					(0.0029)	(0.0174)	(0.0029)	(0.0305)
Married (1 = married)	—	—	—	—	0.2479	0.2440	0.2479	0.2486
					(0.0032)	(0.0049)	(0.0032)	(0.0073)
9 Year-of-birth dummies	Yes	Yes	Yes	Yes	Yes	Yes	Yes	Yes
8 Region-of-residence dummies	No	No	No	No	Yes	Yes	Yes	Yes
Age	—	—	-0.0772	-0.0801	—	—	-0.0760	-0.0741
			(0.0621)	(0.0645)			(0.0604)	(0.0626)
Age-squared	—	—	0.0008	0.0008	—	—	0.0008	0.0007
			(0.0007)	(0.0007)			(0.0007)	(0.0007)
χ^2 [dof]	—	25.4 [29]	—	23.1 [27]	—	22.5 [29]	—	19.6 [27]

a. Standard errors are in parentheses. Sample size is 329,509. Instruments are a full set of quarter-of-birth times year-of-birth interactions. The sample consists of males born in the United States. The sample is drawn from the 5 percent sample of the 1980 Census. The dependent variable is the log of weekly earnings. Age and age-squared are measured in quarters of years. Each equation also includes an intercept.

TABLE VI

OLS AND TSLS ESTIMATES OF THE RETURN TO EDUCATION FOR MEN BORN 1940–1949: 1980 CENSUS[a]

Independent variable	(1) OLS	(2) TSLS	(3) OLS	(4) TSLS	(5) OLS	(6) TSLS	(7) OLS	(8) TSLS
Years of education	0.0573	0.0553	0.0573	0.0948	0.0520	0.0393	0.0521	0.0779
	(0.0003)	(0.0138)	(0.0003)	(0.0223)	(0.0003)	(0.0145)	(0.0003)	(0.0239)
Race (1 = black)	—	—	—	—	−0.2107	−0.2266	−0.2108	−0.1786
					(0.0032)	(0.0183)	(0.0032)	(0.0296)
SMSA (1 = center city)	—	—	—	—	0.1418	0.1535	0.1419	0.1182
					(0.0023)	(0.0135)	(0.0023)	(0.0220)
Married (1 = married)	—	—	—	—	0.2445	0.2442	0.2444	0.2450
					(0.0022)	(0.0022)	(0.0022)	(0.0023)
9 Year-of-birth dummies	Yes	Yes	Yes	Yes	Yes	Yes	Yes	Yes
8 Region-of-residence dummies	No	No	No	No	Yes	Yes	Yes	Yes
Age	—	—	0.1800	0.1325	—	—	0.1518	0.1215
			(0.0389)	(0.0486)			(0.0379)	(0.0474)
Age-squared	—	—	0.0023	0.0016	—	—	0.0019	0.0015
			(0.0006)	(0.0007)			(0.0005)	(0.0007)
χ^2 [dof]	—	101.6 [29]	—	49.1 [27]	—	93.6 [29]	—	50.6 [27]

a. Standard errors are in parentheses. Sample size is 486,926. Instruments are a full set of quarter-of-birth times year-of-birth interactions. Sample consists of males born in the United States. The sample is drawn from the 5 percent samples of the 1980 Census. The dependent variable is the log of weekly earnings. Age and age-squared are measured in quarters of years. Each equation also includes an intercept.

slightly negative and insignificant Wald estimate of the return to education. However, the TSLS estimate of the return to education is positive and statistically significant. Furthermore, in each of the four specifications the return to education estimated by TSLS is statistically indistinguishable from the return estimated by OLS. Including age and age-squared to control for within-year-of-birth earnings trends leads to an even higher TSLS estimate of the return to education.

All of the TSLS estimates we have presented so far are overidentified because several estimates of the return to education could be constructed from subsets of the instruments. For example, one could compare the return to education using variation in education between first and fourth quarter births in 1940, between second and third quarter births in 1940, between second and third quarter births in 1941, etc. The χ^2 statistics presented at the bottom of Tables IV, V, and VI test the hypothesis that the various combinations of instruments yield the same estimate of the return to education. This statistic is calculated as the sample size times the R^2 from a regression of the residuals from the TSLS equation on the exogenous variables and instruments [Newey, 1985]. In spite of the huge sample sizes, the overidentifying restrictions are not rejected in the models in Tables IV and V. The models in Table VI lead to a rejection of the overidentifying restrictions, but the models that include a quadratic age trend are close to not rejecting at the 0.01 level.

In addition to the log weekly wage, we have also examined the impact of compulsory schooling on the log of annual salary and on weeks worked. This exercise suggests that the main impact of compulsory schooling is on the log weekly wage, and not on weeks worked. For example, when the log of weeks worked is used as the dependent variable in column (6) of Table VII instead of the log weekly wage, the TSLS estimate is 0.016 with a standard error of 0.008. This is within sampling variance of the OLS estimate, which is 0.008 with a standard error of 0.0002.

B. Allowing the Seasonal Pattern in Education to Vary by State of Birth

Although most schools admit students born in the beginning of the year at an older age, school start age policy varies across states and across school districts within many states. Therefore, because compulsory schooling constrains some students to remain in school until their birthday, the relationship between education

TABLE VII

OLS and TSLS Estimates of the Return to Education for Men Born 1930–1939: 1980 Census[a]

Independent variable	(1) OLS	(2) TSLS	(3) OLS	(4) TSLS	(5) OLS	(6) TSLS	(7) OLS	(8) TSLS
Years of education	0.0673	0.0928	0.0673	0.0907	0.0628	0.0831	0.0628	0.0811
	(0.0003)	(0.0093)	(0.0003)	(0.0107)	(0.0003)	(0.0095)	(0.0003)	(0.0109)
Race (1 = black)	—	—	—	—	-0.2547	-0.2333	-0.2547	-0.2354
					(0.0043)	(0.0109)	(0.0043)	(0.0122)
SMSA (1 = center city)	—	—	—	—	0.1705	0.1511	0.1705	0.1531
					(0.0029)	(0.0095)	(0.0029)	(0.0107)
Married (1 = married)	—	—	—	—	0.2487	0.2435	0.2487	0.2441
					(0.0032)	(0.0040)	(0.0032)	(0.0042)
9 Year-of-birth dummies	Yes	Yes	Yes	Yes	Yes	Yes	Yes	Yes
8 Region-of-residence dummies	No	No	No	No	Yes	Yes	Yes	Yes
50 State-of-birth dummies	Yes	Yes	Yes	Yes	Yes	Yes	Yes	Yes
Age	—	—	-0.0757	-0.0880	—	—	-0.0778	-0.0876
			(0.0617)	(0.0624)			(0.0603)	(0.0609)
Age-squared	—	—	0.0008	0.0009	—	—	0.0008	0.0009
			(0.0007)	(0.0007)			(0.0007)	(0.0007)
χ^2 [dof]	—	163 [179]	—	161 [177]	—	164 [179]	—	162 [177]

a. Standard errors are in parentheses. Excluded instruments are 30 quarter-of-birth times year-of-birth dummies and 150 quarter-of-birth times state-of-birth interactions. Age and age-squared are measured in quarters of years. Each equation also includes an intercept term. The sample is the same as in Table VI. Sample size is 329,509.

and season of birth is expected to vary among states that have different start age policies. This additional variability can be used to improve the precision of the TSLS estimates.

To incorporate the cross-state seasonal variation in education, we computed TSLS estimates that use as instruments for education a set of three quarter-of-birth dummies interacted with fifty state-of-birth dummies, in addition to three quarter-of-birth dummies interacted with nine year-of-birth dummies.[18] The estimates also include fifty state-of-birth dummies in the wage equation, so the variability in education used to identify the return to education in the TSLS estimates is solely due to differences by season of birth. Unlike the previous TSLS estimates, the seasonal differences are now allowed to vary by state as well as by birth year.

Table VII presents the TSLS and OLS estimates of the new specification for the sample of 40–49 year-old men in the 1980 Census. This is the same sample used in the estimates in Table V. Freeing up the instruments by state of birth and including 50 state-of-birth dummies in the wage equation results in approximately a 40 percent reduction in the standard errors of the TSLS estimates. Furthermore, in the specifications in each of the columns in Table VII, the estimated return to education in the TSLS model is slightly greater than the corresponding TSLS estimate in Table V, whereas in each of the OLS models the return is slightly smaller in Table VII than in Table V. As a consequence, the difference between the TSLS and OLS estimates is of greater significance. For example, the TSLS estimate in column (6) of Table VII is 0.083 with a standard error of 0.010, and the OLS estimate is 0.063 with a standard error of 0.0003: the TSLS estimate is nearly 30 percent greater than the OLS estimate.

One possible explanation for the higher TSLS estimate of the return to education may be that compulsory schooling pushes some students to graduate high school, so that part of the TSLS estimate reflects a high school "completion" effect. On the other hand, using 1980 Census data, Card and Krueger [1992a] find little evidence of nonlinearity in the return to education for middle-aged men with three to fifteen years of education. If the earnings function is

18. In the context of the model, we added a set of state-of-birth dummy variables interacted with quarter-of-birth dummy variables to equation (1), and a set of 50 state-of-birth dummies to equation (2). Although in principle we could also interact the state-of-birth-by-quarter-of-birth effects with year of birth, to have a total of 1,500 exclusion restrictions, estimation of such a model is computationally burdensome.

THE EFFECTS OF COMPULSORY SCHOOL ATTENDANCE   1005

log-linear, then our estimates may be representative of the average return to education in our sample.[19]

To further explore this issue, we computed OLS estimates of the return to education for men with nine to twelve years of schooling, and found little difference between estimates for this subsample and the full sample. For example, the OLS estimate of the return to education for men born 1930–1939 with nine to twelve years of education is 0.059, compared with 0.063 for the full sample in column (5) of Table V. We also note that we obtained similar TSLS estimates of the return to education when our extracts were restricted to men with a high school degree or less.

C. Estimates for Black Men

Using data on men born in the first half of the twentieth century, many researchers find that OLS estimates of the return to education are lower for black men than for white men (e.g., Welch [1973]). At least part of the lower return to education for black men appears to be due to the lower quality schools that were provided for black students in these cohorts (see Card and Krueger [1992b]). If schools attended by black students were of inferior quality, then we would expect to find a lower return to compulsory schooling for black workers than for white workers.

In Table VIII we provide estimates of the return to education for the sample of black men born 1930–1939. As in Table VII the excluded instruments for education are interactions between quarter-of-birth and year-of-birth dummies, and interactions between quarter-of-birth and state-of-birth dummies. Both the OLS and TSLS estimates indicate that the return to education is lower for black men than for the entire male population. In view of the lower quality of schools attended by black students, this finding provides some additional support for the plausibility of the TSLS estimates. Moreover, the TSLS estimates for this subsample are within sampling variance of the OLS estimates. Unlike the estimates for the entire sample, however, the TSLS estimates are slightly less than the OLS estimates.

III. OTHER POSSIBLE EFFECTS OF SEASON OF BIRTH

The validity of the identification strategy used in Section II rests on the assumption that season of birth is a legitimate

---

19. Heckman and Polachek [1974] provide some additional evidence that the earnings function is approximately log-linear.

TABLE VIII

OLS AND TSLS ESTIMATES OF THE RETURN TO EDUCATION FOR BLACK MEN BORN 1930–1939: 1980 CENSUS[a]

Independent variable	(1) OLS	(2) TSLS	(3) OLS	(4) TSLS	(5) OLS	(6) TSLS	(7) OLS	(8) TSLS
Years of education	0.0672 (0.0013)	0.0635 (0.0185)	0.0671 (0.0003)	0.0555 (0.0199)	0.0576 (0.0013)	0.0461 (0.0187)	0.0576 (0.0013)	0.0391 (0.0199)
SMSA (1 = center city)	—	—	—	—	0.1885 (0.0142)	0.2053 (0.0308)	0.1884 (0.0142)	0.2155 (0.0324)
Married (1 = married)	—	—	—	—	0.2216 (0.0193)	0.2272 (0.0136)	0.2216 (0.0100)	0.2307 (0.0140)
9 Year-of-birth dummies	Yes	Yes	Yes	Yes	Yes	Yes	Yes	Yes
8 Region-of-residence dummies	No	No	No	No	Yes	Yes	Yes	Yes
49 State-of-birth dummies	Yes	Yes	Yes	Yes	Yes	Yes	Yes	Yes
Age	—	—	-0.0309 (0.2538)	-0.3274 (0.2560)	—	—	-0.2978 (0.0032)	-0.3237 (0.2497)
Age-squared	—	—	0.0033 (0.0028)	0.0035 (0.0028)	—	—	0.0032 (0.0027)	0.0035 (0.0028)
χ^2 [dof]	—	184 [176]	—	181 [173]	—	178 [176]	—	175 [173]

a. Standard errors are in parentheses. Excluded instruments are 30 quarter-of-birth times year-of-birth dummies and 147 quarter-of-birth times state-of-birth interactions. (There are no black men in the sample born in Hawaii.) Age and age-squared are measured in quarters of years. Each equation also includes an intercept term. The sample is drawn from the 1980 Census. Sample size is 26,913.

instrument for education in an earnings equation. From Section I it would seem that season of birth is related to education because of compulsory schooling requirements. However, for the TSLS estimates to be consistent, it must also be the case that season of birth is uncorrelated with the residual in the earnings equation (μ). In other words, if season of birth influences earnings for reasons other than compulsory schooling, our approach is called into question. Although we believe the evidence in Section I establishes that season of birth influences education exclusively because of compulsory schooling, it is useful to consider the impact of other possible effects of season of birth.

First, several educational psychologists have examined the effect of age at school entry on educational achievement.[20] Most of this literature, however, analyzes extremely small samples, focuses on test scores rather than graduation rates, and takes age at entry to school as exogenous. Furthermore, much of the past literature fails to adequately control for the effects of age.[21] Nevertheless, the previous research indicates that there might be a relationship between age at school entry and academic performance. The consensus in this literature is that, if anything, students who start school at an older age are more mature and perform better in school.

Although we do not find this evidence convincing, it is worth noting what bias the prevailing interpretation of the psychological-season of birth effect might have on our estimates. Assume, for the moment, that children born in the beginning of the year are better students because they are older than their classmates. Men born in the first quarter of the year would therefore have greater unobserved ability for a given level of schooling. However, men born in the first quarter also have less education, probably due to the dominant effect of compulsory education laws. Assuming that this unobserved ability is rewarded in the labor market, any estimator of the return to education that is identified by variations in education due to season of birth would be biased downward.

Second, we note that if season of birth were related to the socioeconomic status of children's parents, one might expect to find a connection between season of birth and education. If this were

---

20. See Halliwell [1966] for a survey of the literature on early school entry and school success; see DiPasquale, Moule, and Flewelling [1980] for a survey of the "birthday effect" on educational achievement.
21. This point is also made by Lewis and Griffin [1981] in the context of season-of-birth effects in diagnoses of schizophrenia.

the case, season of birth would be an unsatisfactory instrumental variable for our purposes. Lam and Miron [1987], however, present a variety of evidence suggesting that season of birth is unrelated to the socioeconomic status (and other characteristics) of parents. For example, they find that the seasonal pattern in births is virtually identical for illegitimate births and legitimate births. In addition, they find that the seasonal pattern of birth is similar across urban and rural families, across regions of the United States that have diverse economic and cultural conditions, and within countries before and after dramatic economic transitions.

Furthermore, both of these alternative explanations are hard pressed to explain why the effect of season of birth on education is smaller for more recent cohorts, as is clear from Table I. There is no obvious reason why the psychological or socioeconomic explanations for the seasonal pattern of education would have less force for the 1940s cohort than for the 1920s cohort. On the other hand, if season of birth influences education because of compulsory schooling, one would expect to find a smaller effect for individuals in more recent cohorts, who are likely to be less constrained by the compulsory schooling requirement.

Third, assuming that the earnings function is consistently estimated by OLS (e.g., no correlation between education and the error) and that the only impact of quarter of birth on earnings is through education, then quarter-of-birth dummies should be insignificant in an earnings equation that also include education. We tested this proposition by adding three quarter-of-birth dummies to the OLS models for the sample of prime-age men in column 5 of Tables IV and V. The prob-value for an F-test of the null hypothesis that the quarter-of-birth dummies jointly equal zero is 0.73 in the 1970 Census and 0.13 in the 1980 Census.

Finally, and perhaps most convincing, we have estimated the effect of season of birth on the earnings of college graduates, a sample whose schooling was not prolonged by compulsory attendance. If season of birth affects education for a reason other than compulsory schooling (e.g., psychological effects of school start age), we would expect season of birth to be related to earnings for this sample. On the other hand, if season of birth only affects education and earnings because of compulsory schooling, we would not expect any relationship in this sample. The estimates suggest that quarter of birth has no effect on earnings for college graduates, a finding which supports the estimation framework employed throughout the paper. For example, using the sample of 40–49-year-old college graduates in the 1970 Census, an F-test of the joint significance of quarter-of-birth dummies in an earnings regression that includes year-of-birth dummies is not rejected at the 25 percent level. Similar results hold for 40–49-year-old men in 1980. We take this as strong evidence that, in the absence of compulsory schooling, season of birth would have no effect on earnings.

IV. Conclusion

Differences in season of birth create a natural experiment that we use to study the effect of compulsory school attendance on schooling and earnings. Because individuals born in the beginning of the year usually start school at an older age than that of their classmates, they are allowed to drop out of school after attaining less education. Our exploration of the relationship between quarter of birth and educational attainment suggests that season of birth has a small effect on the level of education men ultimately attain. To support the contention that this is a consequence of compulsory schooling laws, we have assembled evidence showing that some students leave school as soon as they attain the legal dropout age, and that season of birth has no effect on postsecondary years of schooling.

Variation in education that is related to season of birth arises because some individuals, by accident of date of birth, are *forced* to attend school longer than others because of compulsory schooling. Using season of birth as an instrument for education in an earnings equation, we find a remarkable similarity between the OLS and the TSLS estimates of the monetary return to education. Differences between the OLS and the TSLS estimates are typically not statistically significant, and whatever differences that do exist tend to suggest that omitted variables, or measurement error in education, may induce a downward bias in the OLS estimate of the return to education.[22] This evidence casts doubt on the importance

---

22. Siegel and Hodge [1968] find that the correlation between individuals' education reported in the 1960 Census and in a Post Enumeration Survey is 0.933. This correlation gives an upper bound estimate of the ratio of the variance of true education to the variance of reported education because individuals may consistently misreport their education in both surveys. Moreover, the downward bias in the OLS estimate of the return to education due to measurement error will be exacerbated because the included covariates are likely to explain some of the true variation in education, and because of variability in the quality of education.

of omitted variables bias in OLS estimates of the return to education, at least for years of schooling around the compulsory schooling level.

Our results provide support for the view that students who are compelled to attend school longer by compulsory schooling laws earn higher wages as a result of their extra schooling. Moreover, we find that compulsory schooling laws are effective in compelling some students to attend school. Do these results mean that compulsory schooling laws are necessarily beneficial? A complete answer to this question would require additional research on the social and private costs of compulsory school attendance. For example, compulsory attendance may have the benefit of reducing crime rates. And they may impose a social cost because students who are compelled to attend school may interfere with the learning of other students.

APPENDIX 1: DATA

The empirical analysis draws on a variety of data sets, each constructed from Public Use Census Data. The sample used in Table I to compute quarter-of-birth main effects on educational outcomes consists of all men born 1930–1949 in the 1980 Census 5 percent sample. The sample used to compute the difference-in-differences estimates of the effect of compulsory schooling laws on enrollment in Table II consists of all sixteen-year olds in each of the following Census samples: the 1960 Census 1 percent sample, the two 1 percent State samples from the 1970 Census, and the 1980 Census 5 percent sample. The two samples used to compute the estimates in Tables III–VI consist of men with positive earnings born between 1920–1929 in the three 1970 Census 1 percent samples drawn from the 15 percent long-form, and the sample of men with positive earnings born between 1930–1949 in the 1980 Census 5 percent sample. Information on date of birth in the Censuses is limited to quarter of birth. A more detailed description of the data sets used in the tables and figures is provided below.

A. Samples used in Table I, Tables III–VII, and Figures I–V

1. *1970 Census.* The 1970 Census micro data are documented in *Public Use Samples of Basic Records from the 1970 Census* [Washington, DC: U. S. Department of Commerce, 1972]. Our

THE EFFECTS OF COMPULSORY SCHOOL ATTENDANCE   1011

extract combines data from three separate public-use files: the State, County group, and Neighborhood files. Each file contains a self-weighting, mutually exclusive sample of 1 percent of the population (as of April 1, 1970), yielding a total sample of 3 percent of the population. The data sets we use are based on the questionnaire that was administered to 15 percent of the population.

The sample consists of white and black men born between 1920–1929 in the United States. Birth year was derived from reported age and quarter of birth. In addition, we excluded any man whose age, sex, race, veteran status, weeks worked, highest grade completed or salary was allocated by the Census Bureau. Finally, the sample is limited to men with positive wage and salary earnings and positive weeks worked in 1969.

Weekly earnings is computed by dividing annual earnings by annual weeks worked. Annual earnings is reported in intervals of $100. This variable was converted to a continuous variable by taking the average of the interval endpoints. Weeks worked is reported as a categorical variable in six intervals, and was also converted to a continuous variable by taking the mean of interval endpoints.

Nine region dummies were coded directly from the Census Regions variable in the Neighborhoods 1 percent sample, from state of residence in the State 1 percent sample, and from county locations in the County Group file. If county groups straddled two states, the counties were allocated to the region containing the greatest land-mass of the county group. The education variable is years of schooling completed. The marital status variable equals one if the respondent is currently married with his spouse present. The SMSA variable equals one if the respondent works in an SMSA.

2. *1980 Census.* The 1980 Census micro data are documented in *Census of Population and Housing, 1980: Public Use Microdata Samples* [Washington, DC: U. S. Department of Commerce, 1983]. Our extract is drawn from the 5 percent Public Use Sample (the A Sample). This file contains a self-weighting sample of 5 percent of the population as of April 1, 1980.

The extract we created consists of white and black men born in the United States between 1930–1959. Birth year was derived from reported age and quarter of birth. We excluded respondents whose age, sex, race, quarter of birth, weeks worked, years of schooling, or salary was allocated by the Census Bureau. For the estimates in

1012   *QUARTERLY JOURNAL OF ECONOMICS*

Tables IV–VII and Figure V, the sample is limited to men with positive wage and salary earnings and positive weeks worked in 1979; for the estimates in Table I, the sample includes all men, regardless of whether they worked in 1979.

Weekly earnings in 1979 is computed by dividing annual earnings by weeks worked. Dummies for nine Census regions are coded from state of residence. The education variable is years of completed schooling. The marital status dummy equals one if the respondent is currently married with his spouse present. The SMSA variable equals one if the respondent lives in an SMSA.

B. Samples Used to Compute the Enrollment Estimates in Table II

Table II uses data from the 1960, 1970, and 1980 Censuses. The 1960 Census data are documented in *A Public Use Sample of Basic Records from the 1960 Census* [Washington, DC: U. S. Department of Commerce, 1975]. Our extract for 1960 is drawn from the 1 percent Public Use Sample. The sample used consists of boys and girls born in 1944. The extract of the 1970 Census used in Table II is drawn from the two 1 percent State files (the State samples of the 5 percent Form and of the 15 percent Form) because these files identify state of residence. The sample consists of boys and girls born in 1954. Finally, the sample of boys and girls born in 1964 in the 1980 Census, 5 percent sample are used as well. In each of the three samples, individuals with allocated age or enrollment were excluded.

APPENDIX 2: COMPULSORY SCHOOL ATTENDANCE AGE BY STATE

State	1960	1970	1980	Notes
1 Alabama	16	16	16	
2 Alaska	16	16	16	
4 Arizona	16	16	16	
5 Arkansas	16	16	15	
6 California	16	16	16	
8 Colorado	16	16	16	
9 Connecticut	16	16	16	
10 Delaware	16	16	16	
11 D.C.	16	16	16	
12 Florida	16	16	16	
13 Georgia	16	16	16	
15 Hawaii	16	18	18	Increased to 18 midyear, 1970
16 Idaho	16	16	16	
17 Illinois	16	16	16	

THE EFFECTS OF COMPULSORY SCHOOL ATTENDANCE 1013

APPENDIX 2: (CONTINUED)

State	1960	1970	1980	Notes
18 Indiana	16	16	16	
19 Iowa	16	16	16	
20 Kansas	16	16	16	
21 Kentucky	16	16	16	
22 Louisiana	16	16	16	
23 Maine	15	17	17	
24 Maryland	16	16	16	
25 Massachusetts	16	16	16	
26 Michigan	16	16	16	
27 Minnesota	16	16	16	
28 Mississippi	—	—	—	Age 14 starting 1983
29 Missouri	16	16	16	
30 Montana	16	16	16	
31 Nebraska	16	16	16	
32 Nevada	17	17	17	
33 New Hampshire	16	16	16	
34 New Jersey	16	16	16	
35 New Mexico	16	17	17	
36 New York	16	16	16	May be changed by city districts
37 North Carolina	16	16	16	
38 North Dakota	17	16	16	
39 Ohio	18	18	18	
40 Oklahoma	18	18	18	
41 Oregon	18	18	18	
42 Pennsylvania	17	17	17	
44 Rhode Island	16	16	16	
45 South Carolina	—	16	16	Reinstated in 1967
46 South Dakota	16	16	16	
47 Tennessee	17	17	16	Increased to age 17 in 1983
48 Texas	16	17	17	Must finish school term
49 Utah	18	18	18	
50 Vermont	16	16	16	
51 Virginia	16	17	17	
53 Washington	16	16	18	
54 West Virginia	16	16	16	
55 Wisconsin	16	16	16	Must finish school term
54 Wyoming	17	17	16	

Source: U.S. Office of Education, *Digest of Education Statistics* (Washington, DC: GPO, various years).

HARVARD UNIVERSITY AND NBER
PRINCETON UNIVERSITY AND NBER

REFERENCES

Angrist, Joshua D., and Alan Krueger, "Why do World War Two Veterans Earn More than Nonveterans?" NBER Working Paper No. 2991, May 1989.

____, and ____, "The Effect of Age at School Entry on Educational Attainment: An Application of Instrumental Variables with Moments from Two Samples," NBER Working Paper No. 3571, December 1990.

Card, David, and Alan Krueger, "Does School Quality Matter? Returns to Education and the Characteristics of Public Schools in the United States," *Journal of Political Economy* (February 1992a), forthcoming.

____, and ____, "School Quality and Black/White Earnings: A Direct Assessment," *Quarterly Journal of Economics*, CVII (February 1992b), forthcoming.

Department of Health, Education and Welfare, *State Legislation on School Attendance* (Washington, DC: Circular No. 573, January 1959).

Department of Employment, Education and Training, *School Leavers* (Canberra, Australia: Edition 8, 1987), p. 35.

DiPasquale, Glenn, Allan Moule, and Robert Flewelling, "The Birthdate Effect," *Journal of Learning Disabilities*, XIII (May 1980) 234–37.

Durbin, J. "Errors in Variables," *Review of the International Statistical Institute*, XXII (1954), 23–32.

Edwards, Linda, "An Empirical Analysis of Compulsory Schooling Legislation, 1940–1960," *Journal of Law and Economics*, XXI (April 1978), 203–22.

Ehrenberg, Ronald, and Alan Marcus, "Minimum Wages and Teenagers' Enrollment-Employment Outcomes: A Multinomial Logit Model," *Journal of Human Resources*, XXVII (1982), 39–58.

Griliches, Zvi, "Estimating the Returns to Schooling—Some Econometric Problems," *Econometrica*, XLV (January 1977), 1–22.

Halliwell, Joseph, "Reviewing the Reviews on Entrance Age and School Success," *Journal of Educational Research*, LIX (May–June 1966), 395–401.

Hausman, Jerry, "Specification Tests in Econometrics," *Econometrica*, XLVI (November 1978), 1251–71.

Heckman, James, and Solomon Polachek, "Empirical Evidence on the Functional Form of the Earnings-Schooling Relationship," *Journal of the American Statistical Association*, LXIX (1974), 350–54.

Huntington, Ellsworth, *Season of Birth: Its Relation to Human Abilities* (New York, NY: Wiley, 1938).

Kotin, Lawrence, and William F. Aikman, *Legal Foundations of Compulsory School Attendance* (Port Washington, NY: Kennikat Press, 1980).

Lam, David, and Jeffrey Miron, "The Seasonality of Births in Human Populations," unpublished paper, *Population Studies Center Research Report* No. 87–114, University of Michigan, 1987.

Lewis, Marc, and Patricia Griffin, "An Explanation for the Season of Birth Effect in Schizophrenia and Certain Other Diseases," *Psychological Bulletin*, LXXXIX (1981), 589–96.

Newey, Whitney, "Generalized Method of Moments Specification Testing," *Journal of Econometrics*, XXIX (1985), 229–56.

Organization for Economic Cooperation and Development, *Compulsory Schooling in a Changing World* (Paris: OECD, 1983).

Siegel, Paul, and Robert Hodge, "A Causal Approach to the Study of Measurement Error," *Methodology in Social Research*, Hubert Blalock and Ann Blalock, eds. (New York, NY: McGraw Hill Book Co., 1968), Chapter 2, pp. 29–59.

Spence, Michael, "Job Market Signaling," *Quarterly Journal of Economics*, LXXXVII (1973), 355–75.

Wald, Abraham, "The Fitting of Straight Lines if Both Variables Are Subject to Error," *Annals of Mathematical Statistics*, XI (1940), 284–300.

Welch, Finis, "Education and Racial Discrimination," in *Discrimination in Labor Market*, O. Ashenfelter and A. Rees, eds. (Princeton, NJ: Princeton University Press, 1973), pp. 43–81.

Willis, Robert J., "Wage Determinants: A Survey and Reinterpretation of Human Capital Earnings Functions," *Handbook of Labor Economics*, I, O. Ashenfelter and R. Layard, eds. (Amsterdam: Elsevier Science Publishers BV, 1986), Chapter 10.

[5]

Effects of Family Background on Earnings and Returns to Schooling: Evidence from Brazil

David Lam

University of Michigan

Robert F. Schoeni

RAND

We investigate whether omitted family background variables are responsible for high returns to schooling estimated in Brazil. Returns to schooling fall by about one-third when parental schooling is added to wage equations. Surprisingly, the schooling of fathers-in-law has larger effects on wages than the schooling of fathers. On the basis of a model of assortative mating, we interpret this as evidence that parental characteristics represent unobservable worker attributes rather than nepotism in the labor market. We conclude that the "family background bias" in returns to schooling is modest and need not imply returns to family connections.

Introduction

Two stylized facts about labor markets in developing countries provide a backdrop for this paper. The first, which is supported by extensive empirical research, is that private returns to schooling are sub-

This paper has benefited from comments by Ricardo Barros, T. Paul Schultz, Guilherme Sedlacek, and seminar participants at Berkeley, Brown, Chicago, Michigan, RAND, and Yale. Support from the U.S. National Institutes of Health (National Institute of Child Health and Development grant no. R01-HD19624), the Fulbright Commission, the Program for International Partnerships of the University of Michigan, the Hewlett Foundation, and the Instituto de Pesquisa Econômica Aplicada, Rio de Janeiro, is gratefully acknowledged. Excellent research assistance was provided by Deborah Reed.

[*Journal of Political Economy*, 1993, vol. 101, no. 4]

RETURNS TO SCHOOLING 711

stantially higher in developing countries than in the United States and other high-income countries. The second, which is more impressionistic, is that intergenerational mobility is lower in developing countries, with family background playing a more important role in determining earnings. Many observers have suggested that there are important connections between these two characteristics of developing country labor markets, arguing that omitted family background effects are partly responsible for the apparent high returns to schooling.

This paper analyzes the effects of family background on male labor market earnings in Brazil, a country with unusually high returns to schooling and one of the most unequal distributions of income in the world. We attempt to identify the magnitude of the "family background bias" in conventional estimates of returns to schooling and to identify the direct effect of family background on earnings. We begin with a theoretical model of assortative mating and intergenerational correlations in income-related characteristics. The model demonstrates the potential information contained in characteristics of a worker's parents and parents-in-law about unobserved characteristics of the worker. We show that there are important asymmetries between the characteristics of parents and the characteristics of parents-in-law in relation to workers' earnings, asymmetries that help distinguish among alternative interpretations of observed family background effects.

Building on this model, our econometric approach is straightforward. We sequentially add measures of the schooling of workers' relatives to wage equations, analyzing both the direct effect of these variables on wages and the effect of these variables on the estimated returns to the worker's own schooling. Using a data set with over 40,000 Brazilian males aged 30–55, we are able to identify significant independent effects of the schooling of a worker's parents, wife, and parents-in-law on wages. We find that estimated returns to schooling decline by one-fourth to one-third when family background variables are included in the regression. Direct effects of parental schooling on wages are substantial, though well below the returns to a worker's own schooling. When we control for the worker's own schooling and the schooling of other relatives, for example, having a father with a university education is associated with a 20 percent wage advantage compared to having an illiterate father. Our most intriguing result is that the schooling of a worker's father-in-law has a larger effect on a worker's wage than the schooling of the worker's own father. This surprising result has a clear interpretation in our model of assortative mating and provides support for the interpretation of family background variables as proxies for unobserved worker characteristics, rather than as evidence of returns to nepotistic family connections in the labor market.

Given the high correlations among our family background variables, we pay close attention to the potential role of measurement error bias in our results. We demonstrate that even under modest assumptions about the magnitude of measurement error in schooling, as much as 80 percent of the observed decline in returns to schooling from inclusion of family background variables may be explained by increases in measurement error bias. This factor has been widely ignored in previous studies, and our results suggest that previous researchers may have exaggerated the extent of family background bias in returns to schooling. Even ignoring the increased measurement error bias, we continue to estimate returns to schooling in Brazil of over 10 percent after controlling for a large set of family background variables.

Education, Family Background, and Economic Outcomes

A striking feature of labor markets in many developing countries is the high estimates of returns to schooling in comparison to those of the United States and other industrialized economies. Psacharopoulos (1985), summarizing estimates of returns to education for 60 different countries in the 1970s, reports an average return to schooling in developing countries of about 15 percent, compared to an average of 9 percent for high-income countries. Brazil is no exception to this pattern. Lam and Levison (1992), for example, estimate returns to schooling for separate 3-year age groups of 15–16 percent for Brazilian males, compared to 9–11 percent for the same-age males in the United States. Education alone explains 50 percent of the variation in earnings of 30–33-year-old males in Brazil, compared to less than 10 percent for the same age group of males in the United States.

One natural explanation of these high returns to schooling is that they reflect high rents due to the relative scarcity of human capital, an argument particularly salient in Brazil, where a high degree of industrialization coexists with mean schooling of less than 5 years (see Langoni 1977; Lam and Levison 1992). This interpretation has important policy implications, suggesting that appropriately designed schooling investments can have high social returns and reduce earnings inequality. Critics argue, however, that these high estimates of returns to schooling in developing countries are subject to a variety of biases that cause them to overstate the returns that would be experienced by a randomly drawn individual. Most of these biases are the same ones that have been raised in the debate over the effect of schooling in high-income countries, including the correlation between schooling and ability (Griliches and Mason 1972; Chamberlain and Griliches 1975; Behrman and Taubman 1976) and the correlation between schooling and a variety of family and community background variables (Hauser and Sewell 1986; Corcoran et al. 1990).

Research on the role of family background in explaining earnings and returns to schooling is less extensive for developing countries. Two studies from Latin America are particularly relevant to this study. Behrman and Wolfe (1984) identified strong independent effects of family background in a study of female earnings in Nicaragua. Using a sample of 500 Nicaraguan sister pairs, they difference the data across siblings and find that returns to schooling drop by one-fourth, from 11.4 percent to 8.6 percent, leading them to conclude that standard estimates of returns to schooling are biased upward in the absence of controls for family background and unobserved ability. Heckman and Hotz (1986) estimate earnings equations for Panamanian males that include father's and mother's education as regressors. Parental education is found to have a significant direct effect on earnings, with the point estimates implying that a 1-year increase in mother's education increases the son's annual earnings by 3–5 percent. Heckman and Hotz find that estimated returns to the worker's own schooling drop by about one-third, from 11.9 percent to 8.6 percent, when father's and mother's education is included in the regression.

Assortative Mating and Intergenerational Correlations in Schooling and Earnings

The empirical strategy we adopt below is straightforward. We estimate a series of wage equations in which we begin with the schooling of the worker as a regressor and then sequentially add the schooling of the worker's parents, wife, and parents-in-law. These regressions provide a simple test of the role of "family background" in explaining the relationship between schooling and earnings in Brazil. It is clear ex ante, however, that several alternative interpretations can be given to such regressions. As pointed out by Schultz (1988), a number of researchers have included characteristics of parents in earnings equations, with a variety of interpretations given to the results. The inclusion of characteristics of a worker's wife and parents-in-law is more unusual. We argue that these characteristics of relatives by marriage provide important additional information that helps clarify the interpretation of family background variables.

We begin with a theoretical model of assortative mating and intergenerational correlations in earnings that demonstrates the information captured by characteristics of parents and parents-in-law. Let Y_{hi} denote a measure of lifetime income for the ith potential husband in the population:

$$Y_{hi} = \beta_0 + \beta_s S_{hi} + \beta_a A_{hi} + u_{hi}, \tag{1}$$

where S_{hi} is years of schooling and A_{hi} is a variable that is unobservable and affects income, such as ability.[1] An analogous equation describes income Y_{wi} for the ith potential wife in the population. We are interested in the information that may be captured in wage equations by family background variables such as the schooling of husband i's father, which we shall denote F_{hi}, and the schooling of wife i's father, F_{wi}. Suppose that ability, A_{hi}, has positive returns in the labor market, is unobservable, and is positively correlated with schooling. It is also plausible to expect that husband i's ability is positively correlated with the schooling of his father, F_{hi}. This correlation could result from some more fundamental correlation in ability between generations, with higher ability leading to higher schooling in each generation. Imagine an orthogonal decomposition in which we express ability as a linear function of father's education:

$$A_{hi} = \gamma_f F_{hi} + A_{hi}^u. \tag{2}$$

We could think of this as a crude decomposition of ability into an "inherited" component, $\gamma_f F_{hi}$, and an "uninherited" component, A_{hi}^u. Using equation (2), we can express income as

$$Y_{hi} = \beta_0 + \beta_s S_{hi} + \beta_a (\gamma_f F_{hi} + A_{hi}^u) + u_{hi}. \tag{3}$$

As equation (3) illustrates, parental characteristics such as F_{hi} will typically be indicators of inherited unobservables omitted from the earnings equation. To the extent that the variables they are correlated with are also correlated with schooling, inclusion of these variables in an earnings equation may reduce omitted variable bias in estimates of returns to schooling.[2] From equation (3), the correlation between worker's income and father's schooling will be

$$\rho_{yhfh} = \frac{\beta_s \sigma_{shfh} + \beta_a \gamma_f \sigma_{fh}^2}{\sigma_{yh} \sigma_{fh}}, \tag{4}$$

---

[1] We shall refer to ability here for concreteness, but the same logic applies to any unobservable characteristics that affect labor market productivity such as quality of schooling or education acquired at home.

[2] We shall return below to the issue of how this gain is offset by increased measurement error bias.

where $\sigma_{s_h f_h}$ is the covariance of husband's schooling and father's schooling, and $\sigma_{f_h}^2$ is the variance in father's schooling. Equation (4) implies that father's schooling and son's income will be correlated even after one controls for the correlation in father's and son's schooling, and even if fathers have no direct effect on their sons' earnings. In addition to whatever other direct and indirect effects may be represented by father's schooling, it will also pick up effects of unobserved ability to the extent that γ_f and β_a are greater than zero.

Assume that there is marital sorting with respect to income Y described by the correlation in spouses' incomes $\rho_{y_h y_w}$. This marital sorting may be motivated by an economic model of the marriage market, as in Becker (1981) and Lam (1988), although the behavioral mechanisms generating the correlation in spouses' characteristics are not critical. Lam demonstrates a tendency for positive assortative mating on full income whenever household public goods are an important source of returns to marriage. The role of positive assortative mating will be important to keep in mind in our results below since it clarifies the apparent effect of the wife and wife's parents on wages. We note that spouses' characteristics are very highly correlated in Brazil, with a correlation in spouse's schooling of .77 in the sample used below.

Consider the relationship between the characteristics of a worker and the family background of the worker's spouse. Exploiting the relationship between partial correlations and simple (zero-order) correlations, we can express the correlation between husband's income and wife's family background as

$$\rho_{y_h f_w} = \rho_{y_h y_w} \rho_{y_w f_w} + \rho_{y_h f_w \cdot y_w}[(1 - \rho_{y_h y_w}^2)(1 - \rho_{f_w y_w}^2)]^{1/2}. \tag{5}$$

The first term is the product of the assortative mating correlation, $\rho_{y_h y_w}$, and the intrafamily "inheritability" correlation from parents to daughters, $\rho_{y_w f_w}$, both of which are presumably positive. The second term is an additional positive effect if high-income men tend to marry women with better-educated parents, *with wife's income controlled for*, a partial effect for which we have little prior information. An instructive special case is to assume that while spouses care about their spouses' total income, they are indifferent (and perhaps unknowledgeable) about the role of family background in determining that income. That is, prospective spouses are indifferent between a spouse who has high income because of inherited wealth and a spouse who has high income because of labor market luck that is uncorrelated with family background. Formally, think of this as an assumption that there are zero partial correlations between individuals' incomes and their spouses' family backgrounds, *with total income controlled for*, that is, $\rho_{y_h f_w \cdot y_w} = \rho_{y_w f_h \cdot y_h} = 0$. If we simplify (5) in this way and exploit the symmetry between husbands and wives, it follows that

$$\frac{\rho_{yhfw}}{\rho_{ywfh}} = \frac{\rho_{yhyw}\rho_{ywfw}}{\rho_{yhyw}\rho_{yhfh}} = \frac{\rho_{ywfw}}{\rho_{yhfh}}. \tag{6}$$

This equation can be interpreted as meaning that the ratio of *cross-parent* correlations (husbands to wives' parents over wives to husbands' parents) is equal to the ratio of *own-parent* correlations (husbands to husbands' parents over wives to wives' parents). An intriguing lesson of equation (6) is the demonstration that it is possible, indeed quite plausible, for husbands' incomes to be more highly correlated with their wives' family backgrounds than with their own family backgrounds. This result will hold if the correlation between wives' incomes and wives' family backgrounds is higher than the correlation between husbands' incomes and husbands' family backgrounds. From equation (4), this could occur if the variance in income is greater for men than for women, $\sigma_{yh} > \sigma_{yw}$. This could result from $\sigma_{uh} > \sigma_{uw}$, implying that uninherited ability or luck is a larger component of full income for men than for women, an assumption that might be appropriate in a developing economy with low rates of female labor force participation. Suppose, for example, that $\rho_{ywfw} = .5$, $\rho_{yhfh} = .3$, and $\rho_{yhyw} = .8$. Then ρ_{yhfw}, the correlation between men's incomes and the schooling of their fathers-in-law, is .4, and the correlation between men's incomes and the schooling of their own fathers is only .3.

An interesting way to think about the paradoxical result that there may be a higher correlation between husband's earnings and wife's family background than between husband's earnings and husband's family background is to consider the signals contained in information about characteristics of relatives. Suppose, for example, that you want to guess a man's income and can ask for information about the schooling of his parents, wife, and parents-in-law. Equation (6) implies that there may be more information in the schooling of the man's parents-in-law than there is in the schooling of his parents.[3] This will be especially true if there is a high degree of assortative mating on income-related characteristics. The schooling of a man's father and the schooling of his father-in-law can each be thought of as imperfect signals about unobservable characteristics. The schooling of his father is presumably a better signal about the inherited component of unobservable characteristics such as ability. The schooling of his father-in-law, on the other hand, will tend to be correlated with all inherited

---

[3] This can occur under a wide set of assumptions and does not require the special case of zero partial correlations assumed above for illustration.

and uninherited determinants of earnings, including labor market luck, part of which is revealed by the time of marriage.[4] The magnitude of the correlation will be determined by the strength of assortative mating, the timing of marriage, and the magnitude of the correlation between spouse's family background and the characteristics determining a potential spouse's value in the marriage market.

These correlations imply a variety of direct and indirect mechanisms linking the observed and unobserved characteristics of a worker with those of his parents, wife, and parents-in-law. Since we have data on the schooling of all these individuals, we consider the information provided when we include schooling of other family members in a wage equation. Consider first the schooling of parents. Since data limitations prevent us from controlling for other parental characteristics such as income and wealth, parental schooling is a proxy for a variety of family background variables. On the one hand, we shall expect a positive coefficient on parental schooling if there is a direct return to family connections, as suggested by critics such as Bowles (1972). Given returns to family connections, the inclusion of parental schooling will tend to lower the estimated returns to own schooling as long as parental income increases the schooling of children. A positive coefficient on parental schooling need not imply the kind of labor market imperfections implied by returns to nepotistic family connections, however. It may simply pick up unobserved characteristics directly related to labor productivity. Although these omitted variable effects need not imply labor market imperfections, it will still be true that inclusion of parental schooling will tend to lower the estimated returns to own schooling as long as schooling and these unobserved characteristics are positively correlated.

If we include the schooling of the wife or her parents in the husband's earnings equation, we can expect these variables to have positive coefficients, and to lower estimated returns to own schooling, under several different scenarios. As with the worker's own parents, there is the literal interpretation that increased schooling of these relatives directly increases the worker's labor earnings. This will be true if there is a return to "family connections" and if family connections of the wife and her parents are positively correlated with their schooling. Inclusion of the schooling of the wife and her parents will lower the estimated returns to the earner's own schooling in such a case as long as there is positive assortative mating with respect to

---

[4] Which components of earnings are correlated with characteristics of the wife and her parents will depend on the timing of marriage. The correlation between husband's income and the schooling of parents-in-law will presumably be lower if marriage precedes the completion of schooling or the realization of labor market "luck."

schooling. As in the case of parents, however, we may estimate positive coefficients on the schooling of the wife or her parents even if there are no returns to family connections in the labor market. If husband's ability has a return in the marriage market as well as the labor market, then when one controls for the husband's own schooling, increased schooling of the wife and her parents may indicate higher unmeasured ability for the husband.[5] If ability and schooling are positively correlated, inclusion of these variables will also tend to reduce the estimated returns to own schooling.[6]

If the schooling of the wife's parents reflects returns to "nepotistic" labor market connections, it might seem reasonable to expect that the effects of the schooling of parents-in-law would be smaller than the effects of the schooling of the worker's own parents. That is, we might expect that the worker's own father would be more willing and more able to "pull strings" for the worker than the worker's father-in-law would. Here we see the possibility for an asymmetry between the characteristics of the worker's parents and the characteristics of the worker's parents-in-law. As pointed out in the model of assortative mating above, the correlation between the worker's income and his wife's family background may actually be *higher* than the correlation between the worker's income and his own family background. In a sense, men may be more like their fathers-in-law than their fathers. In this case we might expect the apparent effect of the schooling of parents-in-law on earnings to be greater than the effect of the schooling of parents.

Omitted Variables and Measurement Error in Estimating Returns to Schooling

The previous section demonstrates how the schooling of a worker's parents, wife, and parents-in-law can have significant explanatory power in an earnings equation, even if there is no direct effect of their schooling on earnings. We are especially interested in the interpretation of these variables as proxies for unobserved worker characteristics such as ability and schooling quality. An important econometric consideration is that inclusion of those variables that are correlated with a worker's schooling may increase measurement error bias in the earnings equation, an effect emphasized by Welch (1975) and Griliches (1977). To clarify these points for the kinds of regressions

[5] As shown in Schoeni (1990) and Korenman and Neumark (1991), marital status itself is typically associated with higher earnings, one interpretation of which is that unobserved ability provides returns in both the labor market and the marriage market.

[6] See Behrman, Birdsall, and Deolalikar (1993) for another approach to linking marriage market processes with labor market outcomes.

RETURNS TO SCHOOLING   719

we shall estimate below, we consider the properties of alternative estimates of returns to schooling β_s in the earnings equation (1) using only data on S_i, which may be measured with error, and using additional family background variables that may be correlated with both schooling and ability. Assume that we have a schooling variable S^* measured with error, $S_i^* = S_i + w_i$, where w represents pure measurement error uncorrelated with S. Let $\lambda = V(w)/V(S^*)$ represent the noise-to-signal ratio in measured schooling. If we regress Y on S^*, the probability limit of the estimated effect of schooling on earnings is

$$\text{plim} \quad \hat{\beta}_S = \beta_s - \beta_s\lambda + \beta_a\hat{\beta}_{AS}(1 - \lambda), \tag{7}$$

where $\hat{\beta}_{AS}$ is the coefficient from a hypothetical regression of true ability on true schooling. The bias in the estimate has two well-known components. The first is a downward bias caused by measurement error in schooling, the magnitude of which depends on the proportion of the total variance in observed schooling that is measurement error. The second bias is due to the omitted ability variable and will be positive if $\beta_a > 0$ and if schooling and ability are positively correlated.

If we add some measure of family background F to the regression, the probability limit of the new estimate of returns to schooling is

$$\text{plim} \quad \hat{\beta}_{S \cdot F} = \beta_s - \beta_s \frac{\lambda}{1 - R^2_{S* \cdot F}} + \beta_a\hat{\beta}_{AS}(1 - \lambda)(1 - \rho^2_{AF \cdot S*}), \tag{8}$$

where $R^2_{S* \cdot F}$ is the R^2 from a regression of schooling on family background and $\rho^2_{AF \cdot S*}$ is the squared partial correlation of ability and family background when one controls for schooling. Comparing (7) and (8), we see that adding F as a regressor changes both of the bias terms, in both cases driving the estimate of β_s downward under plausible assumptions. The second term in equation (8) shows that the downward measurement error bias increases in magnitude. As emphasized by Welch (1975) and Griliches (1977), we identify the schooling coefficient from increasingly noisy information as we control for variables that are correlated with schooling. The extent of this increase in measurement error bias will be larger the higher the correlation between schooling and the family background variables. The third term in equation (8) shows that the upward omitted variable bias is reduced by including F, the desired benefit of including proxies for unobservables.

If schooling is measured with error, then we cannot assume that estimates of returns to schooling move closer to the truth when family background variables are used as proxies for unobserved ability, even if they are good proxies. The greater the measurement error in schooling, the more likely that the inclusion of family background variables will lead to underestimates of the returns to schooling. Similarly, the greater the amount of variation in schooling that can be explained by family background, the worse the measurement error bias becomes. It is important to consider the errors-in-variables problem in our analysis of earnings, schooling, and family background in Brazil, since we shall add variables to wage regressions that are highly correlated with the observed schooling of the worker. We do have some information on the extent of the measurement error bias, however. Since we can observe the change in $R^2_{S*.F}$ as we add additional variables, we can at least make educated guesses about the increase in measurement error bias. We shall see below that even modest amounts of measurement error in schooling can translate into substantial increases in bias as we add additional variables to the regression, with important implications for the interpretation of our results.

Parental Schooling, Sons' Schooling, and Wages in Brazil

Our analysis is based on a 1982 survey of over 100,000 Brazilian households.[7] Table 1 provides descriptive statistics for the sample and illustrates the categorical responses used to report parental schooling. The head and spouse report the schooling of their father and mother as one of seven categories: illiterate, literate, 1–3 years, 4 years, 5–8 years, 9–11 years, and university, corresponding to natural breaks in the Brazilian schooling system. For the head and spouse we have more complete data on the highest single year of schooling completed. The wage variable we use throughout the paper is the ratio of monthly earnings from all jobs divided by four times the number of hours worked per week.[8]

As seen in table 1, the sample is very large, with over 40,000 economically active married males aged 30–55 reporting complete parental education data.[9] According to table 1, 39 percent of those sam-

[7] The *Pesquisa Nacional por Amostra de Domicílios* (PNAD) is an annual household survey conducted by the Instituto Brasileiro de Geografia e Estatística (IBGE). It is close to a nationally representative sample, though it is not fully representative of rural areas, especially in the remote frontier regions. The 1982 PNAD added a special supplement on education that included questions on the schooling of the parents of the head and spouse.

[8] Respondents are asked about "normal" monthly earnings and "normal" weekly hours for all jobs they held in the week prior to the survey.

[9] We use the term "married" throughout the paper although formal legal marriage is not required. The sample consists of men with a "spouse" who are heads of their households, from the IBGE definition of a household, which may include consensual unions. The results reported throughout this paper use the sample weights provided by IBGE to produce a representative sample of individuals for the Brazilian population. Sample sizes reported refer to the unweighted number of observations. All regressions and summary statistics are calculated using the sample weights.

TABLE 1

CHARACTERISTICS OF SONS BY FATHER'S SCHOOLING, MARRIED MALES AGED 30–55 WITH POSITIVE EARNINGS, 1982 PNAD

FATHER'S SCHOOLING	UNWEIGHTED N	WEIGHTED PERCENTAGE	SON'S CHARACTERISTICS				
			Mean Schooling	Wife's Schooling	Mean Wage	Percentage White	Percentage Urban
Illiterate	14,864	38.57	1.84	2.11	193.9	46.03	58.23
Literate	8,443	21.10	3.71	3.63	308.6	59.29	68.67
1–3 years	8,082	19.75	4.88	4.64	418.3	72.67	76.93
4 years	6,035	14.22	7.89	7.10	728.6	79.35	89.26
5–8 years	1,373	2.72	10.43	9.05	1,017.8	77.86	94.31
9–11 years	968	1.95	12.53	10.78	1,510.0	84.37	98.28
University	862	1.69	13.75	11.75	1,970.6	87.95	97.53
Total	40,627	100.0	4.34	4.16	416.5	61.15	70.97

NOTE.—Means calculated using PNAD sample weights. Wage calculated as monthly earnings for all jobs in cruzeiros divided by four times weekly hours.

pled have illiterate fathers, and another 40 percent have fathers with less than 4 years of schooling. Although mean schooling remains low in the sons' generation, with mean schooling of only 4.3 years, the table indicates a substantial increase in schooling across generations. For every level of father's education except the small group with university education, the mean years of schooling of the sons are roughly 2 years higher than the education reported for fathers. As shown in Lam and Levison (1991), there have been steady increases in schooling across cohorts in Brazil in recent decades, in spite of what is generally viewed as disappointing performance of the Brazilian educational system. The statistics for schooling of the wives of the men in the sample demonstrate the high degree of assortative mating by schooling in Brazil. Mean schooling for wives is close to the mean schooling for husbands in each of the separate groups of father's education. The correlation between husband's and wife's schooling is 77 in our sample.

Table 1 also shows the strong relationship between fathers' education and the education and earnings of sons. Men with university-educated fathers have, on average, 12 years more schooling and have a mean wage 10 times greater than men with illiterate fathers. The final two columns demonstrate that schooling of fathers and sons is correlated with two other important socioeconomic characteristics in Brazil, race and urban-rural location. Only 46 percent of the men with illiterate fathers are white, compared to over 80 percent of the men whose fathers have more than 8 years of schooling. Only 58 percent of the men with illiterate fathers are urban, compared to 97 percent of the men whose fathers have more than 8 years of schooling. Since an important source of returns to schooling in Brazil occurs through internal migration, we do not include controls for location in the wage equations reported below. Because of the potential confounding influence of the high correlation between education of parents and region, however, we also report results based on regressions that include controls for region and rural-urban residence.[10]

[10] There are several sample selection issues that might introduce bias in our results. The restriction to men with positive earnings is relatively insignificant in this sample of household heads aged 30–55. The restriction to married men is also relatively unimportant quantitatively but may introduce some systematic selection bias as discussed below. The restriction to men with complete data on the schooling of their parents and parents-in-law removes a nontrivial portion of men drawn nonrandomly from the bottom of the schooling and wage distribution. Where possible we have estimated results without restrictions to get information on potential biases. Regressions using data for all men with positive wages produce estimates of returns to schooling similar to those reported here for married men with complete data for all relatives. Regressions for all men with data on the schooling of their parents, independent of marital status, produce estimates for returns to schooling and effects of parental schooling almost identical to those in our sample of married men.

Estimated Effects of Parental Schooling on Earnings and Returns to Schooling

We have two major interests in the regressions reported below. Our first concern lies in the returns to the worker's own schooling and how those returns are affected by the inclusion of various family background variables. Our second concern lies in the direct effects of family background on wages. Social scientists have suggested that family background effects are important in Brazil, but the existence and size of these effects have not been well established empirically. In addition to estimating the magnitude of family background effects on wages, we argued above that the relative magnitude of own father's schooling effects and father-in-law's schooling effects may provide information regarding the cause of measured family background effects. If father-in-law effects are larger than own father effects, this may be evidence that family background variables are proxies for unobserved worker characteristics rather than measures of nepotistic family connections.

In order to formally analyze the strong association between parents' education and sons' wages shown in table 1, we estimate a series of wage equations with and without controls for parental education. Table 2 presents the results of five specifications of wage equations for married Brazilian males in 1982. All specifications include age and age squared and a dummy variable for white.[11] Below we shall also discuss results of regressions that include controls for region and urban-rural residence. In order to have maximum flexibility in the relationship between schooling and earnings, we use 17 dummy variables to represent single years of completed schooling for the worker, a specification that is empirically tractable because of our large sample size and the wide dispersion in schooling in Brazil. Regression 1 includes only the basic controls for age and race and the dummy variables for the worker's schooling. Regression 2 adds the schooling of the worker's father and mother.[12] Regression 3 omits parental schooling but adds the schooling of the wife's parents. Regression 4 uses no parental schooling variables but adds the schooling of the worker's

[11] We use age rather than experience because we have no direct measures of experience and find conventional proxies for potential experience unappealing when the majority of workers leave school at young ages. See Behrman and Birdsall (1983, 1985), Eaton (1985), and Lam and Levison (1992) for analyses of alternative measures of work experience in Brazilian earnings equations.

[12] For parents and parents-in-law we use the categorical data on parental schooling in the most flexible possible way by including the six dummy variables shown, with illiterate as the reference category.

TABLE 2

WAGE EQUATIONS, MARRIED BRAZILIAN MALES AGED 30–55. 1982 PNAD

Dependent Variable: Log of Hourly Wage ($N = 40.627$)

Variable	Regression 1	Regression 2	Regression 3	Regression 4	Regression 5
Own schooling:					
1 year	.2342 (.0172)*	.2140 (.0171)*	.2085 (.0169)*	.1988 (.0168)*	.1824 (.0168)*
2 years	.3650 (.0141)*	.3359 (.0141)*	.3279 (.0140)*	.3038 (.0139)*	.2830 (.0139)*
3 years	.5428 (.0130)*	.4967 (.0132)*	.4835 (.0130)*	.4490 (.0129)*	.4143 (.0131)*
4 years	.8492 (.0110)*	.7676 (.0116)*	.7492 (.0113)*	.7022 (.0113)*	.6396 (.0118)*
5 years	.8542 (.0159)*	.7468 (.0166)*	.7297 (.0162)*	.6654 (.0162)*	.5876 (.0167)*
6 years	1.1981 (.0271)*	1.0667 (.0274)*	1.0505 (.0270)*	.9516 (.0271)*	.8612 (.0274)*
7 years	1.2364 (.0277)*	1.0970 (.0281)*	1.0664 (.0277)*	.9581 (.0279)*	.8593 (.0282)*
8 years	1.4018 (.0170)*	1.2409 (.0181)*	1.2153 (.0176)*	1.0905 (.0182)*	.9805 (.0189)*
9 years	1.4426 (.0436)*	1.2753 (.0437)*	1.2509 (.0433)*	1.1269 (.0433)*	1.0113 (.0433)*
10 years	1.6184 (.0373)*	1.4312 (.0377)*	1.3896 (.0372)*	1.2228 (.0376)*	1.0977 (.0378)*
11 years	1.8246 (.0165)*	1.6114 (.0183)*	1.5786 (.0177)*	1.3982 (.0191)*	1.2571 (.0200)*
12 years	2.0217 (.0572)*	1.7827 (.0573)*	1.7135 (.0570)*	1.5050 (.0573)*	1.3358 (.0572)*
13 years	2.0684 (.0468)*	1.8258 (.0472)*	1.7966 (.0467)*	1.5606 (.0473)*	1.4089 (.0475)*
14 years	2.2191 (.0411)*	1.9512 (.0418)*	1.9166 (.0413)*	1.6602 (.0423)*	1.4920 (.0426)*
15 years	2.4615 (.0206)*	2.1692 (.0230)*	2.1203 (.0224)*	1.8709 (.0245)*	1.6782 (.0257)*
16 years	2.6673 (.0249)*	2.3375 (.0275)*	2.2810 (.0271)*	2.0561 (.0283)*	1.8258 (.0300)*
17 years	2.8127 (.0425)*	2.4613 (.0443)*	2.4001 (.0438)*	2.1367 (.0446)*	1.9005 (.0458)*
Wife's schooling				.0578 (.0014)*	.0451 (.0015)*
Father:					
Literate		.0283 (.0109)*			.0120 (.0108)
1–3 years		.0898 (.0119)*			.0499 (.0119)*
4 years		.1725 (.0157)*			.1005 (.0156)*
5–8 years		.1524 (.0271)*			.0688 (.0268)**
9–11 years		.2654 (.0319)*			.1533 (.0318)*
University		.3073 (.0355)*			.1859 (.0353)*

	(1)	(2)	(3)	(4)	(5)
Mother:					
Literate	.0693 (.0113)*				.0408 (.0113)*
1–3 years	.0716 (.0124)*				.0171 (.0124)
4 years	.0472 (.0161)*				.0652 (.0161)*
5–8 years	.2307 (.0289)*				.1156 (.0287)*
9–11 years	.3172 (.0324)*				.1732 (.0325)*
University	.1825 (.0596)*				.0383 (.0592)
Father-in-law:					
Literate			.0654 (.0106)*		.0401 (.0107)*
1–3 years			.1543 (.0111)*		.1090 (.0112)*
4 years			.2332 (.0143)*		.1470 (.0145)*
5–8 years			.2691 (.0253)*		.1554 (.0254)*
9–11 years			.3729 (.0303)*		.2040 (.0307)*
University			.4189 (.0351)*		.2426 (.0355)*
Mother-in-law:					
Literate			.0784 (.0111)*		.0345 (.0112)*
1–3 years			.0932 (.0115)*		.0313 (.0116)*
4 years			.1660 (.0147)*		.0623 (.0149)*
5–8 years			.2446 (.0275)*		.1031 (.0277)*
9–11 years			.2979 (.0312)*		.1105 (.0315)*
University			.2224 (.0596)*		.0380 (.0593)
Age	.0665 (.0060)*	.0686 (.0060)*	.0668 (.0059)*	.0731 (.0059)*	.0727 (.0059)*
Age squared	−.0007 (.0001)*	−.0007 (.0001)*	−.0007 (.0001)*	−.0007 (.0001)*	−.0007 (.0001)*
White	.2076 (.0087)*	.1832 (.0077)*	.1701 (.0076)*	.1767 (.0075)*	.1510 (.0076)*
Intercept	2.9744 (.1237)*	2.9176 (.1226)*	2.9167 (.1218)*	2.7323 (.1212)*	2.7298 (.1202)*
R^2	.5315	.5404	.5465	.5513	.5594
F-test 1	65.48*	65.48*	111.36*		16.52*
F-test 2					24.47*
F-test 3					2.26**

725

NOTE.—Standard errors are in parentheses. Omitted categories: own schooling; less than 1 year; parents' schooling; illiterate. F-test 1: all 12 own parents' schooling coefficients equal zero; F-test 2: all 24 parents' schooling coefficients equal zero; F-test 3: own father's schooling coefficients equal wife's father's schooling coefficients in each category.

* Significant at the .01 level.
** Significant at the .05 level.

wife, a single variable in years of completed schooling. Regression 5 includes the schooling of all these relatives simultaneously.[13]

Before we discuss specific coefficients, it is worth noting some general points regarding the explanatory power of these regressions. We see the typical result for Brazil that a small set of human capital variables has extremely high explanatory power, with an R^2 of .53 in the simple specification of regression 1. This explanatory power rises very little as we include a variety of family background variables known to be strongly associated with earnings. The R^2 increases only slightly, from .53 in the first regression, which includes only the worker's schooling, to .56 in the last regression, which adds the schooling of the worker's parents, wife, and parents-in-law. Although we clearly have high correlation among the regressors in the final equation, it is noteworthy that the standard errors are in general quite small. Because of the large sample we are remarkably successful in identifying separate effects for these variables.

Effect of Family Background on Estimated
Returns to Schooling

In order to better visualize the returns to schooling, the coefficients on the 17 dummy variables for all five specifications in table 2 are graphed in figure 1. One of the most noteworthy features of this figure is how close the step function used in table 2 is to a simple log-linear wage equation. In fact, the R^2 for a regression that replaces the 17 dummy variables in regression 1 of table 2 with a single variable for years of schooling is .527, compared to .532 for the flexible functional form in table 2.[14] An important deviation from this linearity is what appear to be substantial "sheepskin" effects associated with completion of years 4 and 8, important terminal years in the Brazilian schooling system.[15] Figure 1 also shows clearly that the estimated returns to schooling fall steadily as we move across the five regressions

[13] We restrict the sample to men with spouses (formal or consensual) in order to maintain a consistent sample across the five specifications. As shown in Schoeni (1990) and Korenman and Neumark (1991), marital status itself is typically associated with higher wages, suggesting possible selection biases in a sample of married men. We have estimated regressions 1 and 2, the two specifications that do not use wife's characteristics, on the entire set of male heads with positive wages. The results for these two regressions are robust to this sample selection, with the effects of parents' schooling being almost identical for the sample of all men and the sample of married men.

[14] The results of this log-linear specification are summarized below in table 3.

[15] Similar diploma effects are found by Strauss and Thomas (1991), using the same data set. Strauss and Thomas also estimate similar regressions separately for men and women and for different regions in Brazil.

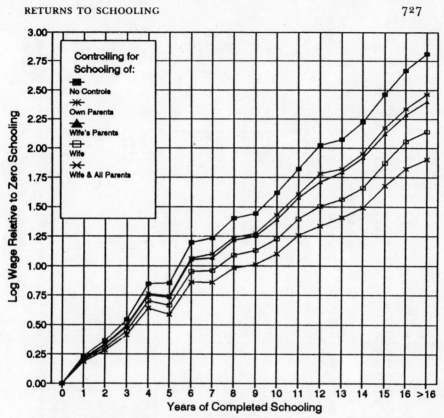

FIG. 1.—Log wage relative to 0 years of schooling, with and without controls for schooling of wife and parents, Brazilian males aged 30–55, 1982 (based on regressions in table 2).

in table 2. The lowest returns, not surprisingly, are estimated in the final regression when the complete set of family background variables is included. The next lowest returns are those estimated with the schooling of the wife included as a regressor. Especially noteworthy is that the returns estimated in regression 3, which includes the schooling of the worker's parents-in-law, are lower than the returns estimated in regression 2, which includes the schooling of the worker's parents.

The magnitude of the reductions in returns to schooling caused by including alternative sets of family background variables is summarized in table 3, which presents returns to the marginal year of schooling for several important years. In addition to the effects implied by the regressions in table 2, we also report the coefficient on years of schooling in the simple specification in which we replace the 17

TABLE 3

PREDICTED RETURNS TO MARGINAL YEAR OF SCHOOLING: PERCENTAGE INCREASE IN WAGES ASSOCIATED WITH COMPLETION OF LAST YEAR OF SCHOOLING WITH AND WITHOUT CONTROLS FOR FAMILY BACKGROUND AND REGION. MARRIED BRAZILIAN MALES AGED 30–55, 1982 PNAD

| YEARS OF SCHOOLING | No BACKGROUND VARIABLES (Reg. 1) | CONTROLLING FOR SCHOOLING OF | | | | PERCENTAGE DECREASE REG. 1 TO REG. 5 |
		Worker's Parents (Reg. 2)	Wife's Parents (Reg. 3)	Worker's Wife (Reg. 4)	Wife and All Parents (Reg. 5)	
		Without Controls for Region				
Year 1	26.39	23.86	23.18	21.99	20.01	24.18
Year 4	35.85	31.11	30.43	28.81	25.27	29.52
Year 8	17.99	15.48	16.06	14.16	12.89	28.36
Year 11	22.90	19.75	20.80	19.17	17.28	24.54
Year 15	27.43	24.36	22.59	23.45	20.47	25.39
Average, 1–16	18.66	16.18	15.74	14.13	12.45	33.26
Linear regression	16.32	14.31	14.02	12.41	11.08	32.11
Percentage increase	17.73	15.38	15.05	13.22	11.72	33.91
		With Controls for Region				
Year 1	17.75	15.32	15.53	14.69	12.84	27.69
Year 4	25.46	21.25	21.24	19.95	16.86	33.77
Year 8	16.78	14.52	15.04	13.43	12.17	27.50
Year 11	22.87	19.98	20.96	19.43	17.71	22.56
Year 15	28.01	25.03	23.62	24.54	21.65	22.70
Average, 1–16	16.26	13.89	13.74	12.45	10.80	33.56
Linear regression	14.26	12.30	12.21	10.85	9.53	33.13
Percentage increase	15.32	13.09	12.98	11.46	10.00	34.72

NOTE.—Based on regressions in table 2 and additional unreported regressions with regional and urban-rural dummies included as regressors, and with single years of schooling variable replacing dummy variables in table 2.

dummy variables with a single variable for completed years of schooling. We also report the results for all specifications when we add a set of controls for region and rural-urban residence. When no background variables are included (regression 1), we see from table 3 that the returns to a year of schooling are 26 percent for the first year, 36 percent for the fourth year, and 27 percent for the fifteenth year, the typical year for completion of college. Note from figure 1 that the diploma years represented here are associated with the largest increases in earnings.

As a summary measure, we present the simple unweighted average of the first 16 years, a figure of 18.7 percent in the specification that does not include family background variables. We also present the estimated returns for the simpler regression using a single continuous years of schooling variable. This linear specification implies returns to schooling of 17.7 percent in regression 1. Adding the schooling of the earner's parents (regression 2) causes a decline in average single-year returns of 2.5 percentage points, ranging up to 4.7 percentage points for the fourth year. Adding the schooling of the wife's parents instead of the worker's own parents causes slightly larger declines on average, with larger declines at many, but not all, levels of schooling. Inclusion of the wife's schooling without controlling for parents' schooling (regression 4) causes a substantially larger decrease in estimated returns to own schooling than the inclusion of parents' schooling. In comparison to the standard estimates in regression 1, estimated returns drop by 4.5 percentage points on average, with a decline of seven percentage points at the fourth year. Using the schooling of all five relatives as regressors (regression 5) causes an average decline of six points, with a decline of over 10 percentage points for the returns to the fourth year.

The final column of table 3 shows the percentage decrease in the estimated returns to schooling from regression 1, the simplest regression, to regression 5, the most inclusive. The declines are remarkably similar across levels of schooling and alternative specifications, typically in the range of 25–35 percent. Regressions that include regional controls, shown in the lower panel of the table, have lower estimated returns to schooling at all levels. In spite of this lower level in the estimated returns, however, the proportional decline in the returns caused by inclusion of family background variables is almost identical in the two sets of regressions. One interpretation of the numbers in the final column of table 3, then, is that the conventional estimates of returns to schooling include a "family background bias" on the order of 25–35 percent. We shall return to this interpretation below when we consider the role of measurement error.

Direct Effects of Family Background on Earnings

We are also interested in the direct effects of family background on wages. It is important to emphasize that in spite of the high correlations between the schooling of all the family members included in the regressions in table 2, we are able to estimate statistically significant independent effects of the separate schooling variables. With the large sample size of the PNAD, we have enough independent variation in the separate schooling variables to overcome what might be expected to be an extreme multicollinearity problem. The data provide strong evidence, for example, that even after one controls for the worker's own schooling, the schooling of his parents, and the schooling of his wife, a man whose father-in-law has a secondary education has significantly higher earnings than a man whose father-in-law is illiterate. While we are left with a number of potential interpretations of this relationship, we can be reasonably confident that it is "real" in a statistical sense.

Regression 2, which includes the schooling of the worker's father and mother, shows a significant wage advantage for men with better-educated parents. When one controls for the earner's own education and that of his mother, having a university-educated father implies more than a 35 percent wage advantage over having an illiterate father.[16] Having a university-educated father implies a 14 percent wage advantage over having a father with 4 years of schooling. Significant wage advantages are also associated with mother's schooling. When one controls for the earner's own schooling and that of his father, having a mother with 9–11 years of schooling implies a 37 percent wage advantage over having an illiterate mother. Several studies, including Heckman and Hotz (1986) for Panamanian males and Behrman and Wolfe (1984) for Nicaraguan females, have found that mother's schooling has a larger effect on earnings than father's schooling. Thomas, Strauss, and Henriques (1990) also find larger effects of mother's schooling on child health outcomes in Brazil. We find mixed results regarding the relative effects of father's and mother's schooling. In regression 2, mother's education has a larger effect at 5–8 years and 9–11 years, whereas father's education has a larger effect at 1–3 years, 4 years, and university.[17]

---

[16] That is, from the coefficient in regression 2 of table 2, a university-educated father implies a wage that is $e^{0.3073} = 1.3597$ times the wage of a man with an illiterate father.

[17] We show low estimates for the effects of university-educated mothers and mothers-in-law in a number of the regressions. We do not attach great significance to these since the number of women in these cells is quite low. Note that the effects of 9–11 years of schooling are generally as large for women as for men.

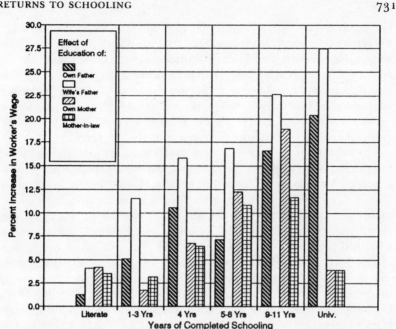

FIG. 2.—Effects of parent's schooling on earnings: percentage wage increase relative to parent being illiterate, with controls for schooling of worker and other relatives, Brazilian males aged 30–55, 1982 (based on regression 5 in table 2).

Regression 3 replaces the schooling of parents with the schooling of parents-in-law. The most striking result is that the coefficients on the schooling of fathers-in-law are larger than the corresponding coefficients on the schooling of fathers in regression 2 for every schooling category. The coefficients on the schooling of mothers-in-law are larger than the coefficients on the schooling of mothers in all but one category. This same result that the schooling of fathers-in-law has a larger effect than the schooling of the fathers is also observed in regression 5, which includes parents and parents-in-law in the same regression. The direct effects of the family background variables estimated in regression 5 are summarized graphically in figure 2. The figure shows the percentage wage increases associated with each category of parental schooling for the worker's father, mother, father-in-law, and mother-in-law, based on the final regression in table 2, the regression that includes the full set of family background variables. The figure shows the consistently larger effect of the schooling of the father-in-law compared to the schooling of the father. The wage increase associated with the father-in-law's schooling is on the order of five percentage points larger than the wage increase associated with the father's schooling. When one controls for the education of the earner, his wife, his parents, and his mother-in-law, having a university-educated father-in-law is associated with 28 percent higher wages than having an illiterate father-in-law. Having a university-educated father is associated with a 20 percent wage advantage compared to having an illiterate father on the basis of the coefficients in regression 5. The third F-test, reported in table 2, shows that we can reject the null hypothesis that the schooling coefficients for father's and father-in-law's schooling are equal at the .05 level.[18]

The relative magnitudes of these coefficients are interesting in their own right. Moreover, we believe that the result that father-in-law's schooling has a larger effect on wages than father's schooling, a result that is very robust to alternative specifications, sheds light on the plausibility of alternative explanations for the strong association between the earnings of a worker and the schooling of his parents, wife, and parents-in-law. Specifically, the relative magnitudes of these effects lead us to believe that the effect of parental schooling is not due solely to "family connections." As demonstrated above in the theoretical model of assortative mating, it is quite plausible that a worker's unobserved wage-related characteristics would be more highly correlated with the schooling of his parents-in-law than with the schooling of his own parents. We argue that the most convincing interpretation of these family background effects is that they are proxies for unobserved worker characteristics. To the extent that these characteristics increase labor productivity, an efficient labor market should be expected to reward them. Our estimates of high returns to family background therefore need not be considered evidence of labor market imperfections.

The role of own schooling and parental schooling in explaining wages is further clarified by table 4. The table summarizes the effect on wages of changing the number of years of schooling for the earner, his wife, his parents, and his wife's parents, on the basis of the regression coefficients in the final regression of table 2. The table

[18] The coefficients on parental schooling in table 2 depend on the arbitrary choice of the omitted schooling category. As inspection of fig. 2 suggests, not every marginal increase in schooling categories gives a bigger wage increase for father-in-law's schooling than for father's schooling. Increasing the father's schooling from 5–8 years to 9–11 years, e.g., implies a larger wage increase than increasing the father-in-law's schooling by the same amount. The tendency for larger effects of increases in father-in-law's schooling is predominant, however. Out of 21 possible pairwise comparisons across schooling categories in regression 5, increases in father-in-law's schooling imply larger wage increases than increases in father's schooling in 16 cases. In separate tests for significance of each of these 21 pairwise comparisons (an extremely demanding test of the data), four imply significantly larger effects for father-in-law's schooling at the .05 level and none implies significantly larger effects for father's schooling. As noted, the joint restriction that the coefficients for fathers and fathers-in-law are equal is rejected.

TABLE 4

PREDICTED WAGE INCREASE FROM INCREASES IN SCHOOLING, MARRIED
BRAZILIAN MALES AGED 30–55, 1982 PNAD

	PERCENTAGE INCREASE IN EARNINGS ASSOCIATED WITH INCREASE IN SCHOOLING FROM		
EFFECT OF	0–4 Years (1)	4–16 Years (2)	0–16 Years (3)
Own schooling	89.57	227.47	520.80
Wife's schooling	19.79	71.90	105.92
Father's schooling	10.57	8.92	20.43
Wife's father's schooling	15.84	10.03	27.46
Mother's schooling	6.74	−2.66	3.91
Wife's mother's schooling	6.43	−2.41	3.87

NOTE.—Based on coefficients in regression 5, table 2. Calculations were made at higher precision than coefficients reported in table 2.

makes it possible, for example, to compare the wage increase associated with increasing the worker's schooling from 0 to 4 years with the wage increase resulting from an increase in his father's education from 0 to 4 years.[19] Consider first increasing various family members' schooling from 0 to 4 years, shown in column 1 of table 4. Raising the worker's own schooling, holding the schooling of other family members constant, raises his wage by 90 percent. Raising his wife's schooling by the same amount, holding constant the schooling of the earner and other family members, is associated with a wage increase of 19.8 percent. Raising his father's schooling from 0 to 4 years, holding the schooling of the earner and other family members constant, implies a wage increase of 10.6 percent. Raising his father-in-law's schooling from 0 to 4 years has a substantially larger effect, implying a wage increase of 15.8 percent. Increases from 0 to 4 years in the schooling of the earner's mother and mother-in-law are associated with wage increases of under 7 percent.

Column 2 shows the effect of moving from 4 to 16 years of schooling, assumed equivalent to the "university" category for parental schooling. An important result of this exercise is that the wage increase associated with having a father with 16 years rather than 4 years of schooling is smaller than the wage increase associated with having a father with 4 years rather than 0 years. We see in column 3 that the wage advantage implied by a university-educated father compared to an illiterate father is 20.4 percent. If we decompose this

[19] For example, wife's father with university compared to wife's father with 4 years implies a predicted log wage difference of .2426 − .1470 = .0956, according to regression 5 in table 2. This implies a wage ratio of $e^{0.0956} = 1.1003$, or a percentage increase in earnings of 10.03 percent, as shown in col. 2 of table 4.

into a portion caused by the father moving from 0 to 4 years and a portion caused by the father moving from 4 to 16 years, those components are 10.6 percent and 8.9 percent, respectively.[20] The additional 12 or so years of schooling from 4 years to university result in a wage increase that is smaller than the increase caused by the first 4 years of the father's schooling. The effects of parental schooling on wages, then, while apparently substantial, are not associated only with those at the top of the schooling and earnings distributions. Sons of fathers with 4 years of schooling have as large a wage advantage over sons of illiterate fathers as the wage advantage that sons of university-educated fathers have over sons of fathers with 4 years of schooling. Table 4 also demonstrates that while the earnings advantages associated with parental education are substantial, they are modest compared to the returns to the worker's own education. Increasing the worker's own schooling from 4 to 16 years, for example, holding the schooling of the other five family members constant, implies a wage increase of over 200 percent. Increasing the schooling of his father or father-in-law from 4 to 16 years, whatever that may represent, implies a wage increase of only about 10 percent.

Interpretation and Consideration of Measurement Error

A number of interpretations can be given to the apparent effects of the schooling of parents, wife, and parents-in-law on wages and returns to schooling. The estimates may represent direct returns to "family connections," presumably implying imperfections in Brazilian labor markets. Alternatively, as demonstrated in our model of assortative mating, the schooling of parents, wife, and parents-in-law may be proxies for unobserved characteristics of the worker such as ability or quality of schooling. Although these two interpretations have quite different implications for labor market imperfections in Brazil, both imply that conventional returns to schooling are overestimated. Under either of these interpretations the returns to schooling estimated with family background variables included are likely to be closer to the returns that would be experienced by a randomly drawn Brazilian worker. The results imply that after controlling for all these family background variables, we are left with returns of over 10 percent at all levels. This is one-fourth to one-third lower than the returns implied by conventional wage equations, but still represent significant private returns to schooling. Our results are similar to those in previous studies from Latin America. Behrman and Wolfe (1984) estimate a family background bias of about one-quarter using sibling

---

[20] That is, from the row for father's schooling in table 4, $1.1057 \times 1.0892 = 1.2043$.

data from Nicaragua, and Heckman and Hotz (1986) observe that returns to schooling drop by one-third when schooling of the mother and father is included in the earnings equation.

One interpretation of our results, then, is that conventional estimates of returns to schooling in Brazil may be roughly one-third family background bias when family background variables are not controlled for. This estimate of one-third may overstate the bias in conventional estimates of returns to schooling, however. As emphasized above, if schooling is measured with error, then inclusion of family background variables that are highly correlated with observed schooling will increase the magnitude of the downward bias due to measurement error. To see how important measurement error can be in our results, consider the case of regressions in which worker's schooling is represented by a single linear schooling variable instead of the 17 dummy variables used in table 2. Drawing on our analysis of measurement error above, and denoting the measurement error bias by m, note from equation (8) that

$$m = \frac{-\lambda\beta_s}{1 - R^2_{S*\cdot F}},$$ (9)

where $\lambda = V(w)/V(S*)$, the proportion of measurement error in observed schooling; β_s is the true returns to schooling; and $R^2_{S*\cdot F}$ is the R^2 from a regression of measured schooling on all other included variables. As we add additional family background variables, the measurement error increases as $R^2_{S*\cdot F}$ increases. Since we can estimate $R^2_{S*\cdot F}$ for any set of independent variables F, we can get some sense of the potential increase in measurement error bias.

Table 5 shows what the measurement error bias would be for our estimates of returns to schooling when different sets of family background variables are used, given alternative assumptions about the noise-to-signal ratio λ and true returns to schooling β_s. As shown in the first row of the table, $\hat{\beta}$ falls by about one-third, from .163 to .111, when the full set of family background variables is included, consistent with our results above. The third row of the table shows $R^2_{S*\cdot F}$ for each set of regressors. For regression 1 the only regressors besides worker's schooling are age, age squared, and race. As shown in the table, a regression of worker's schooling on these variables has an R^2 of .098. If we assume that observed schooling is 15 percent measurement error ($\lambda = .15$) and true returns to schooling $\beta_s = .15$, then from equation (9) we can calculate that the measurement error bias in $\hat{\beta}$ in regression 1 is $-.025$.[21] When dummies for the schooling

[21] We can make only educated guesses about the amount of measurement error in our schooling variable. Ashenfelter and Krueger (1992) estimate measurement error

TABLE 5

INCREASE IN MEASUREMENT ERROR BIAS IN EARNINGS EQUATIONS: ALTERNATIVE SETS OF FAMILY BACKGROUND VARIABLES AND ALTERNATIVE ASSUMPTIONS OF MEASUREMENT ERROR AND RETURNS TO SCHOOLING, MARRIED BRAZILIAN MALES AGED 30–55, 1982 PNAD

	No Background Variables (Reg. 1)	Controlling for Schooling of			
		Worker's Parents (Reg. 2)	Wife's Parents (Reg. 3)	Worker's Wife (Reg. 4)	Wife and All Parents (Reg. 5)
Estimated returns to schooling $\hat{\beta}_i$	.1632	.1431	.1402	.1241	.1108
R^2	.5265	.5360	.5421	.5460	.5550
$R^2_{S \cdot F}$	.0980	.4874	.4430	.6052	.6742
$\Delta\hat{\beta}_i = \hat{\beta}_i - \hat{\beta}_1$		−.0201	−.0230	−.0391	−.0524
$\lambda = .15, \beta_s = .15$:					
Measurement error bias m_i	−.0249	−.0439	−.0404	−.0570	−.0691
$\Delta m_i = m_i - m_1$		−.0189	−.0155	−.0320	−.0441
$\Delta m_i / \Delta\beta_i$		94.28%	67.18%	81.96%	84.19%
$\lambda = .1, \beta_s = .15$: $\Delta m_i / \Delta\beta_i$		62.85%	44.78%	54.64%	56.13%
$\lambda = .1, \beta_s = .1$: $\Delta m_i / \Delta\beta_i$		41.90%	29.86%	36.43%	37.42%
$\lambda = .05, \beta_s = .05$: $\Delta m_i / \Delta\beta_i$		10.48%	7.46%	9.11%	9.35%

NOTE.—All regressions include age, age squared, and race plus family background variables indicated. All changes are relative to regression 1. λ is the noise-to-signal ratio in measured schooling; β_s is the true returns to schooling.

of the worker's father and mother are included, the R^2 of worker's schooling on all other regressors increases dramatically to .487. Including these variables in the earnings equation causes $\hat{\beta}$ to fall from .163 to .143. Continuing to assume that $\lambda = .15$ and $\beta_s = .15$, we calculate from equation (9) that the measurement error bias in $\hat{\beta}$ is $-.044$. The change in measurement error bias from regression 1 to regression 2 is $-.0189$, compared to a change in the estimate of $\hat{\beta}$ of $-.0201$. In other words, 95 percent of the observed change in $\hat{\beta}$ would be due to the increase in measurement error bias if $\lambda = .15$ and $\beta_s = .15$. From the other columns of table 5, over 80 percent of the observed decline in $\hat{\beta}$ as additional family background variables are used would be attributable to increased measurement error bias under the assumption that $\lambda = .15$ and $\beta_s = .15$.

The last three rows of table 5 show the change in measurement error bias across regressions given lower values of λ and β_s. Even given what seem to be conservative estimates for λ and β of .10, measurement error bias accounts for almost 40 percent of the observed decline in $\hat{\beta}$ across regressions. Only when both λ and β approach .05 do we see measurement error explaining less than 10 percent of the observed decline in $\hat{\beta}$. While we have little firm basis for estimating either the proportion of measurement error in schooling or the true returns to schooling, levels of 10–15 percent for both quantities seem plausible. It is clear that even modest levels of measurement error can lead to substantial increases in measurement error bias when family background variables such as the ones we use are added to standard wage equations. The conclusion that conventional estimates of returns to schooling in Latin America are one-third family background bias, then, may be too strong. Previous studies that have reached similar conclusions, such as Behrman and Wolfe (1984) and Heckman and Hotz (1986), may have overstated the extent of the bias, since they did not consider the potentially serious role of measurement error bias.

Conclusions

Using data on the schooling of an earner's parents, wife, and parents-in-law, we identify substantial effects of family background on wages

---

in reported schooling in the United States of about 10 percent. Since the total variance in schooling is much higher in Brazil, the proportion that is measurement error may be smaller (Lam and Levison [1992] show a variance in schooling in Brazil more than twice the variance in the United States, even though the Brazilian mean is less than half the U.S. mean). On the other hand, there may be an overall tendency for greater inaccuracy of reports in Brazil, combined with greater proportional errors due to the restriction that errors will be in integer quantities around a much lower mean.

in Brazil. When one controls for the earner's own schooling and the schooling of the other four relatives, having a father with a university education is associated with a 20 percent wage advantage compared to having an illiterate father, and a 9 percent advantage compared to having a father with 4 years of schooling. Inclusion of family background variables in wage equations lowers estimated returns to schooling by one-fourth to one-third, consistent with previous studies of Latin American labor markets.

Our analysis of the confounding influence of measurement error suggests that our estimate that conventional estimates of returns to schooling in Brazil are one-third family background bias may be overstated. Looking at the components of measurement error bias, we make alternative assumptions about the magnitude of measurement error and the true returns to schooling. Combining these assumptions with estimates of the correlations between observed schooling and our family background variables, we show that even modest assumptions about the degree of measurement error imply that increased measurement error bias accounts for a large proportion of the decline in estimated returns to schooling when family background variables are added to the wage equation. Our results suggest that failing to take account of measurement error may lead to substantial overestimates of the magnitude of the family background bias in estimates of returns to schooling.

While our results are consistent with "structuralist" models of labor markets that emphasize labor market imperfections and an important role for family connections, we find the results more consistent with alternative interpretations. A surprising and substantively important result is that the schooling of fathers-in-law has a greater effect on workers' wages than the schooling of fathers. This result, though counterintuitive, is consistent with our model of intergenerational transmission of schooling and assortative mating. We interpret the result as evidence that family background variables are proxies for unobserved worker characteristics, rather than direct determinants of earnings through nepotistic family connections.

Although we estimate nontrivial effects of the schooling of parents and parents-in-law on wages, it is important to emphasize that the effects are modest in comparison to the effects of the worker's own schooling. While having a father with 4 years of schooling implies a 9 percent wage advantage over having an illiterate father, ceteris paribus, increasing the worker's own schooling from 0 to 4 years implies a 90 percent increase in earnings. Even ignoring the potentially important role of measurement error bias, we continue to estimate returns to schooling of over 10 percent after controlling for the schooling of the worker's parents, wife, and parents-in-law.

References

Ashenfelter, Orley, and Krueger, Alan. "Estimates of the Economic Return to Schooling from a New Sample of Twins." Working Paper no. 304. Princeton, N.J.: Princeton Univ., Indus. Relations Sec., June 1992.

Becker, Gary S. *A Treatise on the Family.* Cambridge, Mass.: Harvard Univ. Press, 1981.

Behrman, Jere R., and Birdsall, Nancy. "The Quality of Schooling: Quantity Alone Is Misleading." *A.E.R.* 73 (December 1983): 928–46.

———. "The Quality of Schooling: Reply." *A.E.R.* 75 (December 1985): 1202–5.

Behrman, Jere R.; Birdsall, Nancy; and Deolalikar, Anil. "Marriage Markets, Labor Markets and Unobserved Human Capital: An Empirical Exploration for South-Central India." Working paper. Philadelphia: Univ. Pennsylvania, 1993.

Behrman, Jere R., and Taubman, Paul. "Intergenerational Transmission of Income and Wealth." *A.E.R. Papers and Proc.* 66 (May 1976): 436–40.

Behrman, Jere R., and Wolfe, Barbara L. "The Socioeconomic Impact of Schooling in a Developing Country." *Rev. Econ. and Statis.* 66 (May 1984): 296–303.

Bowles, Samuel. "Schooling and Inequality from Generation to Generation." *J.P.E.* 80, no. 3, pt. 2 (May/June 1972): S219–S251.

Chamberlain, Gary, and Griliches, Zvi. "Unobservables with a Variance-Components Structure: Ability, Schooling, and the Economic Success of Brothers." *Internat. Econ. Rev.* 16 (June 1975): 422–49.

Corcoran, Mary; Gordon, Roger; Laren, Deborah; and Solon, Gary. "Effects of Family and Community Background on Economic Status." *A.E.R. Papers and Proc.* 80 (May 1990): 362–66.

Eaton, Peter J. "The Quality of Schooling: Comment." *A.E.R.* 75 (December 1985): 1195–1201.

Griliches, Zvi. "Estimating the Returns to Schooling: Some Econometric Problems." *Econometrica* 45 (January 1977): 1–22.

Griliches, Zvi, and Mason, William M. "Education, Income, and Ability." *J.P.E.* 80, no. 3, pt. 2 (May/June 1972): S74–S103.

Hauser, Robert M., and Sewell, William H. "Family Effects in Simple Models of Education, Occupational Status, and Earnings: Findings from the Wisconsin and Kalamazoo Studies." *J. Labor Econ.* 4, no. 3, pt. 2 (July 1986): S83–S115.

Heckman, James J., and Hotz, V. Joseph. "An Investigation of the Labor Market Earnings of Panamanian Males: Evaluating the Sources of Inequality." *J. Human Resources* 21 (Fall 1986): 507–42.

Korenman, Sanders, and Neumark, David. "Does Marriage Really Make Men More Productive?" *J. Human Resources* 26 (Spring 1991): 282–307.

Lam, David. "Marriage Markets and Assortative Mating with Household Public Goods: Theoretical Results and Empirical Implications." *J. Human Resources* 23 (Fall 1988): 462–87.

Lam, David, and Levison, Deborah. "Declining Inequality in Schooling in Brazil and Its Effects on Inequality in Earnings." *J. Development Econ.* 37 (November 1991): 199–225.

———. "Age, Experience, and Schooling: Decomposing Earnings Inequality in the United States and Brazil." *Sociological Inquiry* 62 (Spring 1992): 220–45.

Langoni, Carlos Geraldo. "Income Distribution and Economic Development:

The Brazilian Case." In *Frontiers of Quantitative Economics*, vol. B, edited by Michael Intriligator. Amsterdam: North-Holland, 1977.

Psacharopoulos, George. "Returns to Education: A Further International Update and Implications." *J. Human Resources* 20 (Fall 1985): 583–604.

Schoeni, Robert F. "The Earnings Effects of Marital Status: Results for Twelve Countries." Research Report no. 90-172. Ann Arbor: Univ. Michigan, Population Studies Center, 1990.

Schultz, T. Paul. "Education Investments and Returns." In *Handbook of Development Economics*, vol. 1, edited by Hollis Chenery and T. N. Srinivasan. Amsterdam: North-Holland, 1988.

Strauss, John, and Thomas, Duncan. "Wages, Schooling and Background: Investments in Men and Women in Urban Brazil." Paper presented at the World Bank Conference on Education, Growth, and Inequality in Brazil, Rio de Janeiro, March 1991.

Thomas, Duncan; Strauss, John; and Henriques, Maria-Helena. "Child Survival, Height for Age and Household Characteristics in Brazil." *J. Development Econ.* 33 (October 1990): 197–234.

Welch, Finis. "Human Capital Theory: Education, Discrimination, and Life Cycles." *A.E.R. Papers and Proc.* 65 (May 1975): 63–73.

Part II
Health: Length of Life, Stature and Sickness

[6]

5   Causes and Consequences of Mortality Declines in Less Developed Countries during the Twentieth Century

Samuel H. Preston

Only a few countries of Africa, Asia, and Latin America can supply suitable data for estimating mortality levels in 1900. Many more can supply such data for 1940 or 1950. Without exception, the estimated levels of mortality prevailing in those years are higher than current levels. For those countries that can provide data at both earlier points, most improvement as indexed by life expectancy at birth has been achieved since 1940. It appears from fragmentary records that life expectancy at birth during 1935–39 was about 30 years in Africa and Asia and 40 years in Latin America. The respective levels in 1965–70 were on the order of 43, 50, and 60 (World Health Organization 1974b; United Nations, Population Division 1973).

The magnitude and the demographic character of this improvement have been documented in a number of excellent reviews, and for this reason they need not detain us here (United Nations 1963, 1973, 1974; Stolnitz 1974; Arriaga 1970; World Health Organization 1974b). These works suggest that the mortality improvements, when measured by the absolute decline in age-specific death rates, have tended to be largest at ages under 5 (especially infancy) and above 40. The proportionate declines, on the other hand, have been largest in the older childhood ages. Life expectancy gains for females have been larger than those for males. It is likely that gains have been more rapid in urban than in rural areas. In these matters, mortality experience in less developed countries

Samuel H. Preston is associated with the University of Washington.

The author is grateful to Avery Guest, James McCann, Peter Newman, and Masanori Hashimoto for comments and suggestions and to William Grady and Thomas Revis for research assistance. This research was aided by National Institutes of Health Center Grant 1POL HD 09397–01.

(LDCs) has roughly recapitulated that in more developed countries (MDCs). Life expectancy differences between MDCs and LDCs have narrowed, although the lagging pace of improvement in Africa has produced greater dispersion within LDCs themselves. The decadal rate of mortality decline in many LDCs surpasses that ever observed in populations of the now-developed world.

This paper has two purposes: to identify the factors responsible for these mortality improvements in LDCs and provide estimates of their relative importance; and to begin tracing the effect of these improvements on demographic and economic processes. Less developed countries are defined regionally to comprise Africa, Latin America, and Asia except Japan. Data on mainland China, North Korea, and what was formerly North Vietnam are not available, and for all practical purposes these countries are also excluded from the set under review. Conclusions reached about the importance of various factors in the mortality decline do not appear to conflict with the impressions of informed observers of these matters in China (Wegman, Lin, and Purcell 1973).

5.1 Causes of Declining Mortality

There is much more consensus on the fact of mortality decline in LDCs than on its causes. Considerable dispute remains about whether the decline has been principally a by-product of social and economic development as reflected in private standards of nutrition, housing, clothing, transportation, water supply, medical care, and so on or whether it was primarily produced by social policy measures with an unprecedented scope or efficacy. A third possibility is that technical changes reduced the relative costs of good health. This possibility is usually subsumed within the social policy position because it is clear to most observers that the major technical changes that have occurred—immunization against a host of infectious diseases, vector eradication, chemotherapy —had to be embodied in social programs in order to affect the mortality of the masses in LDCs. Demographers have almost unanimously favored the social policy–technical change interpretation of mortality decline (Davis 1956; Coale and Hoover 1958; United Nations, Population Division 1974; Stolnitz 1974). As evidence, they have principally cited the unprecedented rate of mortality reduction in many LDCs and certain dramatic examples of obviously effective government intervention, most notably in Sri Lanka and Mauritius. Many specialists in international health (Fredericksen 1961, 1966a,b; Marshall, Brown, and Goodrich 1971), medical historians focusing on primarily Western populations (McKeown and Record 1962; McKeown 1965), and some economists (Sharpston 1976) have opposed this interpretation, usually claiming

291   Mortality Declines in Less Developed Countries

that social interventions have been largely ineffective or insufficiently widespread.

Kuznets (1975) and Coale and Hoover (1958) have argued that, in one sense, the distinction between economic development and public health interventions creates a false dichotomy. Development itself strengthens the nation-state, improves communications among nations and hence facilitates the transfer of medical technology, and routinizes scientific advance. While this position is unassailable, it leaves unanswered the question whether the mortality decline was a product of changes in private consumption or of public programs and technical change, regardless of whether the latter were in turn produced by economic development in its broadest sense. Even if public programs and technical changes were merely intervening variables in the relation between mortality and development, the importance of their role remains to be identified.

5.1.1   Effect of Private Income Levels on Mortality

That mortality rates are sensitive to private living standards, independent of the national level of economic development, scarcely needs documentation. Studies of mortality differentials among individuals by social or economic class in countries as disparate as India and the United States consistently reveal lower mortality rates among the upper classes (Kitagawa and Hauser 1973; Vaidyanathan 1972). The role of private living standards in creating the pattern of international mortality differentials is more difficult to assess. Richer countries not only have richer people but, in general, have larger and more effective social programs.

Some indication of the importance of private living standards for international mortality differences may be gained by examining the importance of income distribution as a factor in those differences. The international relation between national income per capita and life expectancy is decidedly nonlinear, with life expectancy showing strongly diminishing returns to increases in income (Preston 1975a; Vallin 1968). It is reasonable to expect that mortality also responds nonlinearly to individual income levels, in which case the distribution of income within a nation should influence its aggregate level of mortality. In particular, suppose that the relation between individual income and life expectancy is log linear:[1]

$$e^o{}_{0i} = a + b \ln Y_i,$$

where $e^o{}_{0i}$ = life expectancy at birth in income group i

Y_i = level of income received by group i

a, b = constants.

If the national level of life expectancy is simply the aggregate of these individual-level relations, with no contribution from the *national* level of income except insofar as it reflects individual incomes, then the life expectancy for the population, $e^o{}_{0p}$, will be equal to

$$e^o{}_{0p} = f[\sum_i (a + b \ln Y_i)]$$

$$= a + b \ln Y + b \times f \times \sum_i \ln (S_i/f),$$

where Y = mean level of income in the population
S_i = share of total national income earned by group i
f = share of total population represented by group i, assumed to be constant among the groups.

Life expectancy will be a function of mean national income, Y, and of the distribution of income as represented by the term $\sum_i \ln(S_i/f)$. This term, which is related to the entropy measure of income distribution, ranges from 0 if income is perfectly evenly distributed to $(-\infty)$ if one group has no income. Strictly speaking, the weights that permit subgroup life expectancies to aggregate into population life expectancy are provided by births rather than by population size, but the two will be very highly correlated.

To examine the importance of private incomes for national life expectancy, the value of this income distribution measure was computed for fifty-two populations on which income shares were estimated in 5% population segments. The values and sources can be found in appendix table 5.A.2, along with values of $e^o{}_0$ and Y. The importance of private incomes can be inferred from the consistency of coefficients on Y and on the income distribution measure. If national life expectancy is simply a function of private income levels, the coefficients on $\sum_i \ln(S_i/.05)$ should be 0.05 of the coefficient on Y. If national income contributes independently of private income, the ratio should be less than 0.05. The equation as estimated by ordinary least squares on the fifty-two observations is

$$e^o{}_0 = 19.105 + 6.984 \ln \overline{Y} + .375 \sum_i \ln(S_i/.05)$$
$$\quad\quad\quad\quad (.859) \quad\quad (.237)$$

$$R^2 = .651$$
$$\overline{R}^2 = .644.$$

The coefficient of the income distribution term is in fact 0.0536 of that of national income, suggesting that relations between mortality and income at the national level are indeed dominated by relations between mortality and income at the individual level. This result should be treated with great caution because of inaccuracy and incomparability in the measure of income distribution and because the log-linear functional form probably simplifies a more complex relationship. Furthermore, the standard error of the income distributional coefficient is large enough to prevent rejection of the hypothesis that the true coefficient is zero. Nevertheless, one direct implication of the result is that the mortality risks facing a family earning $10,000 per year or $100 per year are not strongly influenced by the prevailing level of average income in the nation in which they reside.

The suggestion that private incomes are very influential in determining national levels of life expectancy at a moment in time does not imply, of course, that changes in private incomes have been the dominant factor in mortality changes during this century. The actual changes in income may have been too small, in conjunction with the sensitivity of mortality to income, to account for the observed mortality changes. Before trying to establish the role played by changes in private living standards in LDC mortality declines, it is useful to make an assessment of the causes of death responsible for those declines.

5.1.2   Causes of Death Responsible for Mortality Declines

Interpretation of mortality declines in LDCs would depend on whether the cause of death responsible for the majority of declines were, for example, smallpox, diarrheal disease, or malaria, since it is clear that death rates from these causes are fundamentally responsive to different influences. Unfortunately, the causes of death responsible for mortality change in LDCs have never been documented on a broad scale. A large part of the reason is that most LDCs still cannot supply national-level data on cause patterns, and data for those that can undoubtedly reflect inaccurate diagnoses and incomplete coverage. Problems are magnified when attention is turned to the patterns of earlier years. Nevertheless, it is possible to piece together a picture that provides some useful clues about the order of magnitude of the causes responsible.

First, it is clear that, in high-mortality populations, infectious and parasitic diseases bear almost exclusive responsibility for shortening life below the modern Western standards of 69 years for a male and 75 for a female. Life tables by cause of death have been constructed for 165 populations at varying levels of mortality (Preston, Keyfitz, and Schoen 1972). When the aggregate of infectious and parasitic diseases were hypothetically eliminated from those life tables and life expectancy was recalculated, the common result was to produce a life expectancy between 65 and 70 for males and between 70 and 75 for females, regardless of a population's initial mortality level (Preston, Keyfitz, and Schoen 1973). In 1920, Chilean males would hypothetically have gone from a life expectancy of 28.47 to one of 65.68 and females from 29.85 to 69.76. In Taiwan, males would have enjoyed a life expectancy of

72.27 years instead of 26.68, and females 76.00 instead of 29.18 (Preston, Keyfitz, and Schoen 1972, pp. 150–51, 702–3).[2]

Despite the appeal of life table measures, they are an unnecessarily awkward vehicle for discussing causes of death because the causes are nonadditive in their effect on life table parameters. This problem is averted by the use of age-standardized death rates. Models have been constructed to represent the typical cause-of-death structure for populations at various levels of mortality as indexed by the age-standardized crude death rate from all causes combined (Preston and Nelson 1974). Of the 165 populations supplying data for these models, only 41 were from Africa, Asia, or Latin America, and of these 5 were for Japan and 3 for the Jewish population of Israel. Nevertheless, the results suggest that cause-of-death structures, controlling mortality level, vary less between MDCs and LDCs than they do among regional groups within MDCs. Lower cardiovascular mortality and higher mortality from diarrheal diseases and maternal causes in LDCs represent their only significant divergence from MDC patterns (Preston and Nelson 1974, p. 37). John Gordon, one of the leading epidemiologists whose work focuses on developing countries, states that "infectious disease in the tropics and in some other preindustrial areas is too often viewed elsewhere as a collection of odd processes peculiar to those regions. Such diseases as schistosomiasis, filariasis, paragonimiasis, and all the others do exist. The plight of children, however, [who account for the bulk of annual deaths in LDCs] is the result of the everyday infections of the intestinal and respiratory tracts and with the communicable diseases specific to early life everywhere" (Gordon 1969, p. 218). Even among adults, the exotic tropical diseases are typically much more important sources of morbidity than of mortality.

Thus, there is some justification for allowing LDC cause-of-death patterns to be represented by relationships calculated on the basis of a data set that includes both MDCs and LDCs. The typical cause structures pertaining to populations with age-standardized crude death rates of 0.035 and 0.020 are presented in table 5.1.[3] These are roughly the levels that probably best characterize the average mortality situation in LDCs in 1900 and 1970, since they correspond to life expectancies at birth of 27.5 and 50.[4]

What is perhaps surprising about the table is that the specific "name" infectious and parasitic diseases (the first two listed) account for only an estimated 26.1% of mortality change. More important than all of these diseases combined—tuberculosis, typhoid, typhus, cholera, measles, diphtheria, whooping cough, malaria—is the category of respiratory diseases, which comprises a wide assortment of respiratory difficulties that are concentrated largely in infancy and old age. To be sure, some of the deaths in this category are improperly assigned complications of

Table 5.1   "Normal" Cause-of-Death Patterns at Standardized Crude Death Rates of 35/1,000 and 20/1,000 and Cause-Patterns of Change

Cause of Death	Model Value (Mean, Male and Female) of Age-Standardized Crude Death Rate from Cause at Age-Standardized Crude Death Rate from all Causes Combined of		Percentage of Decline Attributable to Cause
	35/1,000	20/1,000	
Respiratory tuberculosis	3.85	1.42	9.5
Other infectious and parasitic diseases	4.00	1.51	16.6
Influenza/pneumonia/bronchitis	7.85	2.87	33.2
Diarrheal disease	2.32	1.34	6.5
Maternal causes	.27	.14	0.9
Certain diseases of infancy	1.37	.88	3.3
Violence	.89	.78	0.7
All other and unknown	15.45	11.06	29.3
Total			100.0

Source: Preston and Nelson (1974).

specific infectious diseases. After undergoing a careful review of the initial medical certification in 1962–64, death certificates assigned to influenza/pneumonia/bronchitis in ten cities in Latin America, San Francisco, and Bristol, England, suffered a net loss of 1.0% of the original deaths assigned at ages 15–74, while the total of specific infectious and parasitic diseases increased by 5% (Puffer and Griffith 1967, pp. 230, 235). In a similar study of deaths before age 5 in thirteen Latin American and two North American areas between 1968 and 1972, respiratory diseases forfeited 22% of their originally assigned deaths, while the specific infectious diseases gained 23% (Puffer and Serrano 1973, pp. 332, 342). Corresponding adjustment of figures in table 5.1 would equalize the contribution of the specific infectious diseases and of the respiratory diseases to mortality decline at about 28–30%. Nevertheless, the "name" infectious diseases remain relatively submerged compared with popular accounts of their role, a point also stressed by McDermott (1966). Part of the reason for overemphasis on the role of the "name" diseases in mortality decline is probably their preeminent importance in the relatively small-scale English decline from 1851 to 1901, as has been elegantly documented in a widely cited paper by McKeown and Record (1962).

Some indication of whether the patterns depicted in table 5.1 provide a suitable representation for LDCs can be gained by examining the few LDC records that are available. In so doing, it is useful to provide more detail on specific members of the infectious and parasitic set. Mortality changes during long periods will be considered in order to avoid sampling periods during which specific public health interventions may have badly distorted the cause pattern of change.

Table 5.2 presents crude death rates from certain diseases of infectious origin for five populations of LDCs in the early twentieth century and for a more recent year. By and large, they support the previous estimate of the relative importance of respiratory tuberculosis and diarrheal diseases. Influenza/pneumonia/bronchitis is somewhat less important a source of decline than depicted in table 5.1, but the reason is probably that by the latter date each of the four populations supplying information on this cause achieved a mortality level far superior to the 20/1,000 age-standardized rate assumed in table 5.1. This cause is generally a more important source of mortality decline in movements between high and intermediate levels than between intermediate and low ones (Preston and Nelson 1974, pp. 31–33). As a very shaky generalization based on these undoubtedly unrepresentative populations, it may not be too far off the mark to assign 2% of the twentieth-century mortality decline in LDCs as a whole to smallpox, 2% to whooping cough, and 1% each to typhoid, typhus, measles, cholera, and plague (the latter estimate accounting for the disease's heavy concentration in India), and 0.5% to diphtheria. The epidemic nature of typhoid, cholera, and plague add even more uncertainty to these figures.

But the major uncertainty relates to the role of malaria. If estimates for British Guiana and India are to be believed, malaria by itself has accounted for 18–35% of large-scale mortality declines, equaling or exceeding the contribution we have estimated for all infectious and parasitic diseases combined. It should be noted that both estimates are based upon assignment to malaria of an arbitrary portion of deaths originally ascribed to "fever." A less arbitrary approach was pursued by Newman (1965, 1970), who had access to regional mortality data before and after an eradication campaign in Sri Lanka, as well as to regional data on malarial endemicity. Newman estimates by indirect techniques that the malaria eradication campaign in 1946 reduced Sri Lanka's crude death rate (CDR) by 4.2/1,000 between 1936–45 and 1946–60 (1970, p. 157). The relative contribution of such a decline to the total mortality reduction depends, of course, on the size of the latter. Had it been experienced by one of the populations in table 5.2, where the average drop in CDR was 26/1,000, it would account for about 16% of the mortality reduction. As a component of the smaller decline during the shorter period considered by Newman in Sri Lanka, it represented 42%. Simple inspection of time-series data on crude death rates suggests that virtually complete malaria eradication reduced the crude death rate by

297 Mortality Declines in Less Developed Countries

Table 5.2 Crude Death Rates (per 1,000) by Cause in Certain LDCs in the Early Part of the Century and Recently

Cause of Death	Chile, 1920[a]	Chile, 1971[b]	% of Decline	Taiwan, 1920[c]	Taiwan, 1966[d]	% of Decline
Typhoid	.665	.007	2.9	.045	0	.2
Typhus	.439	0	2.0	n.a.	—	—
Malaria	.026	0	0	2.123	0	7.7
Smallpox	.008	0	0	.065	0	.3
Measles	.697	.061	2.8	.358	.039	1.2
Whooping cough	.789	.006	3.5	.046	.004	.2
Diphtheria	.062	.006	.2	.013	.004	0
Influenza/pneumonia/ bronchitis	4.527	1.355	14.1	8.231	.613	27.8
Respiratory tuberculosis	2.404	.209	9.8	1.813	.333	5.4
Diarrhea, dysentery, cholera nostras	2.120	.397	7.7	1.691	.215	5.4
Cholera	n.a.	—	—	.452	0	1.6
Total	30.85	8.389		32.686	5.246	

[a]Chile, Oficina Central de Estadistica, *Annuario Estadistico*, vol. 1 (1920).

[b]World Health Organization, *World Health Statistics Annual*, vol. 1 (1972).

[c]Taiwan, Jinki Dotai Tokei, *Sotoku Kanbo Chosaka* (1920).

[d]United Nations, *Demographic Yearbook* (1967), table 24.

[e]Pani (1917, pp. 192–99).

[f]Mandle (1970, p. 303).

[g]United Nations, *Demographic Yearbook* (1973), table 33.

[h]Compiled from material in Davis (1951, pp. 33–53). The 8.7 malaria estimate assumes that one-third of fever deaths are due to malaria. All estimates are highly suspect because of very deficient coding. Data on cholera, plague, and smallpox are probably most accurate because they were most consistently "notifiable" causes of death at the provincial level. Coale and Hoover (1958, p. 67), using a completely different technique, estimate the pre–spraying program level of malaria death rates in India to be about 6/1,000, including deaths indirectly attributable to the disease.

[i]Crude death rate from United Nations, Population Division, *Selected World Demographic Indicators by Countries, 1950–2000* (1975), p. 125. Average, 1960 and 1965. Distribution of deaths by cause from United Nations, *Demographic Yearbook* (1967), table 24. Data are for medically certified deaths in Poona and Bombay corporations and deaths in public hospitals in Rajasthan. The World Health Organization provides some confirmation of the virtual eradication of malaria from India by noting a hundredfold decline in reported cases between 1952 and 1972. World Health Organization, *Fifth Report on the World Health Situation*, Official Records no. 225 (1975), p. 142.

[j]Bunle (1954).

[k]Deaths under age 2 only.

[l]Malaria and undefined fevers.

[m]Pneumonia and bronchitis.

[n]Tuberculosis, all forms.

298   Samuel H. Preston

Table 5.2 (continued)

Cause of Death	Mexico City, 1904–12[e]	Mexico, 1922–25[j]	Mexico, 1972[b]	% of Difference, Mexico City–Mexico	% of Decline, Mexico
Typhoid	.068	.341	.065	0	1.7
Typhus	1.363	.040	.001	4.1	.2
Malaria	.076	1.471	.001	.2	9.0
Smallpox	.733	.826	0	2.2	5.0
Measles	.290	.427	.219	.2	1.3
Whooping cough	.284	.938	.080	.6	5.2
Diphtheria	.169	.062	.002	.5	.4
Influenza/pneumonia/ bronchitis	7.838	3.213	1.664	18.6	9.4
Respiratory tuberculosis	2.485	.653	.152	7.0	3.1
Diarrhea, dysentery, cholera nostras	9.785	1.861[k]	1.337	25.4	—
Cholera	n.a.	n.a.	—	—	—
Total	42.314	25.489	9.081		

Cause of Death	British Guiana, 1911–20[f]	Guyana, 1967[g]	% of Decline	India, 1898–1907[h]	India, 1963[i]	% of Difference
Typhoid	n.a.	—	—	n.a.	—	—
Typhus	n.a.	—	—	n.a.	—	—
Malaria	4.185[l]	0	18.1	6.0–8.7	0	24.3–35.2
Smallpox	n.a.	—	—	.27	.08	.8
Measles	n.a.	—	—	n.a.	—	—
Whooping cough	n.a.	—	—	n.a.	—	—
Diphtheria	n.a.	—	—	n.a.	—	—
Influenza/pneumonia/ bronchitis	3.680[m]	.055	15.7	n.a.	—	—
Respiratory tuberculosis	1.432[n]	.024	6.1	n.a.	—	—
Diarrhea, dysentery, cholera nostras	2.780	.026	11.9	1.96	.14	7.4
Cholera	n.a.	—	—	1.66	1.18	1.9
Plague	n.a.	—	—	1.82	0	7.3
Total	30.049	6.987		43.5	18.8	

about 3/1,000 in Guatemala (Meegama 1967, pp. 231–33), by 5–9 points in Mauritius (Titmuss and Abel-Smith 1968, pp. 49–50), and by 2–3/1,000 in Venezuela (Pampana 1954, p. 504).

The importance of malaria reduction as a source of declining mortality in a country obviously depends upon initial endemicity and the success of antimalarial campaigns. Southern Africa, southern Latin America, and northern Asia were never seriously afflicted with the disease; malaria in tropical Africa is highly endemic but, with few exceptions, it has not been successfully attacked (World Health Organization 1975*a*). A valuable compilation by Faust (1941, p. 12) suggests that recorded crude death rates from malaria in Mexico, Central America, and the West Indies during the 1930s, before any inroads had been made against the disease in rural areas, was 1.66/1,000. But he considers this "a figure probably far too low." The recorded CDR from malaria in cities of Burma in 1939 was 2.14 (Simmons et al. 1944, p. 11). The preprogram malarial CDR in Venezuela was 1.73/1,000 (Pampana 1954, p. 504). But recorded levels are often greatly in error. Newman calculates for Ceylon that each death assigned to malaria represented approximately four deaths that were directly or indirectly caused by it. But such an inflation factor is simply not tenable in Guatemala or Venezuela, where contemporaneous declines in crude death rates and malarial crude death rates suggest that a 2:1 ratio is the most that could have been sustained. Part of the inflation factor reflects malaria's role as "the great debilitator," but another part may be spurious. Spraying with residual insecticides reduces not only malaria but other vector-borne diseases such as yellow fever, typhus, and especially diarrheal disease. As Newman points out, an indirect approach that bases estimates on relations between regional changes in aggregate mortality and changes in spleen rates may well overascribe mortality decline to malaria reductions (but not to insecticide campaigns themselves). Finally, there is an often-quoted estimate, the basis of which is unknown, that worldwide malarial deaths have declined from 2.5 million per year to less than 1 million (*Lancet* 1970, p. 599), figures suggesting for LDCs a decline in crude death rates on the order of 1/1,000. The 2.5 million estimate evidently first appears in Pampana and Russell (1955) and presumably applies to 1955. Russell put the figure at at least 3 million for 1943 (1943, p. 601).

There is obviously much work to be done on this issue. In the present state of semi-ignorance, it seems judicious to adopt a range of CDR declines of 2–5/1,000, within which the twentieth-century LDC mortality decline attributable to antimalarial programs seems to have a better than even chance of falling. Sri Lanka, the best-documented case, falls within this range, and Sri Lanka was apparently intermediate in terms of initial endemicity, although the program there probably enjoyed unusual success and malaria reduction may not be solely responsible for the mortality decline produced by insecticide spraying. The range is also consistent with the apparently widespread malarial CDR declines of 1.5–2.0/1,000 and with inflation factors of 1.4–2.5.

These assorted scraps of information are pieced together in table 5.3, where diseases that seem in the main to be responsible for mortality declines in LDCs between 1900 and 1970 are classified into three groups according to their dominant mode of transmission. An estimate—obvi-

Table 5.3   Diseases Responsible for LDC Mortality Declines and Methods That Have Been Used against Them

Dominant Mode of Transmission	Diseases	Approximate Percentage of Mortality Decline in LDCs, 1900–1970, Accounted for by Disease[a]	Principal Methods of Prevention Deployed[a]	Principal Methods of Treatment Deployed[a]
Airborne	Influenza/Pneumonia/Bronchitis	30		Antibiotics
	Respiratory tuberculosis	10		Chemotherapy
	Smallpox	2	Immunization; identification and isolation	Chemotherapy
	Measles	1	Immunization	Antibiotics
	Diphtheria / Whooping cough }	2̲	Immunization	Antibiotics
		45	Immunization	
Water-, food-, and fecesborne	Diarrhea, enteritis, gastroenteritis	7	Purification and increased supply of water; sewage disposal; personal sanitation	Rehydration
	Typhoid	1	Purification and increased supply of water; sewage disposal; personal sanitation; partially effective vaccine	Rehydration, antibiotics
	Cholera	1̲	Purification and increased supply of water; sewage disposal; personal sanitation; partially effective vaccine; quarantine	Rehydration
		9		
Insectborne	Malaria	13–33	Insecticides, drainage, larvicides	Quinine drugs
	Typhus	1	Insecticides, partially effective vaccines	Antibiotics
	Plague	1̲	Insecticides, rat control, quarantine	
		15–35		

[a]Major sources: Paul (1964); Morley (1973); Hinman (1966).

ously highly tentative but nevertheless the first that appears to have been offered—of the relative importance of the various diseases in the decline is also supplied. The category totals are somewhat more robust than the figures for individual diseases because diagnostic confusions, disease interactions, and program externalities are more likely to occur within groups than between groups. Since progress was very slow between 1900 and 1935, the listing may serve as an adequate representation of declines between 1935 and 1970 as well. Finally, some indication of the public health and medical instruments that have been deployed against the various diseases is also provided. The modes of transmission that are listed are not mutually exclusive or exhaustive, but the classification is not seriously distortive.

5.1.3 Influences Operating on the Various Causes of Death

Mortality from every disease listed in table 5.3 would be expected to decline when personal living standards rise. Of the many linkages, probably the most important are those between nutritional status and influenza/pneumonia/bronchitis, diarrheal disease, and respiratory tuberculosis. The mechanisms of effect are not well known, but it appears that protein malnutrition impairs the production of circulating antibodies in response to bacterial and viral antigens and that undernutrition can produce atrophy of the organs responsible for the immune response (World Health Organization 1972, pp. 24–25). There is no question of the importance of poor nutrition as a factor underlying high mortality rates in LDCs. The PAHO study of child mortality in thirteen Latin American projects found that immaturity or malnutrition was an associated or underlying cause of 57% of the deaths before age 5 (World Health Organization 1974a, p. 279). Immaturity is in turn a frequent product of maternal malnourishment (Mata et al. 1972). The problem is apparently equally severe in Africa, although the data are much more fragmentary (Bailey 1975). Diet supplementation programs in Peru (Baertl et al. 1970) and Guatemala (Ascoli et al. 1967; Scrimshaw 1970) significantly reduced child mortality in test populations, but, oddly, without having substantial effects on indexes of child physical development. Despite the improvement, mortality and morbidity in the Guatemalan villages remained "shockingly high," which was attributed to irregular participation in the feeding program and to the continued heavy burden of infection to which the children were subject (Scrimshaw 1970, pp. 1689–90).

But nutritional status is not exclusively determined by diet, nor is diet determined only by the availability of calories or protein. There is now extensive evidence that infectious diseases themselves are an extremely important source of malnourishment, independent of the child's nutritional state at the time of attack (Mata et al. 1972; Scrimshaw 1970; World Health Organization 1972, p. 27). Infection increases metabolic demands and often reduces the absorption of nutrients and increases their excretion. Nutritional intake can also be reduced by nausea or through customs denying food to the sick. Infections among pregnant women can reduce birthweights and, among new mothers, milk secretion (Mata et al. 1972; Bailey 1975). Gordon (1969, p. 218) suggests that diet fails by far to explain all the prevalent malnourishment in LDCs. The frequency of inappropriate nutritional practices despite adequate food supplies does not require emphasis (Bailey 1975; Food and Agriculture Organization 1975). The importance of nutritional practices is indicated by the reported reversal of expected social class differences in infant mortality in Chile, a condition attributed to earlier weaning among children of upper-class women (Plank and Milanesi 1973). The point is simply that, even if nutritional status were the only influence on mortality from a disease, mortality declines from that cause do not necessarily imply that an improvement in food supplies has occurred. Nutritional practices and exogenous declines in the incidence of other infections must also be considered candidates for explanation. The "subsistence level" of food production is obviously fictitious if it is presumed to represent a fixed requirement that is independent of the state of prophylactic or nutritional arts.

Despite the undoubted influence of nutritional intake and other components of general living standards on mortality, it is clear from table 5.3 that many other influences have also been at work. Obvious as it may be, it is easy to forget that death from an infectious disease involves an encounter between a pathogenic organism and a vulnerable human host. The rate of death can be altered by changing the rate or terms of the encounter without any prior change in the host. It is not possible and is probably not necessary to document individually the preventive and curative measures that have been utilized for this purpose. With the exception of influenza/pneumonia/bronchitis, it seems likely that preventive measures have been more effective than curative ones.

That preventive measures have been widely deployed in each of the three categories can be demonstrated relatively easily. At the end of 1964, 1.935 billion persons lived in areas that were originally malarious. Of these, 41% were living in areas from which malaria had been eradicated; 16% were living in areas where incidence was very low and was being controlled by case detection and treatment; 24% were living in areas protected by extensive mosquito control measures; and 19% were living in areas without specific antimalarial measures, most of these in tropical Africa (World Health Organization 1975a). The cost of programs producing virtually complete eradication has been estimated at 10–30 cents per capita per year, with programs probably extending over a two- to three-year period and a continuing annual cost of 5 cents per

303   Mortality Declines in Less Developed Countries

capita required for surveillance thereafter (Pampana and Russell 1955, table 1, provides the most complete cost compilation).

India has vaccinated 170 million persons against tuberculosis and in 1968 alone vaccinated 83 million against smallpox (World Health Organization 1975*b*, p. 142). It has finally succeeded in eliminating smallpox completely, as has every other country. Colombia dispensed 5.9 million vaccinations in 1972, one-third of the population size; Egypt vaccinated 15 million persons against cholera in the same year and 25 million against smallpox in 1970. All primary-school entrants in the Philippines are vaccinated against tuberculosis. Barbados has compulsory immunization against diphtheria, polio, smallpox, and tetanus upon school entrance (World Health Organization 1975). An expert committee assembled by WHO estimated that 80% of the 70 million children reaching age one in LDCs each year could be immunized against measles, polio, tuberculosis, pertussis, tetanus, diphtheria, and smallpox at a cost, exclusive of personnel, of $37.5–$60 million, or $0.67–$1.07 apiece (World Health Organization, 1975*c*, p. 2).

Conditions of water supply and sewage disposal have also been markedly improved, despite continued abysmal conditions in many areas. Many of the improvements were normal and integral parts of economic expansion and hence cannot be specifically interpreted as public health interventions of an unprecedented sort. WHO surveys of government officials in 1962 and 1970 indicated that the proportion of LDC urban populations served by house connections to public water supply increased from 0.33 to 0.50 during this eight-year period for the seventy-five countries that replied in both years (World Health Organization 1973, p. 726). No rural population comparisons could be made, but in 1970 only 12% of rural LDC populations had "reasonable access" to community water supply (public fountain or standpipe within 200 meters of a house). The figure was only 6% in India (World Health Organization 1973, pp. 727, 729). New urban house connections were estimated to cost an average of $35 per capita, and providing rural residents with easy access to safe water to cost $12 per capita. In 1970, 69% of LDC urban populations had sewage disposal facilities (27% were connected to public sewerage and 42% had private household systems). New connections to urban public sewerage cost an average of $29 per head. Only 8% of the rural population was judged to have adequate sewage disposal, although the average cost of providing such facilities was estimated at only $4 per capita (World Health Organization 1973, pp. 732–33, 738–43). No trends in sewage facilities could be established, but improvement is probably fairly rapid in urban areas and slow in rural areas. Clearly, the initial cost of such programs is considerably higher than that for programs of vector control and immunization. Water supply improvements were among the very first changes to modify mortality patterns in European countries in the mid-nineteenth century. But they are lagging relative to other improvements in LDCs. This may explain why diarrheal disease remains relatively more prominent as a contributor to total mortality in LDCs than it was in European countries at the same general mortality level (Preston and Nelson 1974).

With the exception of water and sewerage improvements and smallpox vaccination, the techniques of preventive and curative health care that have been widely deployed in LDCs are twentieth-century products. Virtually all were facilitated by ultimate acceptance of the revolutionary germ theory of disease at the turn of the century. Even smallpox eradication has benefited from technical improvements such as freeze-dried vaccine and the forked needle (Foege et al. 1975). The next section attempts to identify the relative importance of these technical improvements, as typically embodied in government health programs enjoying some measure of external assistance or support, in LDC mortality improvements during the last three decades.

5.1.4   Structural Changes in Relations between Mortality and Other Development Indexes

That mortality reductions have not merely been residual by-products of socioeconomic development is best illustrated by showing that major structural changes have occurred in the relationship between mortality and other indexes of development. Important technical changes and exogenous increases in government health commitment or foreign health assistance should result in a shift in the average level of life expectancy that corresponds to a particular level of other development indicators. Preston (1975a) suggested that such a change had occurred in the relation between mortality and national income, and this section will attempt to supplement that observation by introducing new variables and a larger sample of countries. Data have been gathered on national levels of life expectancy, per capita income (in 1970 U.S. dollars), daily calorie consumption, and literacy for thirty-six nations in or about 1940, including seventeen LDCs and several others that today would be classified as LDCs if 1940 conditions had persisted. The LDC estimates of life expectancy are based largely upon indirect demographic techniques such as intercensal survival analysis rather than upon vital statistics. Data on these same variables have been generated for 120 nations in or around 1970. The data and sources are presented in appendix tables 5.A.1 and 5.A.2.

A preliminary indication that structural changes have occurred is presented in table 5.4. Countries are cross-classified by level of per capita national income (in 1970 U.S. dollars) and by daily caloric consumption per head. Complete information was available for only twenty-nine countries in 1940. Nevertheless, it is clear that, within every

305 Mortality Declines in Less Developed Countries

Table 5.4 **Mean Life Expectancy at Birth of Countries in Various Ranges of National Income and Calorie Consumption, 1940 and 1970**

Daily Calories Per Capita	National Income per Capita in 1970 U.S. Dollars				
	<150	150–299	300–699	700+	
<2,100	42.7 (17)	51.5 (8)	53.3 (5)	69.5 (1)	47.5 (31)
	38.3 (5)	36.0 (1)	(0)	(0)	37.9 (6)
2,100–2,399	42.6 (16)	49.9 (14)	56.2 (7)	71.4 (2)	49.1 (39)
	40.0 (1)	43.9 (2)	46.1 (1)	(0)	43.4 (4)
2,400–2,899	45.4 (1)	57.9 (8)	61.3 (10)	68.0 (7)	61.4 (26)
	(0)	44.1 (2)	50.4 (4)	59.6 (2)	51.1 (8)
2,900+	(0)	(0)	(0)	71.6 (24)	71.6 (24)
	(0)	(0)	58.7 (2)	65.2 (9)	64.0 (11)
	42.7 (34)	52.4 (30)	57.8 (22)	70.8 (34)	55.9 (120)
	38.6 (6)	42.4 (5)	52.2 (7)	64.1 (11)	52.2 (29)

Source: Appendix tables 5.A.1 and 5.A.2.
Note: 1970 countries appear in the top rows, 1940 countries in the bottom rows. The number of countries is shown in parentheses.

one of the nine cells where both 1940 and 1970 populations appear, average life expectancy was higher at the later date. The average intra-cell gain is 8.7 years of life expectancy.

A somewhat more precise indication of the magnitude of structural changes can be obtained by regressing life expectancy on income, calories, and literacy separately for 1940 and 1970 observations. Because of nonlinearities expected on obvious inductive and deductive grounds, natural logarithms of calorie consumption and income are used as regressors. Daily calorie consumption is measured from 1,500, approximately the average level required to meet minimum daily metabolic demands. Literacy, a personal dichotomous variable, cannot act nonlinearly at the individual level, since it takes on only two values. Barring spillover effects whose existence in income relations was called into question in section A, the proportion literate should be linearly related to life expectancy at the aggregate level. No claim is made that the resulting equations are perfectly specified, but simply that the socioeconomic variables included are the only ones available in the 1930s. It seems unlikely that relations between terms omitted and terms present would have changed in such as way as to influence the outcomes described below.

The equations as estimated by ordinary least squares are the following:[5]

1970: $e^{o}_{0} = 17.1464 + 4.2488 \times 1n\overline{Y} + .2086 \times LIT$
$\qquad\;\;\; (7.4090)\;\; (.6524) \qquad\qquad (.0212)$

$\qquad\quad + .3170 \times 1n\ CAL$
$\qquad\quad (1.3492)$

$$N = 120, R^2 = .860$$
$$R^2 = .858$$

1940: $e^{o}_{0} = -13.1035 + 5.4352 \times 1n\overline{Y} + .1654 \times LIT$
$\qquad\;\;\; (18.5102)\;\; (2.3860) \qquad\qquad (.0626)$

$\qquad\quad + 2.9470 \times 1n\ CAL$
$\qquad\quad (3.7176)$

$$N = 36, R^2 = .856$$
$$R^2 = .845,$$

where $e^{o}_{0} =$ life expectancy at birth, average male and female
$\qquad\; \overline{Y} =$ national income per capita, 1970 U.S. dollars
$\quad LIT =$ percentage literate of the adult population
$\;\; CAL =$ excess of daily calorie consumption per capita
$\qquad\qquad$ over 1,500.

Coefficients of all three variables in both equations are properly signed. The explanatory power of the regression equations is virtually identical for the two years. Income and literacy terms are highly significant in both periods and retain approximately the same magnitude. This stability was unexpected because of the high degree of colinearity among regressors. The coefficients indicate that a 10 percentage point increase in literacy is associated at both points with a gain in life expectancy of approximately 2 years, and that a 10% gain in national income by itself increases life expectancy by approximately one-half year. Coefficients of the calorie term decrease over time but are insignificant in both periods. It is very unlikely that the availability of calories for daily consumption has no influence on mortality. The calorie variable is probably subject to greater measurement error than the other two, and the influence of calorie availability is probably being reflected through them. The constant term increases by about 30 years between 1940 and 1970, although by itself this change is not readily interpreted, since the zero-points on variables are well below the range of observed experience. The hazards of extrapolation are shown by the negative (though insignificant) intercept for 1940.[6]

The substantive significance of the structural shift, as reflected primarily in the intercept, is probably best illustrated in the following way. Each of the 120 countries in 1970, including 94 LDCs, can supply estimates for each of the three regressors. It is therefore possible to estimate what life expectancy would be for every country at its current developmental level if no structural change had occurred in the relation between mortality and socioeconomic development. This estimate is simply obtained by substituting values of the three regressors for 1970 into the 1940 regression equation. Differences between actual life expectancy and that predicted if 1940 relations had continued to prevail indicate the amount of change in life expectancy attributable to the structural shift. A weighted average of such differences will indicate the importance of the shift for LDCs as a whole.[7] Results of this exercise are presented in table 5.5.

Estimates presented in this table indicate that life expectancy for LDCs as a unit (exclusive of China, North Korea, and North Vietnam) would have been 8.66 years lower in 1970–75 if life expectancy had continued to be related to other development indexes as it was in 1940. Excluding South Vietnam, where special factors were obviously distorting life expectancy, the figure is 8.84. This is an estimate of the amount of increase in life expectancy that is attributable to factors exogenous to national levels of income, literacy, and calorie consumption.[8] What fraction of the total gain in life expectancy during the period this 8.84-year structural shift represents is difficult to assess. WHO estimates that life expectancy in LDCs was 32 years in 1935–39 (30 in Africa and Asia and 40 in Latin America) and 49.6 years in 1965–70 (World Health Organization 1974, p. 23). The earlier figure is based on very little information, but if we accept it, the implication is that the structural change accounts for about half (50.2%) of the total gain in life expectancy during these nearly equivalent 30-year periods. This estimate is lower than the 79.5% (9.7/12.2) figures estimated for MDCs and LDCs combined by Preston (1975, p. 238) not so much because the estimated Δe^o_0 attributed to structural shifts differ (the difference is in fact only 0.86 years) but because the estimated gains in life expectancy differ (12.2 years for the world as a whole between 1938 and 1963 by Preston versus 17.6 years for LDCs between 1935–39 and 1965–70 by WHO). Part of the discrepancy in the estimates probably results from differences in the universe covered. Because MDCs had achieved by 1940 levels of developmental indicators high enough that relatively little gain in life expectancy was to be expected from advances in living standards, it is likely that exogenous factors represented a larger fraction of the gains that occurred there than they did in LDCs. Another part may reflect differences in the periods covered, since the present estimate pertains to a somewhat later period. Suggestions that the pace of mor-

Table 5.5 Life Expectancy in 1970–75 and Life Expectancy Predicted if 1940 Relations between Life Expectancy and Levels of Literacy, Income, and Calorie Consumption Had Continued to Prevail

Africa	Predicted e_0^0*	Actual e_0^0	Difference	Latin America	Predicted e_0^0*	Actual e_0^0	Difference	Asia	Predicted e_0^0*	Actual e_0^0	Difference
Algeria	41.42	53.20	11.78	Argentina	61.84	68.20	6.36	Afghanistan	30.16	40.30	10.14
Angola	37.32	38.50	1.18	Bolivia	39.49	46.80	7.31	Bangladesh	31.49	35.80	4.31
Botswana	34.13	43.50	9.37	Brazil	50.85	61.40	10.55	Burma	41.23	50.00	8.77
Burundi	40.39	39.00	−1.39	Chile	56.62	62.60	5.98	Cyprus	56.21	71.40	15.19
Central African Rep.	35.16	41.00	5.84	Colombia	51.36	60.90	9.54	India	40.11	49.50	9.39
Chad	30.29	38.50	8.21	Costa Rica	56.07	68.20	12.13	Indonesia	39.54	47.50	7.96
Congo	42.47	43.50	1.03	Dominican Rep.	48.38	57.80	9.42	Iran	43.23	51.00	7.77
Dahomey	33.60	41.00	7.40	Ecuador	47.14	59.60	12.46	Iraq	42.57	52.70	10.13
Egypt	41.95	52.40	10.45	El Salvador	45.09	57.80	12.71	Israel	63.10	71.00	7.90
Ethiopia	30.39	38.00	7.61	Guatemala	43.86	52.90	9.04	Jordan	43.59	53.20	9.61
Gabon	41.65	41.00	−.65	Guyana	51.21	67.90	16.69	Khmer Rep.	47.19	45.40	−1.79
Gambia	33.47	40.00	6.53	Haiti	29.48	50.00	20.52	Korea, Rep. of	52.20	60.60	8.40
Ghana	43.10	43.50	.40	Honduras	44.10	53.50	9.40	Laos	32.95	40.40	7.45
Guinea	30.43	41.00	10.57	Jamaica	54.93	69.50	14.57	Lebanon	55.11	63.20	8.09
Ivory Coast	41.97	43.50	1.53	Mexico	55.24	63.20	7.96	Malaysia	50.43	59.40	8.97
Kenya	37.37	50.00	12.63	Nicaragua	48.51	52.90	4.39	Nepal	31.63	43.60	11.97
Liberia	35.68	43.50	7.82	Panama	55.47	66.50	11.03	Pakistan	37.05	49.80	12.75
Libyan Arab Rep.	52.23	52.90	.67	Paraguay	47.84	61.90	14.06	Philippines	47.95	58.40	10.45
Madagascar	39.55	43.50	3.95	Peru	46.72	55.70	8.98	Saudi Arabia	42.56	45.30	2.74
Malawi	33.05	41.00	7.95	Puerto Rico	59.60	72.10	12.50	Singapore	55.22	69.50	14.28
Mali	28.99	38.00	9.01	Trinidad and Tobago	54.17	69.50	15.23	Sri Lanka	46.86	67.80	20.94
Malta	58.07	70.80	12.73	Uruguay	59.54	69.80	10.26	Syria	44.14	54.00	9.86
Maritius	49.47	65.50	16.03	Venezuela	55.14	64.70	9.56	Taiwan	54.32	69.40	15.08
Mauritania	33.50	38.50	5.00					Thailand	48.09	58.00	9.91
								Turkey	49.03	56.90	7.87

Table 5.5 (continued)

Africa	Predicted e_0^0*	Actual e_0^0	Difference
Morocco	39.92	52.90	12.98
Mozambique	38.98	43.50	4.52
Niger	30.20	38.50	8.30
Nigeria	37.52	41.00	3.48
Rhodesia	38.39	51.50	13.11
Rwanda	29.66	41.00	11.34
Senegal	36.25	40.00	3.75
Sierra Leone	35.25	43.50	8.25
Somalia	28.37	41.00	12.63
South Africa	50.59	51.50	.91
Sudan	34.70	48.60	13.90
Togo	33.93	41.00	7.07
Tunisia	42.32	54.10	11.78
Uganda	37.62	50.00	12.38
Cameroon	45.40	41.00	−4.40
Tanzania	32.00	44.50	12.50
Upper Volta	28.92	38.00	9.08
Zaire	37.16	43.50	6.34
Zambia	45.02	44.50	−.52

Mean difference, Africa = 7.05

1970 population-weighted mean difference, Africa = 7.22

Mean difference, Latin America = 10.90

1970 population-weighted mean difference, Latin America = 9.54

Mean, all LDCs = 8.61

1970 Population-weighted mean, all LDCs = 8.66

Asia	Predicted e_0^0*	Actual e_0^0	Difference
Vietnam, Rep. of	49.08	40.50	−8.58
Yemen	31.53	44.80	13.27
Yemen, P.D.R.	31.79	44.80	13.01

Mean difference, Asia = 9.14

1970 population-weighted mean difference, Africa = 8.90

*Based on substitution of 1970 values of literacy, income, and calorie consumption into 1940 regression relating e_0^0 to these variables.

310   Samuel H. Preston

tality decline in LDCs has slowed in the past decade (Hansluwka 1975; World Bank 1975) imply that the shift in the mortality/development relation may have essentially ended by the early 1960s, while gains in living standards continue to exert an influence on mortality. In any case, the estimated amount of the structural shift is consistent between the two estimates at about 9 years of life expectancy at birth.

The structural shift has evidently been least pronounced for African countries and most pronounced for Latin America. Africa has unquestionably experienced the least penetration by modern public health measures of any region. The problem is not simply poverty but also a widely dispersed population that increases program costs (World Health Organization 1975*b*, p. 17). Several of the African countries have lower life expectancies in 1970–75 than could have been expected based on 1940 relations. The apparent advantage enjoyed by Latin American countries may be due to their special relations with the United States. The United States has been by far the largest bilateral donor in international health aid, and the bulk of aid appears to go to Latin American countries, either directly or through the Pan American Health Organization (World Bank 1975, pp. 68–69). It is worth noting that, of the ninety-four LDCs, Sri Lanka and Mauritius are two of the four whose estimated structural changes are largest. It is unfortunate that so much attention has focused on these unusual cases.

Attributing to all countries the relations prevailing in countries for which data are available is always risky. The preceding analysis of change can be complemented by one that focuses exclusively on the cases that can be documented. Each of the thirty-six countries providing data in 1940 can also supply data in 1970. According to the previous formulation, we should expect Δe^o_0 to be linearly related to $\Delta 1nY$, $\Delta 1n$ *CAL*, and ΔLIT, with a relatively large positive intercept reflecting the structural shift. In the first specification of the model, we add three terms believed to reflect factors responsible for a portion of the structural shift. The first (*MAL*) is an estimate of the degree of malarial endemicity in 1940, which is a proxy for the effect of antimalarial programs on Δe^o_0. Each of the thirty-six countries with endemic malaria has had a major antimalarial campaign. It is hoped that the coefficient of this term will provide a clearer indication of the effect of antimalarial activities on gains in life expectancy than was previously available. The second (*AID*) is an estimate of the average annual per capita nonmilitary aid in United States dollars received from bilateral and multilateral donors between 1954 and 1972. The third (*WAT*) is an estimate of per capita aid received for water and sewerage projects between 1965 and 1970 (U.S. dollars). The latter two variables are assumed to be proxies for the amount of total per capita health aid received between 1940

311   Mortality Declines in Less Developed Countries

and 1970. Their values are generally highest for the Latin American countries. Values of these variables are presented in appendix table 5.A.3.

The estimated equation with all six terms present is the following:[9]

$$\Delta e^o{}_0 = 6.5212 + 3.4500 \times \Delta 1n\overline{Y} + .0354 \times \Delta LIT$$
$$\quad (2.8468) \quad (2.4111) \qquad\qquad (.0927)$$

$$+ .5605 \times \Delta 1n\,CAL$$
$$\quad (4.9362)$$

$$+ 3.1328 \times MAL + .1460 \times AID + .1955 \times WAT$$
$$\quad (.9411) \qquad\qquad (.2376) \qquad\qquad (.3668)$$

$$R^2 = .595$$
$$\overline{R}^2 = .506.$$

Each of the coefficients has the expected positive sign. The coefficient of income remains similar in absolute value to that estimated in the cross-sectional regressions, but that of literacy declines by a factor of five and calories remain an insubstantial factor. Receipt of external aid contributes positively but insignificantly to mortality improvement. The most interesting result refers to the constant term. For a country essentially free of malaria in 1940 ($MAL = 0$), it is estimated that life expectancy would have increased by 6.52 years in the absence of socioeconomic development and external aid during the three decades. For a country in which malaria was highly endemic ($MAL = 3$), the corresponding gain is 15.92 years, of which 9.40 is attributable to factors associated with malarial endemicity. The average life expectancy for the seventeen LDCs was 39.29 in 1940 and 59.42 in 1970, giving an average gain of 20.13 years. The average malaria endemicity score for these seventeen was 2.59. Of the total gain in $e^o{}_0$, 8.11 years (3.1328×2.59), or 40%, is attributable to factors associated with malarial endemicity, and the constant term of 6.5 years, or 23%, represents other exogenous factors. The sum of 72% is considerably higher than that implied by the previous procedure. The external aid terms contribute an additional 1.13 years, or 5.6%.[10]

Whether or not antimalarial programs themselves produced the gain of 8.11 years attributed to malarial endemicity remains in serious doubt. The malaria score is correlated with life expectancy in 1940 at −.873. It is thus acting as a proxy for the initial level of mortality from a host of potentially eliminable infectious and parasitic diseases. When the initial level of life expectancy is entered as an independent variable, the magnitude of the structural change remains roughly the same but the portion attributable to the malarial term declines to zero:

$$\Delta e^o_0 = 31.4722 + 3.6048 \times \Delta lnY + .0430 \times \Delta LIT$$
$$\quad\quad (8.5108) \quad (2.0533) \quad\quad\quad\quad (.0790)$$

$$\quad - .9865 \times \Delta CAL$$
$$\quad\;\; (4.2327)$$

$$\quad - .0211 \times MAL + .0750 \times AID + .2939 \times WAT$$
$$\quad\;\; (1.3059) \quad\quad\quad (.2036) \quad\quad\quad (.3139)$$

$$\quad - .4063 \times e^o_0(1940)$$
$$\quad\;\; (.1328)$$

$$R^2 = .720$$
$$R^2 = .643.$$

Other coefficients are not affected in such a way as to substantially alter interpretations, but the coefficient of malarial endemicity becomes effectively zero. The amount of structural change for the seventeen LDCs, the gain that is not accounted for by changes in Y, LIT, or CAL, is 16.46 years of life, or 81.8% of the average gain during the period.[11] The estimated structural change is close to that estimated directly above, but malaria's role in it is now negligible. When malarial endemicity is operationalized as a series of dummy variables, none of the dummy coefficients is significant, and the relation between mortality change and endemicity is nonmonotonic. Other functional forms and variable operationalizations should be investigated; at the moment all we can conclude is that the longitudinal analysis provides no better fix on malaria's role than the largely inconclusive cause-of-death analysis.

Two estimates have been advanced of the fraction of LDC gains in life expectancy between 1940 and 1970 that are attributable to structural change. The first estimate of one-half was based on a regression-decomposition technique that assumed all nations had relations between mortality and development indexes in 1940 identical to those prevailing in nations that could supply data for that year. The second estimate of approximately 80% was based solely upon examination of trends in the latter group. There is an important technical reason to favor the former estimate, namely, that measurement error is likely to be a more important source of distortion in longitudinal than in cross-sectional data. Measurement error biases coefficients toward zero. If random measurement error were all that was reflected in our measured changes in income, literacy, and calorie consumption, then the entire change in life expectancy would be absorbed in the constant term and attributed to structural change, regardless of the actual importance of these factors. Development levels are undoubtedly better measured than development rates, giving greater stability to the analysis based on a comparison of cross sections. There are, however, indications that a fraction of the gain larger than one-half would be attributed to structural shifts if analysis had focused more narrowly on the period between 1940 and 1960.

The estimate of one-half is roughly consistent with the preceding cause-of-death analysis. Influenza/pneumonia/bronchitis has accounted for perhaps a third of the mortality decline. No effective preventive measures have been deployed against these diseases, the effectiveness of immunization being minimal, and there are suggestions that antibiotics, sulfa drugs, and curative services are not widely enough available in LDCs to have substantially altered the disease picture (Sharpston 1976; Bryant 1969, pp. 314–23). Diarrheal diseases probably account for another 9% or so of the decline, and the principal method of control has been improvements in water supply and sewerage that, because of their expense, are closely associated with economic development.[12] It is likely that social and economic development—especially as reflected in water systems, nutrition, housing, and personal sanitary knowledge— have operated largely through these diseases. In the case of other diseases it appears that programs of a narrowly public health nature that have embodied inexpensive new techniques, especially vector control and immunization, have been the decisive forces in mortality reductions.

5.1.5   The Role of MDCs in LDC Gains

Many have argued that MDCs have played a decisive role in the mortality declines experienced by LDCs, although the case has not been well documented. Certain of the influences are clear enough. Sulfa drugs, antibiotics, and most vaccines and insecticides, including DDT, have been developed in laboratories within MDCs. MDCs contributed 5,764 technical assistance workers in health services to LDCs in 1968 (Organization for Economic Cooperation and Development, n.d., pp. 276–77). Governmental health agencies were often created under colonial auspices. The role of external financing has also been stressed, but the accounts have focused on the dramatic examples in relatively small countries where international campaigns have often been undertaken largely for their demonstration value.

Health assistance in the developing world began with the work of medical missionaries, who were established in the Philippines in 1577 and in China by 1835 (Maramag 1965; Bowers 1973).[13] The early efforts of colonial governments were designed primarily to protect the colonials from epidemic diseases (Beck 1970). Correspondingly, cooperative international health efforts principally attempted to protect Europe and North America from imported cholera, plague, and yellow fever (Howard-Jones 1974). An evolving social conscience in the interwar years led to greater concern with the health of the native population itself and to the establishment of local medical colleges (Beck 1970). The most effective international efforts of the period were undoubtedly those of the Rockefeller Foundation, which led a successful campaign to eradicate yellow fever from Latin American cities in 1916–23, repelled the invasion of *Anopheles gambiae* into Brazil in 1938, financed medical schools around the world, and was "probably the largest single factor in improving the public health education of the world up to the creation of the WHO" (Goodman 1971, pp. 381, 266, 377–82). Its antimalarial activities began in 1915 and included demonstrations of the superior cost effectiveness of vector control compared with treatment and the feasibility of complete eradication. The antimalarial activities were considered by Russell, one of the world's leading malariologists, to be of fundamental importance in ultimate control of the disease. "In instance after instance the foundation provided the catalyst, or the inexpensive mainspring, or the seed money that resulted in control of the disease" (Russell 1968, p. 644).

The total amount of money appropriated by the Rockefeller Foundation from 1914 to 1954 for antimalarial activities, exclusive of salaries and overhead was only $5 million (Russell 1968, p. 644). This is a vivid illustration that contributions to mortality change are inaccurately reflected on financial ledgers. International aid for health purposes is a small part of total health expenditures in LDCs and probably always has been. But its cost effectiveness has certainly far surpassed the average for internally financed appropriations, which are too often focused on expensive curative services in urban areas.[14]

Only crude indications are available of the relative magnitudes of internal and external sources of health expenditures in LDCs. In 1970, government health expenditures were estimated for LDCs containing 1.89 billion people. Total government expenditure on health in these areas came to $7.67 billion, or about $4 per capita.[15] Private health expenditures in LDCs are probably slightly larger than public expenditures, judging from comparisons that can be made in seven countries.[16] Addition of private and public expenditure in countries not represented would bring the total annual expenditure perhaps to the range of $20–30 billion.

In contrast, the largest single source of international assistance for health, the World Health Organization, dispersed only $115 million in 1972, a figure that includes family planning activities and some dispersals to MDCs (World Bank 1975, pp. 68–69). The annual budget of the World Health Organization in 1970 was less than that of Massachusetts General Hospital! (Goodman 1971, p. 223). Of its regular budget, the United States contributed 31% and the USSR 13%, with no other country making a contribution larger than 7% (Goodman 1971, p. 220). The second largest source of international assistance in 1972, USAID, contributed $42 million. All together, the ten largest multilateral or bilateral sources of health aid contributed $300.7 million in international assistance for health programs in 1972 (World Bank 1975, p. 68), probably between 1% and 2% of total health expenditures in LDCs. To this should be added a portion of the $79 million in loans and credits made by the World Bank for water supply and sewerage construction in that year (World Bank 1975, p. 48).

It seems very likely, then, that total external health aid received by LDCs is less than 3% of their total health expenditures. The figure may have been somewhat higher earlier in the postwar period. The cumulative United States contribution to antimalarial activities through national research and international assistance has been estimated to be about one-half billion dollars (Russell 1968), but the annual contribution has declined drastically (Weller 1974; World Health Organization 1975a). But even the cumulative total is a paltry figure compared with annual expenditures in LDCs themselves. MDC contributions to mortality declines in LDCs have not been primarily financial; according to the estimates of the preceding section, the financial contributions are associated with an increase in e^o_0 of about one year in the seventeen LDCs between 1940 and 1970. Instead, they seem to have consisted of the development of low-cost health measures exploitable on a massive scale, demonstration of their effectiveness in relatively small areas, training and provision of personnel, and occasionally the initiation of large-scale programs whose major cost was often absorbed by the recipient country.[17] When action appeared to be remarkably cost effective and timely, such as a campaign to eradicate smallpox from West and Central Africa, the entire burden of effort was occasionally absorbed by an MDC (Foege et al. 1975).

5.2 Consequences of Mortality Reductions

In this section we can do no more than begin to sketch in the major influences of these mortality declines on populations of the less developed world, since these declines affect virtually every aspect of individual and collective life in a manner that undoubtedly varies with a host of initial conditions present in the population. It is probably wise to begin with the most concrete and least variable effects, the demographic ones.

Other things remaining the same, mortality declines increase the rate of population growth. The initial effect obviously is to increase the crude rate of natural increase by the absolute amount of the decline in the crude death rate. To a close approximation, the long-run effect of a permanent decline is to increase the rate of natural increase by the average (unweighted) decline in age-specific death rates between age zero and the mean age of childbearing (Preston 1974). This effect is almost fully realized within two generations. In neither case is the growth response strongly conditioned by the prevailing level of fertility. Not a shred of doubt remains that the vast majority of the acceleration in world population growth during the twentieth century is attributable to mortality decline rather than to a rise in fertility.

It is important to recognize that changes in rates of population growth typically have very different effects on demographic, economic, and social processes depending on their source. Coale and Hoover (1958) in their classic study were careful to point out that they were studying the economic implications of variation in fertility, but the study has often been misinterpreted as suggesting the deleterious effects of rapid population growth per se. Application of a modified Coale-Hoover model by Barlow (1967, 1968) demonstrated much more ambiguous economic effects when the source of growth acceleration was mortality decline. Loose discussions of relations between population and economic growth are usually aimed implicitly at the fertility component, even though it is mortality variation that has been the root of trends in population growth.

The fundamental reason why effects differ is a difference in the ages of persons affected. Changes in fertility initially affect only the number of zero-year-olds, and permanent changes permanently affect the age distribution of the population. Mortality changes typically affect all ages, and age distributional changes are relatively minor (Coale 1956; Stolnitz 1956). Such as they are, the short-run age distributional changes induced by mortality decline typically increase the proportion of the population at ages below 5 or 10 and above 40 and decrease the proportion at other ages. The pertinent index is the age-specific death rate, μ_x. When this declines by more than the population-weighted average, the proportion of the population in the immediately succeeding ages will rise. Since mortality declines have tended to be largest in absolute (but not proportional) terms at the extremes of life, the dependency burden initially rises. The long-run effect of a permanent decline in mortality is typically to increase the proportion of the population at ages below 20 and above 75. The pertinent age-specific index here is the cumulative change (unweighted) in age-specific death rates since age zero relative to an appropriately defined average (Preston 1974). The long-run effect on the dependency burden is also positive. With the gross reproduction rate fixed at 2.5, a rise in female life expectancy from 30 to 50 to 70 years in stable populations characterized by "West" mortality patterns increases the ratio of those outside of labor force age (15–64) to those within from 0.635 to 0.764 to 0.847 (Coale and Demeny 1966, pp. 82, 98, 114). All of this increase is sustained in the ages below 15. These changes are not trivial, but they are rather small relative to those induced by movements of fertility within its observed range.

It follows from this discussion and the formal analysis that supports it that if all ages experience an identical decline in death rates (usually

317 Mortality Declines in Less Developed Countries

termed a "neutral" decline), the age composition of the population will be unaffected in both the short run and the long run. The probability of survival from age x *to* age $x + n$ is equal to exp $\{- \int_x^{x+n} \mu(t)dt\}$, where $\mu(t)$ is the death rate at exact age t. A decline in mortality by amount k at all ages will raise all n-year survival probabilities by the factor, exp $\{kn\}$. Since the population at each age grows by the same factor (including infants via the greater survivorship of prospective parents), the proportionate age distribution is unaffected. Barring behavioral changes, a decline that is neutrally distributed among population subgroups, however defined (e.g., occupational or educational groups), will not affect population composition. The point is worth emphasis: it is *differential* mortality change that affects population composition. A change that is equally shared affects only size and growth. To the degree that typical mortality changes have been differentially distributed, the first-order changes induced in population composition have been economically unfavorable. Not only have the very young and the very old profited disproportionately, but so have women and unskilled or semiskilled workers.[18] Unlike programs of human resource development, which usually aim directly at an upgrading of population composition in ways that relate to production, programs of mortality decline have typically increased population size and reduced, at least initially, the desirability of its configuration.

Although mortality and fertility variation have very different effects on population composition, the mechanism by which they influence population size is the same in the long run: changes in the annual number of births. The principal long-run effect of mortality decline on population size arises not from the greater survivorship of persons who would have been born in any event, but from the larger number of births that are produced. To see this clearly, suppose that a neutral mortality change occurs to an initially stable population such that all ages experience a permanent reduction in death rates of .02. If age-specific fertility rates remain unchanged, the rate of population growth will increase by .02 and the rate of increase in the annual number of births will also rise by .02. Consider the number of 20-year-olds in the population 60 years after the mortality decline. The original number born into this cohort will be larger as a result of the mortality decline by $[e^{.02(40)} - 1] = 123\%$, whereas their improved survivorship after birth will have increased their numbers by $[e^{.02(20)} - 1] = 49\%$, a growth factor less than half as large. More than half the members of the cohort would not have been born had mortality not declined. This fraction continues to grow over time, but the improved survivorship factor does not. Stated more vividly, any LDC child "saved" from death today adds only one to the population size for a time. But the progeny of that child will ultimately

318   Samuel H. Preston

be infinite in numbers if current rates of mortality and fertility are maintained by all generations. The prevailing practice in health economics of ignoring the offspring of the population "saved" seriously misrepresents the effect of health programs on populations (see reviews in Weisbrod 1975 and Klarman 1967).

5.2.1   Economic and Behavioral Responses

In discussing aggregate economic and behavioral responses to mortality decline, it is useful to recognize that all of the responses must make themselves felt through one of four indexes. This follows directly from a formal identity:

$$CDR = CBR + CRNM - R_p + R_{pc},$$
where CDR, CBR, $CRNM =$ crude rates of death, birth, and net migration

$R_p, R_{pc} =$ proportionate rate of growth of total production and of production per capita.

When the crude death rate declines, one of the terms on the right side must change to keep the identity in balance. The first three terms on the right side—birthrates, migration rates, and the economic growth rate—primarily reflect behavioral adjustments to mortality change. The fourth —the growth rate of output per capita—is basically a default option, inevitably activated if none of the other three terms change. If none of the four terms on the right can change, or change for very long, the decline in CDR cannot be sustained. This is the basic Malthusian model, in which the "passion between the sexes" placed a floor on the crude birthrate, a subsistence level of production bounded R_{pc} from below, migration was defined as impossible, and slow technical change and rapidly diminishing returns to labor constrained R_p from above.

As an identity, any term in it could be isolated on one side of the equation and the others forced to "respond" to its changes. The justification for isolating the CDR is provided in the first part of the paper: a substantial fraction of changes in CDR have been induced by factors independent of any term on the right side, and it is reasonable to view them as being forced to respond to it. To the extent that declines in CDR have been produced by increases in rates of growth of production per head, the equation as presented is misleading.[19]

In most of the remainder of this section we will consider the various ways populations appear to have responded to mortality declines, taking each of the possibilities in turn. The review attempts to be positive and historical rather than normative.

Declines in Crude Birthrates

There are a multitude of ways that changes in mortality can induce changes in fertility. Three of the effects are quasi-biological. Declines in

mortality change the age structure in such a way as to reduce the proportion of the population in the childbearing years and to reduce crude
birthrates if age-specific fertility rates remain constant. Using the earlier
example, gains in female life expectancy from 30 to 50 to 70 years, with
age-specific fertility held constant at a level that produces a gross reproduction rate of 2.5, changes the crude birthrate from 38.78/1,000 to
37.12 to 35.99. The decline in the crude death rate over this range is
from 33.34 to 5.78, so that the decline in the birthrate compensates for
10.1% of the decline in crude death rates through this age-structural
route (Coale and Demeny 1966).

A second biological mechanism operates through breast-feeding.
Breast-feeding inhibits ovulation, particularly in poorly nourished populations. Survival of the previous birth, by extending lactation, tends to
delay the arrival of the next birth. Estimates of the average amount of
net delay range as high as 12–13 months in Senegal, Bangladesh, and
certain preindustrial European populations, although an estimate of
about 7 months is probably more representative of poor agrarian populations (see the review in Preston 1975*b*). Since average interbirth
intervals in such populations average about 30–35 months, the compensating variation in fertility to a change of infant mortality rates can be
as high as 35% but is more likely to be in the area of 20%. That is, if
all a woman's children die in infancy, her average interbirth intervals
will be shorter by 20% and she will have approximately 20% more
births over her reproductive life than if all had survived. In urban Latin
American settings, where breast-feeding is usually short if it occurs at
all, the compensating variation from this source is negligible (Rutstein
and Medica 1975).

A third quasi-biological influence operates in the opposite direction
but is probably fairly weak. Mortality declines make it more likely that
marriages will survive through the end of the partners' reproductive
periods. In areas such as India where sanctions against widow remarriage are strong, reductions in the incidence of widowhood probably
exert an upward pressure on fertility. Arriaga (1967) has argued that
this mechanism is responsible for substantial postwar increases in child-
woman ratios in certain Latin American populations. However, his argument neglects the age-structural changes that are directly produced by
mortality declines. The maximum effect of mortality changes on a woman's completed fertility can be estimated by assuming that no remarriage
is possible and that childbearing occurs at a constant rate throughout
her reproductive life up to the death of her husband or for 25 years,
whichever comes first. Then her completed fertility is simply proportional to the expected number of years lived by the husband in the first
25 years of marriage. Assuming that males are age 20 at marriage, this
expectation goes from 20.97 years in a population with a male life expectancy at birth of 30.08 to 24.49 when life expectancy is 68.56

(Coale and Demeny 1966, pp. 7, 23). Fertility would increase by 16.8%, or by perhaps 6 points, while the death rate would decline by perhaps 25 points. Complete prohibition of widow remarriage could thus boost the growth acceleration induced by mortality decline by some 25%, making it roughly equivalent to but opposite in sign from the lactational effect. However, it does not appear that taboos on widow remarriage are sufficiently widespread outside of India to have anywhere near this effect.

In addition to the three quasi-biological links, there are many possible behavioral ones. Since these are the subject of another conference paper (chap. 3), they will not be reviewed here (see also O'Hara 1975). Suffice it to say that the magnitude of one relationship has now been investigated rather carefully in a variety of populations in Asia and Latin America, as well as in preindustrial Europe. It has repeatedly been shown that, among women of a particular parity, those who had experienced one additional child death subsequently bore, on average, far fewer than one additional birth. Furthermore, some of the additional childbearing that did occur could be traced indirectly to the biological link identified above. The studies have attempted to control other characteristics of women believed to influence fertility (see studies by Chowdhury, Khan, and Chen; Heer and Wu; Rutstein and Medica; and Knodel in Committee for . . . Demography 1975). The largest "replacement" effect was 0.28 identified in Taiwan by Heer and Wu. It may be that the dead children were replaced in advance, but the simple demography of death makes this an inefficient reproductive strategy. The large majority of children who die before adulthood do so in the first two or three years of life, and their death can be observed and reacted to by parents during their own reproductive period.

The apparent failure of parents in many LDCs to behave as though they were pursuing a single reproductive target framed in terms of surviving children should not be surprising. It is clear that many of the social norms and sanctions that regulate reproductive behavior in LDCs refer to age at entry into union, frequency of intercourse, postnatal abstinence, number of partners, lactation, remarriage, and so on, rather than specifically to the number of children born or surviving (Polgar 1972). It is not necessary to reject the view that reproducers are goal-directed, but only to recognize that social norms and expectations have established other goals than "the" number of children. These norms and expectations are not responsive to an individual's experience with child death, although they may be responsive to aggregate mortality rates. Such conditioning is in fact the basis of functionalist theories of fertility. Davis (1955) has repeatedly argued that high-mortality populations must adopt a set of institutions and customs producing high fertility or else face extinction. The major adaptive institution he points to is the extended family, which encourages early entry into union by arranging marriages and stimulates fertility by removing many of the child-rearing costs from the parents. The expected positive effect of family extension on fertility has not been observed in most empirical studies at the house-hold level (see the review in Burch and Gendell 1970). More to the point, it is not clear how the group-selection processes that are supposed to have created such institutions in the first place would operate to change them when mortality conditions relax.

There is one aggregate-level linkage between death rates and birth-rates that deserves mention because of its apparent importance in pre-industrial Europe. In a spatially limited system where land is the basis of wealth and accession to land the prerequisite for marriage, the rate of marriage and hence childbearing will depend upon the rate at which land becomes available, hence on mortality. Exogenous declines in mor-tality will, more or less automatically, reduce fertility by slowing the turnover of land and delaying marriage. Such a system was apparently an important feature of demographic-economic relations in Western Europe from 1600 to 1800 and may account for the generally late age at marriage in these populations (Habakkuk 1971; Wrigley 1969; see Eversley 1957 for a vivid numerical description of the expected re-sponses to an epidemic). More important, economic historians have suggested that this mechanism, the "European marriage pattern," was a fundamental basis of the industrial revolution since it facilitated capital accumulation by severing the link between the level of mortality and the rate of growth of income per capita (Wrigley 1969; Habakkuk 1971). How important this mechanism is in contemporary less developed coun-tries is unclear. Increased rates of population growth have been accom-panied by declining proportions married throughout much of Asia since 1960 or so (Smith 1976). However, many other modernizing influences have also been at work. In Asia, at least, the prevalence of an extended family system in rural areas reduces the dependence of marriage on individual acquisition of land and presumably attenuates the link be-tween population pressure and individuals' marital behavior. In urban areas, however, a "suitable" job may come to play an analogous, though no doubt less decisive, role.

That the sum of responses of fertility to mortality declines in LDCs has been quantitatively weak is shown clearly in the history of popula-tion growth rates. Durand (1967, p. 7) puts the annual rate of popu-lation growth for LDCs at 0.3% for 1850–1900 and 2.1% for 1950–65. He further suggests that, with few exceptions, birthrates have not de-clined. The United Nations Population Division "estimates and conjec-tures" that CDRs in LDCs were 38/1,000 in 1850–1900 and 17/1,000 in 1960–70, whereas CBRs were 40/1,000 and 41/1,000 in the two periods (United Nations 1971, p. 7). These figures suggest no compen-

sating variation in fertility whatever, although mortality declines may
have reduced the increase in fertility that would otherwise have occurred.
It is true that several of the postulated relations should operate with a
lag, and widespread (but small) declines in fertility since 1970 in LDCs
might be partially attributed to prior mortality decline. But the evidence
is that changes in birthrates have not been a major mechanism of adjustment to date.

Declines in Crude Rates of Net Migration

An increase in out-migration for the world as a whole is clearly impossible, and it has been scarcely more of an option for LDCs as a bloc.
Perceived cultural, economic, and political difficulties attendant upon
migration from LDCs to MDCs have resulted in MDC immigration
quotas that are fixed at a point where they represent a tiny fraction of
annual natural increase in LDCs. International migration among LDCs
faces similar obstacles (see the discussion in Myrdal 1968, pp. 1459–
62). In this matter the present LDC situation is again markedly at variance with that of European populations in the eighteenth and nineteenth
centuries, when a substantial amount of population increase was drained
off via overseas or transcontinental migration. Friedlander (1969)
stresses the importance of this "safety valve" for delaying fertility reductions in England and Sweden. My calculations indicate that 15–25%
of persons born in Sweden in the middle decades of the nineteenth century died outside its borders.

When subnational territories are considered, the migration response
probably becomes more consequential, because the export of population
growth from one area to another faces fewer legal, cultural, and institutional impediments. In Indonesia, the Philippines, and Ceylon, government programs have attempted to redistribute population from dense,
rapidly growing areas to sparsely populated ones, although relative to
natural increase the movements have been small (Myrdal 1968, pp.
2139–49). How important mortality declines in rural areas have been
for rural-urban migration in LDCs has simply not been identified, to my
knowledge. The region with apparently the sharpest mortality decline
since 1900, Latin America, has also had the most rapid rural to urban
migration (United Nations 1971). But both regional peculiarities may
have been caused by its more rapid economic growth. Unlike the European situation, net rural-urban migration is not required to maintain
constant proportions in the two sectors. Rural birthrates are higher, but
so in general are rural death rates. Rates of natural increase are not
widely disparate (Davis 1973). It has often been suggested that, in Asia
at least, a large fraction of rural natural increase (which accounts for
the large bulk of the annual volume) simply cannot be exported to urban
areas because the cities cannot create enough new jobs. Even if these

predictions prove pessimistic, it remains that, for national aggregates, changes in net migration rates have not been and will not be an important response to mortality decline.

Increases in Growth Rates of Total Production

The effect of population growth on economic growth is obviously a topic whose scope and complexity are too vast to be adequately reviewed here. While the effects of changes in death rates on output are difficult to partial out (see Denison 1962 for one attempt), economic history and economic theory are quite consistent with the view that R_p has been the principal respondent to changes in CDR.

A decline in CDR generally increases the growth rate of the labor force in roughly equal measure. As noted above, the labor force growth rate is typically incremented in the short run by a slightly smaller amount than the population growth rate. But even after accounting for this tendency, if we accept standard estimates of the elasticity of production with respect to changes in the quantity of labor input on the order of 0.5 to 0.8, more than half of the "response" can be accounted for without any change in other inputs or in technology.

There are reasons to believe that other inputs have typically changed in a reinforcing fashion. In some instances (South America, Southern Africa, and much of Asia) the growing population has had access to unutilized land not markedly inferior to that already under production (Myrdal 1968). According to D. Gale Johnson (1974, p. 89), between 1935–39 and 1960 approximately 75% of the increased grain output in developing countries resulted from expansion of the planted area. In some cases the mortality reduction campaigns themselves have liberated large areas of previously inhospitable territory. Taylor and Hall (1967) cite examples of such effects from antimalarial programs in Nepal, Sri Lanka, Sardinia, and Mexico (see also Sorkin 1975). Schultz (1964, pp. 63–70) shows that the response is also present when mortality changes in the opposite direction. An estimated 8% fall in the Indian labor force resulting from the 1918–19 influenza epidemic was accompanied by a reduction of 3.8% in acreage sown.

Expansion of land use obviously cannot continue indefinitely, and to the (apparently minor) degree that fixed factors are important in production, the particular effect of accelerated population growth on per capita production will be negative. For most purposes it is more important to know the effects of mortality decline on the capital supply. With one possibly important exception, the effects should not be radically different from those of increased fertility. The age distributional effects are similar in nature, though muted in the case of mortality change. When mortality declines, the proportion of the population in a stage of dissaving increases—permanently. Households face an increased dependency burden and governments a greater press of immediate consumption demands. Business optimism regarding future demand for their products rises with the growth rate of potential consumers. Business profits and internally financed investments may increase as the labor supply curve shifts outward, unless the shift also reduces consumers' purchasing power. These effects have been reviewed elsewhere in conjunction with fertility effects, and it is not profitable to reconsider them here.

The one possibly important difference is that members of a lower-mortality population can look forward to longer lives in which to reap the benefits of personal investment. There is no such effect when fertility is the source of growth acceleration. The present value of investments with a long gestation period, such as extended schooling, retirement equities, or children, necessarily rises when mortality rates fall. Mushkin (1964), Schultz (1975), and others have suggested that such effects may represent an important economic benefit of reduced mortality.

It seems indisputable that such effects operate, and are probably reinforced by the increased proportion of the population who are in the investment stage. Nevertheless, it appears that the effects are relatively small and can be easily overwhelmed by minor variations in discount rates. To illustrate, define the present value of an investment in the standard manner prior to a change in mortality:

$$P.V. = \int_0^\infty p(a) \left[\frac{B(a) - C(a)}{e^{ra}} \right] da,$$

where $p(a)$ = the probability that the investor will survive a years from the time of investment according to the mortality schedule in effect prior to the mortality decline

$B(a), C(a)$ = benefits and costs of the investment realized or incurred in year a

r = subjective rate of discount, continuously applied.

Now superimpose a neutral mortality decline of 0.01 per year, equivalent to a reduction in the CDR of 10/1,000, that is, a large decline. This is the average reduction in age-specific death rates between ages 15 and 50 when male life expectancy at birth increases from 30.1 to 51.8 years (Coale and Demeny 1966, pp. 7, 16). The new present value is

$$P.V.' = \int_0^\infty p(a)\, e^{.01a} \left[\frac{B(a) - C(a)}{e^{ra}} \right] da$$

$$= \int_0^\infty p(a) \left[\frac{B(a) - C(a)}{e^{(r-.01)a}} \right] da.$$

That is, such a major change in mortality conditions has the same effect on present value as reducing the discount rate by only 0.01 and retain-

325   Mortality Declines in Less Developed Countries

ing the initial mortality conditions. In view of the wide variation that seems to prevail in discount rates, as partially reflected in the common analytic practice of applying several that differ by 0.05 or even more, it is readily seen that mortality prospects are a relatively minor influence on present value.

As a more concrete illustration, we will compute the internal rate of return on investment in schooling and show how it is affected by empirically observed variation in mortality. We have chosen Mexico for the illustration because Carnoy (1967) provides all of the necessary information except life tables.[20] We will compute the internal rate of return for a 15-year-old male who has completed grade 8 from his subsequent completion of grades 9, 10, and 11. Three mortality schedules are used: the male life table of Mexico, 1921, having a life expectancy at birth of 33.66 years (Arriaga 1968); the male life table of Mexico, 1966, having a life expectancy at birth of 59.49 years (Keyfitz and Flieger 1971); and immortality. Results are shown in table 5.6.

It is clear from this table that the increment to the private or social rate of return that results from replacing an e^0_0 of 33.7 by immortality is only 1.5 points. This is approximately the difference it makes to use continuous rather than once-a-year compoundings. The reason for the weak effect is simply that mortality rates in young and middle adulthood are not high enough even in very high mortality populations to substantially alter expected payoffs. The large variability in rates experienced in childhood do not figure in the calculation, and the large variability at older ages is heavily discounted.

The effect of mortality variation would be somewhat stronger if individuals were predominantly risk-aversive and made decisions on the basis of the entire distribution of expected outcomes rather than simply on the basis of the mean. Higher mortality adds greater variability to the distribution of expected outcomes as well as reducing the mean. It increases the chance that zero or negative returns will accrue to investment, and this increase is faster than is the reduction in mean. Nevertheless, for the bulk of investors—those in early and middle adulthood

Table 5.6   **Internal Rate of Return from Completing Grades 9, 10, and 11 in Mexico, 1963, under Varying Assumptions about Mortality**

Assumption	Private Rate of Return	Social Rate of Return
Mexican life table of 1921	12.8	9.9
Mexican life table of 1966	13.9	10.9
Immortality	14.3	11.4

Sources: Carnoy (1967); Keyfitz and Flieger (1971); Arriaga (1968).

—it does not appear that even very radical mortality change could exert much influence on perceived investment profitability.

On balance, it does not appear that the effects of population growth acceleration on capital formation when mortality is the source should be markedly different *in nature* from the effects when fertility is the source. The Coale-Hoover model postulates a less-than-proportionate increase in capital supply when the population grows faster via higher fertility, and this feature is retained when the effects of mortality change are simulated (Barlow 1967, 1968). Largely for this reason, Barlow concludes that the antimalarial campaign in Ceylon ultimately had negative effects on per capita income growth, even after the improved health of the labor force is accounted for. Confidence in this conclusion depends on one's confidence in the savings-investment assumptions of the Coale-Hoover model.

It is also possible that mortality reductions foster economies of scale in production and an intensification of individual work effort. Again, the subject is very complex, and in most respects the analysis of mortality variation need not differ from that of fertility variation. A postulated difference is that mortality control programs have an important demonstration effect (Mushkin 1964; Fein 1964; Malenbaum 1970; and others). That is, they demonstrate that individuals can control their own destiny through the rational application of science and technology. They attest to the power of man in contrast to that of the supernatural and hence spark work effort and a stronger motivation toward self-fulfillment. Malenbaum (1970) argues that this is the basis of observed associations between mortality rates and labor productivity, but there are surely other mechanisms that offer more plausible interpretations. The contention has not been put to a rigorous test. It seems inconsistent with observations that poor illiterate farmers in LDCs have always responded quickly to new and profitable opportunities and technologies (Johnson 1974). A sense of personal control over the environment is one of the strongest components of "modern" attitudes (Sack 1974, p. 90). But the importance of mortality declines in the development of this attitude and the influence of the attitude on output remain to be demonstrated, important as the issue may be.

Changes in Growth Rates of Production per Capita

With constant technology and no changes in nonlabor factors of production, it is reasonable to expect that a CDR decline of 10/1,000 would raise the growth rate of total production only by 0.6–0.7% or so. If no birthrate or migration adjustments were forthcoming, the rate of growth of per capita income would decline by 0.3–0.4%. This is not a large amount relative to prevailing growth rates, and it is not surprising that the mortality declines have left no unmistakable imprint on per capita national economic growth rates.

Nevertheless, there are circumstances where the mortality decline has apparently had a decisive negative effect on economic well-being. Perhaps the most vivid account is offered by William Allan (1965, especially chap. 21). Allan outlines a cycle of land degeneration in East Africa that was, he argues, initiated by a mortality reduction. Population pressure at the kin-group level led to land subdivision and fragmentation, since landowners were expected to share their holdings with needy kin. Subdivision led in turn to a shortening of the fallow period and to soil depletion and erosion. Declining yields led to accelerated shortening of the fallow and to ultimate soil exhaustion. "Perhaps the greatest 'sin' of the suzerain powers was the saving of life, the lives of millions of men who under the old conditions would have died in early childhood, or in later life, of famine, disease, and violence" (Allan 1965, p. 338). Ultimately the response was out-migration, but not before a stage of economic misery was encountered. The initial stages of intensified land use are those described by Boserup (1965), but the outcome is very different. Instead of self-sustaining growth supported by a newly developed work ethic, the result was simply impoverishment. Obviously, some soils can support extreme intensification and multiple cropping and others cannot. Population pressure by itself is clearly not sufficient for sustained technological change, nor does it appear to be necessary once the possibilities of trade are opened up.

It is clear that general statements cannot be made about how populations have reacted or will react to exogenous mortality declines. The reaction will depend on a wide variety of initial conditions. In agrarian populations it appears that the most important conditioning factors are type of soil, land tenancy and kinship-marriage systems, density, possibilities for out-migration, savings and investment relationships, and the saliency of surviving-children goals. A great deal of work in recent economic and demographic history remains to be done before the quantitative details of the outline sketched in these sections can be confidently filled in.

328   Samuel H. Preston

Appendix

Table 5.A.1   Estimates of National Indexes about 1940

Country	Life Expectancy at Birth	Year of Estimate	Source	Daily Calories per Capita Available at Retail Level	Year of Estimate	Source: (6) Unless Noted
Australia	66.09	(40)	(2)	3,128	(40)	
Belgium	59.08	(38–40)	(3)	2,885	(40)	
Canada	64.62	(40–42)	(1)	3,109	(40)	
Czechoslovakia	56.79	(37)	(1)	2,761	(40)	
Chile	38.10	(40)	(4)	2,481	(40)	
Colombia	36.04	(38)	(4)	1,860	(38)	(7)
Denmark	66.31	(40)	(2)	3,249	(40)	
Egypt	38.60	(36–38)	(1)	2,199	(40)	
Finland	57.39[a]	(40)	(1)	2,950	(40)	
Greece	54.37	(40)	(1)	2,523	(40)	
Guatemala	30.40	(40)	(4)	—	—	
Honduras	37.50	(40)	(4)	2,079	(40)	
Hungary	56.57	(41)	(1)	2,815	(40)	
India	32.27	(41)	(5)	2,021	(40)	
Ireland	60.02	(40)	(1)	3,184	(40)	
Japan	49.12	(39–41)	(3)	2,268	(40)	
Korea	48.90	(38)	(1)	1,904	(40)	
Luxembourg	60.07	(38–42)	(3)	2,820	(34–38)	(8)
Mexico	38.80	(40)	(4)	1,909	(40)	
Netherlands	65.43	(40)	(2)	2,958	(40)	
New Zealand	67.00	(36)	(2)	3,281	(40)	
Nicaragua	34.50	(40)	(4)	—	—	
Panama	42.40	(40)	(4)	—	—	
Peru	36.50	(40)	(4)	2,090	(40)	
Philippines	46.26	(38)	(1)	2,021	(40)	
Portugal	51.06	(40)	(2)	2,461	(40)	
Puerto Rico	46.09	(39–41)	(1)	2,219	(40)	
Spain	50.18	(40)	(1)	2,788	(40)	
Sweden	66.64	(40)	(1)	3,052	(40)	
Switzerland	64.88	(40)	(2)	3,049	(40)	
Taiwan	47.80	(41)	(1)	2,153	(40)	
Thailand	40.02	(37–38)	(1)	2,173	(40)	
Turkey	33.91	(35–45)	(15)	2,619	(40)	
United Kingdom	61.64	(40)	(2)	3,005	(40)	
United States	63.74	(39–41)	(1)	3,249	(40)	
Venezuela	39.91	(41)	(1)	—	—	

329   Mortality Declines in Less Developed Countries

National Income per Capita in 1970 U.S. Dollars	Year of Estimate	Source: (9) Unless Noted	Percentage Illiterate	Age Range	Year of Estimate	Source: (10) Unless Noted	Population in Thousands (1940)(13)
1,128	(38–40)		2.5	—	(40)	(14)	7,039
715	(38–39)		4.5	—	(40)	(14)	8,301
1,041	(38–40)		3.16	10+	(40)		11,682
438	(38)		3.6	—	(37)	(14)	14,429
371	(38–40)		28.2	10+	(40)		5,063
190	(38–40)		44.10	10+	(38)		8,702
971	(38–40)		1.5	—	(40)	(14)	3,832
167	(39)		84.9	10+	(37)		16,008
419	(39)		8.8	—	(40)	(14)	3,698
187	(38)		34.4	—	(40)	(14)	7,319
78	(40)		65.4	7+	(40)		2,201
109	(41–42)		66.35	10+	(45)		1,146
318	(38–40)		6.0	10+	(41)		9,344
67	(38–39)		86.5	10+	(41)	(10,11)[b]	316,004
665	(40)		1.5	—	(40)	(14)	2,993
260	(39)		—	—	—		71,400
—	—		68.6	10+	(30)		21,817
795	(39)		4.4	—	(40)	(14)	292
138	(40)		51.5	10+	(40)		19,815
889	(38)		1.5	—	(40)	(14)	8,879
1,055	(38–40)		1.5	—	(40)	(14)	1,573
105	(40)		63.0	7+	(40)	(12)	825
374	(40)		35.25	10+	(40)		620
89	(40)	(16)	56.35	10+	(40)		7,033
113	(38)		37.75	10+	(48)		15,814
—	—		48.7	10+	(40)		7,696
413	(38–40)		31.5	10+	(40)		1,880
361	(40)	(16)	23.2	10+	(40)		25,757
1,091	(40)		0.1	10+	(30)		6,356
1,246	(40)		1.5	—	(40)	(14)	4,234
—	—		78.7	5+	(40)		6,163
128	(39)	(11)	46.25	10+	(47)		14,755
212	(39)		79.1	10+	(35)		17,620
1,334	(38–40)		1.5	—	(40)	(14)	41,862
1,549	(40)		4.2	10+	(40)	(13)	132,594
291	(40)		56.50	10+	(41)		3,803

Table 5.A.1 (continued)

Sources: 1. United Nations, *Statistical Yearbook* (1967).
    2. Preston, Keyfitz, and Schoen (1972).
    3. Keyfitz and Fleiger (1968).
    4. Arriaga (1968).
    5. Estimated by Davis (1951, pp. 62–63).
    6. Estimates prepared by the Food and Agriculture Organization of the United Nations, cited in "Food, Income, and Mortality," *Population Index* 13, no. 2 (April 1947): 96–103.
    7. United Nations, *Statistical Yearbook* (1951).
    8. United Nations, Food and Agriculture Organization, *Production Yearbook* (1958).
    9. Estimates prepared by the Technical Group, U.S. Bureau of the Budget; cited in "Food, Income, and Mortality," *Population Index* 13, no. 2 (April 1947): 96–103. All figures have been converted to 1970 U.S. dollars by application of the consumer price index from U.S. Bureau of the Census, *Statistical Abstract of the United States*, various issues.
    10. United Nations, *Statistical Yearbook* (1949–50).
    11. United Nations, *Statistical Yearbook* (1955).
    12. United Nations Educational, Scientific and Cultural Organization, *Basic facts and figures: Illiteracy, libraries, museums, books, newspapers, newsprint, film and radios* (Paris, 1952).
    13. United Nations, *Demographic Yearbook* (1960).
    14. Banks (1971).
    15. Calculated by author from estimates of e_5^0 presented in Shorter (1968). The Coale-Demeny "South" model mortality pattern was assumed to apply.
    16. United Nations, *National Income Statistics of Various Countries, 1938–1948* (Lake Success, N.Y., 1950).

[a]Average 1936–40 and 1941–50.
[b]Interpolated from data for 1931 and 1951.

Table 5.A.2 National Indexes about 1970

	Life Expectancy at Birth 1970–75 (1)	Percentage Illiterate of the Adult Population (2)	Year of Estimate (2)	1970 National Income per Capita (1970 U.S. $) (3)	1970 Daily Calories Available for Consumption, per Capita (4)	1970 Population (in 1,000s) (1)	Index of Income Inequality (5)	Year of Estimate	Coverage
Africa									
Algeria	53.2	52.5	1971	295	1,710	14,330	—		
Angola	38.5	87.5	1973*	280	1,910	5,670	—		
Botswana	43.5	87.0	1971	132	2,040	617	—		
Burundi	39.0	35.0	1974*	68	2,330	3,350	—		
Central African Rep.	41.0	82.0	1975*	122	2,170	1,612	—		
Chad	38.5	90.0	1975*	70	2,060	3,640	—		
Congo	43.5	65.0	1970*	281	2,160	1,191	—		
Dahomey	41.0	80.0	1975*	81	2,250	2,686	—		
Egypt	52.4	62.0	1975*	202	2,360	33,329	−6.5660	1965	Nat. Household
Ethiopia	38.0	93.0	1975*	72	2,150	24,855	—		
Gabon	41.0	88.0	1974*	468	2,210	500	−17.2442	1960	Nat. Population
Gambia	40.0	90.0	1971*	99	2,370	463	—		
Ghana	43.5	56.5	1971	236	2,200	8,628	—		
Guinea	41.0	92.5	1971*	79	2,040	3,291	—		
Ivory Coast	43.5	80.0	1973*	325	2,490	4,310	−9.8088	1970	Nat. Income Recip.
Kenya	50.0	75.0	1975*	130	2,350	11,247	−13.1644	1969	Nat. Income Recip.
Liberia	43.5	88.0	1970	181	2,040	1,523	—		
Libyan Arab Rep.	52.9	68.0	1974*	1,450	2,540	1,938	—		
Madagascar	43.5	60.0	1975*	123	2,350	6,932	−9.8964	1960	Nat. Population
Malawi	41.0	75.0	1976*	68	2,150	4,360	−7.0502	1969	Nat. Household
Mali	38.0	90.0	1972	50	2,170	5,047	—		

Table 5.A.2 (continued)

	Life Expectancy at Birth 1970–75 (1)	Percentage Illiterate of the Adult Population (2)	Year of Estimate (2)	1970 National Income per Capita (1970 U.S. $) (3)	1970 Daily Calories Available for Consumption, per Capita (4)	1970 Population (in 1,000s) (1)	Index of Income Inequality (5)	Year of Estimate	Coverage
Mauritius	65.5	20.0	1974*	223	2,370	824	—		
Mauritania	38.5	95.0	1972*	147	2,060	1,162	—		
Morocco	52.9	78.6	1971	225	2,400	15,126	—		
Mozambique	43.5	80.0	1972	228	2,190	8,234	—		
Niger	38.5	94.0	1973*	70	2,180	4,016	—		
Nigeria	41.0	74.0	1973	135	2,290	55,073			
Rhodesia	51.5	95.0	1972	257	2,550	5,308	−14.8362	1968	Nat. Income Recip.
Rwanda	41.0	90.0	1973*	57	2,160	3,679	—		
Senegal	40.0	95.0	1971*	201	2,300	3,925	−12.1394	1960	Nat. Population
Sierra Leone	43.5	90.0	1974*	150	2,240	2,644	—		
Somalia	41.0	95.0	1974*	85	1,770	2,789	—		
South Africa	51.5	56.0	1974*	680	2,730	21,500	−14.3543	1965	Nat. Population
Sudan	48.6	80.0	1973	109	2,130	15,695	—		
Togo	41.0	90.0	1976*	125	2,160	1,960	—		
Tunisia	54.1	60.0	1972	257	2,060	5,137	−9.7467	1961	Nat. Population
Uganda	50.0	70.0	1976*	127	2,230	9,806	—		
United Rep. of the Cameroon	41.0	35.0	1976*	183	2,230	5,836	—		
United Rep. of Tanzania	44.5	71.0	1967	94	1,700	13,273	−8.1535	1967	Nat. Household
Upper Volta	38.0	90.0	1972	62	1,940	5,384	—		
Zaire	43.5	65.0	1971	118	2,040	21,638	—		
Zambia	44.5	52.7	1969	345	2,040	4,295	—		

Table 5.A.2 (continued)

Asia

	Life Expectancy at Birth 1970–75 (1)	Percentage Illiterate of the Adult Population (2)	Year of Estimate (2)	1970 National Income per Capita (1970 U.S. $) (3)	1970 Daily Calories Available for Consumption, per Capita (4)	1970 Population (in 1,000s) (1)	Index of Income Inequality (5)	Year of Estimate	Coverage
Afghanistan	40.3	92.5	1973	83	1,950	16,978	—		
Bangladesh	35.8	90.0	1973	111	1,860	67,692	−3.5534	1967	Nat. Household
Burma	50.0	30.0	1974*	73	2,230	27,748	—		
Cyprus	71.4	18.0	1973	688	2,460	633	−3.3164	1966	Urban Household
India	49.5	40.0	1971	93	2,060	543,132	−7.6103	1968	Nat. Household
Indonesia	47.5	40.0	1971	98	1,920	119,467	—		
Iran	51.0	65.5	1974	352	2,080	28,359	−8.2776	1968	Urban Household
Iraq	52.7	70.0	1974*	311	2,250	9,356	—		
Israel	71.0	12.8	1974*	1,654	2,970	2,958	−3.1183	1970	Urban Household
Japan	73.3	2.0	1975*	1,636	2,310	104,331	−3.3217	1963	Nat. Household
Jordan	53.2	62.5	1972*	260	2,280	2,280	—		
Khmer Rep.	45.4	15.0	1973	123	2,410	7,060	—		
Korea, Rep. of	60.6	8.5	1970*	252	2,420	30,721	−2.2963	1971	Nat. Household
Laos	40.4	75.0	1970*	71	2,080	2,962	—		
Lebanon	63.2	14.0	1975*	521	2,380	2,469	—		
Malaysia	59.4	24.0	1970	295	2,400	10,466	−10.0406	1970	Nat. Household
Nepal	43.6	86.0	1971	80	2,050	11,232	—		
Pakistan	49.8	83.0	1973	164	2,280	60,449	—		
Philippines	58.4	16.5	1970	225	1,920	37,604	−8.6939	1971	Nat. Household
Saudi Arabia	45.3	75.0	1973*	495	1,920	7,740	—		
Singapore	69.5	24.5	1974	918	2,080	2,075	—		

Table 5.A.2 (continued)

	Life Expectancy at Birth 1970–75 (1)	Percentage Illiterate of the Adult Population (2)	Year of Estimate (2)	1970 National Income per Capita (1970 U.S. $) (3)	1970 Daily Calories Available for Consumption, per Capita (4)	1970 Population (in 1,000s) (1)	Index of Income Inequality (5)	Year of Estimate	Coverage
Asia (continued)									
Sri Lanka	67.8	22.0	1971	160	2,240	12,514	−4.4313	1970	Nat. Household
Syria	54.0	60.0	1970	258	2,530	6,247	—	1964	Nat. Household
Taiwan	69.4(7)	5.0(6)	1965	295(7)	2,662(7)	14,334	−3.6354	1962	Nat. Household
Thailand	58.0	18.0	1970	167	2,330	35,745	−8.3579	1968	Nat. Household
Turkey	56.9	44.0	1970	348	2,770	35,232	−11.6389	1964	Rural Household
Vietnam, Rep. of	40.5	23.0	1971	232	2,340	17,952	−3.8293		
Yemen	44.8	82.5	1975*	77	1,970	5,767	—		
Yemen, P.D.R.	44.8	90.0	1970*	96	2,020	1,436	—		
Latin America									
Argentina	68.2	8.0	1973*	1,065	3,150	23,748	−6.2544	1961	Nat. Household
Bolivia	46.8	58.5	1973	191	1,840	4,780	—		
Brazil	61.4	33.0	1970	376	2,600	95,204	−17.7304	1970	Nat. Household
Chile	62.6	12.0	1970	618	2,460	9,369	−8.4001	1968	Nat. Household
Colombia	60.9	21.5	1973	358	2,250	22,075	−10.6656	1970	Nat. Economic Active Population
Costa Rica	68.2	10.0	1973	522	2,470	1,737	−6.4897	1971	Nat. Household
Dominican Rep.	57.8	32.0	1970	334	2,060	4,343	—		
Ecuador	59.6	30.0	1970	255	2,040	6,031	−17.3614	1970	Nat. Economic Active Population
El Salvador	57.8	40.0	1971	283	1,890	3,516	−8.1625	1969	Nat. Population
Guatemala	52.9	62.0	1974*	343	2,120	5,298	−2.8074	1966	Rural Household

Table 5.A.2 (continued)

	Life Expectancy at Birth 1970–75 (1)	Percentage Illiterate of the Adult Population (2)	Year of Estimate (2)	1970 National Income per Capita (1970 U.S. $) (3)	1970 Daily Calories Available for Consumption, per Capita (4)	1970 Population (in 1,000s) (1)	Index of Income Inequality (5)	Year of Estimate	Coverage
Latin America (continued)									
Guyana	67.9	14.0	1974*	319	2,080	709	—		
Haiti	50.0	90.0	1974*	100	1,720	4,325	—		
Honduras	53.5	53.0	1974*	259	2,180	2,553	−14.9221	1968	Nat. Household
Jamaica	69.5	18.0	1970	600	2,300	1,882	—		
Mexico	63.2	24.0	1970	655	2,560	50,313	—		
Nicaragua	52.9	47.0	1971	423	2,380	1,970	—		
Panama	66.5	21.5	1973	646	2,520	1,458	−11.2564	1969	Nat. Economic Active Population
Paraguay	61.9	38.0	1973	230	2,800	2,301	−14.7827	1971	Nat. Economic Active Population
Peru	55.7	44.3	1970	293	2,310	13,248	—		
Trinidad and Tobago	69.5	30.4	1970	732	2,360	955	—		
Uruguay	69.8	9.0	1975*	799	2,860	2,955	−6.8128	1967	Nat. Household
Venezuela	64.7	35.2	1971	954	2,460	10,559	−10.5676	1962	Nat. Household
North America									
Canada	72.4	1.0	1975*	3,369	3,190	21,406	−4.0518	1965	Nat. Household
United States	71.3	1.0	1969	4,289	3,270	204,879	−6.6384	1966	Nat. Household
Puerto Rico	72.1	27.9	1970	1,744	2,450	2,743	—		

Table 5.A.2 (continued)

	Life Expectancy at Birth 1970–75 (1)	Percentage Illiterate of the Adult Population (2)	Year of Estimate (2)	1970 National Income per Capita (1970 U.S. $) (3)	1970 Daily Calories Available for Consumption, per Capita (4)	1970 Population (in 1,000s) (1)	Index of Income Inequality (5)	Year of Estimate	Coverage
Europe									
Austria	71.2	1.0	1974*	1,730	3,340	7,447	—		
Belgium	72.9	2.0	1975*	2,421	3,390	9,638	—		
Bulgaria	71.8	5.0	1975*	2,726	3,300	8,490	−1.5225	1962	Nat. Workers
Czechoslovakia	69.3	0.0	1974*	3,013	3,190	14,339	−1.1290	1964	Nat. Workers
Denmark	73.9	1.0	1974*	2,898	3,230	4,929	−4.9775	1966	Nat. Income Recip.
Finland	70.4	0.0	1975*	1,998	3,020	4,606	−9.8462	1962	Nat. Income Recip.
France	72.6	3.0	1975*	2,550	3,210	50,670	−11.4365	1962	Nat. Household
Germany, W.	70.6	1.0	1970*	2,752	3,230	60,700	−7.5125	1964	Nat. Income Recip.
Greece	71.8	15.6	1971	1,051	2,900	8,793	—		
Hungary	69.5	2.0	1975*	2,244	3,180	10,338	−2.1548	1969	Nat. Population
Ireland	71.8	1.0	1974*	1,244	3,420	2,954	—		
Italy	72.0	7.0	1975*	1,591	3,170	53,565	—		
Luxembourg	70.8	2.0	1975*	2,613	3,390	339	—		
Malta	70.8	12.0	1974*	721	2,680	326	—		
Netherlands	73.8	2.0	1973*	2,232	3,290	13,032	—		
Norway	74.5	0.0	1974*	2,458	2,920	3,877	—		
Poland	70.1	2.2	1970	5,766	3,270	32,473	−2.2046	1964	Nat. Workers
Portugal	68.0	45.0	1970*	684	2,890	8,628	—		
Spain	72.1	19.9	1970	884	2,620	33,779	−5.1072	1965	Nat. Household
Sweden	73.3	0.1	1975*	3,724	2,800	8,043	−6.1269	1963	Nat. Income Recip.
Switzerland	72.4	0.0	1973*	2,963	3,250	6,267	—		
United Kingdom	72.3	10.0	1975*	1,990	3,140	55,480	−4.0915	1968	Nat. Household

Table 5.A.2 (continued)

	Life Expectancy at Birth 1970–75 (1)	Percentage Illiterate of the Adult Population (2)	Year of Estimate (2)	1970 National Income per Capita (1970 U.S. $) (3)	1970 Daily Calories Available for Consumption, per Capita (4)	1970 Population (in 1,000s) (1)	Index of Income Inequality (5)	Year of Estimate (5)	Coverage
Oceania									
Australia	72.4	1.5	1975*	2,633	3,050	12,552	−3.6895	1968	Nat. Household
New Zealand	72.0	2.0	1975*	2,008	3,330	2,820	—	—	

Sources: (1) United Nations, *Selected World Demographic Indicators by Countries 1950–2000* (Population Division, Department of Economic and Social Affairs of the United Nations, 1975).

(2) Unstarred: United Nations Educational, Scientific, and Cultural Organization, *Statistical Yearbook, 1973* (Paris, 1974), table 1.4; starred: United States, State Department, *Background Notes*, individual country volumes, various years 1970–76.

(3) United Nations, *Statistical Yearbook, 1974*, tables 181, 188.

(4) United Nations, Food and Agriculture Organization, *The State of Food and Agriculture 1974: World Review* (Rome, 1975).

(5) Jain, Shail, "Size Distribution of Income" (International Bank for Reconstruction and Development, Bank Staff Working Paper no. 190, November, 1974).

(6) Kenneth Clark et al., *Area Handbook for the Republic of China* (Washington, D.C.: Department of the Army, 1969), p. viii.

(7) Taiwan, Council for International Economic Cooperation and Development, *Taiwan Statistical Data Book* (1972). All figures refer to 1970.

Table 5.A.3   **National Indexes Used in Analysis of Mortality Change,
                      1940–70**

	Malaria Endemicity in 1943[a] (1)	Annual Average International Economic Aid Received 1954–72[b] [c] (2)	External Assistance Received for Community Water Supply and Sewage Disposal Projects 1966–70[b] (3)
Australia	1	—0	0
Belgium	0	—0	0
Canada	0	—0	0
Chile	1	13.29	.14
Colombia	3	5.13	2.30
Czechoslovakia	0	—0	0
Denmark	0	—0	0
Egypt	2	7.61	.18
Finland	0	—0	0
Greece	2	19.55(4)	0
Guatemala	3	3.35[d]	3.45
Honduras	3	4.05[d]	.90
Hungary	0	—0	0
India	3	1.71	0
Ireland	0	—0	0
Japan	1	—0	0
Korea (South)	1	10.15	.52
Luxembourg	0	—0	0
Mexico	3	1.50	.34
Netherlands	0	—0	0
New Zealand	0	—0	0
Nicaragua	3	5.78[d]	3.40
Panama	3	10.79	19.48
Peru	2	4.13	3.55
Philippines	3	2.02	.58
Portugal	1	—0	0
Puerto Rico	2	—0	0
Spain	1	9.22(4)	0
Sweden	0	—0	0
Switzerland	0	—0	0
Taiwan	3	7.09	0
Thailand	3	1.63	.09
Turkey	3	—0	0
United Kingdom	0	—0	0
United States	0	—0	0
Venezuela	3	2.82	3.71

Sources: (1) Shattuk (1951, p. 4; 1943 map prepared by U.S. Army Medical Intelligence Branch); Faust (1941); Boyd (1949).
(2) United Nations, *Statistical Yearbook* (1958–74).
(3) World Health Organization, *World Health Statistics Report* (1973), vol. 26, no. 11.
(4) Organization for Economic Cooperation and Development, *Development Cooperation: Efforts and Policies of the Members of the Development Assistance Committee, 1973 Review* (Paris, 1973).

339   Mortality Declines in Less Developed Countries

Notes

1. The zero-order correlation between e^0_0 and the natural log of national income per capita for the 120 countries in appendix table 5.A.2 is 0.859; the correlation between e^0_0 and national income itself is only 0.693.

2. Causes eliminated include influenza/pneumonia/bronchitis, diarrheal disease, and maternal mortality, and also a proportion of "other and unknown causes" equal by age to the proportion of known causes assigned to infectious diseases at that age.

3. The age distribution used for direct standardization is that of a female "West" stable population with $e^0_0 = 65$ and $r = .01$ (Coale and Demeny 1966).

4. WHO in conjunction with the United Nations Population Division has estimated that life expectancy for LDCs as a whole was 49.6 in 1965–70 (World Health Organization 1974b, p. 23). Life expectancy in 1900 is the author's guess based upon life tables calculated by Arriaga for Latin America and on life tables for India, Taiwan, and Japan around the turn of the century. Corresponding ASCDRs were computed by the author based on relationships between the two mortality measures in the set of 165 populations employed by Preston and Nelson (1974).

5. Pairwise deletion was employed for missing data in the 1940 regressions. That is, results are based upon correlation matrices computed exclusively on the basis of data that were available. N is taken as 28, the number of cases for which observations were complete. One observation was missing on literacy, three on national income, and four on calorie consumption. For no country was more than one piece of information missing. The data on LDCs were considered too valuable to sacrifice all information because one piece was missing. Standard errors are shown in parentheses.

6. Several alternative specifications of these equations were employed, but results were not appreciably altered. These included polynomial representations of income and calories and measurement of CAL from different base points. The R^2's for equations including first- and second-degree terms for Y and CAL were lower than those for the specification presented in the text despite the addition of two variables. The use of other base points for CAL left R^2 unaffected to four decimals. Population-weighted regressions were rejected on the grounds that they gave too much weight to India, where measurement of variables was believed to be unusually poor, especially in 1940.

7. There are of course many ways to attribute differences to changes in values of variables and to changes in coefficients, none of them clearly preferable. In this instance we are constrained by the unavailability of data for most LDCs in 1940. Substitution of 1970 values of the regressors into the 1970 equation will not, of

---

[a]0 = virtually none; 1 = low; 2 = moderate; 3 = high.

[b]Current U.S. dollars per capita.

[c]Includes net official flow of external resources to individual countries from developed market economies and multilateral agencies and bilateral commitments of capital by centrally planned economies. "Military expenditures and contributions are excluded as far as possible."

[d]Information not available for 1966 through 1968.

[e]Information for 1970–72 from source 4.

340   Samuel H. Preston

course, usually yield the correct 1970 life expectancy for a country. But the predictions must be very nearly correct in the aggregate, since the regression plane must pass through the mean of the variables and since 94 of the 120 observations are LDCs.

8. This figure is close to the 9.7 estimate derived by Preston (1975*a*, p. 238), who considered only income and used cruder, regional income distributions of 1963 to evaluate changes between 1938 and 1963.

9. Once again, pairwise deletion is employed for cases of missing data.

10. The mean values of *AID* and *WAT* for the 17 LDCs were 4.77 and 2.21, respectively.

11. $16.46 = 31.47 - .0211(2.59) - .4063(39.39) + .0750(4.77) + .2939(2.21)$. Of the 16.46 year gain, 1.01 years is attributed to external aid.

12. A large majority of countries in the WHO survey listed lack of financing as the principal barrier to expanded water supply and sewerage systems (World Health Organization 1973).

13. For an account of the impact of the Catholic diocese of Oklahoma on mortality in a Maya village, see Early 1970. The experience was probably repeated hundreds of times.

14. For ample documentation, see World Bank (1975) and Bryant (1969).

15. Compiled from United Nations, *Statistical Yearbook*, 1974, table 197. Figures refer to thirty-nine LDCs.

16. WHO has compiled estimates of private consumption expenditures on health care in certain LDCs (World Health Organization 1970). The percentage of total private consumption that is spent on health can be compared with the proportion of GNP represented by government health expenditure, a procedure that reduces incomparabilities resulting from differences in the years of estimate. The percentages are the following (private consumption appearing first): Sierre Leone, 2.9 and 0.9; Jordan, 0.6 and 2.8; Thailand, 3.6 and 1.2; the Philippines, 1.7 and 0.5; Malaysia, 2.4 and 2.5; Panama, 4.0 and 2.2; Jamaica, 1.1 and 2.7. Government health expenditures are from World Bank (1975, annex 3).

17. WHO, for example, does not absorb any materials costs but views its role exclusively as providing technical, advisory, and educational assistance (Goodman 1971, pp. 203–4). Dispute over the provisions of assistance for material led to the "resignation" from WHO of Soviet-bloc countries between 1949 and 1955.

18. The class distribution of gains in mortality is not well documented. There was a sharp contraction of age-standardized mortality ratios for various classes in England during the twentieth century (Antonovsky 1967, p. 63). Even constant ratios would entail reductions in absolute differences, which is the pertinent index when population composition is considered.

19. This is a less serious problem than it might at first appear. The coefficients of $1nY$ presented earlier range from 3.6 to 7.0 (the latter observed when no other term except income distribution is present in the cross-sectional analysis). A 1-point increase in the rate of per capita economic growth would thus be associated with at most a gain in life expectancy of 0.07 years. A gain in $e^0{}_0$ of 2 years is roughly associated with a drop in CDR of 0.0015. Thus, a 0.01 gain in the rate of economic growth would be expected to reduce the CDR by at most 0.07 $(.0015/2) = 0.000053$, or by 0.53% of the change in R_{pc}.

20. Earnings differentials were obtained from a 1963 survey of 4,000 urban wage earners. Adjusted earnings differentials presented in Carnoy's (1967) table 3 are employed. Retirement was assumed to occur at age 65. The continuously compounded rate of return was calculated using the formula presented in the text, with

P.V. set equal to zero. For calculation of social costs, the average annual public expenditure per student by grade is added to direct personal outlays and income forgone.

Comment J. D. Durand

I will attempt to fit some of Preston's findings with regard to the determinants of mortality, and related results in Ronald Lee's paper (chap. 9), into a sketch of salient features of the evolution of determinants of the overall levels and trends of mortality during recent centuries and decades.

Results of recent work in this field at the University of Pennsylvania suggest that the typical form of the trend of expectation of life in countries making the transition from premodern to modern regimes of mortality may be represented by an essentially logistic curve, which can be divided into fairly distinct phases as follows:

0—pretransitional phase, in which expectation of life fluctuates around a nearly constant long-term level;

1—initial phase of transition, in which expectation of life increases irregularly at a relatively slow long-term average rate;

2—"takeoff" phase, in which expectation of life rises at a steady, rapid rate;

3—final phase, in which expectation of life rises slowly and appears to be approaching a ceiling at a high level.

I will attempt to draw a tentative general sketch of principal causal factors that have contributed to the increases in expectation of life (e) during each of these phases of the transition, in terms of the following simplified formula: $e = f(y, k, s, n, \ldots)$ where y stands for income per head, k for knowledge of the causes of disease and death and methods of prevention and treatment (including what the layman knows as well as what the physician knows), s for social action in the broad field of health protection, and n for natural factors.

This is not a comprehensive formulation of the determinants of mortality. Preston shows that the distribution of income and nutrition are influential; among other factors that may have played significant roles in the gains of life expectancy during modern times are the advance of popular education and the decline of fertility; no doubt urbanization has influenced the trends in various countries, and other factors could be

J. D. Durand is professor of economics and sociology and a research associate of the Population Studies Center, University of Pennsylvania.

mentioned. However, probably the greater part of the increases in expectation of life in most parts of the world during the last two centuries can be attributed to the growth of y, the advances of k and s, and some favorable changes in n. I do not presume that the effects of these factors have been simply additive. It is not to belittle the value of Preston's regression models to postulate, for example, that the effects of given changes in each and all of the factors have varied with the levels of e, as is shown vividly by the smallness of recent gains of life expectancy in countries where the highest levels have been achieved.

Pretransitional Regimes

Lee's study of preindustrial England provides a most valuable example of conditions and factors of mortality in a pretransitional state. In this case, we may disregard factors k and s, assuming that they were constant in effect, at least up to the eighteenth century. From the thirteenth to the eighteenth century, there were important variations of mortality in England, both long-term and short-term, and Lee finds that these were due mainly to noneconomic factors; that is, presumably natural factors in the main. The identification of these natural factors remains an unsolved puzzle. Lee says, "they may have been climatic, or the by-product of independent epidemiological changes, or the result of voyages of exploration."[1] As regards climate, Le Roy Ladurie's work is rather discouraging to hopes of finding in its variations a satisfactory explanation for the long swings in mortality, but the question of its influence on the hazards of disease as well as on agriculture has by no means yet been disposed of. There were also important long- and short-term ups and downs of y, represented in Lee's analysis by indicators of wages and prices, and he finds that their influence on mortality was not negligible, although it was less potent than the influence of n. One of the most interesting features is the low ceiling over e. Apparently even the wealth of kings and dukes would not purchase more than about 25 to 35 years of life expectancy, depending on the conditions of n. The ceiling is much higher today, but it is still firm. Unlimited growth of national income per head seems unlikely under present conditions to bring expectation of life for the two sexes much above 75 years.

England's economic situation during the centuries shortly before the industrial revolution was relatively favorable compared with that of most other countries, as Lee points out. Both e and y were probably considerably lower in most of the rest of the world, and it is likely that the influence of changes of y over time may have been stronger elsewhere than it was in England. Lee suggests this with reference to Goubert's observations on mortality in Beauvais during the seventeenth and eighteenth centuries. However, I would hypothesize that n was a major factor in both temporal variations and international differences in mortality under the pretransitional regimes throughout the world.

Preston (1975) gives a chart of the changing relation between e and y in international cross sections about 1900, 1930, and 1960. If data were available to draw such a chart with reference to conditions around 1750 and earlier dates, I presume that the correlation between e and y would be seen to have been weaker, the curve representing the relation between the two variables would exhibit a less steep positive slope, and it would shift erratically up and down from one date to another under the influence of changing natural factors. A major feature of the transition to modern regimes of mortality has been progressive neutralization of the influences of n as a result of the growth of y and advances of k and s.

First Phase of the Transition

Although it is not easy to define the date of beginning of the mortality transition in any country, the secular trend of slowly rising expectation of life identified with the first phase of the transition was clearly general in Western Europe during the nineteenth century, and indications of accelerating rates of population growth suggest that it was also widespread in Eastern Europe, North Africa, and Latin America. The trend of mortality in the United States before the closing decades of the nineteenth century remains an unresolved question.

In the countries in the vanguard of industrial development during the nineteenth century, the growth of income per head was undoubtedly a major factor contributing to the decline of mortality in this first phase, but the effect of increasing y was reinforced by advances in k and s. Under the heading of k, in addition to the important innovation of smallpox vaccination, I surmise that increasing understanding of the importance of hygiene and proper feeding of children, linked with the advance of popular education in the industrializing countries, played an influential part. Under s were such social actions as protection of water supplies, urban sewerage, swamp drainage, quarantine practices, restriction of child labor, and regulation of conditions of women's employment. Such health-protective social actions were not confined to the wealthiest countries; Sanchez-Albornoz (1974) traces their development in Latin American cities during the nineteenth century.

With regard to the historical antecedents of Preston's (1975) chart of changing relations between e and y during the twentieth century, I postulate, although I cannot provide statistical proof, that the developments related to the first phase of the mortality transition during the nineteenth century had the following effects: making the correlation between e and y stronger than it had been under the pretransitional regimes; gradually shifting upward the curve of *e* values corresponding to given levels of *y*; and making the slope of the curve steeper—that is, widening the differences in *e* between richer and poorer nations.

Second Phase of the Transition

The decided quickening of the rate of gain in life expectancy that marks the beginning of the second phase of the transition took place in the 1890s or about a decade earlier or later in the more developed countries of Europe and America. It seems clear that this turn of the trend was primarily a result of the first revolution in death-control technology produced by the validation and wide acceptance of the germ theory of disease. The effect of this was not limited to the new techniques of immunization and therapy for particular diseases that began to be invented late in the nineteenth century. Meanwhile, increasing income and health-protective social actions continued to contribute to gains in *e*, and it seems a reasonable hypothesis that the tightening control of fertility may also have contributed to the quickening reduction in child mortality.

The less developed countries in Latin America, Asia, and Africa were slow to get much benefit from the advances in *k* at this stage. They were handicapped in applying the new knowledge by low income, low levels of popular education, small resources at the disposal of the governments, and perhaps colonial administrations' lack of interest in taking very costly actions to protect the health of the indigenous people. So the beginnings of the second phase of the transition were delayed in most of these countries until after World War I, and in many until the 1940s or 1950s. As a result, the differences in life expectancy between more and less developed countries widened during the early decades of the present century, and the slope of the curve of *e* in relation to *y* grew steeper as it shifted upward more rapidly in the higher than in the lower brackets of per capita income.

It might be tempting to infer that countries had to reach some threshold of income and development in other respects to be eligible for rapid progress in the reduction of mortality under the conditions of this period. But some observations imply that if this were true, the level of the threshold was not high enough to explain fully why so many less developed countries were so long retarded in entering the second phase of the mortality transition:

1. The case of the eastern and southern European countries: Although they were considerably less developed than the northwestern European countries, they were quick to join their richer neighbors in the sharp acceleration of gains in *e* around the turn of the century or shortly afterward. In spite of handicaps in income, education, and other

aspects of development, the countries in eastern and southern Europe generally managed to keep pace with those of northwestern Europe in rates of gain in life expectancy until about the 1940s, when they began to overtake the lead of the latter.

2. The case of Cuba: In a new study of the trend of mortality in Cuba since the late nineteenth century, Diaz Briquets (1977) shows that a spectacular reduction of mortality was achieved there during the few years of United States military occupation following the Spanish-American War, by a campaign of sanitary reforms and mosquito control instigated and aided by the army of occupation. He estimates that the crude annual death rate in the city of Havana dropped from a prewar average of 32 per 1,000 in 1891–95 to 20 in 1903–7, and a large decrease was achieved in the rest of the country also, in the face of general poverty and illiteracy.

3. The case of Taiwan under Japanese rule during early years of this century is another precocious example of the effective transfer of k and s from a more developed to a less developed country (Barclay 1954). This is even more remarkable than the Cuban case, because when the Japanese arrived Taiwan was a good deal less developed than Cuba, and the Japanese themselves had not yet reached a very high level of either e or y.

4. A decided upturn of the trend of e took place during the 1920s in a number of less developed countries (Cuba, Japan, Taiwan, and others). Diaz Briquets (1977) observes that this seems to have been especially characteristic of countries where export industries were dominant, and he suggests that an economic boom in such countries in the 1920s owing to expanding demand and rising prices for their exports might account for their having entered the second phase of the mortality transition earlier than other less developed countries did. The interest of their more developed trading partners in making these countries healthy places to do business with and in may also have been a factor.

The relevance of the trend of income to the life expectancy gains in less developed countries is illustrated in reverse by the example of Cuba in the 1930s and early 1940s, when the misfortunes of the international market for sugar cast Cuba into economic doldrums. Diaz finds that the decline of mortality in Cuba was checked and probably temporarily reversed during this period, and that worsening nutrition and diminishing public and private expenditures on health services were important factors.

A second revolution in the technology of disease control began about 1935 and progressed rapidly during the 1940s and 1950s, with major advances of k especially in the fields of immunization, chemotherapy, and chemical control of disease vectors. This time, the less developed countries were the principal beneficiaries. Although measures of trends in e since 1940 are lacking for many of these countries, especially among those at the lowest levels of development, it is apparent that substantial gains since that time have been practically universal in the less developed regions of the world. Preston's findings suggest that 50% to 80% of the gains between 1940 and 1970 in less developed countries may be attributable to k and s factors, but advances on these fronts have not gone so far as to make economic factors irrelevant. Gains in e since the 1940s have been less spectacular in the least developed countries, particularly in Africa, than in those that were somewhat more developed, and Preston finds a positive association between rates of increase in e and y among less developed countries.

A tendency toward slackening rates of gain in e in less developed countries is apparent in the 1960s and 1970s. While this might be due partly to slowing economic growth, Preston links it with a diminishing rate of "structural change," that is, slowdown of the advance of k and s. He observes that only a few innovations of major importance to health technology have been made during the last decade. The implication is that upward shifting of e in relation to y may be drawing to an end and that e gains in less developed countries henceforth may depend mainly on their ability to move up on the scales of y and related social developments. This has been suggested in a number of recent studies. However, there may still be a good deal of scope for raising e in less developed countries where it remains relatively low, through the pursuit of s actions to take fuller advantage of existing k at their present levels of y. To cite once again the example of Cuba: the series of Cuban life tables compiled by Diaz Briquets (1977) shows expectation of life at birth for the two sexes increasing from 58.8 years in 1953 to 72.1 in 1971 (70.6 for males, 73.9 for females). The 1971 figure compares favorably with that of the United States, especially for males. Diaz presumes that most of the gain in Cuba since 1953 has taken place since the establishment of the socialist government, and he attributes the high rate of gain since that time mainly to more equal distribution of income and government policies aimed at equalizing access to health services for all categories of the population.

Although the less developed countries were the main beneficiaries of the new advances in k since the 1930s, the more developed countries also benefited to an important extent. Examination of the trends in a number of more developed countries shows that the 1940s were a bumper decade for gains in life expectancy. Preston's analysis indicates that a major share of the gains in more developed as well as less developed countries since 1930 has been due to the upward shifting of the curve of e in relation to y and other indicators of development, which may be attributed to the advances of k and s.

Third Phase of the Transition

In more developed countries, the rates of gain in e have slowed con-spicuously since the 1950s, and in many of them hardly any gains have been registered during the past ten years. The same tendency is notice-able in recent statistics from some less developed countries that have attained levels of e comparable to those of more developed countries. This feature is commonly interpreted as meaning that the expectation of life in countries where it is now highest is approaching a ceiling that cannot be surpassed by increasing income or by other means unless a new revolution in medical technology is achieved—a revolution that would make possible important gains in control over the so-called de-generative diseases. If this interpretation is correct and if the less devel-oped countries where e is still well below such a ceiling manage to continue progress in reducing their mortality rates through economic development and fuller application of the present medical knowledge, the time may come when levels of mortality will be nearly equalized among countries around the world. The advances of k and s would then have neutralized, to a large extent, the influence of y as well as that of n.

An interesting aspect of the recent trends in countries where e is high is that they seem to be leveling off at considerably different values of e. If they are coming up against a ceiling, the level of the ceiling seems not to be the same in all countries. In the United States, for example, e seems to be stagnating some four or five years below the level achieved in the Scandinavian countries. On the surface, these differences do not seem very consistently related to per capita income. I mentioned earlier that Cuba's estimated expectation of life in 1971 compared favorably with that of the United States. The position of Puerto Rico and Hong Kong is similar, although they are far below the United States in per capita income. Perhaps a part of the explanation for such anomalies might be found in factors associated with advanced economic develop-ment that are unfavorable to health and longevity. I think it would be interesting to make a systematic study of factors related to the different levels of e, and of mortality rates for sex and age groups, causes of death, and so forth, at which the trends seem recently to have been stalling in many countries. The distribution of income, governmental action in fields of health care, environmental pollution, diets, and behav-ioral patterns relevant to health are among the factors that might use-fully be examined.

Note

1. McNeill (1976) argues that major factors in the long-range trends of mor-tality and population growth in Europe between the fourteenth and eighteenth centuries were new diseases resulting from increased contacts with the Orient during the Mongol conquests and a subsequent gradual adaptation to these dis-eases, as well as variations of climate.

Comment   Victor R. Fuchs

The paper by Preston has two principal purposes: to explain the increase in life expectancy in the less developed countries over the past several decades and to consider the effect of this increase on population size, output, and output per capita. The bulk of the paper is concerned with the first question, and I shall limit my comment to that. Furthermore, I shall examine only one aspect of Preston's multifaceted discussion—the attempt to partition the gain in life expectancy into the portion attributable to increased per capita income and the portion due to a structural shift in the relationship between life expectancy and per capita income.

Using the data Preston provides, I have run regressions of life expectancy (LE) on the natural logarithm of per capita income (LnY) for four separate groups of countries: LDCs in 1940 ($L40$), MDCs in 1940 ($M40$), LDCs in 1970 ($L70$), and MDCs in 1970 ($M70$).[1] The results are presented in table C5.1. I have also plotted the predicted (from the regressions) relationship between life expectancy and per capita income for each group in figure C5.1. The curves are plotted over the range of per capita income actually observed for each group.

Table C5.1   **Results of Regressing Life Expectancy on Logarithm of per Capita Income across Less Developed and More Developed Countries in 1940 and 1970**

$LE = a + b \ln Y$	L40	M40	L70	M70
b	4.99	6.65	7.82	.13
σ_b	(1.95)	(1.21)	(1.10)	(.85)
a	13.3	17.1	12.5	70.8
σ_a	(10.0)	(8.0)	(6.7)	(6.6)
R^2	.27	.68	.77	−.08
N	16	15	16	15

Inspection of figure C5.1 suggests that the structural relation between life expectancy and per capita income in the LDCs in 1940 was different from that in the MDCs in the same year. Given the level of income, life expectancy seems to have been appreciably higher in the MDCs. It is therefore inappropriate to pool the two groups of countries, as Preston does, without allowing for differences in structure. It should also be

Victor R. Fuchs is professor of economics at Stanford University and is a research associate of the National Bureau of Economic Research.

The author acknowledges the financial support of the Robert Wood Johnson Foundation, the research assistance of Sean Becketti, and the helpful comments of Robert J. Willis.

349   Mortality Declines in Less Developed Countries

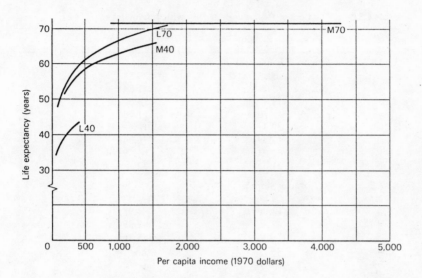

Fig. C5.1   The relationship between life expectancy and per capita
income across less developed and more developed countries
in 1940 and 1970.

noted that in the MDCs in 1970, the relationship between life expectancy and per capita income has disappeared, a phenomenon I have
called attention to before (Fuchs 1965, 1974). There can be no question, therefore, of attempting to assess shifts in the function between the
MDCs in 1940 and 1970 or between the LDCs and MDCs in 1970.

I have run regressions that pool LDCs and MDCs in 1940 and LDCs
in 1940 and 1970 with dummy variables inserted to allow for differences
in intercepts and slopes. These results are reported in table C5.2.

The first regressions (part A) constrain the slopes of the pooled
groups to be equal but allow the intercepts to vary. We see that the shift
coefficients are large and highly significant in both cases. This means
that, compared with the LDCs in 1940, both the MDCs in 1940 and
the LDCs in 1970 had substantially higher life expectancy for any given
level of per capita income. The second set of regressions (part B) constrains the intercepts to be equal and allows the slopes to vary within
each pair of groups. We now find that the slopes do differ significantly.
The third set of regressions (part C) allows both the intercepts and the
slopes to vary, and with this specification none of the interactions are
statistically significant.

If one does not demand statistical significance, it is possible to answer
Preston's question fairly unambiguously along the following lines. The
mean life expectancy of the LDCs rose from 38.8 years in 1940 to 59.6

350   Samuel H. Preston

Table C5.2   Pooled Regression Results with Interactions

	L40 + M40	L40 + L70
A. $LE = a + b\ ln\ Y + c$ Intercept		
b	5.83	6.83
σ_b	(1.14)	(1.04)
c	−13.4	−14.6
σ_c	(2.10)	(1.70)
a	22.4	18.4
σ_a	(7.54)	(6.34)
$\bar{R}^2$	.91	.89
N	31	32
B. $LE = a + b\ ln\ Y + d$ Slope		
b	7.00	7.77
σ_b	(1.00)	(.95)
d	−2.29	−2.69
σ_d	(.35)	(.30)
a	14.7	12.8
σ_a	(6.50)	(5.74)
$\bar{R}^2$	.91	.90
N	31	32
C. $LE = a + b\ ln\ Y + c$ Intercept $+ d$ Slope		
b	6.65	7.82
σ_b	(1.63)	(1.27)
c	−3.79	.78
σ_c	(13.60)	(11.80)
d	−1.66	−2.83
σ_d	(2.31)	(2.15)
a	17.1	12.5
σ_a	(10.7)	(7.73)
$\bar{R}^2$	.91	.90
N	31	32

years in 1970, a rate of increase of 1.4% per annum (see table C5.3).[2] Over that same period the mean per capita income (in 1970 dollars) rose from $194 to $560. We can estimate what the change in life expectancy would have been as a result of income change alone by moving along either the 1940 predicted relation or the 1970 predicted relation. The former tells us that life expectancy would have changed from 39.6 years to 44.8 years, an increase of 0.4% per annum. If we calculate the change along the 1970 curve, we get a predicted increase of 0.5% per annum, from 53.7 years to 62.0 years.

Alternatively, we can look at the implied rates of change attributable to structural shift by comparing predicted life expectancies at the same per capita income in the two years. At $194 the implied change is 1.0% per annum; at $560 it is 1.1% per annum. Thus, either approach indicates that about one-third of the observed change in life expectancy in

351 Mortality Declines in Less Developed Countries

Table C5.3   Life Expectancy in Less Developed Countries in 1940 and 1970: Actual and Predicted Changes

	Mean Life Expectancy (Years)
Actual 1940 (A40)	38.78
Actual 1970 (A70)	59.59
Predicted 1940 (P40:40) (from L40 regression)	39.56
Predicted 1970 (P70:40) (from L40 regression)	44.85
Predicted 1940 (P40:70) (from L70 regression)	53.68
Predicted 1970 (P70:70) (from L70 regression)	61.97

	Rates of Change (Percentage per Annum)
A40 to A70	1.4
P40:40 to P70:40	0.4
P40:70 to P70:70	0.5
P40:40 to P40:70	1.0
P70:40 to P70:70	1.1

the LDCs between 1940 and 1970 can be attributed to the growth of per capita income, and about two-thirds to a shift in the life expectancy–income relationship. Preston presents one estimate of 50% due to structural change and another of 80% due to that source. The results presented here are quite consistent with those estimates.

Notes

1. The LDCs are all in Asia, Africa, and Latin America, and all had life expectancies below 50 years in 1940. The MDCs are all in Europe, North America, and Australia, and all had life expectancies above 50 years in 1940.

2. The change is expressed in percentage per annum in order to minimize the problem of interaction between shifts in the function and movements along the function.

Comment   Richard W. Parks

Preston presents an interesting regression test of the relative importance of private and national income in determining life expectancies. In light of the Kuznets and Fishlow discussions of interaction between the income distribution and the age distribution of the population, it may be useful to point out a possible bias in the Preston regression in section 5.1.1.

The income distribution as commonly measured does not correct for the age distribution of the population. Thus, in a hypothetical world with *no* differences among individuals in their lifetime income streams, we will observe considerable income inequality as conventionally measured if individuals follow the usual life-cycle pattern of earning and saving followed by retirement. For the determination of the effect of income on life expectancy, it appears that a permanent income rather than a measured income concept makes more sense, but given the data available to him, Preston relies on the distribution of measured income.

Preston's distribution measure, which I shall call $D = \Sigma \ln(S_i/.05)$, takes values ranging from $-\infty$ to 0 on a scale representing increasing equality. Thus we can represent the partial relationship between life expectancy $e^o{}_o$, and D as shown in figure C5.2.

We expect a positive association. Suppose we start at point A with given (unequal) distribution and low life expectancy. If incomes were to become more equal (in a life-cycle sense), we would expect to find a new point at B showing greater equality and higher life expectancy. However, even with the pattern of life-cycle income corresponding with point B, there is likely to be an effect on the measured income distribu-

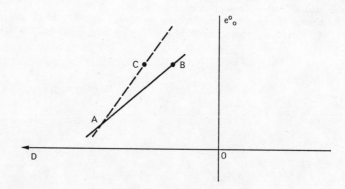

Fig. C5.2

Richard W. Parks is associated with the Department of Economics, University of Washington.

353   Mortality Declines in Less Developed Countries

tion arising from the altered life expectancy. An increase in the share of population in nonproductive years, for example, older age groups, will have the effect of increasing the observed inequality. The observation based on measured income will be at point C, giving an upward bias to the slope coefficient. Since the crucial test of the relative importance of national and private incomes in the determination of life expectancy depends on the size of the slope coefficient, the upward bias would tend to suggest the absence of an effect for national income even when it was in fact important.

References

Allan, William. 1965. *The African husbandman.* London: Oliver and Boyd.

Antonovsky, Aaron. 1967. Social class, life expectancy, and overall mortality. *Milbank Memorial Fund Quarterly* 45: 31–73.

Arriaga, Eduardo. 1967. The effect of a decline in mortality on the gross reproduction rate. *Milbank Memorial Fund Quarterly* 45: 333–52.

———. 1968. *New life tables for Latin American populations.* Berkeley: Institute of International Studies, University of California.

———. 1970. *Mortality decline and its demographic effects in Latin America.* Berkeley: Institute of International Studies, University of California.

Ascoli, Werner; Guzman, Miguel A.; Scrimshaw, Nevin S.; and Gordon, John E. 1967. Nutrition and infection field study in Guatemalan villages, 1959–1964. IV. Deaths of infants and preschool children. *Archives of Environmental Health* 15 (October): 439–49.

Baertl, Juan M.; Morales, Enrique; Verastegui, Gustavo; and Graham, George. 1970. Diet supplementation for entire communities: Growth and mortality of children. *American Journal of Clinical Nutrition* 23(6): 707–15.

Bailey, K. V. 1975. Malnutrition in the African region. *Chronicle of the World Health Organization* 29: 354–64.

Banks, Arthur. 1971. *Cross-polity time-series data.* Cambridge: MIT Press.

Barclay, George W. 1954. *Colonial development and population in Taiwan.* Princeton: Princeton University Press.

Barlow, Robin. 1967. The economic effects of malaria eradication. *American Economic Review* 57(2): 130–48.

———. 1968. *The economic effects of malaria eradication.* Economic Research Series no. 15. Ann Arbor: University of Michigan School of Public Health.

Beck, Ann. 1970. *A history of the British medical administration of East Africa, 1900–1950.* Cambridge: Harvard University Press.

Boserup, Ester. 1965. *The conditions of agricultural growth: The economics of agrarian change under population pressure.* Chicago: Aldine.

Bowers, John. 1973. The history of public health in China to 1937. In *Public Health in the People's Republic of China,* ed. Myron E. Wegman, Tsung-Yi Lin, and Elizabeth F. Purcell, pp. 26–45. New York: Josiah Macy, Jr., Foundation.

Boyd, M. F. 1949. *Malariology.* Vols. 1 and 2. Philadelphia: W. B. Saunders.

Bryant, John. 1969. *Health and the developing world.* Ithaca: Cornell University Press.

Bunle, Henri. 1954. *Le mouvement naturel de la population dans le monde de 1906 à 1936.* Paris: Institut d'études demographiques.

Burch, Thomas K., and Gendell, Murray. 1970. Extended family structure and fertility: Some methodological and conceptual issues. *Journal of Marriage and the Family* 32(2): 227–36.

Carnoy, Martin. 1967. Rates of return to schooling in Latin America. *Journal of Human Resources* 2(3): 359–74.

Coale, Ansley J. 1956. The effects of changes in mortality and fertility on age composition. *Milbank Memorial Fund Quarterly* 34: 79–114.

Coale, Ansley J., and Demeny, Paul. 1966. *Regional model life tables and stable populations.* Princeton: Princeton University Press.

Coale, Ansley J., and Hoover, Edgar M. 1958. *Population growth and economic development in low-income countries.* Princeton: Princeton University Press.

Committee for International Coordination of National Research in Demography. 1975. *Seminar on infant mortality in relation to level of fertility.* Paris.

Davis, Kingsley. 1951. *The population of India and Pakistan.* Princeton: Princeton University Press.

————. 1955. Institutional patterns favoring high fertility in underdeveloped areas. *Eugenics Quarterly* 2: 33–39.

————. 1956. The amazing decline of mortality in underdeveloped areas. *American Economic Review* 46 (May): 305–18.

————. 1973. Cities and mortality. *Proceedings,* International Population Conference, Liège, Belgium, 3: 259–81.

Denison. Edward F. 1962. *The sources of economic growth in the United States and the alternatives before us.* New York: Committee for Economic Development.

Diaz Briquets, Sergio. 1977. Mortality in Cuba: Trends and determinants, 1880 to 1971. Ph.D. diss., University of Pennsylvania.

Durand, John R. 1967. A long-range view of world population growth. *Annals of the American Academy of Arts and Sciences* 369: 1–8.

Early, John. 1970. The structure and change of mortality in a Maya community. *Milbank Memorial Fund Quarterly* 48: 179–201.

Eversley, D. E. C. 1957. A survey of population in an area of Worcestershire from 1660 to 1850 on the basis of parish registers. *Population Studies* 10: 253–79.

Faust, Ernest Carroll. 1941. The distribution of malaria in North America, Mexico, Central America, and the West Indies. In *A symposium on human malaria*, ed. F. R. Moulton, pp. 8–18. Washington, D.C.: American Association for the Advancement of Science.

Fein, Rashi. 1964. Health programs and economic development. In *The economics of health and medical care. Proceedings of the conference on the economics of health and medical care, May 10–12, 1962*, ed. H. E. Klarman. Ann Arbor: Bureau of Public Health Economics and Department of Economics, University of Michigan.

Foege, William H.; Millar, J. D.; and Henderson, D. A. 1975. Smallpox eradication in West and Central Africa. *Bulletin of the World Health Organization* 52: 209–22.

Food and Agriculture Organization of the United Nations. 1975. *Population, food supply, and agricultural development*. Rome: FAO.

Fredericksen, Harald. 1961. Determinants and consequences of mortality trends in Ceylon. *Public Health Reports* 76 (August): 659–63.

———. 1966a. Determinants and consequences of mortality and fertility trends. *Public Health Reports* 81 (August): 715–27.

———. 1966b. Dynamic equilibrium of economic and demographic transition. *Economic Development and Cultural Change* 14 (April): 316–22.

Friedlander, Dov. 1969. Demographic responses and population change. *Demography* 6(4): 359–82.

Fuchs, V. R. 1965. Some economic aspects of mortality in the United States. National Bureau of Economic Research Study Paper.

———. 1974. Some economic aspects of mortality in developed countries. In *The economics of health and medical care*, ed. Mark Perlman, pp. 174–93. Proceedings of a conference held by the International Economic Association at Tokyo. London: Macmillan.

Goodman, Neville M. 1971. *International health organizations and their work*. Edinburgh: Churchill Livingstone.

Gordon, John. 1969. Social implications of nutrition and disease. *Archives of Environmental Health* 18(2): 216–34.

Habakkuk, H. J. 1971. *Population growth and economic development*. New York: Humanities Press.

Hansluwka, Harald. 1975. Health, population, and socio-economic development. In *Population growth and economic development in the Third World*, ed. Léon Tabah, 1: 191–250. Dolhain, Belgium: Ordina.

Hinman, E. Harold. 1966. *World eradication of infectious diseases.* Springfield, Ill.: Charles C. Thomas.

Howard-Jones, N. 1974. The scientific background of the International Sanitary Conferences, 1851–1938. *Chronicle of the World Health Organization* 28(10): 455–70.

Johnson, D. Gale. 1974. Population, food, and economic adjustment. *American Statistician* 28(3): 89–93.

Keyfitz, Nathan, and Fleiger, Wilhelm. 1968. *World population: An analysis of vital data.* Chicago: University of Chicago Press.

———. 1971. *Population: Facts and methods of demography.* San Francisco: W. H. Freeman and Company.

Kitagawa, E. M., and Hauser, P. M. 1973. *Differential mortality in the United States: A study in socioeconomic epidemiology.* Cambridge: Harvard University Press.

Klarman, Herbert E. 1967. Present status of cost-benefit analysis in the health field. *American Journal of Public Health* 57(11): 1948–53.

Kuznets, Simon. 1975. Population trends and modern economic growth: Notes towards an historical perspective. In *The population debate: Dimensions and perspectives*, 1: 425–33. Papers of the World Population Conference, Bucharest: New York: United Nations.

Lancet. 1970. Strategy of malaria eradication: A turning point? *Lancet* editorial. 1970 (21 March): 598–600.

McDermott, W. 1966. Modern medicine and the demographic-disease pattern of overly traditional societies: A technological misfit. *Journal of Medical Education* 41(9): 138–62.

McKeown, Thomas. 1965. Medicine and world population. In *Public health and population change*, ed. Mindel C. Sheps and Jeanne Clare Ridley. Pittsburgh: University of Pittsburgh Press.

McKeown, Thomas, and Record, R. G. 1962. Reasons for the decline of mortality in England and Wales during the 19th century. *Population Studies* 16: 94–122.

McNeill, William H. 1976. *Plagues and peoples.* Garden City, N.Y.: Anchor Press/Doubleday.

Malenbaum, Wilfred. 1970. Health and productivity in poor areas. In *Empirical studies in health economics*, ed. Herbert E. Klarman, pp. 31–57. Baltimore: Johns Hopkins University Press.

Mandle, Jay R. 1970. The decline in mortality in British Guiana, 1911–1960. *Demography* 7, no. 3 (August): 303.

Maramag, Ileana. 1965. The cost of public health programs in the Philippines. *Journal of the American Medical Women's Association* 20 (September): 848–57.

Marshall, Carter L.; Brown, Roy E.; and Goodrich, Charles H. 1971. Improved nutrition vs. public health services as major determinants of world population growth. *Clinical Pediatrics* 10 (July): 363–68.

Mata, Leonardo, et al. 1972. Influence of recurrent infections on nutrition and growth of children in Guatemala. *American Journal of Clinical Nutrition* 25 (November): 1267–75.

Meegama, S. A. 1967. Malaria eradication and its effect on mortality levels. *Population Studies* 26(3): 207–38.

Morley, David. 1973. *Paediatric priorities in the developing world*. London: Butterworth's.

Mushkin, Selma J. 1962. Health as an investment. *Journal of Political Economy* 70 (part 2, supplement): 129–57.

————. 1964. Health programming in developing nations. *International Development Review* 6(1): 7–12.

Myrdal, Gunnar. 1968. *Asian drama: An inquiry into the poverty of nations*. Vols. 1–3. New York: Random House.

Newman, P. 1965. *Malaria eradication and population growth: With special reference to Ceylon and British Guiana*. Research Series no. 10. Ann Arbor, Michigan: Bureau of Public Health Economics, School of Public Health, University of Michigan.

————. 1970. Malaria control and population growth. *Journal of Development Studies* 6: 133–58.

O'Hara, Donald J. 1975. Microeconomic aspects of the demographic transition. *Journal of Political Economy* 83(6): 1203–15.

Organization for Economic Cooperation and Development. N.d. *Resources for the developing world: The flow of financial resources to less developed countries, 1962–1968*. Paris: OECD.

Pampana, E. J. 1954. Effect of malaria control on birth and death rates. *Proceedings of the World Population Conference, 1954*, Rome, pp. 497–508. New York: United Nations.

Pampana, E. J., and Russell, Paul F. 1955. Malaria: A world problem. *Chronicle of the World Health Organization* 9(2–3): 33–100.

Pani, Alberto. 1917. *Hygiene in Mexico*. New York: G. P. Putnam's Sons.

Paul, Hugh H. 1964. *The control of diseases*. 2d ed. Baltimore: Williams and Wilkins.

Plank, S. J., and Milanesi, M. L. 1973. Infant feeding and infant mortality in rural Chile. *Bulletin of the World Health Organization* 48: 203–10.

Polgar, Steven. 1972. Population history and population policies from an anthropological perspective. *Current Anthropology* 13(2): 203–11.

Preston, S. H. 1974. Effect of mortality change on stable population parameters. *Demography* 11(1): 119–30.

————. 1975*a*. The changing relation between mortality and level of economic development. *Population Studies* 29(2): 231–48.

————. 1975*b*. Introduction. In *Seminar on infant mortality in relation to the level of fertility*, pp. 10–22. Paris: Committee for International Coordination of National Research in Demography.

Preston, S. H.; Keyfitz, N.; and Schoen, R. 1972. *Causes of death: Life tables for national populations*. New York: Seminar Press.

————. 1973. Cause-of-death life tables: Application of a new technique to worldwide data. *Transactions of the Society of Actuaries* 25 (December): 83–109.

Preston, S. H., and Nelson, V. E. 1974. Structure and change in causes of death: An international summary. *Population Studies* 28(1): 19–51.

Puffer, R. R., and Griffith, G. W. 1967. *Patterns of urban mortality*. Scientific Publication no. 151. Washington, D.C.: Pan American Health Organization.

Puffer, R. R., and Serrano, C. V. 1973. *Patterns of mortality in childhood*. Scientific Publication no. 262. Washington, D.C.: Pan American Health Organization.

Russell, Paul F. 1943. Malaria and its influence on world health. *Bulletin of the New York Academy of Medicine, September*, pp. 599–630.

————. 1968. The United States and malaria: Debits and credits. *Bulletin of the New York Academy of Medicine* 44(6): 623–53.

Rutstein, Shea, and Medica, Vilma. 1975. The effect of infant and child mortality in Latin America. In *Seminar on infant mortality in relation to the level of fertility*, pp. 225–46. Paris: Committee for International Coordination of National Research in Demography.

Sack, Richard. 1974. The impact of education on individual modernity in Tunisia. In *Education and individual modernity in developing countries*, ed. Alex Inkeles and Donald B. Holsinger, pp. 89–116. Leiden: E. J. Brill.

Sanchez-Albornoz, Nicholas. 1974. *The population of Latin America: A history*. Berkeley: University of California Press.

Schultz, Theodore. 1964. *Transforming traditional agriculture*. New Haven: Yale University Press.

Schultz, T. Paul. 1976. Interrelationships between mortality and fertility. In *Population and development: The search for selective interventions*, ed. Ronald G. Ridker, pp. 239–89. Baltimore: Johns Hopkins University Press.

Scrimshaw, Nevin S. 1970. Synergism of malnutrition and infection. *Journal of the American Medical Association* 212(10): 1685–92.

Sharpston, Michael J. 1976. Health and the human environment. *Finance and Development* 13(1): 24–28.

Shattuk, George. 1951. *Diseases of the tropics.* New York: Appleton-Century-Crofts.

Shorter, Frederick. 1968. Information on fertility, mortality, and population growth in Turkey. *Population Index* 34(1): 5.

Simmons, James Stevens; Whayne, Tom F.; Anderson, Gaylord West; Horack, Harold MacLachian; and collaborators. 1944. *Global epidemiology: A geography of diseases and sanitation.* Vol. 1. Philadelphia: J. B. Lippincott.

Smith, Peter C. 1976. Asian nuptiality in transition. Paper presented at the Seventh Summer Seminar in Population, East-West Population Institute, Honolulu.

Sorkin, Alan L. 1975. *Health economics: An introduction.* Lexington, Mass.: D. C. Heath, Lexington Books.

Stolnitz, George J. 1956. Mortality declines and age distribution. *Milbank Memorial Fund Quarterly* 34: 178–215.

———. 1974. International mortality trends: Some main facts and implications. Background Paper for United Nations World Population Conference E/CONF.60/CBP/17, Bucharest.

Taylor, Carl E., and Hall, Marie-Francoise. 1967. Health population and economic development. *Science* 157 (August): 651–57.

Titmuss, Richard M., and Abel-Smith, Brian. 1968. *Social policies and population growth in Mauritius.* London: Frank Cass.

United Nations, Population Branch. 1963. Population bulletin of the United Nations no. 6 (with special reference to the situation and recent trends of mortality in the world). New York.

United Nations, Department of Economic and Social Affairs. 1971. *The world population situation in 1970.* Population Study no. 49. New York.

———. 1973. *The determinants and consequences of population trends.* Vol. 1. New York: United Nations.

United Nations, Population Division. 1974. Recent population trends and future prospects. World Population Conference Paper E/CONF. 60/3.

Vaidyanathan, K. E. 1972. Some indices of differential mortality in India. In *Studies on mortality in India,* ed. K. E. Vaidyanathan. Gandhigram: Institute of Rural Health and Family Planning.

Vallin, J. 1968. La mortalité dans les pays du Tiers Monde: Evolution et perspectives. *Population* 23: 845–68.

Wegman, Myron E.; Lin, Tsung-yi; and Purcell, Elizabeth F., eds. 1973. *Public health in the People's Republic of China.* New York: Josiah Macy, Jr., Foundation.

Weisbrod, Burton A. 1975. Research in health economics: A survey. *International Journal of Health Services* 5(4): 643–61.

Weller, T. H. 1974. World health in a changing world. *Journal of Tropical Medicine* 77(4), suppl. 54: 54–61.

World Bank. 1975. *Health: Sector policy paper*. Washington, D. C.

World Health Organization. 1970. Special subject: Health expenditure. In *World health statistics annual, 1966–1967* 3: 236–45.

———. 1972. *Human development and public health*. Technical Report Series no. 485. Geneva: WHO.

———. 1973. Community water supply and sewage disposal in developing countries. *World Health Statistics Report* 26(11): 720–83.

———. 1974a. Childhood mortality in the Americas. *Chronicle of the World Health Organization* 28: 276–82.

———. 1974b. Health trends and prospects, 1950–2000. *World Health Statistics Report* 27(10): 672–706.

———. 1975a. The malaria situation in 1974. *Chronicle of the World Health Organization* 29: 474–81.

———. 1975b. *Fifth report on the world health situation*. Official Records of the World Health Organization, no. 225. Geneva: WHO.

———. 1975c. *First WHO seminar on expansion of the use of immunization in developing countries*. Offset Publication no. 16. Geneva: WHO.

———. 1976. Smallpox eradication in 1975. *Chronicle of the World Health Organization* 30: 152–57.

Wrigley, E. A. 1969. *Population and history*. New York: McGraw-Hill.

[7]

Estimating a Household Production Function: Heterogeneity, the Demand for Health Inputs, and Their Effects on Birth Weight

Mark R. Rosenzweig

University of Minnesota

T. Paul Schultz

Yale University

The household production literature emphasizes that technical or biological processes condition input selection by households in their production activities, along with prices and income. Exogenous variations in health, to the extent that they are perceived by individuals (heterogeneity), lead to correlations between inputs and health outcomes that cannot be used to derive causal conclusions. Therefore, estimates of health technology must be obtained from a behavioral model in which health inputs are themselves choices. Consistent estimates are reported of the effect of endogenous inputs, such as medical care, smoking, and fertility, on birth weight and fetal growth in the presence of health heterogeneity.

I. Introduction

In the last decade there has appeared an extensive body of empirical work concerned with the allocation of family resources. The

A preliminary version of this paper was presented at the Fourth World Congress of the Econometric Society, Aix-en-Provence, France, August 1980. The research was supported in part by grants from NIH, Center for Population Research, HD-12172, and NSF, SOC-7814481. We have benefited from the comments on an earlier version of this paper from members of workshops at Johns Hopkins, University of Chicago, Cornell, and University of Minnesota, the referees, and James J. Heckman. Able research assistance was provided by Cynthia Arfken and Thomas Frenkel.

[*Journal of Political Economy*, 1983, vol. 91, no. 5]

framework underlying many of these analyses of the determinants of labor supply, fertility, health, and other family behavior is the household production model introduced by Becker (1965). Despite the emphasis of this framework on the distinction between production technology and preference orderings, none of the empirical studies based on this approach has attempted to disentangle the household's technology from its "tastes." Since the predictions embodied in the reduced-form demand equations for market goods, derived from the household production model, are no different from the predictions contained in demand equations from the conventional multiperson consumer demand model (in which all observable goods enter the utility function directly), the distinct implications of the household production approach have not yet been exploited empirically.

In one field, health, the household production framework appears particularly applicable. The notion of an underlying technology, that is, biological processes, is well accepted, and attention to quantifying health conditions has narrowed the potential set of important health inputs. While economists have employed the household production approach in this domain, the major focus of empirical work has been on the demand for health inputs, chiefly medical services (Goldman and Grossman 1978; Leibowitz and Friedman 1979). Estimates of the technical/biological effects of such inputs on health, constrained by the limited availability of data on inputs, have been obtained from "hybrid" health equations that contain one or two health inputs and prices and income variables on the right-hand side (Edwards and Grossman 1979). Moreover, these latter studies as well as those in the medical literature have ignored the endogeneity of the (self-selected) health inputs and have thereby implicitly assumed that the population does not differ with respect to exogenous health endowments.[1] Yet it would appear that innate differences loom large in the distribution of health across individuals and that at least some of these fixed characteristics are known to individuals, who act upon that knowledge.

In this paper we estimate a (household) health production function using information on one important early health indicator, birth weight, and a set of behavioral variables considered to be the important determinants of birth outcomes in the medical literature—

---

[1] Examples of ordinary least squares (OLS) estimates of hybrid-type functions, in which a measure of child health is the dependent variable and behavioral inputs, prices, education, and income are regressors, are found in Harris (1982) and Lewit (1982). Inman (1976) uses maximum likelihood (ML) logit to estimate child health production functions using dichotomous measures of morbidity. These functions contain, in addition to the use of medical services, measures of lagged child health and family income per person as "inputs." Of the two variables representing the use of doctor care, only number of "curative" doctor visits is treated as endogenous ("preventive" visits, time spent with children, family income, and lagged health are assumed to be exogenous).

prenatal medical care, working and smoking by the mother while pregnant, the number of births of the mother, and her age. In Section II we describe a household production model to interpret the hybrid-type health equation and to assess the effects of health heterogeneity on health behavior and its consequences for the estimation of the health technology. We describe the data and the estimation strategies employed to take into account heterogeneity in Section III. Section IV discusses the estimates of the reduced-form effects of parental income, schooling, race, health programs, and prices on the demand for the health inputs. Section V reports estimates of the birth weight production function. Statistical tests are performed of functional form and of heterogeneity bias as well as of one version of the complete household production-consumption model. Section VI discusses estimates of the effect of child health endowments on input demand behavior. Our results indicate that OLS estimates of the birth weight production function are significantly contaminated by heterogeneity bias. In particular, neglect of heterogeneity appears to lead to a substantial underestimate of the beneficial effects of early prenatal care on the weight of a baby at its birth. The negative effects on fetal growth of the mother's smoking while pregnant are also importantly understated.

II. The Household Production of Health

A. Health Production, Input Demand, and Hybrid Functions

Assume that a household's preference orderings over child health, H, n X-goods, and $m - n$ Y-goods that affect child health can be characterized by the utility function, subject to the usual properties:

$$U = U(X_i, Y_j, H), \quad i = 1, \ldots, n; j = n + 1, \ldots, m. \quad (1)$$

Let the production of child health by the household be described by the production function

$$H = \Gamma(Y_j, I_k, \mu), \quad k = m + 1, \ldots, r, \quad (2)$$

where the $r - m$ I_k are health inputs which do not augment utility other than through their effects on H (e.g., medical care), and μ represents family-specific health endowments known to the family but not controlled by them, for example, genetic traits or environmental factors.[2]

---

[2] Realizations of health outcomes may have a stochastic component, but this will be unknown to the family decision makers at the time when decisions are made. Whether risk enters the process of optimization will thus depend on the form of (1). Variations in

The budget constraint for the household in terms of the r purchased goods is

$$F = \sum_t Z_t p_t, \quad t = 1, \ldots, r, \tag{3}$$

where F is exogenous money income, the p_t are exogenous prices, and $Z = X \cup Y \cup I$. The household model as depicted is characterized by joint production (Pollak and Wachter 1975) in the sense that a subset of goods Y (smoking, e.g.) both affects child health and contributes to utility directly.[3] For simplicity, only one production process is discussed, but the model can be easily generalized to depict many processes without changing its major implications.

The household's reduced-form demand functions for the r goods, including the $r - n$ health inputs, derived from the maximization of (1) subject to (2) and (3), are

$$Z_t = S_t(p, F, \mu), \quad t = 1, \ldots, r. \tag{4}$$

The reduced-form demand function for the health outcome may be written analogously:

$$H = \psi(p, F, \mu). \tag{5}$$

Empirical applications of health production models have chiefly focused on estimating input demand functions, such as (4), or reduced-form health equations, such as (5). Since the properties of (4) are identical to those from models positing no household production of health, and since the reduced-form health equation embodies few, if any, restrictions implied by the model, these studies do not really make use of the notion of an underlying household health technology, nor do they provide information on that technology.

While estimates of reduced forms such as (4) or (5) are useful both in providing policy-relevant parameters and for prediction, econometric applications that have been concerned with the relationships between health and health inputs have been hampered by the limited availability of data on health inputs and have consequently estimated equations (hybrids) with less desirable properties. These hybrid equations have the form

$$H = \theta(Y_m, p_t, \dot{F}, \mu), \quad l = 1, \ldots, m - 1, m + 1, \ldots, r; \tag{6}$$

μ, however, will generally affect decisions and, as shown below, have important econometric implications. Our estimation procedure, described below, is appropriate whether or not household decisions take into account uncertainty.

[3] The model also captures, in its general form, possible interactions between "quality" and quantity of children, as in Becker and Lewis (1973), since one Y_j can represent the number of children. For a discussion of the predictive content of models that assume interactions between family size and investments in children, see Rosenzweig and Wolpin (1980).

that is, one input, say Y_m, and the *determinants* of all other inputs, p_l, F, and μ, are regressed against a measure of health. The "effect" of health input Y_m, usually medical care, estimated from an equation like (6) is interpreted as if it were the relevant production function relation. However, it can be readily shown that the partial θ_{Y_m} in (6) embodies both the technological properties of the health production function and the characteristics of the household's preferences. Thus, the hybrid effect of a health input on health, controlling for prices and income, is generally a biased estimate of the true technical relationship (other inputs held constant) embodied in the health production function, where the sign and magnitude of the bias depend on the properties of (1).[4]

B. *Heterogeneity and the Health Technology*

The data requirements and estimation problems involved in separating out both the characteristics of the utility function and the underlying health technology are clearly formidable (see Barnett 1977; Pollak and Wachter 1977). However, the notion that the health production inputs are behavioral variables also implies that even if only information on the technology of health production were desired, having measures of *all* important behavioral inputs and the health output would not be adequate to describe the health technology. The difficulty arises chiefly from the presence of exogenous health factors that can be known to individual households but that are unobserved by the researcher.[5]

Consider the relationship between a small change in the input Y_m and child health estimated from (2) in a population in which μ is distributed randomly. From (1) and (2), this association can be approximated by

$$\frac{dH}{dY_m} = \Gamma_{Y_m} + \left(\frac{dY_m}{d\mu}\right)^{-1}, \tag{7}$$

---

[4] Ignoring the μ term for a moment, it can be demonstrated that the single-input hybrid relationship between the input Y_m and health from (6) can be written as

$$\theta_{Y_m} = \Gamma_{Y_m} + (S^c_{mm})^{-1}\left(\sum_{n+1}^{m-1} \Gamma_{Y_j}S^c_{jm} + \sum_{m+1}^{r} \Gamma_{I_k}S^c_{km}\right),$$

where S^c_{vm} is the compensated price effect p_m on input v. Since $S^c_{mm} < 0$ and the S^c_{jm} and S^c_{km} terms, j, $k \neq m$, are unlikely to sum to a negative number, given the Cournot aggregation condition, if we define the $r - n$ inputs such that they have nonnegative marginal products, then $\Gamma_{Y_m} > \theta_{Y_m}$.

[5] The problem of heterogeneity in unobserved exogenous factors (not omitted control variables) perceived by decision makers has been well developed in the literature pertaining to the estimation of production functions for farms or firms (Mundlak and Hoch 1965; Fuss and McFadden 1978). This problem has not been treated to our knowledge in estimating household production functions.

where

$$\frac{dY_m}{d\mu} = -\Gamma_\mu\left[\sum_{n+1}^{m} S_{jm}^c(U_{Y_jH} + U_{HHH}\Gamma_{Y_j}) + \sum_{1}^{n} S_{im}^c U_{X_iH} + \sum_{m+1}^{r} S_{km}^c U_{HHH}\Gamma_{I_k}\right]$$
$$- U_{H}\left(\sum_{n+1}^{m} S_{jm}^c\Gamma_{Y_j\mu} + \sum_{m+1}^{r} S_{km}^c\Gamma_{I_k\mu}\right),$$

the S_{ij}^c are the compensated price effects from the relevant demand functions (4), and the Γ_x are the marginal products of the factors in (2). As can be seen, the observed input-constant relationship between Y_m and H will not correspond to the true marginal product, Γ_{Y_m}. Moreover, the "bias," given by the second term in (7), will depend on (i) the properties of the utility function, (ii) the marginal products of all inputs, (iii) how μ affects health directly, and (iv) how μ affects the marginal products of the controllable inputs.

In the study of health, heterogeneity bias is most likely to affect measurements of the effectiveness of "remedial" medical care.[6] Many pregnant women, for example, have information on health endowments from prior histories of pregnancy complications or of prior birth outcomes reflecting low child health, which may alter their use of prenatal care. Indeed, it is not unlikely that women who have prior medical problems may be the ones most likely to be using prenatal medical services and to have such problems again. Inferences from nonexperimental data about the health technology and the value of remedial measures may be misleading, therefore, if these inferences do not take into account the interdependence of the levels of health inputs and preference orderings that occur because of exogenous health heterogeneity.

III. Data and Estimation Strategies

The 1967, 1968, and 1969 U.S. National Natality Followback Surveys (U.S. Department of Health, Education, and Welfare 1978) appear to meet most of the data requirements for estimating the health technology associated with birth outcomes. These national probability samples of approximately 10,000 legitimate live births for the 3 years combined contain information on the birth weight and gestation period for each birth, the schooling attainment of both parents, the income of the husband, and three retrospectively obtained aspects of the mother's behavior while pregnant that are potentially linked to infant health at birth—smoking, working, and prenatal medical care—in addition to data on age at birth and birth order (parity).

---

[6] Inman (1976) found that mothers for whom preventive doctor visits were most effective in reducing the incidence of child morbidity tended to utilize preventive care more often.

While no data on input costs or prices are provided, the survey does provide information on the county of residence of the mother at the time of the birth, enabling us to merge local-area price, health program, and labor force variables with the individual micro data. The sample size for nonmultiple births, available for analysis, is 9,621.

The weight of a child at birth or birth weight and birth weight standardized for gestation length are used in this study as two indicators of child health. Both child health outcome variables are linked in an extensive medical literature to infant survival and to the prospects of subsequent child growth and development.[7] Recently two distinct health effects of low birth weight and prematurity have been noted in the medical literature: a relatively transitory trauma associated with delivery and its immediate consequences and more permanent side effects that contribute to elevated risks of later childhood morbidity and mortality (Beck and van den Berg 1975). The latter, more permanent effect appears to be related to the rate of weight gain of the fetus to birth. To obtain a measure of the latter, an infant's actual birth weight was divided by the expected birth weight conditional on the infant's gestation, predicted by a fetal growth function estimated as a cubic function from the sample data.[8]

The endogenous or behavioral variables considered to have a direct technical or biological relationship with birth weight (the arguments in [2]) are the number of months the mother worked while pregnant, the number of months of elapsed pregnancy before the mother visited a medical doctor (DELAY), the number of cigarettes smoked per day by the mother while pregnant (SMOKING), the order of the current live birth (BIRTHS), and the age of the mother at the birth (AGE).[9] All of these variables have been identified (usually in isola-

---

[7] See, e.g., Beck and van den Berg (1975); Chernichovsky and Coate (1979); and Eisner et al. (1979). The association of birth weight and survival (health) was explored for evidence of a nonlinear, even nonmonotonic, relationship. Chi-squared tests were applied to maximum likelihood probit regressions of child mortality (whether or not the sample child died between its birth and the time of the survey) and transforms of birth weight. The addition of quadratic or higher-order polynomials in birth weight did not significantly alter the explanatory power of the mortality equation, nor the log-linear birth weight coefficient.

[8] The equation is

$$\text{birth weight} = 10,107 - 1,042 \text{ weeks} + 37.8 \text{ weeks}^2 - .398 \text{ weeks}^3, \; R^2 = .227,$$
$$\qquad\qquad (7.7) \qquad (10.0) \qquad\quad (10.4) \qquad\quad (10.9)$$

where the absolute values of t-statistics are reported in parentheses.

[9] The variable DELAY was set equal to the sample mean gestation period (39 weeks) if no prenatal medical care was sought (1 percent of the sample) and to 4 weeks if "immediate" care was received on learning of the pregnancy. The number of cigarettes smoked per day was set equal to one for nonsmoking women in order to avoid undefined log values. Since a large proportion of the sample did not smoke (66 percent), tests of the sensitivity of the estimates to this scaling assumption were performed. While the LSMOKING coefficients did change according to the minimum values se-

tion) as significant correlates of birth weight in the medical literature.[10] We note that the mother's age in this context is a choice variable as it refers to the point in her life cycle at which she is choosing to have a child. In preliminary specifications and tests of the health production function, the number of months the mother worked while pregnant never appeared to be a significant determinant of birth outcomes. In the reported specifications we consequently omit this variable.

To augment the set of exogenous variables in the data, we collected and merged with the household data SMSA- or state-level information on input and goods prices, health infrastructure, public expenditures, and labor market conditions. The added variables are hospital beds per capita; per capita governmental health expenditures; the per capita number of hospitals and health departments with family planning, medical doctors, and obstetrician-gynecologists; the unemployment rate for women aged 15–59; the general unemployment rate; the percentage of persons employed in service, government, and manufacturing industries; the per pack cost (including excise taxes) of cigarettes; the sales tax per pack on cigarettes; the price per quart of milk; and the size of the SMSA for inhabitants of SMSAs. The data sources for these areal variables are described in Rosenzweig and Schultz (1982).

The generalized functional form used for the health production function is the transcendental logarithmic (translog), which can be viewed as a local second-order approximation to any production function. The technological specifications employed also assume that log birth weight and the log of standardized birth weight differ according to whether or not the mother is black. We can thus test for differences in infants' weight at birth by race, conditional on input levels. The generalized birth weight and standardized birth weight production functions are thus given by:

$$\text{LBIRTHWEIGHT} = \gamma_0 + \frac{1}{2} \sum_i \sum_j \beta_{ij} Y_i Y_j + \sum_i \beta_i Y_i$$
$$+ \gamma_1 \text{BLACK} + \mu + \epsilon, \tag{8}$$

where the prefix L denotes the logarithm of the respective variable;

---

lected, statistical significance levels and other input coefficient values were unaltered. The sample mean smoking effects, reported below, conform closely to estimates obtained using linear specifications of the production technology (Leontief and Generalized Leontief-Diewert) (Rosenzweig and Schultz 1982).

[10] Examples, based on univariate associations, are medical care (Shah and Abbey 1971; Rosenwaike 1971; and Iba, Niswander, and Woodville 1973), smoking by mothers (Hebel, Entwisle, and Tayback 1971), and wife's work (Coombs, Freedman, and Namboothiri 1969).

HOUSEHOLD PRODUCTION FUNCTION   731

the Y's are LDELAY, LSMOKING, LBIRTHS, LAGE; μ is the unobserved health endowment effect; ϵ is a random error; the β_{ij} and γ_i are estimated production parameters; and $\beta_{ij} = \beta_{ji}$.

As we have shown, the error term in (8), containing μ, is likely to be correlated with the Y_i, and therefore, OLS estimates of the β_{ij} parameters are inconsistent. Consistent estimates of the health production function (8) could be obtained in a number of ways utilizing information from the full structure of production and utility system, including estimation of a complete structural demand system enabling the identification of the underlying preference parameters (Barnett 1977; Pollack and Wachter 1977). Given the absence of data on (or variation in) the prices of all inputs and of all household expenditures, consistent estimates are obtained here by using two-stage least squares (2SLS), where estimates from the first-stage log-linear input demand equations for the four behavioral input variables, Y_i, are employed to obtain second-stage estimates of the health production parameters.[11] Since the price, income, and education variables that determine input demands are by assumption orthogonal to the exogenous health endowment, they serve as instruments to identify the health technology.[12] For comparative purposes and to perform statistical tests (Durbin 1954) of heterogeneity bias, OLS estimates are also obtained. The log-linear first-stage equations include, in addition to the set of state- and SMSA-level exogenous variables specified, a set of schooling level dummy variables for the husband and wife, the race variable, and a measure of husband's income standardized for years of potential labor market experience.[13] Table 1 defines the variables used and reports their sample means and standard deviations.

[11] An alternative estimation strategy that could provide consistent estimates of the health production function in the presence of heterogeneity would make use of differences in birth outcomes and parental behavior between births within the same family. Such a technique would require longitudinal data or good retrospective information on prior births to implement and requires the assumption that (perceived) μ is constant across all births in the same household, ruling out modifications in expectations through experience. This technique can only be applied, of course, to families with at least two live births and would suffer from the imprecision of estimates obtained from most individual "fixed effects" models.

[12] Controlling for the significant inputs, we assume that education plays no direct role in the production of birth outcomes. Tests of this overidentification restriction with respect to the mother's education, reported elsewhere (Rosenzweig and Schultz 1981), indicate that inclusion of this variable directly in the health production function does not statistically reduce the appropriate standard error of estimate.

[13] The log income measure for each husband was obtained by adding the residual from the estimated log income function

$$\ln Y = 6.65 + .178ED + .0730EX - .00148EX^2,$$
$$\quad\;\; (188.9) \quad (48.6) \qquad\;\; (33.2) \qquad\quad (21.1)$$

$$R^2 = .24; \text{ SEE } .403; \ N = 9{,}621,$$

t values in parentheses, where ED = years of schooling and EX = age + ED − 7, to the predicted value of $\ln Y$ with EX set at 10 years.

TABLE 1

VARIABLE DESCRIPTIONS AND SAMPLE CHARACTERISTICS

Variable	Definition	Mean	Standard Deviation
Health outcomes (ln):			
Birth weight	Weight of infant at birth in grams	8.08	.215
Standardized birth weight	Birth weight divided by predicted birth weight based on gestation ($\times 100$) (see text)	−.0136	.173
Health input behavior (ln):			
Doctor delay	Number of elapsed months of pregnancy before mother consulted a doctor or nurse	.865	.521
Smoking	Number of cigarettes smoked per day by mother while pregnant	.834	1.25
Births	Number of live births born to mother	.713	.638
Age	Age of mother at birth	3.19	.214
Exogenous individual characteristics:			
Mother's education: (less than 9 years omitted)	High school incomplete (9–11 years)	.229	.420
	High school complete (12 years)	.445	.497
	College incomplete (13–15 years)	.143	.350
	College complete (16+)	.088	.283
Father's education: (less than 9 years omitted)	High school incomplete (9–11 years)	.191	.393
	High school complete (12 years)	.378	.485
	College incomplete (13–15 years)	.146	.353
	College complete (16+)	.159	.365
Black	One if mother is black	.185	.388
Income	Log of husband's life cycle (experience equals 10 years) annual income (see n. 13)	8.65	.725
Exogenous area characteristics:			
Metropolitan	One if located in SMSA	.701	.458
City size	Population in SMSA in 1970 ($\times 10^{-3}$)	1,351	2,091
Hospital beds	Number of hospital beds per capita ($\times 10^{2}$), 1965, state level	.465	.109
Health expenditures	Local governmental health and hospital expenditures in thousands of dollars per capita, 1965, at state or SMSA level	.0203	.0226

HOUSEHOLD PRODUCTION FUNCTION   **733**

TABLE 1 *(Continued)*

Variable	Definition	Mean	Standard Deviation
Family planning in health department	Number of health departments with family planning services per capita, 1969, at state or SMSA level ($\times 10^5$)	.486	.871
Family planning in hospitals	Number of hospitals with family planning services per capita, 1969, at state level ($\times 10^5$)	.300	.158
Population per M.D.	Number of persons per medical doctor, 1969, at state or SMSA level	1,422	687
Obstetrician-gynecologists per capita	Number of obstetricians-gynecologists per capita at state or SMSA level ($\times 10^4$)	.801	.234
Female unemployment rate	Proportion of women in labor force, age 15–59, unemployed, 1970, at state level	.0526	.0104
General unemployment rate	Proportion of the labor force unemployed, 1970, at state level	.0476	.0092
Share of jobs in services	Percentage of persons employed in services, 1970, at state level ($\times 10$)	77.8	15.3
Share of jobs in manufacturing	Percentage of persons employed in manufacturing, 1970, at state level ($\times 10$)	260	72.9
Share of jobs in government	Percentage of persons employed in government, 1970, at state level ($\times 10$)	160	29.0
Cigarette price	Price of cigarettes (exclusive of sales tax), cents per pack, 1967–69, at state level	34.6	3.38
Sales tax	Retail sales tax on cigarettes, 1967–69, at state level	.582	.493
Milk price	Retail price of milk per quart, 1970, at state level	27.0	2.23
1967	One if birth occurred in 1967	.330	.470
1968	One if birth occurred in 1968	.331	.471

While the two-stage procedure achieves consistency and allows for flexibility in the specification of the health technology, estimates are not efficient because the reduced-form cross-equation restrictions implied by the model are ignored. Such restrictions, however, cannot be imposed without specifying the exact form of the utility function (1). Moreover, closed-form analytic solutions for the demand equations cannot be obtained without sacrificing the flexibility in either or both of the specifications of the production and utility functions. One production and utility system that yields such solutions, and thus exact cross-equation restrictions, is that in which both functions are described by the Cobb-Douglas form.[14] Since, if the birth weight technology is Cobb-Douglas, $\beta_{ij} = 0$ for all i and j in (8), the translog function can be used to test this restriction on the health technology. Conditional on its acceptance, we can then exploit potential efficiency gains by estimating jointly the production function and the demand system implied by the Cobb-Douglas form of the utility function.

IV. Estimates of the Reduced-Form Demand Equations

The first four columns of table 2 report the first-stage log-linear input demand equations used to estimate the birth weight production functions. While in many cases the estimates are relatively precise, the R^2's of the equations are relatively low, ranging from .033 for smoking to .119 for delay of prenatal care. The input demand equations appear reasonable in the context of prior studies of household behavior, with parental schooling levels and income evidently significant determinants of health-related behavior, along with the local-area health infrastructure. The results indicate that mothers (and fathers) with at least a completed high school education seek prenatal care earlier in their pregnancies than do parents with lower schooling attainment. Husband's income also shortens this delay in care; however, a rise in income by 10 percent reduces the delay by less than 1 percent. Government expenditures on hospitals and health care and urbanization also appear to hasten prenatal care.

Smoking by mothers during their pregnancies is related to the mother's education according to an inverted U-shaped pattern, in which mothers who did not complete high school appear to smoke more frequently than do mothers in other educational groups. Increases in husband's income, however, increase smoking by the wife while she is pregnant, although the income elasticity is again small (.07). Smoking is lower where sales taxes on cigarettes are higher, whereas the effect of the pretax price of cigarettes is weak and nonlinear. Metropolitan residents also tend to smoke more.

[14] When (1) and (2) are Cobb-Douglas, the demand equations for all goods and health inputs have the following form:

$$\ln Z_j = \delta_j + \sum_{k=1}^{r} e_{jk} \ln P_k + f_j \ln F,$$

where $e_{jk} = -1$ for $j = k$; $e_{jk} = 0$ for $j \neq k$; $f_j = f_k = 1$. A subset of the complete Cobb-Douglas utility production demand system is estimated below that includes the production function and the health input demand equations. The cross-equation restrictions for this subsystem are also tested.

The reduced-form equations for number of births and maternal age at birth are consistent with findings obtained in earlier studies of U.S. fertility—more educated women tend to have fewer births and to have them later in their lifetimes, while husband's income is positively and significantly correlated with cumulative fertility and negatively with maternal age. The income elasticity of fertility is comparable in magnitude to that for prenatal care and smoking. Mothers living in urban environments have lower fertility, and in those regions where industries that employ women are concentrated—services, government, and manufacturing—cumulative fertility is also lower. Most interestingly, the local availability of family planning services in health departments (and perhaps in hospitals), while not significantly associated with maternal age of childbearing, is related to lower levels of cumulative fertility. Later childbearing appears to occur in metropolitan areas and regions with greater availability of hospital beds and obstetricians per capita.

The reduced-form input demand equations also indicate statistically significant behavioral differences between black and white mothers with respect to three of the four health-related inputs, which are not accounted for by racial differences in the socioeconomic variables or in the price determinants. Pregnant black women appear to postpone seeking prenatal care about 11 days more than do similarly located white mothers of similar income and educational attainment. However, pregnant black women appear to smoke nearly a third fewer cigarettes than do pregnant white women. Black mothers also appear to have one-fourth more live births but to be only slightly older than white mothers. The extent to which these differences in input demand behavior account for the well-documented lower birth weight of black than of white infants can be ascertained from the production function estimates reported below. Discussion of the reduced-form birth weight equations in columns 5 and 6 of table 2 is postponed until after the presentation of these latter results.

V. Estimates of Infant Health Production Functions

Ordinary least squares (OLS), two-stage least squares (2SLS), and three-stage least squares (3SLS) estimates of the Cobb-Douglas and translog production functions for birth weight and standardized birth weight are reported in table 3. Application of the Durbin (1954) test for the endogeneity of the behavioral inputs indicates that heterogeneity bias in the OLS production function coefficients is statistically significant in all specifications. The computed test statistics for the Cobb-Douglas specification are 3.44 for birth weight and 2.44

TABLE 2

ESTIMATES OF LOG-LINEAR INPUT AND BIRTH CHARACTERISTIC DEMAND EQUATION

Independent Variables	Log of Doctor Delay (1)	Log of Smoking (2)	Log of Births (3)	Log of Age (4)	Log of Birth Weight (5)	Log of Birth Weight Standardized for Gestation (6)
Mother's education:						
High school incomplete	−.0914 (4.46)	.201 (3.91)	−.185 (7.33)	−.0813 (9.59)	−.0109 (1.23)	−.0162 (2.26)
High school complete	−.215 (10.5)	−.0585 (1.14)	−.300 (11.92)	−.0005 (.06)	.00392 (.44)	−.00306 (.43)
College incomplete	−.259 (10.5)	−.0900 (1.46)	−.380 (12.6)	.0148 (1.45)	.00916 (.86)	.000828 (.106)
College complete	−.257 (8.92)	−.145 (2.01)	−.447 (12.6)	.0797 (6.69)	.0135 (1.08)	.00505 (.50)
Father's education:						
High school incomplete	−.0115 (.60)	.192 (3.99)	−.272 (11.47)	−.1144 (14.3)	−.00720 (.86)	−.00606 (.90)
High school complete	−.099 (5.23)	.0441 (.93)	−.355 (15.3)	−.1143 (14.6)	−.00989 (1.21)	−.00829 (1.25)
College incomplete	−.116 (5.14)	−.0366 (.64)	−.387 (13.9)	−.1208 (12.9)	−.00350 (.355)	−.00641 (.81)
College complete	−.149 (5.95)	−.0423 (.08)	−.262 (8.53)	−.0473 (4.57)	−.0144 (1.33)	−.0166 (1.90)
Log of husband's life cycle income	−.079 (9.30)	.0667 (3.12)	.0640 (6.10)	.0107 (3.01)	.00989 (2.67)	.00490 (1.64)
1967	−.084 (6.81)	.149 (4.80)	.0247 (1.62)	.0068 (1.32)	.00658 (1.22)	−1.0157 (3.62)
1968	−.074 (6.00)	.0787 (2.54)	−.0156 (1.03)	−.0049 (.952)	.00536 (1.0012)	−.0124 (.29)
Metropolitan residence	−.052 (3.15)	.0853 (2.04)	−.0342 (1.67)	.00966 (1.40)	−.0169 (2.33)	−.0130 (2.22)
SMSA size ($\times 10^9$)	−.0229 (.01)	27.2 (3.25)	1.03 (.25)	3.10 (2.24)	−.171 (.12)	1.48 (1.26)
Health expenditures	.00815 (.03)	.300 (.37)	−.469 (1.16)	−.240 (1.77)	.155 (1.09)	.0784 (.68)

	(1)	(2)	(3)	(4)	(5)	(6)
Health department family planning	−.2266 (2.40)	4,228 (1.79)	−2,414 (2.08)	−586 (1.50)	−143 (.35)	134 (.41)
Cigarette price (×100)	.186 (.07)	−7.56 (1.06)	8.93 (2.57)	.410 (.35)	1.07 (.87)	2.03 (2.05)
Cigarette price squared (×10⁴)	−.690 (.16)	12.10 (1.11)	−13.6 (2.55)	.339 (.19)	−1.43 (.76)	−3.04 (2.00)
Milk price (×10³)	−.129 (.05)	10.92 (1.51)	.0587 (.016)	.392 (.33)	−1.74 (1.39)	−3.30 (3.26)
Hospital family planning	385.9 (.101)	22,280 (2.37)	−3,942 (.86)	83.3 (.05)	−1,822 (1.12)	−1,316 (1.00)
Population per doctor (×10⁵)	.298 (.371)	−2.74 (1.36)	1.81 (1.83)	.120 (.36)	.141 (.40)	.2851 (1.01)
OB-GYN per capita	604 (1.74)	246 (.28)	98.4 (.23)	302 (2.11)	−98.3 (.65)	202 (1.67)
Manufacturing jobs (×10³)	−.169 (1.15)	−.0612 (.17)	−.484 (2.70)	.0524 (.87)	−.0379 (.60)	−.0702 (1.37)
Black	.142 (10.01)	−.300 (8.40)	.252 (14.4)	.0042 (.72)	−.06701 (10.85)	−.0426 (8.58)
Service jobs (×10³)	−.348 (.61)	−1.55 (1.09)	−1.54 (2.19)	−.675 (2.85)	−.359 (1.42)	−.447 (2.23)
Government jobs (×10³)	−.431 (1.34)	−1.3 (1.40)	−1.151 (2.93)	.0462 (.35)	−.111 (.80)	−.143 (1.27)
General unemployment (×10³)	1.88 (1.48)	5.66 (1.77)	−1.58 (1.01)	−.0664 (1.26)	.250 (.453)	−.392 (.88)
Female unemployment	.017 (.014)	−6.71 (2.26)	1.40 (.96)	−.262 (.53)	.627 (1.22)	1.12 (2.70)
Hospital beds per capita	5.02 (.83)	14.38 (.95)	11.7 (1.58)	9.86 (3.95)	2.47 (.94)	3.60 (1.71)
Sales tax on cigarettes (×100)	−.0126 (.98)	−4.60 (1.42)	−1.30 (.82)	.676 (1.29)	−.842 (1.505)	.00199 (.44)
Intercept	1.89 (3.98)	1.25 (1.05)	−.376 (.65)	3.09 (15.7)	7.88 (38.3)	−.269 (1.62)
R^2	.1188	.0332	.1103	.1070	.0269	.0240
F	43.94	11.18	40.42	39.05	9.03	8.02
SEE	2.266	14,287	3.432	389.1	428.4	277.8
Health endowment elasticity*	.182 (10.4)	−.00643 (.15)	.297 (13.9)	.0754 (10.5)	…	…

NOTE.—Absolute value of t-ratios in parentheses beneath regression coefficient.
* For interpretation of the health endowment elasticity; see Sec. VI of the text and n. 16.

737

TABLE 3

Estimates of Household Production Functions for Birth Characteristics: Translog and Cobb-Douglas Specifications

EXPLANATORY VARIABLES (logs)	Log of Birth Weight					Log of Birth Weight Standardized for Gestation				
	Translog		Cobb-Douglas		Cobb-Douglas System	Translog		Cobb-Douglas		Cobb-Douglas System
	OLS (1)	2SLS (2)	OLS (3)	2SLS (4)	3SLS (5)	OLS (6)	2SLS (7)	OLS (8)	2SLS (9)	3SLS (10)
Delay of doctor (LDELAY)	.0401 (.50)	1.39 (.90)	-.00178 (.41)	-.0682 (2.84)	-.0680 (2.82)	.0448 (.69)	.585 (.37)	.000973 (.28)	-.00216 (.11)	-.00330 (.17)
Smoking (LSMOK)	.0145 (.44)	2.17 (1.82)	-.0241 (13.9)	-.0256 (2.08)	-.0234 (1.88)	.00657 (.25)	2.01 (1.66)	-.0221 (-15.9)	-.0456 (4.59)	-.0469 (4.71)
Births (LPAR)	-.199 (-2.26)	-3.12 (1.77)	.0217 (4.88)	.0413 (2.09)	.0394 (1.97)	-.179 (2.52)	-1.66 (.93)	.0211 (5.87)	.0130 (.81)	.0132 (.82)
Age (LAGE)	.905 (2.66)	9.03 (1.70)	.0125 (.98)	-.0202 (.48)	-.0178 (.42)	.462 (1.69)	5.86 (1.09)	.0148 (1.42)	-.0139 (.40)	-.0191 (.56)
Delay* smoke	.00132 (.38)	.0725 (.57)	...	...	...	-.00115 (.41)	.148 (1.13)	...	...	...
Delay* births	.0165 (1.89)	.333 (1.40)	...	...	...	.0120 (1.71)	-.0207 (.09)	...	...	...

Delay* age	−.0129 (.51)	−.542 (1.12)	⋮	⋮	⋮	−.0147 (.72)	−.209 (−.43)	⋮	⋮	⋮
Smoke* births	−.00166 (.47)	.0535 (.41)	⋮	⋮	⋮	−.00247 (.86)	−.00611 (−.045)	⋮	⋮	⋮
Smoke* age	−.0114 (1.10)	−.797 (1.87)	⋮	⋮	⋮	−.00880 (1.07)	−.813 (1.88)	⋮	⋮	⋮
Births* age	.0729 (2.55)	.958 (1.58)	⋮	⋮	⋮	.0671 (2.91)	.576 (.94)	⋮	⋮	⋮
½ Delay²	−.0121 (.95)	−.0324 (.08)	⋮	⋮	⋮	−.00525 (.51)	−.0328 (−.08)	⋮	⋮	⋮
½ Smoke²	−.00002 (.10)	.166 (.81)	⋮	⋮	⋮	.00179 (.42)	.271 (1.30)	⋮	⋮	⋮
½ Births²	−.0368 (2.50)	−.415 (.85)	⋮	⋮	⋮	−.0338 (2.85)	−.249 (.60)	⋮	⋮	⋮
½ Age²	−.280 (2.67)	2.70 (1.66)	⋮	⋮	⋮	−.147 (1.70)	−1.70 (1.03)	⋮	⋮	⋮
Black	−.0869 (14.8)	−.0314 (1.04)	−.0806 (−15.7)	−.0815 (10.2)	−.0804 (9.99)	−.057 (−12.1)	.0013 (.04)	−.0594 (−12.8)	−.0647 (9.99)	−.0650 (10.0)
Intercept	6.67 (12.3)	−6.66 (.77)	8.06 (199)	8.21 (56.5)	8.20 (56.2)	−.728 (1.57)	−.0992 (1.14)	−.00471 (−1.44)	.0734 (.62)	.0921 (.79)
R²	.0461	...	.0444	...	...	.0458	...	.0444	...	...
F	30.96	7.67	89.47	42.71	64.14*	30.76	3.95	89.07	28.24	61.65*

NOTE.—Absolute value of t-ratios in parentheses beneath regression coefficients.
* F computed for system of four input equations and production function (82 free parameters).

for birth weight standardized for gestation. The appropriate critical F value, assuming that the first-stage input demand and production function residuals are jointly normally distributed (Wu 1973), is 2.37 at the 5 percent level for 4 and 9,000 degrees of freedom. The test statistics are 8.05 and 15.05 for the respective translog specifications, both well exceeding the critical F value of 1.85.

Comparisons of both the OLS and 2SLS residuals across the alternative functional specifications indicate that the ten additional quadratic and interaction terms embodied in the translog functional form are not jointly statistically significant. The F values for birth weight and standardized birth weight computed from the OLS residuals are 1.68 and 1.57, respectively, whereas the critical value at the 5 percent level is 1.85; the additional nonlinear terms increase the magnitude of the residual variance in the 2SLS translog specification.

The existence of bias in the OLS coefficient estimates and the statistical rejection of the more complex functional form in favor of the restrictive Cobb-Douglas specification suggest that there are potential and achievable efficiency gains from estimating the birth weight technology as part of the system of demand equations derived from the Cobb-Douglas utility function. The 3SLS estimates of the Cobb-Douglas function are reported in columns 5 and 10; estimates of the set of demand functions are reported in Rosenzweig and Schultz (1983, tables A and B). While the coefficients and their standard errors are nearly identical to those obtained using the less efficient two-stage procedure, the set of cross-equation restrictions implied by the Cobb-Douglas production utility variant of the model are rejected by the data. All of these tests thus imply that we cannot reject the hypothesis that the birth weight technology is Cobb-Douglas, but we can reject the hypotheses that there is no heterogeneity bias in the production function estimates and that preference orderings are described by the Cobb-Douglas utility function.

Comparison of the OLS and 2SLS Cobb-Douglas birth weight results indicates that the neglect of health heterogeneity can importantly affect the inferences drawn from estimates of the effects of self-selected health inputs. Delay in use of medical care during a woman's pregnancy appears to have no appreciable effect on birth weight according to the OLS estimates (col. 3, table 3), whereas the 2SLS estimates suggest a statistically significant deleterious effect of delay that is almost forty times the OLS point estimate. Parity has almost twice as large a beneficial effect on birth weight according to the 2SLS estimates as indicated by OLS, although the magnitude is small; a fourth birth would weigh 3 percent more than a second birth. Smoking, on the other hand, has a substantial negative effect on birth weight, which is evidently robust to estimation technique.

With respect to the 2SLS point estimates, the Cobb-Douglas smoking effects are slightly higher than those obtained from direct correlational studies for birth weight. The consensus of those studies (U.S. Department of Health and Human Services 1980) attributes a 200 gram deficit to mothers who smoke. In our sample, the one-third who continued to smoke after they knew they were pregnant smoked on average 14 cigarettes a day. According to our estimates, the birth weight of infants for the average smoker would be 7 percent or 230 grams less than that of the nonsmoking mother. A 5-month increase in the sample mean delay in seeking prenatal care has a similar effect on birth weight, decreasing it by 260 grams or 8 percent. Age, however, appears to exert little or no effect on birth weight in the Cobb-Douglas specification.

In the standardized birth weight equations several additional insights emerge. First, the beneficial effects of prenatal care are no longer evident, whether or not heterogeneity is taken into account. Prenatal medical care and associated drug therapies evidently have their primary effect on birth weight by extending gestation, but this care does not have a substantial effect on the rate of growth of the fetus. Second, smoking by the mother while pregnant appears to increase gestation, since when birth weight is standardized for gestation the effect of smoking is increased by 78 percent over its effect on birth weight based on the Cobb-Douglas 2SLS estimates. This pronounced retarding effect of smoking on fetal growth has not been noted in the epidemiological literature and is also nearly masked in our OLS estimates in table 3 (Department of Health and Human Services 1980).

The translog specification, although rejected in favor of the nested Cobb-Douglas form, reveals significant non(log)linear effects of age and substantial age interactions with other inputs that are in accord with the descriptive clinical literature. From the (preferred) 2SLS estimates it appears that the best age for a mother to bear a child is 24, which happens to be the sample mean. At age 20 mothers have babies who have 4.4 percent lower birth weight, while at age 30 mothers have babies who have 6.7 percent lower birth weight. Smoking has an increasing deleterious effect on birth weight among older mothers, probably because of the cumulative nature of smoking on the mother's and child's health and the lifetime persistence of smoking. A larger number of births, according to the translog 2SLS estimates, is associated with lower birth weight, but this is counterbalanced by a large positive age-birth interaction effect. Having a fourth birth at age 20 is not associated with as favorable an outcome as having this fourth birth at age 30. Thus, the age interactions permitted by the translog specification approximate the health effects of different patterns of birth spacing, as well as total number of births and input use.

The 2SLS output elasticities for the health inputs derived from table 3 and the input demand equation estimates together shed some light on the black-white differences in birth weight noted in the literature and evident in the reduced-form demand equations reported in columns 5 and 6 of table 2. Those equations indicate that black infants weigh 6.7 percent less at birth and 4.3 percent less standardized for gestation, conditional on individual socioeconomic characteristics of the mother and father as well as the area-level variables. In the 2SLS Cobb-Douglas specifications of the birth weight production functions, however, blacks have 8 percent lower birth weight and 5–6 percent lower rates of fetal growth, holding constant input behavior.[15] The differentials in smoking, timing of prenatal care, and fertility, net of location and socioeconomic characteristics of blacks and whites also reported in table 2, do not account for black-white differences in birth characteristics. However, it is notable that the more flexible translog 2SLS estimates eliminate half of the black-white birth weight differential and account for nearly all the racial differences in birth weight standardized for gestation. These latter findings suggest that the lower birth weight of black infants, given their mother's input behavior, is due to shorter gestation and not due to lower rates of fetal growth. Methods for increasing gestation for black infants may, therefore, warrant increased study, such as obtaining earlier prenatal care.

VI. The Health Endowment Effect and the Behavior of the Mother

The residuals from the 2SLS birth weight production function estimates, conditioned on the inclusion of all significant inputs, contain the exogenous child health endowment effect and an error component that was unforeseen by the mother and by assumption did not affect her prenatal behavior. Thus, regressions of the health input levels chosen by the mothers on the 2SLS birth weight residuals provide estimates of the effects of the health endowment on input demand behavior, which, though biased to zero because of the measurement error, should yield the correct sign of the relationships.[16] These estimates are reported for each input in the bottom row of table 2.

[15] Separate estimates of white and nonwhite birth weight production functions and separate normalizations of birth weight for gestational age are explored in Rosenzweig and Schultz (1982). Reductions in sample size reduced the precision in estimates for both groups; the hypothesis that input coefficients differed significantly across the two racial groups could not be rejected.

[16] The difference between the actual and predicted health outcome, based on actual input levels and consistent 2SLS estimates of the birth weight production function parameters, approximates the health endowment with a random error. Regressing the logarithms of the behavioral inputs on this calculated residual of the health production

As previously shown, it is difficult to predict how input demand varies with the exogenous component of child health without information both on the health technology and on preference orderings. We conjectured, however, that a major source of bias in the OLS birth weight production function estimates was remedial behavior by mothers who could anticipate a pregnancy that would yield a less healthy (low birth weight) baby. The endowment estimate for the timing of prenatal care (DELAY) supports this interpretation— mothers whose babies have lower than predicted birth weight, given the level of inputs, evidently seek prenatal care earlier. This remedial behavior suggests why epidemiological correlational studies have not always found a beneficial effect of the timing of prenatal care on birth weight (Eisner et al. 1979); indeed our OLS estimates replicate this misleading conclusion.

The endowment-effects estimates also indicate that although the smoking behavior of mothers does not vary significantly with child health endowments, an increase in the birth weight endowment does appear to increase parity. Moreover, while our production function estimates indicate that changes in the age of the mother have only weak effects on the weight of the child at birth, women with more favorable health endowments appear to bear children at significantly later ages. Population heterogeneity may thus wholly account for the observed negative correlations between mother's age over 18 and birth weight reported in epidemiological studies (Eisner et al. 1979).

VII. Conclusion

Much of the information on the human biological mechanisms through which behavior affects health must by necessity come from nonexperimental data that link health-related activities or inputs to health outcomes. The principal insight offered by the household production literature is that these biological processes (the health technology), to the extent that they are perceived, condition health input choices made by households, along with prices and income. As a consequence, if there are exogenous variations in endowment health that are known to individuals but not to the researcher (health heterogeneity), the observed correlations between input behavior and health cannot be used to derive causal conclusions. Estimates of the health technology must therefore be obtained from a behavioral

---

function yields the reported estimate of the elasticity between anticipated exogenous health endowment and the input response of parents. But since the calculated residual measures the health endowment with the error, this estimate of the elasticity of inputs with respect to health endowment is biased toward zero.

model in which inputs affecting health are themselves choice variables. Despite the emphasis of the household production model on the role of technology, econometric applications of this framework have not provided estimates that disentangle the relevant technologies from preference orderings. The medical literature concerned with depicting health technology, on the other hand, has ignored the estimation problems associated with household optimization in the presence of exogenous health heterogeneity.

In this paper we have attempted to bridge these two literatures by directly estimating the health technology pertaining to the "production" of birth weight and fetal growth in a model in which maternal behavior is responsive to variations in prices, income, and exogenous health endowment. The empirical analysis, based on a probability sample of over 9,000 legitimate births in the United States between 1967 and 1969, suggested that inferences concerning the effects of health inputs are sensitive to whether or not heterogeneity is taken into account. In particular, heterogeneity appeared to mask almost completely a significant positive impact on child health of early prenatal medical care and to underestimate the significant negative effects of maternal smoking on the rate of fetal growth, an important indicator of the subsequent health of children. Two important caveats concerning our results must be kept in mind. First, and most obvious, the estimates may be sensitive to the omission of relevant behavioral determinants of birth weight correlated with those included in our data (drugs, consumption of alcohol). More important, the area-level program and price variables used here as instruments to identify the health technology may not be independent of health endowments. Government health programs may be established to serve groups in the population that are known by the government to have distinctly different health endowments or environments. Alternatively, individuals may migrate to regions according to which region has lower prices for preferred inputs or available programs. In either instance, estimates of input productivities and prices and program effects based on regional price and program information could be inconsistent, as the regional variables would no longer be independently distributed with regard to health heterogeneity.

References

Barnett, William A. "Pollak and Wachter on the Household Production Function Approach." *J.P.E.* 85 (October 1977): 1073–82.

Beck, Gerald J., and van den Berg, Bea J. "The Relationship of the Rate of Intrauterine Growth of Low-Birth-Weight Infants to Later Growth." *J. Pediatrics* 86 (April 1975): 504–11.

Becker, Gary S. "A Theory of the Allocation of Time." *Econ. J.* 75 (September 1965): 493–517.

Becker, Gary S., and Lewis, H. Gregg. "On the Interaction between Quantity and Quality of Children." *J.P.E.* 81, no. 2, pt. 2 (March/April 1973): S279–S288.

Chernichovsky, Dov, and Coate, Douglas. "An Economic Analysis of the Diet, Growth, and Health of Young Children in the United States." Working Paper no. 416. Cambridge, Mass.: Nat. Bur. Econ. Res., December 1979.

Coombs, Lolagene; Freedman, Ronald; and Namboothiri, D. Narayanan. "Inferences about Abortion from Foetal Mortality Data." *Population Studies* 23 (July 1969): 247–65.

Durbin, James. "Errors in Variables." *Rev. Internat. Statis. Inst.* 22 (1954): 23–32.

Edwards, Linda N., and Grossman, Michael. "Adolescent Health, Family Background, and Preventive Medical Care." Working Paper no. 398. Cambridge, Mass.: Nat. Bur. Econ. Res., October 1979.

Eisner, Victor; Brazie, Joseph V.; Pratt, Margaret W.; and Hexter, Alfred C. "The Risk of Low Birthweight." *American J. Public Health* 69 (September 1979): 887–93.

Fuss, Melvyn, and McFadden, Daniel. *Production Economics: A Dual Approach to Theory and Applications.* Vols. 1, 2. Amsterdam: North-Holland, 1978.

Goldman, Fred, and Grossman, Michael. "The Demand for Pediatric Care: An Hedonic Approach." *J.P.E.* 86, no. 2, pt. 1 (April 1978): 259–80.

Harris, Jeffrey E. "Prenatal Medical Care and Infant Mortality." In *Economic Aspects of Health,* edited by Victor R. Fuchs. Chicago: Univ. Chicago Press (for Nat. Bur. Econ. Res.), 1982.

Hebel, Richard; Entwisle, George; and Tayback, Matthew. "A Risk Adjustment Technique for Comparing Prematurity Rates among Clinic Populations." *HSMHA Health Reports* 86 (October 1971): 946–52.

Iba, B. Y.; Niswander, J. D.; and Woodville, L. "Relation of Prenatal Care to Birth Weights, Major Malformations, and Newborn Deaths of American Indians." *Health Services Reports* 88 (October 1973): 697–701.

Inman, Robert P. "The Family Provision of Children's Health: An Economic Analysis." In *The Role of Health Insurance in the Health Services Sector,* edited by Richard N. Rosett. New York: Columbia Univ. Press (for Nat. Bur. Econ. Res.), 1976.

Leibowitz, Arleen, and Friedman, Bernard S. "Family Bequests and the Derived Demand for Health Inputs." *Econ. Inquiry* 17 (July 1979): 419–34.

Lewit, E. "The Demand for Prenatal Care and the Production of Healthy Infants." In *Research in Human Capital and Development,* edited by Ismail Sirageldin. Vol. 3. Greenwich, Conn.: JAI, 1982.

Mundlak, Yair, and Hoch, Irving. "Consequences of Alternative Specifications in Estimation of Cobb-Douglas Production Functions." *Econometrica* 33 (October 1965): 814–28.

Pollak, Robert A., and Wachter, Michael L. "The Relevance of the Household Production Function and Its Implications for the Allocation of Time." *J.P.E.* 83 (April 1975): 255–77.

———. "Reply: 'Pollak and Wachter on the Household Production Approach.'" *J.P.E.* 85 (October 1977): 1083–86.

Rosenwaike, Ira. "The Influence of Socioeconomic Status on Incidence of Low Birth Weight." *HSMHA Health Reports* 86 (July 1971): 641–49.

Rosenzweig, Mark R., and Schultz, T. Paul. "Education and Household Production of Child Health." *Proceedings of the American Statistical Association, Social Statistical Section.* Washington: American Statis. Assoc., 1981.

———. "The Behavior of Mothers as Inputs to Child Health: The Determinants of Birth Weight, Gestation, and Rate of Fetal Growth." In *Economic Aspects of Health,* edited by Victor R. Fuchs. Chicago: Univ. Chicago Press (for Nat. Bur. Econ. Res.), 1982.

————. "Estimating a Household Production Function: Heterogeneity, the Demand for Health Inputs and Their Effects on Birthweight." Discussion Paper no. 437. New Haven, Conn.: Yale Univ., Econ. Growth Center, February 1983.

Rosenzweig, Mark, and Wolpin, Kenneth I. "Testing the Quantity-Quality Fertility Model: The Use of Twins as a Natural Experiment." *Econometrica* 48 (January 1980): 227–40.

Shah, Farida K., and Abbey, Helen. "Effects of Some Factors on Neonatal and Postneonatal Mortality." *Milbank Memorial Fund Q.* 49 (January 1971): 33–57.

U.S. Department of Health and Human Services. *The Health Consequences of Smoking for Women: A Report of the Surgeon General.* Washington: Government Printing Office, 1980.

U.S. Department of Health, Education, and Welfare, National Center for Health Statistics. *Standardized Micro-Data Tape Transcripts.* DHEW Publication no. (PHS) 78-1213. Washington: Nat. Center Health Statis., June 1978.

Wu, De-Min. "Alternative Tests of Independence between Stochastic Regressors and Disturbances." *Econometrica* 41 (July 1973): 733–50.

[8]

Does Better Nutrition Raise Farm Productivity?

John Strauss

Yale University

Household-level data from Sierra Leone are used to test whether higher caloric intake enhances family farm labor productivity. This is the notion behind the efficiency wages hypothesis, which has found only weak empirical support. A farm production function is estimated, accounting for the simultaneity in input and calorie choice. Instruments include prices, household demographic characteristics, and farm assets. The latter two sets of instruments are later dropped to explore the robustness of the results to different specifications of exogeneity. The exercise shows a highly significant effect of caloric intake on labor productivity, providing solid support for the nutrition-productivity hypothesis. The marginal effect on productivity falls drastically as calorie consumption rises but remains positive at moderately high levels of intake. One result is a fall in the effective price of food, a decline that is larger for households that consume fewer calories.

I. Introduction

The potential biological relationship that relates current and past nutrition intakes to labor effort per unit of time, or efficiency units of labor, has attracted the interest of economists and nutritionists for some time. Economists have been especially interested in how labor

I gratefully acknowledge the very helpful comments of Jere Behrman, David Feeny, Mark Rosenzweig, T. Paul Schultz, Victor Smith, James J. Heckman, and an anonymous referee. The paper has also benefited from comments from workshop participants at Brown University, McMaster University, North Carolina State University, the University of Toronto, the University of Western Ontario, and the World Bank. Partial support came from the Hewlett Foundation.

[*Journal of Political Economy*, 1986, vol. 94, no. 2]
© 1986 by The University of Chicago. All rights reserved. 0022-3808/86/9402-0008$01.50

markets might adapt to such a relationship, an interest that has spawned the efficiency wages hypothesis. Developed by Leibenstein (1957) and Mazumdar (1959), it has been formalized and extended by Mirrlees (1975), Rodgers (1975), Stiglitz (1976, 1982), Bliss and Stern (1978a), and Gersovitz (1983).[1] This hypothesis has been used to explain (1) why constant real wages in the agricultural sector of a developing economy are part of an equilibrium with involuntary unemployment, (2) the distribution of food within a household, (3) household savings decisions, and (4) shadow wage rates. More recently this idea has even been offered as an explanation of involuntary unemployment in industrial countries (Yellen 1984). While other nonbiological relationships between wages and efficiency units of labor have been suggested,[2] it is the relationship between nutrient intake and labor productivity that remains the primary motivation for the efficiency wages hypothesis as it is applied to developing countries.

Despite this body of theory, the empirical evidence on the existence and shape of a function that relates nutritional status to labor productivity is not abundant, and it is especially lacking for farm labor productivity. Nutritionists and doctors have been interested in this question since before the 1920s. Experiments conducted in Minnesota during the 1940s (Keys et al. 1950) have shown that activity levels drop precipitously when males are subjected to dramatic decreases in caloric intakes from moderate to extremely low ones.[3] What is not clear from this evidence is whether people would not adapt fully to long exposure to low caloric intakes without a decrease in productivity.[4] Also it is not clear whether at higher levels of caloric intake, corresponding to a larger proportion of the developing world, similar relationships would hold.

---

[1] Bliss and Stern (1978a, 1978b) provide an excellent survey, as do Binswanger and Rosenzweig (1984).

[2] For instance, Stiglitz (1982) hypothesizes a morale effect of higher wages, and Weiss (1980) hypothesizes a potential screening effect, that more productive workers have a higher opportunity cost in self-employment activities.

[3] The daily caloric intakes of 32 men were reduced from 3,500 calories to 1,500 over a 24-week period, then increased to 1,800 calories per day. Productivity was not directly measured, but vastly reduced activity levels were one of the adaptive mechanisms observed.

[4] Sukhatme and Margen (1982) argue that over a range of caloric intakes the efficiency with which calories are used by humans may vary positively with the level of intake, gradually adjusting as intake levels change so as to reequilibrate energy intake with energy expenditure. The best evidence on this comes from the Minnesota semi-starvation experiments (Keys et al. 1950), which do show an adjustment in efficiency of calorie use by the body, but not so complete as to prevent a major reduction in activity levels. However, evidence on long-term bodily adaptation at higher levels of caloric intake is extremely scanty.

In other, nonexperimental, evidence from this period Kraut and Muller (1946) report increases in hourly productivity of German coal miners, steelworkers, and workers dumping debris out of railcars when their daily food rations were exogenously increased in special work camps. There were no control groups, however, and no non-labor inputs (or institutional changes) were measured, so some caution has to be used when interpreting the findings. Also the workers presumably knew they were getting the extra rations, which were not tied explicitly to labor supply, so a morale effect is possible.

More recent empirical evidence trying to answer these general questions has severe methodological problems and shows weak or no patterns.[5] One exception is an experimental study (Wolgemuth et al. 1982) that shows a relationship (significant at the .075 level) between current energy supplementation and output of male Kenyan road construction workers.[6] Other less carefully constructed experimental studies have shown no positive effects of current energy intakes on worker productivity (e.g., Immink and Viteri 1981*a*, 1981*b*).[7]

A number of nonexperimental studies exist, but they are plagued by simultaneity problems. Even the experimental studies report certain evidence that is similarly affected. Typically ordinary least squares (OLS) regressions are run that relate individually measured output, often of sugarcane cutters or road construction workers, to such endogenous variables as calorie consumption (Immink and Viteri 1981*a*, 1981*b*; Immink, Viteri, and Helms 1982), blood hemoglobin levels (Popkin 1978; Wolgemuth et al. 1982), dummy variables for current illnesses (Wolgemuth et al. 1982), or weight-for-height mea-

---

[5] Spurr (1983), Martorell and Arroyave (1984), and Latham (1985) provide recent surveys of the nutrition literature. Strauss (1985) gives a far more detailed critique than is given here.

[6] Dirt dug per day increased 12.5 percent for workers with high-calorie supplements (1,000 calories per day) vs. workers with low-level supplements (200 calories per day). The presupplementation daily caloric intake of both groups was approximately 2,000 calories. Because less food was consumed at home, the net increase in daily caloric intake was only 500 calories for the highly supplemented group and almost none for the low-level supplemented group. Workers were randomly assigned to groups; however, attrition was high (the sample size is only 47 workers). Since workers knew which group they were in, it is possible that any selectivity in attrition might have been different for the two groups.

[7] Immink and Viteri (1981*a*, 1981*b*) studied Guatemalan sugarcane cutters, who were provided with a low- and a high-calorie supplement. The different supplements were given to entire villages; thus random assignment of workers to groups was not achieved. Changes in productivity between the two groups showed no differential response, any real differential being swamped by village and seasonal factors. Experimental evidence on iron deficiency as a possible cause of low labor productivity is stronger. Basta et al. (1979) find that anemic Indonesian rubber tree tappers who received an iron supplement were able to catch up in productivity to nonanemic workers, both those receiving a supplement and those receiving a placebo.

surements[8] (six such studies are approvingly cited by Martorell and Arroyave 1984). Using a slightly different twist, Baldwin and Weisbrod (1974) and Weisbrod and Helminiak (1977) regress daily and weekly wages of St. Lucia plantation workers on a set of parasitic disease dummy variables. While the expected positive sign is usually found between productivity and the nutrition or health measures, the attributed causation is in doubt. Unobserved production or earnings function shifters, such as ability or land quality, will also shift food consumption (hence caloric and iron intake) through associated income changes. Health and nutritional status outcomes such as illness and weight for height depend on current and past inputs such as food consumption and time allocation and so will also be endogenous.[9]

The evidence collected to date is overwhelmingly on workers whose individual outputs are easily observed, such as sugarcane cutters or dirt diggers on road construction crews. Labor productivity–nutrition linkages of workers on family farms have been largely unexplored, despite the overwhelming importance of family farms in developing countries.[10] This gap may result from the severe data requirements of such an exercise,[11] including the necessity of having to infer labor productivity instead of directly measuring it. Indeed Bliss and Stern (1978*b*, p. 390) in discussing such a possibility conclude: "We should not be dogmatic. We suggest, however, that an attempt to tease something out of the data, which is much more delicate than the crude production function, with all the problems attendant to that simple exercise, will not be justified." Nonetheless, the gap is sufficiently serious and the hypothesis important enough to warrant more study.

This paper reports an attempt to test and quantify the effects of current nutritional status (measured by annual caloric intake) on annual farm production and, hence, labor productivity using farm

---

[8] Weight for height is often taken as a proxy for current nutritional status and is sometimes hypothesized to play an independent role in raising biological maximum work capacity (Spurr 1983).

[9] Strauss (1982) and Pitt (1983) provide recent evidence of food consumption responses to income and prices for households in poor countries. Pitt and Rosenzweig (1986) report reduced-form responses of adult illness among Indonesian households to food prices and community socioeconomic variables.

[10] A recent exception, in addition to this paper, is Deolalikar (1984). Viteri (1971) reports that a group of Guatemalan farm workers who had a calorie supplementation for 3 previous years could accomplish standardized farm tasks in less time than an unsupplemented group. This study suffers from the same simultaneity problems as discussed previously. The supplemented workers all came from the same farm in a higher-income region, which paid higher than average wages, while the unsupplemented workers were all from one of the poorer areas in Guatemala.

[11] Not only are traditional farm input-output data needed, but also data on nutrient intakes, possibly anthropometric measurements, and potential instrumental variables. Prices are an obvious source of such instruments, which require intertemporal and/or regional variation.

household level data from Sierra Leone. Farm work there—hoe agriculture—is physically demanding. It is thus a good setting in which to test whether nutrition affects labor productivity. This is done by estimating a farm production function in which caloric intake may enhance efficiency units of labor, while accounting for the simultaneity involved in household choices of calorie consumption and in levels of variable farm inputs. A farm household model is outlined, both to motivate the choice of instruments and to provide first-order conditions with which the parameters can be given a more meaningful interpretation. The instrument set includes prices of commodities consumed, output, and variable farm inputs; quasi-fixed farm inputs; and household demographic characteristics. While treating fixed inputs, and perhaps demographics, as predetermined is common when estimating production, cost, or profit functions (Lau 1978), unobserved farm heterogeneity resulting from land or management quality differences may lead to systematic differences between households in levels of those predetermined inputs. The estimates are therefore examined to see how robust they are in reducing the instrument set, and the hypothesis is tested of no correlation between the quasi-fixed factors and random production function disturbances.

The results show a highly significant and sizable effect of caloric intake on farm output, even after accounting for its endogeneity. The effects are greatly attenuated as calorie levels rise but remain positive over a large range of caloric intake. These measured productivity effects can be interpreted as lowering the shadow price of food below the market price. At the sample mean the reduction for rice (the staple) is computed to be between 20 and 40 percent, rising substantially for low-caloric-intake households. Moreover, both the significance and size of the calorie effects are reasonably robust to the ways in which calories enter the production function, to the inclusion of other human capital related variables, to different assumptions concerning the substitutability of family and hired labor, and to assumptions concerning the exogeneity of certain of the instrumental variables.

II. Model

A farm household model (see Singh, Squire, and Strauss 1986) slightly modified to allow nutrient intakes to affect farm output is used to represent household behavior. Households are assumed to choose a consumption bundle of foods (X_a), nonfoods (X_n), and leisure (X_l), input levels of effective family (L_*^f) and hired (L_*^h) labor, and nonlabor variable farm inputs (V) to maximize their utility subject to a farm production function, time, and budget constraints. Since the caloric consumption that potentially matters is at the individual level, a model explaining food consumption of individuals would be better. However, since the available data are at the household level, this is not pursued.

Farm output, Q, is hypothesized to be a function of effective hours of family (L_*^f) and hired (L_*^h) labor, variable nonlabor inputs (V), fixed capital (K), and land cultivated (A):

$$Q = F(L_*^f, L_*^h, V, K, A). \tag{1}$$

Effective labor, both family and hired, is a function of caloric intake (X_c^f, X_c^h) at the individual level and hours worked (L^f, L^h). Individual-level caloric intake in turn is a function of household food consumption, a function that depends on intrahousehold distribution and biological food-calorie conversion rates. It is the inflow of calories during the current year that is hypothesized to affect annual effective labor. No attempt is made to measure effects of deficiencies that occurred long ago, a stock effect, though to the extent that current and past intakes are correlated the joint effects are being captured. Family and hired labor are hypothesized to have the same effective labor function, although they may be at different points on the function because their intakes are different. In specifying effective labor we follow the efficiency wages literature (Bliss and Stern 1978a, 1978b) by making effective labor the product of labor hours and a function relating efficiency per hour worked to caloric intake:[12]

$$L_*^i = h(X_c^i)L^i, \quad i = f, h. \tag{2}$$

The efficiency per hour worked function, $h(\cdot)$, is often hypothesized to have a portion that is increasing at an increasing rate followed by a portion increasing at a decreasing rate. It can begin at the origin or from a positive caloric intake. Figure 1 provides an illustration.

Competitive markets are assumed to exist for all commodities. In principle, provided that a nutrition-productivity relationship exists and perfect information on it exists for both employees and employers, wage per effective hour (the efficiency wage), not clock hour, would be taken as given by family and hired laborers. The associated full income constraint can be written as

$$w_*^f h(X_c^f)T + (p_a Q - w_*^f L_*^f - w_*^h L_*^h - p_v V) + E$$
$$= p_a X_a + p_n X_n + w_*^f h(X_c^f)X_l, \tag{3}$$

---

[12] For simplicity different types of family or hired labor, such as male adult and female adult, are aggregated. In principle each might have a different function relating efficiency per hour worked to caloric intake.

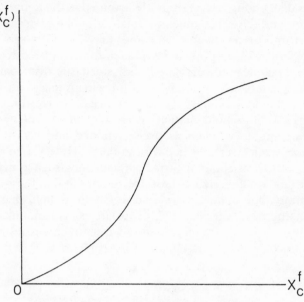

FIG. 1.—Prototype efficiency labor function

where w_*^l is the wage per hour of effective labor hired out—thus $w_*^l h(X_c^f)$ is the wage per clock hour, assuming for simplicity the same efficiency labor function to apply to labor hired out and to family farm labor—w_*^h is the hired-in wage per effective hour, the p's are prices, T is total household clock time available,[13] and E is any non-labor, nonfarm income. The term in parentheses represents the returns to quasi-fixed farm inputs, or profits.

From the first-order conditions it is clear that the real marginal price of foods is less than the market price to the extent that on-farm (and off-farm) labor productivity varies positively with caloric intake.[14] Also the marginal value product of efficiency labor, family or hired in, is equated to the efficiency wage for labor hired out or hired in. Other conditions are standard.

For the purpose of estimating the farm production function, the agricultural household model provides a set of variables that may be

[13] Following Grossman (1972), time available could be modeled as non–sick time available, where morbidity depends in part on nutrient intake. This is not followed here because the necessary data are unavailable.

[14] With interior solutions this condition is

$$\frac{\partial U}{\partial X_a} - \lambda p_a \left[1 - L^f \frac{\partial F}{\partial L_*^f} \frac{dh}{dX_a} - \frac{w_*^f}{p_a} (T - X_l - L^f) \frac{dh}{dX_a} \right] = 0,$$

where $U(\cdot)$ represents the utility function and λ the Lagrange multiplier.

taken as exogenous or at least predetermined to the household, hence that are candidate instrumental variables. These variables can be grouped into prices, farm assets, and quasi-fixed household characteristics. Prices of outputs and inputs and quantities of fixed inputs are often taken as uncorrelated with stochastic disturbances when estimating cost or profit functions of pure firms (e.g., Lau 1978). The farm household model suggests that prices of consumption commodities and household characteristics, such as size and age composition, that might be taken as predetermined and also might enter household utility are additional candidates. However, if there exist unobservable household or farm characteristics, such as management skills or land quality, that persist over time, these will arguably affect the accumulation of farm assets and certain household characteristics, thus making those variables inappropriate as instruments. In view of this potential difficulty, exogeneity of instruments is tested and the robustness of estimates to choice of instruments is examined.

III. The Data and Study Setting

The data are from a cross-section survey of households in rural Sierra Leone taken during the 1974–75 cropping year (May–April). Sierra Leone was divided into eight geographical regions chosen to conform with agroclimatic zones, and they were used to stratify the sample. Within these regions, three enumeration areas were randomly picked and households sampled within them. Households were visited twice in each week to obtain information on production, sales, and labor use, among other variables. Half the households were visited twice during one week per month to obtain market purchase information.

The data set contains details on outputs, family and hired labor use (there is not much use of nonlabor variable inputs in Sierra Leone), capital stock, land use, and household characteristics. It also provides estimates at the household level of food consumption from both market purchases and home production of 196 different foods (see Strauss [1982, 1984] for details of variable construction). From these data, estimates of household caloric availability have been constructed using food composition tables (Food and Agricultural Organization 1968). This data set also has regional average price and wage data with sufficient variation to have supported estimation of a moderately large (seven commodity groups) complete demand system (Strauss 1982). It is then a good data set with which to estimate farm household-level production functions, including a measure of caloric availability, having good data on outputs and inputs as well as data on the type of instrumental variables required for estimation.

The major weaknesses in the data are the absence of individual-

NUTRITION AND FARM PRODUCTIVITY   305

level data on caloric intake and the absence of measures of nutritional
outcomes, especially anthropometric or clinical measures. Anthropometric and clinical variables would be useful to distinguish different
possible effects on productivity of long-term (chronic) and short-term
(acute) deficiencies. Also body size may have an independent effect
from current nutrient intake on labor productivity (Spurr 1983). Ideally the dietary information one would like would include actual intakes for individuals.

The measure available in the Sierra Leone data is availability, not
intake. The two may differ systematically, especially if food waste is
positively related to income levels. However, intake data are difficult
to obtain accurately. Recall methods have potential inaccuracies and,
in addition, may be unrepresentative of average annual intake if the
data come from one or two interviews during the year, as is common
with food recall surveys. The Sierra Leone data were collected
throughout the year, twice weekly for production-related variables
and twice during one week per month for the market purchase information. It is not obvious whether more measurement error is introduced by using annual household availability data or individual
intake data measured infrequently. Clearly, though, the best data
would be frequently measured intakes at the individual level. Since
such data are not available for this sample, the household-level calorie
variable has to be converted into an average per family worker.

Two methods are used to make this conversion to see how robust
the results are. At one extreme one could assume that food is shared
equally among family members and divide household availability by
household size. This seems unreasonable, though, so another assumption used is that individual food consumption is proportional to
approximate caloric "requirements" for a moderately active person of
a given age and sex.[15] This allows adults to get a higher share than
under the equal distribution assumption, though perhaps not as high
as they in fact receive.

Both of these methods assume that intrahousehold allocation of

---

[15] Estimating caloric "requirements" is very imprecise because of wide interindividual
variation in activity levels and digestive efficiency. The weights in this study are taken
from Food and Agricultural Organization (1957):

Sex	Age			
	0–5	6–10	11–15	16+
Male	.2	.5	.75	1.0
Female	.2	.5	.7	.9

Data were unavailable to correct for differential requirements of pregnant or lactating
women.

foods does not vary systematically with socioeconomic factors, such as income or assets, or relative wage rates. There is very little evidence on this question, and none for Sierra Leone. What scanty evidence exists suggests that food sharing between workers and nonworkers may be greater for wealthier households, as might occur if returns from calories are decreasing.[16] In this case the conversions will overstate intakes of workers from higher-income households while understating intakes of workers from poorer households. This should reduce the estimated calorie coefficient.

For hired laborers annual caloric availability data are not directly available. Two approaches are pursued for estimation: the hired labor's calorie consumption is simply omitted, and a regional proxy variable is formed. Given the parameter normalization that is used in estimating the efficiency hours function (see eq. [5]), omitting hired labor's calorie consumption is equivalent to assuming equal consumption at the sample mean by all hired laborers. Forming a regional proxy allows for interregional variation in this measure. Since workers who hire themselves out are identified in the data, this proxy can be calculated as a weighted average of daily caloric availability per consumer equivalent (or per capita) of all households in a region. The weights used are the proportion of total regional hours hired out that comes from each household. This reduces the weighted-average caloric intake for hired laborers beneath the simple regional average since poorer households, which are larger, also tend to provide a proportionately greater amount of labor sold out.

If predicted household and hired labor caloric intakes covary positively within regions and if calories do indeed enhance labor productivity, then estimates of the household's calorie coefficient(s) will be biased upward.[17] Such a positive intraregional sorting of hired and household labor by nutrient intake might arise either if household and hired labor are complements in production, which seems unlikely, or because of a management enhancement effect of current or

---

[16] A study of nutrient consumption of households in Laguna, Philippines (Fabella 1982) reports a negative association between both husband's and wife's caloric intake relative to their children's, and husband's wage rate. This suggests a more egalitarian distribution with higher income. Behrman and Deolalikar (1985) report negligible responses of separate caloric intakes of adult males, adult females, boys, and girls to assets in a set of Indian households. If anything there was a slightly greater response to assets for the children, also consistent with a positive equality-wealth relationship. In a different context both Rosenzweig and Schultz (1982) and Sen and Sengupta (1983) find that landless households in India exhibit greater male-female child mortality rate differentials than do landed households. Other asset variables add very little explanation, however.

[17] Although this strictly applies to only a linear model, the logic seems applicable in this nonlinear model as well. Note that the correlation has to be within regions for the argument to apply to the estimates that use the regional proxy for hired labor's calories.

past nutrition, with management and hired labor being complementary.[18] If positive nutritional sorting did exist, then wage rates should vary positively with current nutrient intake, since there would have to be an incentive for better-fed employers to attract better-fed workers. However, wage differentials need not imply positive sorting. Unfortunately, there is no direct evidence on either the sorting or wage differential question for this sample.[19]

What is known about rural labor markets in Sierra Leone bears indirectly but inconclusively on this question. Sierra Leone is characterized by active rural labor markets (see Spencer [1979] for details) with approximately 15 percent of labor hours hired in. Much hiring is reciprocal, with payment either in cash or in kind (including meals in the field eaten with household workers). Payment in meals could reflect a recognition of nutritional-productivity effects, but it is also consistent with other hypotheses, such as economizing on travel time to and from fields, which are often far from homes. Landless laborers are virtually nonexistent in Sierra Leone, as in much of West Africa, so hired workers are themselves farmers who work only limited amounts of time (under 15 percent of labor supply) for hire. They tend not to work for the same household over long periods of time but move from one farmer's fields to another's (Spencer 1979). Most hired laborers, roughly 87 percent, are paid by the day. Payment by task is not the norm, but is confined to male laborers engaging in brushing, tree felling, or swamp digging, all very physical activities. Wage rates (including in-kind payments) vary by season, by sex, and by region, but not by job performed. Thus if better-fed workers work at more demanding tasks, which are paid better, this does not show up in the data.

IV. Functional Form Specification and Results

The agricultural production function estimated is a Cobb-Douglas function with effective family labor, effective hired labor, capital, and land as inputs (see App. for variable definitions). The production elasticities are allowed to vary linearly with the percentage of cultivated land that is upland. This is an attempt to capture differences in land quality between swamps and uplands and may also capture

---

[18] It seems likely that past nutritional intake, together with education and other human capital investments, would have more of an allocative impact than current intake. However, current intake is likely to proxy for past intake as well.

[19] Using a sample of Indian agricultural workers, Deolalikar (1984) reports a weak correlation between earnings and worker weight for height from a two-stage least-squares (2SLS) regression with demographic variables as instruments.

some output composition effects since swamps tend to produce rice in pure stands while uplands tend to be intercropped (Spencer and Byerlee 1977, p. 18). This specification gives rise to the estimating equation

$$\log Q = \beta_1 + (\beta_2 + \beta_3 U)[\log L^f + \log h(X_c^f)]$$
$$+ (\beta_4 + \beta_5 U)[\log L^h + \log h(X_c^h)] \tag{4}$$
$$+ (\beta_6 + \beta_7 U)\log K + (\beta_8 + \beta_9 U)\log A + \beta_{10} U + \epsilon,$$

where $U \equiv$ upland as a percentage of cultivated acreage, the β's are parameters, and ϵ is an independent, identically distributed (iid) error term with zero mean and constant variance.

The specification reported here for the efficiency per hours worked function is quadratic in daily calories per consumer equivalent (or per capita), normalized so that the function value equals one when calories consumed equals the mean for the sample:

$$h(X_c^i) = 1 + \alpha_1\left(\frac{X_c^i}{\overline{X}_c^f} - 1\right) + \alpha_2\left[\left(\frac{X_c^i}{\overline{X}_c^f}\right)^2 - 1\right], \quad i = f, h. \tag{5}$$

This specification is reasonably flexible, even allowing for a range of negative productivity effects at high levels of food intake. It does not allow for both convex and concave portions, but it is likely that observed values would be on the concave portion of the curve since that is the more relevant economic region. The normalization allows a ready interpretation of the computed value of $h(\cdot)$ at different caloric consumption levels as the efficiency of a labor hour relative to that for the sample representative worker. It has the further advantage that $h(\cdot)$ equals one if the calorie coefficients are zero, so the usual agricultural production function is a special case of the one hypothesized here. Other functional forms for $h(\cdot)$ were used in estimation including a cubic function, which showed very little statistical improvement over the quadratic and log-reciprocal and log-log functions.[20] In addition, a Cobb-Douglas specification was estimated in which family and hired labor are permitted to be perfect substitutes, but with different efficiency weights. All estimates show the same broad patterns.

The basic set of instrumental variables used appears in appendix table A1, along with their summary statistics.[21] The regional average

---

[20] All were normalized in the same way as the quadratic. The log-reciprocal specification, $\log h = -\alpha[(\overline{X}_c^f/X_c^f) - 1]$ reported in Strauss (1984), forces $h(\cdot)$ to be sigmoid in shape.

[21] These instruments are output price, rice price, root crop and other cereal price, oils and fats price, fish and animal product price, miscellaneous foods price, nonfoods price, male adult wage, wage squared, hired labor calorie consumption, hired labor calorie consumption squared, capital stock, upland, land, capital × upland, land × upland, household size, and number of adults.

NUTRITION AND FARM PRODUCTIVITY   309

caloric consumption of hired labor and its square are included in this instrument set, which is equivalent to assuming a pool of labor available to the household for hiring that the household cannot affect. This assumption is relaxed later.

Taking the logarithm of a quadratic function introduces nonlinearity in both parameters and variables into the estimating equation, for which nonlinear two-stage least squares (NL2SLS) is used (see Amemiya 1983).[22] Estimates for the production function (eq. [4]) using the basic instrument set are provided in table 1. The first column gives a linear two-stage least-squares estimate of the Cobb-Douglas function when no calorie variable is included, the family and hired labor variables being treated endogenously. Column 2 contains the NL2SLS estimates with the quadratic effective labor hours function, while the third column repeats the estimation after the jointly insignificant upland and land-upland interaction variables are dropped.[23] Column 4 uses the per capita calorie availability measure for both household and hired labor, but is otherwise the same regression as column 3.

In all three cases in which they are included both the calorie and calorie squared coefficients are significant at more than the .01 level, with calorie consumption contributing positively to output (see table 3). Coefficients of other production function inputs are all significant at the .025 level (col. 3), in contrast to the estimates that omit the calorie variables for which only the family labor and upland variables have asymptotic standard normal statistics of over one.

It is possible that the calorie variables are picking up the effects of other human capital variables. This is explored by repeating the regressions and entering years of English and Islamic education (most respondents had none) into the family effective labor function as well as household head's age and age squared. The coefficients of these human capital variables are completely insignificant, while the calorie coefficients remain highly significant. The remaining coefficients are quite close in magnitude to those reported in table 1.

The fact that only a very crude proxy, percentage upland, is available for land quality could also bias upward the calorie coefficients. Another variable that is related to land quality and available in the data is the average age of bush on fallowed land. To the extent that better-quality land is cultivated more extensively, one would expect that less time in fallow would be allowed, so that a lower average age

[22] Quadratic terms and interactions of exogenous variables can be used as instruments in NL2SLS in addition to levels. The only such term used in this study is wage squared. Other terms resulted in a numerically singular cross-product matrix of instruments. The Davidon-Fletcher-Powell algorithm as available in the Fair-Parke program (see Fair 1984) was used to minimize the objective function.
[23] The Wald test statistic (χ^2 with 2 df) is 1.86.

TABLE 1

AGRICULTURAL PRODUCTION FUNCTIONS: QUADRATIC EFFECTIVE LABOR FUNCTIONS

Variable	(1)	(2)	(3)	(4)*
Constant	−4.21	−.23	1.22	1.39
	(−1.7)	(−.1)	(1.2)	(1.2)
Effective labor function:				
Calories[†]	...	1.35	1.33	1.12
		(4.2)	(4.5)	(4.4)
Calories squared[†]	...	−.41	−.39	−.30
		(−3.2)	(−2.8)	(−4.4)
Family labor[†]	1.61	1.19	.95	.91
	(4.6)	(4.4)	(5.2)	(4.7)
Family labor × upland[†]	−1.89	−1.04	−.53	−.67
	(−3.4)	(−2.3)	(−2.2)	(1.9)
Hired labor[†]	−.27	−.49	−.49	−.41
	(−.9)	(−1.7)	(−2.1)	(−2.3)
Hired labor × upland[†]	.48	1.03	.99	1.15
	(.9)	(2.1)	(2.7)	(2.7)
Capital	.02	.23	.40	.40
	(.1)	(1.1)	(2.7)	(2.3)
Capital × upland	.004	−.38	−.59	−.63
	(.01)	(−1.4)	(−2.9)	(−2.8)
Land	.2	.36	.26	.28
	(.9)	(1.7)	(2.5)	(2.3)
Land × upland	.2	−.14	...	...
	(.6)	(−.5)		
Upland	11.69	3.00	...	...
	(2.8)	(1.1)		
Function value	2.60	2.80	3.33	4.59
Regression standard error	.59	.54	.51	.56
R^2	.35	.47	.52	.42
Minimum χ^2 test	7.47	9.60	12.80	14.64
statistic[‡]	[4]	[7]	[9]	[9]

NOTE.—Asymptotic standard normal statistics in parentheses; degrees of freedom are in square brackets.
* Calories per person used instead of per consumer equivalent.
[†] Endogenous variable.
[‡] Defined as $e'Z(Z'Z)^{-1}Z'e/\hat{\sigma}^2$, where e is the vector of estimated residuals, Z is the matrix of instruments, and $\hat{\sigma}^2$ is the estimated regression variance.

of bush would result. When this variable is entered linearly into an effective land function, similar to the effective labor function, its coefficient is just significant at the .1 level, but once again the other coefficients do not change very much.[24]

The estimates in table 1 all use farm assets, household size, and number of adults as instrumental variables. If there exist time-persistent household effects that are unobserved and are correlated with these variables, then these estimates would be inconsistent. Such

[24] The calorie and calorie squared coefficients are 1.37 and −0.39, respectively, with standard normal statistics of 5.1 and −3.1.

NUTRITION AND FARM PRODUCTIVITY 311

household effects, or heterogeneity, might include managerial ability. Even without this heterogeneity the household size and number of adults variables could possibly be endogenous since households with higher incomes might attract more family members to live with them. Since extended families are important in Sierra Leone, this should be considered. In addition, the proxy variable for hired labor's caloric intake, the regional average variable, and its square were included in the instrument set. This may be objectionable since their inclusion would correspond to the underlying model only if hired labor's calorie consumption were exogenous to the hiring household, which may not be the case.[25]

The existence of correlation between the instruments and residuals is tested by using a generalized method of moments specification test (Hansen 1982; Newey 1983), which examines how close the cross-products of instrumental variables and residuals are to zero when evaluated at the estimated parameter values.[26] If the instruments are truly uncorrelated with the unobserved disturbances, then these cross-products of estimated residuals with instruments ought to be close to zero.[27] This specification test is general in that rejection can occur for more than one reason, for example, endogeneity of instruments or omitted variables. Results from these tests are reported in the last row of table 1 labeled "minimum χ^2 test statistic." The statistics are asymptotically distributed as χ^2 variables with degrees of freedom equal to the number of overidentifying instruments. The statistics from columns 2 and 3, the major ones of interest here, have probability values of roughly .2.[28] They are, therefore, not significant at standard levels. Nevertheless, it is still of some interest to examine the robustness of the results to a reduced instrument set.

Table 2 contains reestimates of column 3 from table 1 while systematically dropping groups of instruments. When the regional hired

[25] Dropping these variables from the instrument list does not solve the problem that hired labor's caloric intake is assumed to be homogeneous within regions, whereas it is almost certainly not. The issue here is still whether systematic sorting of well-nourished hired labor with well-nourished hiring households exists.

[26] The statistic is $e'Z(Z'Z)^{-1}Z'e/\hat{\sigma}^2$, where e is the vector of estimated residuals, Z is the matrix of instrumental variables, and $\hat{\sigma}^2$ is the estimated regression variance. Since the numerator is the minimized value of the objective function used by NL2SLS, this statistic is readily computed from standard computer output. In contrast, a Durbin-Wu-Hausman specification test based on the difference between estimates using the full and reduced instrument sets is complicated to compute for this case. This is because the covariance matrix of the difference is not simply the difference of the two covariance matrices, as in more typical examples, but also depends on the covariance between the two estimators.

[27] Of course, it is necessary that the number of instruments exceed the number of parameters for the cross-products not to be set to zero by the estimation procedure.

[28] The analogous test statistics from the log-reciprocal specifications also have probability levels near .2.

TABLE 2

AGRICULTURAL PRODUCTION FUNCTIONS WITH VARYING INSTRUMENT SET

Variable	(1)	(2)	(3)	(4)
Constant	1.28	1.09	.38	.26
	(1.1)	(.8)	(.2)	(.2)
Effective labor function:				
Calories	1.58*[†]	1.57*[†]	1.05*[†]	.74[†]
	(8.9)	(8.3)	(1.4)	(2.5)
Calories squared	−.49*[†]	−.44*[†]	−.20*[†]	...
	(−8.4)	(−3.0)	(−.4)	
Family labor	.96[†]	1.10[†]	1.00[†]	.97[†]
	(4.9)	(4.8)	(3.4)	(3.2)
Family labor × upland	−.52[†]	−.47[†]	−.22[†]	−.23[†]
	(−1.7)	(−1.4)	(−.4)	(−.4)
Hired labor	−.47[†]	−.67[†]	−.81[†]	−.81[†]
	(−2.0)	(−2.5)	(−2.3)	(−2.2)
Hired labor × upland	.92[†]	.86[†]	1.27[†]	1.31[†]
	(2.1)	(1.8)	(1.9)	(1.9)
Capital	.33	.38	1.16[†]	1.27[†]
	(1.8)	(2.0)	(2.2)	(2.9)
Capital × upland	−.55	−.51	−1.83[†]	−1.88[†]
	(−2.3)	(−2.0)	(−2.5)	(−2.6)
Land	.29	.32	.002[†]	−.05[†]
	(2.4)	(2.6)	(.01)	(−.2)
Function value	3.10	1.33	.02	.09
Regression standard error	.57	.61	.66	.68
R^2	.41	.31	.19	.15
Minimum χ^2 test	9.7	3.55	.05	.2
statistic[‡]	[7]	[5]	[1]	[2]

NOTE.—Asymptotic standard normal statistics in parentheses; degrees of freedom are in square brackets. Instruments dropped from col. 1 are regional hired labor calorie consumption and its square; from col. 2, hired labor calories, household size, and number of adults; from cols. 3 and 4, hired labor calories, capital, land, capital × upland, land × upland, household size, and number of adults.

  * Jointly significant at the .01 level.
  [†] Endogenous variable.
  [‡] See table 1 for formula.

labor calorie variable and its square are dropped from the instrument set (col. 1), the coefficients are not substantially changed, although the fit worsens somewhat. The specification test of orthogonality between residuals and instruments still has a probability value of .2. These estimates are extremely close to those that drop the hired labor calorie variable, which are therefore not reported here. The equation fit worsens still more when the household demographic variables are in addition dropped as instruments (col. 2); however, the coefficient estimates are almost identical to those in column 1, with the calorie coefficients retaining significance at less than the .01 level. Note now that the specification test statistic has become quite insignificant, its probability value rising to .6. Columns 3 and 4 drop the farm asset variables as well. The calorie coefficients remain jointly significant at the .01 level or less (Wald statistic of 9.52), as also evidenced by the linear specification, although the terms in the quadratic specification now lose individual significance. While the magnitudes of the calorie coefficients change for the quadratic $h(\cdot)$ function, the elasticity of $h(\cdot)$ with respect to family calories actually rises a little, compared with the base line estimates from table 1, from .55 to .65 when both farm and household assets are dropped.[29] The land coefficient becomes insignificant and its magnitude drops considerably when the farm asset instruments are omitted. Apparently the remaining instruments predict little of the variation in land input, as evidenced by the large drop in R^2. The hired labor and capital output elasticities change by only a small amount. Dropping both farm asset and demographic variables from the instrument set has lowered the specification test statistic to well under .5.[30]

In sum, the household calorie consumption seems a statistically significant determinant of farm output. While the statistical evidence of possible endogeneity of farm assets and household demographic measures is very weak, even allowing explicitly for that possibility, calorie consumption remains quite significant. How important this relation is in economic terms is the next question to be discussed.

V. Implications

To interpret the coefficients the implied output elasticities and marginal products are first considered. Table 3 reports them using the estimates from column 3 of table 1. Other specifications provide broadly similar patterns. The estimates show roughly constant returns to scale. Interestingly, the 2SLS estimates without the effective labor function (col. 1) imply a returns to scale of .8. The largest change in output elasticities occurs for family labor, which drops to .42. Apparently, with other inputs held constant, households demanding more family labor have a lower equivalent caloric intake per consumer, which biases family labor's coefficients downward.

The marginal products of family and hired labor are fairly close and not significantly different (the standard error of the difference is .45). Both are very close to the sample mean real wage, which is .29.

Family caloric intake has a sizable, statistically significant, output

---

[29] At the sample mean this elasticity equals $\alpha_1 + 2\alpha_2$ (see eq. [5]), where α_1 is the coefficient on calories and α_2 the coefficient on its square.

[30] Estimates were also made by dropping the farm asset variables while retaining household size and number of adults. Coefficient estimates and their standard errors are very close to those of cols. 3 and 4.

TABLE 3

OUTPUT ELASTICITIES AND MARGINAL PRODUCTS AT SAMPLE MEAN

Input	Elasticity	Marginal Product
Household calorie consumption	.33	.19
	(.11)	(.07)
Household labor hours	.60	.32
	(.18)	(.10)
Hired labor hours	.13	.40
	(.15)	(.44)
Capital	.03	2.06
	(.10)	(6.63)
Land	.26	85.40
	(.10)	(34.49)

NOTE.—Asymptotic standard errors in parentheses. Computed using estimates from col. 3 of table 1.

elasticity of .34.[31] The magnitude of this elasticity varies widely from low-consumption to high-consumption households. As the level of caloric intake reaches 4,500 per day, which is roughly the average intake of the upper third of the sample, the output elasticity falls to only .12. However, at a daily intake per consumer equivalent of 1,500 calories, which corresponds to the average for the lower third of the sample, the output elasticity rises to .49. This figure is remarkably close to the calorie output elasticity of .5 found for Kenyan road construction workers, with an average daily intake of 2,000 calories, in the experiment of Wolgemuth et al. (1982) (see n. 6).

The estimated efficiency units of labor function is plotted in figure 2. As indicated, $h(\cdot)$ reveals the relative efficiency of an hour of labor when compared with labor that consumes calories equal to the sample mean. The function reaches a peak at a daily intake per consumer equivalent of 5,200 calories, and thereafter calories have a negative impact on effective labor. The corresponding value of $h(\cdot)$ is 1.2. Roughly 12 percent of the sample (15 households) have an estimated daily caloric intake per consumer equivalent above this level. This is an extremely large intake level for calories to have a positive effect; however, the effective labor function is flat by the level of 4,500 calories per day ($h[\cdot]$ is 1.17), which is roughly the average intake of the upper third of the sample. Indeed this function rises very gently after 3,750 calories (h being 1.1). The flattening of the effective labor function is also apparent by noting the decline in the elasticity of $h(\cdot)$ with respect to calories from .55 at the sample mean intake to .23 at 4,500 calories per day. For households with low levels of calorie con-

[31] Calorie elasticities and marginal products from the log-reciprocal specifications of the effective labor function are lower, .18 and .10, respectively.

NUTRITION AND FARM PRODUCTIVITY

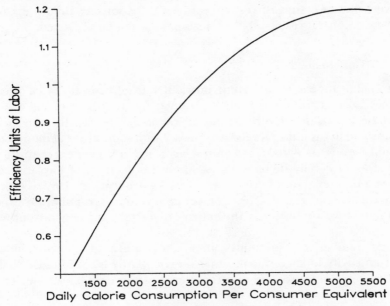

FIG. 2.—Estimated efficiency labor function

sumption per consumer equivalent $h(\cdot)$ rises much more steeply. At an intake of 1,500 calories the calorie elasticity is .75. The level of $h(\cdot)$ is roughly .6, implying that the hourly efficiency of family labor is on the order of 60 percent of the efficiency of a family worker from a representative family.

A different effect may be seen by looking at the first-order condition for food consumption (see n. 14). An increase in caloric intake per consumer equivalent is equivalent to a proportionate reduction in the effective price of food. Taking rice, the staple food in Sierra Leone, and ignoring the effect of higher caloric intake on clock hour wages or on total non–sick time available to the household, these results suggest that at the sample mean a percentage increase in rice consumption will reduce the effective price of rice by 42 percent.[32] Again those percentages vary by level of caloric intake, being in the range of 90 percent for an intake of 1,500 daily calories per consumer equivalent and 15 percent at 4,500 calories. Now clearly these figures are large, especially for the poorer households, although other specifications of $h(\cdot)$ result in somewhat smaller magnitudes.[33] How-

[32] This is calculated assuming a conversion of 3,743 calories per kg of rice, converting this annual figure to a daily per consumer equivalent and multiplying by the marginal product of family calories from table 3.

[33] The log-reciprocal specification of $h(\cdot)$ results in a percentage decline of 22 percent, which still seems large.

ever, they are suggestive, and given the reasonable robustness of these empirical results, these effects should not be dismissed.

VI. Conclusions

It would appear that current nutrient intake, proxied by calories, does raise current farm labor productivity in rural Sierra Leone. These effects seem very strong at low intake levels, dropping off substantially as intake levels rise, but still with some effect at moderate intake levels. As noted, agricultural labor in Sierra Leone is characterized as physically demanding, so these results are not implausible. The effect explored here, however, is a pure worker effect. To the extent that allocative effects of better nutrition are important, the results have understated the impact of better nutrition on output supply.

A number of questions about the nature of the nutrition-productivity linkage remain unanswered, partly because individual-level nutrient intake and anthropometric data were unavailable. The analysis has proceeded on the assumption that current, annual caloric intake directly causes higher productivity. However, current calorie flows are probably correlated with accumulated stocks, such as measured by height or weight, which may have independent effects on productivity. More generally, health may have an impact on productivity and also be correlated with current caloric intake. Thus it is not clear from these estimates how much low-nutrient intake during childhood affects labor efficiency versus current intake or related health outcomes. For policy design this would be useful to know. Individual-level data on nutrient intake and anthropometric or clinical health variables might help economists answer these questions. It is also plausible that the impact of nutrient intake differs by male, female, or child labor and that it has a different impact on home production than on farm production or market earnings. Finally, other studies will have to establish how strong the nutrition-productivity links may be in developing countries with either a greater capital intensity of agriculture production or higher income levels or both.

NUTRITION AND FARM PRODUCTIVITY 317

Appendix

TABLE A1

Sample Summary Statistics

	Mean	Standard Deviation
Endogenous variables:		
Farm output quantity index (kg)	2,295.2	1,844.4
Daily family calories per consumer equivalent	3,061.0	1,811.4
Daily family calories per capita	2,434.7	1,610.9
Hours of family labor	3,898.2	2,122.0
Hours of hired labor	816.5	620.8
Exogenous variables:		
Daily hired labor calories per consumer equivalent	2,788.4	1,242.7
Output price index*	.27	.06
Rice price index*	.24	.05
Root crop and other cereal price index*	.58	.46
Oils and fats price index*	.66	.16
Fish and animal product price index*	.56	.31
Miscellaneous foods price index*	.60	.19
Nonfoods price index*	.64	.09
Male adult wage (leones per hour)	.08	.03
Capital stock (in leones)	34.4	31.6
Land cultivated (in acres)	6.8	4.5
Upland as a percentage of land cultivated	.63	.37
Household size	6.3	3.7
Persons 11 years and older	4.4	2.2
Average age of bush in fields (in years)	7.8	6.8
Number of consumer equivalents	4.7	2.4
Years of English education of household head	.4	1.5
Years of Islamic education of household head	1.6	4.1
Age of household head	50.9	15.0

* Leones per kg. For definitions of commodity groups see Strauss (1982), table A.1.

References

Amemiya, Takeshi. "Nonlinear Regression Models." In *Handbook of Econometrics*, vol. 1, edited by Zvi Griliches and Michael Intriligator. Amsterdam: North-Holland, 1983.

Baldwin, Robert E., and Weisbrod, Burton A. "Disease and Labor Productivity." *Econ. Development and Cultural Change* 22 (April 1974): 414–35.

Basta, Samir S.; Soekirman; Karyadi, Darwin; and Scrimshaw, Nevin S. "Iron Deficiency Anemia and the Productivity of Adult Males in Indonesia." *American J. Clinical Nutrition* 32 (April 1979): 916–25.

Behrman, Jere, and Deolalikar, Anil. "How Do Food and Product Prices Affect Nutrient Intakes, Health and Labor Force Behavior for Different Family Members in Rural India?" Manuscript. Philadelphia: Univ. Pennsylvania, 1985.

Binswanger, Hans P., and Rosenzweig, Mark R. "Contractual Arrangements, Employment, and Wages in Rural Labor Markets: A Critical Review." In *Contractual Arrangements, Employment, and Wages in Rural Labor Markets in*

Asia, edited by Hans P. Binswanger and Mark R. Rosenzweig. New Haven, Conn.: Yale Univ. Press, 1984.

Bliss, Christopher, and Stern, Nicholas. "Productivity, Wages and Nutrition: Part I: The Theory." *J. Development Econ.* 5 (December 1978): 331–62. (*a*)

————. "Productivity, Wages and Nutrition: Part II: Some Observations." *J. Development Econ.* 5 (December 1978): 363–98. (*b*)

Deolalikar, Anil. "Are There Pecuniary Returns to Health in Agricultural Work? An Econometric Analysis of Agricultural Wages and Farm Productivity in Rural South India." Economic Program Progress Report no. 38. Hyderabad, India: Internat. Crops Res. Inst. Semi-Arid Tropics, 1984.

Fabella, Raul. "Economies of Scale in the Household Production Model and Intra-Family Allocation of Resources." Ph.D. dissertation, Yale Univ., 1982.

Fair, Ray C. *Specification, Estimation, and Analysis of Macroeconometric Models.* Cambridge, Mass.: Harvard Univ. Press, 1984.

Food and Agricultural Organization. "Calorie Requirements: Report of the Second Committee on Calorie Requirements." Nutritional Studies no. 15. Rome: Food and Agricultural Org., 1957.

————. *Food Composition Table for Use in Africa.* Rome: Food and Agricultural Org., 1968.

Gersovitz, Mark. "Savings and Nutrition at Low Incomes." *J.P.E.* 91 (October 1983): 841–55.

Grossman, Michael. "On the Concept of Health Capital and the Demand for Health." *J.P.E.* 80 (March/April 1972): 223–55.

Hansen, Lars Peter. "Large Sample Properties of Generalized Method of Moments Estimators." *Econometrica* 50 (July 1982): 1029–54.

Immink, Maarten D. C., and Viteri, Fernando E. "Energy Intake and Productivity of Guatemalan Sugarcane Cutters: An Empirical Test of the Efficiency Wage Hypothesis—Part I." *J. Development Econ.* 9 (October 1981): 251–71. (*a*)

————. "Energy Intake and Productivity of Guatemalan Sugarcane Cutters: An Empirical Test of the Efficiency Wage Hypothesis—Part II." *J. Development Econ.* 9 (October 1981): 273–87. (*b*)

Immink, Maarten D. C.; Viteri, Fernando E.; and Helms, Ronald W. "Energy Intake over the Life Cycle and Human Capital Formation in Guatemalan Sugarcane Cutters." *Econ. Development and Cultural Change* 30 (January 1982): 351–72.

Keys, Ancel B.; Brožek, Josef; Henschel, Austin; Mickelsen, Olaf; and Taylor, Henry L. *The Biology of Human Starvation.* Minneapolis: Univ. Minnesota Press, 1950.

Kraut, H. A., and Muller, E. A. "Calorie Intake and Industrial Output." *Science* 104 (November 29, 1946): 495–97.

Latham, Michael. "The Relationship of Nutrition to Productivity and Wellbeing of Workers." Manuscript. Ithaca, N.Y.: Cornell Univ., 1985.

Lau, Lawrence J. "Applications of Profit Functions." In *Production Economics: A Dual Approach to Theory and Applications*, vol. 1, *The Theory of Production*, edited by Melvyn Fuss and Daniel McFadden. Amsterdam: North-Holland, 1978.

Leibenstein, Harvey. *Economic Backwardness and Economic Growth.* New York: Wiley, 1957.

Martorell, Reynaldo, and Arroyave, Guillermo. "Malnutrition, Work Output and Energy Needs." Manuscript. Stanford, Calif.: Stanford Univ., 1984.

NUTRITION AND FARM PRODUCTIVITY   3¹9

Mazumdar, Dipak. "The Marginal Productivity Theory of Wages and Disguised Unemployment." *Rev. Econ. Studies* 26 (June 1959): 190–97.
Mirrlees, James A. "A Pure Theory of Underdeveloped Economies." In *Agriculture in Development Theory*, edited by Lloyd G. Reynolds. New Haven, Conn.: Yale Univ. Press, 1975.
Newey, Whitney. "Generalized Methods of Moments Specification Testing." Econometric Research Program Memorandum no. 306. Princeton, N.J.: Princeton Univ., Dept. Econ., 1983.
Pitt, Mark M. "Food Preferences and Nutrition in Rural Bangladesh." *Rev. Econ. and Statis.* 65 (February 1983): 105–14.
Pitt, Mark M., and Rosenzweig, Mark R. "Agricultural Prices, Food Consumption and the Health and Productivity of Farmers." In *Agricultural Household Models: Extensions, Applications and Policy*, edited by Inderjit Singh, Lyn Squire, and John Strauss. Baltimore: Johns Hopkins Univ. Press, 1986.
Popkin, Barry M. "Nutrition and Labor Productivity." *Soc. Sci. and Medicine* 12C (November 1978): 117–25.
Rodgers, Gerry B. "Nutritionally Based Wage Determination in the Low-Income Labour Market." *Oxford Econ. Papers* 27 (March 1975): 61–81.
Rosenzweig, Mark R., and Schultz, T. Paul. "Market Opportunities, Genetic Endowments, and Intrafamily Resource Distribution: Child Survival in Rural India." *A.E.R.* 72 (September 1982): 803–15.
Sen, Amartya, and Sengupta, Sunil. "Malnutrition of Rural Children and the Sex Bias." *Econ. and Polit. Weekly* 18 (May 1983): 855–64.
Singh, Inderjit; Squire, Lyn; and Strauss, John, eds. *Agricultural Household Models: Extensions, Applications and Policy.* Baltimore: Johns Hopkins Univ. Press, 1986.
Spencer, Dunstan S. C. "Labour Market Organisation, Wage Rates and Employment in Rural Areas of Sierra Leone." *Labour and Soc.* 4 (July 1979): 293–308.
Spencer, Dunstan S. C., and Byerlee, Derek. "Small Farms in West Africa: A Descriptive Analysis of Employment, Incomes and Productivity in Sierra Leone." Working Paper no. 19. Lansing: Michigan State Univ., African Rural Econ. Program, 1977.
Spurr, G. B. "Nutritional Status and Physical Work Capacity." *Yearbook Physical Anthropology* 26 (1983): 1–35.
Stiglitz, Joseph E. "The Efficiency Wage Hypothesis, Surplus Labour, and the Distribution of Income in L.D.C.s." *Oxford Econ. Papers* 28 (July 1976): 185–207.
———. "Alternative Theories of Wage Determination and Unemployment: The Efficiency Wage Model." In *The Theory and Experience of Economic Development: Essays in Honor of Sir W. Arthur Lewis*, edited by Mark Gersovitz, Carlos Diaz-Alejandro, Gustav Ranis, and Mark R. Rosenzweig. London: Allen & Unwin, 1982.
Strauss, John. "Determinants of Food Consumption in Rural Sierra Leone: Application of the Quadratic Expenditure System to the Consumption-Leisure Component of a Household-Firm Model." *J. Development Econ.* 11 (December 1982): 327–53.
———. "Does Better Nutrition Raise Farm Productivity?" Discussion Paper no. 457. New Haven, Conn.: Yale Univ., Econ. Growth Center, 1984.
———. "The Impact of Improved Nutrition on Labor Productivity and Hu-

man Resource Development: An Economic Perspective." Manuscript. New Haven, Conn.: Yale Univ., 1985.

Sukhatme, P. V., and Margen, Sheldon. "Autoregulatory Homeostatic Nature of Energy Balance." *American J. Clinical Nutrition* 35 (February 1982): 355–65.

Viteri, Fernando E. "Considerations on the Effect of Nutrition on the Body Composition and Physical Working Capacity of Young Guatemalan Adults." In *Amino Acid Fortification of Protein Foods,* edited by Nevin S. Scrimshaw and Aaron M. Altschul. Cambridge, Mass.: MIT Press, 1971.

Weisbrod, Burton A., and Helminiak, Thomas W. "Parasitic Diseases and Agricultural Labor Productivity." *Econ. Development and Cultural Change* 25 (April 1977): 505–22.

Weiss, Andrew. "Job Queues and Layoffs in Labor Markets with Flexible Wages." *J.P.E.* 88 (June 1980): 526–38.

Wolgemuth, June C.; Latham, Michael C.; Hall, Andrew; Chesher, Andrew; and Crompton, D. W. T. "Worker Productivity and the Nutritional Status of Kenyan Road Construction Laborers." *American J. Clinical Nutrition* 36 (July 1982): 68–78.

Yellen, Janet L. "Efficiency Wage Models of Unemployment." *A.E.R. Papers and Proc.* 74 (May 1984): 200–205.

[9]

Economic Growth, Population Theory, and Physiology: The Bearing of Long-Term Processes on the Making of Economic Policy[†]

By ROBERT W. FOGEL*

Economic history has contributed significantly to the formulation of economic theory. Among the economists who have found history an important source for their ideas are Adam Smith, Thomas R. Malthus, Karl Marx, Alfred Marshall, John Maynard Keynes, John R. Hicks, Kenneth J. Arrow, Milton Friedman, Robert M. Solow, and Gary S. Becker. Failure to take account of history, as Simon Kuznets (1941) stressed, has often led to a misunderstanding of current economic problems by investigators who have not realized that their generalizations rested upon transient circumstances. Nowhere is the need to recognize the role of long-run dynamics more relevant than in such pressing current issues as medical care, pension policies, and development policies.

This lecture sketches a theory of the secular decline in morbidity and mortality that takes account of changes induced in physiological functioning since 1700. The synergism between technological and physiological improvements has produced a form of human evolution, biological though not genetic, rapid, culturally transmitted, and not necessarily stable, which is still ongoing in both OECD and developing countries. Thermodynamic and physiological aspects of economic growth are defined and their impact on growth rates is assessed. Implications of this theory for population forecasting, measurement of national income, demand for leisure, pension policies, and demand for health care are considered.

The attempt to explain the secular decline in mortality in a systematic way did not begin until after World War I because before that time it was uncertain whether such a decline was in progress. There were two reasons for the delay in recognizing the phenomenon. First, little was known about mortality rates before the end of the Napoleonic wars. Hardly a dozen life tables had been constructed before 1815 by various pioneers in demography, and they exhibited no clear time trend (Louis I. Dublin and Alfred J. Lotka, 1936; H. Gille, 1949). Second, there was little evidence in the first four official English life tables, covering the years 1831–1880, of a downward trend in mortality.

[†]This article is the lecture Robert W. Fogel delivered in Stockholm, Sweden, December 9, 1993, when he received the Alfred Nobel Memorial Prize in Economic Sciences. The article is copyright © The Nobel Foundation 1993 and is published here with the permission of the Nobel Foundation.

*Graduate School of Business, University of Chicago, 1101 East 58th Street, Chicago, IL 60637. Since this lecture is based on research still in progress, it is important to emphasize that the findings reported here are provisional and are subject to change as the current data bases expand and as the analyses of these data are refined. Nevertheless, I believe that the general outlines of the emerging new theories of mortality, morbidity, and aging are likely to survive further research. Research reported in this paper was supported by grants from the National Institutes of Health (No. PO1-AG10120-02), the National Science Foundation (No. SES-9114981), and the Walgreen Foundation. I have benefited from comments and criticisms by Christopher J. Acito, Robert M. Adams, Gary S. Becker, Christine K. Cassel, Katherine A. Chavigny, Dora L. Costa, William J. Darby, Partha Dasgupta, Sidney Davidson, Stanley L. Engerman, Phyllis Eveleth, Enid M. Fogel, Milton Friedman, Victor R. Fuchs, Zvi Griliches, Robin M. Hogarth, Susan E. Jones, John M. Kim, Peter Laslett, Lionel W. McKenzie, Reynaldo Martorell, Douglass C. North, S. Jay Olshansky, Clayne L. Pope, Samuel H. Preston, Irwin Rosenberg, Roger A. Schofield, Nevin S. Scrimshaw, Robert M. Solow, Richard H. Steckel, David Surdam, Richard Suzman, James M. Tanner, Peter Temin, James Trussell, James W. Vaupel, Hans T. Waaler, Larry T. Wimmer, and E. A. Wrigley.

By the third decade of the 20th century, however, it became obvious that the new declines in British mortality rates were not just a cyclical phenomenon. Between 1871 and 1901 life expectation in Britain increased by four years. During the next three decades there was an additional gain of 16 years. Similar declines in mortality were recorded in other European nations.

The plunge in mortality rates during the early decades of the 20th century delivered a major blow to the Malthusian theory of population. Improvements in mortality were supposed to be short-lived because, under the conditions of population pressure against the food supply that Malthus specified, the elimination of deaths due to one disease would be replaced by those due to some other malady. Efforts to reconcile Malthusian doctrine with the observed mortality decline, to modify it, or to replace it produced a large new literature.

I. Explaining the Secular Decline in Mortality

The drive to explain the secular decline in mortality pushed research in three directions. First, there was a concerted effort to develop time series of death rates that extended as far back in time as possible in order to determine just when the decline in mortality began. Second, the available data on mortality rates were analyzed in order to identify factors that might explain the decline as well as to establish patterns or "laws" that would allow predictions of the future course of mortality.

Third, a widespread effort was undertaken to determine the relationship between the food supply and mortality rates. There were several aspects to this effort. Perhaps the most important was the emergence of a science of nutrition that identified a series of diseases related to specific nutritional deficiencies and discovered the synergy between nutrition and infection (Nevin S. Scrimshaw et al., 1968). Another aspect was the emergence of the field of development economics after World War II as part of the campaign to close the yawning gap in income, health, and life expectancy

between the industrialized nations and the "developing nations." Still another aspect was the combined effort of economic and demographic historians to study the role of mortality crises and their relationship to famines during the 17th and 18th centuries.

Prior to the 1960's, efforts to reconstruct the secular trend in European mortality were focused primarily on notable local communities and parishes. However, developments in statistical techniques and the remarkable reductions in computational costs during the 1960's and 1970's made it possible to draw and process large nationally representative samples. The results of these efforts, combined with official statistics after 1830 in France and after 1871 in England, are displayed in Figure 1. Analysis of the French and English series revealed that the secular decline in mortality took place in two waves. In the English case the first wave began during the second quarter of the 18th century (18-II) and lasted through 19-I after which mortality rates stabilized for half a century. The decline resumed during 19-IV and continues through the present. The French case is similar, except that the first wave of the decline in mortality began about half a century earlier in France, and its rate of decline during the first wave was more rapid.

Perhaps the most surprising aspect of Figure 1 is the implication that the elimination of crisis mortality, whether related to famines or not, accounted for less than 10 percent of the secular decline in mortality rates (Ronald Lee, 1981; E. A. Wrigley and R. S. Schofield, 1981; David R. Weir, 1982, 1989; Toni Richards, 1984; Patrick R. Galloway, 1986; Jacques Dupâquier, 1989; Fogel, 1992b). Similar results were obtained by studies of official statistics for Sweden (Tommy Bengtsson and Rolf Ohlsson, 1984, 1985; Galloway, 1987) (cf. Zvi Eckstein et al., 1984; Gunnar Fridlizius, 1984; Alfred Perrenoud, 1984, 1991). By demonstrating that famines and famine mortality are a secondary issue in the escape from the high mortality rates of the early modern era, these studies shifted attention to the neglected issue of chronic malnutrition as the

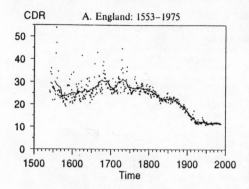

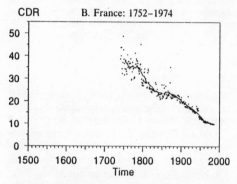

FIGURE 1. THE SECULAR TRENDS IN MORTALITY
RATES IN ENGLAND AND FRANCE

Note: Each diagram shows the scatter of annual death rates around a 25-year moving average. See Fogel and Roderick Floud (1994) for sources and procedures.

principal pathway through which malnutrition contributed to the high mortality rates of the past (cf. Amartya Sen, 1981).

II. The Synergy Between Biomedical and Economic Analyses of the Secular Trend in Chronic Malnutrition

Recently developed biomedical techniques, when integrated with economic techniques, make it possible to probe deeply into the extent of chronic malnutrition from the beginning of the 18th century in Europe and North America, to chart and explain the escape from such malnutrition, and to

consider the impact of improved nutrition on the secular trend in health and life expectation, on labor productivity, and on economic growth. The combination of the economic and biomedical modes of analysis has been synergistic, since it has yielded analytical insights that could not have been obtained merely by relying on the techniques of one of the disciplines.

Malnutrition can be caused either by an inadequate diet or by claims on that diet (including work and disease) so great as to produce malnutrition despite a nutrient intake that in other circumstances might be deemed adequate.[1] There can be little doubt that the high disease rates prevalent during the early modern era would have caused malnutrition even with diets otherwise adequate in calories, protein, and other critical nutrients. However, recent research indicates that, for many European nations before the middle of the 19th century, the national production of food was at such low levels that the poorer classes were bound to have been malnourished under any conceivable circumstance, and that the high disease rates of the period were not merely a cause of malnutrition but undoubtedly, to a considerable degree, a consequence of exceedingly poor diets.

A. Energy Cost Accounting and Secular Trends in Body Size

As a result of the work of agricultural historians we now have estimates of British

---

[1] Before proceeding with the discussion of chronic malnutrition it is necessary to clarify a terminological confusion that has misled some investigators: the distinction between the term "diet" or food intake (which represents gross nutrition) and the term "malnutrition" (which represents net nutrition, the nutrients available to sustain cellular growth). I will not dwell on this distinction here but will only emphasize that when I mean gross nutrition I will use the term "*diet*" and that such other terms as "*malnutrition*," "*undernutrition*," "*net nutrition*," and "*nutritional status*" are meant to designate the balance between the nutrient intake (diet) and the claims on that intake. See Fogel and Floud (1994) for a further elaboration of this distinction.

TABLE 1—ESTIMATED AVERAGE FINAL HEIGHTS OF MEN WHO REACHED
MATURITY BETWEEN 1750 AND 1875 IN SIX EUROPEAN POPULATIONS,
BY QUARTER CENTURIES

	Date of maturity by century and quarter	Height (cm)					
Row		Great Britain	Norway	Sweden	France	Denmark	Hungary
1	18-III	165.9	163.9	168.1	—	—	168.7
2	18-IV	167.9	—	166.7	163.0	165.7	165.8
3	19-I	168.0	—	166.7	164.3	165.4	163.9
4	19-II	171.6	—	168.0	165.2	166.8	164.2
5	19-III	169.3	168.6	169.5	165.6	165.3	—
6	20-III	175.0	178.3	177.6	172.0	176.0	170.9

Sources: Fogel (1987 table 7) for all countries except France. For France, rows 3–5 were computed from M. A. von Meerton (1989) as amended by Weir (1993), with 0.9 cm added to allow for additional growth between age 20 and maturity (Benjamin A. Gould, 1869 pp. 104–5) (cf. Gerald C. Friedman, 1982 p. 510 [footnote 14]). The entry to row 2 is derived from a linear extrapolation of Meerton's data for 1815–1836 back to 1788, with 0.9 cm added for additional growth between age 20 and maturity. The entry in row 6 is from Fogel (1987 table 7).

agricultural production by half-century in-tervals going back to 1700. These provide the basis for national food balance sheets which indicate the secular trend in British caloric consumption (J. A. Chartres, 1985; B. A. Holderness, 1989; R. C. Allen, 1994). Supplemented by household surveys of food purchases (Carole Shammas, 1984, 1990; D. J. Oddy, 1990) (cf. Fogel, 1987), these sources indicate that average daily caloric consumption in Britain circa 1790 was about 2,060 kcal per capita or about 2,700 kcal per consuming unit (equivalent adult males). For France, Jean-Claude Toutain (1971) has constructed estimates from national food balance sheets going back to the decade preceding the French Revolution. His esti-mates indicate that the daily per capita caloric consumption was 1,753 kcal during 1781–1790 and 1,846 kcal during 1803–1812. Converted into calories per consuming unit, these figures become 2,290 kcal and 2,410 kcal, respectively.

One implication of these estimates is that mature adults of the late 18th century must have been very small by current standards. Today the typical American male in his early thirties is about 177 cm (69.7 inches) tall and weighs about 78 kg (172 pounds) (U.S. Department of Health and Human Services [USDHHS], 1987). Such a male

requires daily about 1,794 kcal for basal metabolism (the energy required to keep the body functioning while at rest) and a total of 2,279 kcal for baseline maintenance (the 1,794 kcal required for basal metabo-lism plus 485 kcal for digestion of food and vital hygiene) (M. H. Quenouille et al., 1951; Food and Agriculture Organization of the United Nations, United Nations University, and World Health Organization [FAO/UNU/WHO], 1985). If either the British or the French had been that large during the 18th century, virtually all of the energy pro-duced by their food supplies would have been required for maintenance, and hardly any would have been available to sustain work. To have the energy necessary to pro-duce the national products of these two countries circa 1700, the typical adult male must have been quite short and very light.

This inference is supported by data on stature and weight which have been col-lected for European nations. Table 1 pro-vides estimates of final heights of adult males who reached maturity between 1750 and 1875. It shows that during the 18th and 19th centuries Europeans were severely stunted by modern standards (cf. line 6 of Table 1). Estimates of weights for European nations before 1860 are much more patchy. Those which are available, mostly inferential, suggest that circa 1790 the average weight of English males in their thirties was about 61 kg (134 pounds), which is about 20-percent below current levels. The corresponding figure for French males circa 1790 may have been only about 50 kg (about 110 pounds), which is about a third below current standards.

B. Size Distributions of Calories

The synergy between the economic and biomedical lines of analysis is apparent in the new insights obtained by switching from a reliance on the mean height, the mean weights, and the mean daily consumption of nutrients to the size distributions of these variables. Because of the limits of time, I focus here on the distributions of calories.[2]

Size distributions of caloric consumption are one of the most potent instruments in assessing the plausibility of proffered estimates of average diets. They not only bear on the implications of a given level of caloric consumption for morbidity and mortality rates, but they also indicate whether the calories available for work are consistent with the level of agricultural output and with the distribution of the labor force between agriculture and nonagriculture (Fogel, 1991; Fogel and Floud, 1994) (cf. Wrigley, 1987). Although national food balance sheets, such as those constructed by Toutain (1971) for France over the period 1781–1952, provide mean values of per capita caloric consumption, they do not produce estimates of the size distribution of calories.[3]

Three factors make it possible to estimate the size distributions of calories from the patchy evidence available to historians. First,

studies covering a wide range of countries indicate that distributions of calories are well described by the lognormal distribution. Second, the variation in the distribution of calories (as measured by the coefficient of variation $[s/\overline{X}]$ or the Gini $[G]$ ratio) is far more limited than the distribution of income. Third, when the mean of the distribution is known, the coefficient of variation (which together with the mean determines the distribution) can be estimated from information in either tail of the distribution. Fortunately, even in places and periods where little is known about ordinary people, there is a relative abundance of information about the rich. At the bottom end, it is demographic information, particularly the death rate, which rather tightly constrains the proportion of the population whose average daily consumption of calories could have been below basal metabolic rate (BMR) or baseline maintenance.

Table 2 shows the exceedingly low level of work capacity permitted by the food supply in France and England circa 1790, even after allowing for the reduced requirements for maintenance because of small stature and body mass (cf. Herman Freudenberger and Gaylord Cummins, 1976). In France the bottom 10 percent of the labor force lacked the energy for regular work, and the next 10 percent had enough energy for less than three hours of light work daily (0.52 hours of heavy work). Although the English situation was somewhat better, the bottom 3 percent of its labor force lacked the energy for any work, but the balance of the bottom 20 percent had enough energy for about 6 hours of light work (1.09 hours of heavy work) each day.

Table 2 also points up the problem with the assumption that for ancien régime populations, a daily caloric intake that averaged 2,000 kcal per capita (2,600 kcal per consuming unit) was adequate (Massimo Livi-Bacci, 1990). That average level of consumption falls between the levels experienced by the French and the English circa 1790. In populations experiencing such low levels of average consumption, the bottom 20 percent subsisted on such poor diets that they were effectively excluded from the

---

[2] See the appendix to Floud and Fogel (1994) for the estimated distributions of height, weight, and the body mass index (BMI) in France circa 1790.

[3] In principle it is possible to construct size distributions of calories from household consumption surveys. Inasmuch as most of these surveys during the 19th century were focused on the lower classes, in order to make use of them it is necessary to know from what centiles of either the national caloric or the national income distribution the surveyed households were drawn.

TABLE 2—A COMPARISON OF THE PROBABLE FRENCH AND ENGLISH DISTRIBUTIONS
OF THE DAILY CONSUMPTION OF KILOGRAM CALORIES PER CONSUMING UNIT
TOWARD THE END OF THE 18th CENTURY

Decile	France, circa 1785		England, circa 1790	
	Daily kcal consumption	Cumulative percentage	Daily kcal consumption	Cumulative percentage
Highest	3,672	100	4,329	100
Ninth	2,981	84	3,514	84
Eighth	2,676	71	3,155	71
Seventh	2,457	59	2,897	59
Sixth	2,276	48	2,684	48
Fifth	2,114	38	2,492	38
Fourth	1,958	29	2,309	29
Third	1,798	21	2,120	21
Second	1,614	13	1,903	13
First	1,310	6	1,545	6
$\bar{X}$:	2,290		2,700	
$s/\bar{X}$:	0.3		0.3	

Sources: See Fogel (1993b), especially table 4 and the appendix.

labor force, with many of them lacking the energy even for a few hours of strolling. That appears to be the principal factor explaining why beggars constituted as much as a fifth of the populations of ancien régimes (Pierre Goubert, 1973; Carlo M. Cipolla, 1980; Peter Laslett, 1984). Even the majority of those in the top 80 percent of the caloric distribution were so stunted (height below U.S. standards) and wasted (weight below U.S. standards) that they were at substantially higher risk of incurring chronic health conditions and of premature mortality (see the next section).

III. Waaler Curves and Surfaces: A New Analytical Tool

Extensive clinical and epidemiological studies over the past two decades have shown that height at given ages, weight at given ages, and weight-for-height (a body mass index, or BMI) are effective predictors of the risk of morbidity and mortality. Until recently most of the studies have focused on children under age 5, using one or more of the anthropometric indicators at these ages to assess risks of morbidity and mortality in early childhood, and it was at these ages that the relevance of anthropometric measures originally were established most firmly (Alfred Sommer and Matthew S. Lowenstein, 1975; Lincoln C. Chen et al., 1980; W. Z. Billewicz and I. A. MacGregor, 1982; Arnfried Kielmann et al., 1983; R. Martorell, 1985). During the last few years, however, a considerable body of evidence has accumulated suggesting that height at maturity is also an important predictor of the probability of dying and of developing chronic diseases at middle and late ages (M. G. Marmot et al., 1984; Hans Waaler, 1984; A. Meredith John, 1988; Dora L. Costa, 1993; John M. Kim, 1993). BMI has similar predictive properties (Peter F. Heywood, 1983; Waaler, 1984; Martorell, 1985; P. Payne, 1992; S. R. Osmani, 1992) (cf. T. N. Srinivasan, 1992).

Height and BMI measure different aspects of malnutrition and health. Height is a net rather than a gross measure of nutrition. Moreover, although changes in height during the growing years are sensitive to current levels of nutrition, mean final height reflects the accumulated past nutritional experience of individuals throughout their growing years, including the fetal period. It follows that when final heights are used to explain differences in adult mortality rates, they reveal the effect not of adult levels of nutrition on adult mortality rates, but of nutritional levels during infancy, childhood, and adolescence on adult mortality rates. A weight-for-height index, on the other hand, reflects primarily the current nutritional status. It is also a net measure in the sense that BMI reflects the balance between current intakes and the claims on those intakes.

A. The Relationship Between Body Size and the Risk of Death at Middle and Late Ages

A number of recent studies have established the predictive power of height and BMI with respect to morbidity and mortality at later ages. The results of two of these studies are summarized in Figures 2 and 3. Part A of Figure 2 reproduces a diagram by Waaler (1984). It shows that short Norwegian men aged 40–59 at risk between 1963 and 1979 were much more likely to die than tall men. Indeed, the risk of mortality for men with heights of 165 cm (65.0 inches) was on average 71-percent greater than that of men who measure 182.5 cm (71.9 inches). Part B shows that height is also an important predictor of the relative likelihood that men aged 23–49 would be rejected from the Union Army during 1861–1865 because of chronic diseases. Despite significant differences in ethnicities, environmental circumstances, the array and severity of diseases, and time, the functional relationships between height and relative risk are strikingly similar in the two cases.

Waaler (1984) has also studied the relationship in Norway between BMI and the risk of death in a sample of 1.7 million individuals. Curves summarizing his findings are shown in Figure 3 for both men and women. Although the observed values of the BMI (kg/m^2) ranged between 17 and 39, over 80 percent of the males over age 40 had BMI's within the range 21–29. Within the range 22–28, the curve is relatively flat, with the relative risk of mortality hovering close to 1.0. However, at BMI's of less than 22 and greater than 28, the risk of death rises quite sharply as the BMI moves away from its mean value. It will be noticed that

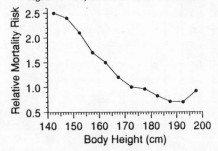

A. *Relative Mortality Risk among Norwegian Men Aged 40–59, Between 1963 and 1979*

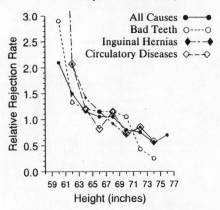

B. *Relative Rejection Rates for Chronic Conditions in a Sample of 4,245 Men Aged 23–49, Examined for the Union Army*

FIGURE 2. COMPARISON OF THE RELATIONSHIP BETWEEN BODY HEIGHT AND RELATIVE RISK IN TWO POPULATIONS

Sources: For part A, Waaler (1984); for part B, Fogel (1993b).

the BMI curves are much more symmetrical than the height curves in Figure 2, which indicates that high BMI's are as risky as low ones.

Although Figures 2 and 3 are revealing, they are not sufficient to shed light on the debate over whether moderate stunting impairs health when weight-for-height is adequate, since Figure 2 is not controlled for weight and Figure 3 is only partially controlled for height (Fogel, 1987; Fogel and

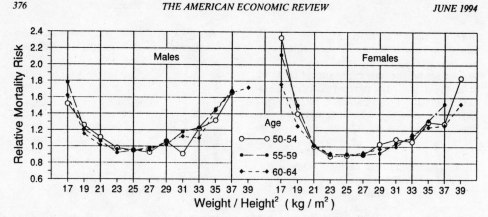

FIGURE 3. RELATIONSHIP BETWEEN BMI AND PROSPECTIVE RISK AMONG NORWEGIAN ADULTS
AGED 50–64 AT RISK, BETWEEN 1963 AND 1979

Source: Waaler (1984).

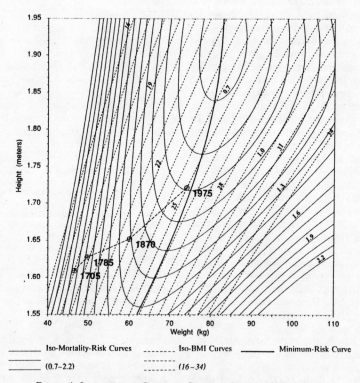

FIGURE 4. ISOMORTALITY CURVES OF RELATIVE RISK FOR HEIGHT AND
WEIGHT AMONG NORWEGIAN MALES AGED 50–64 WITH A PLOT OF THE
ESTIMATED FRENCH HEIGHT AND WEIGHT AT FOUR DATES

Floud, 1994). To get at the "small-but-healthy" issue one needs an isomortality surface that relates the risk of death to both height and weight simultaneously. Such a surface, presented in Figure 4, was fitted to Waaler's data by a procedure described elsewhere (Fogel, 1993b). Transecting the isomortality map are lines which give the locus of each BMI between 16 and 34, and a curve giving the weights that minimize risk at each height.

Figure 4 shows that, even when body weight is maintained at what Figure 3 indicates is an "ideal" level (BMI = 25), short men are at substantially greater risk of death than tall men. Thus, an adult male with a BMI of 25 who is 164 cm tall is at about 55-percent greater risk of death than a male at 183 cm who also has a BMI of 25. Figure 4 also shows that the "ideal" BMI (the BMI that minimizes the risk of death) varies with height. A BMI of 25 is "ideal" for men in the neighborhood of 176 cm, but for tall men (greater than 183 cm) the "ideal" BMI is between 22 and 24, while for short men (under 168 cm) the "ideal" BMI is about 26.

B. Using Waaler Surfaces To Explain the Secular Decline in Mortality

Superimposed on Figure 4 are rough estimates of heights and weights in France at four dates. In 1705, the per capita food supply in France was lower than in Britain, so that average body mass was probably even lower than in Britain. Circa 1705, the French probably achieved equilibrium with their food supply at an average height of about 161 cm and BMI of about 18. Over the next 270 years the food supply expanded with sufficient rapidity to permit both the height and the weight of adult males to increase. Figure 4 indicates that it was factors associated with the gain in BMI that accounted for most of the predicted reduction in the risk of mortality before 1870. After 1870, factors associated with the gain in height explain most of the predicted mortality decline. Figure 4 also implies that, while these factors jointly explain about 90 percent of the actual decline in French mortality rates over the period between circa

1785 and circa 1870, they only explain about 50 percent of the actual decline in mortality rates during the past century. Increases in body size and the factors associated with it continued to have a major impact on the gains in life expectation among persons of relatively good nutritional status, but during the last century factors other than those related to height and BMI became increasingly important.

The analysis in this section points to the misleading nature of the concept of subsistence as Malthus originally used it and as it is still widely used today. Subsistence is not located at the edge of a nutritional cliff, beyond which lies demographic disaster. The evidence outlined in the paper implies that, rather than one level of subsistence, there are numerous levels at which a population and a food supply can be in equilibrium, in the sense that they can be indefinitely sustained. However, some levels will have smaller people and higher "normal" (non-crisis) mortality than others.[4]

C. The Relevance of Waaler Surfaces for Predicting Trends in Chronic Diseases

Poor body builds increased vulnerability to diseases, not just contagious diseases, but chronic diseases as well. This point is implicit in Figure 2, which shows that chronic conditions were much more frequent among

---

[4] Moreover, with a given population and technology, changes in the allocation of labor between agriculture and other sectors may lead to changes in body size and mortality. In an ancien régime economy the lower the share of the labor force that is in agriculture, ceteris paribus, the lower the share of caloric production that can be devoted to baseline maintenance. The reasoning behind this statement is as follows. Assume that one worker in agriculture feeds himself plus three persons outside of agriculture. Hence, a movement of 1 percent of agricultural workers to nonagriculture would reduce the per capita availability of food to the increased nonagricultural sector by about 1.33 percent. If baseline maintenance accounts for 75 percent of caloric consumption and if per capita calories reserved for work remain constant in the nonagricultural sector, calories available for baseline maintenance in that sector would decline by about 1.8 percent (assuming that within the agricultural sector per capita production and consumption are unchanged).

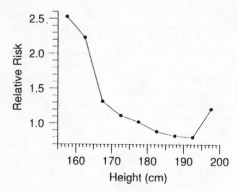

FIGURE 5. THE RELATIONSHIP BETWEEN HEIGHT
AND RELATIVE RISK OF ILL HEALTH IN NHIS
VETERANS AGED 40–59

Source: Fogel et al. (1993).

short young men in the 1860's than among tall men. Figure 5 shows that the same relationship between ill health and stature exists among the males covered by the U.S. National Health Interview Surveys (NHIS) for 1985–1988. Stunting during developmental ages had a long reach and increased the likelihood that people would suffer from chronic diseases at middle and at late ages.

American males born during the second quarter of the 19th century were not only stunted by today's standards, but their BMI's at adult ages were about 15-percent lower than current U.S. levels (Fogel et al., 1993). The implication of the combined stunting and low BMI is brought out by Figure 6, which presents a Waaler surface for morbidity estimated by Kim (1993) from NHIS data for 1985–1988.

The Waaler surface for risk from chronic conditions in Figure 6 is similar to, but not identical with, the Norwegian surface for mortality (see Fig. 4). The isomorbidity curves in ill health rise more steeply than the isomortality curves as one moves away in either direction from the optimal weight curve. Furthermore, the optimal weight curve in Figure 6 usually lies about one iso-BMI curve to the right of the optimal-weight curve computed from the Norwegian mortality data. Thus, both the Norwegian

mortality data and the U.S. health data indicate that for men in the neighborhood of 1.60–1.65 meters the optimal BMI is in the range of 25–27. This is above current levels recommended by FAO/WHO/UNU (1985), falling into the lower ranges of overweight in that standard.

Figure 6 also presents the coordinates in height and BMI of Union Army veterans who were age 65 or older in 1910 and of veterans (mainly of World War II) who were the same ages during 1985–1988. These coordinates predict a decline of about 35 percent in the prevalence of chronic disease among the two cohorts. About 61 percent of the predicted decline in ill health is due to factors associated with the increase in BMI, and the balance is due to factors associated with increased stature.

The decline in the prevalence of chronic diseases predicted by Figure 6 is quite close to what actually occurred. Table 3 compares the prevalence of chronic diseases among Union Army men aged 65 and over in 1910 with two surveys of veterans of the same ages in the 1980's. That table indicates that heart disease was 2.9 times as prevalent, musculoskeletal and respiratory diseases were 1.6 times as prevalent, and digestive diseases were 4.7 times as prevalent among veterans aged 65 or older in 1910 as in 1985–1988. During the 7.6 decades separating the two groups, the prevalence of heart disease among the elderly declined at a rate of 12.8 percent per decade, while musculoskeletal and respiratory diseases each declined at a rate of 5.9 percent per decade.

Young adults born between 1822 and 1845 who survived the deadly infectious diseases of childhood and adolescence were not freer of degenerative diseases than persons of the same ages today, as some have suggested, but more afflicted. At ages 35–39, hernia rates, for example, were more than three times as prevalent in the 1860's as in the 1980's. Of special note is the much higher incidence of clubfoot in the 1860's, a birth anomaly which suggests that the uterus was far less safe for those awaiting birth than it is today.

Those who also survived diseases of middle ages were more afflicted by degenerative

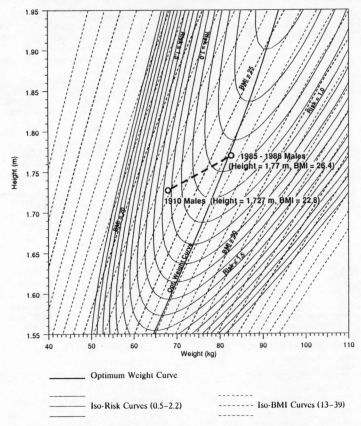

FIGURE 6. HEALTH IMPROVEMENT PREDICTED BY NHIS 1985-1988 HEALTH
SURFACE

Note: All risks are measured relative to the average risk of morbidity (calculated over
all heights and weights) among NHIS 1985-1988 white males aged 45-64.
Source: Kim (1993).

chronic conditions at old ages in the 1910's
than in the 1980's. Nearly 74 percent of the
elderly Union Army veterans suffered from
three or more disabling chronic conditions,
which is much higher than the rate among
elderly veterans in 1983 (Fogel et al., 1993).
It may be true that there were less genetically frail persons among those who survived to age 65 in 1910 than there are today.
If so, that genetic advantage was apparently
offset by a lifetime of socioeconomic and
biomedical stress that left health in old age
badly impaired and that sharply curtailed

the life expectations of the elderly. During
the 1910's the elderly died not from the
infectious diseases that killed the great
majority of their cohorts at relatively young
ages, but primarily from degenerative diseases which, at the two-digit level of the
International Classification of Diseases, are
similar to the distribution of causes of death
during the 1980's, except that deaths from
neoplasms were lower and deaths from tuberculosis were higher than in the 1980's.

The provisional findings thus suggest that
chronic conditions were far more prevalent

TABLE 3—COMPARISON OF THE PREVALENCE OF CHRONIC CONDITIONS
AMONG UNION ARMY VETERANS IN 1910, VETERANS IN 1983
(REPORTING WHETHER THEY EVER HAD SPECIFIC CHRONIC CONDITIONS),
AND VETERANS IN NHIS 1985–1988 (REPORTING WHETHER
THEY HAD SPECIFIC CHRONIC CONDITIONS DURING THE PRECEDING
12 MONTHS), AGED 65 AND ABOVE, PERCENTAGES

Disorder	1910 Union Army veterans	1983 veterans	Age-adjusted 1983 veterans	NHIS 1985–1988 veterans
Musculoskeletal	67.7	47.9	47.2	42.5
Digestive	84.0	49.0	48.9	18.0
Hernia	34.5	27.3	26.7	6.6
Diarrhea	31.9	3.7	4.2	1.4
Genito-urinary	27.3	36.3	32.3	8.9
Central nervous, endocrine, metabolic, or blood	24.2	29.9	29.1	12.6
Circulatory[a]	90.1	42.9	39.9	40.0
Heart	76.0	38.5	39.9	26.6
Varicose veins	38.5	8.7	8.3	5.3
Hemorroids[b]	44.4			7.2
Respiratory	42.2	29.8	28.1	26.5

Notes: Prevailing rates of Union Army veterans are based on examinations by physicians. Those for the 1980's are based on self-reporting. Comparison of the NHIS rates
with those obtained from physicians' examinations in NHANES II indicates that the
use of self-reported health conditions does not introduce a significant bias into the
comparison. See Fogel et al. (1993) for a more detailed discussion of possible biases
and their magnitudes.
Source: Fogel et al. (1993).
[a]Among veterans in 1983, the prevalence of all types of circulatory diseases will be
underestimated because of underreporting of hemorroids.
[b]The variable indicating whether the 1983 veteran ever had hemorroids is unreliable.

throughout the life cycle for those who
reached age 65 before World War I than is
suggested by the theory of the epidemiological transition. Reliance on causes-of-death
information to characterize the epidemiology of the past has led to a significant
misrepresentation of the distribution of
health conditions among the living. It has
also promoted the view that the epidemiology of chronic diseases is more separate
from that of contagious diseases than now
appears to be the case.

IV. Physiological Foundations for Waaler Surfaces and Curves

What is the basis for the predictive capacity of Waaler surfaces and curves? Part of

the answer resides in the realm of human
physiology, which concerns the functioning
of the organs and the organ systems of the
body. Variations in height and weight appear to be associated with variations in the
chemical composition of the tissues that
make up these organs, in the quality of the
electrical transmission across membranes,
and in the functioning of the endocrine
system and other vital systems.

Research in this area is developing rapidly, and some of the new findings are yet
to be confirmed. The exact mechanisms
by which malnutrition and trauma in utero
or early childhood are transformed into
organ dysfunctions are still unclear. What is
agreed upon is that the basic structures
of most organs are laid down early, and it is

reasonable to infer that poorly developed organs may break down earlier than well-developed ones. The principal evidence so far is statistical, and despite agreement on certain specific dysfunctions, there is no generally accepted theory of cellular aging (cf. J. M. Tanner, 1990, 1993).

With these caveats in mind, recent research bearing on the connection between malnutrition and body size and the later onset of chronic diseases can conveniently be divided into three categories. The first category involves forms of malnutrition (including the ingestion of toxic substances) that cause permanent, promptly visible physiological damage, as is seen in the impairment of the nervous systems of fetuses due to excess consumption of alcohol or smoking by pregnant women. Alcohol, for example, induces growth retardation in fetuses and infants and causes atrial septal defect, microcephaly, and other birth anomalies which are collectively labeled Fetal Alcohol Syndrome or Fetal Alcohol Symptoms (S. L. Robbins et al., 1984). It appears that protein calorie malnutrition (PCM) in infancy and early childhood can lead to a permanent impairment of central nervous system function (Scrimshaw and J. E. Gordon, 1968; Martorell et al., 1990; A. Chavez et al., 1994) (cf. J. J. Volpe, 1987). Iodine deficiency in utero and moderate-to-severe iron deficiency during infancy also appear to cause permanent neurological damage (Betsy Lozoff et al., 1991; Scrimshaw, 1993).

Not all damage due to retarded development in utero or infancy caused by malnutrition shows up immediately. In a recent series of studies D. J. P. Barker and his colleagues (Barker et al., 1989, 1990, 1992; Barker, 1991; C. M. Law et al., 1993; D. I. W. Phillips et al., 1993; K. Phipps et al., 1993) have reported that such conditions as coronary heart disease, hypertension, stroke, diabetes, and autoimmune thyroiditis begin in utero or in infancy but do not become apparent until midadult or later ages. In these cases, individuals appear to be in good health and function well in the interim. However, early onset of the degenerative diseases of old age appears to be

linked to inadequate cellular development early in life. Some, but not all, such cases are associated with low birth weight. Some babies are born in the normal weight range but experience below-average infant weight gains. In other instances babies are small relative to the size of their placentas, short in relation to the size of their head, or long but thin (Barker, 1993) (cf. Tanner, 1993).

Certain physiological dysfunctions incurred by persons suffering from malnutrition can, in principle, be reversed by improved dietary intake, but they often persist because the cause of the malnutrition persists. If the malnutrition persists long enough these conditions can become irreversible or fatal. This category of dysfunctions includes the degradation of tissue structure, especially in such vital organs as the lungs, the heart, and the gastrointestinal tract. In the case of the respiratory system, for example, there is not only decreased muscle mass and strength, but also impaired ventilatory drive, biochemical changes in connective tissue, and electrolyte abnormalities. Malnutrition also has been related to the atrophy of the mucosal cells of the gut, the inhibition of wound healing, increased likelihood of traumatic shock and of sepsis, impaired functioning of the endocrine system, increased tendency to edema, electrical instability that can provoke acute arrhythmias, and degenerative joint diseases (Thomas M. Saba et al., 1983; Juan Idiaquez, 1988; G. L. Hill, 1990; M. Molly McMahon and Bruce R. Bistrian, 1990; Janis S. Fisler, 1992) (cf. Kenneth G. Manton, 1993).

Also relevant is the discovery of the relationship between birth weight and the probability of perinatal death. The curves in Figure 7 are U-shaped, indicating that in each population babies significantly heavier than the optimal weight also incur high mortality risks. Moreover the optimal birth weight in the two populations with small mothers was significantly lower than that of the U.S. population, where mothers were relatively large. It appears that prior to high-technology interventions, the size of the mother's pelvis constrained the rate at which birth size (and perhaps the robustness of the vital organs of the baby) could have increased

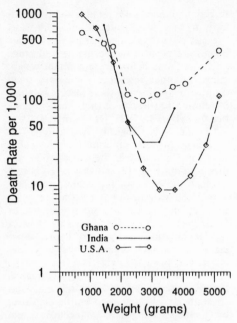

FIGURE 7. PERINATAL DEATH RATE BY BIRTH
WEIGHT IN GHANA, INDIA, AND THE UNITED
STATES

Source: F. E. Hytten and I. Leitch (1971).

with the improvement in intrauterine nutrition. Babies at weights which optimized survival in a relatively tall population were at elevated risks of dying in populations with relatively short mothers, due to delivery distress. There was, in other words, an intergenerational constraint on the rate at which babies could escape from the effects of malnutrition as fetal nutrition improved (cf. R. K. Chandra, 1975).

The recent physiological findings also cast new light on the first phase of the secular decline in mortality. Some investigators have called attention to changes in age-specific mortality rates that may indicate a shift in the balance between pathogens and their human hosts (Fridlizius, 1984; Perrenoud, 1984). Although the shift has been attributed to a decline in the virulence of pathogens, not enough evidence is in hand as yet to assess this possibility. However, the

recent physiological research summarized in this section suggests a new pathway through which the balance between pathogens and human hosts may have turned in favor of the hosts. In addition to the improved operation of the immune system, there is the increased capacity of a vital organ to survive the attack of pathogens as a result of increased tissue resilience, including the improved operation of the nervous system. The process could have been synergistic since the improvement in the operation of the immune system might have interacted with the increased resilience of other vital organs.[5] The last possibility is consistent with the age-specific patterns of decline in mortality rates that have so far been uncovered for the 18th century.

V. Some Implications for Current Policy

Malthus believed that malnutrition manifested itself in the exceptional—in periodic famines and in the excess mortality prevalent among the ultra-poor of his day, who lived in misery and vice. He thought that persons near the middle of the social order, the sturdy agricultural laborer or the town artisan, were generally well fed and healthy and lived normal life spans.

We now know, however, that famines accounted for less than 4 percent of the premature mortality of Malthus's age and that the excess mortality of the ultra-poor (the bottom fifth of society) accounted for another sixth of premature mortality. About two-thirds of all premature mortality in Malthus's time came from the part of society that Malthus viewed as productive and healthy. Yet by current standards, even persons in the top half of the income distribution in Britain during the 18th century were

[5]Such possible synergies call into question the proposition that, because an individual appears to be currently well fed, malnutrition does not affect the outcome of diseases such as influenza, smallpox, or typhoid (cf. S. R. Duncan et al., 1993). Individuals may be more likely to succumb to such infections, even if they are currently well fed, because past malnutrition, either in utero or subsequently, has degraded vital organs (cf. Scrimshaw et al., 1968).

stunted and wasted, suffered far more extensively from chronic diseases at young adult and middle ages than is true today, and died 30 years sooner than today.[6]

A. Implications for Poor Countries

The Malthusian legacy is embodied in such theses as "small-but-healthy" which holds that stunted or moderately wasted individuals may not be more vulnerable to ill health and mortality than those who conform to the U.S. standard. The paucity of life-cycle data sets for developing countries caused investigators to focus only on the early years of the life span, searching for interactions between natal or infant measures of size and measures of health and work capacity later in childhood. Such studies generally picked up the effects of only exceedingly severe stunting and wasting (more than two standard deviations below average), missing the impact of more moderate size effects, many of which do not show up until later in life (David Seckler, 1980; P. V. Sukhatme, 1982; Michael Lipton, 1983) (cf. Patrick West et al., 1990).

However, the information reported in this paper indicates that childhood stunting and wasting has a long reach, predicting chronic disease rates at young-adult and later ages. The higher prevalence of disabling chronic diseases among adults in the developing nations has escaped attention because the relevant information on such conditions is not generally collected. But the long reach of childhood malnutrition in rich countries, both now and when they were much poorer than they are today, suggests that a similar interconnection also exists in developing countries.

[6]Premature mortality is defined here as death rates higher than the 1980 death rates when standardized for the 1700 age structure (cf. Fogel, 1986, 1992b). Estimates of the overall death rate circa 1790 are from Wrigley and Schofield (1981). Estimates of the relative death rates by deciles of the caloric consumption distribution were based on the estimated average heights and BMI in these deciles and on the relative mortality risks that they imply, as indicated in Figure 4. For further details on the computations see the appendix in Fogel and Floud (1994) and table A2 in Fogel (1993b).

Chronic diseases are not the only way that chronic malnutrition reduces the productivity of the labor force. When the mean amounts of calories are as low as they are in the poor nations of the world, labor-force participation rates and measures of labor productivity are bound to be low, especially when the hours of labor are adjusted for the intensity of labor (see Fogel, 1991) (cf. Partha Dasgupta, 1993). Elsewhere (Fogel, 1991), I have estimated that when the labor input is adjusted for intensity (measured by calories), improved gross nutrition accounts for roughly 30 percent of the growth of per capita income in Britain between 1790 and 1980.

B. Implications for Rich Countries

Between 1850 and 1950 U.S. life expectation at birth increased from about 40 to 68 years. Then for the next two decades further progress in longevity came to a virtual halt. During and following this interregnum, investigators who reviewed the progress in mortality over the preceding century tended toward a consensus on three propositions:

(i) The century-long decline in mortality rates was unique and could not be repeated because virtually all of the gains made through the elimination of death from contagious diseases below age 60 had been made.

(ii) Deaths, now concentrated at older ages, were due to degenerative diseases that were unrelated to the contagious diseases that they superseded. The degenerative diseases were caused by accelerated organ losses that were part of the natural process of aging.

(iii) There was an upper limit to life expectation that was genetically determined. One influential paper put that limit at 85 ± 7 years (James F. Fries, 1980) (cf. Fries, 1989).

More recent studies, responding to the renewed decline in mortality, which this time is concentrated at ages 65 and over, have uncovered evidence that militates against the notion of a genetically fixed life span or, if it is fixed, suggests that the upper limit is well above 85. James W. Vaupel's (1991a) study of Danish twins indicates that genetic factors account for only about 30 percent of the variance in age of death. His study of Swedish males who lived to age 90 indicates that the death rate at that age has declined at a rate of about 1 percent per annum since 1950, a finding that is contradictory to the rectangularization of the survivorship curve (Vaupel, 1991b) (cf. A. R. Thatcher, 1992; Vaupel and H. Lundström, 1994; V. Kannisto et al., 1994). Two recent studies of insect populations (James R. Carey et al., 1992; James W. Curtsinger et al., 1992) indicated that variation in environmental conditions had a much larger effect on the life span than genetic factors and revealed no pattern suggestive of a fixed upper limit. Collectively, these studies do not rule out genetic factors but suggest something much less rigid than the genetic programming of absolute life spans. An emerging theory combines genetic susceptibility of various organs with cumulative insults as a result of exposure to risk.

Recent studies also indicate that age-specific rates of chronic conditions above age 65 are generally falling. According to Manton et al. (1993) the rate of disability among the elderly in the United States declined by 4.7 percent between 1982 and 1989. Put on a decade basis, this rate of decline is quite similar to the long-term rates of decline between 1910 and 1985–1988 in chronic conditions among elderly veterans (Fogel et al., 1993). The finding is consistent with the growing body of evidence (reported in Sections III and IV above) indicating that chronic diseases at later ages are, to a considerable degree, the result of exposure to infectious diseases, malnutrition, and other types of biomedical and socioeconomic stress early in life. It is also consistent with the predicted decline of about 6 percent per decade in chronic diseases based on the Waaler surface in ill health displayed in Figure 6 (cf. Steven N. Blair et al., 1989; Manton et al., 1992; Manton and Beth J. Soldo, 1992).

Much current research is now focused on explaining the decline in chronic conditions. Part of the emerging explanation is a change in life styles, particularly reduced smoking,

improved nutrition, and increased exercise, which appear to be involved in reducing the prevalence of coronary heart disease and respiratory diseases. Another part of the explanation is the increasing effectiveness of medical intervention. This point is strikingly demonstrated by comparing the second and last columns of the line on hernias in Table 3, above. Prior to World War II, hernias, once they occurred, were generally permanent and often exceedingly painful conditions. However, by the 1980's about three-quarters of all veterans who ever had hernias were cured of them. Similar progress over the seven decades is indicated by the line on genito-urinary conditions. Other areas where medical intervention has been highly effective include control of hypertension and reduction in the incidence of stroke, surgical removal of osteoarthritis, replacement of knee and hip joints, curing of cataracts, and chemotherapies that reduce the incidence of osteoporosis and heart disease (Manton et al., 1993).

The success in medical interventions combined with rising incomes has naturally led to a huge increase in the demand for medical services. Econometric estimates suggest a long-run income elasticity in the demand for medical services across OECD nations in the neighborhood of 1.5 and indicate that 90 percent of the variance in medical expenditures across OECD countries is explained by variations in income (William J. Moore et al., 1992). The rapidly growing level of demand, combined with the egalitarian policy of providing medical care at highly subsidized prices, has created the crisis in health-care costs that is now such a focus of public-policy debates across OECD nations, with various combinations of price and governmental rationing under consideration (*The Economist*, 1990; William B. Schwartz and Henry J. Aaron, 1991; Joseph P. Newhouse, 1992; George J. Schieber et al., 1993).

Whatever the eventual outcome of these policy debates, it is clear that we are in a much different world than that of Malthus. Instead of debating whether to provide food to paupers who might otherwise die, we are now debating how to distribute services that have proved successful in raising the quality of life of the aged and in extending life expectation. And we are now struggling with entirely new ethical issues such as whether it is right to restrict medical services that extend life of a low quality (Barbara L. Wolfe, 1986; John Sterling Shuttleworth, 1990; Edmund D. Pellegrino, 1993).

Growing opportunity to improve health at young ages, to reduce the incidence of chronic diseases at late ages, and to cure or alleviate the disabilities associated with chronic diseases raises two other post-Malthusian population issues. One is the impact of improved health on population size. A recent paper by Dennis A. Ahlburg and Vaupel (1990) pointed out that if mortality rates at older ages continue to decline at 2 percent per annum, the U.S. elderly population of 2050 would be 36 million larger than forecast by the Census Bureau (cf. Samuel H. Preston, 1993). That possibility poses policy issues with respect to health-care costs (because total medical costs may rise sharply even if cure rates continue to improve) and to pension costs (because the number of persons eligible for benefits under present proposed rules and projected levels of compensation will become so large that outpayments will exceed planned reserves).

Some policymakers have sought to meet the pension problem by delaying retirement. Such schemes are based on the proposition that improved health will make it possible for more people to work past age 65. However, the recent findings on the secular improvement in health at older ages make it clear that worsening health is not the explanation for the steep decline since 1890 in labor-force participation rates of males over age 65. As Costa (1993) has reported, the U.S. decline in participation rates of the elderly over the past century is largely explained by the secular rise in income and a decline in the income elasticity of the demand for retirement. It is also related to the vast increase in the supply and the quality of leisure-time activities for the laboring classes.

In Malthus's time, and down to the opening of this century, leisure was in very short supply in the OECD countries and, as T. Veblen (1934) pointed out, it was conspicu-

ously consumed by a small upper class. The typical person labored over 60 hours per week for wages, and many had chores at home which consumed an additional 10 or 12 hours (Kuznets, 1952; John F. Olson, 1992; Fogel, 1993a) (cf. Jeremy Atack and Fred Bateman, 1992). Aside from sleep, eating, and hygiene, such workers usually had barely two hours a day for leisure. Although opera, theater, and ballet were available, they were too expensive to be consumed ordinarily by the laboring classes.

Over the 20th century, hours of work have fallen by nearly half for typical workers. Ironically, those in the top decile of the income distribution have not shared much in this gain of leisure since the highly paid professionals and businessmen who populate the top decile work closer to the 19th-century standard of 3,200 hours per year than the current working-class standard of about 1,800 hours. There has also been a vast increase in the supply of leisure-time activities (movies, radio, television, amusement parks, participant and spectator sports, and travel) and a decline in the relative price of such activities. Many firms cater especially to the tastes of the elderly, offering reduced prices and special opportunities. As a result, the typical worker spends two-thirds as much time in leisure activities as in work and looks forward to retirement (Fogel, 1992a, 1993a).

Given the growing and income-inelastic demand for leisure that characterizes the post-Malthusian milieu of the OECD nations, it remains to be seen to what extent the demand for leisure and retirement can be throttled. Policymakers may encounter as much resistance to efforts to reduce the implicit subsidies for leisure as they have had recently in raising the taxes on work.

VI. Some Implications for the Theory and Measurement of Economic Growth

Recent findings in the biomedical area call attention to what may be called the thermodynamic and physiological factors in economic growth. Although largely neglected by theorists of both the "old" and the "new" growth economics, these factors can easily be incorporated into standard growth models. Viewed in the human-capital context, both factors may be thought of as labor-enhancing technological changes that were brought about by developments in the agricultural, public-health, medical-services, and household sectors. They may also be thought of as adjustments for the mismeasurement of the labor input, when labor is measured only in person-hours.

I referred to the thermodynamic factor indirectly in Section V-A, when I indicated that about 30 percent of the British growth rate over the past 200 years was attributable to improvements in gross nutrition. That computation was based on the first law of thermodynamics, which holds that energy output cannot exceed energy input. Since that law applies as much to human engines as to mechanical ones, it is possible to use energy-cost-accounting techniques to estimate the increase in the energy available for work over the past two centuries. In the British case that increase had two effects. It raised the labor-force participation rate by bringing into the labor force the bottom 20 percent of consuming units in 1790 who had, on average, only enough energy for a few hours of strolling. Moreover, for those in the labor force, the intensity of work per hour has increased because the number of calories available for work increased. This change in the intensity of effort, by itself, appears to have accounted for about 20 percent of the long-term growth rate.

The contention that the British intensity of effort increased over time may seem dubious since the work day, week, and year (measured in hours) declined significantly over the past two centuries. However, the British (and other Europeans) could not have worked at the same average intensity *per hour* in 1790 as they do today, since that would have required a considerably larger supply of dietary energy per capita than was actually available. Increases in the intensity of labor per hour were also a factor in the American case, where food supplies were far more abundant than in Europe. Even if it is assumed that the daily number of calories available for work was the same in the United States in 1860 as today, the intensity of work per hour would have been well

below today's levels, since the average number of hours worked in 1860 was about 1.75 times as great as today. During the mid-19th century, only slaves on southern gang-system plantations appear to have worked at levels of intensity per hour approaching current standards (cf. Fogel, 1991, 1993a; Fogel and Stanley L. Engerman, 1992; Olson, 1992).

The physiological factor pertains to the efficiency with which the human engine converts energy input into work output. Nutritionists, physiologists, and development economists have contributed to the extensive literature on this topic. Since some important issues are still unresolved, a firm assessment of the physiological contribution to economic growth is not yet possible. However, some aspects of the contribution can be indicated.

Changes in health, in the composition of diet, and in clothing and shelter can significantly affect the efficiency with which ingested energy is converted into work output.[7] Reductions in the incidence of infectious diseases increase the proportion of ingested energy that is available for work, both because of savings in the energy required to mobilize the immune system and because the capacity of the gut to absorb nutrients is improved, especially as a consequence of a reduction in diarrheal diseases. Thermodynamic efficiency has also increased because of changes in the composition of the diet, including the shift from grains and other foods with high fiber content to sugar and meats. These dietary changes raised the proportion of ingested energy that can be metabolized (increased the average value of the "Atwater factors," to use the language of nutritionists). Improvements in clothing and shelter have also increased thermodynamic efficiency by reducing the amount of energy lost through radiation.

Individuals who are stunted but otherwise healthy at maturity will be at an increased

---

[7] The discussion in this paragraph draws on Dasgupta (1993) and the sources cited there.

risk of incurring chronic diseases and of dying prematurely. To evaluate the significance of changes in the rate of deterioration of the capacity to work over the life cycle, one needs to calculate the effect of changes in stature and weight on the discounted present value of the difference between earnings and maintenance over the life cycle (cf. Dasgupta, 1993). A procedure for estimating this effect is set forth in the notes, along with illustrative estimates of the key variables.[8] The exercise indicates that the discounted revenues would have increased by about 37 percent. This last figure, combined with a guess on the effect

[8]The discounted present value of the age–earnings profile for n years beginning with the age at which earnings peak is given by

$$(1) \qquad P_x = E_x \int_0^n e^{-(\mu + \phi + r)t} dt$$

where μ is the rate of decline in the survivorship function (the l_x curve of the life table), ϕ is the rate of decline in annual net earnings after age x, r is the discount rate (which, for convenience, is set at 6 percent), x is the age at which earnings peak, E_x is net earnings at that age, n is the average number of years that elapsed between x and the average age at which a living male ceased to be in the labor force regularly (which, for convenience, will be taken to be equal to 35), and P_x is the discounted present value of the net earnings stream.

The value of μ for 1790 was computed from Wrigley and Schofield (1981), taking the average of their e_0 for 1786–1795 (which is 36.63) and interpolating between levels 8 and 9 in their family of English life tables to obtain the proper l_x curve for circa 1790. The value of μ over ages 35–70 in that schedule is 0.0289.

The projected shift in the l_x curve was based on the Waaler surface in table A1 in Fogel (1993b). Using 1.68 m and 61 kg for 1790, and 1.76 m and 76 kg for 1980, yields a predicted decline of 31 percent in the mortality rate. The corresponding l_x schedule was obtained from Princeton-model North tables at male level 14, using $0.69(_{35}m_{35})$ as the basis for the fit. The value of μ between ages 35–70 in that l_x schedule is -0.0202.

The changes in E_x associated with changes in height and weight were estimated from an equation reported by Robert A. Margo and Richard H. Steckel (1982). The data they used pertained to slaves seized as booty of war by the Union Army in 1863. The traders who related the value of slaves to their height and weight appear to have focused only on the differences in the location (not the slope) of the age–earnings profile, showing no apparent awareness of the relationship of stature and BMI to mortality and chronic diseases (cf.

of the shifting of Atwater factors, suggests that the average efficiency of the human

Fogel, 1992c). The Margo-Steckel equation is:

$$(2) \quad \ln V = 2.73 + 0.032S + 0.17A - 0.005A^2$$
$$\quad (1.47) \quad (0.92) \quad (2.22) \quad (-2.23)$$

$$+ 0.000046A^3 + 0.053H$$
$$(2.10) \qquad (2.16)$$

$$+ 0.019W - 0.00027(H \times W)$$
$$(1.79) \qquad (-1.73)$$

($N = 523$, $\overline{R}^2 = 0.20$), where V is the value of a slave, S is a dummy for skin color, A is age, H is height (in inches), and W is weight (in pounds); t statistics are in parentheses. For 1790, I used 66.1 inches and 134 pounds; for 1980, I used 69.3 inches and 167 pounds. These figures indicate that E_x increased by about 7 percent as a result of changes associated with body size.

The value of ϕ for 1790 between ages 35 and 70 was computed from data reported in Fogel and Engerman (1974). These data indicate that net earnings at age 70 were about 17 percent of peak earnings, which was attained at age 35.

With the foregoing information and an initial assumption that ϕ remained constant, the increase in P_x can be computed from the data shown in equations (3) and (4):

$$(3) \quad P_{x,1790} = \frac{E_x[1 - e^{-(0.0289 + 0.0494 + 0.06)35}]}{0.1383} = 7.17E_x$$

$$(4) \quad P_{x,\text{p}} = \frac{1.07E_x[1 - e^{-(0.0202 + 0.0494 + 0.06)35}]}{0.1296} = 8.17E_x$$

where $P_{x,1790}$ is the present value of the 1790 earnings profile and $P_{x,\text{p}}$ is the present value of the profile projected from the changes in height and BMI. Equations (3) and (4) imply that P_x increased by 14 percent ($[8.17/7.17] - 1 = 0.14$).

It is now necessary to take account of the effect of changes in body size on the rate of decline in the net earnings function (the value of ϕ). If it is assumed that net earnings at age 70 rose from 17 percent to 40 percent of peak-age earnings as a result of physiological improvements, P_x increases by 37 percent. However, even the last figure is probably too low since it does not take account of the secular shift in the peak of the age–earnings profile from the mid-thirties to the mid-forties. Moreover, studies of the profiles of manual workers in recent times suggest that net earnings now decline much more slowly after the peak than in past times (cf. Fogel and Engerman, 1974; Mary Jablonski, et al., 1988; Kevin Murphy and Finis Welch, 1990).

engine in Britain increased by about 53 percent between 1790 and 1980. The combined effort of the increase in dietary energy available for work, and of the increased human efficiency in transforming dietary energy into work output, appears to account for about 50 percent of the British economic growth since 1790.[9]

Focusing on the thermodynamic and physiological aspects of economic growth calls attention to the long lags that frequently occur between the time that certain investments are made and the time that their benefits occur. Much of the gain in thermodynamic efficiency that occurred in Britain and other OECD countries between 1910 and 1980 was due to a series of investments made as much as a century earlier. Failure to take account of these extremely long lags between investments and payoffs leads to puzzling paradoxes. During the Depression decade of the 1930's, for example, the U.S. unemployment rate was never less than 16 percent; for half the period unemployment ranged between 20 percent and 25 percent. Yet life expectation between 1929 and 1939 increased by four years, and the

heights of men reaching maturity during this period increased by 1.6 cm (Bernard D. Karpinos, 1958; U.S. Bureau of the Census, 1975).

The resolution of the paradox turns, I believe, on the huge social investments made between 1870 and 1930, whose payoffs were not counted as part of national income during the 1920's and 1930's even though they produced a large stream of benefits during these decades. I refer, of course, to the social investment in biomedical research (which included the establishment and expansion of modern teaching and research hospitals) whose largest payoffs came well after the investment was made. Also included in this category are such public-health investments as the construction of facilities to improve the supply of water, the cleaning up of the milk supply, the draining of swamps, the development of effective systems of quarantines, and the cleaning up of the slums.

VII. Concluding Comment

Keynes said, "In the long run we are all dead" (1971 p. 65). That was an appropriate point to make during the interwar period, which included the severe inflations of the 1920's and the worst depression in history during the 1930's. Urgent, forceful action was needed to regain control of the money supply, to take care of the millions of unemployed, and to prevent the collapse of the democracies.

We live in another era. The major issues of economic policy in OECD nations today cannot be understood from a purely short-run perspective. The crisis in medical care, the pension crisis, and the challenges of globalization are governed by long-run processes that policymakers need to understand. As I have tried to point out in this lecture, we have not yet completed the escape from hunger and premature death that began nearly three centuries ago. Chronic diseases and death are still occurring prematurely even in the rich countries. If the reforms of health care and pension programs now being considered by policymakers are to be successful, they must be con-

---

[9]The following procedure was used to arrive at this estimate: Bringing the bottom 20 percent of the caloric distribution of circa 1790 into the labor force increased the labor-force participation rate by 25 percent. Among those in the labor force, the average number of calories available for work increased by 56 percent between circa 1790 and 1980. Hence, the total increase in output per capita as a result of the increased availability of calories for work was 95 percent $(1.25 \times 1.56 = 1.95)$. Dasgupta's (1993) discussion suggests that reductions in diarrheal and other diseases combined with a shift in the composition of the diet increased the Atwater factors by about 12 percent. Since the exercise based on the equation in footnote 8 implies that the reduction in chronic diseases and premature mortality increased thermodynamic efficiency by 37 percent, the combined increase in thermodynamic efficiency is about 53 percent $(1.12 \times 1.37 = 1.53)$. In combination, then, increased calories available for work and the increased thermodynamic efficiency increased per capita income between circa 1790 and 1980 by 198 percent $(1.95 \times 1.53 = 2.98)$ or by 0.58 percent per annum $(2.98^{1/190} - 1 = 0.0058)$, which is about half of the annual British growth rate $(0.58/1.15 = 0.50)$. For further details, including discussion of possible upward and downward biases in this computation, see Fogel (1987) and Fogel and Floud (1994).

sistent with the long-term physiological changes governing the decline in chronic diseases and the increase in longevity. Long-term forecasts that do not take account of the dynamics of these changes over the past century, and of the socioeconomic, biomedical, and other environmental improvements that made them possible, are liable to be far off the mark.

At the outset of this lecture I stressed the need for economists to take account of long-run dynamic processes through a study of history. Uncovering what actually happened in the past requires an enormous investment in time and effort. Fortunately for theorists, that burden is borne primarily by economic historians. Theorists only need to spend the time necessary to comprehend what the historians have discovered. A superficial knowledge of the work of economic historians is at least as dangerous as a superficial knowledge of theory.

REFERENCES

Ahlburg, Dennis A. and Vaupel, James W. "Alternative Projections of the U.S. Population." *Demography*, November 1990, *27*(4), pp. 639–52.

Allen, R. C. "Agriculture during the Industrial Revolution, 1700–1850," in Roderick Floud and Donald McCloskey, eds., *The economic history of Britain since 1700*, 2nd Ed. Cambridge: Cambridge University Press, 1994 (forthcoming).

Atack, Jeremy and Bateman, Fred. "How Long Was the Work Day in 1880?" *Journal of Economic History*, March 1992, *52*(1), pp. 129–60.

Barker, D. J. P. "The Intrauterine Environment and Adult Cardiovascular Disease," in Gregory R. Bock and Julie Whelan, eds., *The childhood environment and adult disease*, Ciba Foundation Symposium 156. Chichester, U.K.: Wiley, 1991, pp. 3–16.

_____. "Fetal Origins of Coronary Heart Disease." *British Heart Journal*, March 1993, *69*(3), pp. 195–96.

Barker, D. J. P.; Meade, T. W.; Fall, C. D. H.; Lee, A.; Osmond, C.; Phipps, K. and Stirling, Y. "Relation of Fetal and Infant Growth to Plasma Fibrinogen and Factor VII Concentrations in Adult Life." *British Medical Journal*, 18 January 1992, *304*(6820), pp. 148–52.

Barker, D. J. P.; Osmond, C. and Golding, J. "Height and Mortality in the Counties of England and Wales." *Annals of Human Biology*, January-February 1990, *17*(1), pp. 1–6.

Barker, D. J. P.; Osmond, C.; Golding, J.; Kuh, D. and Wadsworth, M. E. J. "Growth in Utero, Blood Pressure in Childhood and Adult Life, and Mortality from Cardiovascular Disease." *British Medical Journal*, 4 March 1989, *298*(6673), pp. 564–67.

Bengtsson, Tommy and Ohlsson, Rolf. "Population and Economic Fluctuations in Sweden, 1749–1914," in Tommy Bengtsson, Gunnar Fridlizius, and Rolf Ohlsson, eds., *Pre-industrial population change*. Stockholm: Almquist and Wiksell, 1984, pp. 277–97.

_____. "Age-Specific Mortality and Short-Term Changes in the Standard of Living: Sweden, 1751–1859." *European Journal of Population*, November 1985, *1*(4), pp. 309–26.

Billewicz, W. Z. and MacGregory, I. A. "A Birth to Maturity Longitudinal Study of Heights and Weights in Two West African (Gambian) Villages, 1951–1975." *Annals of Human Biology*, July-August 1982, *9*(4), pp. 309–20.

Blair, Steven N.; Kohl, Harold W., III; Paffenbarger, Ralph S., Jr.; Clark, Debra G.; Cooper, Kenneth H. and Gibbons, Larry W. "Physical Fitness and All-Cause Mortality: A Prospective Study of Healthy Men and Women." *Journal of the American Medical Association*, 3 November 1989, *262*(17), pp. 2395–2401.

Carey, James R.; Liedo, Pablo; Orozco, Dina and Vaupel, James W. "Slowing of Mortality Rates at Older Ages in Large Medfly Cohorts." *Science*, 16 October 1992, *258*(5081), pp. 457–61.

Chandra, R. K. "Antibody Formation in First and Second Generation Offspring of Nutritionally Deprived Rats." *Science*, 17 October 1975, *190*(4211), pp. 289–90.

Chartres, J. A. "The Marketing of Agricultural Produce," in Joan Thirsk, ed., *The agrarian history of England and Wales*,

Vol. 5 (*1640–1750*, Part 2: *Agrarian change*). Cambridge: Cambridge University Press, 1985, pp. 406–502.

Chavez, A.; Martinez, C. and Soberanes, B. "The Effect of Malnutrition on Human Development," in Nevin S. Scrimshaw, ed., *Longitudinal community based studies of the impact of early malnutrition on child health and development*. Boston, MA: International Nutrition Foundation for Developing Countries, 1994 (forthcoming).

Chen, Lincoln C.; Chowdhury, A. K. M. Alauddin and Huffman, Sandra L. "Anthropometric Assessment of Energy-Protein Malnutrition and Subsequent Risk of Mortality Among Pre-School Aged Children." *American Journal of Clinical Nutrition*, August 1980, *33*(8), pp. 1836–45.

Cipolla, Carlo M. *Before the industrial revolution: European society and economy, 1000–1700*, 2nd Ed. New York: Norton, 1980.

Costa, Dora L. "Health, Income, and Retirement: Evidence from Nineteenth Century America." Ph.D. dissertation, University of Chicago, 1993.

Curtsinger, James W.; Fukui, Hidenori H.; Townsend, David R. and Vaupel, James W. "Demography of Genotypes: Failure of the Limited Life-Span Paradigm in *Drosphila melanogaster*." *Science*, 16 October 1992, *258*(5081), pp. 461–63.

Dasgupta, Partha. *An inquiry into well-being and destitution*. Oxford: Clarendon, 1993.

Dublin, Louis I. and Lotka, Alfred J. *Length of life: A study of the life table*. New York: Ronald, 1936.

Duncan, S. R.; Scott, Susan and Duncan, C. J. "The Dynamics of Smallpox Epidemics in Britain, 1550–1800." *Demography*, August 1993, *30*(3), pp. 405–23.

Dupâquier, Jacques. "Demographic Crises and Subsistence Crises in France, 1650–1725," in John Walter and Roger Schofield, eds., *Famine, disease and the social order in early modern society*. Cambridge: Cambridge University Press, 1989, pp. 189–99.

Eckstein, Zvi; Schultz, T. Paul and Wolpin, Kenneth I. "Short-Run Fluctuations in Fertility and Mortality in Pre-industrial Sweden." *European Economic Review*,

December 1984, *26*(3), pp. 297–317.

The Economist. "Squeezing in the Next Five Billion." 20–26 January 1990, *314*(7638), pp. 19–20, 22.

Fisler, Janis S. "Cardiac Effects of Starvation and Semistarvation Diets: Safety and Mechanisms of Action." *American Journal of Clinical Nutrition*, July 1992, *56*(supplement 1), pp. 230S–34S.

Fogel, Robert William. "Nutrition and the Decline in Mortality Since 1700: Some Preliminary Findings," in Stanley L. Engerman and Robert E. Gallman, eds., *Long-term factors in American economic growth*. Chicago: University of Chicago Press, 1986, pp. 439–555.

_____. "Biomedical Approaches to the Estimation and Interpretation of Secular Trends in Equity, Morbidity, Mortality, and Labor Productivity in Europe, 1750–1980." Unpublished manuscript, University of Chicago, 1987.

_____. "New Findings on Secular Trends in Nutrition and Mortality: Some Implications for Population Theory." Unpublished manuscript, University of Chicago, 1991.

_____. "Egalitarianism: The Economic Revolution of the Twentieth Century." The 1992 Simon Kuznets Memorial Lectures presented at Yale University, 22–24 April 1992a.

_____. "Second Thoughts on the European Escape from Hunger: Famines, Chronic Malnutrition, and Mortality," in S. R. Osmani, ed., *Nutrition and poverty*. Oxford: Clarendon, 1992b, pp. 243–86.

_____. "The Body Mass Index of Adult Male Slaves in the U.S. c. 1863 and Its Bearing on Mortality Rates," in Robert William Fogel, Ralph A. Galantine, and Richard L. Manning, eds., *Without consent or contract*, Vol. 2 (*Evidence and methods*). New York: Norton, 1992c, pp. 311–18.

_____. "A Comparison of Biomedical and Economic Measures of Egalitarianism: Some Implications of Secular Trends for Current Policy." Unpublished manuscript presented at the Workshop on Economic Theories of Inequality, Stanford University, 11–13 March 1993a.

_____. "New Sources and New Techniques for the Study of Secular Trends in Nutritional Status, Health, Mortality, and the Process of Aging." *Historical Methods*, Winter 1993b, *26*(1), pp. 5–43.

Fogel, Robert William; Costa, Dora L. and Kim, John M. "Secular Trends in the Distribution of Chronic Conditions and Disabilities at Young Adult and Late Ages, 1860–1988: Some Preliminary Findings." Unpublished manuscript presented at the NBER Summer Institute, Economics of Aging Program, 26–28 July 1993.

Fogel, Robert William and Engerman, Stanley L. *"Time on the cross: The economics of American slavery*, 2 vols. Boston: Little, Brown, 1974.

_____. "The Slave Diet on Large Plantations in 1860," in Robert William Fogel, Ralph A. Galantine, and Richard L. Manning, eds., *Without consent or contract*, Vol. 2 (*Evidence and methods*). New York: Norton, 1992, pp. 291–304.

Fogel, Robert William and Floud, Roderick. "Nutrition and Mortality in France, Britain, and the United States." Unpublished manuscript, University of Chicago, 1994.

Food and Agriculture Organization of the United Nations, World Health Organization, and United Nations University. *Energy and protein requirements. Report of a joint FAO / WHO / UNU expert consultation*, Technical Report Series No. 724. Geneva: World Health Organization, 1985.

Freudenberger, Herman and Cummins, Gaylord. "Health, Work, and Leisure Before the Industrial Revolution." *Explorations in Economic History*, January 1976, *13*(1), pp. 1–12.

Fridlizius, Gunnar. "The Mortality Decline in the First Phase of the Demographic Transition: Swedish Experiences," in Tommy Bengtsson, Gunnar Fridlizius, and Rolf Ohlsson, eds., *Pre-industrial population change*. Stockholm: Almquist and Wiksell, 1984, pp. 71–114.

Friedman, Gerald C. "The Heights of Slaves in Trinidad." *Social Science History*, Fall 1982, *6*(4), pp. 482–515.

Fries, James F. "Aging, Natural Death, and the Compression of Morbidity." *New England Journal of Medicine*, 17 July 1980, *303*(3), pp. 130–36.

_____. "The Compression of Morbidity: Near or Far?" *Milbank Quarterly*, 1989, *67*(2), pp. 208–32.

Galloway, Patrick R. "Differentials in Demographic Responses to Annual Price Variations in Pre-Revolutionary France: A Comparison of Rich and Poor Areas in Rouen, 1681–1787." *European Journal of Population*, May 1986, *2*(3–4), pp. 269–305.

_____. "Population, Prices and Weather in Preindustrial Europe." Ph.D. dissertation, University of California, Berkeley, 1987.

Gille, H. "The Demographic History of Northern European Countries in the Eighteenth Century." *Population Studies*, June 1949, *3*(1), pp. 3–70.

Goubert, Pierre. *The ancien régime* [Steven Cox, transl.]. New York: Harper, 1973.

Gould, Benjamin Apthorp. *Investigations in the military and anthropological statistics of American soldiers*. New York: Hurd and Houghton, 1869.

Heywood, Peter F. "Growth and Nutrition in Papua New Guinea." *Journal of Human Evolution*, January 1983, *12*(1), pp. 131–43.

Hill, G. L. "Some Implications of Body Composition Research for Modern Clinical Management." *Infusionstherapie*, April 1990, *17*(supplement 3), pp. 79–80.

Holderness, B. A. "Prices, Productivity, and Output," in G. E. Mingay, ed., *The agrarian history of England and Wales*, Vol. 6 (*1750–1850*). Cambridge: Cambridge University Press, 1989, pp. 84–189.

Hytten, F. E. and Leitch, I. *The physiology of human pregnancy*, 2nd Ed. Oxford: Blackwell, 1971.

Idiaquez, Juan. "Nutritional Status and Autonomic Nervous System Function." *Functional Neurology*, April–June 1988, *3*(2), pp. 205–9.

Jablonski, Mary; Rosenblum, Larry and Kunze, Kent. "Productivity, Age, and Labor Composition Changes in the U.S." *Monthly Labor Review*, September 1988, *111*(9), pp. 202–29.

John, A. Meredith. *The plantation slaves of*

Trinidad, 1783–1816. A mathematical and demographic inquiry. Cambridge: Cambridge University Press, 1988.

Kannisto, V.; Lauritsen, J.; Thatcher, A. R. and Vaupel, J. W. "Reductions in Mortality at Advanced Ages." *Population and Development Review*, 1994 (forthcoming).

Karpinos, Bernard D. "Height and Weight of Selective Service Registrants Processed for Military Service during WW II." *Human Biology*, December 1958, *30*(4), pp. 292–321.

Keynes, John Maynard. *Collected writings of John Maynard Keynes*, Vol. 4 (*A Tract on Monetary Reform*). London: Macmillian, 1971 [1923].

Kielmann, Arnfried A.; DeSweemer, Cecile; Chernichovsky, Dov; Uberoi, Inder S.; Masih, Norah; Taylor, Carl E.; Parker, Robert L.; Reinke, William A.; Kakar, D. N. and Sarma, R. S. S. *Child and maternal health services in rural India: The Narangwal experiment*, Vol. 1 (*Integrated nutrition and health*). Baltimore, MD: Johns Hopkins University Press, 1983.

Kim, John M. "Economic and Biomedical Implications of Waaler Surfaces: A New Perspective on Height, Weight, Morbidity, and Mortality." Unpublished manuscript, University of Chicago, 1993.

Kuznets, Simon. "Statistics and Economic History." *Journal of Economic History*, May 1941, *1*(1), pp. 26–41.

_____. "Long-Term Changes in the National Income of the United States of America Since 1879," in Simon Kuznets, ed., *Income and wealth of the United States: Trends and structure*. International Association for Research in Income and Wealth, Income and Wealth Series 2. Baltimore, MD: Johns Hopkins University Press, 1952, pp. 2–241.

Laslett, Peter. *The world we have lost: England before the industrial age*, 3rd Ed. New York: Scribner's, 1984.

Law, C. M.; de Swiet, M.; Osmond, C.; Fayers, P. M.; Barker, D. J. P.; Cruddas, A. M. and Fall, C. H. D. "Initiation of Hypertension in Utero and Its Amplification Throughout Life." *British Medical Journal*, 2 January 1993, *306*(6869), pp. 24–27.

Lee, Ronald. "Short-Term Variation: Vital Rates, Prices, and Weather," in E. A. Wrigley and R. S. Schofield, eds. *The population history of England, 1541–1871: A reconstruction*. Cambridge, MA: Harvard University Press, 1981, pp. 356–401.

Lipton, Michael. "Poverty, Undernutrition and Hunger." World Bank (Washington, DC) Staff Working Paper No. 597, 1983.

Livi-Bacci, Massimo. *Population and nutrition: An essay on European demographic history*. New York: Cambridge University Press, 1990.

Lozoff, Betsy; Jimenez, Elias and Wolf, Abraham W. "Long-Term Developmental Outcome of Infants with Iron Deficiency." *New England Journal of Medicine*, 5 September 1991, *325*(10), pp. 687–95.

Manton, Kenneth G. "Biomedical Research and Changing Concepts of Disease and Aging: Implications for Long-Term Forecasts for Elderly Populations," in Kenneth G. Manton, Burton H. Singer, and Richard M. Suzman, eds., *Forecasting the health of elderly populations*. New York: Springer-Verlag, 1993, pp. 319–65.

Manton, Kenneth G.; Corder, Larry S. and Stallard, Eric. "Estimates of Change in Chronic Disability and Institutional Incidence and Prevalence Rates in the U.S. Elderly Population from the 1982, 1984, and 1989 National Long-Term Care Survey." Mimeo, Center for Demographic Studies, Duke University, 1993.

Manton, Kenneth G. and Soldo, Beth J. "Disability and Mortality among the Oldest Old: Implications for Current and Future Health and Long-Term Care Service Needs," in Richard M. Suzman, Kenneth G. Manton, and David P. Willis, eds., *The oldest old*. New York: Oxford University Press, 1992, pp. 199–250.

Manton, Kenneth G.; Stallard, Eric and Singer, Burt. "Projecting the Future Size and Health Status of the U.S. Elderly Population." *International Journal of Forecasting*, November 1992, *8*(3), pp. 433–58.

Margo, Robert A. and Steckel, Richard H. "The Heights of American Slaves: New Evidence on Slave Nutrition and Health." *Social Science History*, Fall 1982, *6*(4), pp. 516–38.

Marmot, M. G.; Shipley, M. J. and Rose, Geoffrey. "Inequalities in Death—Specific Explanations of a General Pattern?" *Lancet*,

5 May 1984, (8384), pp. 1003–6.

Martorell, R. "Child Growth Retardation: A Discussion of Its Causes and Its Relationship to Health," in Sir Kenneth Blaxter and J. C. Waterlow, eds., *Nutritional adaptation in man*. London: Libby, 1985, pp. 13–29.

Martorell, R.; Rivera, J. and Kaplowitz, H. "Consequences of Stunting in Early Childhood for Adult Body Size in Rural Guatemala." *Annales Nestlé*, 1990, *48*, pp. 85–92.

McMahon, M. Molly and Bistrian, Bruce R. "The Physiology of Nutritional Assessment and Therapy in Protein-Calorie Malnutrition." *Disease-a-Month*, July 1990, *36*(7), pp. 373–417.

Meerton, M. A. von. "Croissance économique en France et accroissement des Française: Une analyse 'Villermetrique'." Unpublished manuscript, Center voor Economische Studiën, Louvain, Belgium, 1989.

Moore, William J.; Newman, Robert J. and Fheili, Mohammad. "Measuring the Relationship between Income and NHEs." *Health Care Financing Review*, Fall 1992, *14*(1), pp. 133–39.

Murphy, Kevin M. and Welch, Finis. "Empirical Age–Earnings Profiles." *Journal of Labor Economics*, April 1990, *8*(2), pp. 202–29.

Newhouse, Joseph P. "Medical Care Costs: How Much Welfare Loss?" *Journal of Economic Perspectives*, Summer 1992, *6*(3), pp. 3–21.

Oddy, D. J. "Food, Drink and Nutrition," in F. M. L. Thompson, ed., *The Cambridge social history of Britain, 1750–1950*, Vol. 2 (*People and their environment*). New York: Cambridge University Press, 1990, pp. 251–78.

Olson, John F. "Clock Time versus Real Time: A Comparison of the Lengths of the Northern and Southern Agricultural Work Years," in Robert William Fogel and Stanley L. Engerman, eds., *Without consent or contract*, Vol. 3 (*Markets and production: Technical Papers*, Vol. 1). New York: Norton, 1992, pp. 216–40.

Osmani, S. R. "On Some Controversies in the Measurement of Undernutrition," in S. R. Osmani, ed., *Nutrition and poverty*. Oxford: Clarendon, 1992, pp. 121–64.

Payne, P. "Assessing Undernutrition: The Need for a Reconceptualization," in S. R. Osmani, ed., *Nutrition and poverty*. Oxford: Clarendon, 1992, pp. 49–96.

Pellegrino, Edmund D. "The Metamorphosis of Medical Ethics: A 30-Year Retrospective." *Journal of the American Medical Association*, 3 March 1993, *269*(9), pp. 1158–62.

Perrenoud, Alfred. "The Mortality Decline in a Long-Term Perspective," in Tommy Bengtsson, Gunnar Fridlizius, and Rolf Ohlsson, eds., *Pre-industrial population change*. Stockholm: Almquist and Wiksell, 1984, pp. 41–69.

_____. "The Attenuation of Mortality Crises and the Decline of Mortality," in R. Schofield, D. Reher, and A. Bideau, eds., *The decline of mortality in Europe*. Oxford: Clarendon, 1991, pp. 18–37.

Phillips, D. I. W.; Cooper, C.; Fall, C.; Prentice, L.; Osmond, C.; Barker, D. J. P. and Rees Smith, B. "Fetal Growth and Autoimmune Thyroid Disease." *Quarterly Journal of Medicine*, April 1993, *86*(4), pp. 247–53.

Phipps, K.; Barker, D. J. P.; Hales, C. N.; Fall, C. H. D.; Osmond, C. and Clark, P. M. S. "Fetal Growth and Impaired Glucose Tolerance in Men and Women." *Diabetologia*, March 1993, *36*(3), pp. 225–28.

Preston, Samuel H. "Demographic Changes in the United States, 1970–2050," in Anna M. Rappaport and Sylvester J. Schieber, eds., *Demography and retirement: The twenty-first century*. Westport, CT: Praeger, 1993, pp. 19–48.

Quenouille, M. H.; Boyne, A. W.; Fisher, W. B. and Leitch, I. *Statistical studies of recorded energy expenditure in man*." Technical Communication No. 17. Aberdeenshire, Scotland: Commonwealth Bureau of Animal Nutrition, 1951.

Richards, Toni. "Weather, Nutrition and the Economy: The Analysis of Short Run Fluctuations in Births, Deaths and Marriages, France 1740–1909," in Tommy Bengtsson, Gunnar Fridlizius, and Rolf Ohlsson, eds., *Pre-industrial population change*. Stockholm: Almquist and Wiksell, 1984, pp. 357–89.

Robbins, S. L.; Cotran, R. S. and Kumar, V. *Pathologic basis of disease*, 3rd Ed.

Philadelphia: Saunders, 1984.

Saba, Thomas M.; Dillon, Bruce C. and Lanser, Marc E. "Fibronectin and Phagocytic Host Defense: Relationship to Nutritional Support." *Journal of Parenteral and Enteral Nutrition*, January-February 1983, *7*(1), pp. 62–68.

Schieber, George J.; Poullier, Jean-Pierre and Greenwald, Leslie M. "Health Care Systems in Twenty-Four Countries." *Health Affairs*, Fall 1993, *10*(3), pp. 22–38.

Schwartz, William B. and Aaron, Henry J. "Must We Ration Health Care?" *Best's Review*, January 1991, *91*(9), pp. 37–41.

Scrimshaw, Nevin S. "Malnutrition, Brain Development, Learning and Behavior." The Twentieth Kamla Puri Sabharwal Memorial Lecture presented at Lady Irwin College, New Delhi, 23 November 1993.

Scrimshaw, Nevin S. and Gordon, J. E., eds. *Malnutrition, learning and behavior*. Cambridge, MA: MIT Press, 1968.

Scrimshaw, Nevin S.; Taylor, C. E. and Gordon, J. E. *Interactions of nutrition and infection*. Geneva: World Health Organization, 1968.

Seckler, David. "'Malnutrition': An Intellectual Odyssey." *Western Journal of Agricultural Economics*, December 1980, *5*(2), pp. 219–27.

Sen, Amartya. *Poverty and famines: An essay on entitlement and deprivation*. Oxford: Clarendon, 1981.

Shammas, Carole. "The Eighteenth-Century English Diet and Economic Change." *Explorations in Economic History*, July 1984, *21*(3), pp. 254–69.

_____. *The pre-industrial consumer in England and America*. Oxford: Clarendon, 1990.

Shuttleworth, John Sterling. "Ethical Issues in Long-Term Care." *Journal of the Medical Association of Georgia*, November 1990, *79*(11), pp. 843–45.

Sommer, Alfred and Lowenstein, Matthew S. "Nutritional Status and Mortality: A Prospective Validation of the QUAC Stick." *American Journal of Clinical Nutrition*, March 1975, *28*(3), pp. 287–92.

Srinivasan, T. N. "Undernutrition: Concepts, Measurement, and Policy Implications," in S. R. Osmani, ed., *Nutrition and poverty*. Oxford: Clarendon, 1992, pp. 97–120.

Sukhatme, P. V. "Poverty and Malnutrition," in P. V. Sukhatme, ed., *Newer concepts in nutrition and their implications for policy*. Pune, India: Maharashtra Association for the Cultivation of Science Research Institute, 1982, pp. 11–63.

Tanner, J. M. *Foetus into man: Physical growth from conception to maturity*, Rev. Ed. Cambridge, MA: Harvard University Press, 1990.

_____. Review of D. J. P. Barker's *Fetal and infant origins of adult disease*. *Annals of Human Biology*, September-October, 1993, *20*(5), pp. 508–9.

Thatcher, A. R. "Trends in Numbers and Mortality at High Ages in England and Wales." *Population Studies*, November 1992, *46*(3), pp. 411–26.

Toutain, Jean-Claude. "La consommation alimentaire en France de 1789 à 1964." *Economies et Sociétés, Cahiers de l'ISEA*, November 1971, *5*(11), pp. 1909–2049.

U.S. Bureau of the Census. *Historical statistics of the United States, colonial times to 1970*. Washington, DC: U.S. Government Printing Office, 1975.

U.S. Department of Health and Human Services. *Anthropometric Reference Data and Prevalence of Overweight*, Vital and Health Statistics, Series 11 No. 238. Washington, DC: U.S. Government Printing Office, 1987.

Vaupel, James W. "The Impact of Population Aging on Health and Health Care Costs: Uncertainties and New Evidence About Life Expectancy." Unpublished manuscript, Center for Health and Social Policy, Odense University, Denmark, 1991a.

_____. "Prospects for a Longer Life Expectancy." Unpublished manuscript presented to the annual meeting of the Population Association of America, Washington, DC, 21–23 March 1991.

Vaupel, James W. and Lundström, H. "Prospects for Longer Life Expectancy," in David Wise, ed., *Economics of aging*. Chicago: University of Chicago Press, 1994 (forthcoming).

Veblen, T. *The theory of the leisure class: An*

economic study of institutions. New York: Modern Library, 1934 [1899].

Volpe, J. J. "Hypoxic-Ischemic Encephalopathy—Clinical Aspects," in *Neurology of the newborn*, 2nd Ed. Philadelphia: Saunders, 1987, pp. 236–79.

Waaler, Hans Th. "Height, Weight and Mortality: The Norwegian Experience." *Acta Medica Scandinavica*, Supplement 1984, (679), pp. 1–51.

Weir, David R. "Fertility Transition in Rural France, 1740–1829." Ph.D. dissertation, Stanford University, 1982.

_____. "Markets and Mortality in France, 1600–1789," in John Walter and Roger Schofield, eds., *Famine, disease and the social order in early modern society*. Cambridge: Cambridge University Press, 1989, pp. 201–34.

_____. "Parental Consumption Decisions and Child Health during the Early French Fertility Decline, 1790–1914." *Journal of Economic History*, June 1993, *53*(2), pp. 259–74.

West, Patrick; Macintyre, Sally; Annandale, Ellen and Hunt, Kate. "Social Class and Health in Youth: Findings from The West of Scotland Twenty-07 Study." *Social Science and Medicine*, 1990, *30*(6), pp. 665–73.

Wolfe, Barbara L. "Health Status and Medical Expenditures: Is There a Link? *Social Science and Medicine*, 1986, *22*(10), pp. 993–99.

Wrigley, E. A. "Urban Growth and Agricultural Change: England and the Continent in the Early Modern Period," in *Peoples, cities and wealth: The transformation of traditional society*. Oxford: Blackwell, 1987, pp. 157–93.

Wrigley, E. A. and Schofield, R. S, eds. *The population history of England, 1541–1871: A reconstruction*. Cambridge, MA: Harvard University Press, 1981.

Part III
Individual and Household Behaviour: Production and Consumption

[10]

THE ECONOMIC JOURNAL

SEPTEMBER 1965

A THEORY OF THE ALLOCATION OF TIME

I. INTRODUCTION

THROUGHOUT history the amount of time spent at work has never consistently been much greater than that spent at other activities. Even a work week of fourteen hours a day for six days still leaves half the total time for sleeping, eating and other activities. Economic development has led to a large secular decline in the work week, so that whatever may have been true of the past, to-day it is below fifty hours in most countries, less than a third of the total time available. Consequently the allocation and efficiency of non-working time may now be more important to economic welfare than that of working time; yet the attention paid by economists to the latter dwarfs any paid to the former.

Fortunately, there is a movement under way to redress the balance. The time spent at work declined secularly, partly because young persons increasingly delayed entering the labour market by lengthening their period of schooling. In recent years many economists have stressed that the time of students is one of the inputs into the educational process, that this time could be used to participate more fully in the labour market and therefore that one of the costs of education is the forgone earnings of students. Indeed, various estimates clearly indicate that forgone earnings is the dominant private and an important social cost of both high-school and college education in the United States.[1] The increased awareness of the importance of forgone earnings has resulted in several attempts to economise on students' time, as manifested, say, by the spread of the quarterly and tri-mester systems.[2]

Most economists have now fully grasped the importance of forgone earnings in the educational process and, more generally, in all investments in human capital, and criticise educationalists and others for neglecting them. In the light of this it is perhaps surprising that economists have not been

---

[1] See T. W. Schultz, "The Formation of Human Capital by Education," *Journal of Political Economy* (December 1960), and my *Human Capital* (Columbia University Press for the N.B.E.R., 1964), Chapter IV. I argue there that the importance of forgone earnings can be directly seen, *e.g.*, from the failure of free tuition to eliminate impediments to college attendance or the increased enrolments that sometimes occur in depressed areas or time periods.

[2] On the cause of the secular trend towards an increased school year see my comments, *ibid.*, p. 103.

equally sophisticated about other non-working uses of time. For example, the cost of a service like the theatre or a good like meat is generally simply said to equal their market prices, yet everyone would agree that the theatre and even dining take time, just as schooling does, time that often could have been used productively. If so, the full costs of these activities would equal the sum of market prices and the forgone value of the time used up. In other words, indirect costs should be treated on the same footing when discussing all non-work uses of time, as they are now in discussions of schooling.

In the last few years a group of us at Columbia University have been occupied, perhaps initially independently but then increasingly less so, with introducing the cost of time systematically into decisions about non-work activities. J. Mincer has shown with several empirical examples how estimates of the income elasticity of demand for different commodities are biased when the cost of time is ignored;[1] J. Owen has analysed how the demand for leisure can be affected;[2] E. Dean has considered the allocation of time between subsistence work and market participation in some African economies;[3] while, as already mentioned, I have been concerned with the use of time in education, training and other kinds of human capital. Here I attempt to develop a general treatment of the allocation of time in all other non-work activities. Although under my name alone, much of any credit it merits belongs to the stimulus received from Mincer, Owen, Dean and other past and present participants in the Labor Workshop at Columbia.[4]

The plan of the discussion is as follows. The first section sets out a basic theoretical analysis of choice that includes the cost of time on the same footing as the cost of market goods, while the remaining sections treat various empirical implications of the theory. These include a new approach to changes in hours of work and " leisure," the full integration of so-called " productive " consumption into economic analysis, a new analysis of the effect of income on the quantity and " quality " of commodities consumed, some suggestions on the measurement of productivity, an economic analysis of queues and a few others as well. Although I refer to relevant empirical

---

[1] See his " Market Prices, Opportunity Costs, and Income Effects," in *Measurement in Economics: Studies in Mathematical Economics and Econometrics in Memory of Yehuda Grunfeld* (Stanford University Press, 1963). In his well-known earlier study Mincer considered the allocation of married women between " housework " and labour force participation. (See his " Labor Force Participation of Married Women," in *Aspects of Labor Economics* (Princeton University Press, 1962).)

[2] See his *The Supply of Labor and the Demand for Recreation* (unpublished Ph.D. dissertation, Columbia University, 1964).

[3] See his *Economic Analysis and African Response to Price* (unpublished Ph.D. dissertation, Columbia University, 1963).

[4] Let me emphasise, however, that I alone am responsible for any errors.

I would also like to express my appreciation for the comments received when presenting these ideas to seminars at the Universities of California (Los Angeles), Chicago, Pittsburgh, Rochester and Yale, and to a session at the 1963 Meetings of the Econometric Society. Extremely helpful comments on an earlier draft were provided by Milton Friedman and by Gregory C. Chow; the latter also assisted in the mathematical formulation. Linda Kee provided useful research assistance. My research was partially supported by the IBM Corporation.

work that has come to my attention, little systematic testing of the theory has been attempted.

II. A Revised Theory of Choice

According to traditional theory, households maximise utility functions of the form

$$U = U(y_1, y_2, \ldots, y_n) \quad \cdots \quad \cdots \quad (1)$$

subject to the resource constraint

$$\sum p_i' y_i = I = W + V \quad \cdots \quad \cdots \quad (2)$$

where y_i are goods purchased on the market, p'_i are their prices, I is money income, W is earnings and V is other income. As the introduction suggests, the point of departure here is the systematic incorporation of non-working time. Households will be assumed to combine time and market goods to produce more basic commodities that directly enter their utility functions. One such commodity is the seeing of a play, which depends on the input of actors, script, theatre and the playgoer's time; another is sleeping, which depends on the input of a bed, house (pills?) and time. These commodities will be called Z_i and written as

$$Z_i = f_i(x_i, T_i) \quad \cdots \quad \cdots \quad (3)$$

where x_i is a vector of market goods and T_i a vector of time inputs used in producing the ith commodity.[1] Note that, when capital goods such as refrigerators or automobiles are used, x refers to the services yielded by the goods. Also note that T_i is a vector because, *e.g.*, the hours used during the day or on weekdays may be distinguished from those used at night or on week-ends. Each dimension of T_i refers to a different aspect of time. Generally, the partial derivatives of Z_i with respect to both x_i and T_i are non-negative.[2]

In this formulation households are both producing units and utility maximisers. They combine time and market goods via the " production functions " f_i to produce the basic commodities Z_i, and they choose the best combination of these commodities in the conventional way by maximising a utility function

$$U = U(Z_i, \ldots Z_m) \equiv U(f_1, \ldots f_m) \equiv U(x_1, \ldots x_m; T_1, \ldots T_m) \quad (4)$$

---

[1] There are several empirical as well as conceptual advantages in assuming that households combine goods and time to produce commodities instead of simply assuming that the amount of time used at an activity is a direct function of the amount of goods consumed. For example, a change in the cost of goods relative to time could cause a significant substitution away from the one rising in relative cost. This, as well as other applications, are treated in the following sections.

[2] If a good or time period was used in producing several commodities I assume that these " joint costs " could be fully and uniquely allocated among the commodities. The problems here are no different from those usually arising in the analysis of multi-product firms.

subject to a budget constraint

$$g(Z_t, \ldots Z_m) = Z \qquad . \quad . \quad . \quad . \quad . \quad (5)$$

where g is an expenditure function of Z_i and Z is the bound on resources. The integration of production and consumption is at odds with the tendency for economists to separate them sharply, production occurring in firms and consumption in households. It should be pointed out, however, that in recent years economists increasingly recognise that a household is truly a "small factory":[1] it combines capital goods, raw materials and labour to clean, feed, procreate and otherwise produce useful commodities. Undoubtedly the fundamental reason for the traditional separation is that firms are usually given control over working time in exchange for market goods, while "discretionary" control over market goods and consumption time is retained by households as they create their own utility. If (presumably different) firms were also given control over market goods and consumption time in exchange for providing utility the separation would quickly fade away in analysis as well as in fact.

The basic goal of the analysis is to find measures of g and Z which facilitate the development of empirical implications. The most direct approach is to assume that the utility function in equation (4) is maximised subject to separate constraints on the expenditure of market goods and time, and to the production functions in equation (3). The goods constraint can be written as

$$\sum_1^m p_i x_i = I = V + T_w \bar{w} \qquad . \quad . \quad . \quad . \quad (6)$$

where p_i is a vector giving the unit prices of x_i, T_w is a vector giving the hours spent at work and $\bar{w}$ is a vector giving the earnings per unit of T_w. The time constraints can be written as

$$\sum_1^m T_i = T_c = T - T_w \qquad . \quad . \quad . \quad . \quad (7)$$

where T_c is a vector giving the total time spent at consumption and T is a vector giving the total time available. The production functions (3) can be written in the equivalent form

$$\left.\begin{aligned} T_i &\equiv t_i Z_i \\ x_i &\equiv b_i Z_i \end{aligned}\right\} \qquad . \quad . \quad . \quad . \quad . \quad (8)$$

where t_i is a vector giving the input of time per unit of Z_i and b_i is a similar vector for market goods.

The problem would appear to be to maximise the utility function (4) subject to the multiple constraints (6) and (7) and to the production relations (8). There is, however, really only one basic constraint: (6) is not independent of (7) because time can be converted into goods by using less time

---

[1] See, *e.g.*, A. K. Cairncross, "Economic Schizophrenia," *Scottish Journal of Political Economy* (February 1958).

at consumption and more at work. Thus, substituting for T_w in (6) its equivalent in (7) gives the single constraint [1]

$$\sum p_i x_i + \sum T_i \bar{w} = V + T\bar{w} \quad \ldots \quad \ldots \quad (9)$$

By using (8), (9) can be written as

$$\sum (p_i b_i + t_i \bar{w}) Z_i = V + T\bar{w} \quad \ldots \quad \ldots \quad (10)$$

with

$$\left. \begin{array}{l} \pi_i \equiv p_i b_i + t_i \bar{w} \\ S' \equiv V + T\bar{w} \end{array} \right\} \quad \ldots \quad \ldots \quad (11)$$

The full price of a unit of Z_i (π_i) is the sum of the prices of the goods and of the time used per unit of Z_i. That is, the full price of consumption is the sum of direct and indirect prices in the same way that the full cost of investing in human capital is the sum of direct and indirect costs.[2] These direct and indirect prices are symmetrical determinants of total price, and there is no analytical reason to stress one rather than the other.

The resource constraint on the right side of equation (10), S', is easy to interpret if $\bar{w}$ were a constant, independent of the Z_i. For then S' gives the money income achieved if all the time available were devoted to work. This achievable income is " spent " on the commodities Z_i either directly through expenditures on goods, $\sum p_i b_i Z_i$, or indirectly through the forgoing of income, $\sum t_i \bar{w} Z_i$, *i.e.*, by using time at consumption rather than at work. As long as $\bar{w}$ were constant, and if there were constant returns in producing Z_i so that b_i and t_i were fixed for given p_i and $\bar{w}$ the equilibrium condition resulting from maximising (4) subject to (10) takes a very simple form:

$$U_i = \frac{\partial U}{\partial Z_i} = \lambda \pi_i \qquad i = 1, \ldots m \quad . \quad . \quad (12)$$

where λ is the marginal utility of money income. If $\bar{w}$ were not constant the resource constraint in equation (10) would not have any particularly useful interpretation: $S' = V + T\bar{w}$ would overstate the money income achievable as long as marginal wage-rates were below average ones. Moreover, the equilibrium conditions would become more complicated than (12) because marginal would have to replace average prices.

The total resource constraint could be given the sensible interpretation of the maximum money income achievable only in the special and unlikely case when average earnings were constant. This suggests dropping the approach based on explicitly considering separate goods and time constraints and substituting one in which the total resource constraint necessarily equalled the maximum money income achievable, which will be simply called " full income." [3] This income could in general be obtained by devoting all the

---

[1] The dependency among constraints distinguishes this problem from many other multiple-constraint situations in economic analysis, such as those arising in the usual theory of rationing (see J. Tobin, " A Survey of the Theory of Rationing," *Econometrica* (October, 1952)). Rationing would reduce to a formally identical single-constraint situation if rations were saleable and fully convertible into money income.

[2] See my *Human Capital, op. cit.*

[3] This term emerged from a conversation with Milton Friedman.

time and other resources of a household to earning income, with no regard for consumption. Of course, all the time would not usually be spent " at " a job: sleep, food, even leisure are required for efficiency, and some time (and other resources) would have to be spent on these activities in order to maximise money income. The amount spent would, however, be determined solely by the effect on income and not by any effect on utility. Slaves, for example, might be permitted time " off " from work only in so far as that maximised their output, or free persons in poor environments might have to maximise money income simply to survive.[1]

Households in richer countries do, however, forfeit money income in order to obtain additional utility, *i.e.*, they exchange money income for a greater amount of psychic income. For example, they might increase their leisure time, take a pleasant job in preference to a better-paying unpleasant one, employ unproductive nephews or eat more than is warranted by considerations of productivity. In these and other situations the amount of money income forfeited measures the cost of obtaining additional utility.

Thus the full income approach provides a meaningful resource constraint and one firmly based on the fact that goods and time can be combined into a single overall constraint because time can be converted into goods through money income. It also incorporates a unified treatment of all substitutions of non-pecuniary for pecuniary income, regardless of their nature or whether they occur on the job or in the household. The advantages of this will become clear as the analysis proceeds.

If full income is denoted by S, and if the total earnings forgone or " lost " by the interest in utility is denoted by L, the identity relating L to S and I is simply

$$L(Z_1, \ldots, Z_m) \equiv S - I(Z_1, \ldots, Z_m) \quad . \quad . \quad . \quad (13)$$

I and L are functions of the Z_i because how much is earned or forgone depends on the consumption set chosen; for example, up to a point, the less leisure chosen the larger the money income and the smaller the amount forgone.[2] Using equations (6) and (8), equation (13) can be written as

$$\sum p_i b_i Z_i + L(Z_1, \ldots, Z_m) \equiv S \quad . \quad . \quad . \quad . \quad (14)$$

[1] Any utility received would only be an incidental by-product of the pursuit of money income. Perhaps this explains why utility analysis was not clearly formulated and accepted until economic development had raised incomes well above the subsistence level.

[2] Full income is achieved by maximising the earnings function

$$W = W(Z_1, \ldots Z_m) \quad . \quad . \quad . \quad . \quad . \quad . \quad . \quad . \quad (1')$$

subject to the expenditure constraint in equation (6), to the inequality

$$\sum_{1}^{m} T_1 \leq T \quad . \quad . \quad . \quad . \quad . \quad . \quad . \quad . \quad . \quad (2')$$

and to the restrictions in (8). I assume for simplicity that the amount of each dimension of time used in producing commodities is less than the total available, so that (2') can be ignored; it is not

This basic resource constraint states that full income is spent either directly on market goods or indirectly through the forgoing of money income. Unfortunately, there is no simple expression for the average price of Z_i as there is in equation (10). However, marginal, not average, prices are relevant for behaviour, and these would be identical for the constraint in (10) only when average earnings, $\bar{w}$, was constant. But, if so, the expression for the loss function simplifies to

$$L = \bar{w}T_c = \bar{w}\sum t_i Z_i \; . \; . \; . \; . \; . \; . \; (15)$$

and (14) reduces to (10). Moreover, even in the general case the total marginal prices resulting from (14) can always be divided into direct and indirect components: the equilibrium conditions resulting from maximising the utility function subject to (14) [1] are

$$U_i = T(p_i b_i + L_i), \quad i = 1, \ldots, m \; . \; . \; . \; (16)$$

where $p_i b_i$ is the direct and L_i the indirect component of the total marginal price $p_i b_i + L_i$.[2]

Behind the division into direct and indirect costs is the allocation of time and goods between work-orientated and consumption-orientated activities. This suggests an alternative division of costs; namely, into those resulting from the allocation of goods and those resulting from the allocation of time. Write $L_i = \partial L / \partial Z_i$ as

$$L_i = \frac{\partial L}{\partial T_i} \frac{\partial T_i}{\partial Z_i} + \frac{\partial L}{\partial x_i} \frac{\partial x_i}{\partial Z_i} \; . \; . \; . \; . \; . \; (17)$$

$$= l_i t_i + c_i b_i \; . \; . \; . \; . \; . \; . \; . \; (18)$$

where $l_i = \dfrac{\partial L}{\partial T_i}$ and $c_i = \dfrac{\partial L}{\partial x_i}$ are the marginal forgone earnings of using more time and goods respectively on Z_i. Equation (16) can then be written as

$$U_i = T[b_i(p_i + c_i) + t_i l_i] \; . \; . \; . \; . \; (19)$$

The total marginal cost of Z_i is the sum of $b_i(p_i + c_i)$, the marginal cost of using goods in producing Z_i, and $t_i l_i$, the marginal cost of using time. This division would be equivalent to that between direct and indirect costs only if $c_i = 0$ or if there were no indirect costs of using goods.

---

difficult to incorporate this constraint. Maximising (1′) subject to (6) and (8) yields the following conditions

$$\frac{\partial W}{\partial Z_i} = \frac{p_i b_i \sigma}{1 + \sigma} \; . \; . \; . \; . \; . \; . \; . \; . \; . \; (3')$$

where σ is the marginal productivity of money income. Since the loss function $L = (S - V) - W$, the equilibrium conditions to minimise the loss is the same as (3′) except for a change in sign.

[1] Households maximise their utility subject only to the single total resource constraint given by (14), for once the full income constraint is satisfied, there is no other restriction on the set of Z_i that can be chosen. By introducing the concept of full income the problem of maximising utility subject to the time and goods constraints is solved in two stages: first, full income is determined from the goods and time constraints, and then utility is maximised subject only to the constraint imposed by full income.

[2] It can easily be shown that the equilibrium conditions of (16) are in fact precisely the same as those following in general from equation (10).

The accompanying figure shows the equilibrium given by equation (16) for a two-commodity world. In equilibrium the slope of the full income

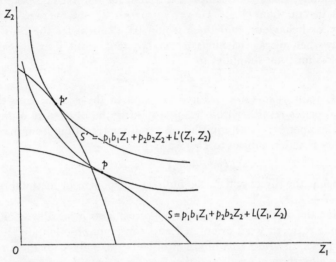

opportunity curve, which equals the ratio of marginal prices, would equal the slope of an indifference curve, which equals the ratio of marginal utilities. Equilibrium occurs at p and p' for the opportunity curves S and S' respectively.

The rest of the paper is concerned with developing numerous empirical implications of this theory, starting with determinants of hours worked and concluding with an economic interpretation of various queueing systems. To simplify the presentation, it is assumed that the distinction between direct and indirect costs is equivalent to that between goods and time costs; in other words, the marginal forgone cost of the use of goods, c_i, is set equal to zero. The discussion would not be much changed, but would be more cumbersome were this not assumed.[1] Finally, until Section IV goods and time are assumed to be used in fixed proportions in producing commodities; that is, the coefficients b_i and t_i in equation (8) are treated as constants.

III. APPLICATIONS

(a) *Hours of Work*

If the effects of various changes on the time used on consumption, T_c, could be determined their effects on hours worked, T_w, could be found residually from equation (7). This section considers, among other things, the effects of changes in income, earnings and market prices on T_c, and thus on T_w,

[1] Elsewhere I have discussed some effects of the allocation of goods on productivity (see my "Investment in Human Capital: A Theoretical Analysis," *Journal of Political Economy*, special supplement (October 1962), Section 2); essentially the same discussion can be found in *Human Capital, op. cit.*, Chapter II.

using as the major tool of analysis differences among commodities in the importance of forgone earnings.

The relative marginal importance of forgone earnings is defined as

$$\alpha_i = \frac{l_i t_i}{p_i b_i + l_i t_i} \quad \cdots \cdots \quad (20)$$

The importance of forgone earnings would be greater the larger l_i and t_i, the forgone earnings per hour of time and the number of hours used per unit of Z_i respectively, while it would be smaller the larger p_i and b_i, the market price of goods and the number of goods used per unit of Z_i respectively. Similarly, the relative marginal importance of time is defined as

$$\gamma_i = \frac{t_i}{p_i b_i + l_i t_i} \quad \cdots \cdots \quad (21)$$

If full income increased solely because of an increase in V (other money income) there would simply be a parallel shift of the opportunity curve to the right with no change in relative commodity prices. The consumption of most commodities would have to increase; if all did, hours worked would decrease, for the total time spent on consumption must increase if the output of all commodities did, and by equation (7) the time spent at work is inversely related to that spent on consumption. Hours worked could increase only if relatively time intensive commodities, those with large γ, were sufficiently inferior.[1]

A uniform percentage increase in earnings for all allocations of time would increase the cost per hour used in consumption by the same percentage for all commodities.[2] The relative prices of different commodities would, however, change as long as forgone earnings were not equally important for all; in particular, the prices of commodities having relatively important forgone earnings would rise more. Now the fundamental theorem of

---

[1] The problem is: under what conditions would

$$\frac{-\partial T_w}{\partial V} = \frac{\partial T_c}{\partial V} = \Sigma t_i \frac{\partial Z_i}{\partial V} < 0 \quad \cdots \cdots \quad (1')$$

when

$$\Sigma(p_i b_i + l_i t_i) \frac{\partial Z_i}{\partial V} = 1 \quad \cdots \cdots \quad (2')$$

If the analysis were limited to a two-commodity world where Z_1 was more time intensive, then it can easily be shown that $(1')$ would hold if, and only if,

$$\frac{\partial Z_1}{\partial V} < \frac{-\gamma_2}{(\gamma_1 - \gamma_2)(p_1 b_1 + l_1 t_1)} < 0 \quad \cdots \cdots \quad (3')$$

[2] By a uniform change of β is meant

$$W_1 = (1 + \beta) W_0(Z_1, \ldots Z_n)$$

where W_0 represents the earnings function before the change and W_1 represents it afterwards. Since the loss function is defined as

$$L = S - W - V$$
$$= W(\acute{Z}) - W(Z),$$

then

$$L_1 = W_1(\acute{Z}) - W_1(Z)$$
$$= (1 + \beta)[W_0(\acute{Z}) - W_0(Z)] = (1 + \beta)L_0$$

Consequently, all opportunities costs also change by β.

demand theory states that a compensated change in relative prices would induce households to consume less of commodities rising in price. The figure shows the effect of a rise in earnings fully compensated by a decline in other income: the opportunity curve would be rotated clockwise through the initial position p if Z_1 were the more earnings-intensive commodity. In the figure the new equilibrium p' must be to the left and above p, or less Z_1 and more Z_2 would be consumed.

Therefore a compensated uniform rise in earnings would lead to a shift away from earnings-intensive commodities and towards goods-intensive ones. Since earnings and time intensiveness tend to be positively correlated,[1] consumption would be shifted from time-intensive commodities. A shift away from such commodities would, however, result in a reduction in the total time spent in consumption, and thus an increase in the time spent at work.[2]

The effect of an uncompensated increase in earnings on hours worked would depend on the relative strength of the substitution and income effects. The former would increase hours, the latter reduce them; which dominates cannot be determined *a priori*.

The conclusion that a pure rise in earnings increases and a pure rise in income reduces hours of work must sound very familiar, for they are traditional results of the well-known labour–leisure analysis. What, then, is the relation between our analysis, which treats all commodities symmetrically and stresses only their differences in relative time and earning intensities, and the usual analysis, which distinguishes a commodity having special properties called " leisure " from other more commonplace commodities? It is easily shown that the usual labour–leisure analysis can be looked upon as a special case of ours in which the cost of the commodity called leisure consists entirely of forgone earnings and the cost of other commodities entirely of goods.[3]

---

[1] According to the definitions of earning and time intensity in equations (20) and (21), they would be positively correlated unless l_i and t_i were sufficiently negatively correlated. See the further discussion later on.

[2] Let it be stressed that this conclusion usually holds, even when households are irrational; sophisticated calculations about the value of time at work or in consumption, or substantial knowledge about the amount of time used by different commodities is not required. Changes in the hours of work, even of non-maximising, impulsive, habitual, etc., households would tend to be positively related to compensated changes in earnings because demand curves tend to be negatively inclined even for such households (see G. S. Becker, " Irrational Behavior and Economic Theory," *Journal of Political Economy* (February 1962)).

[3] Suppose there were two commodities Z_1 and Z_2, where the cost of Z_1 depended only on the cost of market goods, while the cost of Z_2 depended only on the cost of time. The goods-budget constraint would then simply be

$$p_1 b_1 Z_1 = I = V + T_w \bar{w}$$

and the constraint on time would be

$$t_2 Z_2 = T - T_w$$

This is essentially the algebra of the analysis presented by Henderson and Quandt, and their treatment is representative. They call Z_2 " leisure," and Z_1 an average of different commodities. Their

As a description of reality such an approach, of course, is not tenable, since virtually all activities use both time and goods. Perhaps it would be defended either as an analytically necessary or extremely insightful approximation to reality. Yet the usual substitution and income effects of a change in resources on hours worked have easily been derived from a more general analysis which stresses only that the relative importance of time varies among commodities. The rest of the paper tries to go further and demonstrate that the traditional approach, with its stress on the demand for " leisure," apparently has seriously impeded the development of insights about the economy, since the more direct and general approach presented here naturally leads to a variety of implications never yet obtained.

The two determinants of the importance of forgone earnings are the amount of time used per dollar of goods and the cost per unit of time. Reading a book, taking a haircut or commuting use more time per dollar of goods than eating dinner, frequenting a night-club or sending children to private summer camps. Other things the same, forgone earnings would be more important for the former set of commodities than the latter.

The importance of forgone earnings would be determined solely by time intensity only if the cost of time was the same for all commodities. Presumably, however, it varies considerably among commodities and at different periods. For example, the cost of time is often less on week-ends and in the evenings because many firms are closed then,[1] which explains why a famous liner intentionally includes a week-end in each voyage between the United States and Europe.[2] The cost of time would also tend to be less for commodities that contribute to productive effort, traditionally called " productive consumption." A considerable amount of sleep, food and even " play " fall under this heading. The opportunity cost of the time is less because these commodities indirectly contribute to earnings. Productive consumption has had a long but bandit-like existence in economic thought; our analysis does systematically incorporate it into household decision-making.

Although the formal specification of leisure in economic models has ignored expenditures on goods, cannot one argue that a more correct specification would simply associate leisure with relatively important forgone earnings? Most conceptions of leisure do imply that it is time intensive and does not indirectly contribute to earnings,[3] two of the important

equilibrium condition that the rate of substitution between goods and leisure equals the real wage-rate is just a special case of our equation (19) (see *Microeconomic Theory* (McGraw-Hill, 1958), p. 23).

[1] For workers receiving premium pay on the week-ends and in the evenings, however, the cost of time may be considerably greater then.

[2] See the advertisement by United States Lines in various issues of the *New Yorker* magazine: " The S.S. *United States* regularly includes a week-end in its 5 days to Europe, saving [economic] time for businessmen " (my insertion).

[3] For example, *Webster's Collegiate Dictionary* defines leisurely as " characterized by leisure, taking *abundant time* " (my italics); or S. de Grazia, in his recent *Of Time, Work and Leisure*, says, " Leisure is a state of being in which activity is performed for its own sake or as its own end " (New York: The Twentieth Century Fund, 1962, p. 15).

characteristics of earnings-intensive commodities. On the other hand, not all of what are usually considered leisure activities do have relatively important forgone earnings: night-clubbing is generally considered leisure, and yet, at least in its more expensive forms, has a large expenditure component. Conversely, some activities have relatively large forgone earnings and are not considered leisure: haircuts or child care are examples. Consequently, the distinction between earnings-intensive and other commodities corresponds only partly to the usual distinction between leisure and other commodities. Since it has been shown that the relative importance of forgone earnings rather than any concept of leisure is more relevant for economic analysis, less attention should be paid to the latter. Indeed, although the social philosopher might have to define precisely the concept of leisure,[1] the economist can reach all his traditional results as well as many more without introducing it at all!

Not only is it difficult to distinguish leisure from other non-work [2] but also even work from non-work. Is commuting work, non-work or both? How about a business lunch, a good diet or relaxation? Indeed, the notion of productive consumption was introduced precisely to cover those commodities that contribute to work as well as to consumption. Cannot pure work then be considered simply as a limiting commodity of such joint commodities in which the contribution to consumption was nil? Similarly, pure consumption would be a limiting commodity in the opposite direction in which the contribution to work was nil, and intermediate commodities would contribute to both consumption and work. The more important the contribution to work relative to consumption, the smaller would tend to be the relative importance of forgone earnings. Consequently, the effects of changes in earnings, other income, etc., on hours worked then become assimiliated to and essentially a special case of their effects on the consumption of less earnings-intensive commodities. For example, a pure rise in earnings would reduce the relative price, and thus increase the time spent on these commodities, *including the time spent at work*; similarly, for changes in income and other variables. The generalisation wrought by our approach is even greater than may have appeared at first.

Before concluding this section a few other relevant implications of our

[1] S. de Grazia has recently entertainingly shown the many difficulties in even reaching a reliable definition, and *a fortiori*, in quantitatively estimating the amount of leisure. See *ibid.*, Chapters III and IV; also see W. Moore, *Man, Time and Society* (New York: Wiley, 1963), Chapter II; J. N. Morgan, M. H. David, W. J. Cohen and H. E. Brazer, *Income and Welfare in the United States* (New York: McGraw-Hill, 1962), p. 322, and Owen, *op. cit.*, Chapter II.

[2] Sometimes true leisure is defined as the amount of discretionary time available (see Moore, *op. cit.*, p. 18). It is always difficult to attach a rigorous meaning to the word " discretionary " when referring to economic resources. One might say that in the short run consumption time is and working time is not discretionary, because the latter is partially subject to the authoritarian control of employers. (Even this distinction would vanish if households gave certain firms authoritarian control over their consumption time; see the discussion in Section II.) In the long run this definition of discretionary time is suspect too because the availability of alternative sources of employment would make working time also discretionary.

theory might be briefly mentioned. Just as a (compensated) rise in earnings would increase the prices of commodities with relatively large forgone earnings, induce a substitution away from them and increase the hours worked, so a (compensated) fall in market prices would also induce a substitution away from them and increase the hours worked: the effects of changes in direct and indirect costs are symmetrical. Indeed, Owen presents some evidence indicating that hours of work in the United States fell somewhat more in the first thirty years of this century than in the second thirty years, not because wages rose more during the first period, but because the market prices of recreation commodities fell more then.[1]

A well-known result of the traditional labour–leisure approach is that a rise in the income tax induces at least a substitution effect away from work and towards " leisure." Our approach reaches the same result only via a substitution towards time-intensive consumption rather than leisure. A simple additional implication of our approach, however, is that if a rise in the income tax were combined with an appropriate excise on the goods used in time-intensive commodities or subsidy to the goods used in other commodities there need be no change in full relative prices, and thus no substitution away from work. The traditional approach has recently reached the same conclusion, although in a much more involved way.[2]

There is no exception in the traditional approach to the rule that a pure rise in earnings would not induce a decrease in hours worked. An exception does occur in ours, for if the time and earnings intensities (*i.e.*, $l_i t_i$ and t_i) were negatively correlated a pure rise in earnings would induce a substitution towards time-intensive commodities, and thus away from work.[3] Although this exception does illustrate the greater power of our approach, there is no reason to believe that it is any more important empirically than the exception to the rule on income effects.

(b) *The Productivity of Time*

Most of the large secular increase in earnings, which stimulated the development of the labour–leisure analysis, resulted from an increase in the productivity of working time due to the growth in human and physical capital, technological progress and other factors. Since a rise in earnings resulting from an increase in productivity has both income and substitution

---

[1] See *op. cit.*, Chapter VIII. Recreation commodities presumably have relatively large forgone earnings.

[2] See W. J. Corbett and D. C. Hague, " Complementarity and the Excess Burden of Taxation," *Review of Economic Studies*, Vol. XXI (1953–54); also A. C. Harberger, " Taxation, Resource Allocation and Welfare," in the *Role of Direct and Indirect Taxes in the Federal Revenue System* (Princeton University Press, 1964).

[3] The effect on earnings is more difficult to determine because, by assumption, time intensive commodities have smaller costs per unit time than other commodities. A shift towards the former would, therefore, raise hourly earnings, which would partially and perhaps more than entirely offset the reduction in hours worked. Incidentally, this illustrates how the productivity of hours worked is influenced by the consumption set chosen.

effects, the secular decline in hours worked appeared to be evidence that the income effect was sufficiently strong to swamp the substitution effect.

The secular growth in capital and technology also improved the productivity of consumption time: supermarkets, automobiles, sleeping pills, safety and electric razors, and telephones are a few familiar and important examples of such developments. An improvement in the productivity of consumption time would change relative commodity prices and increase full income, which in turn would produce substitution and income effects. The interesting point is that a very different interpretation of the observed decline in hours of work is suggested because these effects are precisely the opposite of those produced by improvements in the productivity of working time.

Assume a uniform increase only in the productivity of consumption time, which is taken to mean a decline in all t_i, time required to produce a unit of Z_i, by a common percentage. The relative prices of commodities with large forgone earnings would fall, and substitution would be induced towards these and away from other commodities, causing hours of work also to fall. Since the increase in productivity would also produce an income effect,[1] the demand for commodities would increase, which, in turn, would induce an increased demand for goods. But since the productivity of working time is assumed not to change, more goods could be obtained only by an increase in work. That is, the higher real income resulting from an advance in the productivity of consumption time would cause hours of work to *increase*.

Consequently, an emphasis on the secular increase in the productivity of consumption time would lead to a very different interpretation of the secular decline in hours worked. Instead of claiming that a powerful income effect swamped a weaker substitution effect, the claim would have to be that a powerful substitution effect swamped a weaker income effect.

Of course, the productivity of both working and consumption time increased secularly, and the true interpretation is somewhere between these extremes. If both increased at the same rate there would be no change in relative prices, and thus no substitution effect, because the rise in l_i induced by one would exactly offset the decline in t_i induced by the other, marginal forgone earnings ($i_i t_i$) remaining unchanged. Although the income effects would tend to offset each other too, they would do so completely only if the income elasticity of demand for time-intensive commodities was equal to unity. Hours worked would decline if it was above and increase if it was below unity.[2] Since these commodities have probably on

---

[1] Full money income would be unaffected if it were achieved by using all time at pure work activities. If other uses of time were also required it would tend to increase. Even if full money income were unaffected, however, full real income would increase because prices of the Z_i would fall.

[2] So the " Knight " view that an increase in income would increase " leisure " is not necessarily true, even if leisure were a superior good and even aside from Robbins' emphasis on the substitution effect (see L. Robbins, " On the Elasticity of Demand for Income in Terms of Effort," *Economica* (June 1930)).

the whole been luxuries, such an increase in income would tend to reduce hours worked.

The productivity of working time has probably advanced more than that of consumption time, if only because of familiar reasons associated with the division of labour and economies of scale.[1] Consequently, there probably has been the traditional substitution effect towards and income effect away from work, as well as an income effect away from work because time-intensive commodities were luxuries. The secular decline in hours worked would only imply therefore that the combined income effects swamped the substitution effect, not that the income effect of an advance in the productivity of working time alone swamped its substitution effect.

Cross-sectionally, the hours worked of males have generally declined less as incomes increased than they have over time. Some of the difference between these relations is explained by the distinction between relevant and reported incomes, or by interdependencies among the hours worked by different employees;[2] some is probably also explained by the distinction between working and consumption productivity. There is a presumption that persons distinguished cross-sectionally by money incomes or earnings differ more in working than consumption productivity because they are essentially distinguished by the former. This argument does not apply to time series because persons are distinguished there by calendar time, which in principle is neutral between these productivities. Consequently, the traditional substitution effect towards work is apt to be greater cross-sectionally, which would help to explain why the relation between the income and hours worked of men is less negatively sloped there, and be additional evidence that the substitution effect for men is not weak.[3]

Productivity in the service sector in the United States appears to have advanced more slowly, at least since 1929, than productivity in the goods sector.[4] Service industries like retailing, transportation, education and health, use a good deal of the time of households that never enter into input, output and price series, or therefore into measures of productivity. Incorporation of such time into the series and consideration of changes in its productivity would contribute, I believe, to an understanding of the apparent differences in productivity advance between these sectors.

An excellent example can be found in a recent study of productivity

[1] Wesley Mitchell's justly famous essay " The Backward Art of Spending Money " spells out some of these reasons (see the first essay in the collection, *The Backward Art of Spending Money and Other Essays* (New York: McGraw-Hill, 1932)).

[2] A. Finnegan does find steeper cross-sectional relations when the average incomes and hours of different occupations are used (*see* his " A Cross-Sectional Analysis of Hours of Work," *Journal of Political Economy* (October, 1962)).

[3] Note that Mincer has found a very strong substitution effect for women (see his " Labor Force Participation of Married Women," *op. cit.*).

[4] See the essay by Victor Fuchs, " Productivity Trends in the Goods and Service Sectors, 1929–61: A Preliminary Survey," N.B.E.R. Occasional Paper, October 1964.

trends in the barbering industry in the United States.[1]   Conventional productivity measures show relatively little advance in barbers' shops since
1929, yet a revolution has occurred in the activities performed by these shops.
In the 1920s shaves still accounted for an important part of their sales, but
declined to a negligible part by the 1950s because of the spread of home safety
and electric razors.   Instead of travelling to a shop, waiting in line, receiving
a shave and continuing to another destination, men now shave themselves at
home, saving travelling, waiting and even some shaving time.   This considerable advance in the productivity of shaving nowhere enters measures
for barbers' shops.   If, however, a productivity measure for general
barbering activities, including shaving, was constructed, I suspect that it
would show an advance since 1929 comparable to most goods.[2]

(c) *Income Elasticities*

Income elasticities of demand are often estimated cross-sectionally from
the behaviour of families or other units with different incomes.   When these
units buy in the same market-place it is natural to assume that they face the
same prices of goods.   If, however, incomes differ because earnings do,
and cross-sectional income differences are usually dominated by earnings
differences, commodities prices would differ systematically.   All commodities prices would be higher to higher-income units because their forgone
earnings would be higher (which means, incidentally, that differences in real
income would be less than those in money income), and the prices of earnings-
intensive commodities would be unusually so.

Cross-sectional relations between consumption and income would not
therefore measure the effect of income alone, because they would be affected
by differences in relative prices as well as in incomes.[3]   The effect of income
would be underestimated for earnings-intensive and overestimated for other
commodities, because the higher relative prices of the former would cause a
substitution away from them and towards the latter.   Accordingly, the
income elasticities of demand for " leisure," unproductive and time-intensive
commodities would be under-stated, and for " work," productive and other
goods-intensive commodities over-stated by cross-sectional estimates.   Low
apparent income elasticities of earnings-intensive commodities and high
apparent elasticities of other commodities may simply be illusions resulting
from substitution effects.[4]

---

[1] See J. Wilburn, " Productivity Trends in Barber and Beauty Shops," mimeographed report,
N.B.E.R., September 1964.

[2] The movement of shaving from barbers' shops to households illustrates how and why even in
urban areas households have become " small factories."   Under the impetus of a general growth
in the value of time they have been encouraged to find ways of saving on travelling and waiting time
by performing more activities themselves.

[3] More appropriate income elasticities for several commodities are estimated in Mincer,
" Market Prices . . .," *op. cit.*

[4] In this connection note that cross-sectional data are often preferred to time-series data in
estimating income elasticities precisely because they are supposed to be largely free of co-linearity

Moreover, according to our theory demand depends also on the importance of earnings as a source of income. For if total income were held constant an increase in earnings would create only substitution effects: away from earnings-intensive and towards goods-intensive commodities. So one unusual implication of the analysis that can and should be tested with available budget data is that the source of income may have a significant effect on consumption patterns. An important special case is found in comparisons of the consumption of employed and unemployed workers. Unemployed workers not only have lower incomes but also lower forgone costs, and thus lower relative prices of time and other earnings-intensive commodities. The propensity of unemployed workers to go fishing, watch television, attend school and so on are simply vivid illustrations of the incentives they have to substitute such commodities for others.

One interesting application of the analysis is to the relation between family size and income.[1] The traditional view, based usually on simple correlations, has been that an increase in income leads to a reduction in the number of children per family. If, however, birth-control knowledge and other variables were held constant economic theory suggests a positive relation between family size and income, and therefore that the traditional negative correlation resulted from positive correlations between income, knowledge and some other variables. The data I put together supported this interpretation, as did those found in several subsequent studies.[2]

Although positive, the elasticity of family size with respect to income is apparently quite low, even when birth-control knowledge is held constant. Some persons have interpreted this (and other evidence) to indicate that family-size formation cannot usefully be fitted into traditional economic analysis.[3] It was pointed out, however, that the small elasticity found for children is not so inconsistent with what is found for goods as soon as quantity and quality income elasticities are distinguished.[4] Increased expenditures on many goods largely take the form of increased quality–expenditure per pound, per car, etc.—and the increase in quantity is modest. Similarly, increased expenditures on children largely take the form of increased expenditures per child, while the increase in number of children is very modest.

---

between prices and incomes (see, *e.g.*, J. Tobin, " A Statistical Demand Function for Food in the U.S.A.," *Journal of the Royal Statistical Society*, Series A (1950)).

[1] Biases in cross-sectional estimates of the demand for work and leisure were considered in the last section.

[2] See G. S. Becker, "An Economic Analysis of Fertility," *Demographic and Economic Change in Developed Countries* (N.B.E.R. Conference Volume, 1960); R. A. Easterlin, "The American Baby Boom in Historical Perspective," *American Economic Review* (December 1961); I. Adelman, "An Econometric Analysis of Population Growth," *American Economic Review* (June 1963); R. Weintraub, " The Birth Rate and Economic Development: An Empirical Study," *Econometrica* (October 1962); Morris Silver, *Birth Rates, Marriages, and Business Cycles* (unpublished Ph.D. dissertation, Columbia University, 1964); and several other studies; for an apparent exception, see the note by D. Freedman, " The Relation of Economic Status to Fertility," *American Economic Review* (June 1963).

[3] See, for example, Duesenberry's comment on Becker, *op. cit.*   [4] See Becker, *op. cit.*

Nevertheless, the elasticity of demand for number of children does seem somewhat smaller than the quantity elasticities found for many goods. Perhaps the explanation is simply the shape of indifference curves; one other factor that may be more important, however, is the increase in forgone costs with income.[1] Child care would seem to be a time-intensive activity that is not " productive " (in terms of earnings) and uses many hours that could be used at work. Consequently, it would be an earnings-intensive activity, and our analysis predicts that its relative price would be higher to higher-income families.[2] There is already some evidence suggesting that the positive relation between forgone costs and income explains why the apparent quantity income elasticity of demand for children is relatively small. Mincer found that cross-sectional differences in the forgone price of children have an important effect on the number of children.[3]

(d) Transportation

Transportation is one of the few activities where the cost of time has been explicitly incorporated into economic discussions. In most benefit-cost evaluations of new transportation networks the value of the savings in transportation time has tended to overshadow other benefits.[4] The importance of the value placed on time has encouraged experiment with different methods of determination: from the simple view that the value of an hour equals average hourly earnings to sophisticated considerations of the distinction between standard and overtime hours, the internal and external margins, etc.

The transport field offers considerable opportunity to estimate the marginal productivity or value of time from actual behaviour. One could, for example, relate the ratio of the number of persons travelling by aeroplane to those travelling by slower mediums to the distance travelled (and, of course, also to market prices and incomes). Since relatively more people use faster mediums for longer distances, presumably largely because of the greater importance of the saving in time, one should be able to estimate a marginal value of time from the relation between medium and distance travelled.[5]

[1] In *Ibid.*, p. 214 fn. 8, the relation between forgone costs and income was mentioned but not elaborated.

[2] Other arguments suggesting that higher-income families face a higher price of children have generally confused price with quality (see *ibid.*, pp. 214–15).

[3] See Mincer, " Market Prices . . .," *op. cit.* He measures the price of children by the wife's potential wage-rate, and fits regressions to various cross-sectional data, where number of children is the dependent variable, and family income and the wife's potential wage-rate are among the independent variables.

[4] See, for example, H. Mohring, " Land Values and the Measurement of Highway Benefits," *Journal of Political Economy* (June 1961).

[5] The only quantitative estimate of the marginal value of time that I am familiar with uses the relation between the value of land and its commuting distance from employment (see *ibid.*). With many assumptions I have estimated the marginal value of time of those commuting at about 40% of their average hourly earnings. It is not clear whether this value is so low because of errors in these assumptions or because of severe kinks in the supply and demand functions for hours of work.

Another transportation problem extensively studied is the length and mode of commuting to work.[1] It is usually assumed that direct commuting costs, such as train fare, vary positively and that living costs, such as space, vary negatively with the distance commuted. These assumptions alone would imply that a rise in incomes would result in longer commutes as long as space ("housing") were a superior good.[2]

A rise in income resulting at least in part from a rise in earnings would, however, increase the cost of commuting a given distance because the forgone value of the time involved would increase. This increase in commuting costs would discourage commuting in the same way that the increased demand for space would encourage it. The outcome depends on the relative strengths of these conflicting forces: one can show with a few assumptions that the distance commuted would increase as income increased if, and only if, space had an income elasticity greater than unity.

For let Z_1 refer to the commuting commodity, Z_2 to other commodities, and let

$$Z_1 = f_1(x, t) \qquad \cdots \cdots \cdots \quad (22)$$

where t is the time spent commuting and x is the quantity of space used. Commuting costs are assumed to have the simple form $a + l_1 t$, where a is a constant and l_1 is the marginal forgone cost per hour spent commuting. In other words, the cost of time is the only variable commuting cost. The cost per unit of space is $p(t)$, where by assumption $p' < 0$. The problem is to maximise the utility function

$$U = U(x, t, Z_2) \qquad \cdots \cdots \cdots \quad (23)$$

subject to the resource constraint

$$a + l_1 t + px + h(Z_2) = S \qquad \cdots \cdots \quad (24)$$

If it were assumed that $U_t = 0$—commuting was neither enjoyable nor irksome—the main equilibrium condition would reduce to

$$l_1 + p'x = 0 \,[3] \qquad \cdots \cdots \cdots \quad (25)$$

which would be the equilibrium condition if households simply attempt to minimise the sum of transportation and space costs.[4] If $l_1 = kS$, where k

---

[1] See L. N. Moses and H. F. Williamson, "Value of Time, Choice of Mode, and the Subsidy Issue in Urban Transportation," *Journal of Political Economy* (June 1963), R. Muth, "Economic Change and Rural–Urban Conversion," *Econometrica* (January 1961), and J. F. Kain, *Commuting and the Residential Decisions of Chicago and Detroit Central Business District Workers* (April 1963).

[2] See Muth, *op. cit.*

[3] If $U_t \neq 0$, the main equilibrium condition would be

$$\frac{U_t}{U_x} = \frac{l_1 + p'x}{p}$$

Probably the most plausible assumption is that $U_t < 0$, which would imply that $l_1 + p'x < 0$.

[4] See Kain, *op. cit.*, pp. 6–12.

is a constant, the effect of a change in full income on the time spent commuting can be found by differentiating equation (25) to be

$$\frac{\partial t}{\partial S} = \frac{k(\epsilon_x - 1)}{p''x} \quad \ldots \ldots \quad (26)$$

where ϵ_x is the income elasticity of demand for space. Since stability requires that $p'' > 0$, an increase in income increases the time spent commuting if, and only if, $\epsilon_x > 1$.

In metropolitan areas of the United States higher-income families tend to live further from the central city,[1] which contradicts our analysis if one accepts the traditional view that the income elasticity of demand for housing is less than unity. In a definitive study of the demand for housing in the United States, however, Margaret Reid found income elasticities greater than unity.[2] Moreover, the analysis of distance commuted incorporates only a few dimensions of the demand for housing; principally the demand for outdoor space. The evidence on distances commuted would then only imply that outdoor space is a " luxury," which is rather plausible [3] and not even inconsistent with the traditional view about the total elasticity of demand for housing.

(e) *The Division of Labour Within Families*

Space is too limited to do more than summarise the main implications of the theory concerning the division of labour among members of the same household. Instead of simply allocating time efficiently among commodities, multi-person households also allocate the time of different members. Members who are relatively more efficient at market activities would use less of their time at consumption activities than would other members. Moreover, an increase in the relative market efficiency of any member would effect a reallocation of the time of all other members towards consumption activities in order to permit the former to spend more time at market activities. In short, the allocation of the time of any member is greatly influenced by the opportunities open to other members.

IV. Substitution Between Time and Goods

Although time and goods have been assumed to be used in fixed proportions in producing commodities, substitution could take place because different commodities used them in different proportions. The assumption of fixed proportions is now dropped in order to include many additional implications of the theory.

It is well known from the theory of variable proportions that households

[1] For a discussion, including many qualifications, of this proposition see L. F. Schnore, " The Socio-Economic Status of Cities and Suburbs," *American Sociological Review* (February 1963).

[2] See her *Housing and Income* (University of Chicago Press, 1962), p. 6 and *passim*.

[3] According to Reid, the elasticity of demand for indoor space is less than unity (*ibid.*, Chapter 12). If her total elasticity is accepted this suggests that outdoor space has an elasticity exceeding unity.

would minimise costs by setting the ratio of the marginal product of goods to that of time equal to the ratio of their marginal costs.[1] A rise in the cost of time relative to goods would induce a reduction in the amount of time and an increase in the amount of goods used per unit of each commodity. Thus, not only would a rise in earnings induce a substitution away from earnings-intensive commodities but also a substitution away from time and towards goods in the production of each commodity. Only the first is (implicitly) recognised in the labour–leisure analysis, although the second may well be of considerable importance. It increases one's confidence that the substitution effect of a rise in earnings is more important than is commonly believed.

The change in the input coefficients of time and goods resulting from a change in their relative costs is defined by the elasticity of substitution between them, which presumably varies from commodity to commodity. The only empirical study of this elasticity assumes that recreation goods and " leisure " time are used to produce a recreation commodity.[2] Definite evidence of substitution is found, since the ratio of leisure time to recreation goods is negatively related to the ratio of their prices. The elasticity of substitution appears to be less than unity, however, since the share of leisure in total factor costs is apparently positively related to its relative price.

The incentive to economise on time as its relative cost increases goes a long way towards explaining certain broad aspects of behaviour that have puzzled and often disturbed observers of contemporary life. Since hours worked have declined secularly in most advanced countries, and so-called " leisure " has presumably increased, a natural expectation has been that " free " time would become more abundant, and be used more " leisurely " and " luxuriously." Yet, if anything, time is used more carefully to-day than a century ago.[3] If there was a secular increase in the productivity of working time relative to consumption time (see Section III (*b*)) there would be an increasing incentive to economise on the latter because of its greater expense (our theory emphatically cautions against calling such time " free "). Not surprisingly, therefore, it is now kept track of and used more carefully than in the past.

Americans are supposed to be much more wasteful of food and other

---

[1] The cost of producing a given amount of commodity Z_i would be minimised if

$$\frac{\partial f_i/\partial x_i}{\partial f_i/\partial T_i} = \frac{P_i}{\partial L/\partial T_i}$$

If utility were considered an indirect function of goods and time rather than simply a direct function of commodities the following conditions, among others, would be required to maximise utility:

$$\frac{\partial U/\partial x_i}{\partial U/\partial T_i} \equiv \frac{\partial Z_i/\partial x_i}{\partial Z_i/\partial T_i} = \frac{p_i}{\partial L/\partial T}$$

which are exactly the same conditions as above. The ratio of the marginal utility of x_i to that of T_i depends only on f_i, x_i and T_i, and is thus independent of other production functions, goods and time. In other words, the indirect utility function is what has been called " weakly separable " (see R. Muth, " Household Production and Consumer Demand Functions," unpublished manuscript).

[2] See Owen, *op. cit.*, Chapter X.   [3] See, for example, de Grazia, *op. cit.*, Chapter IV.

goods than persons in poorer countries, and much more conscious of time: they keep track of it continuously, make (and keep) appointments for specific minutes, rush about more, cook steaks and chops rather than time-consuming stews and so forth.[1] They are simultaneously supposed to be wasteful—of material goods—and overly economical—of immaterial time. Yet both allegations may be correct and not simply indicative of a strange American temperament because the market value of time is higher relative to the price of goods there than elsewhere. That is, the tendency to be economical about time and lavish about goods may be no paradox, but in part simply a reaction to a difference in relative costs.

The substitution towards goods induced by an increase in the relative cost of time would often include a substitution towards more expensive goods. For example, an increase in the value of a mother's time may induce her to enter the labour force and spend less time cooking by using pre-cooked foods and less time on child-care by using nurseries, camps or baby-sitters. Or barbers' shops in wealthier sections of town charge more and provide quicker service than those in poorer sections, because waiting by barbers is substituted for waiting by customers. These examples illustrate that a change in the quality of goods [2] resulting from a change in the relative cost of goods may simply reflect a change in the methods used to produce given commodities, and not any corresponding change in *their* quality.

Consequently, a rise in income due to a rise in earnings would increase the quality of goods purchased not only because of the effect of income on quality but also because of a substitution of goods for time; a rise in income due to a rise in property income would not cause any substitution, and should have less effect on the quality of goods. Put more dramatically, with total income held constant, a rise in earnings should increase while a rise in property income should decrease the quality chosen. Once again, the composition of income is important and provides testable implications of the theory.

One analytically interesting application of these conclusions is to the recent study by Margaret Reid of the substitution between store-bought and home-delivered milk.[3] According to our approach, the cost of inputs into the commodity " milk consumption at home " is either the sum of the price of milk in the store and the forgone value of the time used to carry it home or simply the price of delivered milk. A reduction in the price of store relative to delivered milk, the value of time remaining constant, would reduce the cost of the first method relatively to the second, and shift production towards the first. For the same reason a reduction in the value of time, market prices

---

[1] For a comparison of the American concept of time with others see Edward T. Hall, *The Silent Language* (New York: Doubleday, 1959), Chapter 9.

[2] Quality is usually defined empirically by the amount spent per physical unit, such as pound of food, car or child. See especially S. J. Prais and H. Houthakker, *The Analysis of Family Budgets* (Cambridge, 1955); also my " An Economic Analysis of Fertility," *op. cit.*

[3] See her " Consumer Response to the Relative Price of Store versus Delivered Milk," *Journal of Political Economy* (April 1963).

of milk remaining constant, would also shift production towards the first method.

Reid's finding of a very large negative relation between the ratio of store to delivered milk and the ratio of their prices, income and some other variables held constant, would be evidence both that milk costs are a large part of total production costs and that there is easy substitution between these alternative methods of production. The large, but not quite as large, negative relation with income simply confirms the easy substitution between methods, and indicates that the cost of time is less important than the cost of milk. In other words, instead of conveying separate information, her price and income elasticities both measure substitution between the two methods of producing the same commodity, and are consistent and plausible.

The importance of forgone earnings and the substitution between time and goods may be quite relevant in interpreting observed price elasticities. A given percentage increase in the price of goods would be less of an increase in commodity prices the more important forgone earnings are. Consequently, even if all commodities had the same true price elasticity, those having relatively important forgone earnings would show lower apparent elasticities in the typical analysis that relates quantities and prices of goods alone.

The importance of forgone earnings differs not only among commodities but also among households for a given commodity because of differences in income. Its importance would change in the same or opposite direction as income, depending on whether the elasticity of substitution between time and goods was less or greater than unity. Thus, even when the true price elasticity of a commodity did not vary with income, the observed price elasticity of goods would be negatively or positively related to income as the elasticity of substitution was less or greater than unity.

The importance of substitution between time and goods can be illustrated in a still different way. Suppose, for simplicity, that only good x and no time was initially required to produce commodity Z. A price ceiling is placed on x, it nominally becomes a free good, and the production of x is subsidised sufficiently to maintain the same output. The increased quantity of x and Z demanded due to the decline in the price of x has to be rationed because the output of x has not increased. Suppose that the system of rationing made the quantity obtained a positive function of the time and effort expended. For example, the quantity of price-controlled bread or medical attention obtained might depend on the time spent in a queue outside a bakery or in a physician's office. Or if an appointment system were used a literal queue would be replaced by a figurative one, in which the waiting was done at " home," as in the Broadway theatre, admissions to hospitals or air travel during peak seasons. Again, even in depressed times the likelihood of obtaining a job is positively related to the time put into job hunting.

Although x became nominally a free good, Z would not be free, because the time now required as an input into Z is not free. The demand for Z

would be greater than the supply (fixed by assumption) if the cost of this time was less than the equilibrium price of Z before the price control. The scrambling by households for the limited supply would increase the time required to get a unit of Z, and thus its cost. Both would continue to increase until the average cost of time tended to the equilibrium price before price control. At that point equilibrium would be achieved because the supply and demand for Z would be equal.

Equilibrium would take different forms depending on the method of rationing. With a literal " first come first served " system the size of the queue (say outside the bakery or in the doctor's office) would grow until the expected cost of standing in line discouraged any excess demand;[1] with the figurative queues of appointment systems, the " waiting " time (say to see a play) would grow until demand was sufficiently curtailed. If the system of rationing was less formal, as in the labour market during recessions, the expected time required to ferret out a scarce job would grow until the demand for jobs was curtailed to the limited supply.

Therefore, price control of *x* combined with a subsidy that kept its amount constant would not change the average private equilibrium price of Z,[2] but would substitute indirect time costs for direct goods costs.[3] Since, however, indirect costs are positively related to income, the price of Z would be raised to higher-income persons and reduced to lower-income ones, thereby redistributing consumption from the former to the latter. That is, women, the poor, children, the unemployed, etc., would be more willing to spend their time in a queue or otherwise ferreting out rationed goods than would high-earning males.

V. SUMMARY AND CONCLUSIONS

This paper has presented a theory of the allocation of time between different activities. At the heart of the theory is an assumption that households are producers as well as consumers; they produce commodities by combining inputs of goods and time according to the cost-minimisation rules of the traditional theory of the firm. Commodities are produced in quantities determined by maximising a utility function of the commodity set subject to prices and a constraint on resources. Resources are measured by what is called full income, which is the sum of money income and that forgone or " lost " by the use of time and goods to obtain utility, while commodity prices are measured by the sum of the costs of their goods and time inputs.

[1] In queueing language the cost of waiting in line is a " discouragement " factor that stabilises the queueing scheme (see, for example, D. R. Cox and W. L. Smith, *Queues* (New York: Wiley 1961)).

[2] The social price, on the other hand, would double, for it is the sum of private indirect costs and subsidised direct costs.

[3] Time costs can be criticised from a Pareto optimality point of view because they often result in external diseconomies: *e.g.*, a person joining a queue would impose costs on subsequent joiners. The diseconomies are real, not simply pecuniary, because time is a cost to demanders, but is not revenue to suppliers.

The effect of changes in earnings, other income, goods prices and the productivity of working and consumption time on the allocation of time and the commodity set produced has been analysed. For example, a rise in earnings, compensated by a decline in other income so that full income would be unchanged, would induce a decline in the amount of time used at consumption activities, because time would become more expensive. Partly goods would be substituted for the more expensive time in the production of each commodity, and partly goods-intensive commodities would be substituted for the more expensive time-intensive ones. Both substitutions require less time to be used at consumption, and permit more to be used at work. Since the reallocation of time involves simultaneously a reallocation of goods and commodities, all three decisions become intimately related.

The theory has many interesting and even novel interpretations of, and implications about, empirical phenomena. A few will be summarised here.

A traditional " economic " interpretation of the secular decline in hours worked has stressed the growth in productivity of working time and the resulting income and substitution effects, with the former supposedly dominating. Ours stresses that the substitution effects of the growth in productivity of working and consumption time tended to offset each other, and that hours worked declined secularly primarily because time-intensive commodities have been luxuries. A contributing influence has been the secular decline in the relative prices of goods used in time-intensive commodities.

Since an increase in income partly due to an increase in earnings would raise the relative cost of time and of time-intensive commodities, traditional cross-sectional estimates of income elasticities do not hold either factor or commodity prices constant. Consequently, they would, among other things, be biased downward for time-intensive commodities, and give a misleading impression of the effect of income on the quality of commodities consumed. The composition of income also affects demand, for an increase in earnings, total income held constant, would shift demand away from time-intensive commodities and input combinations.

Rough estimates suggest that forgone earnings are quantitatively important and therefore that full income is substantially above money income. Since forgone earnings are primarily determined by the use of time, considerably more attention should be paid to its efficiency and allocation. In particular, agencies that collect information on the expenditure of money income might simultaneously collect information on the " expenditure " of time. The resulting time budgets, which have not been seriously investigated in most countries, including the United States and Great Britain, should be integrated with the money budgets in order to give a more accurate picture of the size and allocation of full income.

GARY S. BECKER

Columbia University.

[11]

Leisure, Home Production, and Work— the Theory of the Allocation of Time Revisited

Reuben Gronau

The Hebrew University of Jerusalem and
National Bureau of Economic Research, Stanford

The paper tries to formalize the trichotomy of work in the market, work at home, and leisure. Time is used at home to produce home goods that are perfect substitutes for market goods, where home production is subject to diminishing marginal productivity. An increase in the market wage rate is expected to reduce work at home, while its effect on leisure and work in the market is indeterminate. An increase in income increases leisure, reduces work in the market, and leaves work at home unchanged. These conclusions are supported by empirical tests based on the Michigan Income Dynamics data, as well as by previous time budget studies. Further implications for labor supply, fertility, gain from marriage, demand for child care, and the measurement of home output are investigated.

I. Time Budget Evidence—Data in Search of a Theory

The household production function is by now an established part of economic theory. As formulated by Becker, Lancaster, Muth, and others, the new consumption theory emphasizes the fact that market goods and services are not themselves the agents which carry utility but are rather inputs in a process that generates commodities (or characteristics) which, in turn, yield utility. A second feature, introduced into the analysis by

This paper was written while I was on sabbatical at the National Bureau of Economic Research. It has not undergone the full critical review accorded the NBER studies. Research on this paper was supported by a grant to the National Bureau of Economic Research from the Rockefeller Foundation. The paper was inspired by discussions with Yoram Weiss and Robert J. Willis. I am grateful to Orley Ashenfelter, Gary Becker, Victor Fuchs, Zvi Griliches, Robert Michael, Jacob Mincer, Donald Parsons, and Shmuel Sharir for their comments on earlier drafts on this paper and to Kris Chinn and Kyle Johnson for computational assistance.
[*Journal of Political Economy*, 1977, vol. 85, no. 6]

Becker, is that market goods and services are not the only input in this process, the other input being the consumer's time. According to this approach (Becker 1965) the consumer maximizes welfare subject to the time and budget constraints where welfare is a function of commodities, which are produced using market goods and time.

The new approach has been put to wide use in the analysis of fertility, health, consumption, labor supply, and transportation demand (to name just a few). A fact that seemed to have been overlooked is that the theory does not really deal with household production in the common sense of the term.[1] It does deal with (to use Lancaster's terminology) consumption technology, but has very little to say (in its current form) on home production. It was Mincer (1962) who first pointed out that, at least in the case of women, one should distinguish between work at home and leisure, but this distinction (so common in everyday language) disappeared in Becker's more general formulation. This omission was partly due to practical difficulties in distinguishing between the two, given the large number of borderline cases (e.g., is playing with a child leisure or work at home?), but partly because it has not been shown that our understanding of household behavior would be enriched by the distinction. Whatever the reason, the theory of the allocation of time in its current form is of little help where it is most needed, namely, in the analysis of time-budget data.

From the theoretical point of view, the justification for aggregating leisure and work at home into one entity, nonmarket time (or home time), can rest on two assumptions: (*a*) the two elements react similarly to changes in the socioeconomic environment and therefore nothing is gained by studying them separately; and (*b*) the two elements satisfy the conditions of a composite input, that is, their relative price is constant and there is no interest in investigating the composition of the aggregate since it has no bearing on production and the price of the output. Both assumptions are suspect. Recent time-budget findings have established that work at home and leisure are not affected in the same way by changes in socioeconomic variables, and this paper shows that the composition of the aggregate affects many facets of household behavior, such as labor supply, specialization in the household, and demand for children.

A great deal is known about the household's labor force behavior but only little about how the family allocates its time within the home. It therefore seems worth recapitulating some of the major findings on the latter. The time-use patterns of American and Israeli families have been

[1] One exception is Perlman (1969, chap. 1). Since writing the first draft of this paper, I have become aware of two others, Bloch (1973) and Sharir (1975). Both suggest models that are in many respects similar to the one suggested here but do not analyze all the implications.

LEISURE, HOME PRODUCTION, AND WORK   1101

TABLE 1

THE DETERMINANTS OF THE ALLOCATION OF TIME: UNITED STATES AND ISRAEL

	WIFE			HUSBAND		
	Work in the Market	Work at Home	Leisure	Work in the Market	Work at Home	Leisure
U.S. (1964):[a]						
Husband's wage	−	0	+	+	−	+(?)
Wife's wage	+	−	−	0	+	−(?)
Nonwage income	−(?)	−	+	−	0	+
Total N children	−	+	−	+	+(?)	−
Existence of preschool children	−(?)	+	0	+	+(?)	−
Israel (1968):[b]						
Husband's schooling	...	...	...	0	0	0
Wife's schooling	+	−	+(?)			
Total N children	−	+	−	+	+	−
N preschool children	−	+	−	0(?)	0(?)	0(?)

[a] The results are based on Bloch (1973). Question marks denote cases where the direction of the effect depended on the functional form of the regression equations.
[b] Based on Gronau (1976a). Question marks denote cases where the regression coefficients are barely significant.

studied by Bloch (1973) and myself (Gronau 1976a). These findings are summarized in table 1, which presents the signs of the regression coefficients of the major determinants of the allocation of time. In spite of the differences in methodology and in the nature of the data used,[2] the two studies agree in pointing out that changes in the socioeconomic environment (e.g., changes in the wage rate, income, education, and the number of children) differ in their effects on work at home and leisure and on the allocation of time of husbands and wives.

According to the Israeli data, an increase in the wife's education results in an increase in the time she spends in the labor market. This time is withdrawn primarily from work at home, leaving leisure unaffected (and perhaps even increased). The U.S. findings are much more specific, distinguishing between income and price effects. An increase in the wife's wage rate increases her supply of labor and reduces both work at home

---

[2] The U.S. and Israeli data differ both in the nature of the dependent variables and in the degree of detail of the explanatory variables. In the American survey (the 1964 *Productive American* study), people were asked how much time they spent annually in regular and irregular housework and how much in market work. Leisure was defined in this study as the residual. In the Israeli survey (conducted by the Israel Institute of Applied Social Research in Jerusalem), people were asked how they had spent each hour of the preceding day. The survey included 48 activities which I classified into four major groups (work in the market, work at home, leisure, and physiological needs, only the first three of which are reported in table 1). The respondents' background data are much more detailed in the American survey. The Israeli survey does not contain any information on the person's wage rate, and one has to use education as a very imperfect proxy.

and leisure. A change in the wife's wage does not affect her husband's work in the market but is positively correlated with his work at home and, as a result, negatively correlated with his leisure. An increase in the husband's wage rate increases his own supply of labor (mainly at the expense of his work at home), but reduces his wife's. This change does not affect the wife's work at home, and consequently it increases her leisure. An increase in unearned income reduces the supply of labor of both husband and wife, it reduces work at home (at least in the case of women), and it thus increases leisure.

Finally, both studies concur that children cause their mother to transfer time from the market to home tasks. However, the amount of time transferred falls short of the additional time required to care for children, so that leisure is reduced. Children have the same downward effect where the father's leisure is concerned, but in this case the father increases both work at home and work in the market.

The total time available for work at home and leisure depends to a large extent on the person's employment status. Comparing the allocation of time of employed and nonemployed Israeli married women (table 2), one can observe that, when education is controlled for, the employed have less leisure than the nonemployed. The employed Israeli married woman worked on the average 4.3 hours in the market. She saved 2.8 hours by cutting her work at home, but 1.5 hours had to come at the expense of leisure and time spent on physiological needs.

Married men work more in the market than the unmarried, and married women spend more time than the unmarried in work at home (and somewhat less in the market). Consequently, it is observed (Gronau 1976a) that married people have less leisure than the unmarried, and the difference is greater for men than for women. These differences are explained by two factors—marriage and the existence of children. To isolate the effect of marriage, I ran separate regressions for all men and for all women who had no young children (i.e., children in age group 0–5, or alternatively in the age group 0–12). The dependent variable is the time spent on the activity, and the explanatory variables include the person's age, schooling, continent of birth, length of residence, and number of older children; marital status is represented by a dummy variable. (For lack of space, I do not present the detailed regressions here.)

Controlling for the number of children (and the other socioeconomic variables), I found that marriage reduces the Israeli wife's supply of work to the market and increases her work at home. The decline in work in the market (about 1.5 hours a day) is somewhat smaller than the increase in work at home (about 2 hours), but the difference is too small to be significant (time spent on physiological needs and, to a lesser extent, time spent on leisure decline, but the decline is not statistically significant).

TABLE 2

TIME-BUDGET SURVEY—AVERAGE TIME USES OF ISRAELI MARRIED WOMEN, BY EDUCATION AND EMPLOYMENT STATUS (1968)

| | YEARS OF SCHOOLING | | | | | | | | | | | |
| | 0-8 | | | 9-12 | | | 13+ | | | Total | | |
	Employed	Not Employed	Total	Employed	Not Employed	Total	Employed	Not Employed	Total	Employed	Not Employed	Total
Age (years)	40.2	42.8	42.1	40.2	40.2	40.2	38.5	38.2	38.4	39.8	41.4	40.8
Schooling (years)	4.80	4.92	4.89	10.63	10.52	10.56	14.13	13.57	13.94	9.58	7.83	8.46
Continent of birth[a]	61	58	59	19	28	25	4	8	6	29	42	38
Number of children:												
Aged 0-5	0.46	0.74	0.66	0.41	0.68	0.58	0.44	0.70	0.53	0.43	0.71	0.61
Aged 6-12	0.98	0.93	0.94	0.24	0.51	0.42	0.34	0.49	0.39	0.51	0.73	0.65
Aged 13-17	0.85	0.90	0.89	0.38	0.35	0.36	0.34	0.35	0.34	0.53	0.64	0.60
Monthly income (IL)	670	546	578	990	843	896	1,380	915	1,221	983	694	797
Labor force participation (%)[b]	...	...	26	...	...	36	...	...	66	...	...	36
Time use (hours):[b]												
Total work	9.18	7.79	8.15	8.82	6.84	7.55	7.87	6.28	7.32	8.70	7.29	7.79
Work at home	4.85	7.67	6.94	4.30	6.71	5.84	3.97	6.26	4.75	4.40	7.18	6.19
Work in the market	4.34	0.12	1.21	4.52	0.13	1.71	3.90	0.02	2.57	4.30	0.11	1.60
Physiological needs	9.95	10.30	10.21	9.49	10.36	10.04	9.78	10.62	10.06	9.71	10.35	10.12
Leisure	4.63	5.27	5.10	5.16	6.14	5.78	5.86	6.50	6.08	5.16	5.71	5.52
N observations	93	265	358	117	208	325	71	37	108	281	510	791

a Percent of cell born in Asia-Africa.
b Because of missing data the time uses do not always add up to 24 hours.

As for men, they hardly increase their work at home but significantly increase their supply of labor to the market (by about 2 hours). This results in a significant drop in married men's leisure.

These findings give rise to several questions: Why do education, the wage rate, and income differ in their effect on work at home and leisure? What explains the effect of children? What explains the differences in the allocation of time between labor force participants and nonparticipants? What explains the differences between men's and women's time-use patterns? How can one explain the effect of marriage, and what is the source of the asymmetry in the effect of marriage on the husband's and wife's time-use patterns? In answering these questions, we shall see that the distinction between consumption time and production time (i.e., leisure and work at home) has implications reaching far beyond the analysis of home time use, embracing such topics as labor supply, fertility, marital stability, consumption (and in particular the demand for substitutes for the person's home services), and the reevaluation of the contribution of housewives to total economic welfare.

The paper opens with a description of a theoretical model that seems to provide us with a unifying explanation of the observed time-use patterns. Some of the crucial assumptions of this model are tested in Section III. The implications of the model for the analysis of fertility, marital stability, the demand for housemaids and child care, and the evaluation of the output of the home sector are investigated in Section IV. A summarizing section discusses some qualifications and suggests some future research.

II. The Model

An intuitive distinction between work at home (i.e., home production time) and leisure (i.e., home consumption time) is that work at home (like work in the market) is something one would rather have somebody else do for one (if the cost were low enough), while it would be almost impossible to enjoy leisure through a surrogate. Thus, one regards work at home as a time use that generates services which have a close substitute in the market, while leisure has only poor market substitutes. In the extreme, though by no means unusual, case, work at home and work in the market are perfect substitutes as far as the direct utility they generate is concerned, and a person is indifferent to the composition of the goods and services he consumes, that is, to whether they are produced at home or purchased in the market.

Formally, let there be a single-person household. The person maximizes the amount of commodity Z, which is a combination of goods and services

(X) and consumption time (L),

$$Z = Z(X, L). \tag{1}$$

The goods can either be purchased in the market or produced at home, but the composition of X does not affect Z.[3] I shall measure the value of home goods and services (X_H) in terms of their market equivalents (i.e., the cost of the quality-corrected good in the market). Let X_M denote market expenditures; then total consumption is composed of the consumption of goods purchased in the market and those produced at home,

$$X = X_M + X_H. \tag{2}$$

Home goods are produced by work at home (H),

$$X_H = f(H), \tag{3}$$

subject to decreasing marginal productivity $(f' > 0, f'' < 0)$.[4] The decline in the value of marginal productivity at home is due not only to fatigue or changes in input proportions but also to a change in the composition of X_H—a shift, as H increases, toward activities that have a cheaper market substitute.

The maximization of Z is bound by two constraints: the (endogenous) budget constraint

$$X_M = WN + V, \tag{4}$$

where W is the person's wage rate (assumed to be constant), N denotes market work, and V other sources of income; and the time constraint[5]

$$L + H + N = T. \tag{5}$$

The necessary conditions for an interior optimum call for the marginal product of work at home to equal the marginal rate of substitution between goods and consumption time, which in turn equals the shadow price of time, W^* (eq. [6]). If the person works in the market $(N > 0)$, they

---

[3] This assumption is crucial to the model and distinguishes it from previous formulations such as $Z = Z(X_M, X_H, L)$ which had only very limited predictive power (Gronau 1973).

[4] For simplicity I ignore the market goods that enter into the production of home goods.

[5] Thus one can easily rewrite eq. (1) as

$$Z = Z(X, L) = Z'(X, L, T - L) = Z'(X, L, H + N), \tag{1a}$$

i.e., eq. (1) does not imply that work at home and work in the market do not affect welfare, but merely that H and N are perfect substitutes as far as the consumption technology (Z) is concerned.

will also equal the real wage rate, W (eq. [6a]).[6]

$$\frac{\partial Z/\partial L}{\partial Z/\partial X} = f' = W^*, \tag{6}$$

$$\frac{\partial Z/\partial L}{\partial Z/\partial X} = f' = W^* = W. \tag{6a}$$

These conditions are depicted in figure 1. The home production function is described by the concave curve $TB_0'A_0C_0$. The more time the individual spends working at home (as measured by the horizontal distance from point T), the greater the amount of home goods produced. If the individual spends all his time in work at home, he can produce an amount of OC_0 units of goods. In the absence of market opportunities, the curve $TB_0'A_0C_0$ is the opportunity frontier enclosing the set of all feasible combinations of X and L. The existence of a market where the person can sell his working time and buy market goods expands this set. Thus, given the real wage rate W (described by the slope of the line A_0E_0), the person can trade his time for goods along the price line A_0E_0 (the line tangent to the production curve $TB_0'A_0C_0$). At the optimum the person may choose a goods-intensive combination of X and L, such as B_0, where he enjoys OL_0 units of consumption time, spends L_0N time units on work in the market, and spends NT time units on work at home. Alternatively, the person may have a high preference for leisure (i.e., a leisure-intensive consumption technology), choosing as his optimum combination the point B_0'. In this case he does not work in the market, but splits his time between leisure (OL_0') and work at home ($L_0'T$).

Note that the person may adopt a goods-intensive technology, such as B_0, but it may still be home-time intensive in the sense that a large part of the goods are produced at home. Thus, leisure intensive and home-time intensive are not synonymous. Note further that if the marginal productivity of work at home at the point T falls short of the real wage rate, there is no home production and we are faced with the familiar Robbins diagram and the dichotomy of work (in the market) and leisure.

To analyze the properties of this model, let it be assumed that there is an increase in other sources of income by an amount of ΔV. An increase in other sources of income secures for the person the amount of OX_0 of

---

[6] Eqq. (6) and (6a) are derived by maximizing the Lagrangian function $G = Z\{[X_M + f(H)], L\} + \lambda(WN + V - X_M) + \mu(T - L - H - N)$ with respect to L, H, N, and X_M. The shadow price of time (measured in real terms) equals $W^* = \mu/\lambda$, where μ and λ are the marginal utilities of time and income, respectively. The wage rate may fall short of the value of marginal productivity at home ($W < f'$), either because of the person's reluctance to perform the home services outside of his own home or because of differences in the value of marginal productivity between home and the outside, due to transport costs, monitoring costs, and efficiency (the person being self-employed in his own home).

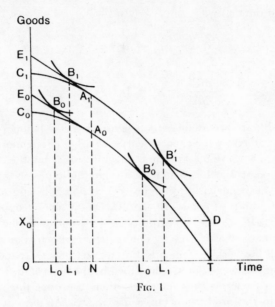

FIG. 1

market goods even if he spends all his time in consumption. The change is reflected, therefore, in a vertical shift of the production curve $TB'_0 A_0 C_0$ to $TDB'_1 A_1 C_1$. The change does not affect the marginal productivity of work at home—it does not affect the shape of the curve but only its location. Since the real wage rate is given, there is no change in the point at which the person finds it cheaper to buy the goods in the market than to produce them at home. If the person prefers a goods-intensive consumption technology which makes him work in the market (combination B_0), he does not change the amount of time he spends working at home (NT) and, given the pure income effect, he increases his amount of leisure (if leisure is not an inferior input) at the expense of work at the market (consumption time increases from OL_0 to OL_1 and work in the market is reduced from $L_0 N$ to $L_1 N$).[7]

If, on the other hand, the person does not initially work in the market (point B'_0), the increase in income and the resulting increase in Z call for an increase in consumption time which can come only at the expense of work at home.

Let there be an increase in the real wage rate W (fig. 2). If the person works in the market (point B_0), a change in wages affects both the rate of substitution between consumption time and goods and the profitability of home production. The increase in wages lowers the price of goods in terms of time, thereby making home production less profitable and

[7] The decline in work in the market may result in the person's dropping out of the labor force altogether.

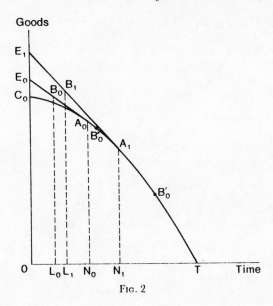

FIG. 2

inducing substitution of goods for consumption time. This change will, therefore, definitely cut work at home (from $N_0 T$ to $N_1 T$), while its effect on leisure is indeterminate. The substitution effect tends to reduce leisure, while the expansion effect tends to raise it. As for work in the market, it depends on the extent of the reduction of work at home and on the change in consumption time. If the reduction in work at home exceeds the increase in leisure (if there is one), the supply of work to the market increases. The tendency of this supply curve to be positively sloped increases, the greater the rate of substitution between goods and consumption time, the less sensitive the marginal productivity in home production to changes in the amount of work, and the smaller the income elasticity of leisure.

If the person initially does not work, the change in wages may lure him into the market (point B_0''), or he may be completely unaffected (point B_0').

A third kind of change worth examining is a change in productivity. It is impossible to predict the implications of this change without specifying the exact nature of the changes in home productivity (i.e., changes in f) and consumption technology (i.e., changes in Z). In the absence of the necessary information, one's predictions are limited to the case where the person works in the market. In this case a change in consumption technology would affect work in the market and leisure but would leave work at home unchanged. On the other hand, an increase in the productivity of work at home is associated with an increase in real income and an

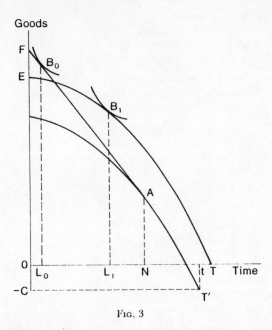

Fig. 3

increase in leisure, but its effect on work at home and work in the market is indeterminate.

Up to this point, it has been assumed that entry into the market is costless. In practice, work in the market involves costs in terms of both money and time. Let these costs be C and t, respectively, and let them be independent of the amount of work N (e.g., transportation costs and time).[8] The introduction of these costs calls for some modification of the budget and time constraints

$$X_M + \delta C = WN + V, \tag{4a}$$

$$L + H + N + \delta t = T, \tag{5a}$$

where δ is a dummy variable that describes the person's employment status

$$\delta = \begin{cases} 1 \text{ when } N > 0 \\ 0 \text{ when } N = 0. \end{cases} \tag{7}$$

The person is faced by two alternative opportunity sets (fig. 3). If he stays out of the labor force and confines himself to home production, he can choose any point on the boundary TB_1E. On the other hand, if he decides to join the labor force, he suffers a loss of t units of time and C

[8] Variable time and money costs (i.e., costs that vary with N) can easily be treated by an appropriate modification of the wage rate.

units of X, but his opportunity locus becomes $T'AF$. Given these opportunity sets, a person with a greater preference for goods will join the labor force (point B_0), spending OL_0 units of time on leisure, working in the market for L_0N units, working at home for Nt units, and, say, traveling to work for tT units of time. A person with a greater taste for leisure will decide to stay out of the market (point B_1), dividing his time between leisure and work at home (OL_1 and L_1T, respectively). Given the opportunity set, labor force participation is therefore associated with a decline both in leisure and in work at home.[9] The existence of entry costs does not, however, affect our previous conclusions about the effect of changes in the socioeconomic characteristics on the allocation of time.

The predictions of this simple model are by and large consistent with the reported findings. An increase in the wage rate should not affect the allocation of time of the nonemployed but should reduce the work at home of the employed. Thus, on the whole, one would expect the wage rate and work at home to be negatively correlated. The effect of a change in the wage rate on leisure depends on the relative magnitudes of the income effect and the substitution effect. The tendency for the income effect to dominate increases with the number of hours worked in the market. Thus, it is not surprising that the substitution effect is the dominant factor in the case of the wife's leisure, but the two effects cancel out (or even the income effect dominates) in the case of the husband's. An increase in nonwage income should not affect the work at home of employed persons but should reduce the work at home of the nonemployed. Consequently, one expects nonwage income and the wife's work at home to be negatively correlated. On the other hand, in the case of men, who are mostly employed, the negative effect should be much less pronounced and may be nonsignificant. In either case, one expects nonwage income and leisure to be positively correlated. Finally, in the presence of market entry costs, employed persons should spend less time on work at home than the unemployed, but this difference is swamped by the difference in the market hours. Consequently, one expects the employed to work longer hours (in the market and at home) and enjoy less leisure, other things being equal.

The model can easily be extended to the case of two commodities. In this case the person maximizes the welfare function $U(Z_1, Z_2)$ subject to the constraints imposed by the transformation curve between the two commodities. The latter depends on the consumption technology of each commodity (eq. [1]), the home production function (eq. [3]), and the time and budget constraints. The comparative-static properties of the extended model are very similar to those of the one presented earlier and

---

[9] An alternative interpretation of the different patterns of time use of the employed and nonemployed traces them to differences in productivity at home, the less productive person having a stronger inclination to join the labor force.

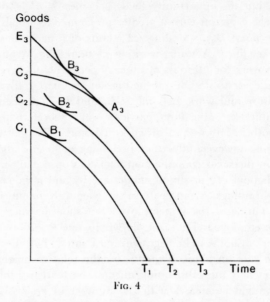

Fig. 4

will therefore not be discussed here.[10] However, the extended model sheds new light on the effect of children on the allocation of time.

An increase in the number of children (or the introduction of children) is associated with a transfer of time to child-related activities. The additional time units devoted to children are spent on work at home and leisure (a horizontal shift from $T_1B_1C_1$ to $T_2B_2C_2$ in fig. 4). Eventually the opportunities for profitable home production are exhausted, and any additional units of time spent on the commodity of children will be spent on work in the market (which will permit the purchase of child-related market goods) and leisure, leaving work at home unchanged (curve $T_3A_3B_3E_3$).

When the person participates in the labor force, the time withdrawn from other activities is initially withdrawn from work in the market and leisure, curtailing the market goods and consumption time associated with these activities. If the person is not a labor-force participant, the entire time is naturally withdrawn from work at home and leisure.

The overall effect on the allocation of time of introducing children (or of an increase in their number) depends on the leisure intensity of child-related in comparison with other activities and on the profitability of home production of child-related services. It is my contention that children are less leisure intensive (i.e., more goods intensive) than other activities. Thus an increase in the number of children at the expense of other

10 For a detailed discussion see an earlier version of this paper (Gronau 1976b).

activities should reduce the person's leisure. The effect of children on work at home and in the market depends on the profitability of home production. Women are, usually, offered lower wages than their husbands, and they may also be more productive in home production. An increase in the number of children therefore leads working mothers to work less in the market and more at home. Similarly, nonparticipants shift time from less goods-intensive to more goods-intensive activities, increasing their work at home. The scope for profitable child-related home production is much more limited for the husband. In his case one can therefore expect to observe that the shift to the more goods-intensive commodity (i.e., children) results primarily in increased work in the market (though there may also be an increase in work at home).

The price of market substitutes (maids, nursery school, kindergarten, school) declines as the child grows older. Put differently, as the child grows older, the real wage of the mother (in terms of market substitutes) increases. This increase leads to a decline in work at home and an increase in work at the market, but need not increase the demand for leisure much.[11]

Similarly, it seems that in Israel the prices of market substitutes (maids, nursery school) are cheaper than in the United States.[12] Thus, an Israeli mother should find it less profitable than an American one to divert time from work in the market to work at home when she has a child. The supply of labor of Israeli women, in particular the more educated ones, should therefore be less affected by young children than that of their American counterparts (Gronau 1976*a*).

Additional insights are gained by extending the model to the multiperson case and, in particular, the case of the married couple. Marriage introduces into people's choice set a new activity, "married life." The new activity uses home-produced goods in its production and thus involves an increase in work at home at the expense of work in the market. Furthermore, to the extent that this loosely defined activity is more goods intensive than the other activities, it should also reduce leisure. Marriage may, however, have a more fundamental effect on household members' allocation of time by allowing for specialization within the family. Much of the preceding discussion is based on the proposition that a person is reluctant (or finds it unprofitable) to sell his home goods outside the household. This assumption is, however, relaxed in the family context. Greater market involvement and discrimination result in the husband's

---

[11] The goods intensity of children may decline and thus leisure may increase as the child grows older. However, as long as children are more goods intensive than other activities, they should be associated with a decline in leisure.

[12] In Israel many of the 2-year-olds and most of the 3–4-year-olds attend a nursery for at least 4 hours a day. In 1968 over 40 percent of the working mothers with a child of less than 3 years old employed a maid (the fraction for working mothers with 13+ years of schooling was two-thirds).

wage rate being higher than his wife's; on the other hand, on-the-job training may make women more efficient in home production. There is therefore an incentive within the family to trade goods for time. Leisure is, by definition, an input which the person has to provide himself. Thus, there is no way in which the wife can save leisure for her husband. She can, however, save him work-at-home time. Indeed, the woman who is reluctant to sell her home goods (e.g., serve as a maid) is willing to exchange them within the family for market goods. The extent to which such an exchange takes place and the terms of the exchange depend to a large degree on her marginal costs of producing these goods.

If before marriage a woman obtained some of the goods solely through home production, the price she places on them is below that paid by her husband in the market. Specialization and trade within the family should increase the family members' welfare. The wife expands her home production while the husband increases his work in the market.[13] On the other hand, if both participate in the labor force and there is no good or service which is supplied solely though home production (i.e., $X_M > 0$ for all goods for both husband and wife), then it can be shown (Gronau 1976b) that before marriage both members face the same set of prices and marriage does not yield any gains of trade.

III. Some Empirical Tests

The model gives rise to a wealth of testable hypotheses. Although many of these hypotheses could have been generated also by other models, which use a weaker set of assumptions (e.g., the models discussed in my 1973 and 1976a papers), none of them generates this model's prediction concerning the income effect on work at home. A crucial test of our analysis focuses, therefore, on this effect: Does an increase in unearned income reduce the work at home of the nonemployed while leaving the work at home of the employed unaffected? The examination of this hypothesis is the subject of this section.

The data used are the 1972 panel of the Michigan Study of Income Dynamics. Given the peculiar characteristics of the subsample of nonemployed men (e.g., a mean age of 68), I confine the discussion to the time usage of white married women. The sample included 1,281 women, of whom 660 were employed at some time during the preceding year and 621 reported that they did not work in 1971. The dependent variables consisted of the time spent working in the market (including travel to

---

[13] The wife's tendency to specialize in work at home is reinforced if work in the market involves fixed entry costs. Marriage offers the woman a job which does not involve these fixed costs at terms which may not be much inferior to her market wage rate. As a result, the wife may be tempted to drop out of the labor force and concentrate on work at home.

work), the time spent in housework, and leisure.[14] The explanatory variables included the wife's age, education, and labor force experience (i.e., full-time work) since the age of 18, the husband's education and wage, the family's unearned income, the number of children below the age of 18, the number of children at school, and the number of rooms in the home. The regressions were estimated for the whole sample and separately for the employed and the nonemployed.[15]

The findings for the whole sample closely resemble those reported earlier in Section I and are therefore not presented here. Table 3 presents the results for the two subsamples separately. The results confirm the predictions of the model. When the wife is not employed, her work at home is negatively affected (and her leisure is positively affected) by her unearned income and her husband's wage rate. Children tend to increase her home tasks, but schoolchildren less so than younger ones. Her work at home is negatively associated with her education, but positively associated with the size of her house. As predicted, her potential wage rate (as approximated by her past labor force experience) does not affect her allocation of time.

When the woman is employed, a major determinant of her allocation of time is her wage rate. This variable explains the negative effect of labor force experience on work at home and leisure and the negative effect of the wife's education on her work at home (education and leisure are positively correlated in this regression, but the regression coefficient is nonsignificant). Children have a negative effect on their mother's leisure, the time withdrawn from the market falling short of the increase in housework. As the child grows older and enters school, housework diminishes, but this change results in hardly any gains in leisure—the time saved in work at home is diverted back to the market.[16] Most important for our analysis is the income effect. The husband's wage has a significant positive effect on leisure, but no effect on work at home.

[14] The families reported on the number of weeks worked, the number of hours the wife worked per week, and the number of hours spent in housework in an average week. (Housework is not defined in the questionnaire, but the examples mentioned are cooking, cleaning, and other work around the house. Thus, it is not known whether the families included such activities as child care and shopping in housework.) I defined leisure as the difference between 8,760 hours per annum and the number of hours reported worked in the market and at home.

[15] Separating the sample by employment status may give rise to selectivity biases. I tried to correct for these, but had very little success because of the strong multicollinearity between the correction coefficient and the rest of the explanatory variables. It is comforting to learn that a recent attempt to correct selectivity biases in labor supply (Cogan 1976) has generated results that do not differ much from simple OLS estimates based on a sample of working wives.

[16] The effect of children on leisure, as presented in table 3, is significant at the conventional 5 percent level only if one uses a one-tailed test. However, if one removes the variable schoolchildren from the regression, the variable number of children turns out to be highly significant by any standard (i.e., *t*-values that exceed 3).

TABLE 3

The Determinants of the Allocation of Time of Married Women in the United States, by Employment Status[a]

	NOT EMPLOYED		EMPLOYED					
	Work at Home	Work at Home	Work in the Market	Work at Home	Leisure	Work in the Market	Work at Home	Leisure
Constant	1,669.40 (6.74)	1,677.29 (6.69)	1,953.51 (8.44)	1,155.30 (5.32)	5,651.19 (21.37)	−9,310.70 (9.14)	3,213.34 (3.30)	14,857.36 (12.61)
Wife's age	−1.165 (0.37)	−1.312 (0.41)	−15.745 (5.01)	3.895 (1.32)	11.850 (3.30)	−14.965 (5.08)	4.084 (1.45)	10.881 (3.19)
Wife's education	−53.469 (3.28)	−53.811 (3.29)	20.740 (1.36)	−36.262 (2.53)	15.522 (0.89)	−241.312 (8.47)	11.883 (1.45)	229.429 (6.97)
Husband's education	22.668 (1.82)	22.511 (1.81)	−32.781 (2.38)	14.412 (1.12)	18.369 (1.17)	−31.028 (2.30)	14.000 (1.09)	17.028 (1.09)
Husband's wage ($/hour)	−16.129 (2.21)	−16.199 (2.22)	−24.017 (1.80)	−8.048 (0.64)	32.065 (2.11)	−151.896 (8.89)	15.264 (0.93)	136.632 (6.91)
Unearned income ($10/year)	−0.441 (2.23)	−0.445 (2.24)	−0.660 (2.39)	0.210 (0.81)	0.451 (1.43)	−0.598 (2.21)	0.197 (0.76)	0.401 (1.28)
Children aged 0–17	327.654 (6.94)	327.843 (6.94)	−198.781 (4.94)	278.141 (7.37)	−79.359 (1.73)	−189.559 (4.81)	276.025 (7.31)	−86.466 (1.90)
Children at school	−125.196 (2.86)	−124.926 (2.85)	123.216 (3.24)	−104.465 (2.93)	−18.752 (0.43)	98.394 (2.64)	−100.098 (2.81)	1.704 (0.04)
Rooms	83.251 (3.17)	83.207 (3.16)	6.446 (0.28)	27.467 (1.29)	−33.912 (1.31)	−3.502 (0.16)	29.148 (1.37)	−25.646 (1.00)
Wife's experience	...	0.808 (0.21)	38.498 (9.57)	−6.244 (1.65)	−32.254 (7.02)	...	...	...
Wife's expected wage (log; ¢/hour)	...	...	...	...	...	2,810.95 (11.11)	−514.77 (2.13)	−2,296.18 (7.85)
R^2	.26	.26	.19	.17	.11	.23	.17	.12
N observations	621	621	660	660	660	660	660	660

[a] Numbers in parentheses = t-ratios.

Similarly, work at home is not affected by changes in unearned income; their effect on leisure is positive, though weak. It is also worth noting that the work at home of employed women is not correlated with the size of their house—presumably any extra work associated with extra rooms is done by maids (or other market substitutes).

To isolate the wage effect from other effects associated with education, I introduced this variable directly into the regression. Since the survey does not include direct information on the hourly wage rate, hourly earnings are computed by dividing annual earnings by annual hours (i.e., by the product of weeks worked and weekly hours). This procedure generates serious measurement errors which bias the estimate of the wage effect. To overcome this problem, I used an indirect approach: At the first stage I estimated the wage function; at the second stage I introduced the imputed (log) wage in the time use functions. The estimated wage function was of the semilog variety, the explanatory variables being the wife's education (ED), her labor force experience (EX), and her husband's wage rate (W_h)

$$\log W = -0.5955 + 0.0905ED + 0.0302EX - 0.0006(EX)^2$$
$$\qquad\qquad\quad (9.18)\qquad\quad (4.72)\qquad\quad (2.99)$$
$$+ \ 0.0442W_h$$
$$\quad (4.75)$$

$$R^2 = .20$$

where the wages are measured in dollars and the numerals in parentheses denote the corresponding t-values.

The results of the second stage (table 3) do not diverge much from our previous findings. The wage rate has a strong negative effect on both leisure and work at home. Education is positively correlated with leisure, but its effect on work at home (though positive) is not significant. (The direct effect of education on number of hours worked in the market is therefore negative.) Finally, the pure income effect is as predicted: neither unearned income nor the husband's wage rate affect the employed woman's work at home.[17] Our model also passes this test successfully.

IV. So, What's New?

The model has been shown to yield a comprehensive yet concise interpretation of the findings on the allocation of time between work in the market, work at home, and leisure. It explains the different behavior

[17] Comparing the regression coefficients of unearned income in the work-at-home, leisure, and work-in-the-market equations, one observes that the first two are nonsignificant while the last is significant. This difference is explained by the better fit of the last equation. The difference between the husband's wage effect and the effect of unearned income is due primarily to differences in the units of measurement (dollars per hour and dollars per annum, respectively).

patterns of people with different incomes, wages, and education, and the effect of children on the allocation of time. It accounts for the different patterns observed for men and women, the married and unmarried, the employed and nonemployed; and it appears, on the whole, to provide the economist with more refined tools for analyzing time-budget data. But does the theory extend our understanding of household behavior beyond this goal? In this section I shall try to show that the ramifications of the theory reach far beyond the analysis of time use.

The Supply of Labor

The most direct application of our model is, of course, to the analysis of labor supply. In the short run the two most important economic factors affecting the supply of labor of married women are income and wage rates. According to our analysis, the income effect works primarily through its effect on leisure. On the other hand, wage increases tend to increase the supply of labor by reducing work at home, but their effect on leisure is indeterminate. Given the wage effect on leisure, the labor supply is more elastic the greater the sensitivity of work at home to changes in the wage rate (i.e., the smaller the effect of H on f'). For that reason alone, one would expect the supply of labor of married women to be more elastic than that of men. But the analysis brings up a further point: A wage increase may result not merely in a shift from work at home to work in the market but also in reduced leisure—employed women have less leisure than the nonemployed. Indeed, according to the estimates presented in table 3, the marginal effect of a wage change on the leisure of the employed is more than four times that on work at home, although the wage elasticities are almost identical (about 0.4). Admittedly, some of these changes in leisure may be due to changes in activities which are normally regarded as work at home but were not defined as housework by the respondent,[18] but it is hard to believe that this misclassification explains such a great difference.

Recent decades have witnessed a great expansion in the labor supply of married women. Still, with only about half of married women participating in the labor force, and with the number of working hours of employed women equaling the number of hours they put in on work at home, it looks as if this resource has only been partly tapped for future expansion. A natural question is to what extent will the labor-supply function of married women resemble that of their husbands once they reach similar labor force participation rates? Right now any answer to this question should be regarded as sheer speculation, since so much depends on changes in role differentiation and on reallocation of work

[18] See n. 14. According to the Israeli data, housework (not including child care) accounts for only two thirds of the time defined by me as work at home.

at home within the family. It is, however, worth noting that right now women are more willing to dispense with leisure in response to wage increases than men (the change in leisure induced by a 1 percent change in wages is almost twice as great for employed wives as for their husbands) and that men are apt to increase their leisure in response to an increase in income much more than women (the ratio of the income effects is about 5:1).[19]

In the long run, changes in wages are associated with changes in education. But while in the short run wage increases, education given, reduce both work at home and leisure, changes in education (when the wage is not held constant) affect only work at home. The long-run prospects for increased labor supply due to increases in education are therefore much more limited. On the other hand, one can expect further expansion in labor supply if the increase in education and wages is associated with a decline in fertility.

The Demand for Children

It is customary for economists (e.g., Willis 1973) to argue that children are a home-time-intensive activity and that an increase in children therefore reduces work in the market. A corollary of this contention is that since children are time intensive, an increase in their mother's wage rate should raise their price relative to that of other commodities. Given our analysis, one has to distinguish between home-time intensity and leisure intensity (or average and marginal home-time intensity). Children may be home time intensive when they are introduced into the household, since some of the goods used in the activity can be profitably produced at home. However, as the activity increases, the profitability of home production diminishes and eventually the family relies solely on market goods (on the margin). At this point the goods-intensive nature of children becomes apparent. Thus a wage increase raises the price of children in the range where children's goods are produced at home; but when these goods are market produced, the price of children is reduced by a wage increase. The tendency to replace home goods by market goods increases with the mother's wage rate. Thus, one would expect that the price of children increases with the mother's wage for low-wage mothers but that this relationship is reversed as the mother's wage increases. Ben-Porath (1973) observes a transposed J-shaped relationship between fertility and education for Israeli women: Fertility declines with education, but there is a slight inflection at the top. These findings are consistent with the

---

[19] The findings for the employed married men (not presented here) are based on the same sample as those for the women.

prediction of the model.[20] The price of housemaids relative to the wife's wage seems to be lower in Israel than in the United States, and the tendency to substitute housemaid services for wife's time is therefore greater in Israel. Consequently, the transposed J-shaped relationship between fertility and wife's education should be more pronounced in the Israeli data.

The price of market substitutes relative to the wife's wage declines as the child gets older, and the goods-intensive nature of children therefore becomes more explicit. The relative price of "older children" has a greater tendency to decline as the parent's wage increases. The overall effect of changes in the wage rate on the present value of the cost of children is therefore indeterminate and depends on the price of market substitutes, the rate of discount, etc.

Gains from Marriage

Previous studies (e.g., Becker 1973) have asserted that gains from marriage depend on the husband-wife wage ratio. Other things being equal, the higher the husband's wage rate relative to his wife's the greater the opportunity for specialization within the household and the greater the gains from trade. This conclusion must be somewhat modified if one realizes that there exists no direct way of trading leisure and that the exchange is confined to home goods. The scope for gains from exchange within the household is limited by the profitability of home production. The latter in turn depends on the wife's home productivity and the price of market substitutes. Given the wife's home productivity and the price of market substitutes, the higher the wife's wage the greater the probability that any change in her activities will not affect her home production. In this case the prices of goods confronting men and women are the same and there are no gains to be reaped from trade. The gains from trade therefore decline as the wife's wage increases irrespective of the husband's. The increase in marital instability which has accompanied the increase in women's real wage rates and their increased labor-force participation is consistent with the prediction of the model, though one does not observe any substantial narrowing of the sex wage gap (Fuchs 1974).[21]

[20] Ben-Porath (1973) explained this relationship in a somewhat similar fashion, arguing that if the elasticity of substitution between time and goods in the production of children exceeds unity, children may be a time-intensive commodity for low-wage mothers but a goods-intensive commodity for high-wage mothers.

[21] Fuchs (1974) reports that the sex differential in hourly earnings of white nonfarm employed hardly changed in the last decade (from 0.61 in 1959 to 0.64 in 1969). Moreover, the differential for the young (below 35) married (the group most prone to divorce) has even slightly increased (from 0.73 to 0.70).

Taxes, Child-Care Programs, and the Demand for Domestic Help

It is often claimed that the wife's entry into the labor force involves costs such as child-care and housemaid services which by far exceed the husband's cost of entry. According to this argument, child-care services should be tax deductible, as are books or other costs a person must undertake in order to work. This argument has been accepted by many legislators and incorporated into the tax laws.

The economic validity of such deductions apart, it seems that this popular argument is wrong. An increase in expenditures on child-care services is associated with the wife's work in the same way an increase in the expenditures on a gardener is associated with the husband's work. Unlike expenditures on books or commuting costs (and time), which are a prerequisite for work, they are a cost which the family willingly undertakes because it finds that it is unprofitable for the wife to spend her time in child-care activities.

The analysis emphasizes, however, an additional point. In evaluating the various child-care programs which have been proposed or enacted in recent years, one has to distinguish between their effect on the marginal rate of substitution between goods and leisure and their effect on the profitability of home production. Assume a one-commodity world where the only commodity is children. A program which gives the mother a fixed child-care subsidy for every hour worked is equivalent to a wage increase and affects both the profitability of home production and the price of leisure. On the other hand, a fixed cash rebate or free child-care services which are conditional on a minimum number of working hours do not affect the profitability of home production of working women and may only affect their demand for leisure. When it comes to nonemployed women, this kind of program encourages labor force participation (in particular if entry into the market involves fixed costs) and may affect both home production and leisure. Finally, a tax deduction for child-care expenditures which declines gradually with earnings may affect home production but need not affect the price of leisure.

It has been argued (Heckman 1974) that to evaluate and compare the impact of various programs on labor supply and welfare it is sufficient to know the indifference curves between market goods and nonmarket time. Our analysis indicates that this knowledge may not be sufficient and that a thorough evaluation may require specific information on both the household production function $f(H)$ and consumption technology (Z).[22]

Finally, it seems at first puzzling that work at home is so insensitive

[22] One can easily incorporate in the analysis additional proposals (e.g., a subsidy confined to institutional forms of child care) and complicate it by introducing additional activities or exchange within the household, but this would not change our basic conclusion.

to changes in income, given the high income elasticity of the demand for housemaids.[23] The puzzle is solved, however, if one realizes that the demand for housemaid services (like that for many other services) is an excess demand. An increase in income does not increase the profitability of producing these services at home when a person is employed and reduces the profitability when he is not employed (the shadow price of time increasing). Thus, changes in income may have a strong effect on the excess demand for these market services and no effect (or even a negative one) on home services.

The Evaluation of Home-Sector Output

A long-standing complaint against the current national accounting system is its omission of the output of the nonmarket sector and, specifically, the output of wives at home, which according to some estimates (Morgan, Sirageldin, and Baerwaldt 1966) constitutes close to 40 percent of measured GNP. Several attempts have been made to correct this shortcoming (Morgan et al. 1966; Nordhaus and Tobin 1973; Sirageldin 1969), but these attempts were accompanied by controversy over which prices should be used to evaluate the wife's output. Should one infer the value women assign to their time and use that (Gronau 1973), or should one use the market prices of the services rendered by the wives (Walker and Gauger 1973)? The present model provides an analytical tool to resolve this controversy.

If the wife works in the market and at least some of each good is purchased ($X_{Mi} > 0$), her value of marginal productivity at home equals her wage rate ($f_i' = W$). Since most of the goods produced at home are services, she assigns to them a value that equals the wage she would have to pay somebody else to do the work for her divided by the average productivity of that person ($= W_H/AP_{Hi}$). The value placed on the last unit of work at home is therefore $W = W_H f_i'/AP_{Hi}$. Using the wage W_H of the services worker who can replace the wife in home production serves as a good approximation for the value of her time only if his or her average productivity equals the wife's marginal productivity. If $f_i' > AP_{Hi}$, the wage of the services worker will understate the price the wife assigns to her marginal unit of time in work at home.

Similarly unsatisfactory seems to be the method that uses the person's wage rate for the imputation. Women who do not participate in the labor force assign to their time a price that exceeds the wage they expect to get in the market. More important, the wage rate may serve as a close approximation to marginal, but not average, productivity at home. The

[23] Using Israeli data (the Family Expenditure Survey 1968–69), I found that even when one controls for the wife's education and employment status, the income elasticity of housemaids exceeds unity.

product of the average wage rate and the number of hours worked at home therefore understates the value of home production to the extent that diminishing marginal productivity prevails. This imputation does not account for the rent (i.e., the producer's surplus) accruing to a person who is self-employed in his own home.

V. What Next?

I believe that this paper provides ample evidence for establishing the distinction between work at home and leisure as an integral part of the theory of the allocation of time and household production. It has been shown that this distinction is a prerequisite for any further investigation of time-use patterns and is highly useful in the analysis of fertility, marriage, child-care programs, labor force participation, and the evaluation of the output of the nonmarket sector. I am confident the model will also be found fruitful for the analysis of problems in other fields, such as medical economics or transport demand, in which the household production model has been put to good use.

It is clear that the model is incomplete. I expect major criticism to be launched against the assumption that work at home involves the same marginal utility as work in the market. Child care, cooking, gardening, etc., clearly create direct utilities (positive or negative). The psychic income derived from these activities relative to that derived from work in the market may vary with the person's socioeconomic characteristics and affect his behavior. Admitting the validity of this criticism, I contend that it is not more serious than in the case of the dichotomy of home time versus work in the market. Psychic income (or leisure on the job) is an important determinant of investment in human capital, occupational choice, and the supply of labor. Economists so far have not been able to derive a satisfactory method of isolating this factor. This has not prevented research on the determinants of the supply of work to the market, and it should not block research on the supply of work at home.

A second point of criticism may focus on the neglect of joint production and joint consumption. These are important features of human behavior which are not adequately treated by our analysis.[24] But in this respect our model does no worse (and no better) than the current model of household production (Pollak and Wachter 1975).

Finally, in the empirical part of this paper I have explored only a small fraction of the implications of the model for the allocation of time and consumption patterns of the household. Topics such as the interaction

---

[24] It may very well be that the observed goods intensity of children can be traced to joint consumption and production. Much of the satisfaction derived from children and much child-care activity involves just having children around while doing other things, such as cooking or watching TV.

between work at home and substitute market services or the interaction between entry costs (time and money) and time use have only been touched upon. More ambitious endeavors, such as the estimation of the household production function and the value of home output, are still in a preliminary stage. However, given the right data, it is hoped that this paper will facilitate their realization.

References

Becker, Gary S. "A Theory of the Allocation of Time." *Econ. J.* 75 (September 1965): 493–517.

———. "A Theory of Marriage: Part I." *J.P.E.* 81, no. 4 (July/August 1973): 813–46.

Ben-Porath, Yoram. "Economic Analysis of Fertility in Israel: Point and Counterpoint." *J.P.E.* 81, no. 2, pt. 2, suppl. (March/April 1973): S202–S233.

Bloch, F. "The Allocation of Time to Market and Non-Market Work within a Family Unit." Technical Report no. 114. Inst. Math. Studies Soc. Sci., Stanford Univ., November 1973.

Cogan, John. "Labor Supply with Time and Money Costs of Participation." Rand Corp. R-2044-HEW, August 1976.

Fuchs, Victor R. "Recent Trends and Long-Run Prospects for Female Earnings." *A.E.R. Papers and Proceedings* 64 (May 1974): 236–42.

Gronau, Reuben. "The Intrafamily Allocation of Time: The Value of the Housewives' Time." *A.E.R.* 68 (September 1973): 634–51.

———. "The Allocation of Time of Israeli Women." *J.P.E.* 84, no. 4, pt. 2, suppl. (August 1976): S201–S220. (*a*)

———. "Leisure, Home Production and Work—the Theory of the Allocation of Time Revisited." Mimeographed. Nat. Bur. Econ. Res. Working Paper no. 137. Stanford, Calif., May 1976. (*b*)

Heckman, James J. "Effects of Child-Care Programs on Women's Work Effort." *J.P.E.* 82, no. 2, pt. 2, suppl. (March/April 1974): S136–S263.

Mincer, Jacob. "Labor Force Participation of Married Women." In *Aspects of Labor Economics*, edited by H. Gregg Lewis. Universities-National Bureau Conference Series, no. 14. Princeton, N.J.: Princeton Univ. Press, 1962.

Morgan, James N.; Sirageldin, Ismail A.; and Baerwaldt, Nancy. *Productive Americans: A Study of How Individuals Contribute to Economic Progress.* Ann Arbor: Univ. Michigan Press, 1966.

Nordhaus, William D., and Tobin, James. "Is Growth Obsolete?" In *The Measurement of Economic and Social Performance*, edited by M. Moss. Nat. Bur. Econ. Res. Studies in Income and Wealth, no. 38. New York: Columbia Univ. Press, 1973.

Perlman, R. *Labor Theory.* New York: Wiley, 1969.

Pollak, Robert A., and Wachter, Michael L. "The Relevance of the Household Production Function and Its Implications for the Allocation of Time." *J.P.E.* 83, no. 2 (April 1975): 255–77.

Sharir, S. "The Income Leisure Model: A Diagrammatic Extension." *Econ. Rec.* (March 1975): 93–98.

Sirageldin, I. A. *Non-Market Components of National Income.* Ann Arbor: Univ. Michigan Press, 1969.

Walker, K. E., and Gauger, W. H. "The Dollar Value of Household Work." Mimeographed. New York State Coll. Human Ecology, Cornell Univ., 1973.

Willis, Robert J. "A New Approach to the Economic Theory of Fertility Behavior." *J.P.E.* 81, no. 2, pt. 2, suppl. (March/April 1973): S14–S64.

[12]

1

The Basic Model: Theory, Empirical Results, and Policy Conclusions

Inderjit Singh, Lyn Squire, and John Strauss

THE BASIC MODEL PRESENTED HERE is the analytical framework used in most of the early empirical efforts to investigate the behavior of agricultural households. A more general analytical framework is described in the appendix to part I. Many of the case studies presented in part II illustrate how the basic model can be expanded to treat a wider range of policy issues and how it can be modified to reflect more accurately the realities of agricultural production. For the present, however, attention is focused on fundamentals.

The Basic Model

For any production cycle, the household is assumed to maximize a utility function:

$$(1\text{-}1) \qquad U = U(X_a, X_m, X_l)$$

where the commodities are an agricultural staple (X_a), a market-purchased good (X_m), and leisure (X_l). Utility is maximized subject to a cash income constraint:

$$p_m X_m = p_a(Q - X_a) - w(L - F)$$

where p_m and p_a are the prices of the market-purchased commodity and the staple, respectively, Q is the household's production of the staple (so that $Q - X_a$ is its marketed surplus), w is the market wage, L is total labor input, and F is family labor input (so that $L - F$, if positive, is hired labor and, if negative, off-farm labor supply).

17

The household also faces a time constraint—it cannot allocate more time to leisure, on-farm production, or off-farm employment than the total time available to the household:

$$X_l + F = T$$

where T is the total stock of household time. It also faces a production constraint or production technology that depicts the relation between inputs and output:

$$Q = Q(L, A)$$

where A is the household's fixed quantity of land.

In this presentation, various complexities have been omitted. For example, other variable inputs—fertilizer, pesticide—have been omitted and the possibility that more than one crop is being produced has also been ignored. In addition, it has been assumed that family labor and hired labor are perfect substitutes and can be added directly. Production is also assumed to be riskless. Finally, and perhaps most importantly, it will be assumed that the three prices in the model—p_a, p_m, and w—are not affected by actions of the household. That is, the household is assumed to be a price-taker in the three markets and, as argued in the Introduction, this will result in a recursive model. At various points in this volume, each of these assumptions will be abandoned, but for much of the discussion in this chapter they will be retained.

The three constraints on household behavior can be collapsed into a single constraint. Substituting the production constraint into the cash income constraint for Q and substituting the time constraint into the cash income constraint for F yields a single constraint of the form

(1-2) $$p_m X_m + p_a X_a + w X_l = wT + \pi$$

where $\pi = p_a Q(L, A) - wL$ and is a measure of farm profits. In this equation, the left-hand side shows total household "expenditure" on three items—the market-purchased commodity, the household's "purchase" of its own output, and the household's "purchase" of its own time in the form of leisure. The right-hand side is a development of Becker's concept of full income in which the value of the stock of time (wT) owned by the household is explicitly recorded. The extension for agricultural households includes a measure of farm profits ($p_a Q - wL$) with all labor valued at the market wage, this being a consequence of the assumption of price-taking behavior in the labor market. Equations 1-1 and 1-2 are the core of all the studies of agricultural households reported in this volume.

In these equations, the household can choose the levels of consumption for the three commodities and the total labor input into agricultural production. We therefore need to explore the first-order conditions for maximizing each of these choice variables. Consider labor input first. The first-order condition is:

(1-3) $p_a \partial Q / \partial L = w.$

That is, the household will equate the marginal revenue product of labor to the market wage. An important attribute of this equation is that it contains only one endogenous variable, L. The other endogenous variables—X_m, X_a, X_l—do not appear and therefore do not influence the household's choice of L. Accordingly, equation 1-3 can be solved for L as a function of prices (p_a and w), the technological parameters of the production function, and the fixed area of land. This result parallels that described in the Introduction in that production decisions can be made independently of consumption and labor-supply (or leisure) decisions.

Let the solution for L be

(1-4) $L^* = L^*(w, p_a, A).$

This solution can then be substituted into the right-hand side of the constraint (equation 1-2) to obtain the value of full income when farm profits have been maximized through an appropriate choice of labor input. We could, therefore, rewrite equation 1-2 as

$$p_m X_m + p_a X_a + w X_l = Y^*$$

where Y^* is the value of full income associated with profit-maximizing behavior. Maximizing utility subject to this new version of the constraint yields the following first-order conditions:

(1-5) $\partial U / \partial X_m = \lambda p_m$

$$\partial U / \partial X_a = \lambda p_a$$

$$\partial U / \partial X_l = \lambda w$$

and

$$p_m X_m + p_a X_a + w X_l = Y^*$$

which are the standard conditions from consumer-demand theory.

The solution to equation 1-5 yields standard demand curves of the form

(1-6) $X_i = X_i(p_m, p_a, w, Y^*)$ $i = m, a, l.$

That is, demand depends on prices and income. In the case of the agricultural household, however, income is determined by the household's production activities. It follows that changes in factors influencing production will change Y^* and hence consumption behavior. Consumption behavior, therefore, is not independent of production behavior. This establishes the recursive property of the model described in the Introduction.

To complete this section, we derive the "profit effect" also mentioned in the Introduction. Assume that the price of the agricultural staple is increased. What is the effect on consumption of the staple? From equation 1-6,

$$(1\text{-}7) \qquad \frac{dX_a}{dp_a} = \frac{\partial X_a}{\partial p_a} + \frac{\partial X_a}{\partial Y^*}\frac{\partial Y^*}{\partial p_a}.$$

The first term on the right-hand side is the standard result of consumer-demand theory and, for a normal good, is negative. The second term captures the profit effect. A change in the price of the staple increases farm profits and hence full income. From equation 1-7,

$$\frac{\partial Y^*}{\partial p_\alpha}\,dp_\alpha = \frac{\partial \pi}{\partial p_\alpha}\,dp_\alpha = Q\,dp_\alpha.$$

That is, the profit effect equals output times the change in price and is, therefore, unambiguously positive. As noted in the Introduction, the positive effect of an increase in profits—an effect that is totally ignored in traditional models of demand—will definitely dampen and may outweigh the negative effect of standard consumer-demand theory.

Estimation Issues

Given a recursive model, a set of output-supply and variable input-demand functions (equation 1-4) and a set of commodity-demand equations including leisure or labor supply (see equation 1-6) can be derived from the household's equilibrium. The output supplies and input demands are functions of input and output prices and of farm characteristics (including fixed inputs). They are derived from a profit function that obeys the usual constraints from the theory of the firm: homogeneity of degree one in prices, and convexity with respect to prices. The commodity demands are functions of commodity prices, full income, and possibly household characteristics (see below). When full income is held constant, these demands satisfy the usual constraints of demand theory: adding up to total expenditure; zero homogeneity with respect to prices and exogenous income; and symmetry and negative semidefiniteness of the Slutsky-substitution matrix. These results can be used as a guide when specifying the model for estimation.

If estimation is to be carried out by econometric means, errors have to be added to the model. The issues involved in specifying a sensible error structure are outside the scope of this chapter. For simplicity, suppose the errors are added to the demand and output-supply equations. If for a given household the errors on the input-demand and output-supply equations are uncorrelated with the errors on the commodity-demand equations, the entire system of equations is statistically block recursive. In this case, profits will be uncorrelated with the commodity-demand disturbances so that the latter equations may be consistently estimated as a system independent from the output-supply and input-demand equations. The practical advantage of estimating the demand and production sides of the model separately is that far fewer parameters need to be estimated for each. This can be important if the equations are nonlinear in parameters and have to be estimated using numerical algorithms, since expense is greatly reduced and tractability increased. Thus models with greater detail can be estimated.

Even though demand-side and production-side errors are uncorrelated, errors on different commodity-demand equations may still be correlated, as might errors of different output-supply and input-demand equations. This is intuitively plausible. Moreover, it is a necessary condition for the commodity-demand equations, since they must satisfy the adding-up constraint; that is, expenditures must add up to full income. If this constraint is to be met for every household, the errors, or a linear combination of them, must add up to zero for each household so that the result is nonzero correlations. This result is well known and is one reason for estimating either the commodity-demand equations or the output-supply and input-demand equations as a system: accounting for the error covariances will improve the statistical efficiency of the estimates. A second reason for estimating these equations as a system (or, more properly, two separate systems, one for the commodity demands and one for the output supplies and input demands) is to account for cross-equation parameter restrictions. These will occur because these equations are derived from a common optimizing problem. In particular, the adding up and the Slutsky symmetry constraints will impose certain cross-equation constraints on commodity-demand parameters, which, if used (and if they are correct), will again improve the statistical efficiency of the estimates. These advantages are well known and have given rise to an econometric literature on estimation of demand systems (see, for example, Brown and Deaton 1972; Barten 1977; Deaton and Muellbauer 1980).

One does not have to estimate a system of equations, since single, reduced-form equations can be consistently estimated as well. This will be advantageous when the underlying model is not recursive (see chapter 2).

The disadvantage of this approach is that it is usually not possible to solve for the reduced form analytically. Consequently, one cannot take full advantage of economic theory in imposing (or testing) parameter restrictions, although some of the restrictions may be readily apparent. Nevertheless, it is possible to specify what variables belong in the reduced form and thus to estimate a least squares approximation to it. In general, by not imposing parameter restrictions one sacrifices only statistical efficiency, and not consistency.

Even if the underlying model is recursive, estimating a single equation may be advantageous because it can economize data requirements. To estimate a complete set of commodity-demand, output-supply, and input-demand equations requires an enormous amount of data on consumption expenditures and prices for farm and nonfarm commodities; on household time allocation to on-farm and off-farm work and related wages; and on inputs and outputs of the production activities. To estimate a single equation, however, the analyst needs data on only one endogenous variable and the proper exogenous variables, but not on all the endogenous variables. (Other aspects of estimation—data requirements, specification of variables—are discussed in chapter 2.)

Empirical Results

The first empirical studies to give estimates of agricultural household models (Lau, Lin, and Yotopoulos 1978; Yotopoulos, Lau, and Lin 1976; Kuroda and Yotopoulos 1978, 1980; Adulavidhaya and others 1979; Adulavidhaya, Kuroda, Lau, and Yotopoulos 1984; and Barnum and Squire 1978, 1979a, b) are econometric studies that specify separable models and that estimate commodity demands and either output supply and input demands or a production function. They are highly aggregative on the demand side and use one agricultural commodity produced and consumed by the household (our X_a), one nonagricultural commodity that can only be purchased (our X_m), and leisure (our X_l). Kuroda and Yotopoulos decompose leisure into leisure of family members who work on the farm and leisure of these working off the farm. Those working off the farm are therefore different people with different labor quality than those working on the farm. To make the model separable they also implicitly assume hired labor is used on the farm. All the studies provide more detail on the production side and thus allow for several variable and fixed inputs.

Lau, Lin, and Yotopoulos (1978) look at Taiwanese household data averaged by farm size and by region for each of two years. Kuroda and Yotopoulos (1978, 1980) use cross-sectional household data from Japan, also grouped by farm size and by region. Adulavidhaya and others (1979, 1984) use cross-sectional household data from Thailand, but the cross sections differ for the production and consumption sides of the model. This approach considers that the two sets of households behave identically and is possible only because the model is recursive. Otherwise, data on the same set of households would be necessary. Barnum and Squire (1978, 1979a, b) use cross-sectional household data from the Muda River Valley in Malaysia. Both the Malaysian and Thai households practice monoculture (rice cultivation), so that aggregation on the production side is not a problem. It was possible to estimate price elasticities for Taiwan, Japan, and Thailand because prices vary by region (and over time in Taiwan). In Malaysia only, wages vary. By making sufficiently strong assumptions about preferences, however, price elasticities could be calculated.

These four studies use the systems approach to estimate commodity demands. Lau, Lin, and Yotopoulos (1978), Kuroda and Yotopoulos (1980), and Adulavidhaya and others (1984) use the Linear Logarithmic Expenditure System (LLES), whereas Barnum and Squire (1979a, b) use a Linear Expenditure System (LES). The LLES is derived from a translog indirect utility function that is homogeneous of degree minus one in prices. This implies that every expenditure elasticity with respect to full income is one—which is a restrictive assumption, particularly if one specifies many commodities. That fact that LLES is linear in parameters, however, makes estimation simpler. The LES is derived from an additive utility function, the Stone-Geary. It has fewer parameters to estimate than an LLES, but is nonlinear in parameters. Since the system is additive, Engel curves must be linear and no Hicks-complementarity between commodities is allowed for. As is true for the LLES, these conditions become less restrictive when commodities are highly aggregated. According to Deaton (1978), however, additivity should be rejected even then.

In all of these studies, household characteristics such as total size and its distribution are regarded as fixed, but they do affect commodity demands. The effects of demographic variables on demand can be modeled in different ways. Lau, Lin, and Yotopoulos (1978), for example, enter household characteristics as separate arguments into the utility function. This implies that they will be independent variables in the expenditure as well as indirect utility functions. Barnum and Squire use linear translation (see Pollak and Wales 1981) to enter household characteristics. This involves subtracting commodity-specific indices from each commodity in the utility function—that is, $U(X_0 - \gamma_0, \ldots, X_n - \gamma_n)$, where the X_i's are consumption of commodity i, and the γ's are the translation parameters that depend linearly on household characteristics. The associated indirect utility function looks like $V(p, Y - \Sigma^n_{i=1} p_i \gamma_i)$. In other words, everywhere that full income, Y, appears, one subtracts the sum of the values of these commodity indices (the p_i's being prices). Consequently, in this specification, the effect of household characteristics comes through full income. Other specifications of household characteristics are possible and perhaps are preferable. (For an excellent review, see Pollak and Wales 1981.

When demographic variables are used, an LLES share equation is given by

$$-\frac{p_j X_j}{Y} = \alpha_j + \sum_{k=1}^{n} \beta_{jk} \ln \frac{p_j}{Y} + \sum_{l=1}^{r} \sigma_{jl} \ln a_l$$

$$\sum_{j=1}^{n} \alpha_j = -1; \quad \sum_{k=1}^{n} \beta_{jk} = 0, \forall_j; \quad \sum_{j=1}^{n} \sigma_{jl} = 0, \forall_l$$

where p_j, X_j, and Y are defined as before, a_l is the lth household characteristic, and the α's, β's, and σ's are parameters to be estimated. An LES expenditure equation with linear translating is given by

$$p_j X_j = p_j(\theta_j + \gamma_j) + \beta_j[Y - \sum_{i=1}^{n} p_i(\theta_i + \gamma_i)], \quad \sum_{j=1}^{n} \beta_j = 1.$$

Here the β's are the (constant) marginal budget shares, the θ's are parameters, and the γ's are the translation parameters that are a linear function of household characteristics, that is, $\gamma_i = \Sigma^r_{l=1} \sigma_{il} a_l$.

For the production side, Yotopoulos, Lau, and Lin (1976), Kuroda and Yotopoulos (1978), and Adulavidhaya and others (1979) estimate a profit function and associated input demand functions, which are derived from a Cobb-Douglas production function. Barnum and Squire (1978, 1979a) estimate a Cobb-Douglas production function directly since they do not have the necessary price data to estimate the dual functions.

Two other studies must be included here since they also estimate complete systems on both the demand and production sides. One, by Singh and Janakiram (see chapter 3), is based on Korean and Nigerian data, and the other, by Strauss (chapter 4), looks at data from Sierra Leone. Singh and Janakiram specify a linear expenditure system for the consumption side and use a linear program to model the production side; Strauss characterizes consumption behavior by a quadratic expenditure system and production behavior by a multiple output production function in which outputs are related by a constant elasticity of transformation and inputs by a Cobb-Douglas function.

As can be seen from table 1-1, the seven studies are nearly evenly split in their findings concerning the consumption of the agricultural commodity: four report a positive own-price elasticity and three a negative one. The magnitudes of both positive and negative elasticities are small. The positive response indicates that the profit effect has more than offset the traditional negative effect predicted by standard consumer-demand theory. For consumption of market-purchased goods, the most important result is the strongly positive cross-price elasticities. This result also attests to the strength of the profit effect in increasing total expenditure. The reported elasticities suggest that the level of farm incomes and the availability of nonfarm goods are important determinants of responsiveness. Sierra Leone, for example, has a much lower elasticity than the East Asian economies.

Elasticities of marketed surplus are strongly positive, whereas those for labor supply are negative. The positive elasticities of marketed surplus indicate that, even where the profit effect is strong enough to make consumption response positive, the total output response is always large enough to offset increased household consumption. The negative responses for labor supply suggest a strong profit effect and reflect the empirical fact that leisure is a normal good. (Other results are summarized in appendix tables 1A-1–1A-4.)

Table 1-1. *Selected Elasticities: Response to Changes in the Price of the Agricultural Commodity*

Economy	Agricultural commodity	Consumption of agricultural good	Consumption of market-purchased goods	Marketed surplus	Labor supply
Taiwan	Farm output	0.22	1.18	1.03	−1.54
Malaysia	Rice	0.38	1.94	0.66	−0.57
Korea, Rep. of	Rice	0.01	0.81	1.40	−0.13
Japan	Farm output	−0.35	0.61	2.97	−1.01
Thailand	Farm output	−0.37	0.51	8.10	−0.62
Sierra Leone	Rice	−0.66	0.14	0.71	−0.09
Northern Nigeria	Sorghum	0.19	0.57	0.20	−0.06

Do Agricultural Household Models Matter?

Agricultural household models integrate production and consumption decisions in rural farm households. As a result, they require a complex theoretical structure as well as a considerable amount of data for empirical estimation. The studies summarized here attest to the fact that, both theoretically and empirically, such models are difficult and costly to estimate. Is the effort justified? Can practitioners make do with far simpler techniques that have been traditionally used to model farm behavior—that is, with techniques that do not allow for even a recursive relation between the supply and demand sides? If our interest is empirical, we must ask whether agricultural household models, which account for the interdependence of production and consumption decisions, provide estimates of elasticities that are quite different from what could have been obtained otherwise. If we are interested in policy, we must ascertain whether the differences in these elasticity estimates have different policy implications from those that would have been arrived at by traditional methods. In this section we consider the empirical significance of agricultural household models.

As noted earlier, the distinctive feature of agricultural household models is that they include the profit effect (equation 1-7). When we compare elasticities with and without the profit effect (see table 1-2), the results clearly establish the empirical significance of agricultural household models. The estimates of the elasticity of demand with respect to

Table 1-2. *Selected Response Elasticities under Varying and Constant Profits*

	Agricultural commodity		Nonagricultural commodity		Labor supply	
Economy	A^a	B^b	A^a	B^b	A^a	B^b
With respect to agricultural price						
Taiwan	−0.72	0.22	0.13	1.18	0.21	−1.59
Malaysia	−0.04	0.38	−0.27	1.94	0.08	−0.57
Korea, Rep. of	−0.18	0.01	−0.19	0.81	0.03	−0.13
Japan	−0.87	−0.35	0.08	0.61	0.16	−1.00
Thailand	−0.82	−0.37	0.06	0.51	0.18	−0.62
Sierra Leone	−0.74	−0.66	−0.03	0.14	0.01	−0.09
Northern Nigeria	−0.05	0.19	−0.14	0.57	0.03	−0.06
With respect to wage rate						
Taiwan	0.14	−0.03	0.05	−0.12	−0.12	0.17
Malaysia	0.06	−0.08	0.29	−0.35	−0.07	0.11
Korea, Rep. of	0.16	0.01	0.77	0.05	0.00	0.11
Japan	0.29	0.15	0.39	0.25	0.15	0.45
Thailand	0.57	0.47	0.62	0.52	0.08	0.26
Sierra Leone	0.47	0.37	0.78	0.57	0.14	0.26
Northern Nigeria	0.06	0.02	0.04	0.01	0.01	0.01

a. Holding profits constant.
b. Allowing profits to vary.

own-price not only differ significantly in the cases of Japan, Thailand, and Sierra Leone, for example, but they also change sign in the case of Taiwan, Malaysia, Korea, and northern Nigeria. Thus, whereas traditional models of demand, as we would expect, predict a decline in own-consumption in response to an increase in agricultural commodity prices, for four cases, the agricultural household models predict an increase. This is because the profit effect—which is the result of the increase in income when crop prices are raised—offsets the negative price effects. Farm households end up increasing their own consumption as prices are raised. Whether or not the amounts they offer on the market will be reduced will depend on the elasticity of output, which we know remains positive in these cases (see table 1-1). The marketed surplus response, however, is dampened by the profit effect.

The differences in the elasticity of demand for nonagricultural goods with respect to the price of agricultural goods are also striking. The elasticities change sign in four cases, and in the other three cases the magnitudes are much larger when the profit effect is included. Whereas cross-price elasticities estimated using traditional demand models tend to be low or negative because of negative income effects, the estimates obtained with the agricultural household model are positive and large because of the positive profit effect. The elasticities of household labor supply with respect to the price of the agricultural good also differ greatly. In the traditional demand models, an increase in the price of the agricultural good reduces the consumption of both that good and leisure, and thus implies an increase in the family work effort (table 1-2). In contrast, agricultural household models predict a negative response of household labor supply to increased output prices because households are willing to take a part of their increased incomes in increased leisure, thereby reducing their work effort. Consequently, any increase in the demand for labor in agricultural production will have considerable spillover effect on the demand for hired labor.

Although fewer signs change when responses to agricultural wage rates are examined, the magnitudes change. In traditional demand models, an increase in the wage rate implies an increase in real household incomes, which induces a positive-demand response with respect to agricultural and nonagricultural goods and a negative or inelastic response where household labor supply is concerned. In agricultural household models these effects are partly offset because an increase in wages also affects the production side and reduces total farm incomes. As a result, demand responses for both agricultural and nonagricultural goods are either dampened or totally offset (as in Taiwan and Malaysia), and labor supply response becomes positive or more elastic.

Looking at the market (or off-farm) labor-supply responses of landed and landless households in rural India, Rosenzweig (1980) provides a different type of evidence that agricultural household models matter. After separately estimating reduced-form market-supply equations for landless and agricultural households, Rosenzweig compares coefficients between the two groups and finds that twenty-one out of twenty-two comparisons conform to the predictions of the agricultural household framework. For instance, the off-farm male labor response of landless households to increases in the market male wage is less than for agricultural households, as would be predicted because of the negative profit effect of raising male wages.

Furthermore, agricultural household models provide other elasticities that are not even defined for models that focus exclusively on consumption behavior. These are the elasticities of demand with respect to nonlabor input prices and stocks of fixed factors of production, including land and farm technology (see table 1-3). Although the absolute magnitudes are small in most cases, the important point is that they have no counterpart in models that do not integrate production and consumption. Thus, despite the fact that traditional demand models can predict demand responses to output prices, they tell us nothing about such responses to changes in the fixed factors of product or technology. Similarly, traditional supply models can predict supply responses to changes in output

Table 1-3. *Selected Response Elasticities with Respect to Variable Input Prices and Fixed Factors*

Economy	Agricultural commodity	Nonagricultural commodity	Marketed surplus	Labor supply
With respect to fertilizer price[a]				
Taiwan	−0.11	−0.11	−0.24	0.18
Malaysia	−0.03	−0.18	−0.15	0.05
Korea, Rep. of	−0.05	−0.23	−0.34	0.04
Japan	−0.03	−0.03	−0.09	0.07
Thailand	−0.03	−0.03	−0.41	0.05
With respect to land				
Taiwan	0.46	0.46	1.00	−0.77
Malaysia	0.26	1.37	1.15	−0.41
Korea, Rep. of	0.10	0.49	0.81	−0.08
Japan	0.19	0.19	0.96	−0.43
Thailand	0.11	0.11	1.48	−0.19
Sierra Leone	0.01	0.02	0.02	−0.01
Northern Nigeria	0.10	0.16	0.06	−0.08

a. Fertilizer is barely used in the Sierra Leone and northern Nigeria samples and therefore was not modeled.

and input prices or in fixed factors of production and technology, but they fail to tell us anything about the demand responses to these exogenous factors. Agricultural household models therefore provide a vital link between the demand and supply-side responses to exogenous policy changes. Although these links can be established informally between traditional supply-and-demand models, in agricultural household models they are handled directly within a consistent theory and framework of estimation.

When should a full agricultural household model be used? The answer is that, since the profit effect is its distinguishing feature, such a model is appropriate when the profit effect is likely to be important. Notice, however, that changes in some exogenous prices have a small effect on farm profits. The profit effect is much more important in Malaysia than in Sierra Leone (table 1-6), for example, partly because the effect of a price change on profits is much larger in Malaysia, where a 10 percent increase in output price results in a 16 percent increase in profits. In Sierra Leone, the same percentage increase in output price increases profits by only 2 percent.

Second, even if profits are affected by an exogenous price increase, they may be only a small part of full income (equation 1-2), and it is full income that appears in the demand equations. For our sample of economies, the share of profits in full income ranges from 0.5 in Malaysia to only 0.2 in Thailand. It follows that a given percentage increase in profits will have a much greater impact on total income in Malaysia than in Thailand.

Finally, the effect of full income on demand varies among commodities. It is much more important in the case of nonagricultural commodities than agricultural ones, for example, since the demand for agricultural commodities tends to be inelastic with respect to income. In Malaysia, the elasticity of demand for rice with respect to full income is only 0.52 compared with 2.74 for market-purchased goods. As a result, the profit effect is much more significant in the case of nonagricultural goods (table 1-6).

These remarks suggest that, if profits are relatively insensitive to producer prices and constitute a relatively small part of full income and if consumption of a particular item is relatively insensitive to full income, then an agricultural household model will not necessarily make our analysis more accurate. This proves to be the case, for example, with the elasticity of demand for agricultural goods with respect to changes in producer prices in Sierra Leone, although it is not true for low-income households in that study (see chapter 4). If these three conditions are reversed, however, a full agricultural household model is of critical importance, as the elasticity of demand for nonagricultural goods with respect to producer prices in Malaysia reveals.

Policy Results

Agricultural household models provide insight into three broad areas of interest to policymakers: the welfare or real incomes of agricultural households; the spillover effects of agricultural policies onto the rural, nonagricultural economy; and, at a more aggregate level, the interaction between agricultural policy and international trade or fiscal policy. The potential role of agricultural household models in this respect becomes evident when we look at these three dimensions in a "typical" agricultural policy such as taxing output (either through export taxes or marketing boards) in order to generate revenue for the central exchequer and simultaneously subsidizing a significant input (usually fertilizer) to restore, at least in part, producer incentives. The model could just as easily be applied to other policies, but this particular combination has been adopted by many developing countries and illustrates well the type of issue that can be analyzed within the framework of the agricultural household model.

Consider, first, the effect of pricing policy on the welfare or real full income of a representative agricultural household. For some price changes—for example, a change in the price of fertilizer—the resulting change in nominal full income is an accurate measure of the change in real income since the prices of all consumer goods have remained unchanged. In other cases, however, the commodity in question may be both a consumer good and a farm output or input. If the price of, say, an agricultural staple is increased, the household will benefit as a producer but lose as a consumer. As long as the household is a net producer of the commodity, its net benefit will be positive (see the appendix to part I). Nevertheless, to quantify the net gain to the household, one must allow for both the positive effect coming through farm profits and the negative effect coming through an increase in the price of an important consumer good.

Table 1-4 presents estimates of the elasticities of real full income with respect to changes in output price and fertilizer price for the six studies examined earlier. For marginal changes, the decrease in real income following an increase in the price of the agricultural output equals marketed surplus times the price increase, and the increase following a reduction in the price of an input equals the quantity of the input times the price reduction. Thus, if prices, marketed surplus, and full income are known, these elasticities can be calculated without reference to price and income elasticities. For nonmarginal changes, however, it would be necessary to

Table 1-4. *Effect on Real Income of Changes in Output and Fertilizer Prices*

Economy	Response to output price	Response to fertilizer price
Taiwan	0.90	−0.11
Malaysia	0.67	−0.07
Korea, Rep. of	0.40	−0.10
Japan	0.34	−0.03
Thailand	0.10	−0.03
Sierra Leone	0.09	—
Northern Nigeria	0.12	—

— Not applicable. Fertilizer is barely used in the Sierra Leone and northern Nigeria samples and therefore was not modeled.

use information on the underlying structure of preferences to calculate equivalent or compensating variation.

The percentage change in real income among the six countries under consideration is less than the percentage change in either the output price or the fertilizer price (table 1-4). In addition, it appears that the loss in real income arising from a given percentage reduction in the output price can be offset only if the price of fertilizer is reduced by a much larger percentage. In Malaysia, for example, a 10 percent reduction in output price would reduce real income by almost 7 percent, whereas a 10 percent reduction in the price of fertilizer would increase real income by only about 1 percent. This difference arises from the relative magnitudes of marketed surplus and fertilizer use. Thus, if policymakers are interested primarily in the welfare of agricultural households, intervention in output markets is likely to be much more important than intervention in the markets for variable, nonlabor inputs.

Policymakers are also concerned with the welfare of rural households that do not own or rent land for cultivation. Landless households either sell their labor to land-operating households or else engage in nonfarm activities (see, for example, Anderson and Leiserson 1980). Although governments have few policy instruments by which to improve the welfare of these households directly, price interventions and investment programs directed at land-operating households have spillover effects that may (or may not) be beneficial for these households. What can agricultural household models tell us about these effects?

An increase in the price of an important agricultural staple will obviously hurt households that are net consumers of that item. The direct effect of a price increase will therefore be unambiguously negative for landless households and nonfarm households. The policymaker thus faces a dilemma: if he wants to improve incentives and increase the incomes of agricultural households, he does so at the expense of other rural households. There are, however, offsetting indirect effects. If the price of the agricultural commodity is increased, for example, agricultural households increase their demand for total—hired and family—farm labor and reduce the supply of family labor; that is, they increase their leisure time (see table 1-5). As a result, the demand for hired labor can be expected to increase substantially to the benefit of landless households. In Malaysia, the reported elasticities of labor demand (1.61) and labor supply (0.57) imply an elasticity of demand for hired labor of 10.9. Although this figure in part reflects the initial small percentage of hired labor in total labor (19 percent), it nevertheless implies a substantial change in labor market conditions and would undoubtedly exert upward pressure on rural wage rates and would thereby offset, at least to some extent, the negative consequences, among landless households, of higher prices for agricultural commodities.

The policy implications of these findings are particularly significant because they also shed light on the extent to which the positive gains from technological improvements trickle down via the labor market to the rural landless. It is now widely accepted that the technological innovations associated with the green revolution (improved seeds, increased use of fertilizers and pesticides, increased irrigation and cropping intensity) have

Table 1-5. *Spillover Effects of Changes in Output and Fertilizer Price*

Economy	Labor demand	Labor supply	Consumption of nonagricultural goods
Output price			
Taiwan	2.25	−1.54	1.18
Malaysia	1.61	−0.57	1.94
Korea, Rep. of	0.57	−0.13	0.81
Japan	1.98	−1.01	0.61
Thailand	1.90	−0.62	0.51
Sierra Leone	0.14	−0.09	0.14
Northern Nigeria	0.12	−0.06	0.23
Fertilizer price[a]			
Taiwan	−0.23	0.18	−0.22
Malaysia	−0.12	0.05	−0.18
Korea, Rep. of	−0.12	0.04	−0.23
Japan	−0.13	0.07	−0.03
Thailand	−0.11	0.05	−0.03

a. Fertilizer is barely used in the Sierra Leone and northern Nigeria samples and therefore was not modeled.

had a great deal to do with increasing the demand for total labor, but the concern has been whether this increased demand would do much for hired labor, most of which comes from the smallest farms and the landless. The empirical findings show that it could. When an increase, either in the fixed factors of production or technologies, boosts farm incomes, the amount of family (household's own) labor effort tends to decline (see table 1-7). Therefore any increase in the demand for total labor means an even larger increase in the demand for hired labor. The labor supply-and-demand elasticities emerging from empirical applications of agricultural household models provide strong support for the view that trickle-down effects are both positive and significant.

A second indirect effect of increased output prices is a significant increase in the demand for nonagricultural goods (see table 1-5). The response elasticity is positive and greater than 1 in two economies (Taiwan and Malaysia) and is positive and greater than 0.5 in all economies except Sierra Leone, though for low-income households in Sierra Leone it is also high (0.9). Some of this demand will be for imports and urban-produced commodities. But a large part will be for rurally produced goods and services and will therefore increase demand for the output of nonfarm, rural households. Any increase in farm profits, whether caused by a price change or a technological improvement, can be expected to lead to a substantial increase in the demand for goods and services produced by non-agricultural households. Thus, spillover effects through output markets will, at least in part, offset the negative effects on nonfarm households of an increase in agricultural prices and will ensure that the benefits of technological improvements are dispensed throughout the rural community.

Table 1-5 also traces through the effects of a change in the price of fertilizer. The results suggest that changes in fertilizer prices can be made without generating large negative or positive spillover effects.

As mentioned earlier, governments often tax agricultural output in order to generate revenue and at the same time subsidize essential inputs such as fertilizer in order to restore production incentives. In this way, they hope to achieve self-sufficiency or earn foreign exchange. Can agricultural household models shed light on these and other policy options? Indeed, the information they provide with respect to the effect of pricing policy on marketed surplus and fertilizer demand can be used as inputs in calculations of self-sufficiency, balance of payment effects, and budgetary effects.

If a government's primary concern is self-sufficiency, it needs to know the marketed surplus available for procurement. When we look at the elasticity estimates for agricultural production, consumption, and marketed surplus (table 1-6), two points become clear. First, even where con-

Table 1-6. *Response of Output, Consumption, Marketed Surplus, and Input Demand to Price Changes*

Economy	Agricultural output	Agricultural consumption	Marketed surplus	Fertilizer demand
Output price				
Taiwan	1.25	0.22	1.03	2.25
Malaysia	0.61	0.38	0.66	1.61
Korea, Rep. of	1.56	0.01	1.40	1.29
Japan	0.98	−0.35	2.97	1.98
Thailand	0.90	−0.37	8.10	1.90
Sierra Leone	0.11	−0.66	0.71	—
Northern Nigeria	0.30	0.19	0.20	—
Fertilizer price[a]				
Taiwan	−0.23	−0.11	−0.23	−1.23
Malaysia	−0.13	−0.03	−0.15	−1.13
Korea, Rep. of	−0.30	−0.05	−0.34	−1.10
Japan	−0.13	−0.03	−0.09	−1.13
Thailand	−0.11	−0.03	−0.41	−1.11

— Not applicable.

a. Fertilizer is barely used in the Sierra Leone and northern Nigeria samples and therefore was not modeled.

sumption responds positively to an increase in the price of the agricultural commodity because of the profit effect, marketed surplus still responds positively. Where the consumption response is negative, the elasticities of marketed surplus are positive and large (see, for example, the case of Thailand). Governments can therefore use pricing policy in the output market to increase the marketed surplus even when it is unable to set consumer and producer prices independently. Second, efforts to offset disincentives in output markets through fertilizer subsidies will not be effective unless the fertilizer price is reduced by a much greater percentage than the output price.

Rough estimates of the effect of pricing policies on budget revenues and foreign exchange can also be derived from table 1-6. Assume, for example, that the output is exported and that the fertilizer is imported. According to table 1-10, an increase in output price will induce an increase in marketed surplus available for export, but only at the expense of increased use of fertilizer. The net foreign exchange effect, therefore, is given by the difference between the revenues from exporting the agricultural output and the costs of importing additional fertilizer. Similarly, if the output is taxed and fertilizer is subsidized, one can perform a similar calculation to arrive at a rough estimate of the net impact on the budget. In fact, the framework of the agricultural household model is highly flexible and can be adapted to fit many other circumstances and issues. One of the purposes of this volume is to present some of the extensions that have recently been tested (see chapters 3, 4, 5, 6, and 7).

Some Extensions

Most of the early work on agricultural household models ignored questions of choice among competing crops. These studies either examined monocultures or else treated farm output as an aggregate. Several important policy issues, however, are concerned with the *choice among alternative crops*. Many governments, for example, are concerned with the effect of export taxation on production when export crops compete with food crops destined for the domestic market. Similarly, if fertilizer intensity varies among crops, price-induced changes in the composition of output may have significant effects on the demand for fertilizer. The demand for hired labor can also be influenced by changes in crop composition.

The basic agricultural household model can be modified easily to accommodate multiple crops. Thus a production function for a single crop can be replaced with an implicit production function linking inputs and outputs:

$$G(Q_1, \ldots Q_n, V_1, \ldots V_m, A_1, \ldots A_k) = 0$$

where Q represents output, V is variable inputs, and A is fixed factors. Provided the household is a price-taker in the relevant markets, the introduction of multiple outputs does not affect the recursive property of the model. Two of the studies covered in this volume—those by Singh and Janakiram and by Strauss—allow specifically for multiple crops.

This is an important policy extension since pricing policies are often oriented around specific commodities, but other crops will likely be affected as well. These studies cover three countries: the Republic of Korea, Nigeria, and Sierra Leone, and in each case cover crops grown primarily for consumption, for sale, and crops both consumed and exchanged. The countries cover three dissimilar environments. In Korea, farm households are well integrated into product and factor markets. Crops are grown under irrigated conditions and in single stands. Considerable technological advance has occurred in rice production, with a consequent high-level use of purchased inputs. In addition, there are many sources for nonfarm incomes. Households in Sierra Leone are also fairly well integrated into product and labor markets, but the level of income is far lower than for Korean households. There has been little technological change in paddy rice (or other crop) production so there is little use for nonpurchased inputs. Irrigation is nonexistent and crops are grown in mixtures. Households in the state of Kaduna in northern Nigeria are far more isolated from factor and product markets. Production is mostly for subsistence, and intercropping is widespread. Northern Nigeria is also a semiarid area, in contrast to Korea and Sierra Leone, so production risk is important (see chapter 9).

Table 1-7 reports own- and cross-price elasticities both for output supplies and marketed surpluses for households in the three countries. In all cases, the cross-price elasticities of output supply are very small, despite the crop disaggregation. For these studies, then, the need for comprehensive pricing policies is not evident. Korean households show a far greater own price output responsiveness than their northern Nigerian or Sierra Leone counterparts, which may be partly explained by the higher level of infrastructural development and the greater market integration in Korea.

The cross-price responses of marketed surpluses are small for the Sierra Leone case, but not negligible, and they are miniscule for the Korean and northern Nigerian samples. This reflects the very small cross-price elasticities both of output supply and commodity demands in the latter two studies. Again, the overwhelming impact of a commodity pricing policy is predicted by these studies to be on that commodity, without large spillover effects. It was necessary to disaggregate commodities in order to reach such a conclusion.

Table 1-7. *Cross-Price Elasticities of Supply and Marketed Surplus*

Economy	With respect to price of	Supply			Marketed surplus		
Korea,		Rice	Barley	Soybeans	Rice	Barley	Soybeans
Rep. of	Rice	1.56	−0.00[a]	0.00[a]	1.4	−0.00[a]	−0.00[a]
	Barley	−0.00[a]	0.50	−0.00[a]	−0.00[a]	0.50	−0.00[a]
	Soybeans	0.04	−0.10	−0.10	−0.03	−0.15	0.06
Nigeria		Sorghum	Millet	Groundnuts	Sorghum	Millet	Groundnuts
	Sorghum	0.30	−0.00[a]	−0.20	0.25	−0.00[a]	0.04
	Millet	−0.00[a]	0.25	−0.05	−0.00[a]	0.18	−0.07
	Groundnuts	−0.00[a]	−0.00[a]	0.18	−0.00[a]	−0.00[a]	0.09
Sierra Leone		Rice	Rootcrops	Oil palm	Rice	Rootcrops	Oil palm
	Rice	0.11	0.01	0.00[a]	0.71	0.06	−0.03
	Root crops and other cereals	0.02	0.10	0.00[a]	−0.08	0.46	−0.29
	Oil palm products	0.00[a]	0.00[a]	0.02	−0.05	−0.02	0.44

a. Insignificantly small.

Commodity disaggregation may also be important if calorie content varies among commodities and if governments are interested in the *nutritional status* of agricultural households. Strauss (chapter 4) shows how the basic model can be elaborated to investigate the effect of pricing policy on caloric intake. In his model, the utility function (see equation 1-1) becomes

$$U = U(X)$$

where X is a vector of consumer goods, including food items, nonfood items, and leisure. Caloric intake (K) can then be calculated from

$$K = \sum_i a_i X_i \qquad\qquad i = 1 \cdots m$$

where a_i is the calorie content of a unit of the ith food and $X_i, i = 1 \cdots m$ are quantities of different food items.

With this extension, Strauss demonstrates that price changes exert a considerable effect on caloric intake and that the profit effect plays a significant role. One might expect that an increase in the price of an important food item would probably have a negative impact on caloric intake. According to table 1-8, however, in most cases, an increased price results in increased caloric intake because of an increase in profits. That is to say, even if the consumption of such a commodity declines, the extra profits can be used to purchase increased quantities of other foodstuffs, with the result that overall caloric intake will respond positively. Strauss is also able to demonstrate an important point regarding the distribution of calories among income groups in Sierra Leone: even if a price increase causes a reduction in the caloric intake of middle-income and high-income households (see the case of rice in table 1-8), the intake of low-income households is increased. This suggests that, if policymakers are concerned primarily with the nutritional status of low-income households, price increases for major food items may prove to be beneficial. Increases in the prices of food items toward, say, world prices may improve the nutri-

Table 1-8. *Response of Caloric Intake to Price Changes in Sierra Leone*

Food	Elasticity of caloric intake		
	Low income	Middle income	High income
Rice	0.19	−0.24	−0.20
Root crops and other cereals	0.43	0.13	0.11
Oils and fats	0.27	−0.03	−0.21
Fish and animal products	0.48	0.23	0.05
Miscellaneous foods	0.14	0.01	−0.01

tional status of low-income households and provide appropriate signals for resource allocation. The usual equity-growth tradeoff may be absent in this case.

Policymakers are interested in nutritional status presumably because it affects health and may also affect productivity at the individual level. Pitt and Rosenzweig (chapter 5) take the analysis one step further, therefore, and examine the interaction between *prices, health, and farm profits* in the context of an agricultural household model. To do so, they incorporate a health variable directly in the utility function (people prefer to be healthy) and in the production function (a healthy individual is more productive). To complete their model, they introduce a production function for health:

$$H = H(X_a, X_m, X_l, Z)$$

which says that health (H) depends on consumption (X_a and X_m) and hence on nutrition, leisure (or work effort, X_l), and a vector (Z) of other factors that affect health, some of which are chosen by the household (boiling water) and some of which are community-level services (well water).

When this model is applied to data from Indonesia, it is found that a 10 percent increase in the consumption of fish, fruit, and vegetables reduces the probability of illness by 9, 3, and 6 percent, respectively, whereas a 10 percent increase in the consumption of sugar increases the probability of illness by almost 12 percent. These results suggest that increases in consumption cannot automatically be assumed to contribute to health since the composition of consumption may also change in a manner detrimental to health.

In addition to estimating the health production function, Pitt and Rosenzweig also estimate a reduced-form equation that produces a direct link between prices and health. They show that a 10 percent reduction in the prices of vegetables and vegetable oil will decrease the probability of the household head being ill by 4 and 9 percent, respectively, whereas the same percentage reduction in the prices of grains and sugar will increase the probability of illness by 15 and 20 percent, respectively, albeit from a very low base. These results are calculated with profits held constant, however. In principle, when profits are allowed to vary, some of these results may be modified. In this particular application the coefficient on farm profits proved statistically insignificant. The results reported above are therefore reasonably accurate measures of the total effect of price changes on health.

Changes in health may also affect productivity and farm profits. Pitt and Rosenzweig demonstrate for their sample, however, that the effects of ill-health on labor supply are not reflected in reduced farm profits when households have recourse to an active labor market. Thus, although family labor supply is significantly reduced by illness, total labor input, and hence farm profits, remain unaffected. In other words, in this Indonesian sample the benefits of improved health (or the costs of a deterioration in health) in agricultural households will be reflected in household income— if at all—only through labor-market supply.

Most of the policy issues mentioned thus far have been static in nature and have been couched in a single-period framework. Iqbal's work (chapter 6) represents a significant departure from previous studies in that it introduces another period to accommodate *borrowing, saving, and investment* decisions. Since governments and multinational agencies devote substantial quantities of funds to rural credit programs, this particular extension makes it possible to apply agricultural household models to a new set of policy issues of considerable importance in many countries.

In the first period of Iqbal's two-period model, the household may borrow and invest in farm improvements. In the second period, the loan must be repaid with interest and the household enjoys higher farm profits as a result of its investment in period one. Accordingly, the single full-income constraint is replaced by two full-income constraints, one for each period:

$$\Pi(K_1) + w_1 T_1 + B = C_1 + I$$

and

$$\Pi(K_1 + I) + w_2 T_2 = C_2 + B(1 + r[B])$$

where K_1 is capital in period one and I is investment, so that $K_1 + I$ is capital in period two. B is borrowing in period one and $B(1 + r[B])$ is repayment in period two. C is the value of consumption of goods and leisure. Iqbal draws a parallel between his treatment of household savings and borrowing and the treatment of own-consumption and marketed surplus or family labor supply and hired labor in the standard agricultural household model. He notes that the recursive property of the standard model carries over to his two-period extension, provided the household can borrow at a fixed rate of interest. In his application to Indian households, Iqbal argues that the interest rate is influenced by household borrowing decisions (r is a function of B in the second-period constraint) and therefore he adopts a nonrecursive specification.

Iqbal finds that borrowing is significantly reduced by increases in the interest rate, the elasticity being -1.2. His results support the view that interest rate policy can have a marked effect on the level of debt held by farmers. Iqbal also shows that farmers owning more than three hectares are highly sensitive to the interest rate, whereas the coefficient on borrowing by farmers owning less than three hectares is statistically insignificant. It follows that the elimination or reduction of subsidies to programs providing agricultural credit may serve the dual purpose of increasing efficiency in the capital market and simultaneously improving equity, since the reduction in borrowing by "large" farmers will exceed that by "small" ones.

As noted earlier, governments are also interested in the effects of agricultural pricing policy on more aggregate economic variables such as *budget deficits and foreign exchange earnings*. In Senegal, for example, agricultural products generate 70 percent of total export earnings, and deficits arising from the government's policy on agricultural pricing amount to more than 20 percent of government expenditure and 2 percent of GDP. Changes in agricultural prices can therefore be expected to have a considerable impact on these aggregates. Indeed, concern with the existing levels of foreign exchange earnings and a budget deficit may be the primary motivation for changing pricing policy in many countries. The government of Senegal has explored a number of ways, including pricing policy, to promote the production and consumption of millet in order to reduce imports of rice and hence improve the country's balance of payments.

The effect of pricing policy on foreign exchange and budget revenues discussed earlier in the chapter is further illuminated by Braverman and Hammer (chapter 8) through their addition of market-clearing conditions (for the major outputs and inputs) to the basic model. The changes in consumption, production, or labor supply at the household level following any change in an exogenous variable can then be aggregated and fed into the market-clearing equations. In some cases, the market is cleared through adjustments in international trade, and prices remain fixed at levels determined by the government, that is,

$$Q(\bar{p}_a) = X_a(\bar{p}_a) + E$$

where E represents net exports. In this event, a change in production or consumption has an immediate effect on foreign exchange earnings. Alternatively, the market may clear through adjustments in price, that is,

$$Q(p_a) = X_a(p_a).$$

Now a policy-induced change in production or consumption will bring about a change in price, which will generate second-round effects on production and consumption.

In their application to Senegal, Braverman and Hammer assume the first form of marketing clearing (quantity adjustment) for cotton, ground-

nuts, and rice and the second form (price adjustment) for maize and millet. The second-round effects flowing from induced changes in the prices
of maize and millet are captured fully in their model. Table 1-9 provides a
sample of their policy results. Compare, first, the effect of reducing the
price of groundnuts or increasing the price of fertilizer on the deficit arising from the government's agricultural pricing policy. Both policies reduce the deficit. The reduction in the price of groundnuts, however, has a
relatively small effect on net foreign exchange earnings (mainly because a
reduction in rice imports offsets reduced exports), although it reduces the
real incomes of farmers in the groundnut basin by almost 6 percent. Although an increase in the price of fertilizer causes a larger fall in net export earnings (in reflection of the fertilizer intensity of export crops), farm
incomes are reduced by only 1 percent. This example illustrates the policy
tradeoffs that can be explored within the framework of Braverman and
Hammer's extension. It also confirms a point made earlier—that to be
effective, changes in the prices of inputs such as fertilizer must be much
larger than changes in the prices of the main outputs.

Another important point regarding the formulation of policy in Senegal is that the government has been eager to reduce imports of rice and
hence save foreign exchange by increasing domestic production of rice
and increasing consumption of domestic substitutes such as millet. How
can this goal be achieved? One possibility is to increase the producers'
price of rice. Such a measure does indeed reduce rice imports (by 7 percent), but net foreign exchange earnings fall (by 4.5 percent), because in
order to increase rice production, farmers switch out of export crops (see
table 1-9). The desired result, an increase in net foreign exchange earnings, fails to materialize because of substitution possibilities in production. In this case, failure to recognize substitution possibilities produces a

Table 1-9. *Effect of Agricultural Pricing Policy in Senegal*
(percentage change)

Policy	Real income, groundnut basin	Export earnings	Government deficit
15 percent decrease in producer price of groundnuts	−5.7	−1.9	−18.1
100 percent increase in price of fertilizer	−1.1	−5.2	−10.4
50 percent increase in producer price of rice	0.2	−4.5	−0.1
50 percent increase in consumer price of rice	−4.7	−0.2	−34.8

perverse result. In other situations, however, policy may be designed to take advantage of substitution possibilities. The government might increase the consumer price of rice in the hope that people would change their pattern of consumption in favor of millet. According to Braverman and Hammer's analysis, however, such a policy would have little impact on net export earnings, so that in this case a reliance on substitution possibilities would have been misplaced (see table 1-9).

These examples from the work of Braverman and Hammer illustrate the importance of placing agricultural household models in a multimarket framework, particularly where foreign exchange earnings and government revenues are of concern. Because the expansion of one crop is usually detrimental to another crop, changes in the quantities of internationally traded items and in the quantities of taxed or subsidized items will influence the overall impact of policy on foreign exchange and government revenue even if a change in a government-controlled price in one market leaves the prices in all other agricultural markets unchanged. More generally, changes in government-controlled prices will induce changes in other prices so that even measures of output response, labor supply response, consumer response, and changes in farm profits will have to allow for general equilibrium effects (see chapter 2). Thus the multimarket extension may well emerge as the most useful vehicle for generating relevant policy results from agricultural household models.

Appendix: Detailed Elasticities from Studies of Agricultural Household Models

The four tables in this appendix are on the following pages.

Table 1A-1. *Elasticities of Agricultural Commodity Consumption*

Economy	Commodity	Total expenditure	Commodity price		Wage	Fertilizer price	Fixed factors				
			Own	Nonfarm			Workers	Dependents	Land	Capital	Scale technology factor
Taiwan	Farm goods	n.a.	0.22	0.29	−0.03	−0.11	0.84	0.43	0.46	0.04	n.a.
Malaysia	Rice	n.a.	0.38	−0.15	−0.08	−0.03	0.44	0.23	0.26	n.a.	0.42
Japan	Farm goods	n.a.	−0.35	0.31	0.15[a]	−0.03	0.07[b]	0.14	0.19	0.07[c]	n.a.
Thailand	Farm goods	n.a.	−0.37	0.05	0.47	−0.03[d]	0.70	−0.16	0.11	0.10	n.a.
Korea, Rep. of	Rice	0.57	0.01	n.a.	0.01	−0.05	n.a.	n.a.	0.10[e]	n.a.	0.002[f]
Sierra Leone	Rice	0.52	−0.66	0.13	0.37	—	0.26[g]	0.13[h]	0.01	0.04	0.11
Northern Nigeria	Sorghum	1.80	0.19	n.a.	0.02	—	n.a.	n.a.	n.a.	n.a.	n.a.

n.a. Not available.
— Not applicable. Fertilizer was barely used by the Sierra Leone and northern Nigeria samples and therefore was not modeled.
a. Farm wages.
b. On-farm workers.
c. Machinery.
d. Price index of fertilizer, seed, and chemicals.
e. Average farm size.
f. With respect to increased tiller capacity.
g. Males 15 years and older.
h. Children 10 years and younger.

Table 1A-2. *Elasticities of Nonagricultural Commodity Consumption*

		Commodity prices			Fixed factors					
Economy	*Total expenditure*	*Own*	*Agricultural commodity*	*Wage*	*Fertilizer price*	*Workers*	*Dependents*	*Land*	*Capital*	*Scale technology factor*
Taiwan	n.a.	−0.58	1.18	−0.12	−0.11	0.84	0.0	0.46	0.04	n.a.
Malaysia	n.a.	−0.77	1.94[a]	−0.35	−0.18	−0.06	−0.05	1.37	n.a.	2.21
Japan	n.a.	−0.97	0.61	0.25[b]	−0.03	−0.12[c]	0.02	0.19	0.07[d]	n.a.
Thailand	n.a.	−0.89	0.51	0.52	−0.03[e]	0.69	−0.29	0.11	0.10	n.a.
Korea, Rep. of	2.76	−0.87	0.81[a]	0.05	−0.23	n.a.	n.a.	0.49[f]	n.a.	0.01[g]
Sierra Leone	1.18	−0.93	0.14[a]	0.57	n.a.	0.41[h]	0.09[i]	0.02	0.10	0.27
Northern Nigeria	3.30	n.a.	0.57[j]	0.01	n.a.	n.a.	n.a.	n.a.	n.a.	n.a.

n.a. Not available.
a. Price of rice.
b. Farm wage.
c. On-farm workers.
d. Machinery.
e. Price index of fertilizer, seed, and chemicals.
f. Average farm size.
g. With respect to tiller capacity.
h. Males 15 and older.
i. Children 10 and younger.
j. With respect to sorghum price.

Table 1A-3. *Elasticities of Agricultural Commodity-Marketed Surplus*

		Commodity prices				Fixed factors				
Economy	*Commodity*	*Own*	*Nonfarm*	*Wage*	*Fertilizer price*	*Workers*	*Dependents*	*Land*	*Capital*	*Scale technology factor*
Taiwan	Farm goods	1.03	-0.05	-0.95	-0.24	-0.13	-0.07	1.00	0.08	n.a.
Malaysia	Rice	0.66	n.a.	-0.55	-0.15	0.09	-0.50	1.15	n.a.	1.85
Japan	Farm goods	2.97	-0.13	-0.77[a]	-0.09	-0.03[b]	-0.06	0.96	0.37[c]	n.a.
Thailand	Farm goods	8.10	-0.12	-3.62	-0.41[d]	-1.72	0.39	1.48	1.44	n.a.
Korea, Rep. of	Rice	1.40	n.a.	n.a.	-0.34	n.a.	n.a.	0.81	n.a.	n.a.
Sierra Leone	Rice	0.71	-0.12	-0.49	n.a.	-0.21[e]	-0.12[f]	0.02	0.11	0.32
Northern Nigeria	Sorghum	0.20	n.a.	n.a.	n.a.	n.a.	n.a.	0.06	n.a.	n.a.

n.a. Not available.
a. Farm wage.
b. On-farm workers.
c. Machinery.
d. Price index of fertilizer, seed, and chemicals.
e. Males 15 and older.
f. Children 10 and younger.

Table 1A-4. Elasticities of Labor Supply

Economy	Type of labor	Commodity prices					Fixed factors				
		Agricultural commodity	Nonfarm commodity	Farm wage	Off-farm wage	Fertilizer price	Workers	Dependents	Land	Capital	Scale technology factor
Taiwan	Total	-1.54	0.58	0.17	n.a.	0.18	1.27	0.20	-0.77	-0.06	n.a.
Malaysia	Total	-0.57[a]	0.24	0.11	n.a.	0.05	0.62	0.12	-0.41	n.a.	-0.65
Japan	Farm	-1.01	0.30	0.45	-1.97	0.07	-0.89[b]	0.34	-0.43	-0.17[c]	n.a.
Thailand	Total	-0.62	0.10	0.26	n.a.	0.05[d]	0.94	-0.28	-0.19	-0.19	n.a.
Korea, Rep. of	Total	-0.13[a]	n.a.	0.11	n.a.	0.04	n.a.	n.a.	-0.08[c]	n.a.	-0.002[f]
Sierra Leone	Total	-0.09[a]	-0.05	0.26	n.a.	n.a.	0.55[g]	0.13[h]	-0.01	-0.05	n.a.
Sierra Leone	Off-farm	-4.42[c]	-1.85	17.18	n.a.	n.a.	14.36[g]	3.78[h]	-0.94	-4.90	n.a.
Northern Nigeria	Total	-0.06	n.a.	0.10	n.a.	n.a.	n.a.	n.a.	n.a.	n.a.	n.a.

n.a. Not available.
a. Price of rice.
b. On-farm workers.
c. Machinery.
d. Price index of fertilizer, seed, and chemicals.
e. Average farm size.
f. With respect to tiller capacity.
g. Males 15 and older.
h. Children 10 and younger.

References

Adulavidhaya, Kamphol, Yoshimi Kuroda, Lawrence Lau, Pichit Lerttamrab, and Pan Yotopoulos. 1979. "A Microeconomic Analysis of the Agriculture of Thailand." *Food Research Institute Studies*, vol. 17, pp. 79–86.

Adulavidhaya, Kamphol, Yoshimi Kuroda, Lawrence Lau, and Pan Yotopoulos. 1984. "The Comparative Statics of the Behavior of Agricultural Households in Thailand." *Singapore Economic Review*, vol. 29, pp. 67–96.

Anderson, Dennis, and Mark Leiserson. "Rural Nonfarm Employment in Developing Countries." *Economic Development and Cultural Change*, vol. 28, pp. 227–48.

Barnum, Howard, and Lyn Squire. 1978. "Technology and Relative Economic Efficiency." *Oxford Economic Papers*, vol. 30, pp. 181–98.

––––––. 1979a. "An Econometric Application of the Theory of the Farm Household." *Journal of Development Economics*, vol. 6, pp. 79–102.

––––––. 1979b. *A Model of an Agricultural Household*. Washington, D.C.: World Bank.

Barten, Anton. 1977. "The Systems of Consumer Demand Functions Approach: A Review." *Econometrica*, vol. 45, pp. 23–52.

Brown, Alan, and Angus Deaton. 1972. "Surveys in Applied Economics: Models of Consumer Behavior." *Economic Journal*, vol. 82, pp. 1145–1236.

Deaton, Angus, and John Muellbauer. 1980. *Economics and Consumer Behavior*. Cambridge, Mass.: Cambridge University Press.

Kuroda, Yoshimi, and Pan Yotopoulos. 1978. "A Microeconomic Analysis of Production Behavior of the Farm Household in Japan: A Profit Function Approach." *The Economic Review* (Japan), vol. 29, pp. 116–29.

––––––. 1980. "A Study of Consumption Behavior of the Farm Household in Japan: An Application of the Linear Logarithmic Expenditure System." *The Economic Review* (Japan), vol. 31, pp. 1–15.

Lau, Lawrence, Wuu-Long Lin, and Pan Yotopoulos. 1978. "The Linear Logarithmic Expenditure System: An Application to Consumption Leisure Choice." *Econometrica*, vol. 46, pp. 843–68.

Pollak, Robert, and Terence Wales. 1981. "Demographic Variables in Demand Analysis." *Econometrica*, vol. 49, pp. 1533–51.

Yotopoulos, Pan, Lawrence Lau, and Wuu-Long Lin. 1976. "Microeconomic Output Supply and Factor Demand Functions in the Agriculture of the Province of Taiwan." *American Journal of Agricultural Economics*, vol. 58, pp. 333–40.

2

Methodological Issues

Inderjit Singh, Lyn Squire, and John Strauss

A NUMBER OF IMPORTANT METHODOLOGICAL ISSUES arise from the empirical literature on agricultural household models. Perhaps foremost among these is the question of the empirical validity of recursive models. Some would argue (see Lopez chapter 11) that the principle of separability cannot be applied in some cases. (Separable and recursive are used interchangeably here.) Nonseparability may be important when modeling certain phenomena, for instance when sales and purchase prices differ for the same commodity, or when markets are incomplete, as they might be in the face of risk and incentive problems. The first question to consider, then, is to what extent nonseparability is justified in agricultural household modeling.

Nonseparability

Nonseparability affects empirical farm-household modeling in two ways: it changes the comparative statics, and it renders statistically inconsistent the usual demand-and-supply parameter estimates. The comparative statics of a general, one-period nonseparable model are derived in the appendix to part I, where it is shown that a virtual (or shadow) price will exist if a commodity has an incomplete market or if the household is at a corner (that is, if it consumes all of its output). This virtual price will be endogenous to the household, and, if the commodity is both produced and consumed, the shadow price will be a function of both preferences and technology.

In Lopez's model (chapter 11), for instance, on-farm and off-farm labor are imperfect substitutes in the household utility function. Members care differentially whether they work for themselves or for others. In addition, Lopez assumes that family and hired labor are imperfect substitutes in the farm production function. Because of these two assumptions, his model is nonseparable; households have a supply of on-farm and off-farm labor, but, at the given market farm wage rate, it is unlikely that the supply of household on-farm labor will equal the demand for household farm labor. Since households will equate the two, they will act as if they faced a virtual farm wage different from the market wage. This virtual farm wage is derived implicitly from equating household on-farm household labor supply and demand. It is therefore a function of both consumption-related and production-related variables and is endogenous to the household. Meanwhile, if interior solutions are assumed, off-farm labor-supply decisions will respond to the market off-farm wage, and hired-in farm labor demand will respond to the market farm wage. Hence, the virtual farm wage will be a function of both market-farm and off-farm wages.

The comparative statics will have extra terms similar to those derived in the appendix to part I because the virtual farm wage will now change in response to exogenous variables. If the researcher wrongly believed the model to be separable, elasticity calculations would be in error, even if utility and production function parameters were known, because the virtual price would be wrongly treated as constant. How important this omission will be depends on the responsiveness of the virtual price to the changing exogenous variable and on the responsiveness of the variable of policy interest to changes in the virtual price. These magnitudes can often be guessed.

In Lopez's model, for example, the response of the uncompensated virtual farm wage (see the appendix for the distinction between uncompensated and compensated virtual prices) to an exogenous change in, say, the off-farm wage is likely to be positive. As the off-farm wage increases, there will be a positive substitution effect on the virtual farm wage, provided off-farm and on-farm work are substitutes in the utility function. This results from an upward shift of the on-farm labor-supply function (if utility is held constant) that accompanies the increase in the off-farm wage. In addition, full income rises with the off-farm wage rate, which, if we assume negative income effects on labor supply, should shift the on-farm labor-supply function still further upward. The responsiveness of the virtual farm wage will depend on the magnitudes of the shifts of the on-farm labor-supply function and on the steepness of the household farm-labor-demand functions. If family and hired labor are close substitutes, farm demand for household laborers should be elastic, and the resulting effect of the off-farm wage on the virtual farm wage should be small. This is clearly an empirical question, however.

If the policymaker is interested in the effect of a change in the off-farm wage on off-farm labor supply, the next step is to investigate the responsiveness of off-farm labor supply to a rise in the virtual farm wage. This should be negative because, if utility is held constant, off-farm labor supply will respond negatively to the virtual farm wage (if we assume substitutability). Income effects will be nonexistent because household farm-labor demand equals on-farm labor supply. This suggests that ignoring the endogeneity of the virtual farm wage in Lopez's model will create an upward bias in the off-farm labor-supply elasticity with respect to the off-farm wage rate, providing the true model parameters are known.

True model parameters are not known, however, and if a nonseparable model is wrongly estimated as separable, parameter estimates will be inconsistent. In general, the magnitude of the inconsistency cannot be determined analytically and as yet there is no Monte Carlo experimental evidence in this regard. Consequently, the magnitude of the statistical bias for estimating a separable model when a nonseparable model is valid is not known. Of course, the combined effects of parameter inconsistency and missing terms in the comparative statics may reinforce or offset each other. The one piece of evidence on the combined effect—that provided by Lopez—suggests that total labor supply (off-farm plus on-farm labor) is much less responsive to a simultaneous change in off-farm and on-farm market wage rates when a nonseparable model is being used. This finding is consistent with the previous arguments concerning off-farm elasticity. The nonseparable model yields a total labor-supply elasticity of 0.04, whereas the separable model indicates an elasticity of 0.19. Standard errors are not provided, however, so it is not clear how much of the difference is attributable to imprecision in the estimates.

It seems intuitively clear that, if the changing exogenous variable and the variable of policy interest are far removed from the market that is cleared by a virtual price, the issue of separability becomes less important. In the above example, the exogenous variable was a wage rate, the variable of policy interest was labor supply, and the virtual price was also a wage rate. In these circumstances, the difference between a separable specification and a nonseparable specification is likely to be at its greatest. Consider a different example, say, the consequences for marketed surplus when the price of the agricultural output changes. Output price will have three effects on the virtual farm wage rate. First, the farm-labor-demand schedule will be raised, and this will put upward pressure on the virtual wage. Second—provided on-farm labor and the agricultural commodity are substitutes—the income-compensated on-farm labor-supply schedule will be raised. This shift will probably be small, however, since the degree of substitutability between on-farm labor and food, far removed variables, is likely to be low. Third, an increased farm output price will have an effect on real full income in proportion to the marketed surplus of output. Provided this surplus is positive, the labor-supply schedule will shift upward still further. All three effects will tend to push the virtual on-farm wage higher.

The higher virtual farm wage will reduce output supply and increase consumption of the farm output. The effect on consumption is likely to be small, however, coming as it will through substitution effects between farm-labor and farm-output consumption. (Remember there will be no income effects from the induced rise in the virtual farm wage since on-farm labor demand equals its supply in this model.) Consequently, the difference between a separable and nonseparable specification, when we are considering the effect of the price of the agricultural output on marketed surplus, is likely to be confined to the effect on output of an induced rise in the on-farm virtual wage. The size of the increase will depend largely on the responsiveness of labor demand to output price and of on-farm labor supply to income. Accordingly, before abandoning separability, the analyst should carefully consider the interaction among changes in exogenous variables, changes in the virtual price, and changes in the variables of policy interest.

A few more points should be noted concerning potential generalizations from Lopez's paper. First, the data are aggregate, being at the level of the census division in Canada. To treat an average of households as if it were a single household requires special assumptions concerning the utility function. Lopez assumes quasi homotheticity, which results in linear Engel curves. Likewise, the commodities are highly aggregated, with all consumption (both food and nonfood) being grouped together; off-farm and on-farm labor constitute the other groups.

One reason for the limited commodity disaggregation on the demand side is the high cost of estimating such a nonseparable model, even with only three commodities. Lopez's model is highly nonlinear in parameters; thus, if many equations were involved, it would be very difficult to estimate them with maximum likelihood techniques. As an alternative, equations could be consistently estimated by subgroups, for instance, by those from the production side and those from the consumption side, provided instrumental variables techniques (such as nonlinear three-stage least squares) were used to account for endogeneity of certain variables (for example, profits in the commodity-demand equations). The use of subgroups could reduce the expense of estimation at the cost of some statistical efficiency, but the procedure would still be expensive. Estimating separable models is in general a much more tractable problem; hence it is useful to know roughly what is lost by incorrectly specifying a separable model.

Unfortunately, it is impossible to assess the overall importance of separability, and, even in a specific case such as Lopez's, a useful prognosis is not readily apparent to practitioners. For some types of analyses, the basic model will probably be a good approximation, but under what conditions? The most that can be said at present is that it may be possible to assess the bias in comparative statics caused by ignoring nonseparability, as was done in this section, but even then, the potential bias depends upon the hypothetical sources of the nonseparability, which the analyst will in general know only imperfectly.

Applications of Nonseparability: Differing Sales and Purchase Prices

Given the strong policy and empirical focus of the agricultural household literature, it makes sense that methodological interest in nonseparability should be directed at specific circumstances in which reasonable models ought to be nonseparable. The example of differing preferences for on-farm and off-farm work is a possible source of nonseparability, but its empirical relevance in developing countries is not clear. As Lopez argues, differential preferences for on-farm and off-farm labor can arise from transportation costs of off-farm labor. Although Lopez does not use some of the testable implications of that idea (such as differing transportation costs across households leading to differing labor supply decisions), he does illustrate how differences between sales and purchase prices can affect the basic assumptions used in formulating a model.

Differences between sales and purchase prices can arise because of commodity heterogeneity. For instance, the quality of food consumed out of home production may differ from that of market-purchased food. Some of these differences may be related to different degrees of processing or other embodied market services. In a dynamic model under risk, demands for home-produced and market-purchased food might differ because of differing attitudes toward risk. Allowing this kind of commodity heterogeneity seems to be a reasonable way to model the household effects of certain government infrastructural investments such as roads.

Alternatively, sales and purchase prices might differ for labor. One potential reason might be the higher costs of supervising hired labor because of incentive problems connected with short-run fixed wage contracts. Such moral-hazard problems could give rise to imperfect substitutability between hired and family labor. Though it need not. Quality-adjusted units of labor could be perfect substitutes. In this case, quality-adjusted sales and purchase prices do not differ, and separability of the basic agricultural household model is unaffected.

Whether commodity heterogeneity results in nonseparability depends on whether the household chooses a corner solution for which supply equals demand. For instance, if a household consumes its entire food production, market-purchased food being an imperfect substitute, then a virtual price for home-produced food exists, which in general will be higher than the sales price of food. This will affect the comparative statics, as explained earlier (also see the appendix). If the household sells some of its food output, however, the market sales price is the appropriate opportunity cost. The same idea is applicable in the hired-versus-family labor case. In many data sets, there will be households both at corners and at interior solutions. Since being at corners is a household choice, it must be modeled as such statistically (see Wales and Woodland 1983; Lee and Pitt 1984). Given current econometric theory and software, only a few corner solutions (two to three per household, at the most) can be handled simultaneously.

Another view is that different sales and purchase prices do not result from commodity heterogeneity, since the commodities are perfect substitutes without adjusting for quality. This might result from transport costs, abstracting from any quality differential caused by the transport. In this case, the budget constraint has a different slope, depending upon whether the commodity is to be sold or purchased on net balance.

The two cases are portrayed in figure 2-1. Take first the case that family labor is an imperfect substitute for hired labor. Output is also consumed. In this case, family labor cannot be purchased, so the budget constraint is the segment BD, just being tangent from the right to the production possibilities frontier at point B. There exists a virtual, or shadow, wage that would cause the household to supply labor just up to point B. If this virtual price is greater than the market wage, then the household will not sell any labor on the market, choosing a point on the segment OB of production function at which its marginal rates of substitution and marginal product are equated.

In the case in which a price wedge exists between sales and hiring wage of labor (there being no quality differences between hired and family labor), the budget constraint will look like the segments CA and BD. The smaller the price wedge, the closer the two segments will lie, joining as one line in the limit with no price differential. In this case, a household may be on the budget segment CA as a net hirer of labor, on the segment BD as a net seller of labor, or on the portion AB of the production func-

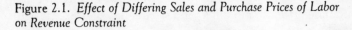

Figure 2.1. *Effect of Differing Sales and Purchase Prices of Labor on Revenue Constraint*

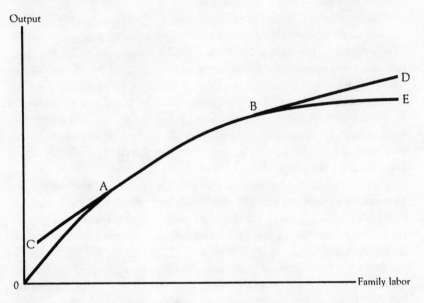

tion. Thus three regimes exist, whereas in the imperfect substitutes case, there are only two. Now two comparisons of virtual with market wages must be made to determine which segment the household chooses.

If the virtual price of labor at point A is greater than the market wage, then labor will be hired, the household being on the CA segment. If the virtual wage at point B is less than the market wage, then labor will be sold, and the household located on segment BD. Otherwise the household will be self-sufficient in labor, equating marginal rates of substitution with marginal product.

This problem resembles the nonconvex budget constraint arising from nonproportional income taxes, which has been described in the literature. Some of the econometric methods that exist to handle this case (see Heckman and MaCurdy 1981) are applicable here.

Applications of Nonseparability:
Incomplete and Interlinked Markets and Risk

Despite the growing literature on interlinkage (for example, Bardhan 1984; Binswanger and Rosenzweig 1984), studies of empirical modeling of agricultural households have not yet considered the interlinking of markets that may result from incomplete markets. The fact that households may be rationed in the credit market because of potential default (Stiglitz and Weiss 1981) will affect their behavior in other markets. Credit rationing may give rise to share tenancy (Jaynes 1982), with tenants borrowing from landlords. Access to land rental markets may be constrained by ownership of draft animals in cases where no rental markets exist for such animals. Renting out land may serve to secure more draft animals. The nonseparability thereby induced will give rise to several phenomena: for example, land lease or rental decisions may be affected by the stock of household laborers as households adjust land holdings to family size, or labor-supply decisions may be affected by land ownership through virtual prices as well as through income.

In the case of credit rationing, the interest rate charged to the household will be a function of how much has been borrowed, as well as of other household characteristics (see chapter 6). Furthermore, the effective wage rate may be affected by the number of hired laborers if supervision costs per worker are not constant. Such imperfections in markets will also result in nonseparability.

Underlying many of the discussions of incomplete markets and market interlinkages is the notion of risk. Although risk in one market is not a sufficient condition to cause such linkages, it is an important ingredient in the case of share tenancy (Newbery and Stiglitz 1979). Bardhan and Srinivasan (1971) use an agricultural household model in which land can be sharecropped and households maximize expected utility. Their model, although it incorporates risk, has a one-period framework, as do most models in the market-linkage literature. Yet, this approach ignores the time dimension that is crucially related to risk.

The only truly dynamic model under risk is that formulated by Roe and Graham-Tomasi (chapter 9), who model risks in farm production, not in prices. The separability results they obtain are not only instructive, but they also alert one to certain strong assumptions that have to be made if the result is to stand. Clearly, if perfectly competitive markets exist for future contingencies as well as for other markets, and given product homogeneity, risk can be completely diversified away and so does not present a problem. If contingent markets do not exist, then special assumptions must be made about preferences and about the distribution of yields in addition to markets before separability can result. Given their multiperiod framework, Roe and Graham-Tomasi must assume a perfectly competitive market to exist for a financial asset. This assumption, on top of the assumptions for one-period static models, would result in separability in an intertemporal model without risk, as Iqbal (chapter 6) points out. Adding risk, however, requires further assumptions concerning preferences. Providing households maximize expected utility, risk neutrality along with the previously maintained assumptions plus a perfectly competitive financial market would ensure separable production and consumption decisions.

Under risk aversion, Roe and Graham-Tomasi show that if the utility function is additively separable over time, with each period's subutility function being of negative exponential form (as is often assumed in the risk literature), if the exponents are functions that are homothetic with respect to consumption bundles (including leisure) and if production risk is multiplicative and normally distributed, then separability results. In this very special case, the household behaves as if it first maximizes certainty equivalent full income with respect to input and output choices (which is equivalent to maximizing expected utility of full income), and then maximizes utility subject its budget constraint, in which certainty equivalent full income appears.

In this special case, the profit effect of a change in farm output price has two counteracting components, since it is certainty equivalent full income that is changing in response to output price. An increase in farm output price raises mean profits but also increases its variance. The first effect is analogous to the usual profits effect. The second effect, however, acts to reduce certainty equivalent full income for risk averters, thus counteracting the positive effect on mean profits. Indeed, the combined profit effect of an increase in output price is no longer unambiguously positive, particularly if yields are sufficiently risky.

Past literature on the behavior of the pure firm under risk (for instance, Roumasset, Boussard, and Singh 1979) assumed that firms maximize expected utility of profits; this idea is consistent with a farm household framework, given risk aversion, under these special assumptions, but not necessarily under more general conditions. Without any restrictions on preferences other than a utility function—which is additively separable over time—Roe and Graham-Tomasi show that, conditional upon the optimal consumption bundle, the first-order conditions for expected utility maximization are identical to those of the pure firm maximizing expected utility of profits. Embedded in these first-order conditions, however, are the levels of optimal commodity consumption, which are unknown, and therefore input choices do depend in general upon consumption bundles.

As noted, markets for contingent claims (that is, for consumption in each period as a function of the realized state of the world), are absent in this model. Given possibilities for complete diversification of production risk, attitudes toward risk will not matter in the determination of production choices (whereas they do in Roe and Graham-Tomasi's model). Although complete risk diversification may not be possible in developing country agriculture, some means of diversification do exist; these range from investment in human capital (through education and migration) to investment in livestock or other physical assets to the formation of larger households, and so on. Clearly, this initial attempt at incorporating risk does not allow for such possibilities.

The assumption of a perfect financial asset market is one of the points of departure for the literature on incomplete and interlinked markets discussed above. If the interlinkage literature is correct, then the separability assumption under risk will not apply. Since much of this literature is theoretical, further empirical research is needed to define the nature of interlinked markets.

A second set of problems arises when we consider the particular specification of Roe and Graham-Tomasi's model, especially their assumption that the period-specific subutility function is homothetic. This restriction on preferences is implied by either constant absolute or constant relative risk aversion (Stiglitz 1969). Although this may be an empirically tractable assumption, the homotheticity assumption is overly strong since it restricts all income elasticities to unity.

Furthermore, this model overlooks possible randomness in future prices. Roe and Graham-Tomasi assume that future prices are known by households but that future production is random. Yet there may be circumstances in which production instability will cause price instability. In all agricultural household modeling, the data on relative prices must vary over observations, say, regions, if commodity-demand systems are to be estimated. If markets are well integrated so that local production disturbances do not affect local prices and regional price variation is sufficiently great, then local production uncertainty is consistent with local price certainty. Regional prices may vary because of other factors, however, such as government prescriptions on interregional trade or extremely poor transportation facilities, which may make invalid a small region assumption (so that local production does affect local prices).

Incorporating random prices into the agricultural household model is likely to be a more complicated task and will probably involve private storage decisions (see Wright 1979) as well as price expectations formation (see Eckstein 1983).

In addition, just as in the literature on the pure firm under risk, assumptions concerning what decisions can be made before uncertainty is resolved may vary and thus can greatly affect the analytical results. In Roe and Graham-Tomasi's model, all input decisions are made before the uncertainty is resolved.

Applications of Nonseparability: Household Production Activities

For many policy applications, it will be necessary to consider both household production activities and agricultural production activities. When this new dimension is added to the model, separability will in some cases be affected. Pitt and Rosenzweig (chapter 5) argue that whether farm production decisions can be modeled independently of other decisions—such as health inputs, consumption, and labor supply—depends on the nature of the hired labor market and the degree of substitutability between hired and family labor. Provided the two types of labor are perfect substitutes, separability between farm production and other decisions still holds because household demand for a certain quantity of a particular quality of labor can be met by hiring at a constant wage in the market. Consequently, the health of family laborers does not affect demand for healthy labor time. Clearly this would not be true if family and hired labor were imperfect substitutes.

A current concern of many policymakers is how to estimate the impacts of policy instruments such as food prices and health and education projects on health outcomes of individual farm-household members. For some policies, it may be important to estimate certain household production processes empirically, such as the relationship between food intakes, other health inputs, and health outcomes (see chapter 5). If estimates of the health technology are to be consistent, attention must be given to the fact that certain health inputs—such as food consumed, time devoted to health care, or boiling water—are household decisions. This is an important area for future research.

Even if policymakers only need reduced-form estimates of policy impacts, it will be important to disaggregate male and female time use and wages. This has not been done in typical farm-household modeling (Rosenzweig 1980 is an exception), but is important in this context because of specialization by gender in certain household activities. If health time care is female-labor intensive, for example, the effects on health outcomes within the household will differ between a rise in female wages and a rise in male wages. The substitution effect of an increase in female wages should lead to a greater decline in health than would the substitution effect of an equivalent increase in male wages. Of course, income effects will also be important and will tend to raise the demand for health. The importance of distinguishing male and female wages when evaluating impacts of policies on household nonmarket, nonfarm activities is one of the principal messages of the literature on the so-called new household economics that needs to be incorporated into household production activities of farm households as well.

Multimarket Analysis

If agricultural household models are to be used for policy analysis, inter-market relations need to be accounted for because of their potential importance. Such an accounting requires moving toward a general equilibrium analysis. Yotopoulos and Lau (1974) suggested some types of macrolevel models that might be useful, but they did not have the data needed to test their ideas. Barnum and Squire (1979) and Smith and Strauss (chapter 7) allow rural wages to be endogenously determined by equilibrating net labor demand (supply) among agricultural households with net labor supply (demand) in the rest of the economy.

Even if a limited amount of market interaction is allowed, certain results are significantly affected. Barnum and Squire find that in Malaysia increases in the price of rice cause such a large increase in the rural wage rate that output supply and marketed surplus of rice are both lowered in response. Consumption of paddy still increases, but by a smaller amount than when wages are exogenous. Smith and Strauss show that the partial equilibrium results for Sierra Leone stand up in sign but not in magnitude. Marketed surplus of rice remains positive, but the magnitude of the arc elasticity is more than halved, from 0.75 to 0.3.

Of course, the wage rate may not be the only endogenous price. Other prices may be endogenous as a result of government trade policies (for example, import or export quotas) or because of high transportation costs. Which prices should be allowed to equilibrate will differ, of course, for each application.

Braverman, Ahn, and Hammer (1983) examine agricultural pricing policies in Korea that were expected to reduce deficits in the government's Grain Management Fund and Fertilizer Fund. This study allows the price of the traditional variety of rice and rural wages to be endogenous while prices of high-yielding rice, barley, and fertilizer are government controlled. Effects of policy changes are traced through to government budgets, incomes of different classes of rural and urban households, national income, and marketed surpluses. The model's equations are based on agent optimizing behavior. For the rural sector, there are commodity and labor-demand and labor-supply equations derived from an agricultural household model using the Almost Ideal Demand System (Deaton and Muellbauer 1980) and the translog profit function. Urban commodity demands are also derived using an Almost Ideal Demand System. Finally, market-clearing equations are specified, and it is through these that specific government policies can be analyzed. For instance, the traditional rice market in Korea is modeled as a closed system in which urban demand equals rural marketed surplus. For a high-yielding variety of rice, imports are allowed, and the government supports the producer price above the world market price and subsidizes urban consumers. Because the structure of the model is general, it can be adapted to a variety of country and policy contexts. Indeed, a number of such adaptations have been reported: in Senegal (see chapter 8), Sierra Leone (Braverman, Hammer, and Jorgenson 1983), Cyprus (Braverman, Hammer, and Jorgenson 1984), and Malawi (Kirchner, Singh, and Squire 1984).

Several problems with respect to specification and data arise in those models. The basic model demands a great deal of data, as does the agricultural household model. Ideally, parameters should be econometrically estimated before being used in the simulation, but this ideal will not always be feasible because of the poor quality or lack of data. Hence, in practice, parameters are estimated, borrowed from other studies, or assumed. The system of equations is then solved at one point in time, and the solved values are compared with actual values for the economy at that particular moment. If the difference is too large in some sense, parameters are then changed iteratively until a desired closeness of simulated to actual values is achieved. Once a baseline simulation has been achieved, policy experiments can be simulated and sensitivity analysis of some small number of parameters performed. The lack of appropriate data manifests itself in parameters that may be imprecise. The sensitivity of the model's policy should therefore be carefully investigated. The Korea study, for example, has a relatively large number of parameters estimated from real world data. In the Senegal study, by contrast, many parameters are assumed and others (for instance, the price elasticities) are drawn from weak sources. This situation is largely a reflection of the stage of development of the data collection agencies in Korea versus those in Senegal. The assessment of the sensitivity of policy results to unprecise parameters is therefore especially important in the Senegalese model. This analysis of sensitivity leads to different conclusions for different variables of policy interest, and for different parameters. Parameters more directly related to the policy outcomes of interest will need to be estimated more precisely. In Senegal, for example, the effect of a 50 percent increase in the consumer price of rice on net foreign exchange earnings from agriculture depends critically on the assumed cross-price elasticity between the price of rice and millet consumption. Under high elasticity, much more millet is consumed, millet prices go up, and acreage is switched from groundnuts, the export crop, to domestically consumed millet. A low elasticity raises foreign exchange from agriculture, as tariffs from rice are increased, whereas rice consumption falls off only slightly. For government deficits in the agricultural sector, the elasticity assumptions make much less difference. Although less government tariff revenue is gained from increased consumer prices of rice when rice price elasticities are assumed to be high, the subsidies to groundnut producers drop because fewer groundnuts are produced—more acreage being switched over to millet than in the low-elasticity case.

Another practical problem has to do with how these models are solved numerically. If the model is set up in levels—for instance, if the quantities of rice demanded by rural households are a function of prices, wage, full income, and so on—the system of equations is highly nonlinear, and requires a great deal of time and expertise to solve. If the nonlinear system is totally differentiated, however, the resulting linear approximation will be relatively easy to solve with existing computer hardware. Nonetheless there is a tradeoff here because the approximation will be good only for variable values close to the baseline values, and policy analysts may be interested in the effects of large changes in certain variables, in which case the differentiated system may approximate the real world poorly. It is obviously a relatively simple matter to test the reliability of linear approximations by comparing their results with those of fully specified models. This is a high priority for future research and could be easily accomplished using some of the existing multimarket models.

A further problem that arises in model specification but that is not peculiar to multimarket models has to do with the Almost Ideal Demand System, which allows commodities to be inferior goods, but only permits a limited amount of nonlinearity in the Engel curves. It also restricts Engel curves to zero intercepts. Although this might be intuitively acceptable, real world incomes, appropriately measured, are sufficiently far from zero so that extending an approximation to an Engel curve in the relevant region will generally result in a nonzero intercept. If the functional form used to fit the Engel curve has sufficient curvature, this will be less of a problem. As already noted, however, the Almost Ideal Demand System does not have much curvature. The consequences of this are twofold: Engel curve slopes may be badly estimated even at the sample mean, and changes in the slopes as income changes may be missed. These consequences will be most damaging when the real Engel curves are very nonlinear, as might be expected when commodities are more highly disaggregated. This problem can be solved by using Engel curves with more curvature or by introducing nonzero intercepts, or both. Clearly both can be easily incorporated into multimarket analysis. Deaton (1982) has introduced quadratic income terms into the Almost Ideal Demand System, and Strauss (1982) has used the quadratic expenditure system of Howe, Pollak, and Wales (1979). Moreover, Gorman (1981) has shown that, in general, a second-order polynomial in income is as general as one can be in modeling Engel curves and yet still be consistent with utility maximization.

A common approach in macroeconomic work, also followed by Braverman and Hammer in their analyses, is to treat an aggregate of consumers (and producers) as an individual. For example, to relate aggregate commodity consumption to prices and average income, individual Engel curves must be both linear and parallel, as is well known. Otherwise the distribution of income will also affect aggregate consumption. If the concept of representative income (which is not average income) is used, where representative income depends on the income distribution and possibly on prices, then somewhat more general behavior can be accommodated.

Smith and Strauss (chapter 8) simulate outcomes for individual households in the Sierra Leone sample, as do Lau and others (1981) for the Taiwan sample. Knowledge of the regional sampling proportions allows the authors to convert the outcomes for individual households into regional and finally national aggregates. Comparing arc elasticities between this method of microsimulation and that using the representative household, Smith and Strauss find some large differences for both commodity-demand and output-supply elasticities. For example, a 10 percent increase in the price of rice raises the total national production of rice by only 1 percent when a representative household approach is used, compared with 3.4 percent under microsimulation. Rural rice consumption drops 6½ percent with the representative household approach, but only 5 percent with microsimulation. Although the results depend on both the data and the commodity-demand and output-supply specifications, they suggest that care should be taken when simulations are performed with functional forms that do not admit of perfect aggregation. As Smith and Strauss also point out, microsimulation allows the analyst to examine distributional effects of policies more readily. Braverman and Hammer come part way toward distributional disaggregation by allowing for representative households of different income classes (for Korea) or for different regions (Senegal).

Data Requirements and Implications for Data Collection

To estimate a complete agricultural household model, the analyst must have an extensive set of data on consumption expenditures (market purchased and subsistence), labor supply (possibly broken down by sex), farm and nonfarm outputs, purchased and household-supplied variable inputs, fixed farm assets, basic demographic characteristics, and prices, both for consumption and production inputs, including wages. It is obviously a massive undertaking to obtain data of reasonable quality on this scale for a single household. That is why comparatively few such data sets have been collected. Sample size clearly has to be traded off against both data comprehensiveness and quality. Empirical studies conducted to date indicate, however, that massive sample sizes, which many cross sections contain, are not needed to obtain plausible estimates of the structure of the basic farm household.

The precise nature of the potential tradeoffs between sample size, comprehensiveness, and quality is not entirely clear. In separable models, for example, commodity-demand and production-side equations can be estimated on different sets of data as long as each can be considered representative of the area in question, as would be the case if each were from a probability sample. Adulavidhaya and others (1984) did precisely this in the Thailand study. Such a data collection strategy may be more expensive than using common households, however, if increasing returns to scale exist in the collection techniques. Nevertheless, existing, less comprehensive sets of data can be combined. In particular, it is possible to supplement prototypical farm management surveys with a special household budget survey in which prices are also collected.

If complete nonseparable models are to be estimated, then this collection strategy is no longer viable because data are needed for both consumption and production activities on identical households. Many countries today conduct household budget surveys and farm management surveys. If the surveys could be coordinated so that household coverage could at least overlap, and if some price and wage data could be added, the information available for policy analysis would greatly increase. The payoff would be sizable—since such policy analyses could be built on much better quality data.

One potential way to reduce the costs of collecting comprehensive data on a moderately sized group is to obtain samples from only a limited number of geographical areas. This would be a grave mistake in farm-household modeling because then very little price variation would appear in the data. Yet the analyst relies on just such a variation in prices to explain differing consumption and production patterns. Unfortunately, many existing farm management surveys suffer from this very problem. Although household budget surveys may cover an adequate number of geographic regions, they often omit any price or wage data.

If longitudinal data are collected, then less geographical dispersion will be necessary because prices will vary over time. Indeed, longitudinal data on households circumvent a possible problem in the use of purely cross-sectional data—that is, that geographical price variation will be a proxy for other regional variables that might affect consumption or production outcomes. Collecting such panel data can be expensive, and some house-holds may drop out of the survey in a systematic way.

Alternatively, for separable models, it would be possible to use time-series cross-sectional data (which do not follow identical households over time) as long as each cross section was from a representative sample. In that case, households would have to be averaged in groups, for example, by size of land owned within each geographic region. The observations for analysis would then be the group averages. Such a procedure was used by Lau, Lin, and Yotopoulos (1978). The problem with this approach is that the group average may no longer behave as if it were a single house-hold; that is, the distribution of income or assets within the group may also matter. This problem was covered above (see also Deaton and Muellbauer 1980 for an excellent survey).

A different type of aggregation problem has to do with the grouping of commodities and the computation of group price indices. Several stud-ies—for instance those in Taiwan, Japan, and Thailand—assume that all households in a region face the same prices for disaggregated commodi-ties, but allow the weights used in forming the indices to vary for each observation (household group). This technique enables the analyst to de-rive household (or household group) specific prices. At the same time, it introduces two potentially serious problems: a spurious variation in prices, and a price index endogenous to the household. Suppose that every household in a market area (say, a region) faced the same set of prices for each disaggregated commodity (that is, for different qualities of the same aggregate commodity). Even with a common utility function, different households will buy different amounts of each quality of the ag-gregate commodity because of differences in full income and in household characteristics. Since the weights used are the share of household expend-iture on a particular commodity, the weights will differ by household. Thus the price variation seen by the researcher will be spurious. In addi-tion, these aggregate prices are endogenous to the household since ex-penditure decisions are endogenous. The endogeneity of prices would have to be accounted for in the estimation procedure in order to produce consistent statistical estimates, but the identifying instruments are lack-ing. All the variables that might affect the choice of quality are already included in the demand equations, so there would not seem to be any instruments left. Consequently, the analytical framework would have to be reformulated, for instance, into a model of probabilistic choice (see, for example, McFadden 1981). A more practical approach, if choice of qual-ity is not the main focus of the research, is to use regional average weights rather than household specific weights when constructing the price indi-ces. This approach is used in the Sierra Leone and Indonesian studies, among others. Even by averaging the expenditure-share weights over a region, however, it may not be possible to eliminate endogeneity if regions and full incomes are highly correlated.

Although, ideally, prices should be collected for all items consumed by a sample's households, this is both an impractical and unnecessary step in many cases. For the empirical analysis, the researcher will decide on the level of commodity disaggregation and will compute price indices for each group. In practice, prices will probably be required only for the most important items (with respect to budget shares) for each group, but all groups must be covered. If price indices cannot be computed for some groups, price and income elasticities can still be estimated in separable models, but strong assumptions will then have to be made about household preferences. If, for instance, we assume additivity of the direct utility function, as the Linear Expenditure System does, then all price elasticities can be estimated, although not every parameter will be identified. Barnum and Squire (1979) use this property of the LES to estimate all the price and income elasticities in a separable model for data from the Muda River valley in Malaysia when the only price variation in the data set applies to wages. Given the empirical evidence that contradicts some of the implications of the LES (such as additivity of the utility function and linear Engel curves), this is arguably a poor substitute for complete group price coverage. (See Deaton 1978 for a discussion of empirical evidence on additivity; Strauss 1982 for a strong rejection of linear Engel curves for farming households.)

Some comprehensiveness of data may be sacrificed if estimating a complete agricultural household model is not the objective of the analysis. It may be that only one or a few structural or reduced-form equations are of interest. To estimate reduced-form equations, the analyst needs data on all the exogenous variables, of course, but not on all endogenous variables. Moreover, certain details may not be necessary. To estimate health reduced-form equations, for instance, Pitt and Rosenzweig only need data on farm profits (subtracting out the value of family labor as well as purchased inputs), and not on specific input usage. Provided it is easier to obtain expenditure data on inputs rather than quantity data, this is a smaller information requirement. Note, however, that data on consumption prices are needed, even though the focus is on health outcomes. Consequently, it is not enough to collect data on only health outcomes, prices of health inputs (for example, doctor's fees, distance to health facilities, and so on), and an appropriate definition of income such as farm profits (that part of income uncorrelated with that equation's statistical error term) in order to obtain consistent estimates of the reduced-form health equation.

Iqbal, for example, does not need detailed data on consumption expenditure or input usage to estimate his reduced-form borrowing function. Of course, more complete data would have aided the analysis since fewer proxy variables would have been needed, and the interpretation of the coefficients of those contaminated variables would have been cleaner (for instance, the family size variable represents life cycle decisions, but it also affects current full income).

Furthermore, the traditional farm production, cost, or profit-function analysis is concerned only with a subset of the relevant household equations. This traditional analysis, as already noted, is acceptable as long as one is working with a separable farm-household model. In that case, detailed consumption expenditure and price data are not needed. If one is dealing with a nonseparable model, however, estimating even reduced-form output-supply equations will require prices of consumption commodities.

How comprehensive the data set should be depends on whether the goal is to estimate the complete farm-household system or just some parts of it. What data can be reasonably omitted also depends on whether structural or reduced-form equations are being estimated, and whether the household model assumes separability.

As for what can be accomplished with different degrees of shortfall from an ideal quality of data, that question has been only partly answered in the existing studies. Clearly, data sets do not have to be perfect—they never are—and in fact much insight has been gained from data that are far from perfect in quality. Yet even these imperfect data sets are extensive in their variable coverage and contain geographical, and in some instances time-series variations in prices.

Agenda for Future Research

To organize an agenda for future research, we must first distinguish between issues of household behavior and issues of policy analysis. (In making this delineation, we are not judging the relative importance of each group of issues, both of which are very important.) The first question in the household behavior category is what difference it makes if basic elasticity calculations wrongly assume separability. As we have seen, there is little evidence with which to answer this question. Moreover, the question itself is inherently difficult because the answer is likely to depend on how nonseparability enters the model, and there are many possible ways. Thus it may be more fruitful to pursue certain types of nonseparability that are suggested by the policy issue of interest and by the economic institutions that characterize the data set.

With respect to the basic, static model, one of the most important sources of nonseparability is likely to involve commodity heterogeneity, whether for consumption commodities or labor inputs. Such heterogeneity may lead to differing sales and purchase prices for the same commodity (whether there is a quality difference will need to be carefully considered since it leads to differences in modeling, as argued earlier). For labor, potential differences between family and hired labor, or between male, female, and child labor may be important (the latter distinction approaches the issue of intrahousehold distribution, treated below).

In some cases, but not all, it will be important to consider household production activities, not only for health issues, as noted earlier, but also for issues such as fertility and household composition. Although household production activities need not lead to nonseparability between farm production and household consumption, they may. Even if they do not, problems may arise in dealing with intrahousehold distribution, whether a reduced-form, or black box, approach is used in which the intrahousehold allocation mechanisms are not modeled explicitly, or whether more structural approaches are employed. In the black box approach, it will be crucial to account differentially for the effect of male and female opportunity costs on intrahousehold distribution (at least between sexes), as do Pitt and Rosenzweig.

One of the weak areas in the overall farm-household literature is the lack of empirical results on savings and investments. The little work that has been done (for example, that of Iqbal) has used a static framework. No study, except the one by Roe and Graham-Tomasi, has attempted a truly dynamic analysis, and very few longitudinal data sets exist to analyze these issues. Although this type of dynamic analysis could be carried out by ignoring risk, this consideration surely adds a great deal. Within such a framework, the analyst is able to consider not only issues connected with savings and investments (and perhaps their composition), but also those having to do with the adoption of new technologies. Most work on technology adoption under risk (for example, Feder, Just, and Zilberman 1985) has ignored the composition side of household activities and has modeled the household as maximizing expected utility of wealth or income. As Roe and Graham-Tomasi show, the assumptions justifying this approach may be rather restrictive. Much remains to be done in this area; to begin with, much more empirical work is needed, some of the rather restrictive assumptions such as homothetic preferences need to be relaxed, and price risk should be added. Unfortunately, the empirical work will not be easy and may well involve tackling the household model by parts rather than estimating a giant model, which is bound to be enormously expensive to test.

Just how restrictive are the assumptions underlying separability in dynamic models under production risk? This is an area in which the market interlinkage literature and the agricultural household literature intersect. Much more empirical work needs to be done on the true nature of rural labor, credit, and land markets in developing countries. In some areas of the world, farm-household models having a fixed land area will be very poor approximations. Investigating the determinants of land lease and sales behavior within the framework of an agricultural household model is likely to prove highly interesting, even if only reduced-form equations or a subset of structural equations are estimated. In other areas, credit may be rationed for some households and the effects of this on consumption and investment will have to be accounted for. All these issues are theoretical possibilities. Just how prevalent they are empirically is an important question with important consequences for farm-household modeling.

These aspects of household behavior must be considered whether one is attempting to improve the realism of agricultural household models or to model certain policy issues. Some other important research issues have to do with multimarket modeling and tradeoffs that can be made between the quality of data and cost.

A high priority for multimarket policy analysis will be to experiment with less costly solution algorithms and to investigate the adequacy of approximation with a fully differentiated system. In the absence of better-quality data, sensitivity analysis will remain quite important, but it would also be interesting to see just how much difference better-quality data would make.

The realism of the farm-household models used in multimarket analyses could be enhanced by introducing more highly nonlinear Engel curves, for example, and this would be a useful extension, although probably a less important one than the extensions noted above. Somewhat lower on the priority list would be experimenting with disaggregation (microsimulation). Since microsimulation will raise the computational costs of finding equilibrium, it will be important to have some idea of what is lost by wrongly treating groups of households as if they are individual households.

Finally, we need to know whether better-quality data would greatly affect elasticity estimates and which types of data are most crucial. If data on farm profits are gathered in one-time retrospective interviews, for example, will this vastly reduce the quality of estimates compared with a much more intensive (for example, biweekly or monthly) effort to obtain detailed input data, including information on family labor, and output data? These questions have been addressed to some extent by those who collect farm management or household expenditure surveys separately. They are of particular concern in agricultural household modeling since the expense of past surveys has discouraged many from undertaking this kind of analysis.

References

Adulavidhaya, Kamphol, and others. 1984. "The Comparative Statics of the Behavior of Agricultural Households in Thailand." *Singapore Economic Review*, vol. 29, pp. 67–96.

Bardhan, Pranab. 1984. *Land, Labor and Rural Poverty*. New York: Columbia University Press.

Bardhan, Pranab, and T. N. Srinivasan. 1971. "Cropsharing Tenancy in Agriculture: A Theoretical and Empirical Analysis." *American Economic Review*, vol. 51, pp. 48–64.

Barnum, Howard, and Lyn Squire. 1979. *A Model of an Agricultural Household*. Washington, D.C.: World Bank.

Binswanger, Hans, and Mark Rosenzweig, eds. 1984. *Contractual Arrangements, Employment, and Wages in Rural Labor Markets in Asia*. New Haven, Conn.: Yale University Press.

Braverman, Avishay, C. Y. Ahn, and Jeffrey Hammer. 1983. *Alternative Agricultural Pricing Policies in Korea: Their Implications for Government Deficits, Income Distribution, and Balance of Payments*. World Bank Staff Working Paper no. 621. Washington, D.C.

Braverman, Avishay, Jeffrey Hammer, and Erika Jorgenson. 1983. "Agricultural Taxation and Trade Policies in Sierra Leone." World Bank Country Policy Department Paper. Washington, D.C.

_____. 1984. "An Economic Analysis of Reducing Input Subsidies to the Livestock Sector in Cyprus." World Bank Country Policy Department Paper. Washington, D.C.

Deaton, Angus. 1978. "Specification and Testing in Applied Demand Analysis." *Economic Journal*, vol. 88, pp. 524–36.

Deaton, Angus, and John Muellbauer. 1980. *Economics and Consumer Behavior*. Cambridge, Mass.: Cambridge University Press.

Eckstein, Zvi. 1984. "A Rational Expectations Model of Agricultural Supply." *Journal of Political Economy*, vol. 92, pp. 1–19.

Feder, Gershon, Richard Just, and David Zilberman. 1985. "Adoption of Agricultural Innovations in Developing Countries: A Survey." *Economic Development and Cultural Change*, vol. 33, pp. 255–98.

Heckman, James J., and Thomas MaCurdy. 1981. "New Methods for Estimating Labor Supply Functions: A Survey." In *Research in Labor Economics*, vol. 4. Edited by R. Ehrenberg. New York: JAI Press.

Jaynes, Gerald, 1982. "Production and Distribution in Agrarian Economies." *Oxford Economic Papers*, vol. 34, pp. 346–67.

Kirchner, James, I. J. Singh, and Lyn Squire. 1984. "Agricultural Pricing and Marketing Policies in Eastern Africa." World Bank. Processed.

Lau, Lawrence, Wuu-Long Lin, and Pan Yotopoulos. 1978. "The Linear Logarithmic Expenditure System: An Application to Consumption Leisure Choice." *Econometrica*, vol. 46, pp. 843–68.

Lau, Lawrence, Pan Yotopoulos, Erwin Chou, and Wuu-Long Lin. 1981. "The Microeconomics of Distribution: A Simulation of the Farm Economy." *Journal of Policy Modeling*, vol. 3, pp. 175–206.

Lee, Lung-Fei, and Mark Pitt. 1984. "Microeconometric Models of Consumer and Producer Demand with Limited Dependent Variables." Economic Development Center Bulletin no. 84-4. University of Minnesota, Minneapolis.

McFadden, Daniel. 1981. "Econometric Models of Probabilistic Choice." In *Structural Analysis of Discrete Data with Econometric Applications*. Edited by C. Manski and D. McFadden. Cambridge, Mass.: MIT Press.

Muth, Richard. 1966. "Household Production and Consumer Demand Functions." *Econometrica*, vol. 34, pp. 699–708.

Newbery, David, and Joseph Stiglitz. 1979. "Sharecropping, Risk Sharing, and the Importance of Imperfect Information." In *Risk, Uncertainty and Agricultural Development*. Edited by J. Roumasset, J. M. Boussard, and I. J. Singh. New York: Agricultural Development Council.

Pollak, Robert, and Michael Wachter. 1975. "The Relevance of the Household Production Function for the Allocation of Time." *Journal of Political Economy*, vol. 83, pp. 255–77.

Roumasset, James, Marc Boussard, and Inderjit Singh. 1979. *Risk, Uncertainty and Agricultural Development*. New York: Agricultural Development Council.

Stiglitz, Joseph. 1969. "Behavior toward Risk with Many Commodities." *Econometrica*, vol. 37, pp. 660–67.

Stiglitz, Joseph, and Andrew Weiss. 1981. "Credit Rationing in Markets with Imperfect Information." *American Economic Review*, vol. 71, pp. 393–410.

Strauss, John. 1982. "Determinants of Food Consumption in Rural Sierra Leone: Application of the Quadratic Expenditure System to the Consumption-Leisure Component of a Household-Firm Model." *Journal of Development Economics*, vol. 11, pp. 327–53.

Wales, Terence, and A. D. Woodland. 1983. "Estimation of Consumer Demand Systems with Binding Non-Negativity Constraints." *Journal of Econometrics*, vol. 21, pp. 263–285.

Wright, Brian. 1979. "Effects of Ideal Production Stabilization: A Welfare Analysis under Rational Behavior." *Journal of Political Economy*, vol. 87, pp. 1011–33.

Yotopoulos, Pan, and Lawrence Lau. 1974. "On Modeling the Agricultural Sector in Developing Economies." *Journal of Development Economics*, vol. 1, pp. 105–27.

Appendix

The Theory and Comparative Statics of Agricultural Household Models: A General Approach

John Strauss

THIS APPENDIX DEVELOPS the basic model of the agricultural household introduced in chapter 1. The recursive property and comparative statics are derived first. The concept of a shadow or virtual price is then explicitly defined, and it is shown how the response of the virtual price to exogenous variables can be obtained. It turns out that with a minimum of assumptions this response can be signed. Next, these results are used to examine the comparative statics of various farm-household models, when the household faces virtual rather than parametric prices. During this exercise, the difference in the comparative statics between recursive and nonrecursive models becomes clear. The next section presents the outline of a model in which the market for labor is absent. This follows the earliest modeling of an agricultural household, by Chayanov, and its later technical development by Japanese economists (for example, Nakajima). Models that incorporate Z-goods are subsequently discussed, along with the previously neglected topic of models with certain types of commodity heterogeneity, which lead to corner solutions. Finally, conditions under which agricultural household models are recursive are summarized.

A Basic Model: The Household as Price-Taker

All prices in the static model developed here are taken as exogenous. Assume the household maximizes its utility subject to its constraints. Three constraints are specified at first: a production function, a time, and a budget constraint. Since agricultural household models have not generally been used to address issues of intrafamily distribution (Pitt and Rosenzweig explore some of the conceptual problems involved), a household utility function is assumed to exist. Let

(IA-1) $$U(X_1, \ldots, X_L)$$

be the utility function, which is well behaved: quasi-concave with positive partial derivatives. The arguments are household consumption of commodity i, with X_L denoting total leisure time. Clearly, the X_i's can be a vector of commodity consumption for different members of the family as well. For instance, we might want X_L to include male, female, or children's leisure time separately. We could also allow household characteristics such as number of members to enter the utility function separately. As long as these are viewed as fixed, this will not change the analysis.

Utility is maximized subject to a budget constraint:

(IA-2) $$Y = \sum_{i=1}^{L} p_i X_i$$

where Y is the household's full income (see equation [IA-3]), and the p_i's are commodity prices (p_L being the wage rate). Full income of an agricultural household equals the value of its time endowment, plus the value of the household's production less the value of variable inputs required for production of outputs, plus any nonwage, nonhousehold production income such as remittances:

(IA-3) $$Y = p_L T + \sum_{j=1}^{M} q_j Q_j - \sum_{i=1}^{N} q_i V_i - p_L L + E$$

where

T = time endowment
Q_j = output, for $j = 1, \ldots, M$
V_i = nonlabor variable inputs, for $i = 1, \ldots, N$
L = labor demand
q_j = price of Q_j
q_i = price of V_i
E = exogenous income.

For the moment, it is assumed that L is total labor demanded by the household, both family and hired, which are assumed to be perfect substitutes, an assumption we relax later in the discussion on partly absent markets.

Outputs and inputs are related by an implicit production function

(IA-4) $$G(Q_1, \ldots, Q_M, V_1, \ldots, V_N, L, K_1, \ldots, K_0) = 0$$

where K_i's are fixed inputs. This is a general specification that allows for separate production functions for different outputs, or for joint production. G is assumed to satisfy the usual properties for production functions: it is quasi-convex, increasing in outputs and decreasing in inputs.

If the household maximizes utility (IA-1) subject to its full-income (IA-2 and IA-3) and production-function (IA-4) constraints and to prices (p, q) being fixed, then the household's choices can be modeled as recursive decisions, even though the decisions are simultaneous in time (Jorgenson and Lau 1969; Nakajima 1969). The household behaves as though it maximizes the revenue side of its full income, equation (IA-3), subject to its production-function constraint, and then maximizes utility subject to its full-income constraint, equation (IA-2). Since neither the value of endowed time nor exogenous income are household choice variables, maximizing full income is equivalent to maximizing the value of outputs less variable inputs (that is, profits).

To see that the model is separable between revenue and expenditure, the comparative statics are examined. Let the household consume three commodities: leisure, X_L; a good that is purchased on the market, X_m; and a good, X_a, produced by the household. (Obviously all these scalars could just as well be vectors.) The household uses labor, L, another variable input, V, and a fixed input K to produce both Q_a and another crop, Q_c. All Q_c is sold on the market (a commercial crop). The Lagrangian function can be written as

(IA-5) $\mathcal{L} = U(X_L, X_m, X_a) + \lambda[p_L T + (q_c Q_c + p_a Q_a - p_L L - q_v V)$
$+ E - p_L X_L - p_m X_m - p_a X_a] + \mu G(Q_c, Q_a, L, V, K).$

If we assume interior solutions, the first-order conditions are:

(IA-6)
$$\frac{\partial \mathcal{L}}{\partial X_L} = U_L - \lambda p_L = 0$$

$$\frac{\partial \mathcal{L}}{\partial X_m} = U_m - \lambda p_m = 0$$

$$\frac{\partial \mathcal{L}}{\partial X_a} = U_a - \lambda p_a = 0$$

$$\frac{\partial \mathcal{L}}{\partial \lambda} = p_L(T - X_L - L) + q_c Q_c + p_a(Q_a - X_a)$$
$$- q_v V - p_m X_m + E = 0$$

$$\frac{1}{\lambda} \frac{\partial \mathcal{L}}{\partial Q_c} = q_c + \frac{\mu}{\lambda} G_c = 0$$

$$\frac{1}{\lambda}\frac{\partial \pounds}{\partial Q_a} = p_a + \frac{\mu}{\lambda} G_a = 0$$

$$\frac{1}{\lambda}\frac{\partial \pounds}{\partial L} = -p_L + \frac{\mu}{\lambda} G_L = 0$$

$$\frac{1}{\lambda}\frac{\partial \pounds}{\partial V} = -q_v + \frac{\mu}{\lambda} G_v = 0$$

$$\frac{\partial \pounds}{\partial \mu} = G(Q_c, Q_a, L, V, K) = 0.$$

Totally differentiating (IA-6),

(IA-7)

$$
\begin{bmatrix}
U_{LL} & U_{Lm} & U_{La} & -p_L & 0 & 0 & 0 & 0 & 0 \\
U_{mL} & U_{mm} & U_{ma} & -P_m & 0 & 0 & 0 & 0 & 0 \\
U_{aL} & U_{am} & U_{aa} & -p_a & 0 & 0 & 0 & 0 & 0 \\
-p_L & -p_m & -p_a & 0 & 0 & 0 & 0 & 0 & 0 \\
0 & 0 & 0 & 0 & \frac{\mu}{\lambda}G_{cc} & \frac{\mu}{\lambda}G_{ca} & \frac{\mu}{\lambda}G_{cL} & \frac{\mu}{\lambda}G_{cv} & G_c \\
0 & 0 & 0 & 0 & \frac{\mu}{\lambda}G_{ac} & \frac{\mu}{\lambda}G_{aa} & \frac{\mu}{\lambda}G_{aL} & \frac{\mu}{\lambda}G_{av} & G_a \\
0 & 0 & 0 & 0 & \frac{\mu}{\lambda}G_{Lc} & \frac{\mu}{\lambda}G_{La} & \frac{\mu}{\lambda}G_{LL} & \frac{\mu}{\lambda}G_{Lv} & G_L \\
0 & 0 & 0 & 0 & \frac{\mu}{\lambda}G_{vc} & \frac{\mu}{\lambda}G_{va} & \frac{\mu}{\lambda}G_{vL} & \frac{\mu}{\lambda}G_{vv} & G_v \\
0 & 0 & 0 & 0 & G_c & G_a & G_L & G_v & 0
\end{bmatrix}
\begin{bmatrix}
dX_L \\ dX_m \\ dX_a \\ d\lambda \\ dQ_c \\ dQ_a \\ dL \\ dV \\ d\left(\frac{\mu}{\lambda}\right)
\end{bmatrix}
=
\begin{bmatrix}
\lambda dp_L \\ \lambda dp_m \\ \lambda dp_a \\ \psi \\ -dq_c \\ -dp_a \\ dp_L \\ dq_v \\ 0
\end{bmatrix}
$$

where $\psi = -(T - X_L - L)dp_L + X_m dp_m - (Q_a - X_a)dp_a - dE - Q_c dq_c + V dq_v - \mu/\lambda\, G_k dk$. When differentiating the budget constraint we have substituted

$$-\frac{\mu}{\lambda}(G_c dQ_c + G_a dQ_a + G_L dL + G_v dV)$$

for

$$q_c dQ_c + p_a dQ_a - p_L dL - q_v dV.$$

This equals $\mu/\lambda \, G_k dK$ since $G(\cdot) = 0$. This system of equations is block diagonal, as can easily be seen from equation system (IA-7). The first set of equations, corresponding to the upper left block of the bordered Hessian matrix, gives the solution for commodity demands and the marginal utility of full income. The second (lower right) set of equations gives the solution for output supplies, variable input demands, and the associated multiplier. The assumptions concerning the utility and production functions ensures that second-order conditions are met. Hence, the two decision problems can indeed be solved recursively, despite their simultaneity in time.

Equation (IA-7) demonstrates the principal message of the farm-household literature, that farm technology, quantities of fixed inputs, and prices of variable inputs and of outputs do affect consumption decisions. Given recursiveness, however, the reverse is not true. Preferences, prices of consumption commodities, and income do not affect production decisions. Output supply responds positively to own-price at all times owing to the quasi-convexity assumption on the production function, $\partial Q_c/\partial q_c > 0$. The price of the cash crop, q_c, will be related to consumption of the purchased commodity, X_m, through changed income. From equation (IA-7) it can be seen that

$$\frac{\partial X_m}{\partial q_c} = Q_c \frac{\partial X_m}{\partial E}.$$

Likewise, changes in quantities of fixed inputs, K, will affect income, hence the consumption of X_m:

$$\frac{\partial X_m}{\partial K} = \frac{\mu}{\lambda} G_K \frac{\partial X_m}{\partial E}.$$

Assuming X_m is a normal commodity, increments to fixed inputs or to the cash crop price will induce higher consumption of X_m. For commodities that are also produced by the household, own-price effects are

(IA-8) $$\frac{\partial X_a}{\partial p_a} = \frac{\partial X_a}{\partial p_a}\bigg|_U + (Q_a - X_a)\frac{\partial X_a}{\partial E}.$$

Thus, a change in the price of X_a has the usual negative substitution effect, and an income effect that is weighted by net sales (or marketed surplus) of X_a, not consumption of X_a. The income effect is positive for a net seller and negative for a net buyer. In consequence, for net sellers, consumption of X_a might respond positively to changes in its own price even though it is a normal good.

The income effect for a farm household has an extra term, $Q_a(\partial X_a/\partial E)$, as compared with the pure consuming household. This extra effect is introduced when the profits component of full income is raised; hence it can be referred to as a profit effect. To see this, note that from equation (IA-3) $dY = T dp_L + d\pi + dE$, where π = profits, the value of outputs less the value of variable inputs. From equation (IA-3) and the first-order conditions,

$$d\pi = Q_c dq_c + Q_a dp_a - L\, dp_L - V\, dq_v + \frac{\mu}{\lambda}\, G_k dK.$$

Thus, the fourth element of the right-hand side of equation (IA-7) may be expressed as

$$\psi = -(T - X_L) dp_L + X_m dp_m + X_a dp_a - d\pi - dE.$$

It is then clear that the Marshallian demand for food can be written as

$$X_a(p_L, p_m, p_a, q_c, q_v, K, E) \quad \text{or as} \quad X_a(p_L, p_m, p_a, \pi, E)$$

with profits replacing nonlabor variable input prices and fixed inputs. The comparative statics are then

$$(IA\text{-}8a) \qquad \left.\frac{\partial X_a}{\partial p_a}\right|_\pi = \left.\frac{\partial X_a}{\partial p_a}\right|_U - X_a \frac{\partial X_a}{\partial Y}$$

which is identical to the pure consumer case, while

$$(IA\text{-}8b) \qquad \frac{\partial X_a}{\partial p_a} = \left.\frac{\partial X_a}{\partial p_a}\right|_U - X_a \frac{\partial X_a}{\partial Y} + \frac{\partial X_a}{\partial Y} \frac{\partial \pi}{\partial p_a}.$$

Since $\partial \pi / \partial p_a = Q_a$, from above, the extra effect does indeed come through changing farm profits. The comparative statics for leisure

$$(IA\text{-}9) \qquad \frac{\partial X_L}{\partial p_L} = \left.\frac{\partial X_L}{\partial p_L}\right|_U + (T - X_L - L) \frac{\partial X_L}{\partial Y}$$

are similar. The income effect is weighted by household labor supply minus labor demand (marketed surplus of labor), not by household labor supply. Assuming that leisure is a normal good makes a backward-bending supply curve less likely than if the household were solely a supplier of labor.

Deriving Virtual (Shadow) Prices

To explore the consequences of making prices endogenous to the household, it will be convenient to use duality results to express the equilibrium of the household. We can define the full-income function as the maximization of equation (IA-3) with respect to outputs and variable inputs subject to the production function, (IA-4), and can write

(IA-10)

$$Y = \Lambda(q_c, p_a, p_L, q_v, K, T, E) = p_L T + \pi(q_c, p_a, p_L, q_v, K) + E.$$

The full-income function is the sum of the value of endowed time, a restricted (or short-run) profits function, and exogenous income. The profits function has the usual properties—for example, it is convex in all prices. For the expenditure side of full income, we can define an expenditure function as the minimum expenditure (equation IA-2) required to meet a specified level of utility, $e(p_L, p_m, p_a, U)$. It obeys the usual properties; in particular it is concave in prices, and the partial derivatives with respect to price are the Hicksian (compensated) demand functions.

Now we are in a position to relax our assumption that prices are fixed market prices. The household's equilibrium is characterized by equality between the household's full-income function, Λ, and its expenditure function, e, where the expenditure function is evaluated at the utility level achieved at the household's optimum. This condition will hold whether or not households face given market prices. Now suppose that a household is constrained to equate consumption with production for some commodity(ies). One possible reason for this would be nonexistence of a market. Consequently, the household's equilibrium will be characterized by a set of additional conditions—equality of household demand and household supply for each commodity for which there is no market (see Dixit and Norman 1980, who use these conditions to characterize an economy under autarky). This second set of equilibrium conditions implicitly defines a set of virtual prices—or shadow prices (Neary and Roberts 1980; Deaton and Muellbauer 1980, chapter 4.3), which, if they existed, would induce the household to equate supply and demand for these commodities.

These virtual prices are not taken parametrically by the household as market prices are; rather, they are determined by the household's choices. From the household's equilibrium, it can be seen that they will be a function of market prices, time endowment, fixed inputs, and either exogenous income or utility. (They will also be a function of fixed household characteristics if these are introduced into the model.) Consequently, these prices depend on both the household's preferences and its production technology. Changes in market prices will now affect behavior directly, as before, and indirectly through changes in the virtual prices. Some mechanism of identifying the consequences of this additional effect is therefore needed to illuminate the significance of one's assumptions regarding price formation. That mechanism will be the comparative statics of the virtual price, which will now be developed.

Suppose, for the moment arbitrarily, that there exists no market for labor. The household equilibrium is characterized by

(IA-11) $e(\bar{p}_L^*, p_m, p_a, \bar{U}) = \bar{p}_L^* T + \pi(q_c, p_a, \bar{p}_L^*, q_v, K) + E$

$\qquad e_L(\bar{p}_L^*, p_m, p_a, \bar{U}) = T + \pi_L(q_c, p_a, \bar{p}_L^*, q_v, K)$

where $e_L = \partial e / \partial p_L^*$ and likewise $\pi_L = \partial \pi / \partial p_L^*$. The second equation gives the Hicksian leisure demand on the left-hand side and time endow-ment minus labor demand on the right. From this equation, $\bar{p}_L^*$, the com-pensated virtual price, can be solved for as

(IA-12) $\qquad \bar{p}_L^* = \bar{p}_L^*(p_m, p_a, q_c, q_v, K, U).$

Note that the utility level is being held constant, and not exogenous in-come. Alternatively, the Marshallian leisure demand

$$X_L(p_L^*, p_m, p_a, p_L^* T + \pi + E)$$

can be set equal to time minus labor demand, and a solution obtained:

(IA-13) $\qquad p_L^* = p_L^*(p_m, p_a, q_c, q_v, K, E).$

To relate the functions $\bar{p}_L^*$ and p_L^*, a somewhat different expenditure function is needed. Let

$e'(p_L, p_m, p_a, q_c, q_v, K, T, \bar{U}) =$

(IA-14) $\displaystyle \min_{\substack{X_L, X_m, X_a \\ Q_c, Q_a, L, V}} p_L X_L + p_m X_m + p_a X_a - p_L T - q_c Q_c - p_a Q_a$

$\qquad\qquad + p_L L + q_v V \quad \text{st } U(\cdot) = \bar{U} \text{ and } G(\cdot) = 0.$

This represents the minimum exogenous income, E, necessary to achieve utility level $\bar{U}$, given the production function and prices. It is clear that e' meets all the conditions that a regular expenditure function does, and that

(IA-15) $e'(p_L, p_m, p_a, q_c, q_v, K, T, \bar{U}) =$

$\qquad\qquad e(p_L, p_m, p_a, \bar{U}) - p_L T - \pi(q_c, p_a, p_L, q_v, K).$

In equation (IA-13), if exogenous income E is evaluated at e' (hence full income, Y, at e) then Marshallian leisure demand equals the Hicksian demand and $p_L^* = \bar{p}_L^*$. Using this equality

(IA-16) $\qquad \dfrac{\partial \bar{p}_L^*}{\partial Z} = \dfrac{\partial p_L^*}{\partial Z}\bigg|_E + \dfrac{\partial p_L^*}{\partial E} \dfrac{\partial e'}{\partial Z} \qquad Z = p_m, p_a, q_c, q_v, K.$

With utility constant, the response of the virtual price can be expressed in terms of second partial derivatives of the expenditure and profit func-tions. Using the implicit function rule and equation (IA-11),

(IA-17) $\dfrac{\partial \bar{p}_L^*}{\partial Z} = -(e_{LZ} - \pi_{LZ})/(e_{LL} - \pi_{LL}) \qquad Z = p_m, p_a, q_c, q_v, K.$

The denominator is unambiguously negative owing to the concavity of the expenditure function and the convexity of the profits function. The numerator can be either sign, but often the sign will be determinate if one is willing to assume that commodities are substitutes or complements in consumption or production. For instance, if $Z = p_m$, the price of the market-purchased commodity, X_m, the numerator is $-e_{Lm}$, which is negative if leisure and X_m are substitutes. If $Z = p_a$, the numerator is $\pi_{La} - e_{La}$. The first term is the response of output of X_a to wage, which should be negative. The second term is negative if leisure and X_a are substitutes. For an input price, q_v, the numerator is π_{Lv}, which can be positive or negative, depending on whether labor and input V are gross substitutes or complements.

Equation (IA-17) is a basic result that will be used repeatedly in the subsequent discussion to illuminate the effects of totally or partly absent markets. It allows one to sign the partial derivatives of the compensated virtual price, making this device useful in looking at the comparative statics. Moreover, it allows one to compare directly models that make differing assumptions about the nature of prices the household faces.

The sign of the response of the compensated virtual price, $\bar{p}_L^*$, to exogenous variables can be given an intuitive interpretation. If, for instance, the price of the cash crop rises, the demand schedule for labor should shift upward. Given that other market prices, fixed inputs, and utility are constant, the virtual wage has to rise in order to reequate compensated labor supply with demand. Such a rise will lower labor demand along the new schedule, while raising compensated, or Hicksian, labor supply.

The virtual prices are functions of both household preferences and production technology. Because these prices help to determine both consumption and production choices—they belong in both the expenditure and the full-income functions—the household commodity demands will depend on production technology, both through the virtual price and through full income. Output supplies and input demands will depend on preferences through the virtual price. If, however, the household faces only market prices or if it faces a virtual price for a commodity that is consumed but not produced (or vice versa), then production choices will not depend on household preferences, but consumption choices will depend on production technology through full income. The model is then recursive.

Models with Absent Markets: Labor

In the historical development of agricultural household models, partially autarkic behavior has been very important. One of the earliest models can be traced to the Russian economist A. V. Chayanov (1925) (see Millar 1970 for a reinterpretation). Chayanov was concerned with explaining the allocation of labor between work and leisure in Russian peasant households given his observation that virtually no hired labor was used in farm production activities. He recognized that such households were not simply maximizing profits as in the theory of the firm; rather, they had a subjective equilibrium in which they equated the marginal utility of household consumption with the marginal utility of leisure. His analysis was embellished by a group of Japanese economists, notably Tanaka (1951) and Nakajima (1957), during the 1950s and 1960s. Nakajima (1969), in particular, gave the model currency among English-speaking economists. He not only gave a mathematical formulation to Chayanov's model, but also proposed some additional models. Nakajima's (1969) model of a pure commercial family farm without a labor market assumed that households sold all of their output and purchased commodities from the market, and that they produced the output with family labor and a fixed amount of land. He also allowed for the possibility of a minimum subsistence consumption requirement as well as a target income. In a different version (his semisubsistence family farm), he allows the family to consume some of its output, and in another version introduces two outputs. Similar models of peasant households were advanced by Mellor (1963) and Sen (1966) and by economic anthropologists such as Fisk and Shand (1969). These models are thus special cases of the general form of the agricultural household model developed here.

These models in which the family supplied all of its labor were used primarily to explore the effects on labor supply (and hence output, since family labor was assumed to be the only variable input) of changes in different variables. The effect of output price was of particular interest because of the seemingly perverse possibility that output might respond negatively to output price. This might occur if the income effect, resulting in more leisure demand, was large enough. Nakajima showed that an exogenous increase in land input might also reduce output, because it too would have an income effect on leisure. Nakajima separated the response of labor supply to output price into substitution and income effects, showing that the income-compensated response of labor supply to output price was positive. Sen showed that output response to output price could be negative, and that there could be no output response to the withdrawal of family workers if the remaining family laborers worked sufficiently hard to offset the reduced number of hours worked as workers were withdrawn. This required that the virtual wage (or its ratio to output price, Sen's real cost of labor) be constant, as would be the case in

Sen's model if the marginal utilities of both income and leisure were roughly constant.

The possibility of a negative response of labor demand (and of output supply) to output price at the household level is dependent on the constrained equality of labor demand and labor supply. At the market level labor demand might respond negatively to output price if wage is bid up sufficiently (see Barnum and Squire 1980). If markets exist for all commodities, then the model is recursive and labor demand will respond positively to output price as long as it is not an inferior input. Nakajima noted this when discussing his model with a labor market and a cash crop. Both Jorgenson and Lau (1969) and Krishna (1964, 1969) proposed separable semisubsistence models in which labor is marketed and output is partly consumed at home. Jorgenson and Lau's study has formed the basis on which most of the empirical work to date has been conducted.

Consumption and Leisure Responses

The difference that absence of a labor market makes to the comparative statics of leisure and commodity demand can easily be seen by using the notion of a virtual wage. Write the Marshallian demand as

$$X_i[p_L^*, p_m, p_a, p_L^* T + \pi(q_c, p_a, p_L^*, q_v, K) + E], \quad i = L, M.$$

Differentiate this with respect to q_c to obtain

$$\text{(IA-18)} \qquad \frac{\partial X_i}{\partial q_c} = \frac{\partial X_i}{\partial p_L^*} \frac{\partial p_L^*}{\partial q_c} + Q_c \frac{\partial X_i}{\partial Y} \qquad i = L, M.$$

Cash output price has two effects on the demand for leisure or for the market purchased good: it has an income effect by changing profits (the second term), and it changes the virtual price for labor. Clearly, when the household is a price-taker in the labor market, the latter effect is zero.

Equation (IA-18) can be decomposed into substitution and income effects, which will help in signing the uncompensated changes in the demand for leisure and the market-purchased commodity. First, it can be shown that the uncompensated effect with respect to the virtual wage equals the compensated effect. To do this, it will be useful to equate Marshallian and Hicksian demands by evaluating full income, Y, and e and the virtual wage at $\bar{p}_L^*$ (that is, if both hold utility constant):

$$\text{(IA-19)} \quad X_i[\bar{p}_L^*, p_m, p_a, e(\bar{p}_L^*, p_m, p_a, U)] = X_i^c(\bar{p}_L^*, p_m, p_a, U)$$
$$i = L, M.$$

Differentiating both sides of (IA-19) with respect to the cash crops price, q_c, and using $\partial e / \partial \bar{p}_L^* = X_L$ results in

(IA-20) $$\left.\frac{\partial X_i}{\partial p_L^*}\right|_Y \frac{\partial \bar{p}_L^*}{\partial q_c} + X_L \frac{\partial X_i}{\partial Y} \frac{\partial \bar{p}_L^*}{\partial q_c} = \frac{\partial X_i^c}{\partial p_L^*} \frac{\partial \bar{p}_L^*}{\partial q_c} \qquad i = L, M.$$

Since

(IA-21) $$\frac{\partial X_i}{\partial p_L^*} = \left.\frac{\partial X_i}{\partial p_L^*}\right|_Y + (T - L) \frac{\partial X_i}{\partial Y}$$

and since labor supply equals labor demand, so that $X_L = T - L$, it can be shown by means of equation (IA-20) that $\partial X_i/\partial p_L^* = \partial X_i^c/\partial p_L^*$. Thus the income effect of a change in the virtual wage equals zero, which is intuitive since the net marketed surplus is zero when no labor market exists.

The term $\partial p_L^*/\partial q_c$ in equation (IA-18) can be made more transparent by noting from (IA-16) that

$$\frac{\partial p_L^*}{\partial q_c} = \frac{\partial \bar{p}_L^*}{\partial q_c} + Q_c \frac{\partial p_L^*}{\partial E} \qquad \text{(recall that } \frac{\partial e'}{\partial q_c} = -Q_c\text{).}$$

When this is substituted into (IA-18), one obtains

(IA-22) $$\frac{\partial X_i}{\partial q_c} = \frac{\partial X_i^c}{\partial p_L^*} \frac{\partial \bar{p}_L^*}{\partial q_c} + Q_c \left(\frac{\partial X_i}{\partial Y} + \frac{\partial X_i}{\partial p_L^*} \frac{\partial p_L^*}{\partial E} \right) \qquad i = L, M$$

(IA-22a) $$= \frac{\partial X_i^c}{\partial p_L^*} \frac{\partial \bar{p}_L^*}{\partial q_c} + Q_c \frac{\partial X_i}{\partial E} \qquad i = L, M.$$

Equations (IA-22) and (IA-22a) show the decomposed income and substitution effects. They also clarify the significance of one's view regarding the labor market. If the labor market does exist, then the household faces market prices so the substitution effect—the first term in (IA-22a)—is zero and the entire effect of the change in output price is captured by the income effect $[Q_c(\partial X_i/\partial Y)]$. This is positive, providing leisure or the purchased commodity are normal goods. When the labor market is absent, a substitution effect is caused by the change in the income-compensated virtual wage. Using equation (IA-17), we can rewrite this substitution effect as

(IA-23) $$\frac{\partial X_i^c}{\partial p_L^*} \frac{\partial \bar{p}_L^*}{\partial q_c} = e_{Li} \pi_{Lc}/(e_{LL} - \pi_{LL}) \qquad i = L, M.$$

If the compensated virtual wage rises—that is, if $\pi_{Lc} < 0$, in equation (IA-23)—then there is a substitution away from leisure or toward the purchased commodity (if it is a substitute for leisure). The income effect comes in two parts: first, a traditional looking income effect, and, second, a substitution-type effect due to an induced change in the uncompensated virtual wage, p_L^*. This two-part income effect is identical to equation (IA-24) of Neary and

Roberts (1980), once their equation (IA-19) has been substituted in. From equation (IA-22), we can see that when leisure is normal, $\partial p_L^*/\partial E > 0$, the income effect is smaller for leisure and larger for purchased goods (if we assume substitutability with leisure) when the labor market does not exist than when it does. An increase in exogenous income raises the uncompensated virtual wage, and this increase induces a substitution away from leisure or toward the purchased commodity. If we assume that the entire income effect is positive, the net effect of a rise in output price q_c on leisure is indeterminant, but it will be positive for the purchased commodity. This is the same result, of course, as is obtained by both Nakajima (1969) and Sen (1966).

Output Responses

If labor is the only variable input, then the sign of output response to output price must be the opposite to the leisure response. More generally, we can write output supply Q_c as

$$Q_c = \frac{\partial \pi}{\partial q_c} (q_c, p_a, p_L^*, q_v, K)$$

consequently,

(IA-24)
$$\frac{\partial Q_c}{\partial q_c} = \pi_{cc} + \pi_{cL} \frac{\partial p_L^*}{\partial q_c}.$$

The first term is the output-supply response when the virtual wage is fixed, and is positive. The second term is negative, if we assume that output responds negatively to the virtual wage ($\pi_{cL} < 0$), so that the sign of the entire expression is indeterminant. It is possible to show that when household utility is held constant, the response is positive. (See Lopez 1980 for a somewhat different demonstration of this.) Substituting for $\partial p_L^*/\partial q_c$ from equation (IA-16),

(IA-25)
$$\frac{\partial Q_c}{\partial q_c} = \left(\pi_{cc} + \pi_{cL} \frac{\partial \bar{p}_L^*}{\partial q_c} \right) + Q_c \pi_{cL} \frac{\partial p_L}{\partial q_c}.$$

The first two terms are the response of output supply when utility is held constant. The third term is an income effect, which is negative if π_{cL} is negative. The second term equals $\pi_{cL}^2/(e_{LL} - \pi_{LL})$, so it is negative. However, summing it with π_{cc} gives a nonnegative quantity because the function e' (equation [IA-15]) is concave in prices, so that

$$\frac{\partial^2 e'}{\partial q_c^2} \frac{\partial^2 e'}{\partial p_L^{*2}} - \left(\frac{\partial^2 e'}{\partial q_c \partial p_L^*} \right)^2 \geq 0.$$

Straightforward algebra shows that this expression is simply the first two terms in equation (IA-25) multiplied by $-\partial^2 e'/\partial p_L^{*2}$. The magnitude of π_{cL} and consequently the likelihood of a negative output response will be influenced by the number of variable inputs and the partial elasticity of substitution between labor and these other inputs. Presumably, the more inputs and the more substitutable they are, the less negative π_{cL} will be and the more likely will be a positive response to output price. Clearly, when the virtual wage is exogenous to the household, output response will be positive and greater than when the virtual wage is endogenous.

If the household consumes some of the output for which price is changing, Q_c, the comparative statics have an additional substitution effect, and the income effect is weighted by net output sold (marketed surplus) and not by total output:

$$(IA\text{-}26) \qquad \frac{\partial X_i^c}{\partial p_a} = \left.\frac{\partial X_i^c}{\partial p_a}\right|_{\bar{p}_L^*} + \frac{\partial X_i^c}{\partial p_L^*}\frac{\partial \bar{p}_L^*}{\partial p_a} \qquad i = L, M, A.$$

Again using equation (IA-17), $\partial \bar{p}_L^*/\partial p_a = (\pi_{aL} - e_{aL})/(e_{LL} - \pi_{LL})$, which is positive if Q_a and leisure are substitutes. Deriving the comparative statics as before, one finds

$$(IA\text{-}27) \quad \frac{\partial X_i}{\partial p_a} = \left(\left.\frac{\partial X_i^c}{\partial p_a}\right|_{\bar{p}_L^*} + \frac{\partial X_i^c}{\partial p_L^*}\frac{\partial \bar{p}_L^*}{\partial p_a}\right)$$

$$+ (Q_a - X_a)\left(\frac{\partial X_i^c}{\partial p_L^*}\frac{\partial p_L^*}{\partial E} + \frac{\partial X_i}{\partial Y}\right) \qquad i = L, M, A$$

$$(IA\text{-}27a) \qquad \frac{\partial X_i}{\partial p_a} = \frac{\partial X_i^c}{\partial p_a} + (Q_a - X_a)\frac{\partial X_i}{\partial E} \qquad i = L, M, A.$$

The substitution effect for leisure demand can be of either sign. It is not necessarily positive, even if X_a and leisure are substitutes holding the virtual wage constant. The income-compensated response of X_a can also be of either sign when the wage is virtual, since an increase in the price, p_a, will increase the compensated virtual wage leading to a substitution toward X_a. The substitution effect for X_a will be less negative than when the labor market exists, as Neary and Roberts (1980) found in the pure rationing case. The income effect has an extra term, which for X_a and X_m is positive if leisure is a substitute and is negative for leisure demand.

Marketed Surplus Responses

If we examine the response of marketed surplus of X_a, $Q_a - X_a$, to change in p_a, we obtain from (IA-25), (IA-16), and (IA-27)

$$\frac{\partial(Q_a - X_a)}{\partial p_a} = \left(\frac{\partial Q_a}{\partial p_a} \bigg|_{\bar{p}_L^*} + \frac{\partial Q_a}{\partial p_L^*} \frac{\partial \bar{p}_L^*}{\partial p_a} - \frac{\partial X_a^c}{\partial p_a} \bigg|_{\bar{p}_L^*} - \frac{\partial X_a^c}{\partial p_L^*} \frac{\partial \bar{p}_L^*}{\partial p_a} \right)$$

(IA-28)
$$+ (Q_a - X_a) \left(\frac{\partial Q_a}{\partial p_L^*} \frac{\partial p_L^*}{\partial E} - \frac{\partial X_a^c}{\partial p_L^*} \frac{\partial p_L^*}{\partial E} - \frac{\partial X_a}{\partial Y} \right).$$

The first four terms (in brackets) hold utility constant, and therefore comprise the substitution effect. It is straightforward to see that this effect equals

$$- \frac{\partial^2 e'}{\partial p_L^{*2}} \left[\frac{\partial^2 e'}{\partial p_a^2} \frac{\partial^2 e'}{\partial p_L^{*2}} - \left(\frac{\partial^2 e'}{\partial p_a \partial p_L^*} \right)^2 \right]$$

and consequently is nonnegative (remember that e' is concave in prices). The last term equals

$$(Q_a - X_a) \left(\frac{\partial Q_a}{\partial E} - \frac{\partial X_a}{\partial E} \right)$$

and so is the income effect that should be negative if marketed surplus is positive and X_a is a normal good. Consequently, marketed surplus of X_a might respond positively or negatively to an increase in its own price. Comparing this result with that when the labor market exists, one can see that the extra substitution effects will be negative if X_a and leisure are substitutes, since the compensated virtual wage will then rise. The extra income effects should also be negative, so that a greater possibility exists of obtaining a negative own-price response of marketed surplus of X_a.

The comparative statics with respect to changes in p_m, q_v, K, and T are similar to equation (IA-22), except that the response of the compensated virtual wage is different, as is the term weighting the income effect. Specific formulae are left for the interested reader to derive.

Models with Absent Markets: Z-Goods

The market that one assumes not to exist clearly does not affect the foregoing argument. Hence, the existence of a labor market is a necessary but not a sufficient condition for an agricultural household model to be separable. *All markets must exist for separability*, although this is not a sufficient condition, as is discussed in the next section. Historically, economists thought that the labor market was the one least likely to exist for peasant farms. That view has been changing, however, since active rural labor markets have been found according to several studies (Rosenzweig 1978; Spencer and Byerlee 1977; Bardhan 1979; Squire 1981; Binswanger and Rosenzweig 1984), although they are not necessarily perfectly competitive ones. More recent studies have focused on the nonexistence of a market for so-called Z-goods. This was first formalized by Hymer and Resnick (1969), who refer to Z-goods as nonagricultural, nonleisure activities. In general the commodities Hymer and Resnick refer to, such as food processing and metalworking, are commodities for which small-scale rural industries have been found to exist (Anderson and Leiserson 1980; and Liedholm and Chuta 1976). Z-goods, however, refer equally as well to nontraded outputs of household production activities such as the number and quality of children, home maintenance, or food preparation. In this way, the household production models of Becker (1965) and Gronau (1973, 1977) can be incorporated into agricultural household models.

Hymer and Resnick (1969) were concerned with the increasing specialization of agricultural household activities, which they saw as occurring over time and resulting in an increasing marketed surplus from agricultural households. Rather than focus on the leisure-labor tradeoff, they concentrated on the Z-goods-food tradeoff. In terms of the general model specified here, households produce foods, Q_a, which they consume and sell the surplus in exchange for manufactured commodities, X_m. They produce Z-goods, our L, which they consume entirely at home, $L = X_L$. Labor supply does not enter their model, but implicitly it is assumed to be fixed in amount and to be equal to labor demand; thus it is not a choice variable. In terms of this model, labor is one of the fixed inputs, K, and it does not appear in the utility function. Alternatively, leisure can enter the utility as a fixed factor, similar to other fixed household characteristics such as household size and age distribution. In this case, the expenditure function will include leisure as a conditioning variable just as a short-run cost or profit function includes fixed inputs.

There are no other variable inputs, $V = 0$, nor does there exist a cash crop, $Q_c = 0$. These assumptions imply that the product transformation curve between foods and Z-goods has the usual downward-sloping, concave shape. Consequently, to find the sign of the effect of a change in the price of foods, p_a, on the output of foods, only the effect on demand (hence supply) of Z-goods needs to be considered, $\partial X_L / \partial p_a$, which is given by equation (IA-27). The substitution effect can be of either sign. If Z-goods and foods are substitutes, a rise in food prices will increase Z-goods consumption when the compensated virtual price of Z-goods is held constant. This will force up the virtual price, however, and lead to a substitution away from Z-goods consumption. The income effect is weighted by the marketed surplus of foods, which is presumed to be positive. Hymer and Resnick assume that Z-goods consumption is inferior and that the combined substitution effect is small, so that the net effect of a rise in the price of foods will be a fall in the consumption (and production) of Z-goods, and hence a rise in food production. Of course, if foods are consumed by the household, the food consumption response to food price needs to be examined before what happens to marketed surplus of foods can be judged. As seen from equation (IA-28), marketed surplus of food can either rise or fall in response to an increase in food price, provided the household has a positive marketed surplus and Z-goods are normal (so $\partial p_{\bar{z}}^*/\partial E > 0$). However, if Z-goods are inferior, then its virtual price falls when exogenous income rises, so that production of foods rises and compensated consumption of foods falls (provided foods and Z-goods are substitutes), making it more likely that the response of marketed surplus is positive.

The Hymer and Resnick assumption that leisure and labor demand are not choice variables can be relaxed. If it is assumed that no labor market exists, then two virtual prices exist, one for labor and one for household Z-goods. There are thus two equality constraints on supply and demand rather than one. Alternatively, the labor market may be assumed to exist.

As an alternative to the Hymer and Resnick interpretation, Z-goods might be interpreted as being synonymous with household production activities. The original work of Becker (1965), Lancaster (1966), and Muth (1966) emphasizes that the commodities that yield household utility are produced within the household by goods purchased in the market and by labor. In terms of this general model, X_c is a vector of commodities consumed and produced in the home. Market-purchased inputs are denoted by V ($X_m = 0$), and labor demand, L, is a vector of time allocated to the production of each commodity. Leisure usually is not considered, so total time is the sum of time spent in household production, plus market work. It is often assumed that Z-goods production is not joint and that it exhibits constant returns to scale. If no fixed inputs exist, the supply (and profit) functions will be ill-defined so that shadow (or implicit) prices cannot be defined in terms of equality between household supply and demands. Rather, they are defined implicitly by the partial derivatives of the cost functions with respect to output (Pollak and Wachter 1975). However if fixed inputs do exist, or the production functions are strictly convex, shadow (or virtual) prices can be implicitly defined from the equality of household demand and supply functions.

An elaboration of the household production framework by Gronau (1973) provides results almost identical to the model of Hymer and Resnick. Gronau's model amounts to relabeling food consumption as leisure and food production as labor demand. He, too, has a market-purchased and a home-produced (Z) commodity, with home production using labor and purchased inputs. As in the Hymer and Resnick model, a virtual

price exists for the home-produced (Z) good. If no labor is supplied to the
market, there will exist a virtual (shadow) wage as well, and the analysis is
comparable to the Hymer and Resnick model when labor is a choice variable but no market for it exists. In a subsequent study, Gronau (1977)
assumes that the market-purchased and the household-produced commodities are perfect substitutes in consumption and so may be added. As
long as market purchases are positive and labor is sold on the market, this
model is recursive. If labor is not sold on the market, a virtual (shadow)
price for labor exists, and if market purchases of the home-produced commodity are zero, a virtual price for it exists. Huffman and Lange (1982)
have a slightly different version of Gronau's model in which the household is explicitly an agricultural household. The household jointly produces a farm and a household commodity (X_c and X_a), selling the former
and consuming the latter. Labor is sold on the market, but the only market purchases are for production inputs. A virtual price exists for the
household commodity and the model is not separable. If, however, the
farm and household commodities have separate production functions
and fixed inputs could only be allocated to one enterprise, the model
would be recursive between farm production decisions and the rest.

Partly Absent Markets: Commodity Heterogeneity

Even if all markets exist, households may face a virtual price that depends on both production technology and household preferences, so that
again an agricultural household model would not be recursive. This can
occur because markets are partly absent or because constraints are insti-
tutionally imposed (see Sicular, chapter 10, for an analysis of such constraints imposed on a production team in the People's Republic of
China). In particular, a household may be able to sell a commodity but
not buy it, or vice versa. If this commodity is both consumed and produced by the household, then the household's optimum may be at a corner at which consumption equals production. Such corner solutions are
likely to occur especially when commodities are heterogeneous. For example, hired and family labor may be imperfect substitutes because of
extra monitoring or search costs of hired labor. On-farm and off-farm
labor may give different levels of disutility (see Lopez, chapter 11). Alternatively, a commodity consumed out of home production may have a
different quality than the same commodity purchased on the market, and
thus sales and purchase prices may differ.

Households can sell and consume family labor or home production,
but they cannot purchase them. This suggests that, at the market price,
supply might be less than demand, which is not possible. For such corner

solutions, the commodity in question has a virtual price that would equate supply and demand. The virtual price will be higher than the market price provided that the compensated marketed surplus responds positively to price.

If households have preferences between on-farm and off-farm labor, then even if hired and family labor are perfect substitutes in production there may exist excess supply of on-farm labor at the market wage, in which case the virtual wage will be lower.

It should be clear that the comparative statics for these equilibria are identical to those considered earlier for the cases in which no market exists. Also, if these corner solutions are not binding, then the model is separable, the market prices being the opportunity costs. This will complicate empirical work since, if such heterogeneity exists, a sample is likely to include both households at corners and households at interior solutions.

Recursive Conditions Summarized

This appendix has reviewed the comparative statics of some basic, static agricultural household models. A key modeling issue is under what circumstances a model is recursive. This is very important for applied empirical work since it makes the problem far more tractable (see chapter 1). It has been shown that a sufficient condition for recursiveness is that all markets exist for commodities that are both produced and consumed, with the household being a price-taker in each one, and that such commodities are homogeneous. As long as households can buy or sell as much as they want at given prices, production and consumption decisions can be treated as if they were sequential, production decisions being made first, even though they may be made simultaneously. Such strong conditions are not necessary, however. In particular, the homogeneity assumption can be dropped. In this case, however, the agricultural household model remains recursive only if the household does not choose to be at a corner for a commodity that it both produces and consumes (for example, consuming all of its output). If a corner solution is chosen, then a virtual price exists, which is a function of both preferences and technology, so that the household's decision is no longer separable. Note that even in the case of heterogeneity, it is still necessary to assume that all markets exist and that prices are given to households to achieve recursiveness. If even one market does not exist (for a commodity that is consumed and produced), then recursiveness from production to consumption decisions breaks down.

Historically, nonrecursive agricultural household models were thought to be relevant, primarily because labor markets were presumed not to exist. As more has been learned about rural labor markets in developing countries, this assumption has become increasingly questioned. This does not mean that empirically relevant models have to be recursive, but the reasons for nonrecursiveness need to be clearly spelled out (see chapter 2).

References

Anderson, Dennis, and Mark Leiserson. 1980. "Rural Nonfarm Employment in Developing Countries." *Economic Development and Cultural Change*, vol. 28, pp. 227-48.

Bardhan, Pranab. 1979. "Wages and Unemployment in a Poor Agrarian Economy: A Theoretical and Empirical Analysis." *Journal of Political Economy*, vol. 87, pp. 479-500.

Barnum, Howard, and Lyn Squire. 1980. "Predicting Agricultural Output Response." *Oxford Economic Papers*, vol. 32, pp. 284-95.

_____. 1979. *A Model of an Agricultural Household*. Washington, D.C.: World Bank.

Becker, Gary. 1965. "A Theory of the Allocation of Time." *Economic Journal*, vol. 75, pp. 493-517.

Binswanger, Hans, and Mark Rosenzweig, eds. 1984. *Contractual Arrangements, Employment and Wages in Rural Labor Markets: A Critical Review*. New Haven, Conn.: Yale University Press.

Chayanov, A. V. 1925. "Peasant Farm Organization." Moscow: Cooperative Publishing House. Translated in *A. V. Chayanov: The Theory of Peasant Economy*, ed. D. Thorner, B. Kerblay, and R. E. F. Smith. Homewood, Ill.: Richard Irwin, 1966.

Deaton, Angus, and John Muellbauer. 1980. *Economics and Consumer Behavior*. Cambridge, Mass.: Cambridge University Press.

Dixit, Avinash, and Victor Norman. 1980. *Theory of International Trade: A Dual, General Equilibrium Approach*. Cambridge, Mass.: Cambridge University Press.

Fisk, E. K., and K. T. Shand. 1969. "The Early Stages of Development in a Primitive Economy: The Evolution from Subsistence to Trade and Specializations." In *Subsistence Agriculture and Economic Development*, ed. C. F. Wharton, Jr. Chicago: Aldine.

Gronau, Reuben. 1973. "The Intrafamily Allocation of Time: The Value of the Housewives' Time." *American Economic Review*, vol. 68, pp. 634-51.

_____. 1977. "Leisure, Home Production and Work: The Theory of the Allocation of Time Revisited." *Journal of Political Economy*, vol. 85, pp. 1099-1124.

Huffman, Wallace, and Mark Lange. 1982. "Farm Household Production: Demand for Wife's Labor, Capital Services and the Capital-Labor Ratio." Yale University Economic Growth Center Discussion Paper no. 408. New Haven, Conn.

Hymer, Stephan, and Stephen Resnick. 1969. "A Model of an Agrarian Economy with Nonagricultural Activities." *American Economic Review*, vol. 59, pp. 493-506.

Jorgenson, Dale, and Lawrence Lau. 1969. "An Economic Theory of Agricultural Household Behavior." Paper read at 4th Far Eastern Meeting of the Econometric Society.

Krishna, Raj. 1964. "Theory of the Firm: Rappoteur's Report." Indian Economic Journal, vol. 11, pp. 514–25.

———. 1969. "Comment: Models of the Family Farm." In Subsistence Agriculture and Economic Development, ed. C. F. Wharton, Jr. Chicago: Aldine.

Lancaster, Kelvin. 1966. "A New Approach to Consumer Theory." Journal of Political Economy, vol. 74, pp. 132–57.

Liedholm, Carl, and Enyinya Chuta. 1976. The Economics of Rural and Urban Small-Scale Industry in Sierra Leone. African Rural Economy Working Paper no. 14. East Lansing: Michigan State University.

Lopez, Ramon. 1980. "Economic Behaviour of Self-Employed Farm Producers." Ph.D. dissertation, University of British Columbia, Vancouver.

Mellor, J. 1963. "The Use and Productivity of Farm Labor in Early Stages of Agricultural Development." Journal of Farm Economics, vol. 45, pp. 517–34.

Millar, J. 1970. "A Reformulation of A. V. Chayanov's Theory of the Peasant Economy." Economic Development and Cultural Change, vol. 18, pp. 219–29.

Muth, Richard. 1966. "Household Production and Consumer Demand Functions." Econometrica, vol. 34, pp. 699–708.

Nakajima, Chihiro. 1957. "Over-Occupied and the Theory of the Family Farm." Osaka Daigaku Keizaigaku, vol. 6.

———. 1969. "Subsistence and Commercial Family Farms: Some Theoretical Models of Subjecture Equilibrium." Subsistence Agriculture and Economic Development. Edited by C. F. Wharton, Jr. Chicago: Aldine.

Neary, J., and K. Roberts. 1980. "The Theory of Household Behavior under Rationing." European Economic Review, vol. 13, pp. 25–42.

Pollak, Robert, and Michael Wachter. 1975. "The Relevance of the Household Production Function for the Allocation of Time." Journal of Political Economy, vol. 83, pp. 255–77.

Rosenzweig, Mark. 1978. "Rural Wages, Labor Supply, and Land Reform." American Economic Review, vol. 68, pp. 847–61.

———. 1982. "Agricultural Development, Education and Innovation." In The Theory and Experience of Economic Development. Edited by M. Gersovitz and others. London: George Allen & Unwin.

Sen, Amartya K. 1966. "Peasants and Dualism with and without Surplus Labor." Journal of Political Economy, vol. 74, pp. 425–50.

Spencer, Dunstan, and Derek Byerlee. 1977. Small Farms in West Africa: A Descriptive Analysis of Employment, Incomes and Productivity in Sierra Leone. African Rural Economy Program Working Paper no. 19. East Lansing: Michigan State University.

Squire, Lyn. 1981. Employment Policy in Developing Countries: A Survey of Issues and Evidence. New York: Oxford University Press.

Tanaka, Osamu. 1951. "An Equilibrium Analysis of Peasant Economy." Nogyo Keizai Kenkyu (Journal of Rural Economics), vol. 22.

World Bank. 1983. World Development Report. New York: Oxford University Press.

Part IV
Family Coordination: Unified and Bargaining Approaches

[13]

INTERNATIONAL ECONOMIC REVIEW
Vol. 22, No. 2, June, 1981

NASH-BARGAINED HOUSEHOLD DECISIONS: TOWARD A GENERALIZATION OF THE THEORY OF DEMAND*

By Marjorie B. McElroy and Mary Jean Horney[1]

1. INTRODUCTION

The theoretical underpinnings of much empirical work in economics is, either implicitly or explicitly, *individual* constrained utility maximization and the resulting system of demand equations. Often times, however, the behavior being modeled is the outcome of *group*, not *individual*, decisions. Recent studies of the allocation of the time of individual family members between home and the market are a case in point: Ashenfelter and Heckman [1974], Heckman [1974, 1977], and Wales and Woodland [1976, 1977]. In this paper we present alternative theoretical underpinnings for such studies, a Nash-bargained system of demand equations and the comparative statics of the associated demand system. Attention is focused on contrasting the empirical implications of the Nash bargaining model with those of neoclassical individual utility maximization.

To be concrete, we work with a two-person household, a "married couple," and their joint allocation of money-income and time. The model, however, is applicable to outcomes of any decisions that can be structured as a constrained, static, two-person, non-zero-sum game. The model can also be generalized to more than two players. Although we analyze only the outcome of a two-person cooperative game with a Nash [1953] solution, our goal is broader: to illuminate the general characteristics of the empirically observable differences between bargained and individual decision making. Our approach contrasts with those of Becker [e.g., 1973] and Samuelson [1956]. They place sufficient *a priori* structure (in the form of "full caring" and a "marginal-ethical-worth" rule, respectively) on "family" decisions so that the outcomes are empirically indistinguishable from those of constrained individual utility maximization. We refer to these and other approaches which explicitly or implicitly reduce family decisions to individual decisions as "neoclassical."

The empirical distinctions between Nash-bargained and neoclassical household decisions are highlighted in the explicit expressions we derive for Nash generalizations of the neoclassical Slutsky equation, of neoclassical substitution symmetry, and of Engel aggregation.[2] The Nash generalization of Engel aggregation arises

* Manuscript received July 5, 1978; revised August 19, 1980.
  [1] For useful comments and criticisms, we are indebted to M. Brown, S. Clemhout, J. Gates, T. Kniesner, and H. G. Lewis. The first author received financial support from the Duke University Research Council, the National Bureau of Economic Research at Stanford, and the National Opinion Research Center, University of Chicago.
  [2] Many of the comparative static results were presented in Horney [1977]. If nonwage income were not an argument of the threat points but prices remained so, then our model would be a special case of (conditional) price dependent preferences as surveyed by Pollak [1977].

because, in contrast to a neoclassical household, for a Nash household male and female nonwage incomes are distinct arguments of each demand equation. Since the usual neoclassical comparative static results are nested in their Nash generalizations, we propose empirical tests that the Nash demand system collapses to a neoclassical one. In a companion paper, Horney and McElroy [1980], using a three equation linear expenditure system on married, working couples from the 1967 National Longitudinal Survey of Mature Women, we find evidence to reject the proposition that the Nash comparative statics collapse to the neoclassical ones.

The work of Manser and Brown [1978, 1980] and Brown and Manser [1977, 1978] is both parallel and complementary to ours. Using a Nash bargaining specification similar to ours, they demonstrate the existence of household demand functions. Their work is broader than ours in that they analyze bargaining rules other than the Nash type, and look at the empirical distinctions among these as well as between these and the neoclassical demand system. In addition, Manser and Brown analyze the demand for marriage. In contrast, our work is more narrowly focused on the Nash household model and a detailed and explicit analysis of the comparative statics, empirical implications, and specification of tests of the hypothesis that the Nash model collapses to the neoclassical demand model. In related work, Clemhout and Wan [1977] use a Nash solution to a differential game to determine income shares which, in turn, dictate the allocation of household expenditures through a Lindahl equilibrium. Thus, changes in relative income shares explain changes in consumption and work patterns.

Section 2 presents the Nash model and the associated complete system of demand equations. Section 3 presents the Nash analogue to neoclassical indifference curves and their relationship to prices and incomes. Section 4 derives the comparative statics of the Nash model, including the Nash generalizations of the Slutsky equation, of substitution symmetry and of Engel aggregation. In this section, the usual neoclassical comparative static results are shown to be nested in those of the Nash model; based on this nesting, empirical tests are proposed. In Section 5 a graphical analysis is used to summarize the relationship between the Nash model and neoclassical model. Section 6 contains brief concluding remarks.

2. THE NASH HOUSEHOLD OBJECTIVE FUNCTION AND DEMAND SYSTEM

Assume that a household consists of two people, m and f. Their objects of choice are $x = (x_0, x_1, x_2, x_3, x_4)'$ with given market prices $p = (p_0, p_1, p_2, p_3, p_4)'$. Here x_1 is a market good consumed by the husband; x_2 is a market good consumed by the wife; x_3 is the quantity of "leisure" of the husband; x_4 is the quantity of "leisure" of the wife; and x_0 is a "household good."[3] The household good is defined as a pure public good within the household: consumption of x_0 by one

---

[3] It is straightforward to generalize the theory that follows by taking each x_t to be a vector. Few, if any, insights are lost by ignoring this complication.

NASH-BARGAINED HOUSEHOLD DECISIONS   335

household member does not reduce the amount available to the other.   "Leisure" time includes all time not spent at market work.   It will prove convenient to classify goods and prices as those of direct interest to m,

$$x_m = (x_0, x_1, x_3)', \quad \text{at} \quad p_m = (p_0, p_1, p_3)';$$

and those of direct interest to f,

$$x_f = (x_0, x_2, x_4)', \quad \text{at} \quad p_f = (p_0, p_2, p_4)'.$$

We assume that if m and f were not married, each would behave as if to maximize a twice continuously differentiable, nondecreasing, quasiconcave utility function, subject to that individual's budget restraint,

(1) $I_m + p_3(T - x_3) = p_0 x_{0_m} + p_1 x_1, \quad \text{for} \quad m \quad \text{and}$

(2) $I_f + p_4(T - x_4) = p_0 x_{0_f} + p_2 x_2, \quad \text{for} \quad f.$

Here x_{0_k} is the amount of the "household" good each consumes; I_k is nonwage income for $k = m, f$; and T is total time to be allocated between market and nonmarket pursuits.   Consequently, each person has a well defined continuous, strictly quasiconvex indirect utility function giving the maximum attainable utility level as a function of prices and nonwage income:

(3) $V_0^m = V_0^m(p_m, I_m) \quad \text{and} \quad V_0^f = V_0^f(p_f, I_f).$

Duality insures that the partial derivatives of the indirect utilities have the indicated signs:[4]

TABLE 1

	$\dfrac{\partial V_0^k}{\partial p_0}$	$\dfrac{\partial V_0^k}{\partial p_1}$	$\dfrac{\partial V_0^k}{\partial p_2}$	$\dfrac{\partial V_0^k}{\partial p_3}$	$\dfrac{\partial V_0^k}{\partial p_4}$	$\dfrac{\partial V_0^k}{\partial I_m}$	$\dfrac{\partial V_0^k}{\partial I_f}$
$k=m$	$-$	$-$	0	$+$	0	$+$	0
$k=f$	$-$	0	$-$	0	$+$	0	$+$

For a couple, however, the utility of each is assumed to depend not only on own goods, own leisure, and the household good, but also upon the nonmarket time and the consumption of the spouse as well.   Thus their individual utility functions are given by

(4) $U^k = U^k(x),$ for $k = m, f.$

Hence, the gain from being married as opposed to single, assumed non-negative for existing marriages,[5] is

(5) $U^k(x) - V_0^k(p_k', I_k)$ for $k = m, f.$

[4] For convenience, we define as zero the partial of V_0^k with respect to a variable which is not an argument of V_0^k, e.g., $\dfrac{\partial V_0^m}{\partial p_2} \equiv 0.$

[5] See Manser and Brown [1980] for an elaboration of this point.

336   M. B. McELROY AND M. J. HORNEY

In this model, a married couple is not necessarily distinguished from two single individuals on legal grounds, but rather on the basis of pooling resources and allocating them jointly.[6] Thus, total expenditures on the household good, own goods and leisures equals "full income," or

(6) $p_0 x_0 + p_1 x_1 + p_2 x_2 + p_3 x_3 + p_4 x_4 = (p_3 + p_4)T + I_m + I_f.$

We assume that bargaining over the allocation óf x achieves the Nash solution to a two-person, nonzero-sum game. As is well known, this solution is characterized by invariance with respect to linear transformations of individual utility functions, Pareto efficiency of the allocation of resources, independence of irrelevant alternatives and symmetry (in terms of utilities) with respect to the roles of the players. We will not debate here the merits of this particular set of criteria, but refer the reader to Manser and Brown [1980]. However, we would emphasize that we think the most serious deficiency of the Nash solution as applied to this household game may lie not in the assumption of the independence of irrelevant alternatives or symmetry but rather in the inadmissibility of interpersonal comparisons of utility.[7]

Thus, we assume the couple chooses x to maximize, subject to (6), what we call the "utility-gain product function," a special case of the Nash product function,

(7) $N = [U^m(x) - V_0^m(p_m', I_m; \alpha_m)] [U^f(x) - V_0^f(p_f', I_f; \alpha_f)].$

Each term in brackets is the gain from marriage over the next best alternative; V_0^k is reinterpreted as the threat point of the k-th individual and represents the best he could expect to do if he were to withdraw from the household.[8] The threat points may shift because the opportunities outside of the marriage change. We define the α_k's as the relevant shift parameters. For example, α_k might be a search parameter such as the ratio of males to females in the relevant marriage market.[9] Setting the first partials of the appropriate Lagrangian function equal to zero yields the necessary conditions for a maximum. These are unique up to linear transformations of the $(U^k - V_0^k)$:

(8) $N_i \equiv U_i^m(U^f - V_0^f) + (U^m - V_0^m)U_i^f = \lambda p_i,$ $i = 0, 1, 2, 3, 4,$

---

[6] The class of admissible utility functions is restricted. For example, let m's utility function as a single person be $U^m(x)$ with x_2 and x_4 constrained to be zero. Then clearly certain functions such as $U^m = x_0^{r_0} x_1^{r_1} x_2^{r_2} x_3^{r_3} x_4^{r_4} \equiv 0$ for all (x_0, x_1, x_3) are inadmissible for then $V_0^m \equiv 0$ for all (p_m, I_m).

[7] Luce and Raiffa [1957, pp. 130–132] briefly discuss the possible advantages of admitting interpersonal comparisons at the expense of independence. In the broader context of collective choice Sen [1977, pp. 1550–1552] gives references to rules incorporating both independent and interpersonal comparisons, neither one, and independence without interpersonal comparisons. He then gives the first discussion of the remaining combination: rules using interpersonal comparisons without independence.

[8] This maximum is not necessarily associated with being single, but instead with attaining the highest level of utility among all alternatives to the marriage.

[9] In an interesting elaboration of this point, Manser and Brown [1980] take the threat point to be the expected utility from continued search for a partner.

NASH-BARGAINED HOUSEHOLD DECISIONS 337

(9) $\quad -N_\lambda \equiv p_0 x_0 + p_1 x_1 + p_2 x_2 + p_3 x_3 + p_4 x_4 - T(p_3 + p_4) - I_m - I_f = 0,$

where $N_i = \dfrac{\partial N}{\partial x_i}$, $U_i^k = \dfrac{\partial U^k}{\partial x_i}$ for $k = m$, f and $i = 0, 1, ..., 4$; $N_\lambda = \dfrac{\partial N}{\partial \lambda}$, and λ is the Lagrange multiplier. Solving (8) and (9) (locally) for the optimal x as a function of prices and nonwage incomes[10] yields the demand system and the associated optimal value of the Lagrange multiplier:

(10) $\quad\quad\quad\quad\quad\quad\quad\quad x_i = h_i(p', I_m, I_f), \quad\quad\quad\quad\quad i = 0, 1, 2, 3, 4,$

(11) $\quad\quad\quad\quad\quad\quad\quad\quad \lambda = h_\lambda(p', I_m, I_f).$

The multiplier, λ, is the increase in the utility-gain product due to a unit increase in full income, evaluated at the optimal x. Since V_0^m and V_0^f are homogeneous of degree zero in prices and income, (8) guarantees that the demand functions (10) are homogeneous of degree zero in prices and incomes.

3. ISO-GAIN PRODUCT CURVES AND THE FAMILY RATE OF SUBSTITUTION

In the comparative statics of the neoclassical utility model, changes in prices and income change the optimal bundle only via twists and shifts in the budget restraint while the indifference map remains fixed. In the comparative statics of a bargaining model there is an additional complication: changes in prices and nonwage incomes not only twist and shift the budget restraint but also change the objective function itself. These changes in the objective function are easily characterized as twists and shifts in the "iso-gain product curves" (the bargaining analogue of neoclassical indifference curves): the twists are changes in the "family rate of substitution" (the bargaining analogue of neoclassical marginal rates of substitution); the shifts are changes in the level of the value attached to an iso-gain product curve.

3.1. *Definition of IGPC.* Define an iso-gain product curve (IGPC) as the locus of bundles, x, for which the utility-gain product function is constant. For given prices and incomes, there is a family of iso-gain product curves which share the following properties with neoclassical indifference curves: (a) two curves cannot intersect; (b) an IGPC with a higher value lies everywhere to the northeast of any IGPC with a lower value; (c) there is an IGPC passing through every point in the nonnegative orthant of the space in which the x's lie.

3.2. *Changes in FRS_{ij}.* The "family" rate of substitution of x_i for x_j is defined as minus the slope of the IGPC at x, or

(12) $\quad FRS_{ij} = -\dfrac{dx_j}{dx_i}\bigg|_N = \dfrac{N_i}{N_j}$, and $dx_k = 0$ for $k \neq i$, $k \neq j$, $i \neq j$,

$$k, i, j = 0, 1, 2, ..., 4.$$

---

[10] We assume that the U^k and V_0^k are such that N is a quasiconcave function and that the implicit function theorem holds.

338   M. B. McELROY AND M. J. HORNEY

At x, FRS_{ij} depends upon the arguments of the threat points: p, I_m, I_f, α_m and α_f. Let z stand for any particular one of these arguments. Then[11]

$$(13) \quad \frac{\partial FRS_{ij}}{\partial z} = \frac{U_j^m U_j^f}{N_j^2}\left(\frac{U_i^f}{U_j^f} - \frac{U_i^m}{U_j^m}\right)\left[\frac{\partial V_0^f}{\partial z}(U^m - V_0^m) - \frac{\partial V_0^m}{\partial z}(U^f - V_0^f)\right]$$

$$\equiv -\frac{U_j^m U_j^f}{N_j^2}(\Delta MRS_{ij})[W], \text{ say, } \quad \text{for } i,j = 0, 1, 2, 3, 4 \text{ and } i \neq j.$$

Since $U_j^m U_j^f / N_j^2 > 0$, the sign of $\dfrac{\partial FRS_{ij}}{\partial z}$ depends on those of ΔMRS_{ij} and of W.

If z is any one of the following, p_1, p_2, p_3, p_4, I_m, or I_f, then the sign of W is determined. For in these cases, one of the terms $\dfrac{\partial V_0^f}{\partial z}$, $\dfrac{\partial V_0^m}{\partial z}$ will have a known sign (see Table 1 above), and the other will be zero. Finally if $z \equiv \alpha_m \equiv \alpha_f$ but $\dfrac{\partial V_0^m}{\partial \alpha_m}$ and $\dfrac{\partial V_0^f}{\partial \alpha_m}$ have opposite signs, then once again the sign of W is determined. For example, let $z \equiv \alpha_m \equiv \alpha_f$ be the ratio of the number of males to the number of females in the relevant marriage market. Then $\dfrac{\partial V_0^m}{\partial \alpha_m} < 0$, $\dfrac{\partial V_0^f}{\partial \alpha_m} > 0$ and W is positive. Hence the sign of W is determined in all but two cases: when z is p_0 and when z is $\alpha_m = \alpha_f$ and sign $\dfrac{\partial V_0^m}{\partial \alpha_m} = $ sign $\dfrac{\partial V_0^f}{\partial \alpha_f}$.

ΔMRS_{ij} is the difference in the spouses' individual marginal rates of substitution at x. If $\Delta MRS_{ij} > 0$, then she places a higher relative value on x_i (in terms of x_j) than he does.

DEFINITION. If x_i and x_j, with $i \neq j$, are both of direct interest to her (him), then he (she) is said to be *nonjudgmental* with respect to x_i and x_j at x if at x,

$$(14) \qquad \frac{U_i^m}{U_j^m} = \frac{U_i^f}{U_j^f}.$$

If the relationship (14) is changed to inequality, say $>$, then he is *paternalistic* and pushing x_i at the expense of x_j (she is *maternalistic* and pushing x_j at the expense of x_i); or, he (she) views x_i (x_j) as a *merit* good.

DEFINITION. If x_i is of direct interest to him (her) and x_j, only of indirect interest to him (her), then *they are selfish* at x

$$(15) \qquad \text{if } \frac{U_i^f}{U_j^f} < \frac{U_i^m}{U_j^m} \quad \left(\text{if } \frac{U_i^f}{U_j^f} > \frac{U_i^m}{U_j^m}\right).$$

They are altruistic if the opposite relationship holds, and *neutral* in the case of equality.

---

[11] Since $\dfrac{\partial FRS_{ij}}{\partial z} = \dfrac{N_j \dfrac{\partial N_i}{\partial z} - N_i \dfrac{\partial N_j}{\partial z}}{N_j^2}$, (for $i, j - 0, 1, 2, 3, 4$ and $i \neq j$), then substituting in (8) as well as $\dfrac{\partial N_i}{\partial z} = -\left(\dfrac{\partial V_0^m}{\partial z}U_i^f + \dfrac{\partial V_0^f}{\partial z}U_i^m\right)$ gives (13).

For the many cases where we can sign W and make an assumption with respect to ΔMRS_{ij} (e.g., selfishness), we can sign $\dfrac{\partial FRS_{ij}}{\partial z}$ and thereby know, for a region of the space in which the x's lie, the direction of the twist in the IGPC map. For example, let $(x_i, x_j) = (x_1, x_2)$, his and her consumption goods. Assume selfishness at x, i.e., $\Delta MRS_{12} < 0$. Then $W < 0$ and $\dfrac{\partial FRS_{12}}{\partial I_m} > 0$ in a neighborhood of x. In words, selfishness implies that an increase in his nonwage income changes the family decision function to reflect a relatively higher value placed on his consumption good.

3.3. *Changes in the IGP level.* Changes in z also change the value attached to the IGPC through any point, x. In general

(16)
$$\frac{\partial N}{\partial z} = -(U^m - V_0^m)\frac{\partial V_0^f}{\partial z} - (U^f - V_0^f)\frac{\partial V_0^m}{\partial z}.$$

From Table 1 above, we can sign $\partial N/\partial z$ when z is any price, including p_0, and when z is I_m or I_f. In Section 5 below, we use these changes in the numerical value assigned to an IGPC through x for expositing the effect of income-compensated price changes. As the reader may suspect, however, such changes do wash out of the empirical implications.

4. COMPARATIVE STATICS OF THE NASH MODEL: A GENERALIZATION OF THE NEOCLASSICAL MODEL

In this section we present the uncompensated effects of price changes, the compensated effects of price changes, and the effects of income changes on both the optimal bundle (x) and the Lagrange multiplier (λ). These effects lead naturally to a Nash generalization of Engel aggregation, of the Slutsky equation, and of substitution symmetry. The derivations of many of the relationships in this section are relegated to the Appendix.

4.1. *Notation.* The vector of excess demands for x is

$$\underset{(5\times 1)}{q} = x' - (0, 0, 0, T, T)' = (x_0, x_1, x_2, x_3 - T, x_4 - T)'.$$

The last two elements of q are the negatives of his and her excess supply of hours of market work. The j-th column of the following X-matrices and the j-th element of the λ-vectors contain the partial derivatives of the optimal bundle (x) and of λ with respect to the j-th price:

$$\underset{(5\times 5)}{X_p} = [\partial x_i/\partial p_j], \qquad \underset{(5\times 1)}{\lambda_p} = \left(\frac{\partial \lambda}{\partial p_0}, \frac{\partial \lambda}{\partial p_1}, \dots, \frac{\partial \lambda}{\partial p_4}\right)',$$

$$\underset{(5\times 5)}{X_p^*} = [\partial x_i^*/\partial p_j], \qquad \underset{(5\times 1)}{\lambda_p^*} = \left(\frac{\partial \lambda^*}{\partial p_0}, \frac{\partial \lambda^*}{\partial p_1}, \dots, \frac{\partial \lambda^*}{\partial p_4}\right)'.$$

Here an asterisk indicates that N is being held constant. The partials of the optimal x and λ with respect to I_m and I_f are in

$$\underset{(5\times 2)}{X_I} = [X_{I_m}, X_{I_f}] = \left[\frac{\partial x}{\partial I_m}, \frac{\partial x}{\partial I_f} \right], \qquad \underset{(1\times 2)}{\lambda_I} = \left[\frac{\partial \lambda}{\partial I_m}, \frac{\partial \lambda}{\partial I_f} \right].$$

The effect of prices and incomes on m's and f's threat points are captured in

$$\underset{(2\times 5)}{V_p} = \begin{bmatrix} \dfrac{\partial V_0^m}{\partial p_0} & \dfrac{\partial V_0^m}{\partial p_1} & 0 & \dfrac{\partial V_0^m}{\partial p_3} & 0 \\[2ex] \dfrac{\partial V_0^f}{\partial p_0} & 0 & \dfrac{\partial V_0^f}{\partial p_2} & 0 & \dfrac{\partial V_0^f}{\partial p_4} \end{bmatrix}, \qquad \underset{(2\times 2)}{V_I} = \begin{bmatrix} \dfrac{\partial V_0^m}{\partial I_m} & 0 \\[2ex] 0 & \dfrac{\partial V_0^f}{\partial I_f} \end{bmatrix}.$$

The effects on the threat point of one spouse will usually be weighted by *either* the marginal utilities of the opposite spouse which appear in the columns of

$$\underset{(5\times 2)}{D} = \begin{bmatrix} U_0^f & U_1^f & U_2^f & U_3^f & U_4^f \\ U_0^m & U_1^m & U_2^m & U_3^m & U_4^m \end{bmatrix}',$$

or by the "gain from marriage" of the opposite spouse which appears in

$$\underset{(2\times 1)}{g} = (U^f - V_0^f, U^m - V_0^m)' > (0, 0)'.$$

Finally, b, c, and B are the (5×1), (1×1), and symmetric (5×5) submatrices of the inverse of the appropriate bordered Hessian for the optimization problem; I_5 is the identity matrix of size 5; and ι is a 2×1 vector of ones.

4.2. *Comparative Statics of the Nash Model.* The *uncompensated effects of changing the j-th price* — other prices and incomes constant — on the optimal (x, λ) are the j-th column of

$$(17) \qquad \begin{bmatrix} X_p \\ -\lambda_p' \end{bmatrix} = \begin{bmatrix} B(\lambda I_5 + DV_p) - bq' \\ b'(\lambda I_5 + DV_p) + c^{-1}q' \end{bmatrix},$$

which is obtained by partial differentiation of (8) and (9) with respect to each p_j and then solving for X_p, λ_p. (Details of the derivation are contained in the Appendix.)

The *income compensated effects of changing the j-th price* — holding other prices and the level of N constant — are the j-th column of

$$(18) \qquad \begin{bmatrix} X_p^* \\ -\lambda_p^{*'} \end{bmatrix} = \begin{bmatrix} B(\lambda I_5 + DV_p) + \lambda^{-1}bg'V_p \\ b'(\lambda I_5 + DV_p) - (c\lambda)^{-1}g'V_p \end{bmatrix}$$

which is obtained by partial differentiation of (7) and (8) with respect to each p_j and then solving for X_p^*, λ_p^*. As noted in Section 3.3 above, the level of N is of no intrinsic interest. Equation (18) is, however, essential to understanding the Nash generalization of the Slutsky equation and the like.

Equal changes in male and female incomes have different effects on the Nash

NASH-BARGAINED HOUSEHOLD DECISIONS 341

objective function (7) and, consequently, on the optimal bundle. The *effects of changing the k-th spouse's income* I_k — all prices and the other spouse's income $I_{k'}$ constant — on the optimal (x, λ) are the k-th column of

$$(19) \qquad \begin{bmatrix} X_I \\ -\lambda_I \end{bmatrix} = \begin{bmatrix} BDV_I + b\iota' \\ b'DV_I - c^{-1}\iota' \end{bmatrix}$$

which is obtained via partial differentiation of (8) and (9) with respect to I_m and I_f — and then solving for X_I, λ_I.

To emphasize the separate impacts of I_m and I_f on the optimal x, write the first line of (19) as,

$$(20) \qquad X_I = [X_{I_m}, X_{I_f}] = \left[BDe_m \frac{\partial V_0^m}{\partial I_m}, \; BDe_f \frac{\partial V_0^f}{\partial I_f} \right] + [b, b],$$

where $e_m = (1, 0)'$ and $e_f = (0, 1)'$. These separate impacts also show up in the Nash generalization of *Engel aggregation*,[12]

$$(21) \qquad p'X_I = \iota', \quad \text{or} \quad \text{both} \; p'X_{I_m} = 1 \; \text{and} \; p'X_{I_f} = 1.$$

The *Nash generalization of the Slutsky equation* is obtained by substitution of (18) and (19)[13] into (17) to get

$$(22) \qquad \begin{bmatrix} X_p \\ \lambda_p' \end{bmatrix} = \begin{bmatrix} (X_p^* - \lambda^{-1}bg'V_p) - \dfrac{1}{2}(X_I - BDV_I)\iota q' \\ (\lambda_p^{*'} - (c\lambda)^{-1}g'V_p) + \dfrac{1}{2}(\lambda_I - bDV_I)\iota q' \end{bmatrix}.$$

Further substitutions yield the *Nash generalization of substitution symmetry,*[14]

$$(23) \qquad \left(X_p + \frac{1}{2}X_I\iota q' \right)G^{-1} = (G^{-1})'\left(X_p + \frac{1}{2}X_I\iota q' \right)'.$$

Note that $\frac{1}{2}X_I\iota = \frac{1}{2}(X_{I_m} + X_{I_f})$ is the average of his and her income effects. Equation (23) provides ten linear restrictions among the observable partial derivatives of (10) with respect to price (X_p) and income (X_I). The weights in these restrictions are taken from G^{-1} whose columns are identified only up to a scalar multiple:

---

[12] This statement of Engel aggregation falls out of the derivation of the income effects. See equation (A. 7) in the Appendix.

[13] Post-multiplying the first line in (19) by ι 1/2 allows one to solve for b which is used in the substitution: $b = 1/2 (X_I - BDV_I)\iota$.

[14] Using (18), the first line of (22) may be written as

$$X_p = B(\lambda I_s + DV_p) - 1/2(X_I - BDV_I)\iota q'.$$

Solving for B yields, $B = (X_p + 1/2X_I\iota q')G^{-1}$, where $G \equiv (\lambda I_s + DV_p) + 1/2 DV_I\iota q'$. Since $B = B'$, (23) follows.

(24) $$G^{-1} = \hat{p}\left(X_p + \frac{1}{2}X_I \iota q'\right)',$$

where $\hat{p}$ is any diagonal matrix of order 5.

Finally, we note that the matrix B contained in equation (18) is *symmetric, negative semidefinite* and that *Cournot aggregation* is given by

(25) $$p'X_p = -q'.$$

These propositions are proved in the Appendix.

4.3. *Comparison with the neoclassical comparative statics.* Direct substitution of $V_p = 0$ and $V_I = 0$ shows that the uncompensated price effects (17), the compensated price effects (18) and the income effects (19), as well as the Nash generalizations of both the Slutsky equation (22) and substitution symmetry (23) collapse to their neoclassical counterparts when both threat points are independent of prices and nonwage incomes. These substitutions yield the neoclassical equations of comparative statics:

(17a) Uncompensated price effects: $\begin{bmatrix} X_p \\ -\lambda_p \end{bmatrix} = \begin{bmatrix} \lambda B - bq' \\ \lambda b' - c^{-1}q' \end{bmatrix}$,
              $(V_p = 0)$

(18a) Compensated price effect: $\begin{bmatrix} X_p^* \\ -\lambda_p^* \end{bmatrix} = \begin{bmatrix} \lambda B \\ \lambda b' \end{bmatrix}$,
              $(V_p = 0)$

(19a) Income effects: $\begin{bmatrix} x_I \\ l_I \end{bmatrix} = \begin{bmatrix} b \\ c^{-1} \end{bmatrix}$,
              $(V_I = 0)$

(22a) Slutsky equation: $\begin{bmatrix} X_p \\ \lambda_p \end{bmatrix} = \begin{bmatrix} S - x_I q' \\ \lambda_p^* + l_I q' \end{bmatrix}$,
              $(V_I = 0 \text{ and } V_p = 0)$

(23a) Substitution symmetry: $(X_p + x_I q') = (X_p + x_I q')$.

In (19a), (22a), and (23a) x_I stands for the common value, $x_I = X_{I_m} = X_{I_f} = b$, and l_I for the common value, $l_I = \lambda_{I_m} = \lambda_{I_f} = c^{-1}$. Likewise, in (22a) and (23a) S replaces X_p^*, i.e., for $V_p = 0$ and $V_I = 0$, the neoclassical substitution matrix is

$$\lambda B = \left(X_p + \frac{1}{2}X_I \iota q'\right) = (X_p + x_I q') \equiv S.$$

Finally, note the Nash and neoclassical Cournot aggregation conditions (25), are identical (i.e., (25) is unaffected by $V_p = 0$). In contrast, when $V_I = 0$, the Nash generalization of Engel aggregation (21), reduces to neoclassical Engel aggregation,

(21a) $p'x_I = 1$.

Hence, when V_p and V_I are null, the generalized Nash comparative statics and restrictions collapse to their neoclassical counterparts. This suggests testing the following hypotheses:[15]

(i) $H_0: X_{I_m} = X_{I_f}$ versus $H_A: X_{I_m} \neq X_{I_f}$,
or the effect on the demand for x_i of a change in male nonwage income is identical to the effect of a change in female nonwage income (19a).

(ii) $H_0: (X_p + x_i q') = (X_p + x_i q')'$ versus $H_A: \left(X_p + \frac{1}{2} X_I \iota q' \right) G^{-1}$

$$= (G^{-1})' \left(X_p + \frac{1}{2} X_I \iota q' \right)',$$

or neoclassical substitution symmetry (23a) holds; and

(iii) $H_0: X_p + x_I q'$ is negative semidefinite,
or the neoclassical substitution matrix is negative semidefinite.

A necessary condition for (iii) is

(iii') $H_0: [X_p + x_I q']_{ii} < 0$ versus $H_A: [X_p + x_I q']_{ii} \geq 0$,
or, neoclassical own substitution terms are negative.

Rejection of any of these hypotheses would be rejection of the neoclassical restrictions and would contradict the notion that the Nash demand model collapses to the neoclassical one. Of course, the aggregation conditions (25) and (21a) provide no further tests since any system of demand equations which identically satisfies the budget restraint will identically satisfy Cournot aggregation and our generalized Nash-Engel aggregation condition.

5. GRAPHICAL RELATIONSHIP BETWEEN THE NASH AND NEOCLASSICAL MODELS

5.1. *Nash income effects.* Figure 1 depicts IGPC's for his leisure, x_3, versus hers, x_4. For purposes of exposition, assume that in the relevant region the couple is selfish, i.e., $\Delta MRS_{34} < 0$, so that, by (13), an increase in his income, I_m, increases the family's valuation of his leisure in terms of hers, i.e., $\frac{\partial FRS_{34}}{\partial I_m} > 0$. Suppose initially the budget restraint is KL, the representative IGPC's are the (boldfaced) curves (labeled N'), and the optimal bundle is C. An increase in I_m shifts the budget restraint out to WR and twists a representative IGPC to one such as the dotted curve (labeled N''); consequently, the final optimal bundle is F. Comparison of (19) and (19a) shows that the total Nash income effect, CF in Figure 1, can be resolved into a neoclassical income effect, CE, and an effect, EF, due to the tilt in the family of IGPC's:

	total income effect	=	neoclassical income effect	+	IGP income tilt
Figure 1	CF	=	CE	+	EF
Equation (19)	$[X_{I_m}, X_{I_f}]$	=	$[b, b]$	+	BDV_I
Equation (19a)	x_I	=	b		$(V_I = 0)$

[15] Manser and Brown [1978] suggest similar tests.

344   M. B. McELROY AND M. J. HORNEY

5.2. *Nash uncompensated and income-compensated price effects.* Continue with the assumption of selfishness in the relevant region so that, by (13), an increase in his wage, p_3, increases the family's valuation of his leisure in terms of hers, i.e., $\dfrac{\partial FRS_{34}}{\partial p_3} > 0$. Assume initially that the budget restraint is QR, the family of IGPC's is represented by the curve labeled $N = a$, and the optimal bundle is A. An increase in his wage, p_3, rotates the budget line to WR and twists the family of IGPC's to the family of (boldfaced) curves (labeled N'); consequently the final optimal bundle is at E. Thus AE is the Nash uncompensated price effect.

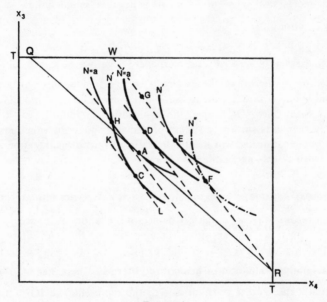

FIGURE 1

THE NASH UNCOMPENSATED AND INCOME-COMPENSATED EFFECTS OF AN
INCREASE IN p_3 ON THE OPTIMAL QUANTITIES OF x_3 AND x_4.

For this change in p_3 the corresponding income-compensated price effect is AD, where D is the tangency of the new IGPC with value $N' = a$ to a budget line reflecting the new price ratio. This Nash income-compensated price effect may be resolved into three components as follows:

			income compensated price effect	=	neoclassical substitution effect	+	IGP price tilt effect	+	relabeling effect
Figure 1	AD	=	AH	+	HC	+	CD
Equation (18)	X_p^*	=	λB	+	BDV_p	+	$\lambda^{-1}bg'V_p$
Equation (18a)	S	=	λB		$(V_p = 0)$		

NASH-BARGAINED HOUSEHOLD DECISIONS   345

Comparing (18) with (18a) and Figure 1, it is easily seen that the change in the optimal bundle AH can be identified with the term λB which is the neoclassical substitution effect. Furthermore, let C be the tangency of the new (boldfaced) IGPC through H tangent to a (dashed) budget line reflecting the new price ratio. Then we can identify the term BDV_p with the change in the optimal bundle, HC, which is due to the tilt in the IGPC's associated with the increase in p_3.[16]

Finally the residual component of the compensated price effect is CD which corresponds to $\lambda^{-1}bg'V_p$ in (18) and is called the "relabeling effect." By (16), the new $N'=a$ curve lies everywhere to the northeast of the old $N=a$ curve and does not intersect it. Since a monotone transformation (or relabeling) of IGPC's cannot affect choice, this relabeling effect will drop out of the Nash generalization of the Slutsky equation.

5.3. *Nash generalization of the Slutsky equation.* Combining the above effects gives us the Nash generalization of the Slutsky equation which resolves the total effect of a price change into appropriately adjusted substitution and income effects:

	total price effect	=	(compensated price effect − relabeling)	+	(income effect − IGP income tilt)
Figure 1	AE	$=$	$(AD-CD)$	$+$	$(CF-EF)$
	AE	$=$	AC	$+$	CE
Equation (22)	X_p	$=$	$(X_p^* - \lambda^{-1}bg'V_p)$	$-$	$\frac{1}{2}(X_I - BDV_I)\iota q'$
Equation (22a)	X_p	$=$	S	$-$	$x_I q'$

Notice that the substitution term is adjusted by subtracting off the relabeling effect (CD, or $\lambda^{-1}bg'V_p$). Similarly, the income term is adjusted by subtracting off the effect on the optimal bundle of the income-compensation (i.e., subtracting off BDV_I or deleting the move EF). Consequently, in Figure 1, if she rather than he had received the income compensation associated with the change in p_3, the total income effect would have been, say, CG, but the adjusted income effect would have remained unchanged, CE. Thus, both the adjusted income effect and the Nash generalization of the Slutsky equation are invariant with respect to the recipient of the (hypothetical) income compensation. This makes sense: for the total price effect, X_p, the net change in the IGPC's should reflect only the price changes and not a change in I_m or I_f.

6. CONCLUDING REMARKS

This paper presents a theory of demand associated with a Nash bargaining model of decision-making for a two-person household. The Nash objective

---

[16] The i, h element of DV_p is $\frac{\partial N_i}{\partial p_h}$. When $\frac{\partial N_i}{\partial p_h}=0$ for all i and h then, by (13), $\frac{\partial FRS_{ij}}{\partial p_h}=$ 0 for all i, j and h. Thus, $DV_p=0$ implies $\frac{\partial FRS_{ij}}{\partial p_h}=0$.

function depends upon individual utilities. It also depends upon the maximum value of (indirect) utility each person can obtain outside of the household and it is hence dependent upon prices and nonwage incomes. Consequently the non-wage income of *each* spouse appears as an independent variable in each demand equation. The Nash demand system retains the neoclassical properties of homogeneity and Cournot aggregation. It also exhibits what we call the Nash generalizations of Engel aggregation, of the Slutsky equation and of substitution symmetry. These three generalizations lead naturally to tests of the hypotheses that the Nash demand restrictions collapse to the corresponding neoclassical ones.

In a companion paper (Horney and McElroy [1980]), we specified a three commodity (male leisure, female leisure, and a Hicksian composite commodity) Nash linear expenditure system and estimated it for the 1967 National Longi-tudinal Survey of Mature Women. On the whole, the results were reasonable and there were indications that the Nash linear expenditure system does not collapse to the neoclassical one. Brown and Manser [1978], using a somewhat different Nash bargaining specification and a Rotterdam-type demand system, also found evidence to reject the hypothesis that a Nash demand system collapses to a neoclassical one. These studies point to the empirical enrichment available from bargaining models as opposed to individual decision models. The empirical payoff includes both richer functional forms for demand systems and additional explanatory variables incorporated via the threat points.

This richer analytical framework has many potential applications. For ex-ample, the Nash model provides for the first time an analytical framework for examining the effect of the "marriage tax" on the joint labor supply of husbands and wives: her current, married after-tax marginal wage rate is an argument of the family full income constraint; whereas her hypothetical unmarried after-tax marginal wage rate is an argument of her threat point. This is only one of a general class of applications where, due to taxes and transfers, the prices and nonwage incomes faced by an individual differ according to his or her marital status.

Duke University and the University of Chicago
Furman University

APPENDIX

In this Appendix we derive the comparative static equations of the bargaining model — equations (17), (18), and (19) of the text.

Uncompensated price effects. Partial differentiation of each equation in (8) and (9) with respect to each price, holding other prices and nonwage income con-stant yields the matrix equation,

NASH-BARGAINED HOUSEHOLD DECISIONS 347

(A.1)
$$\begin{bmatrix} J & p \\ p' & 0 \end{bmatrix} \begin{bmatrix} X_p \\ -\lambda_p' \end{bmatrix} = \begin{bmatrix} \lambda I_s + DV_p \\ -q' \end{bmatrix},$$

where

$$\underset{5 \times 5}{J} = [N_{ij}] = [U_i^m U_j^f + U_j^m U_i^f + U_{ij}^m(U^f - V_0^f) + U_{ij}^f(U^m - V_0^m)].$$

The partitioned inverse of the leftmost matrix in (A.1) is

(A.2)
$$\begin{bmatrix} J & p \\ p' & 0 \end{bmatrix}^{-1} = \begin{bmatrix} J^{-1} - (p'J^{-1}p)^{-1}J^{-1}pp'J^{-1} & J^{-1}p(p'J^{-1}p)^{-1} \\ (p'J^{-1}p)^{-1}p'J^{-1} & -(p'J^{-1}p)^{-1} \end{bmatrix}$$

$$\equiv \begin{bmatrix} B & b \\ b' & -c^{-1} \end{bmatrix}.$$

Premultiplication of (A.1) by (A.2) yields the matrix of uncompensated price effects on the optimal x and λ,

(A.3)
$$\begin{bmatrix} X_p \\ -\lambda_p' \end{bmatrix} = \begin{bmatrix} B & b \\ b' & -c^{-1} \end{bmatrix} \begin{bmatrix} \lambda I_s + DV_p \\ -q' \end{bmatrix} = \begin{bmatrix} B(\lambda I_s + DV_p) - bq' \\ b'(\lambda I_s + DV_p) + c^{-1}q' \end{bmatrix},$$

which is equation (17) in the text. Finally, note that (A.1) contains the Cournot aggregation condition,

(A.3)
$$p'X_p = -q',$$

which is equation (25) in the text.

Compensated price effects. For a fixed value of N in (7), partial differentiation of (7) and (8) with respect to each price, holding all other prices constant, (and substituting from (8)) yields

(A.5)
$$\begin{bmatrix} J & p \\ p' & 0 \end{bmatrix} \begin{bmatrix} X_p^* \\ -\lambda_p^{*'} \end{bmatrix} = \begin{bmatrix} \lambda I_s + DV_p \\ \lambda^{-1}g'V_p \end{bmatrix},$$

Premultiplication of (A.5) by (A.2) yields the matrix of compensated price effects,

(A.6)
$$\begin{bmatrix} X_p^* \\ -\lambda_p^{*'} \end{bmatrix} = \begin{bmatrix} B & b \\ b' & -c^{-1} \end{bmatrix} \begin{bmatrix} \lambda I_s + DV_p \\ \lambda^{-1}g'V_p \end{bmatrix}$$

$$= \begin{bmatrix} B(\lambda I_s + DV_p) + \lambda^{-1}bg'V_p \\ b'(\lambda I_s + DV_p) - (c\lambda)^{-1}g'V_p \end{bmatrix},$$

which is equation (18) in the text.

By Young's theorem, J is symmetric and therefore B is symmetric. From the first line of (A.6) we can see that λB is negative semi-definite: In the neoclassical case, V_p is null and the substitution matrix $S = \lambda B$. Then, since the J matrix is

348   M. B. McELROY AND M. J. HORNEY

just a matrix of second partials of a quasiconcave objective function the standard proof of the negative semidefiniteness of S holds. Therefore λB is negative semidefinite whether or not V_p is null.

Income effects. Finally, holding prices constant, partial differentiation of (8) and (9) with respect to I_m and I_f yields

$$(A.7) \qquad \begin{bmatrix} J & p \\ p' & 0 \end{bmatrix} \begin{bmatrix} X_I \\ -\lambda_I \end{bmatrix} = \begin{bmatrix} DV_I \\ \iota' \end{bmatrix}.$$

Premultiplying (A.7) by (A.2), yields the matrix of Nash income effects,

$$(A.8) \qquad \begin{bmatrix} X_I \\ -\lambda_I \end{bmatrix} = \begin{bmatrix} B & b \\ b' & -c^{-1} \end{bmatrix} \begin{bmatrix} DV_I \\ \iota' \end{bmatrix} = \begin{bmatrix} BDV_I + b\iota' \\ b'DV_I - c^{-1}\iota' \end{bmatrix},$$

which is equation (19) in the text.

REFERENCES

ASHENFELTER, O. AND J. HECKMAN, "The Estimation of Income and Substitution Effects in a Model of Family Labor Supply," *Econometrica*, 42 (January, 1974), 73–85.

BECKER, G. S., "A Theory of Marriage: Part I, *Journal of Political Economy*, 81 (July-August 1973), 813–846.

BROWN, M. AND M. MANSER, "Neoclassical and Bargaining Approaches to Household Decision-Making-with Application to the Household Labor Supply Decision," Discussion Paper, No. 401, State University of New York at Buffalo (March, 1977, revised January, 1978).

——— AND ———, "Estimation of the Demand for Marriage Based on a Bargaining Model," Discussion Paper, No. 419, State University of New York at Buffalo (October, 1977).

CLEMHOUT, S. AND H. Y. WAN, Jr., "Symmetric Marriage, Household Decision Making and Impact on Fertility," Working Paper, No. 152, Cornell University (September, 1977).

HECKMAN, J., "Shadow Prices, Market Wages, and Labor Supply," *Econometrica*, 42 (July, 1974), 679–694.

———, "Sample Selection Bias as a Specification Error," NBER Working Paper, No. 172 (1977).

HORNEY, M. J., *Household Decision Making: A Game Theoretic Approach,* Ph. D. Dissertation, Duke University (1977).

——— AND M. B. McELROY, "A Nash-Bargained Linear Expenditure System: The Demand for Leisure and Goods," Duke University (1980).

LUCE, R. D. AND H. RAIFFA, *Games and Decisions*, 2nd edition, (New York: Wiley, 1957).

MANSER, M. AND M. BROWN, "Marriage and Household Decision-Making: A Bargaining Analysis," Discussion Paper, No. 376, State University of New York at Buffalo (March, 1976, revised January, 1978).

——— AND ———, "Bargaining Analysis of Household Decisions," Discussion Paper, No. 423, State University of New York at Buffalo (November, 1977, revised March, 1978).

NASH, J. F., "Two-Person Cooperative Games," *Econometrica*, 21 (January, 1953), 128–140.

POLLAK, R. A., "Price Dependent Preferences," *American Economic Review*, 67 (March, 1977), 64–74.

SAMUELSON, P. A., "Social Indifference Curves," *Quarterly Journal of Economics*, 70 (February, 1956), 1–22.

NASH-BARGAINED HOUSEHOLD DECISIONS 349

SEN, A., "On Weights and Measures: Information Constraints in Social Welfare Analysis," *Econometrica* 45 (October, 1977), 1539–1572.

WALES, T. J. AND A. D. WOODLAND, "Estimation of Household Utility Functions and Labor Supply Response," *International Economic Review*, 17 (June, 1976), 397–410.

———— AND ————, "Estimation of the Allocation of Time for Work, Leisure, and Housework," *Econometrica*, 45 (January, 1977), 115–132.

[14]

Marriage and Divorce:
Informational Constraints and Private Contracting

By H. Elizabeth Peters*

Accompanying the striking rise in U.S. divorce rates during the last several decades have been changes in the laws regulating divorce. One of the more pervasive changes is the move towards "no-fault" divorce. Since 1970, more than half of the states have adopted a rule which basically allows divorce at the demand of either spouse.[1] The remaining states require either mutual agreement (explicitly or in practice) or—in the case of a contested divorce—a costly legal battle. The constraints imposed by the law and any shift in the law could have behavioral and distributional consequences. The rules might influence an individual's decisions about whether or not to divorce or to marry, and how much to invest in the marriage relationship. The law's impact on the nature of the marriage agreement might also affect the distribution of income within marriage and the terms of the divorce settlement.

This paper is an empirical study that utilizes a contract-theoretic framework to ex-amine the impact of both legal and informational constraints on several aspects of the marriage relationship: 1) the probability of divorce; 2) compensation at divorce (i.e., the terms of the divorce settlement); 3) the probability of entering marriage; and 4) incentives for investment in marriage-specific capital. Two models of contracting that differ most fundamentally in their assumptions about information are contrasted. The first assumes that *ex post* information about the value of each spouse's opportunities at divorce is symmetric. The model predicts that costless bargaining could redistribute the gains to marriage in such a way that divorce only occurs when the joint benefits exceed the joint costs. Thus the law would have no effect on the divorce rate. The compensation scheme would, however, vary with the law to achieve efficiency. This argument is a form of the Coase Theorem. A second model asserts that the existence of asymmetric information might lead to a fixed wage marriage contract. This model predicts that the divorce rate would be higher in states that allow unilateral divorce.

The empirical investigation is based on data from a special 1979 *Current Population Survey* that contains information on marital history and financial settlements at divorce. Evidence that divorce is no more likely to occur for women living in unilateral divorce states, but that divorce settlement payments are lower for those women, supports the symmetric information hypothesis.

I. Marriage Contracts

This section presents two models of marital contracting. For each model, empirical implications are derived that specify the effects of different divorce laws (one law allows either spouse to initiate divorce *unilaterally*, the other law requires *mutual consent* before

*Assistant Professor, Department of Economics, and Research Associate, Research Program on Population Processes, Institute of Behavioral Science, University of Colorado, Boulder, CO 80309. I thank Gary Becker, Charles Kahn, Edward Lazear, Dorothy Maddi, Robert Michael, Donald Parsons, Sherwin Rosen, Lawrence Summers, Donald Waldman, and Franklin Zimring for helpful comments and encouragement. The paper has also benefited from comments by Orley Ashenfelter, two anonymous referees, and seminar participants at the University of Chicago, and Yale, Columbia, Michigan State, and Ohio State universities. Research support from the Economics Research Center/NORC, the Earhart Foundation, and the U.S. Department of Labor, Employment and Training Administration is gratefully acknowledged. I remain solely responsible for the paper's content.

[1] By this date, almost every state has adopted some form of no-fault divorce. However, only some of these no-fault laws allow for unilateral divorce. The classification scheme that I utilize is discussed later in the paper. See Doris Freed and Henry Foster (1979) for more details concerning the laws.

divorce can occur) on the probability of marriage and divorce and on the structure of the compensation scheme in the marriage contract. The first model assumes that information about the value of opportunities that would exist should divorce occur is symmetric, that is, the husband and wife have the same information. This model predicts that marriage contracts will be efficient: divorce only occurs when the joint value of the marriage is less than the sum of the values of opportunities that face each spouse at divorce. Thus, the probability of divorce will be independent of the divorce law, but the compensation scheme will vary with the law to induce efficient separation decisions. These results are a form of the Coase Theorem.

There are several reasons why this model might fail. One reason refers to the problem of imperfect state verification. Each spouse may not be able to determine the value of opportunities at divorce that face the other spouse. Incentives then exist for each spouse to misrepresent the value of alternatives that he or she faces and engage in costly strategic bargaining. The second model illustrates one possible solution to this asymmetric information problem: a fixed marriage wage contract. The contrasting empirical implications of this kind of contract are presented later.

The symmetric information model might also fail because of the problem of moral hazard. It may be difficult to determine each spouse's inputs to the marriage and to pay each the full return on his or her investment. Thus there exist incentives to invest in less than the optimal amount of marriage-specific capital. These incentives can be affected by the different constraints imposed by the divorce law.

The general structure and notation common to these models of marriage contracts is outlined below. Marriage is viewed as a long-term match between two individuals that produces a valuable, though partially intangible, output. Examples of this output include children, love, security, companionship, money income from market work, and household goods from home production.[2]

Decisions about marriage and divorce are made as follows. Each individual who contemplates marriage has certain implicit expectations about the value of the marriage, the composition of the output, and the inputs required in the production of that output. That individual also has some idea about the probability of divorce, and the costs and consequences associated with the divorce. If the expected gains to marriage exceed the expected losses due to the possibility of future divorce, the marriage occurs. As the marriage continues over time, information about the value of alternatives, should divorce occur, becomes available. Examples of alternatives include the value of a potential new relationship (i.e., remarriage after divorce), and the value of market opportunities which might be different at divorce for women who were homemakers during marriage. Given this knowledge, the couple then decides whether to continue the marriage or to divorce.

To simplify the model, assume there are only two periods. At the beginning of the first period, the contract is negotiated. If it is acceptable to both, the couple marries and each spouse invests in the specified amount of marriage-specific capital. The information that is available at the time the contract is negotiated includes the present value to each individual of remaining single (S_w for the female and S_h for the male),[3] the joint probability *distribution* of possible divorce alternatives facing each spouse should marriage occur but later end in divorce ($g(A_w, A_h)$), and the joint value of marriage in each period (M_1 and M_2). At the beginning of the second period, the actual values of each spouse's opportunities outside the marriage are realized (A_w and A_h for the wife and husband, respectively), and a decision is made about whether to continue the marriage or to divorce. The expected joint value of the contract, R, can be expressed as the sum of the values of the possible outcomes in the two periods where each outcome is weighted by

---

[2] See Gary Becker (1974) for the development of this idea.

[3] In a more general model with more than two periods, the value of being single also includes the value of continuing to search for a marriage match.

the probability of its occurrence:

$$(1) \quad R = M_1 + b\big[M_2(1-p)$$
$$+ E(A_w + A_h|divorce)\cdot p\big],$$

where p is the probability of divorce, E is the expectation operator, and b is a discount factor. In this framework the stochastic variables are A_w, A_h, and p, where p is a function of A_w and A_h. The variables M_1 and M_2 are assumed to be fixed and known with certainty at the time the couple decides to marry. This last assumption implies that the inputs or marriage-specific capital investments of the husband and wife are fixed. Thus, the possibility of moral hazard is ignored in this specification. Later, the implications of relaxing this assumption are discussed. Because the true values of A_w and A_h are not revealed until period two, decisions about divorce are independent of M_1.[4] In the subsequent analysis of divorce rates and compensation, I ignore the first period and drop the discount factor and the subscript on M.

The inequality $R > S_w + S_h$ implies that there is a net gain to entering marriage, and some allocation of that gain is possible which would make both parties agree to marry. The *ex ante* division of the total product of the contract is determined in the marriage market. It will depend on such variables as the value to each of remaining single (i.e., the reservation wage), and the expected contribution (i.e., marginal product) and investment of each spouse in the marriage. The allocation of total compensation between a wage during marriage and compensation at divorce (possibly zero) depends on the probability of divorce, the distribution of alternatives available to each spouse at divorce, attitudes toward risk, and the legal constraints imposed on the contract.[5]

One assumption in the results derived below is that M, A_w, and A_h are perfectly divisible, that is, convertible into monetary units. Therefore the distribution to the husband and wife of the gains to marriage or divorce will fully exhaust those gains. This may not be an entirely plausible assumption in the analysis of marriage contracts because children are a major component of the gains to marriage, and they also play an important role in any divorce settlement.[6] One solution would be to posit a more general utility function that includes as separate arguments money and nonmonetary goods such as children. Incorporation of these issues in the present analysis, however, is beyond the scope of this paper.

In the following, I use this basic contract framework, which integrates the various aspects of the marriage relationship, to derive empirically testable implications for the two models.

A. Symmetric Information

1. Divorce and Compensation. Efficiency requires that resources be used in their highest valued activity. Because a husband and wife work together to produce the marriage output, joint wealth is maximized by a rule which compares the sum of each spouse's alternatives at divorce with the joint product of the marriage. Thus divorce in period two is efficient when

$$(2) \qquad M < A_w + A_h.$$

Figure 1 represents the joint distribution of all potential A_w and A_h.[7] The wife's opportunities at divorce get better the further from the origin is the realized value of A_w, whereas

---

[4] This result is crucially dependent on the assumption of no moral hazard problems.

[5] The nature of this contractual relationship is partly determined from the body of family law. Husbands have certain legal obligations towards their wives and vice versa. Lenore Weitzman (1980) examines the marriage contract implied by these laws. In this paper I focus on

the particular aspect of the law that specifies which party can initiate divorce.

[6] Robert Mnookin and Lewis Kornhauser (1979) speculate about the possibility of a tradeoff between financial settlements at divorce and child custody arrangements.

[7] I have modified a figure which is presented in Masanori Hashimoto and Ben Yu (1980) and Robert Hall and Edward Lazear (1984) to fit this analysis of marriage.

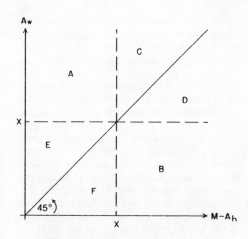

FIGURE 1. DISTRIBUTION OF ALTERNATIVES AT DIVORCE RELATIVE TO THE VALUE OF MARRIAGE

TABLE 1 — INCOME UNDER DIFFERENT LEGAL REGIMES

Period Two Income	Mutual	Unilateral
Wife's		
If Married	X	$A_w + \alpha(M - (A_w + A_h))$
If Divorced	$A_w + C_w = X + \alpha(A_w + A_h - M)$	A_w
Husband's		
If Married	$M - X$	$A_h + (1 - \alpha)(M - (A_w + A_h))$
If Divorced	$A_h + C_h = (M - X) + \alpha(A_w + A_h - M)$	A_h

the husband has better divorce opportunities the closer $M - A_h$ is to the origin. Divorce is optimal anywhere to the left of the 45° line (areas A, C, and E) where $M - A_h < A_w$.

Now assume that the outcome of the contracting process specifies an initial marriage wage, X, for the wife and the residual, $M - X$ (which is fixed because by assumption M is fixed), for the husband. The wife then wants to divorce in period two when her realization of A_w is greater than X (areas A, C, and D). The husband wants to divorce when $A_h > M - X$ or $M - A_h < X$ (areas A, E, and F). The two agree to divorce in area A but disagree about divorce elsewhere (they both, however, want to stay married in area B). If the contract can be costlessly renegotiated in period two, *and* if each spouse has the same information about A_w and A_h, a compensation scheme exists such that only joint wealth-maximizing separations will occur.[8] The nature of the scheme depends on the rules under which divorce can be obtained.

If the law requires mutual consent, some kind of severance pay or compensation at divorce will be necessary to convince the wife

[8] See Becker et al. (1977).

(area E.) or the husband (area C) to agree to a divorce. A divorce compensation formula like the following would induce efficient divorce:

$$(3) \quad C_w = (X - A_w) + \alpha(A_w + A_h - M).$$

$$(4) \quad C_h = -C_w = ((M - X) - A_h) + (1 - \alpha)(A_w + A_h - M),$$

where C_w is what the wife receives (or pays out) and C_h is what the husband pays out (or receives). Then income at divorce is $A_w + C_w$ for the wife and $A_h + C_h$ for the husband (see Table 1). The first term in the compensation formulas is required to make each spouse indifferent between divorce and continuing the marriage. The second term represents the net gain to divorce, and α, the wife's share of that gain, is determined in the *ex ante* negotiations of the contract. Only when the second term is greater than zero will both husband and wife agree to divorce. Thus, efficiency and the requirement of mutual consent imposed by the law will jointly be satisfied.

If the law allows unilateral divorce, then either spouse can walk out of the marriage *without compensating the other*. In essence, both must agree for the marriage to continue. A *marriage* compensation scheme like the following would induce the wife (area D) or the husband (area F) to remain married. The wife receives

$$(5) \quad X = A_w + \alpha(M - (A_w + A_h))$$

and the husband receives the residual

$$(6) \quad M - X = A_h + (1-\alpha)(M-(A_w + A_h)).$$

Analogous to the above discussion, the first term is the payment that makes each spouse indifferent between continuing the marriage and divorcing. The second term is the net gain from the marriage. If that gain is negative, then, as efficiency dictates, at least one spouse will decide to become divorced.

Under both laws divorce occurs when $A_w + A_h > M$. Thus the constraints imposed by the legal rules about the right to divorce do not affect the divorce rate. By contrast, the actual wage payments or income streams in the married and divorced states do depend on the divorce rule.[9] The compensation (in marriage or divorce) fluctuates so as to maximize the *ex post* value of the contract.

The relationship between the variance in divorce compensation payments under different legal regimes is straightforward. In this simple model, a mutual divorce law requires that C_w is paid before divorce can occur, and the variance of C_w is

$$(7) \quad \mathrm{Var}(C_w) = (\alpha-1)^2\mathrm{Var}(A_w|Z)$$

$$+ \alpha^2\mathrm{Var}(A_h|Z) + \alpha(\alpha-1)\mathrm{Cov}(A_w, A_h|Z),$$

where Z is the condition that $A_w + A_h > M$. In unilateral divorce states, no divorce compensation payments are required: $C_w = 0$ and $\mathrm{Var}(C_w) = 0$.

In a more complicated model there may be other reasons for divorce compensation payments to exist in unilateral as well as in mutual states. One reason is compensation for observable marriage-specific investments.

A second reason relates to the division of tangible marital capital that is left after the marriage dissolves. As long as divorce compensation payments due to these other reasons are uncorrelated both with the unilateral/mutual divorce law and with A_w and A_h, then it still is true that the variance in the total divorce compensation payments under a mutual law is greater than the variance in those payments under a unilateral law.

The relationship between the variance in income at divorce under different legal regimes is more complex. Under a mutual divorce law regime, the first term of C_w guarantees that the wife will be no worse off at divorce than she was in marriage (see Table 1). This contract thus provides insurance against the possibility of receiving low values of A_w at divorce. The second term of C_w allocates the gains to divorce. Under a unilateral divorce law regime, income is just A_w.

Because of the insurance component of C_w in mutual divorce states, it seems intuitive that incomes at divorce should be less variable under mutual law than under unilateral law. Because of the variation caused by the second term of C_w, however, this intuition only holds under certain conditions. The variance in income at divorce in mutual law states is defined as follows:

$$(8) \quad \mathrm{Var}(A_w + C_w|Z) = \alpha^2\left[\mathrm{Var}(A_w|Z)\right.$$

$$\left. + \mathrm{Var}(A_h|Z) + 2\mathrm{Cov}(A_w, A_h|Z)\right].$$

Assume that the gains to divorce are split equally (i.e., $\alpha = 1/2$) and that A_w and A_h have a bivariate normal distribution with $\rho = 0$.[10] Then $\mathrm{Var}(A_w + C_w|Z) < \mathrm{Var}(A_w|Z)$

---

[9] If the law allows unilateral separation but also will enforce a compensation scheme where there is a separation penalty such as specified in equations (3) and (4), then individuals will behave as if mutual agreement is required, and the results for unilateral and mutual states will not be empirically differentiable. Thus it is important to examine the effect of the law on both the divorce rate and the compensation at divorce.

[10] Zero correlation between A_w and A_h is a convenient and not unreasonable assumption. The common idea in the marriage literature of positive assortative mating leads to a correlation between the traits that were observable when the couple married. There is no compelling reason, however, to assume that the random values of A_w and A_h would be correlated, because these values were not known when the couple married.

if $\text{Var}(A_h) < 3\,\text{Var}(A_w)$.[11,12] The intuition that the variance in divorce income under mutual law is less than the variance in divorce income under unilateral law holds as long as the relative variances of A_w and A_h are not too different.

2. *Marriage.* As seen in equation (1), the likelihood of entering marriage depends on the *ex ante* value of the contract, which, in turn, is a function of the probability of divorce and the value of alternatives at divorce. In the symmetric information model, the probability of divorce and $E(A_w + A_h|\text{divorce})$ do not depend on the divorce law. Therefore the initial constraints to the contract imposed by these different divorce laws will not affect the likelihood of entering marriage. The possibility of risk aversion, however, could induce differences in the propensity to marry because the variance in the value of the contract is a function of the divorce rule.

B. *Asymmetric Information*

This section focuses on contracting problems caused by bilateral asymmetric information. If neither spouse knows the value of the divorce opportunity facing the other, a rule relating compensation to these outside opportunities may not be viable. Each spouse would have an incentive to misrepresent his own opportunities or to participate in excess

search for alternatives to the current marriage in order to gain a larger share of the marital wealth.[13] Behavior to support these claims can be costly and unproductive.

Because these incentives can be anticipated at the time the contract is made, an alternative to the *ex post* compensation scheme may be devised. One solution is a fixed wage contract which prohibits *ex post* bargaining.[14,15] The cost of this solution is the possibility of inefficient separations.[16]

1. *Divorce and Compensation.* Implications from this model for the divorce rate can be obtained from Figure 1. If the wife's marriage wage is fixed at X and bargaining is successfully prevented, a mutual divorce law will allow divorce only in area A where both agree. Since divorce is efficient in areas $A + C + E$, the mutual rule allows *fewer* divorces than is optimal. A unilateral rule leads to divorce in areas $A + C + E + F + D$ where either spouse wants to divorce. This rule produces *more* divorces than is optimal. Thus the fixed wage model would predict a higher divorce rate in unilateral states than in mu-

---

[11] Given the assumptions in the text, the relationship between the conditional and unconditional variance can be calculated as follows:

$$\alpha^2 \left[\text{Var}(A_w + A_h | Z) \right] = \alpha^2 \left[\text{Var}(A_w) + \text{Var}(A_h) \right] \cdot Q_1$$

and $\text{Var}(A_w|Z) = \text{Var}(A_w) \cdot Q_2$, where $Q_1 = 1 - q(a)(q(a) - a)$; $Q_2 = 1 - \rho_T^2 q(a)(q(a) - a)$; $a = M \cdot (\text{Var}(A_w + A_h))^{-.5}$; $q(a)$ is the inverse Mills ratio evaluated at a; and ρ_T is the correlation between A_w and the truncated variable $A_w + A_h$ (see Jagdish Patel and Campbell Read, 1982, p. 320). It is obvious that $Q_1 < Q_2$. Therefore the sufficient condition in the text will be a lower bound on the variance of A_h relative to A_w.

[12] Given the same assumptions, a similar condition holds for the variance in husband's income at divorce: $\text{Var}(A_h + C_h | Z) < \text{Var}(A_h | Z)$ if $\text{Var}(A_w) < 3\text{Var}(A_h)$.

[13] Dale Mortensen (1978) discusses a related problem of excess job search in response to an offer matching scheme when search effort cannot be verified.

[14] Becker (1964) discusses the implications of a fixed wage contract for the incidence of quits and layoffs when the worker-firm match involves specific capital. More recently, Hashimoto and Yu and Hall and Lazear explore various motivations for fixed wage contracts.

[15] An important consideration in determining the feasability of fixed wage contracts is whether the no *ex post* bargaining stipulation can be enforced. As long as there is a positive benefit to strategic *ex post* bargaining, an incentive for that behavior exists. The multiperiod aspect of the marriage relationship may, however, reduce incentives for strategic bargaining. The mistrust and ill-feelings engendered by strategic bargaining can be detrimental to a relationship based on trust and intimacy. The greater the reduction in the value of marriage in future periods, the less bargaining that will occur.

[16] The fixed wage contract is not the only solution that addresses the problems caused by asymmetric information. More complicated game theoretic schemes have been proposed which can lead to optimal separations (see Michael Riordan, 1984). These schemes do not appear to be reflected in real world marriage contracts, however. Therefore these first-best contracts will be ignored in the subsequent analysis.

tual states. Because the amount of efficient divorce is independent of X (i.e., it occurs when $M < A_w + A_h$), this result will hold for any value of X.[17]

The determination of X is based on *ex ante* information,[18] and is calculated to minimize the potential inefficiencies—areas C and E where divorce should occur but does not under the mutual rule, or areas D and F where marriage should continue but does not under the unilateral rule. In this model the marriage wage plays the same role as the optimal sharing of investment costs in Gary Becker's (1964) model of specific human capital investment. The sharing rule (i.e., the compensation scheme) depends in part on the distribution of each party's alternatives to the match (for example, the relative variances and covariances) and on the separation rule imposed by the law (see Masanori Hashimoto and Ben Yu; Robert Hall and Edward Lazear).

2. Marriage. Joint incentives to marry depend on the expected value of the contract. The existence of *ex ante* rents to marriage is important because the divorce rate differs under the two laws. If $E(M) > E(A_w + A_h)$, the expected value of the marriage contract will be higher under the law that minimizes the number of inefficient divorces. Thus, more couples may be expected to marry in a mutual law state.

C. *Moral Hazard*

The previous analysis dealt primarily with the issue of the availability of information about *alternatives*. When the effort or other

inputs of each party can affect the value of the relationship, however, information about the *inputs* is also necessary to avoid the problems associated with moral hazard. In the labor market literature, it has sometimes been assumed that it is easier to verify the value of alternatives (for example, an alternative wage offer) than to observe the amount of effort on the job. This same kind of problem can exist in marital relationships as well.[19]

A woman who invests in marriage by working in the household may face a lower market wage in the future. Because she only receives a fraction of the value of her investment in marriage, but bears the full cost of the lower wages at divorce, she has an incentive to self-insure against these potentially negative consequences by working more in the labor market during marriage. Marital fertility is another kind of behavior that can alter both the value of marriage and the value of alternatives at divorce. Divorced women with children have a higher cost of entering the labor market and also are less likely to remarry. Women who foresee the possibility of divorce might decide to have fewer children than they would otherwise.

To the extent that this behavior can be anticipated or observed, the structure of the initial contract will be altered to provide incentives which mitigate the problem. Constraints imposed by the law that limit the contracting responses reduce the value of the relationship and increase the likelihood of this kind of strategic behavior.

Divorce settlement payments are one way to compensate the wife for her previous marital investments. However, when the law allows either spouse to dissolve the marriage unilaterally, it may be more difficult to enforce this kind of payment. The unilateral divorce rule might therefore lead to an increase in the divorce rate as the value of marriage falls relative to the value of alternatives at divorce. Conversely, if the potential

---

[17] The value of X will influence the magnitude of the difference in divorce rates between the two legal regimes because it influences the relative amount of efficient vs. inefficient decisions. But the direction of the difference is independent of X.

[18] It is possible to have partially contingent payments that are based on jointly observable *ex post* information such as age and education of each spouse, number of children, etc.. Thus the contract could vary among observationally distinct couples. In this case, A_w and A_h might be viewed as the residual divorce alternatives obtained after controlling for observable characteristics.

[19] See Elisabeth Landes (1978) and William Johnson and Jonathan Skinner (1986) for more formal treatments of moral hazard problems in marital relationships.

TABLE 2 — VARIABLE DEFINITIONS

Ever Divorced	= 1 if the woman became divorced during 1975–78.	SMSA	= 1 if the woman lived in a standard metropolitan statistical area in 1979.
Remarried	= 1 if a divorced woman was remarried by April 1979.		
Time Since Divorce:		In Labor Force 1978	= 1 if the woman had positive earnings in 1978.
< 1 year	= 1 if divorce occurred less than 1 year before April 1979.	Husband's Earnings	= husband's earnings in 1978 in 1000's of dollars.
< 2 years	= 1 if divorce occurred 1 to 2 years before April 1979.	Earnings	= woman's earnings in 1978 in 1000's of dollars.
< 3 years	= 1 if divorce occurred 2 to 3 years before April 1979.	Family Income	= total family income in 1978 in 1000's of dollars.
< 4 years	= 1 if divorce occurred 3 to 4 years before April 1979.	Unilateral	= 1 if the woman lived in a unilateral state at the time of divorce (or remarriage).
Age	= age of woman in 1979.		
Age at Divorce	= age at divorce for women who became divorced.	State Divorce Rate 1970	= number of divorces per 100 women at risk of divorce in 1970 in the state in which the woman lives.
Education	= number of years of education completed as of 1979.		
White	= 1 if woman is white.	State Catholic 1970	= percent Catholic in 1970 in the state in which the woman lives.
Kids under 18	= number of children younger than 18 in the household in 1979; for ever-divorced women this number only includes children from the former marriage.	Alimony Received	= amount of alimony received in 1978.
		Child Support Received	= amount of child support received in 1978.
Kids Squared	= Kids under 18 × Kids under 18.	Support	= Alimony Received + Child Support Received
Kids under 6	= number of children younger than 6 in the household in 1979; the number is not calculated for remarried women because it is difficult to separate children from the former marriage.	Settlement Value	= value of the property settlement received.
		Proportion Eligible	= proportion of 1978 a woman was eligible to receive payments; if divorced or remarried during 1978, Proportion Eligible is the time after the divorce or before remarriage; otherwise Proportion Eligible = 1.
Kids 6–18	= number of children ages 6 to 18 in the household; the same restriction applies as for kids under 6.		

for moral hazard can be anticipated, only those marriages with expected returns that are high enough to offset these costs will occur. The impact of the unilateral rule would then be seen as a fall in the rate of marriage rather than as an increase in the rate of divorce.

D. *Summary of Theoretical Results*

The most clearly distinguishing implication of the two contract models concerns the divorce rate. If information about alternatives for each spouse at divorce is symmetric, a contingent compensation scheme can be devised such that divorce only occurs when it is *ex post* efficient. Thus the divorce rate will be the same regardless of the constraints imposed by law. The compensation scheme, however, would vary with the law to enable this efficient outcome. If a problem of asymmetric information leads to the development of fixed wage contracts, the divorce rate would be higher when unilateral dissolution is allowed.

The impact of the law on other aspects of the marital relationship—for example, the propensity to marry and the compensation at divorce—is less easy to predict. Assumptions about the distribution of divorce opportunities for the husband and wife, and the sharing ratio, α, of the rents from marriage and divorce, as well as the extent of asymmetric information about the *ex post* divorce alternatives are crucial. The issue of whether either spouse can influence the value of the

TABLE 3—MEANS FROM 1979 *Current Population Survey* DATA

Variable	All		Ever Divorced		Remarried	
	Unilateral	Mutual	Unilateral	Mutual	Unilateral	Mutual
Ever Divorced (percent)	6.2[a]	5.3[a]	100.	100.	100.	100.
Remarried (percent)	–	–	31.6	33.2	100.	100.
Age	43.3[a]	44.0[a]	35.5	36.1	33.9	34.2
Education	12.9[a]	12.8[a]	13.1	12.9	13.0	12.7
White (percent)	91.7[a]	89.3[a]	90.3	89.3	92.9	94.1
Kids under 18	1.0[a]	1.0[a]	1.0	0.9	0.8[a]	0.6[a]
SMSA (percent)	50.9[a]	58.8[a]	54.7	57.8	53.6	51.2
In Labor Force 1978 (percent)	56.6[a]	54.0[a]	82.4[a]	77.5[a]	75.0[b]	67.1[b]
Earnings	3,626.	3,594.	6,407.	5,974.	5,004.	4,427.
Family Income	20,731.	20,815.	14,242.	14,015.	22,670.	21,213.
Alimony Received[c]	–	–	200.[a]	505.[a]	–	–
Child Support Received[c]	–	–	1,070.[a]	1,472.[a]	–	–
Settlement Value[c]	–	–	6,752.	6,605.	–	–
Sample Size	11,500	9,714	709	512	224	170

Note: Those excluded from the analysis are women who had moved from another state since 1975 and either were married or became divorced in 1975–78. A second group of women who were excluded from the analysis includes never married women, widows, and those women who became divorced before 1975.

[a] Mutual and unilateral means are not equal at the 5 percent significance level.

[b] Mutual and unilateral means are not equal at the 10 percent significance level.

[c] Only 7.2 percent of the sample of ever-divorced women received any alimony in 1978. For those with positive amounts, the mean alimony payment was $3456. In 1978, 62.6 percent of eligible women received child support and 58.1 percent received a property settlement at the time of divorce. The mean values for those with positive amounts were $2145 and $11,522 for child support and property settlements, respectively.

marriage as a means of gaining an advantage at divorce may also be important.

II. Empirical Analysis

The data consist of observations from the March/April 1979 *Current Population Survey* that includes demographic variables such as state of residence, age, current marital status, number of children, and economic variables such as income, labor force behavior, and education. Additional information on marital history, type and amount of child and spousal support payments, and the value of any property settlement is available for those women who have ever been divorced.

To study the division of family resources at divorce and the probability of remarriage (used to investigate the implications for marriage in general), I use the sample of 1,221 women who became divorced between 1975 and 1978, and who indicated that they had lived in the same state in 1975 as in 1979. These requirements are so that I can make some inference about the state in which a

woman became divorced.[20] For estimates of the divorce rate, this ever-divorced sample is combined with the sample of currently married, never-divorced women who lived in the same state in 1975 as in 1979. Table 2 gives the variable definitions and Table 3 presents the means for the variables.

Information on state divorce laws during 1975–79 is also available. States are grouped according to whether they fit in the following categories (Table 4 lists the states in each):

1) Pure unilateral—either spouse can dissolve the match by saying there are "irreconcilable differences," or that the marriage is "irretrievably broken." This is commonly

---

[20] The possibility exists that a woman may obtain a divorce in a state other than the one in which she resides. The problem of "migratory divorce" is briefly examined in Hugh Carter and Paul Glick (1976). Their estimates of out-of-state divorces range from one-in-ten to one-in-twenty in the period before the easing of divorce laws in the early 1970's. Presumably migratory divorce would be much less frequent today.

TABLE 4—CLASSIFICATION OF STATES BY 1978 DIVORCE LAW

Unilateral[a]

Arizona	Michigan	New Hampshire	Alaska
California	Montana	New Mexico	Georgia
Colorado	Nebraska	Indiana	Oklahoma
Florida	Oregon	Connecticut	Kansas
Iowa	Washington	North Dakota	Hawaii
Kentucky	Wyoming	Maine	Idaho
Minnesota	Nevada	Rhode Island	Texas
Alabama	Massachusetts		

Mutual[b]

Illinois	Ohio	West Virginia	Missouri
Pennsylvania	Tennessee	New Jersey	Virginia
South Dakota	Utah	Louisiana	Arkansas
North Carolina	Mississippi	Wisconsin	Maryland
New York	South Carolina	Vermont	Washington, D.C.
Delaware			

Source: Freed and Foster (1979).

[a] Includes states with only irretrievable breakdown and incompatability grounds for divorce and states where these grounds have been added to traditional fault grounds.

[b] Includes states with only fault grounds for divorce, states that explicitly stipulate mutual agreement, and states where divorce is not allowed until the couple has been separated for a specified period of time.

called no-fault. (Included in this group are states which allow unilateral no-fault divorce but have still retained the traditional fault grounds. In practice, however, in these states the unilateral rule dominates.)

2) Mutual divorce with binding arbitration should no agreement be reached. What usually happens in "fault only" states is that if the couple agrees to divorce there is collusion. One spouse claims the other is guilty of one of the traditional grounds (usually cruelty) and no defense is made by the other spouse. If they cannot agree and one spouse sues for divorce, the court decides whether or not to grant the divorce. A second type of mutual divorce occurs in states which use no traditional fault grounds but require that the couple reach an agreement about the division of marital resources before a divorce is granted. If no agreement is reached, the court may stipulate the division and grant the divorce.

3) Unilateral divorce is possible but requires a large cost. States which fit this category are those, for example, which allow divorce on the grounds of unilateral separation for periods ranging from one to seven years. If these costs are large enough it will be cheaper to agree than to divorce unilaterally. Thus in the empirical analysis I have included these states under the mutual divorce category.

A. _Divorce Rate_

The theory presented earlier predicted that if there were an effective constraint to the spouses' _ex post_ bargaining about the individual returns to marriage or the division of resources at divorce, the divorce rate would be higher in states that allowed unilateral divorce. Popular wisdom agreed with that prediction. Much of the opposition to the legal change from mutual to unilateral divorce was based on the belief that if either spouse could walk out of the marriage, divorce would be easier and thus more likely to occur. A second model predicted that costless bargaining could redistribute the gains to marriage or divorce in such a way that divorce only occurred when the joint benefits exceeded the joint cost. Thus the law would have no effect on the divorce rate. In this section I present evidence about the relationship between the law and the divorce rate.

TABLE 5—PROBABILITY OF DIVORCE AND REMARRIAGE

| | Divorce | | |
	(A)	(B)	Remarriage
Intercept	-3.44^b	-2.81^b	27.69^b
	(5.15)	(4.91)	(4.27)
Age^c	-0.26^b	-0.26^b	-1.23^b
	(403.95)	(405.05)	(65.04)
Education	-0.19^b	-0.19^b	0.23
	(8.57)	(8.95)	(0.13)
White	-0.38	-0.33	19.49^b
	(0.48)	(0.37)	(9.95)
Kids under 18	-1.53^b	-1.55^b	-7.49^b
	(20.80)	(21.33)	(5.16)
Kids Squared	0.07	0.07	0.70
	(0.54)	(0.56)	(0.48)
SMSA	0.61^a	0.56^a	-0.25
	(3.25)	(2.87)	(0.01)
South	1.05	1.81^b	22.50^b
	(1.67)	(12.47)	(19.72)
West	1.70^b	3.12^b	20.46^b
	(4.57)	(30.21)	(13.50)
North Central	1.41^b	1.91^b	15.87^b
	(5.32)	(13.86)	(9.90)
In Labor Force 1978	–	–	-17.96^b
			(21.65)
Time Since Divorce:			
<1 year	–	–	-41.65^b
			(38.08)
<2 years	–	–	-26.15^b
			(21.73)
<3 years	–	–	-16.35^b
			(9.13)
<4 years	–	–	-4.36
			(0.70)
State Divorce Rate 1970	0.96^b	–	
	(17.36)		
State Catholic 1970	-0.23	–	
	(0.01)		
Unilateral	-0.32	0.01	-9.77^b
	(0.70)	(0.00)	(8.29)
Sample Size	21,214	21,214	1,153
Percent	5.76	5.76	28.27

Note: The estimates reported are $\partial \text{Percent}/\partial X = \beta(\bar{P} \cdot (1 - \bar{P})) \cdot 100$ from the logit $P = 1/(1 + e^{-X\beta})$. *Chi*-square statistics are in parentheses.
^{a}Significantly different from zero at the 5 percent level.
^{b}Significantly different from zero at the 10 percent level.
^{c}In the remarriage regression this variable is age at divorce.

The dependent variable in these logit regressions is the probability of becoming divorced during 1975–78 given no previous divorces. Parameter estimates are reported in Table 5. As found in other studies (see, for example, Becker et al.), divorce is less likely to occur if a woman is older, more educated, has more children, and does not live in an urban area. The unilateral divorce rule is found to have no relationship to the probability that a woman becomes divorced.[21]

[21] To test whether this result is an artifact of the classification scheme, the same regression was run using a subsample of women living only in states with divorce

The state divorce rate in 1970 (a time period *before* the changes in divorce laws) is included as a proxy for an unobserved state-specific propensity to divorce. The coefficient is, as expected, positive and highly significant—the higher the 1970 state divorce rate, the more likely is a woman living in that state to become divorced during 1975–78. My earlier analysis (1983) found that states with higher 1970 divorce rates were more likely later to adopt a unilateral divorce rule. Thus leaving out the 1970 divorce rate would result in an upward bias on the estimated effect of unilateral divorce (compare regressions A and B in Table 5). The legal variable is, however, insignificant under either specification.

The *CPS* sample that I use is not representative of the population as a whole because it only includes women who lived in the same state in 1975 and 1979. Both theoretical and empirical research have found that geographic mobility is positively correlated with divorce (see Bill Fenelon, 1971; Jacob Mincer, 1978). Therefore it is important to determine whether this sample selection criterion seriously affects the conclusions drawn from Table 5 that the probability of divorce is independent of the law regulating divorce.

If migration is a *consequence* of divorce (for example, divorced individuals may tend to move to avoid bad memories and associations), and if, for some exogenous reason, interstate migration is higher for unilateral states, then omitting migrants from the analysis would cause a downward bias on the coefficient on unilateral divorce. This could explain why the results show that the divorce rate is not higher in unilateral states. Alternatively, if migration is a factor that *precipitates* divorce (for example, conflicting location choices for the husband and wife leading to marital breakdown), then omitting migrants from the sample would not alter the

conclusion that, *ceteris paribus*, the probability of divorce is independent of the law regulating divorce.

Results from aggregate state analyses can be used to resolve this issue. Several univariate and multivariate time-series studies have examined changes in state aggregate divorce rates before and after the changes in the law that occurred during the 1970's (Gerald Wright and Dorothy Stetson, 1978; Harvey Sepler, 1981; Robert Schoen et al., 1975; Becker, 1981; and myself, 1983). For the most part, these studies found that the trend in the divorce rates was unaffected by the change in the law. A study of several Scandanavian countries that had implemented what were essentially unilateral divorce rules shows similar results (Annemette Sorensen, 1980). These studies, in conjunction with the results reported in Table 5, provide evidence in support of the symmetric information model.

B. *Compensation at Divorce*

The empirical test of the effect of the law depends crucially on the assumption that the actual practice in states with mutual divorce laws differs from that in states with unilateral divorce laws. For example, if the law allows unilateral separation but also enforces a scheme where the injured party is compensated for unanticipated loss at divorce, then individuals would behave as if mutual agreement were required. In this case it would be the compensation scheme rather than the separation rule which influences behavior. Thus it is important to examine jointly the law on the books and the compensation scheme which is practiced. This subsection explores the effect of the law on the levels of the divorce settlement and on the variability of the settlement.

The divorce settlement can consist of three kinds of payments: 1) alimony; 2) child support; and 3) property settlement. Although in theory the purpose for each payment is different, in practice they should be fungible. The weight given to each, however, will vary according to the importance of such factors as the differential tax structure applied to each type of payment, the fact that alimony

---

laws that could be unambiguously classified as unilateral or mutual. In these regressions, the probability of divorce is not higher in unilateral divorce states, and there is some evidence that the rate may be slightly lower.

TABLE 6—*OLS* REGRESSIONS OF AMOUNT OF DIVORCE SETTLEMENT RECEIVED

	Alimony Received	Child Support Received	Support Received	Settlement Value
Intercept	−1,423.22[b]	−4,265.92[b]	−3,323.69[b]	−21,614.50[b]
	(4.26)	(4.59)	(5.83)	(7.66)
Age of Divorce	22.20[b]	55.38[b]	39.63[b]	248.34[b]
	(5.77)	(4.27)	(6.04)	(7.37)
Education	59.47[b]	115.95[b]	113.91[b]	1056.90[b]
	(3.43)	(2.46)	(3.85)	(6.96)
White	247.72[a]	710.41[b]	689.89[b]	4317.20[b]
	(1.75)	(2.13)	(2.85)	(3.48)
Kids under 18	23.16	971.30[b]	1085.10[b]	3883.78[b]
	(0.27)	(3.35)	(7.38)	(5.14)
Kids Squared	−1.80	−138.87[b]	−154.23[b]	−607.07[b]
	(0.08)	(2.34)	(3.86)	(2.96)
SMSA	97.86	73.64	141.66	1642.55[b]
	(1.15)	(0.36)	(0.98)	(2.21)
In Labor Force 1978	−205.81[a]	241.30	−15.00	1284.10
	(1.86)	(0.88)	(0.08)	(1.32)
Proportion Eligible	321.45[a]	1225.39[b]	689.88[b]	–
	(1.71)	(2.33)	(2.15)	
Time Since Divorce	−65.19	−204.84	−120.85	−930.96[b]
	(1.41)	(1.65)	(1.53)	(2.95)
Unilateral	−185.65[b]	−462.36[b]	−448.54[b]	−137.19
	(2.19)	(2.25)	(3.10)	(0.18)
R^2	.048	.078	.105	.110
Sample Size	1,221	636[c]	1,221	1,221

Note: *T*-statistics are shown in parentheses.

   [a] Significantly different from zero at the 5 percent level.

   [b] Significantly different from zero at the 10 percent level.

   [c] The regression is run on the sample of women with children who are eligible to receive child support.

and child support are usually periodic payments and the property settlement is lump sum, and the restriction that alimony ends at remarriage.

Table 6 presents the regression estimates. The regressions include several socioeconomic variables to control for the influence of the woman's observable characteristics on the divorce settlement. The estimates of these parameters are consistent with the expectation that compensation at divorce is positively related to the value of the marriage and to the amount of marriage-specific investment by the wife (see Landes for similar results concerning alimony).

Table 6 also shows that the amounts of alimony and child support received are significantly lower in unilateral states.[22,23] Evi-

dence that the divorce rate does not differ between the two regimes but that the compensation schemes do differ supports the symmetric information model—separations are efficient, but the constraints imposed by the law require different compensation schemes to achieve that efficiency.

---

make the argument that unilateral divorce was accompanied by other changes in marriage property law which tended to raise the property settlement and offset the lower levels of child support and alimony payments.

   [23] A few studies have examined changes in divorce settlement payments in a single state before and after the adoption of a unilateral divorce rule (Ruth Dixon and Weitzman, 1980; K. Seal, 1983; Charles Welch and Sharon Price-Bonham, 1983). In general, these studies are consistent with the cross-state results reported in this paper. No-fault (or unilateral divorce) is associated with lower amounts of alimony and child support payments (although the differences were not always significant in the Welch and Price-Bonham study). Two of the studies also showed significant changes in property settlements.

   [22] The amount of the property settlement seems to be unrelated to the unilateral/mutual law. Thus one cannot

TABLE 7—MEASURES OF THE DISPERSION OF THE DIVORCE SETTLEMENT AND FAMILY INCOME BY STATE LAW
(Shown in thousands of dollars)

		Variance	Coefficient of Variation[e]	Unexplained Variance[c]	Unexplained Coefficient of Variation[d,e]
Alimony Due	M[b]	6.28[a]	486.98	5.98[a]	475.43
	U	0.87	506.38	0.83	494.88
Alimony Received	M	4.11[a]	558.44	3.92[a]	545.39
	U	0.82	544.22	0.79	534.19
Child Support Due	M	14.60[a]	195.43	13.99[a]	191.29
	U	2.38	92.33	2.08	86.32
Child Support Received	M	13.54[a]	228.02	13.09[a]	224.21
	U	2.19	128.08	1.92	119.91
Support	M	12.42[a]	298.72	11.37[a]	285.87
	U	2.76	212.54	2.37	196.79
Settlement Value	M	204.14[a]	216.32	177.30[a]	201.59
	U	165.65	190.61	151.78	182.45
Family Income	M	124.45	77.53	114.70	73.95
	U	137.00	78.76	114.16	73.64

[a] Variances are not equal at 5 percent significance level.
[b] M = Mutual Divorce Law Sample; U = Unilateral Divorce Law Sample.
[c] Unexplained Variance is the sum of squared residuals divided by the degrees of freedom from a regression of the divorce settlement payment on individual characteristics.
[d] From previous column—see note c.
[e] Tests of significance are not calculated for coefficient of variation.

C. Variance in Payments

The variance in settlement payments in a symmetric information model is a function of the divorce law. Mutual divorce requires that these payments vary to compensate the spouse that is worse off at divorce. Compensating payments are not required under unilateral divorce. Thus the variance in settlement payments will be higher under a mutual divorce law if the information is symmetric.

To test for a difference in variances, a simple F-distribution is used on the ratio of the two variances. In all of the six measures of divorce payments in Table 7, the variance under mutual divorce is significantly greater than that under unilateral divorce. Because the distribution of observed characteristics may differ in states with the two laws, I also calculate F-tests on the residual variances from regressions of the settlement payments on the characteristics of divorced women. Again, variance is significantly higher in mutual divorce states. These tests are on absolute variances. The mean payment also

differs by the divorce law, therefore a measure of relative variance—the coefficient of variation—is calculated. Using this measure reduces the differential in variances, but in only one case is the direction of that inequality reversed.

If divorce payments under a mutual law compensate for a low draw of A_w, under certain distributional assumptions, they should reduce the variance in total income. However, an F-test shows no significant difference in the variance of total income between unilateral and mutual states. The results from the F-tests on equality of variances of divorce payments tend to support the symmetric information model, and the results about variances in income are not inconsistent with the model.

D. Remarriage

The CPS data do not allow a test of the relationship between unilateral divorce law and first marriages. Some information, however, exists about remarriage of those previously divorced. The kind of contract made at remarriage may differ in some significant ways from one made at first marriage (for example, the presence of children from a previous marriage may alter the nature of the agreement). I do not, however, expect the qualitative effect of the divorce rule on the contract to differ between marriage and remarriage. The effect may, in fact, be stronger because women who have already been divorced are more aware of any potential consequences of divorce laws.

The dependent variable in the last logit regression in Table 5 is the probability that a woman remarried by April 1979, given that she became divorced sometime between 1975 and 1978. The effects of the socioeconomic variables in this regression are consistent with other results (see Becker et al.). Older women and women with children are less likely to remarry. Whites are more likely to remarry. The date of divorce in this sample ranges from 1975 to 1978. The coefficients on the dummy variables indicating time since divorce are negative compared to the omitted category of divorce occurring more than 4 years before 1979. As expected, the probability of being remarried by April 1979 increases as time since divorce increases. Unilateral divorce lowers the probability of remarriage by a little more than nine percentage points.[24]

E. *Moral Hazard*

The largest source of income for divorced women who have not remarried is earnings. Staying in the home and caring for the children during marriage will lower future potential earnings. If this marriage-specific investment is not fully compensated for at divorce, there exists an incentive for married

---

[24] Because all individuals in this sample have not had the same amount of time in which to become remarried, the logit estimates of the probability of remarriage within a given time period will not be entirely correct. The use of hazard rate models might be more appropriate. However, the coefficient estimate on the variable of interest, the divorce law, is robust across logit specifications that both included and excluded the time since divorce control variables. Therefore, the limitations imposed by the specification in the paper are probably not too severe.

TABLE 8—LABOR FORCE AND FERTILITY BEHAVIOR OF NEVER-DIVORCED MARRIED WOMEN

	Labor Force Participation[c]	Children Less than 6[d,e]
Intercept	71.98[b]	1.91[b]
	(426.38)	(25.73)
Age	−1.92[b]	−0.04[b]
	(2,119.43)	(22.81)
Kids under 6	−30.84[b]	−
	(752.80)	
Kids 6–18	−8.80[b]	−
	(99.30)	
Kids Squared	1.42[b]	−
	(54.94)	
Education	3.46[b]	−0.01[b]
	(452.74)	(3.23)
White	−12.52[b]	−0.11[b]
	(71.21)	(3.64)
Husband's Earnings	−0.39[b]	0.01[b]
(in thousands)	(98.21)	(5.52)
SMSA	−0.31	−0.03[b]
	(0.14)	(1.98)
South	−0.08	−0.02
	(0.00)	(0.80)
West	−0.71	0.06[b]
	(0.28)	(2.19)
North Central	2.54[b]	0.04[a]
	(4.98)	(1.74)
Unilateral	2.22[b]	−0.02
	(6.34)	(1.23)
Percent	53.64	−
R^2		0.06
Sample Size	19,501	8,413

[a] Significantly different from zero at the 5 percent level.

[b] Significantly different from zero at the 10 percent level.

[c] The estimates reported are ∂ Percent/$\partial X = \beta(\bar{P} \cdot (1 - \bar{P})) \cdot 100$ from the logit $P = 1/(1 + e^{-X\beta})$. Chi-square statistics are in parentheses.

[d] T-statistics for the *OLS* regression are in parentheses.

[e] The sample is restricted to women younger than 40.

women to reduce their time spent in the home and increase their more general market capital by entering the labor force.

In Table 8, I examine the effect of unilateral divorce laws on the labor force participation of married women. The independent variables have the usual effect on labor force participation. Older women, white women, and women with young children are less likely to participate. The marginal effect of a child declines with the number of children. Husband's earnings are also negatively related to the likelihood of participation. Living in a unilateral state, however, increases the probability of participation by two percentage points. This may be indicative of the incentive for married women to enter the labor force to self-insure against becoming divorced without compensation.[25]

The analysis of fertility tells a somewhat different story. Table 8 reports a regression of the number of children younger than age 6 living in the households of never divorced, married women. The effect of the independent socioeconomic variables is consistent with other research. Fertility is lower for older, more educated, and white women, and is positively related to the earnings of the husband. The coefficient on the legal variable is negative, but not significantly different than zero.

Thus it seems that differences in law are associated with differences in labor force behavior, but not with differences in fertility behavior. There are several possible explanations for these results. First, the measure of fertility, the number of children younger than 6, represents fertility decisions made over a period in the past. It would take some time for changes that occurred in the legal environment during the mid-1970's to have their full impact on that measure. The labor force variable, however, measures a single year's participation decision. A response in labor force behavior to a change in the law would therefore be observed sooner.

A second explanation may involve the relationship between children and labor market opportunities and the amount of the divorce settlement for women. Better labor market opportunities raise the income for divorced women but do not consistently lower the divorce settlement (see Table 6). Children may increase the cost of being divorced; however, this is partly offset by the positive effect that children have on the divorce settlement. Thus a change in labor force behavior may be a more effective method for a woman to self-insure against the negative consequences at divorce.

It may seem surprising that this moral hazard problem does not lead to higher divorce rates in unilateral states. If, however, the problems can be anticipated, individuals may respond, instead, by marrying less or by searching longer for a better match. This may explain the results from the remarriage regressions.[26]

III. Conclusions

This paper presents empirical evidence about the impact of two types of divorce laws on various aspects of the marriage contract. One law specifies that either spouse can initiate divorce (unilateral), the other requires that both agree to divorce (mutual). Two models of contracting are proposed that differ in their assumptions about the information set available to each spouse. One model assumes that *ex post* information about the value of opportunities outside the marriage is symmetric. The other model assumes that information is asymmetric. The clearest distinction between the two models concerns predictions about divorce rates and divorce settlement payments. The empirical results show that the divorce rates are not significantly different in unilateral and mutual consent states, but that divorce settlement payments are lower in unilateral states. This evidence supports the hypothesis of the symmetric information model that divorce

[25]A second specification of this regression included the 1970 state married female labor force participation rate as an exogenous variable. While this variable was highly correlated with the dependent variable, its inclusion had a trivial impact on the coefficient for unilateral divorce. The participation rate for married women living in unilateral states in 1979 remained almost 2 percentage points higher. A similar kind of variable, 1970 state marital fertility rate was included in the fertility equation. Again, this specification did not affect the coefficient on unilateral divorce.

[26]Johnson and Skinner develop a model where women who anticipate a higher probability of divorce will invest more in the labor market to insure against lower earnings at divorce. The evidence presented in this paper suggests that it is the nature of the compensation scheme that is important. If a scheme could be enforced that insured women against the negative consequences of divorce, incentives for providing less than optimal investment in marriage would be reduced.

occurs when it is efficient, but the compensation scheme depends on the divorce law. Findings of lower remarriage rates and lower variance in compensation at divorce for women living in unilateral states are also consistent with this hypothesis.

Despite the recent emphasis in the contract literature on the constraints of asymmetric information (see the survey by Oliver Hart, 1983), there are several reasons why the above results may not seem unreasonable for the case of marriage. First, the nature of the interaction in marriage makes it more difficult to conceal information than would be true of more impersonal relationships. Second, there may be ties such as the presence of children that continue after the relationship has terminated. These ties may create incentives to reveal information by inducing each party to consider the joint, rather than the individual, gain to any action.[27]

[27] These results concerning marriage contracts could be relevant to certain labor market relationships with similar characteristics. These include jobs where there is a close working relationship between employer and employee, jobs with a high degree of firm-specific capital, and jobs which induce the individual to consider the profit of the company even after job separation through compensation such as stock options. Employees in a small firm and specialized executives and managers are some examples of the kinds of relationships to which the analysis and conclusions presented in this paper might be applicable.

REFERENCES

Becker, Gary S., *Human Capital*, NBER, New York: Columbia University Press, 1964.

———, "A Theory of Marriage: Part II," *Journal of Political Economy*, March/April 1974, *82*, 11–26.

———, *A Treatise on the Family*, Cambridge: Harvard University Press, 1981.

———, Landes, Elisabeth M. and Michael, Robert T., "An Economic Analysis of Marital Instability," *Journal of Political Economy*, December 1977, *85*, 1141–88.

Carter, Hugh and Glick, Paul C., *Marriage and Divorce: A Social and Economic Study*, Cambridge: Harvard University Press, 1976.

Dixon, Ruth B. and Weitzman, Lenore J., "Evaluating the Impact of No-Fault Divorce in California," *Family Relations*, No. 3, 1980, *29*, 297–307.

Fenelon, Bill, "State Variations in United States Divorce Rates," *Journal of Marriage and the Family*, May 1971, *33*, 321–27.

Freed, Doris Jonas and Foster, Henry H., Jr., "Divorce in the 50 States: An Overview as of 1978," *Family Law Quarterly*, Spring 1979, *13*, 105–28.

Hall, Robert E. and Lazear, Edward P., "The Excess Sensitivity of Layoffs and Quits to Demand," *Journal of Labor Economics*, April 1984, *2*, 233–57.

Hart, Oliver D., "Optimal Labor Contracts Under Asymmetric Information: An Introduction," *Review of Economic Studies*, January 1983, *50*, 3–35.

Hashimoto, Masanori and Yu, Ben T., "Specific Capital, Employment Contracts and Wage Rigidity," *Bell Journal of Economics*, Autumn 1980, *11*, 536–49.

Johnson, William R. and Skinner, Jonathan, "Labor Supply and Marital Separation," *American Economic Review*, June 1986, *76*, 455–69.

Landes, Elisabeth M., "Economics of Alimony," *Journal of Legal Studies*, January 1978, *7*, 35–63.

Mincer, Jacob, "Family Migration Decisions," *Journal of Political Economy*, October 1978, *86*, 749–73.

Mnookin, Robert H. and Kornhauser, Lewis, "Bargaining in the Shadow of the Law: The Case of Divorce" *Yale Law Journal*, April 1979, *88*, 950–97.

Mortensen, Dale, "Specific Capital and Labor Turnover," *Bell Journal of Economics*, Autumn 1978, *9*, 572–86.

Patel, Jagdish K. and Read, Campbell B., *Handbook of the Normal Distribution*, New York: Marcel Dekker, 1982.

Peters, H. Elizabeth, "The Impact of Regulation of Marriage, Divorce and Property Settlements in a Private Contracting Framework," unpublished doctoral dissertation, University of Chicago, December

1983.

Riordan, Michael H., "Uncertainty, Asymmetric Information and Bilateral Contracts," *Review of Economic Studies*, January 1984, *51*, 83–93.

Schoen, Robert, Greenblatt, Harry N. and Mielke, Robert B. "California's Experience with Non-adversary Divorce," *Demography*, May 1975, *12*, 223–44.

Seal, K., "A Decade of No-fault Divorce: What It Has Meant Financially for Women in California," *Family Advocate*, Spring 1983, *1*, 10–15.

Sepler, Harvey J., "Measuring the Effects of No-Fault Divorce Laws Across Fifty States: Quantifying a Zeitgeist," *Family Law Quarterly*, Spring 1981, *15*, 65–102.

Sorensen, Annemette, "Flight from Unhappiness: Causes and Implications of the Recent Upturn in Divorce, The Case of Denmark," unpublished doctoral dissertation, University of Wisconsin-Madison, 1980.

Weitzman, Lenore J., *The Marriage Contract: Couples, Lovers, and the Law*, New York: Free Press, 1980.

Welch, Charles E. III and Price-Bonham, Sharon, "A Decade of No-fault Divorce Revisited: California, Georgia, and Washington," *Journal of Marriage and the Family*, May 1983, *45*, 411–18.

Wright, Gerald C., Jr. and Stetson, Dorothy M., "The Impact of No-Fault Divorce Law Reform on Divorce in the American States," *Journal of Marriage and the Family*, August 1978, *40*, 575–80.

U.S. Bureau of the Census, BLS, *Current Population Survey*, Match File, Washington, March/April 1979.

[15]

Testing the Neoclassical Model of Family Labor Supply and Fertility

T. Paul Schultz

ABSTRACT

The McElroy-Horney Nash-bargaining model of family demand behavior relaxes the restriction that nonearned income of husband and wife has the identical effect on family labor supply and commodity demands. This restriction of the neoclassical model of family behavior is tested for the determination of husband and wife labor supply and fertility based on the 1981 Socioeconomic Survey of Thailand. The neoclassical restriction is rejected for female labor supply and fertility. Another unexplored limitation of family demand studies, due to the sample self selection of intact marriages, is empirically treated through alternative estimation strategies. In this case, a more sharply focused theory of marital behavior is needed to identify family demand models.

I. Introduction

For several decades, the neoclassical model of individual consumer choice has guided empirical analysis of behavior within the family. In one form or another, the family is central in virtually all socie-

The author is a professor of economics at Yale University. A draft of this paper was presented at meetings of the Population Association of America in Baltimore, MD, on March 30, 1989 and at workshops at Yale, Brown and VPI. The research underlying this paper has been partly supported by the Women in Development Division, Population and Human Resource Division of The World Bank. The author appreciates in particular the comments of J. Berhman, B. Herz, S. Khandkar, J. Strauss, D. Thomas, and the computational assistance of P. McGuire. Permission to study these Thai surveys was generously granted by Dr. Duangchai Poomchusri of the Thailand National Statistical Office.

ties, coordinating not only consumption and production, but, equally important, reproduction and child rearing. This neoclassical framework helps to explain the increase in female labor supply to the market and the decrease in fertility in terms of the increase in women's market wage opportunities or the opportunity cost of women's time in nonmarket production (Layard and Mincer 1985). Conversely, at least in poorer agricultural societies where unskilled child labor remains a valuable family resource, the neoclassical framework provides an interpretation for why child wage rates and adult male wage rates are both positively associated with fertility and negatively related to the time women allocate to market production (Rosenzweig and Evenson 1977). To forecast how wages for men, women, and children affect fertility and the allocation of a population's time to taxable forms of market production requires a model that encompasses production and consumption behavior of family members. This neoclassical model of family labor supply and fertility has thus become a common tool for evaluating many public finance issues involving welfare policies and labor markets.

But because the functions performed by the family are varied and in flux in many industrially advanced and low-income countries, the neoclassical framework that is often formulated in terms of the nuclear conjugal family may not always prove suitable. Cross-cultural comparisons of family behavior, including fertility, investment in children, and time allocation, span many functions of the family that encompass different degrees of coordination along varied lines of kinship and responsibility. Flexible models of family decision-making are thus needed that can discriminate between alternative definitions of the family, some of which will be more extensive than the nuclear family or coresidential household. A variety of resource pooling arrangments may also coexist and they need not be coincident across different family functions, such as production, consumption, investments in child health, schooling, and migration (e.g., Pollak 1985, Lundberg 1988, Rosenzweig and Stark 1989, Schultz 1989).

This paper reports empirical evidence drawn from a survey of Thailand. In distinction to the neoclassical model of the family that implies families act according to a common set of preferences and thus have no reason not to pool the resource of their individual members, the Thai evidence suggests that family members exercise a self-interest in family resource allocations. These findings are not, therefore, consistent with the standard neoclassical model of integrated family utility maximization that has guided much recent research on family behavior. The Nash-bargained model of family decisionmaking (McElroy and Horney 1981) is an alternative framework to guide research on family and individual behavior that can accommodate these empirical results. Although it embodies a specific bargaining rule associated with cooperative game-theoretic conventions, it can also be interpreted as a generalization of the neoclassical family demand model. It directs particular attention to the resources the individual would control, *if* the marriage had not formed in the past, or *if* it were to dissolve in the future. These "partible" resources are assumed to strengthen the partner's bargaining power by increasing her or his opportunity cost of being married and thus to shift outward their "threat point." The natural counterpart to partible family resources in the neoclassical demand model is nonearned income.[1]

The distribution of earned income in the family is a choice variable, and thus it is not legitimately treated as an exogenous determinant of household behavior or demands. Not only is the choice of labor supply a determinant of current market earnings of family members, but the shadow value of each member's time (or wage if a market worker) can also affect the composition of household demands for market goods and how they are combined to produce final consumption commodities in the neoclassical household production framework (Becker 1965). For example, if more educated (or higher wage) women are observed to invest more in child health inputs and produce healthier children, it cannot be concluded that more educated women have stronger preferences for healthy children than do less educated women. The more educated (higher wage) women could have a comparative advantage in producing child health, and only because they can produce child health at lower cost do they demand more health inputs and produce a higher level of child health.

The challenge to the neoclassical model of household demand arises if *nonearned income* of different family members is observed to affect differently the household's allocation of resources. If nonearned income (or ownership of the underlying physical asset) influences family demand behavior differently depending on who in the family controls the income (or owns the asset), then the preferences for that demand must differ

---

1. In principle, the measurement of nonearned income is to capture an exogenous difference across persons in their budget constraint that does not also induce a change in money or time prices of various types of consumption or behavior. In practice, nonearned income (rents, dividends, interest, and capital gains) could arise from inheritances that are similar to schooling, in that they are largely financed by parents and family, and can be viewed as exogenous at the start of adult life. But nonearned income also represents returns on a person's lifecycle accumulation of savings, and hence captures in part the person's behavior. It then becomes, for some purposes, an endogenous choice variable. Hence, it is desirable for survey questionnaires to pursue the sources of current nonearned income, current assets, date of receipts of bequest that led to these current assets, and whether they came from the husband's or wife's side of the family. This analysis disaggregates nonearned income to treat separately property and transfer payments (see Table A-1) that probably includes pensions to those who are retired. Exclusion of persons over age 54 attempts to minimize this source of simultaneous equation bias.

across individuals and such families must not completely pool nonearned income. This test of the neoclassical model of the family is qualified by two further working assumptions: differential individual sources of nonearned income must be indistinguishable in terms of what they can purchase in the market and produce in the household, and these sources of nonearned income must be exogenous or not affected by other household choices.

This approach to testing the neoclassical model of the family should be more robust to misspecification of functional forms than is the alternative that tests the equality of symmetric income-compensated cross-price effects. In the case of the nuclear family, the practice has been to test for the equality of cross-compensated wage effects on the labor supplies of husband and wife (Heckman 1971, Ashenfelter and Heckman 1974, Kniesner 1976, Killingsworth 1983). The effect on husband's labor supply of an income compensated change in the wife's wage tends to be less negative than the effect on wife's labor supply of a compensated change in the husband's wage. The testing of such symmetry restrictions becomes more complicated, of course, if the income effects of husband- and wife-specific nonearned income differ.

This paper first reviews the standard individual and family models of economic and demographic behavior and the bargaining models derived from the two-person cooperative game theory of Nash (1950, 1953). It should be noted that this bargaining approach does *not* prescribe why one family member prefers a certain allocative outcome whereas another family member prefers another. It does allow, however, for individual preferences to differ and for it to influence observed family behavior. Some of the empirical behavioral regularities examined below can be interpreted by appeal to intuition.

Many aspects of household economic and demographic behavior are currently studied to inform public policy and guide resource allocations. Forecasts of household behavior may be improved by conditioning that behavior on individually disaggregated household resources (as implied by the bargaining model) or by the inclusion of the economic resources of "relatives" in other households (that are omitted in regular household-based surveys). In this manner, the bargaining approach to family decisionmaking could be compared to the neoclassical framework over time as a forecasting model (e.g., Heckman and Walker 1989).

II. Models of Marriage and Family Behavior

If both partners to a union derive some part of the net gains from marriage, in addition to the opportunity costs given up by each from foregoing alternative arrangements, the union has at least an economic basis for continuation (Becker 1974). Market forces or personal endowments of family members might affect the division of family output between partners (Becker 1981, p. 42). The allocation of consumption among members in a family is, however, rarely studied, probably because it is hard to measure the consumption of particular family members. Moreover, neoclassical demand models of the family do not formally prescribe how distributional patterns accommodate these market forces and personal endowments.

The neoclassical model of the family assumes that the family behaves as if it were trying to allocate the time of its members and other endowments to satisfy a common set of "family" preferences (Becker 1965, 1981). This process involves pooling resources and agreeing on the form of the family's preferences. The simplest way this might occur is if couples share the same preferences. More realistic is the assumption that a dominant family decision-maker allocates gains from marriage to reward the other spouse with more than she or he expects to receive as a single person or in an alternative union. Incentives are also needed to encourage the nondominant members of the marriage to allocate their time along with other family resources to accomplish the production solution chosen by the dominant member (Becker 1981). Although more plausible, the second set of assumptions still does not imply any testable predictions about intrafamily allocations of resources.

If the family demand model is modified to accommodate the distinct preferences of family members, these conflicts of interest must be resolved by a specified bargaining mechanism. Because many game theoretic models of this form do not imply a unique equilibrium, they are rarely tested with empirical evidence (Harsanyi 1977, Harsanyi and Selten 1987). However, the cooperative Nash-bargained framework, as stated by McElroy and Horney (1981), nests the neoclassical family demand system within it as a special case. Statistical tests can be implemented, therefore, to determine whether data on observable family behavior satisfy the added restrictions implied by the neoclassical model of the family (e.g., Jones 1986, Carlin 1990).

These tests are simple and intuitive. As stated in the introduction, they imply that exogenous nonearned income of the husband and wife may influence family consumption differently in a bargaining model, whereas within the neoclassical model of the family, these spouse-specific sources of nonearned income must exert the same effects on family allocative behavior. If this empirical test rejects the neoclassical family demand model, more complex tests of the demand system can be implemented (McElroy and Horney 1981, Horney and McElroy 1988), but they may be sensitive to the choice of functional form as in the conventional models of demand (Deaton and Muellbauer 1980).

Other models of bargaining may be developed which are less restrictive than the cooperative Nash-bargained solution. They may permit partners to know different amounts of information, choose among a wider range of Pareto allocations, and engage in strategic planning (Chiappori 1988). However, the Nash-bargained allocative solution can also be reached through other, more complex, negotiating procedures. For example, uncertainty and risk can be introduced by allowing partners to maximize their expected utility based on the subjective probability that their offer of a "distribution of marital gains" will be accepted, or alternatively, that they will receive their initial endowment as a single person. Under quite general conditions, a couple engaging in this sequential form of bargaining over offers of how to distribute marital gains will eventually arrive at the Nash-bargained solution, if one exists (Harsanyi and Selten 1987). Even this simplest form of game-theoretic model of the family adds flexibility to the neoclassical framework by dealing more realistically with the distinct interests of family members and their potential retention of control over economic resources in marriage.

Consider, for example, the individual model of consumer choice and labor supply. The individual maximizes utility in a single period by purchase of X market goods and production at home of Z commodities,

(1) $U_i = U(X_i, Z_i)$

subject to a full income budget constraint and technical opportunities to produce Z. Market prices, P, and individual wages, W_i, and nonearned income, V_i, then determine individual demand for X and Z. One form of Z could be called leisure, L_i, which is the mirror image of labor supply, H_i.

A linear approximation for the labor supply function for individuals can be written:

(2) $H_i = a_o + a_1 W_i + a_2 P_i + a_3 V_i + e_i$

where e is a random disturbance due to stochastic variation and also undoubtedly includes errors in measurement and functional form, and the a's are parameters to be estimated.

This approach is adapted to analyze labor supply behavior of wives (Mincer 1962, Kosters 1966, Smith 1980) and then generalized to all family members (Heckman 1971):

(3) $H_i = b_o + b_i W_i + b_2 W_j + b_3 P + b_4 \bar{V}_i + u_i \quad i, j = 1, 2$

where $i \neq j$ and only husband and wife couples are analyzed who both earn a wage (Ashenfelter and Heckman 1974). Leisure of each working family member has been added as an argument to the unified family utility function, but family nonearned income is aggregated into $\bar{V} = V_i + V_j$.

Although nonmarket time is more than leisure, since some of it may be used to produce Z for the benefit of other family members, it is common to assume that the hours of labor supplied to the labor force decreases with an increase in family nonearned income. Nonearned income is assumed to be unaffected by past or current time allocation choices or household demands in general. Nonmarket time is thus assumed to be a "normal good," just as leisure is expected to be. In sum, this neoclassical approach implies that nonearned income has the identical effect on household demands and labor supply regardless of the source of the nonearned income.

In contrast, in the Nash-bargained model (Manser and Brown 1979, 1980, McElroy and Horney 1981) it is assumed that partners cooperatively maximize W, a product of the differences in each individual's utility from belonging to the family, U_i^f, and the individual's reservation utility sacrificed outside of the family or an alternative union, U_i^a:

$$(4) \quad W = [U_i^f(X, Z) - U_i^a(P, W_i, V_i)] \cdot [U_j^f(X, Z) - U_j^a(P, W_j, V_j)].$$

The utility in the alternative state represents a "threat point" that limits consumption allocations within marriage to those which benefit, and hence are acceptable to, both spouses. Increases in nonearned income of the husband or of the wife are expected to increase the "threat point" of that spouse and thereby increase that spouse's bargaining power. This could potentially change the distribution of consumption in the family.

Consequently, nonearned income is divided into those elements brought to the marriage or accumulated during the marriage through the individual's activities, the receipt of bequests or transfers, and by means of personal connections. A wife might reduce her market labor supply by a specific number of hours per week if she had inherited wealth or brought to her marriage a dowry that earned a given flow of nonearned income. Her labor supply response might be systematically different, plausibly less, if the same nonearned income accrued from her husband's inherited property. Conversely, the payment of a bride price in many areas of Sub-Saharan Africa by the groom to the bride's parents may be associated with the bride increasing her supply of time to the labor force. The implicit assumption that a dowry is controlled by the bride after marriage or that a brideprice adds to her financial indebtedness may not accurately describe how these transfers at the time of marriage are viewed by the couple and their families, or how they cement the union or subjugate a partner.

However, nonearned income can come from many sources and its effect on labor supply or consumption patterns could differ. Unexpected bequests or gifts that increase the property of the individual should relax the budget constraint but not alter the prices facing the individual or be biased toward a particular pattern of consumption or behavior. Alternatively, property income can be accumulated by the savings of an individual out of past earnings. In this case, property income may be related to prior labor supply behavior. If preferences for work and savings are persistent over time for individuals, current property income could become positively associated with labor supply behavior, because property income is endogenous or determined in part by the family.

Another source of nonearned income is private and public transfer. These transfers from outside the coresidential family may be viewed as consumption-smoothing, and may involve obligations to reciprocate in other time periods. Other items of nonearned income may appear to be more similar to a transfer than a return from property, such as insurance payments, scholarships, and grants. All of these sources of nonearned income may perform a variety of functions in a poor society where credit markets are imperfect, or transaction costs are substantial, or weather-induced variability in agricultural incomes are important. These varied forms of "transfer" nonearned income could respond to shocks in labor supply caused by unemployment, illness, disability, or even unwanted pregnancy and thus also be endogenous to family consumption behavior.

Between the two types of nonearned income, "property" income is more likely to be exogenous for younger persons, and if endogenous, to be positively correlated with labor supply. "Transfers," on the other hand, may be increased by depressed labor supply or unemployment, bad health, or family support problems. If transfer and property nonearned income exerted the same effects on family time allocation and consumption behavior, the case would be strengthened for treating them as an aggregate. If the behavioral effects of transfer and property nonearned income are identical, regardless of whether they are received by male and female members of the family, the pooling of family resources assumed in the neoclassical model of family decisionmaking would be confirmed.

III. Data and Empirical Model Specification

The analysis is based on the Socio Economic Survey of Thailand for 1980-81, a national stratified probability sample of households. The survey collects information on household expenditures, labor force activities, and income sources, and is used by the National Statistics Office to adjust periodically the weights for price indices. Income is reported by type for all adults, with about 20 percent of males and 16 percent of females over age 14 reporting some nonearned income in the last month (see Appendix A). The survey provides a sample of 8,816 women and 7,986 men between the ages of 25 and 54. These age restrictions are designed to exclude most persons not working because they are investing in schooling or are retired.

The estimation strategy involves several steps. Alternative specifications are reported to assess the sensitivity of the findings. First, market wage rates are estimated for men and women, correcting for the selective sample of wage earners (Heckman 1979). Second, the response of labor supply behavior to wife and husband transfer and property nonearned income is estimated, to test the equality restriction on the impacts of spouse-specific nonearned income implied by the neoclassical model of family labor supply (Horney and McElroy 1988). Third, fertility is analyzed to test another dimension of the neoclassical model of the family. Finally, marriage is introduced as a further sample selection criterion and added as another interrelated decision process that might respond to sex-specific amounts of nonearned income. The inclusion of husband nonearned income and wage rate opportunities in the female labor supply and fertility equations requires that either the presence of the husband and their endowments are taken as exogenous as is common in the empirical literature, or these husband endowment variables are treated as jointly determined and endogenous. Adopting the latter specification, the sample is restricted to those women with husbands, and a further Heckman-type sample selection correction regressor is added to the family labor supply and fertility models.

IV. Labor Supply Tests of Family Decisionmaking

Hourly wage rate functions are estimated for men and women separately, correcting for the selective sample of wage earners. Although an unusually large fraction of women in Thailand participates in the labor force (83 percent of those age 25 to 54), the fraction of women in wage employment is much lower, 28 percent. Virtually all men in these age groups are in the labor force (98 percent), whereas 57 percent work for wages (see Appendix B). The probit sample selection equation for the wage employment status includes all of the variables in the semilogarithmic wage function: years of schooling at three levels, a quadratic in post-schooling experience, and four regional strata variables that may capture regional differences in the cost of living, or interregional costs of migration, or disequilibrium rents. The wage earner status probit equation also includes the husband- and wife-specific property and transfer nonearned income and the number of hectares of irrigated or dry farm land owned by the family. These latter identifying variables are assumed to raise the shadow value of a person's time in nonmarket and self-employment activities and thereby reduce the probability that that person will be a wage earner.[2] The wage equations and the wage status probit equations are jointly estimated by maximum likelihood methods for women and men and are shown in Appendixes C and D in columns 2 and 3.

In Tables 1 and 2 labor supply equations are reported for women and men in what has become called a generalized Tobit model (Heckman 1976). The probit equation for participation in the labor force last week, and the linear equation for hours worked per week among participants are estimated jointly by maximum likelihood methods. In columns (1) and (2) no correction is attempted for the selective nature of the sample of women with husbands present in Table 1, or men with wives present in Table 2. A likelihood ratio test is first performed to assess if coefficients on the transfer and property nonearned income are equal, though possibly different for nonearned income owned by husbands and wives. The null hypothesis of equality cannot be rejected at the 5 percent level of confidence, with the Chi-squared statistics for women's labor supply being 2.04, with 4 degrees of freedom, and the analogous test statistic for men's labor supply of 1.60. However, the null hypothesis of equality on the coefficients on the male and female nonearned income can be rejected at the 1 percent level of confidence for women's labor supply, where the Chi-squared statistic is 7.17, with 2 degrees of freedom. For men's labor supply, the Chi-square statistic remains insignificant at 1.66. The neoclassical model of family labor supply is thus rejected for women. The significant difference found between the spouse-specific nonearned income effects on women's labor supply behavior is interpreted as due to a shift in the "threat point" within the bargaining model of family decisionmaking (McElroy and Horney 1981).

Furthermore, the pattern of coefficients is intuitively suggestive. The individual's own nonearned income has a larger effect reducing his or her labor supply than an equal amount of nonearned income controlled by one's spouse. This pattern is clearest in the case of Thai women, where the own nonearned income effect on participation is six times as large as that of their spouse's nonearned income. The preponderant sign of all of the labor supply effects of transfer and property nonearned income is negative, as anticipated.

Future research is planned to disaggregate family nonearned income by its ownership in order to explain the allocation of labor supply by

2. For Thai women a double sample selection decision rule may be justified, by which one selection equation determines labor force participation and a second selection equation determines wage earner status. This double selection specification of the wage function is reported in Schultz (1989) for women, but here the analysis of wages provides for only a single source of sample selection bias (i.e., wage earner status) and treats men and women in a parallel specification.

family members among alternative types of jobs, such as wage employment, self-employment, and family unpaid work. In many parts of the world women engage in separate jobs from their husbands. This may occur to increase women's control over family resources and thereby influence to a greater extent family consumption patterns. This tendency is particularly notable in Sub-Saharan Africa and Southeast Asia, although even in these regions, women still work primarily as unpaid family workers. In parts of Africa, husband and wife often cooperate in the joint production of some crops, while other crops or parts of the production process—such as marketing—are entirely the responsibility of one person. The neoclassical model of the family leads to the expectation that the wife allocates her time between the joint crops and her own crops to equalize the value of her marginal product across all activities. The bargaining model, however, would suggest that she would work more than expected on the basis of the neoclassical model on her own fields. Jones (1986) confirmed these predictions of the bargaining model with survey data collected from North Cameroon. Allocative incentives within these Cameroon families, therefore, do not appear to allocate labor to maximize family income, but seek other objectives that involve the competing interests of family members.[3]

To evaluate the partial effects of husband and wife nonearned income on household time allocation and expenditure patterns, the wage rates of both partners should be held constant. It is often suggested that increases in women's productive endowments increase expenditures on children's nutrition, health, and education (e.g., Senauer, Garcia, and Jacinto 1988). Unfortunately, the Thai Socio Economic Survey does not describe sufficiently nutrition, health, and educational investments allocated to children, to test these implications of the bargaining approach. One interesting household "demand" that can be studied in the survey is fertility.

V. Fertility and Investment in Children

The pattern of consumer demands may be especially sensitive to variation in market wage rates available to men and women in cases where the good demanded requires a disproportionate amount of production time from either the husband or the wife. The care of children in many cultures occupies much of their mother's time and this describes

---

3. In principle there might be a superior Pareto-efficient allocation of husband and wife labor that would yield a larger output for both members of the family. But in practice, there are costs in monitoring labor inputs over scattered plots and transaction costs in exchange of inputs and outputs that might be required to provide both persons with the incentives needed to achieve Pareto efficiency. These transaction costs might absorb the output gains.

Table 1
Jointly Estimated Participation and Hours of Work and Marriage of Women Age 25–54 in Thailand, 1981[a]

Dependent Variable: Joint Maximum Likelihood:	Participate (Probit)	Hours per Week (OLS)	Husband Present (Probit)	Participate (OLS)	Husband and Participant (Probit)	Hours per Week (OLS)	Sample Means All Women[b]
	(1)	(2)	(3)	(4)	(5)	(6)	(7)
Explanatory Variables							
Market opportunity wage							
Women's wage[c]	.619	-10.3	2.76	.196	.953	-7.16	1.45
	(10.6)	(8.63)	(4.92)	(9.23)	(1.66)	(7.36)	(1.24)
Women's wage squared[c]	—	—	.0252	—	.153	—	—
			(.67)		(4.15)		
Husband's wage[c]	-.404	-1.07	—	-.131	—	-3.57	.812
	(11.2)	(8.63)		(9.36)		(4.72)	(.728)
Husband present	.483	.748	—	—	—	—	.699
	(4.89)	(.54)					(4.59)
Unearned income: (baht/month)							
Women's transfer ($\times 10^{-4}$)	-.170	.137	-.663	-.0241	-.592	.964	.163
	(15.9)	(.31)	(26.5)	(.92)	(20.5)	(.82)	(.954)
Women's transfer squared ($\times 10^{-9}$)	—	—	.251	—	.0225	—	—
			(13.8)		(10.2)		
Women's property ($\times 10^{-4}$)	-.263	-1.98	-.534	-.0343	-.510	-.294	.0249
	(3.99)	(1.62)	(4.98)	(1.85)	(4.24)	(.08)	(.367)
Women's property squared ($\times 10^{-9}$)	—	—	.463	—	.0202	—	—
			(3.41)		(.68)		

Table 1 (continued)

Dependent Variable: Joint Maximum Likelihood:	Participate (Probit)	Hours per Week (OLS)	Husband Present (Probit)	Participate (OLS)	Husband and Participant (Probit)	Hours per Week (OLS)	Sample Means All Women[b]
Men's transfer ($\times 10^{-4}$)	-.0359 (1.76)	-.188 (.45)	—	-.0113 (2.49)	—	-.212 (.51)	.0863 (.614)
Men's property ($\times 10^{-4}$)	-.0246 (.62)	.451 (.74)	—	-.00689 (.83)	—	.459 (.74)	.0312 (.431)
Other adults ($\times 10^{-4}$)	-.0618 (3.45)	-.763 (2.65)	—	.00042 (.02)	—	.0002 (.05)	.136 (.799)
Age of woman	.130 (5.94)	1.40 (4.46)	.0282 (.57)	.0250 (2.21)	.157 (3.14)	.848 (1.60)	36.1 (8.13)
Age squared ($\times 10^{-2}$)	-.181 (6.33)	-.154 (3.67)	-.133 (2.70)	-.0333 (2.24)	-.246 (4.93)	-.798 (1.15)	13.7 (6.18)
Schooling years of woman:							
Primary			-.242 (4.85)	—	-.0926 (1.81)	—	
Secondary			-.475 (6.58)	—	-.224 (3.04)	—	
Higher			-.158 (5.01)	—	-.0821 (2.74)	—	
Hectares of land owned							
Irrigated land			-.0018 (.94)	—	.00455 (2.54)	—	
Dry land			-.00094 (.72)	—	.00386 (3.14)	—	

Residential area:							
Bangkok	−.655 (13.4)	.681 (.54)	−1.20 (5.86)	−.194 (12.7)	−.885 (4.23)	1.90 (1.95)	.267 (.442)
Municipal	−1.03 (12.7)	11.2 (6.06)	−3.07 (5.76)	−.271 (10.5)	−1.83 (3.37)	11.4 (7.11)	.364 (.481)
Sanitary district	−.544 (8.35)	4.54 (4.57)	−1.64 (5.40)	−.108 (5.85)	−.875 (2.83)	5.69 (5.93)	.154 (.361)
Northeast region	−.288 (5.84)	.409 (.60)	.166 (3.70)	.0958 (6.37)	.0184 (.42)	−1.74 (2.54)	.274 (.446)
Intercept	−.612 (1.54)	29.7 (5.04)	2.06 (1.72)	.664 (2.94)	1.50 (1.22)	45.2 (4.22)	
Sigma (σ_{11})	15.9 (128.9)			.352 (44.0)		16.1 (45.0)	
Rho (λ/σ_{12})	−.0481 (.17)			−.0849 (.50)		−.223 (1.30)	
Log likelihood	32,444.6			6,759.89		25,032.16	
Sample size	8,380	6,994	8,380	5,858	8,380	4,793	
Dependent variable means	.835	54.8	.699	.818	.572	55.0	
(Standard deviation)	(.371)	(16.5)	(.459)	(.386)	(.475)	(16.4)	

a. Absolute values of asymptotic *t* ratios are reported beneath coefficients in parentheses.
b. Means of variables in sample of all women aged 24 to 54 in the Thai 1981 SES.
c. Hourly wage rates imputed from wage equations estimated by a sample selection model and reported in Appendixes C and D.

Thailand as well. An increase in the market earnings potential of women relative to men may increase what parents perceive as being the cost to bear and rear children. This perception is likely to decrease fertility among better educated women who are offered higher wages in the labor force, even though at the same time the woman's earning potential increases the family's income opportunities. Increases in wages of women relative to men are generally associated with a reduction in fertility and with a reallocation of women's time from nonmarket to market work. Alternatively, increases in the labor productivity and wage rates of men can enhance the attractions of a large family and often are associated with higher levels of fertility, at least in low-income agricultural countries such as Thailand (Schultz 1981, Levy 1985).

The labor supply and fertility patterns derived from this conventional economic model of the family are based on the assumption that the nuclear family pools resources. Consequently, a married woman is assumed to rely in part on the earnings of her husband for the purchase of market goods consumed by her children and herself. Where wives engage in economic activities oriented toward market exchange as well as family consumption, such as in rural Sub-Saharan Africa, Thailand, and Malaysia, it is not clear whether the human and physical wealth of a husband are pooled with those of a wife to support all members of their nuclear family.

Table 3 reports ordinary least squares estimates of the number of living children under age 5 residing with their mother age 15 to 49 in Thailand, as recorded in the 1981 Socioeconomic Survey. Fertility has been declining at about 2 percent per year since the 1960s in Thailand. This measure of surviving fertility and the basis for this specification of the fertility equation are discussed more fully elsewhere (Schultz 1988). As already noted, the bargaining model of family decision-making does not inform us as to why the preferences of husband and wife might be different for children. However, the neoclassical model of the family implies that the distribution of ownership of nonearned income should be irrelevant to its impact on fertility. As seen from column (1) of Table 3 only nonearned income of the woman, and primarily transfer income, is associated with her recent fertility. Nonearned income owned by the woman is significantly related to higher fertility, and this effect is not evident for male nonearned income. Based on the joint F test of equality of the coefficients on nonearned income of the woman and man, the null hypothesis consistent with the neoclassical model of family demand is rejected at a confidence level of 1 percent.[4]

---

4. The nonnegative integer forms of the fertility variable led to parallel estimates of these equations using a Poisson specification of the model (see Schultz 1988). The likelihood ratio

Table 2

Jointly Estimated Participation and Hours of Work and Marriage of Men Age 25–54 in Thailand, 1981[a]

Dependent Variable: Joint Maximum Likelihood:	Participate Women[b] (Probit)	Hours per Week (OLS)	Wife Present (Probit)	Participate (OLS)	Wife and Participant (Probit)	Hours per Week (OLS)	Sample Means All
	(1)	(2)	(3)	(4)	(5)	(6)	(7)
Explanatory Variables							
Market opportunity wage							
Men's wage[c]	.0373	-9.69	11.9	-.00003	33.6	-9.82	1.47
	(.44)	(17.4)	(.93)	(.01)	(2.56)	(13.3)	(1.14)
Men's wage squared[c]	—	—	.0332	—	.0772	—	—
			(1.67)		(3.00)		
Wife's wage[c]	.179	-2.49	—	-.00240	—	1.45	.584
	(2.05)	(4.56)		(.78)		(1.79)	(.683)
Wife present	1.01	4.70	—	—	—	—	.805
	(7.81)	(6.09)					(.396)
Unearned income: (baht/month)							
Men's transfer ($\times 10^{-4}$)	-.115	-.242	.192	-.0148	.169	-.768	.114
	(4.07)	(.79)	(4.04)	(21.2)	(3.03)	(2.83)	(.718)
Men's transfer squared ($\times 10^{-9}$)	—	—	.0394	—	-.00887	—	—
			(1.60)		(1.76)		
Men's property ($\times 10^{-4}$)	-.0628	-.115	.189	-.00904	.368	-.972	.0383
	(1.96)	(.24)	(.76)	(15.5)	(1.89)	(1.51)	(.484)
Men's property squared ($\times 10^{-9}$)	—	—	-.0702	—	.0164	—	—
			(.32)		(1.03)		

Table 2 (continued)

Dependent Variable: Joint Maximum Likelihood:	Participate Women[b] (Probit)	Hours per Week (OLS)	Wife Present (Probit)	Participate (OLS)	Wife and Participant (Probit)	Hours per Week (OLS)	Sample Means All
Women's transfer	−.0181	.748	—	−.00162	—	.682	.0293
($\times 10^{-4}$)	(.09)	(1.61)		(.32)		(1.37)	(.283)
Women's property	−.0937	.276	—	−.00600	—	−.587	.0116
($\times 10^{-4}$)	(1.57)	(.13)		(8.72)		(1.85)	(.305)
Other adults	−.0563	.272	—	.00330	—	1.79	.111
($\times 10^{-4}$)	(2.45)	(1.25)		(2.37)		(2.52)	(.794)
Age of man	.155	1.09	.683	−.0185	.445	.152	38.3
	(3.84)	(4.52)	(1.86)	(9.23)	(1.17)	(.37)	(8.41)
Age squared ($\times 10^{-2}$)	−.207	−1.10	−.418	.0197	−.517	.00247	15.3
	(4.10)	(3.67)	(7.85)	(8.35)	(10.5)	(.51)	(6.57)
Schooling years of man							
Primary			1.42		−3.96		
			(.94)		(2.52)		
Secondary			1.52		−4.61		
			(.90)		(2.63)		
Higher			.0703		−.386		
			(.69)		(3.45)		
Hectares of land owned							
Irrigated land			.00374		−.0021		
			(1.09)		(.76)		
Dry land			.00307		−.0011158		
			(1.65)		(.98)		

Residential area:							
Bangkok	-.141 (1.61)	.0992 (.17)	5.24 (.92)	-.00331 (1.00)	-15.4 (2.61)	-.640 (.93)	.268 (.443)
Municipal	-.301 (2.12)	12.0 (12.6)	14.2 (.92)	.00401 (.76)	-41.8 (2.59)	11.9 (10.5)	.356 (.479)
Sanitary district	-.124 (.95)	5.58 (7.89)	8.30 (.92)	.00087 (.18)	-24.1 (2.58)	5.16 (6.15)	.153 (.360)
Northeast region	-.0237 (.23)	-2.54 (4.68)	-6.44 (.91)	-.00451 (1.11)	19.0 (2.58)	2.71 (4.06)	.273 (.446)
Intercept	-1.14 (1.46)	46.1 (9.81)	-7.46 (8.37)	1.41 (35.3)	7.70 (8.99)	79.5 (9.45)	
Sigma (σ_{11})		15.64 (109.)		.104 (.174)		16.9 (92.6)	
Rho (λ/σ_{12})		.460 (4.11)		-.996 (585.)		-.461 (7.76)	
Log likelihood		30,198.8	3,398.0	3,398.0		27,458.0	
Sample size	7,278	7,081	5,858	5,858	7,278	5,858	
Dependent variable means	.973	57.4	.805	.988	.805	57.7	
(Standard deviation)	(.162)	(16.7)	(.396)	(.108)	(.396)	(17.6)	

a. Absolute values of asymptotic t ratios are reported beneath coefficients in parentheses.

b. Means of variables in sample of all women aged 24 to 54 in the Thai 1981 SES.

c. Hourly wage rates imputed from wage equations estimated by a sample selection model and reported in Appendixes C and D.

Sociological studies of contemporary Thailand also suggest that if women had more wealth, they would want to have more children (Chamrathrithirong 1984). The common survey response is that women would desire more children, were it not for the rising cost of rearing and educating them. Mothers remain primarily responsible for childcare in Thai society, but they also appear to reap more of the economic benefits from their children in the form of old age support than do fathers (e.g., Knodel, Chamrathrithirong, and Debavalya 1987). These observations are consistent with the positive effect of women's nonearned income on the demand for children shown in Table 3, even though the effects of women's market wage opportunities (and indirectly their education) is nonetheless to reduce their fertility.

VI. Marriage and Sample Selection Bias

One way that people express their demands for consumption patterns is in the form of families they create. Both the neoclassical (Becker 1974, 1981, Freiden 1974) and the bargaining (Manser and Brown 1980, McElroy 1988) approach to family decisionmaking suggest that the productivity and endowments of men and women may influence the timing and frequency of marriage. Cross-sectional patterns and some time series evidence in industrially advanced countries suggest that if male and female productivity increase at the same rate, women's participation in the labor market increases, the onset of marriage is delayed, and lifetime fertility decreases (Layard and Mincer 1985). This cluster of developments are thought to be related to the reduced net gains from specialization by husband and wife in market and nonmarket production, respectively, within lifetime marriages (Becker 1981). Although it has not been subsequently replicated in other U.S. social experiments, women who were given independent financial support (i.e., nonearned income) for their children in the Seattle negative income tax experiment opted with increased frequency to separate from their husbands (U.S. Department of Health and Human Services 1983). In those societies where women's earnings approach more nearly those of men, there are fewer women married at each age, and there may be more female-headed households. This latter development may be partially attributed to the greater life expectancy of women than of men in the more industrially advanced

---

test of the equality restriction on the coefficients for the husband's and wife's nonearned income in this Poisson model is rejected by the Thai survey data in both years. Increases in the woman's nonearned income is associated with higher levels of fertility. In the cases of increases in the husband's nonearned income, fertility tends to be somewhat lower but this tendency is statistically significant only in the case of children under age 5.

618   The Journal of Human Resources

Table 3
Fertility of Women Aged 15–49 in Thailand, 1981[a]

Dependent Variable Estimation Method	Number of Own Coresidential Children Age 0–4 per Woman		Sample Means[b] All Women
	(OLS)	(ML)	
Explanatory Variables	(1)	(2)	(3)
Market opportunity wages (in baht/hours)			
Woman[c]	−.126	.606	.663
	(7.18)	(4.81)	(.773)
Man[c]	−.0491	−.0803	1.06
	(4.73)	(1.93)	(1.21)
Husband present	.608		.545
	(24.7)		(.498)
Husband (mills ratio)$^{-1}$		−1.74[d]	
		(6.09)	
Unearned income (baht/month $\times$ 10^{-4})			
Woman's transfer	.0449	.554	.118
	(6.56)	(5.09)	(.801)
Woman's property	.0201	.154	.0148
	(.84)	(.87)	(.225)
Man's transfer	.0058	.0145	.0556
	(.54)	(.75)	(.498)
Man's property	−.0154	.0053	.0152
	(.56)	(.12)	(.199)
Other adults	−.00843	−.0281	.201
	(1.46)	(1.11)	(.907)
Age of woman	.0685	−.495	30.4
	(13.6)	(5.33)	(9.32)
Age squared ($\times$ 10^{-2})	−.119	.664	10.1
	(15.7)	(4.94)	(6.02)
Residential area			
Bangkok	.0827	−.0663	.265
	(5.12)	(1.10)	(.441)
Municipal	.142	−.365	.357
	(5.43)	(3.02)	(.479)
Sanitary district	.0468	−.322	.152
	(2.37)	(3.89)	(.359)

Table 3 (*continued*)

Dependent Variable Estimation Method	Number of Own Coresidential Children Age 0–4 per Woman		Sample Means[b] All Women
	(OLS)	(ML)	
Northeast region	.0843	.0706	.277
	(6.25)	(1.53)	(.447)
Intercept	−.770	10.2	
	(10.2)	(6.19)	
R^2	.233	.155	
χ^2 (14)		1,077.0	
F (15)	253.9		
Sample size	11,708	6,386/11,708	
Dependent variable mean	.410	.665	
(Standard deviation)	(.663)	(.746)	

a. Dependent variables is the number of coresidential children age 0–4 of women age 15 to 49. Estimates in column (1) are ordinary least squares coefficients with the absolute value of the *t* ratios reported in parentheses beneath the coefficients. Poisson and Tobit regressions have also been estimated for the fertility relationship by maximum likelihood methods without altering any of the signs or the significance of the OLS coefficients reported here. The estimates in column (2) are two-step Heckman (1979) estimates, where the standard error are adjusted for consistency, but joint ML estimates did not converge to a optimum after 100 iterations.

b. Means of entire sample of 1981 SES used in estimation; standard deviations reported in parentheses.

c. Endogenous variables imputed from wage equations corrected for sample selection bias. See Appendixes C and D.

d. Husband present and sample selection criteria is determined by probit equation that includes only woman's characteristics plus quadratic forms in her predicted wage and own property and transfer nonearned income.

countries, but it could also reflect the choices made by women (and men) of marriage and household arrangements.[5]

Data have also been analyzed to estimate the determinants of age-at-

5. Aggregate data on the proportion of women married are analyzed to make this point, for example, in Chile in 1960 (DaVanzo 1972), relative education of men and women in Thailand as of 1960 (Maurer, Ratajiczak, and Schultz 1973), the U.S. in 1960 (Frieden 1974), and in Puerto Rico in 1950 and 1960 (Nerlove and Schultz 1970).

marriage among individual women in low-income countries. More educated women marry later, even in cases where marriage is sufficiently
delayed in the overall society to avoid overlapping with school attendance, as in East and Southeast Asia (Montgomery and Sulak 1988, Anderson and Hill 1980, King et al. 1986, Casterline and Reynes 1990).

The family bargaining model may clarify the gains to marriage and the
resulting prevalence of marriage in contemporary Thai society. Demographic and anthropological studies of Thailand document that marriage
was until recently nearly universal. About 95 percent of men and women
reported themselves as having been married (once) by age 35 (in the 1960
census cited by Knodel, Chamrathrithirong, and Debavalya 1987, Table
5.1). An informal process of divorce has also been traditionally common
with frequent remarriage. Seventy percent of the women and 81 percent
of the men between the ages of 25 and 54 are living in the same household
as their spouse in the 1981 Survey of Thailand. To explain who is in this
sense "currently married," the specialization model of Becker as well as
the bargaining model would predict a decrease in marital gains with an
increase in women's predicted market wage opportunities, holding men's
expected wage opportunities equal. These predictions as to the sign of
wage effects are ambiguous if education is also treated as a marriage
determinant, because of the strong correlation between wages and
schooling (see Appendixes C and D). At the individual level, however,
the "expected" spouse's characteristics are not observed, and thus it is
not possible to hold constant for the characteristics of potential spouses
in the entire population.

Table 4 therefore reports the probit equation for the likelihood of being
married, conditional on the individual's own characteristics, including
quadratic terms in instrumented wage rates and nonearned income. It is
notable that both nonearned income from property and transfer sources
contribute to increased marriage among men and decreased marriage
among women. The size of the coefficients on property and transfer income is many times larger in absolute value in the case of women than
of men. However, the coefficients on property and transfer sources of
nonearned income are of roughly similar magnitude. The statistical restriction of equality of coefficients can be accepted at the 5 percent confidence level, using the likelihood ratio test. In sum, marriage in Thailand
is not a "normal" good for Thai women: marriage is less attractive to
the wealthier Thai women than remaining single, other things being equal.

If nonearned income is an important determinant of marriage in Thailand, just as are wage opportunities, schooling, and urbanization, how
can the sample of married couples be assumed a representative sample
for the purposes of estimating family labor supply and fertility relationships? If it is not, can the selection bias correction terms (i.e., the inverse

Table 4

*Probit Estimates of the Probability that a Spouse Is Present
in a Household, Women and Men in Thailand, 1981*[a]

Dependent Variable: (Age of Sample)	Women Fertility (17–49)	Women Labor (25–54)	Men Labor (25–54)
Explanatory Variables	(1)	(2)	(3)
Market opportunity wage[b]	−.801	−.443	−.478
(log baht per hour)	(12.0)	(4.45)	(3.68)
Wage squared[b]	.0613	.0293	.0389
	(2.75)	(.95)	(1.73)
Unearned income by source (baht per month)			
Property	−.326	−.508	.299
($\times 10^{-4}$)	(2.26)	(4.09)	(2.66)
Property squared	.0160	.0445	−.0121
($\times 10^{-8}$)	(.69)	(2.97)	(2.18)
Transfer	−.619	−.648	.162
($\times 10^{-4}$)	(15.2)	(16.7)	(2.59)
Transfer squared	.0232	.0245	−.00873
($\times 10^{-8}$)	(10.3)	(11.6)	(2.17)
Age	.555	.309	.557
	(47.0)	(16.5)	(25.0)
Age squared	−.799	−.399	−.643
($\times 10^{-2}$)	(45.7)	(16.4)	(22.5)
Residential area			
Bangkok	.183	.0321	.0177
	(4.82)	(.74)	(.33)
Municipal	.544	.131	.0639
	(8.69)	(1.72)	(.68)
Sanitary district	.376	.132	.143
	(7.46)	(2.11)	(1.85)
Northeast region	.0199	.0405	−.0295
	(.64)	(1.08)	(.49)
Intercept	−8.46	−4.81	−9.67
	(45.3)	(14.0)	(22.4)
χ^2	3,217.73	1,028.9	1,577
Sample size	11,708	8,380	7,278
Mean of dependent variable	.545	.699	.805

a. Absolute values of asymptotic *t* ratios are reported beneath ML coefficients in parentheses.

b. Hourly wage rates imputed from wage equations estimated by a sample selection model and reported in Appendixes C and D.

of the Mill's ratio in Heckman's 1976, 1979 terms) be incorporated into the family labor supply and fertility relationships? These estimates are reported in the second half of Tables 1, 2, and 3. The previously reported specification in these tables assumed that the presence of a spouse is an exogenous event and can be approximately held constant by the introduction of a dummy variable for a husband (or wife). The second specification allows for the covariation between the error in the marital status equation and the labor supply and fertility equations. A variety of methods might be proposed to deal with this potential simultaneity bias. The estimation strategy followed here is to analyze the censored sample of married couples and include in these family "demand" equations a sample selection bias correcting term derived from the probit equation for marital status and participation, parallel to those as reported in Table 4. The labor supply equations are estimated jointly by maximum likelihood methods in columns (3), (4), (5), and (6) in Tables 1 and 2, as is the fertility equation in column (2) in Table 3 and column (1) in Table 4. Consequently, the standard errors and reported asymptotic t ratios are consistent and appropriate for hypothesis testing.

A comparison of the estimates based on these two model specifications confirms that the differential effects of male and female nonearned income are not changed. Indeed the same coefficient restriction tests reported earlier continue to reject the neoclassical model for female labor supply and fertility, but do not reject the restriction for male labor supply. However, certain other response coefficients are more sensitive to the assumptions about the determinants of marital status (compare columns 2 and 6 in Tables 1 and 2). The impact of the woman's wage opportunities on her fertility changes sign when the estimation is restricted to the sample of married women and corrected for this selective sampling. The own-wage effect of the married women on fertility is positive (Table 3, column 2), because her market wage opportunities also influence marital status through the sample selection rule (Table 4). The exclusion restriction that identifies these marriage sample selection corrections assumes that the quadratic (nonlinear) effects of own wages and nonearned income influence marital status but do not influence fertility (or labor supply). Until a stronger theoretical basis for the marriage selection rule is provided, all estimates of models of family labor supply and fertility must be viewed with some skepticism.

In the 1981 survey of Thailand there is no information on the individual's migration, occupational, or marital history. There is little information, therefore, that might have a particular bearing on marital status compared with other current conditions that could affect last week's labor supply or fertility during the last five years. Ultimately disentangling the effect of marital status on fertility and female labor supply will require a more fully articulated model of life cycle behavior of women and men in Thailand and a richer source of data to implement that model.

In this single cross-sectional survey support has been found, nonetheless, for the hypothesis that the ownership of nonearned income in the Thai family has a distinct association with that family's labor supply and reproductive behavior. The differences in the effect of husband- and wife-owned sources of nonearned income on these forms of behavior did not prove particularly sensitive to the two specifications considered for dealing with the marriage decision rule. However, other important response coefficients do appear to be more sensitive to the statistical methods employed to hold constant for the likelihood that a husband resides in a woman's household. There is much room here for further research.

VII. Conclusions

This paper has rejected one of the restrictions implied by the neoclassical model of family demand behavior, that for female labor supply. However, the evidence does not actually accept the "bargaining" model. If nonearned income is assumed to be a proxy for bargaining power of the person who owns or controls that income, then the empirical results obtained here for the Thai population in 1981 imply that women with more "bargaining power" prefer to increase their own consumption of leisure or time in nonmarket activities. Correspondingly, these same women prefer to have more children, though this conclusion is more qualified, because the finding is due predominantly to the positive partial correlation between transfer income to the woman and her recent fertility, and the correlation is not statistically significant with respect to her property nonearned income. Consequently, the connection between transfer income and fertility may reflect the reverse causation to that hypothesized here, where women with more children to support are more likely to receive transfers from their family and other groups in society. In the case of men, their nonearned income is also associated with their preference for more leisure or time out of the labor force. But in the case of men's joint decisions of participation and hours worked, the impact of their wife's nonearned income exerts a weaker effect. The difference between the effects of the spouse's nonearned income on male labor supply is not statistically significant.

A limitation of previous tests of the family demand model that focus on the equality of compensated cross-wage effects (Cain and Watts 1973, Heckman 1971, Kalachek and Raines 1970, Ashenfelter and Heckman 1974, Olsen 1977, Killingsworth 1983) is that the estimates are for samples of married couples or couples both of whom are working in the labor force. The resulting selectivity of the sample of married couples may bias estimates, and this potential source of parameter bias should be eliminated to test the family demand model (Heckman 1979). In the final section of this paper, quadratic terms for the own wage and own nonearned income are added to other individual characteristics to predict the probability of marriage, and this probit model is used to add a regressor in the family demand system (i.e., the inverse of the Mills ratio). This alternative censored specification to the conventional family demand model does not change the previously summarized conclusion—fertility and female labor supply behavior reject the neoclassical restriction that nonearned income is pooled and partners exhibit the same behavioral preferences.

However, the spouse cross-wage effects do, in some cases, change substantially in magnitude when the marriage sample selection is included in the specification of the family demand model. A better model is needed to forecast marriage that will provide a theoretical basis for the exclusion restrictions needed to correct for the source of sample selection bias in models of family demands. In other words, variables are needed for partners that have an impact on their likelihood of being currently married but are deemed theoretically irrelevant in directly affecting family labor supply and fertility.

Whether this family demand model is viewed as neoclassically pooled or individualistically bargained, the basis for identifying the family demand model must start with a better theory of marriage. These Thai survey data suggest that such an adjustment for the bias of being included in the selective sample of intact marriages can change appreciably population parameter estimates and thereby modify economic inferences about the behavioral responses of individuals and families.

Appendix A

Percentage of Persons with Various Sources of Nonearned Income in Thailand 1981 SES, by Sex and Age of Recipient (Mean amount in Bahts per Month for Persons with Source)

Sex and Age of Income Recipient (Total Size of Sample)	Property Income	Rentals	Interest	Transfers Public & Private	Grants, Insurance, and Sales	Total Nonearned Income
	(1)	(2)	(3)	(4)	(5)	(1)+(4)+(5) =(6)
Women						
All ages	3.14	1.04	1.53	11.12	4.05	15.87
(17,002)	(6,954)	(5,484)	(4,263)	(9,952)	(3,769)	(9,309)
Age 15–24	.42	.02	.35	6.30	1.77	8.05
(5,763)	(2,015)	(1,000)	(974)	(6,472)	(2,166)	(5,644)
Age 25–39	3.16	.49	2.07	7.08	4.99	13.30
(5,566)	(3,271)	(3,179)	(2,182)	(17,233)	(3,650)	(11,324)
Age 40–54	4.57	1.50	2.30	13.84	5.59	20.28
(3,525)	(10,090)	(8,788)	(8,197)	(10,809)	(4,955)	(11,015)
Age 55+	8.05	4.47	2.05	30.07	5.17	36.31
(2,148)	(8,467)	(4,354)	(3,959)	(6,819)	(3,435)	(8,014)
Men						
All ages	4.40	1.50	2.07	10.79	8.08	20.01
(15,304)	(7,818)	(6,299)	(5,239)	(7,469)	(5,517)	(7,975)
Age 15–24	.36	.02	.26	5.80	2.08	7.68
(5,001)	(2,016)	(750)	(516)	(6,308)	(2,208)	(5,456)
Age 25–39	3.88	.47	2.58	6.18	10.53	18.33
(4,851)	(3,884)	(3,293)	(2,950)	(5,255)	(5,441)	(5,722)
Age 40–54	6.76	2.41	3.05	12.43	12.40	27.43
(3,314)	(9,601)	(8,416)	(7,649)	(6,071)	(5,188)	(7,463)
Age 55+	11.37	5.85	3.65	30.40	9.82	41.16
(2,138)	(9,648)	(5,542)	(6,575)	(9,896)	(7,983)	(11,878)

Appendix B
*Labor Force and Wage Employment Participation Rates in Thailand
1976, 1981, and 1986 SES, by Sex and Education, Ages 25 to 54*

Year, Sex, and Education Group	Percent of Persons Aged 25 to 54	Percent of Education Group	
		in Labor Force	in Wage Employment
1976			
Male			
0– 3 years	16.7	95.	32.
4– 6 years	62.7	98.	37.
7– 9 years	4.8	96.	50.
10–12 years	9.4	95.	71.
12 + years	6.4	95.	85.
All	100.0	97.	43.
Female			
0– 3 years	24.7	72.	13.
4– 6 years	64.0	73.	11.
7– 9 years	3.0	60.	14.
10–12 years	4.6	70. .	45.
12 + years	3.7	87.	82.
All	100.0	73.	16.
1981			
Male			
0– 3 years	12.3	97.	45.
4– 6 years	63.3	99.	53.
7– 9 years	12.8	97.	66.
10–12 years	8.8	95.	82.
12 + years	2.9	92.	86.
All	100.0	98.	57.
Female			
0– 3 years	18.9	82.	24.
4– 6 years	66.1	84.	22.
7– 9 years	7.2	71.	31.
10–12 years	5.9	86.	73.
12 + years	1.9	93.	88.
All	100.0	83.	28.

Economic Demography I

Appendix B (*continued*)

Year, Sex, and Education Group	Percent of Persons Aged 25 to 54	Percent of Education Group	
		in Labor Force	in Wage Employment
1986			
Male			
0– 3 years	8.6	94.	46.
4– 6 years	63.8	98.	49.
7– 9 years	5.3	97.	52.
10–12 years	8.8	96.	68.
12 + years	13.4	95.	80.
All	100.0	97.	55.
Female			
0– 3 years	14.0	83.	29.
4– 6 years	67.4	85.	27.
7– 9 years	4.3	71.	23.
10–12 years	4.0	74.	32.
12 + years	10.4	84.	73.
All	100.0	83.	32.

Appendix C
Sample Selection Corrected Wage Function for Women Age 25–54 in Thailand, 1981[a]

Dependent Variable: Estimation Method	Participation Probit	Wage Earner Status Probit	Log of Hourly Wage Rate	
			ML-Linear	Heckman
	(1)	(2)	(3)	(4)
Explanatory Variables				
Schooling in Years				
Primary	.00410	−.0429	.0969	.111
	(.36)	(3.74)	(4.55)	(4.84)
Secondary	.0985	.213	.166	.120
	(7.44)	(15.6)	(6.01)	(3.41)
Higher	.165	.104	−.0424	−.0605
	(3.60)	(2.46)	(.70)	(1.45)
Post-schooling experience in years	.14	.00446	.0310	.0287
	(7.32)	(.44)	(1.73)	(1.76)
Experience squared ($\times 10^{-2}$)	−.189	−.0387	−.0237	−.0112
	(7.41)	(2.17)	(.74)	(.37)
Unearned income by source (baht per month $\times 10^{-4}$)				
Women–property	−.182	−.0747		
	(3.04)	(.80)		
Women–transfer	−.105	−.0356		
	(6.50)	(2.43)		
Men's–property	−.0744	−.119		
	(2.55)	(3.79)		
Men's–transfer	−.0799	−.0179		
	(3.63)	(1.05)		

Appendix C (*continued*)

Other persons–total	.000213 (.01)	−.0647 (2.94)		
Land owned in hectares				
Irrigated	.0247 (5.54)	−.0220 (11.5)		
Dry	.0180 (7.68)	−.0203 (14.6)		
Residential areas				
Bangkok	.495 (12.0)	−.0223 (.54)	.807 (9.72)	.798 (11.6)
Municipal	−.692 (16.1)	−.423 (10.2)	1.49 (18.3)	1.55 (19.1)
Sanitary districts (suburban)	−.361 (6.94)	−.0417 (.95)	.836 (12.1)	.832 (10.6)
Northeast region	.171 (3.77)	−.272 (7.04)	−.0614 (.94)	.0198 (.24)
Intercept	−1.25 (3.35)	−.0448 (.31)	−.0191 (.07)	.304 (1.03)
Wage earner status (lambda)				−1.45 (7.49)
Rho (Equations 2 and 3)			−.755 (21.9)	
Sigma			1.46 (29.4)	
Log likelihood	4,029.0		8,290.6	3,476.9
χ^2 (df)	1,166.7 (16)			2,264.3 (10)
Sample size	8,816			

a. Absolute values of asymptotic t ratios are reported beneath coefficients in parentheses.

Appendix D
Sample Selection Corrected Wage Function for Men Age 25–54 in Thailand, 1981[a]

Dependent Variable: Estimation Method	Participation Probit	Wage Earner Status Probit	Log of Hourly Wage Rate	
			ML-Linear	Heckman
	(1)	(2)	(3)	(4)
Explanatory Variables				
Schooling in Years				
Primary	.0598	.00966	.145	.146
	(2.27)	(.79)	(8.03)	(7.04)
Secondary	−.0375	.0923	.160	.123
	(1.67)	(7.26)	(8.75)	(6.16)
Higher	.0521	.0331	.0355	.0255
	(1.19)	(.93)	(.75)	(.68)
Post-schooling experience in years	.101	.0270	.0280	.0167
	(5.83)	(2.85)	(2.14)	(1.16)
Experience squared ($\times 10^{-2}$)	−.182	−.0722	−.00265	.0269
	(5.89)	(4.38)	(.12)	(.99)
Unearned income by source: (baht per month $\times 10^{-4}$)				
Men–property	−.0656	−.00376		
	(1.74)	(.16)		
Men–transfer	−.121	−.000205		
	(4.69)	(.01)		
Women–property	−.104	−.0506		
	(2.16)	(.55)		
Women–transfer	.00333	.0936		
	(.02)	(2.55)		

Appendix D (*continued*)

	(1)	(2)	(3)	(4)
Other persons–total	-.0959 (4.33)	-.0276 (1.74)		
Land owned in hectares:				
Irrigated	.0112 (1.54)	-.0205 (18.5)		
Dry	.00582 (1.52)	-.0201 (23.0)		
Residential areas:				
Bangkok	-.0405 (.50)	.176 (4.34)	.449 (7.00)	.369 (5.56)
Municipal	-.298 (3.38)	-.277 (6.84)	1.22 (19.5)	1.28 (20.8)
Sanitary districts (suburban)	-.0883 (.81)	.0305 (.72)	.710 (13.1)	.673 (9.57)
Northeast region	-.0196 (.22)	.0502 (1.49)	-.557 (12.6)	-.552 (9.47)
Intercept	.827 (3.21)	.0179 (.52)	.128 (.66)	.669 (2.58)
Wage earner status (lambda)				1.90 (10.8)
Rho (Equations 2 and 3)			-.845 (62.4)	
Sigma			1.45 (60.5)	
Log likelihood	837.9		11,972.00	6,961.0
χ^2 (df)	176.9 (16)			3,637.2 (10)
Sample size	7,986		7,986	7,986

a. Absolute values of asymptotic t ratios are reported beneath coefficients in parentheses.

References

Anderson, K. H., and M. A. Hill. 1980. "Determinants of Age at Marriage in Malaysia and Japan." Economic Growth Center Discussion Paper, Yale University.

Ashenfelter, O., and J. J. Heckman. 1974. "The Estimation of Income and Substitution Effects in a Model of Family Labor Supply." *Econometrica* 42(1):73–76.

Becker, G. S. 1965. "A Theory of the Allocation of Time." *Economic Journal* 75 (December):493–519.

———. 1974. "A Theory of Marriage." In *Economics of the Family*, T. W. Schultz. Chicago: University of Chicago Press.

———. 1981. *A Treatise on the Family*. Cambridge, Mass.: Harvard University Press.

Cain, G., and H. Watts, eds. 1973. *Income Maintenance and Labor Supply*. New York: Academic Press.

Carlin, P. S. 1990. "IntraFamily Bargaining and Time Allocation." In *Research in Population Economics*, vol. 7, ed. T. W. Schultz. Greenwich, Conn.: JAI Press.

Casterline, J. B., and J. F. Reynes. 1990. "Women's Schooling and Marriage in Low Income Countries." Presented at American Association for the Advancement of Science, New Orleans (February).

Chamratrithirong, A., ed. 1984. *Perspectives on the Thai Marriage: A Review of Demographic Evidence*. Institute for Population and Social Research, Mahidol University, Salaya, Thailand.

Chiappori, D. A. 1988. "Nash-Bargained Household Decisions." *International Economic Review* 29 (September):791–96.

DaVanzo, J. 1972. *Determinants of Family Formation in Chile, 1960*. Santa Monica, Calif.: The Rand Corporation (August).

Deaton, A., and J. Muellbauer. 1980. *Economics of Consumer Behavior*. Cambridge University Press.

Engel, E. 1895. "Die Lebenskosten Belgischer Arbeiter-Familien fruher and jetzt." *International Statistical Institute Bulletin* 9:1–74.

Freiden, A. 1974. "The U.S. Marriage Market." In *Economics of the Family*, ed. T. W. Schultz. Chicago: University of Chicago Press.

Harsanyi, J. C. 1977. *Rational Behavior and Bargaining Equilibrium*. Cambridge, Mass.: MIT Press.

———, and R. Selten. 1987. *A General Theory of Equilibrium Selection in Games*. Cambridge, Mass.: MIT Press.

Heckman, J. J. 1971. "Three Essays on the Supply of Labor and the Demand for Goods." Ph.D. dissertation, Princeton University (May).

———. 1974. "Shadow Prices, Market Wages and Labor Supply." *Econometrica* 42:679–94.

———. 1976. "A Common Structure of Statistical Models of Truncation, Sample Selection and Limited Dependent Variables and a Simple Estimator for Such Models." *Annals of Economic and Social Measurement* 5(4):475–502.

————. 1979. "Sample Bias as a Specification Error." *Econometrica* 47 (January):153–62.

————, and J. R. Walker. 1989. "Forecasting Aggregate Period Specific Birth Rates." *Journal of American Statistical Association* 84 (December):958–65.

Horney, M. J., and M. B. McElroy. 1988. "The Household Allocation Problem: Empirical Results from a Bargaining Model." In *Research in Population Economics* vol. 6, ed. T. P. Schultz. Greenwich, Conn.: JAI Press.

Jones, C. N. 1986. "Intra-Household Bargaining in Response to the Introduction of New Corps." In *Understanding Africa's Rural Households and Farming Systems,* ed. J. L. Moock. Boulder, Colo.: Westview Press.

Kalachek, E. D., and F. Q. Raines. 1970. "Labor Supply of Lower Income Workers." In *Technical Studies,* Presidents' Commission on Income Maintenance Programs, 159–86. Washington, D.C.: G.P.O.

Killingsworth, M. 1983. *Labor Supply.* Cambridge: Cambridge University Press.

King, E. M., J. R. Peterson, S. M. Adioetomo, L. J. Domingo, and S. H. Syed. 1986. *Change in the Status of Women Across Generations in Asia.* Santa Monica, Calif.: The Rand Corporation (December).

Kneisner, T. J. 1976. "An Indirect Test of Complementarity in a Family Labor Supply Model." *Econometrica* 44 (July):651–59.

Knodel, J., A. Chamrathrithirong, and N. Debavalya. 1987. *Thailand's Reproductive Revolution.* Madison: University of Wisconsin Press.

Kosters, M. 1966. *Income and Substitution Effects in a Family Labor Supply Model.* P-3339. Santa Monica, Calif.: The Rand Corporation.

Layard, R., and J. Mincer, eds. 1985. "Trends in Women's Work, Education, and Family Building." *Journal of Labor Economics* 3 (January).

Levy, V. 1985. "Cropping Pattern, Mechanization, Child Labor and Fertility in a Farming Economy: Rural Egypt." *Economic Development and Cultural Change* 33(4):777–92.

Lundberg, S. 1988. "Labor Supply of Husbands and Wives: A Simultaneous Equation Approach." *Review of Economics and Statistics* 70 (May):224–35.

McElroy, M. B. 1988. "The Empirical Content of Nash-Bargained Household Behavior." Economics Department Discussion Paper No. 88-08, Duke University (September).

————, and M. J. Horney. 1981. "Nash Bargained Household Decisions." *International Economic Review* 22 (June):333–50.

Manser, M., and M. Brown. 1979. "Bargaining Analysis of Household Decisions." In *Women in the Labor Force,* eds. C. B. Lloyd, E. S. Andrews, and C. L. Gilroy. New York: Columbia University Press.

————, and ————. 1980. "Marriage and Household Decisionmaking." *International Economic Review* 21 (February):31–44.

Maurer, J., R. Ratajiczak, and T. P. Schultz. 1973. *Marriage, Fertility and Labor Force Participation of Thai Women.* Santa Monica, Calif.: The Rand Corporation.

Mincer, J. 1962. "Labor Force Participation of Married Women." In *Aspects of Labor Economics,* Princeton, N.J.: Princeton University Press.

Montgomery, M., and D. Sulak. 1988. "Female First Marriage in East and Southeast Asia." *Journal of Development Economics.*

Nash, J. F. 1950. "The Bargaining Problem." *Econometrica* 18:155–62.
———. 1953. "Two-Person Cooperative Games." *Econometrica* 21:128–40.
Nerlove, M., and T. P. Schultz. 1970. "Love and Life Between the Censuses," RM-6322, Santa Monica, Calif.: The Rand Corporation.
Olsen, R. J. 1977. "An Econometric Model of Family Labor Supply." Ph.D. dissertation, University of Chicago Press.
Pollak, R. A. 1985. "A Transactions Cost Approach to Families and Households." *Journal of Economic Literature* 23:581–608.
Rosenzweig, M. R., and R. E. Evenson. 1977. "Fertility, Schooling and the Economic Contribution of Children in Rural India." *Econometrica* 45 (July):1065–80.
———, and O. Stark. 1989. "Consumption Smoothing, Migration, and Marriage: Evidence from India." *Journal of Political Economy* 97 (August):905–26.
Senauer, B., M. Garcia, and E. Jacinto. 1988. "Determinants of the Intrahousehold Allocation of Food in Rural Philippines." *American Journal of Agricultural Economics* 70(1):170–80.
Schultz, T. P. 1981. *Economics of Population*. Reading, Mass.: Addison-Wesley.
———. 1988. "The Relationship between Local Family Planning Expenditures and Fertility in Thailand, 1976–1981." Yale University.
———. 1989. "Women in Development: Objectives, Framework and Policy Interventions." Yale University (April).
Smith, J. P., ed. 1980. *Female Labor Supply*. Princeton, N.J.: Princeton University Press.
Thomas, D. 1989. "Intrahousehold Resource Allocation: An Inferential Approach." Economic Growth Center Discussion Paper 586, Yale University (February).
Treas, J. 1988. "Money in the Bank: Transaction Costs and Privatized Marriage." *American Sociological Review* (forthcoming).
U.S. Department of Health and Human Services. 1983. *Final Report of the Seattle-Denver Income Maintenance Experiment*, vol. 1, part 5. Washington, D.C.: G.P.O.

[16]

Like Father, Like Son; Like Mother, Like Daughter
Parental Resources and Child Height

Duncan Thomas

ABSTRACT

Using household survey data from the United States, Brazil, and Ghana, I examine the relationship beween parental education and child height, an indicator of health and nutritional status. In all three countries, the education of the mother has a bigger effect on her daughter's height; paternal education, in contrast, has a bigger impact on his son's height. There are, apparently, differences in the allocation of household resources depending on the gender of the child and these differences vary with the gender of the parent. These results are quite robust and persist even after including controls for unobserved household fixed effects. In Ghana, relative to other women, the education of a woman who is better educated than her husband has a bigger impact on the height of her daughter than her son. In Brazil, women's nonlabor income has a positive impact on the health of her daughter but not on her son's health. If relative education of parents and nonlabor income are indicators of power in household allocation decisions, then these results, along with difference-in-diference of estimated income effects, suggest that gender differences in resource allocations reflect both technological differences in child rearing and differences in the preferences of parents.

> All women become like their mothers. That is
> their tragedy. No man does. That's his.
> Oscar Wilde, *The Importance of Being Earnest*, Act 1.

The author is a senior economist at the RAND and an associate professor of economics at the University of California, Los Angeles. He acknowledges the very helpful comments of Jere Behrman, Janet Currie, Jacques van der Gaag, Paul Gertler, Al Klevorick, David Lam, Marjorie McElroy, John Newman, Ariel Pakes, Mark Pitt, Mark Rosenzweig, T. Paul Schultz, Jody Sindelar, James P. Smith, John Strauss, and David Weiman.

I. Introduction

How are resources allocated within the household? Whereas sociologists and anthropologists have attempted to peer into this black box, economists have paid less attention to the question. In almost every study of household behavior, economic models, implicitly or explicitly, treat resource allocations as the outcome of maximizing a well-behaved household welfare function (Becker 1964, 1981) without specifying the mechanisms underlying the allocation process.[1]

Economists have paid more attention to a second, related issue: is there evidence for gender bias in the allocation of resources? A mini-industry revolves around discrimination in the labor market and, within the household economics literature, several studies have looked at gender differences in human capital investments. In South and, possibly, Southeast Asia, girls tend to fare worse than boys,[2] but the evidence elsewhere seems quite weak.[3]

My aim is to determine whether there is evidence for differences by gender in the allocation of household resources. I will focus on child health, as measured by height for age. Among nutritionists, it is considered a long-run measure of nutritional status (Waterlow et al. 1977) reflecting accumulation over the child's lifetime. It has been shown to be related to mental development, to mortality, and to wages as an adult and, in fact, both nutritionists and economists have suggested that height is also a useful indicator of child health and welfare. I expect it to be related to indicators of long-run resource availability within the household, and I focus the spotlight here on parental education.[4]

---

1. McElroy and Horney (1981) and Manser and Brown (1980) propose alternative models of household decision-making and recently there has been a resurgence of interest in these models; see Browning and Chiappori (1993), Chiappori (1988a, 1992), Lundberg and Pollak (1993), McElroy (1990, 1994), McElroy and Horney (1988), Ulph (1988). Behrman (1994) reviews the economics literature; Blumberg (1988) discusses several studies in sociology.

2. D'Souza and Chen (1980) and Rosenzweig and Schultz (1982) find infant and child mortality in India is lower among boys; Sen (1984), Sen and Sengupta (1983) and Behrman (1988) argue, on the basis of anthropometric indicators, that boys receive preferential treatment in India. Several studies indicate that boys tend to be favored in the intrahousehold distribution of nutrients (Rosenzweig and Schultz 1982, and Behrman and Deolalikar 1989 for India; Evenson et al. 1980, and Senauer et al. 1988 for the Philippines; Chen, Huq, and D'Souza 1981 for Bangladesh; Chernichovsky et al. 1983 for India) although at least part of these differences can be ascribed to different activity levels (Pitt, Rosenzweig, and Hassan 1990, using data from Bangladesh). Alderman and Gertler (1989) report the income and price elasticities of the demand for health care are larger for girls than boys in Pakistan; see also Behrman and Deolalikar (1990). Finally, Subramanian and Deaton (1990) argue there is evidence in Indian NSS data that parents make more room in their household expenditures for boys rather than girls.

3. There is little evidence other than in Asia for gender differences in infant and child mortality outcomes; gender differences in levels of anthropometric outcomes are small and often not significant; see, for example, Strauss (1990), and Svedberg (1990) on Africa, and Schofield (1979), on Latin America. In many countries, school enrollment ratios are higher for boys: Schultz (1987) argues that gender bias in schooling enrollments and attainments tends to decline with income. Psacharopolous and Arriagada (1989) present evidence for discrimination against boys in school attendance and performance in Brazil; Chernichovsky (1985) argues there is discrimination against girls in school attendance in Botswana. In the equivalence scale literature, there is little evidence for gender bias in the allocation of expenditures in the Côte d'Ivoire and Thailand (Deaton 1989), or in the United States (Gronau 1991). See Behrman (1992) for a comprehensive review.

4. It has been demonstrated that parental education and, to a less extent, household income, often have a significant positive impact on child height for age even after controlling for genetic endowment; see

Tests for gender differences based on anthropometric data typically compare the mean standardized *levels* of boys with girls, where the standards take account of differential growth patterns over age. Since these growth patterns also distinguish boys from girls, gender differences can only be identified *relative* to the standards.[5] Rather than follow this approach, I will examine the *determinants* of child anthropometric outcomes and test for differential impacts of mother's and father's education on the heights of sons and daughters. Our results will be suggestive of how resources are allocated within a household.

The data are drawn from four household surveys carried out in the United States, Africa, and Latin America. It turns out that in a variety of cultural and economic settings, the effect of a mother's education is larger on the health of her daughters than her sons, and that the education of the father has a bigger impact on the health of his sons than his daughters. There are, then, gender differences in the allocation of household resources to child health and these differences vary with the gender of the parent.

This may simply reflect differences in the technology of child rearing; for example, it may be efficient for mothers to spend more time with daughters and fathers with sons. It turns out, however, that relative to other women, the education of a woman who is better educated than her husband has a bigger impact on the health of her daughters. Nonlabor income in the hands of women has a positive effect on daughter's height but no effect on that of a son and this difference is significant. If nonlabor income and education differences between husbands and wives are indicative of power in asserting one's preferences in the allocation of household resources, then this additional evidence suggests that the gender differences reflect *both* differences in the technology of child rearing *and* differences in the preferences of parents.

Public policy can change the balance of power within the household. Government transfer programs may be directed at particular individuals within the household. Development programs and public investments may favor one gender over another (see, for example, Boserup 1970). Our results suggest that the impact on child health of a change in household resource allocation mechanisms is unlikely to be gender neutral.

II. Theoretical Model

The model motivating this study integrates a health production function with a model of household decision making to develop a reduced form demand for child health function. Assume child health, θ, depends on a set of inputs, M (such as nutrient intake and the quantity and quality of child care), individual characteristics, μ_i (including age and sex), family characteristics, μ_f

---

Horton (1986), Behrman and Deolalikar (1990), Barrera (1990), Behrman (1988), Thomas, Strauss, and Henriques (1990). For reviews of the determinants of child anthropometric indicators, see Cochrane, Leslie, and O'Hara (1982); Martorell and Habicht (1986); and Strauss and Thomas (1994).

5. These are usually the National Center for Health Statistics standards for a well-nourished child in the United States (NCHS 1976). Sample based standardization obviously preclude even these simple sorts of tests for gender differences.

(such as parental human capital), and community characteristics, μ_c (such as the healthiness of the environment):

(1) $\theta_i = \theta_i(M, \mu_i, \mu_f, \mu_c, \eta_i)$.

η_i represents individual-specific unobserved heterogeneity in health. The technology underlying the health production function may vary with the gender and age of the child and so gender specific differences in the impact of parental education on child height may simply reflect this technology.

Next, assume each household member, $m = 1, \ldots, M$, wishes to maximize his own utility given by:

(2) $v_m(x, l, \theta; \mu, \varepsilon)$,

where x is a vector of goods demanded by each individual in the household and l is a vector of leisure of each individual. θ can be thought of as a vector of home produced commodities, in general, although in this paper I am particularly concerned with child health. μ represents the background characteristics, such as education, of all household members and ε is a vector representing the unobserved tastes of members. Virtually every economic model of the household assumes that it may be treated as a single individual (or as a set of individuals with *common preferences*)[6] in which case (2) is the household welfare function and it is maximized subject to a single budget constraint:

$$px = \sum_m w_m(T_m - l_m) + y_m.$$

T is the amount of time available for work, w is a vector of wages and y_m is each individual's nonlabor income which I assume to be exogenous.[7]

As an outcome of this household optimization program, there is a household demand for each element of x, l, and θ. I focus here on one element of θ, namely child height, h, which depends on exogenous child, family, and community characteristics, $\bar{\mu}_i$, $\bar{\mu}_f$, and $\bar{\mu}_c$, respectively. Under the assumptions of the common preference model, child height also depends on *total* household nonlabor income, Σy_m:

(3) $h_i = h_i(\bar{\mu}_i, \bar{\mu}_f, \bar{\mu}_c, \Sigma y_m, \xi_i)$.

ξ_i represents individual specific heterogeneity, part of which may be common across individuals within a household because of, for example, family specific health variation.

Maternal (or paternal) education may have a bigger impact on the height of her daughter, relative to a son for two reasons. First, the technology underlying the health production function, (1), may differ for boys and girls. Second, the mother (or father) may prefer to allocate more time to the daughter. Estimates of the impact of parental education on child height in the reduced form (3) do not permit empirically distinguishing these explanations.

---

6. Implicitly or explicitly, these models assume that all household members have the same preferences or that one member dictates all resource allocation decisions; these assumptions are observationally equivalent for our purposes. See Folbre (1986) and Fapohunda and Todaro (1988) for a critical discussion.
7. This is a strong assumption since current nonlabor income reflects, in part, past labor supply. The issue will be discussed in detail below.

In order to disentangle the role of preferences from technology I need a richer specification of household choices and consider two classes of models which relax the assumption of common preferences.[8] The first relies on notions of bargaining and, following McElroy and Horney (1981) and Manser and Brown (1980), I assume that Nash equilibrium is the appropriate concept (although the particular choice of equilibrium is not critical for our results). Each individual seeks to maximize the difference between utility achieved by cooperating within the household and the threat point or reservation utility, V_m, which may be utility outside of the household (McElroy 1990) or that achieved in a noncooperative equilibrium (Ulph 1988; Lundberg and Pollak 1993). The household will maximize the product of these differences:

$$\prod_{i}^{m=1} v_m(x, l, \theta; \mu, \varepsilon) - V_m(p, y_m, \bar{\mu}_m),$$

where $\bar{\mu}_m$ are any characteristics that would affect member m's ability to assert his or her preferences. The demand for health function will depend on the same individual, family, and community characteristics, μ, in (3) but also anything that affects a member's bargaining power; this will include *individual* nonlabor income together with any elements of $\bar{\mu}$ not already in the demand function.

Chiappori (1988a, 1988b) has argued that imposing an equilibrium concept places more structure than is necessary on the model and suggests, instead, that households be assumed to make Pareto efficient allocations. Let household members' preferences be altruistic in the sense that each cares about the others' consumption of private goods; they may also consume public goods. Browning and Chiappori (1993) show that for all Pareto efficient allocations, there exists a set of individual welfare weights, ω, such that the household welfare function may be written as the weighted sum of all individual utility functions, (2). This household welfare function is then optimized subject to total expenditures equaling total household income. In this model, child height will depend on prices, incomes, and these welfare weights which, in turn, depend on prices, *individual* incomes, and other factors that might affect a member's ability to assert his or her preferences in the household allocation process. The key insight for our purposes is that it is, once again, *individual* and not household nonlabor income that affects child height in this model.

This class of models can also be given an income sharing interpretation in which the household optimization problem is modelled as a two stage budgeting problem (Browning, Bourguignon, Chiappori, and Lechene 1993, 1994). In the first stage, members allocate total resources amongst themselves and in the second stage each member maximizes utility, v_m, subject to the budget constraint

---

8. The restrictions of the common preference model have been empirically tested in only a small number of cases. Ashenfelter and Heckman (1974) reported one of the first tests of Slutsky symmetry for labor force participation of men and women using aggregate data from the United States; McElroy and Horney (1981) performed similar tests with individual survey data. In both cases, the common preference assumption is not rejected. In contrast, household survey data from several other countries indicates that the common preference assumption is violated by the data (Browning, Bourguignon, Chiappori, and Lechene 1993, 1994; Schultz 1990; Thomas 1990; Thomas and Chen 1993).

associated with his (her) income share. The welfare weights, ω, and the income share all have a simple intuitive relationship with the bargaining model: those characteristics which affect a member's bargaining power, $\bar{\mu}$, will presumably also affect that person's share in the first stage.

Relaxing the assumptions of the common preference model in the direction of either of these two classes of models leads to the empirical prediction that child height depends on *individual* nonlabor income together with any elements of $\bar{\mu}$, call them $\bar{\mu}'$, that are not already in the demand function:

$$(4) \quad h_i = h_i(\bar{\mu}_i, \bar{\mu}_f, \bar{\mu}_c, y_1, \ldots, y_M', \mu^{-'}, \xi_i).$$

I present estimates of (4) below which include the child's gender and age, $\bar{\mu}_i$, together with parental education and height, $\bar{\mu}_f$. The inclusion of wages complicates the reduced form model and in the absence of instruments to control for selection into the labor market, the impact of education must be interpreted as incorporating the role of time allocation decisions including labor force outcomes. In addition, I include measures of individual nonlabor income as well as other indicators of "bargaining strength" (discussed below). To control, albeit crudely, for community heterogeneity, $\bar{\mu}_c$, the functions will be estimated separately for rural and urban sectors or, in one case, the race of the child.

If nonlabor income is exogenous and it has a different effect on the height of boys relative to girls then this must reflect preferences, rather than technology, since income does not enter the health production function (1). I will test for differential effects of nonlabor income in the hands of mothers and fathers on sons and daughters. Secondly, education is highly correlated with potential earnings and so, ceteris paribus, a parent who is better educated than his or her spouse is likely to have more power in the determination of household resource allocations. In game-theoretic terms, the better educated spouse may be able to extract more of the gains from the marriage or, in the context of the income-sharing interpretation, that spouse may be able to demand a bigger share of income in the first stage budgeting. I will compare the estimated education effects on child height of women who are better educated than their husbands with the estimated effects for all other women. As long as this does not simply reflect non-linearities in the effect of education on child height, then it may also be interpreted as reflecting differences in preferences. I will also compare the evidence for Brazil in 1974 with 1986, a period during which women's opportunities outside the home have increased substantially.

These are more subtle tests for gender differences in resource allocations than simply comparing mean (standardized) heights of boys and girls or, analogously in the multivariate regression context, testing for the significance of a gender dummy in (4). Whereas the conventional tests can only identify gender differences relative to some (arbitrarily chosen) standards, the tests proposed here are independent of standards (the effects of which are captured in gender and age dummies). Instead, I look at interactions between family characteristics and child gender.

There is some evidence from several countries that suggests there may be gender differences in the allocation of resources within the household, with mothers devoting more resources towards their daughters and fathers towards their sons.[9] Why might mothers (or fathers) have different preferences with respect to the health of their daughters and sons? From an economic point of view, it is possible that the returns to investments in daughters and sons differ for mothers and fathers. For example, in many societies, children participate in work within the family and typically sons work with their fathers, daughters with their mothers. Furthermore, in the United States, there is some evidence that in old age, women tend to have more contact with their daughters than sons (Spitze and Logan 1990; Hess and Waring 1978). Under these circumstances, it would not be surprising for mothers to prefer to allocate more resources to their daughters than to their sons and for fathers to want to invest more in their sons than daughters. A fuller description of this literature is deferred to the final section.

III. Empirical Results

There are a limited number of surveys which include information on both child anthropometry and household socioeconomic characteristics. Four household surveys will be analyzed in this paper: one each from the United States and Ghana and two from Brazil. All of the analyses draw on the theoretical model outlined above and estimate the demand for height function, (4), following a similar empirical strategy. Heights are converted to age and gender specific z-scores using the NCHS (1976) standards for a population of well-nourished children in the United States:[10] these z-scores are used in all the analyses below. Since each survey involves its own peculiar empirical issues, the data and results are described separately in the next four sub-sections.

A. National Longitudinal Survey: Mother and Child Sample, 1986

In the United States, information has been collected on the labor market, education, training, and marital experiences of young men and women since 1979, on an annual basis, as part of the National Longitudinal Survey (NLS) Youth Cohort.

---

9. Using data on weight for age, another indicator of child health, Bhuiya et al. (1986) find that in Matlab, Bangladesh, mother's education has a significant positive effect on daughter's weight but not on son's. King and Lillard (1987) report that among Malays in Malaysia, mother's and father's education has a significant effect on daughter's schooling attainment, but not on son's. Among the Chinese in Malaysia, mother's education has a positive effect on both but father's education affects only son's schooling attainment. King and Bellew (1989) report that, in Peru, both parents' education significantly raises the probability a child (aged eight through 19) attends school. Maternal education has a bigger effect on the probability a daughter is at school, relative to a son; paternal education has a bigger impact on the son. Using data from the United States, Desai et al. (1989) find that a mother's education significantly affects her daughter's intellectual ability (measured by the Peabody Picture Vocabulary Test) but not her son's ability. However, none of Bhuiya et al., King and Lillard, King and Bellow, or Desai et al. report whether the effect of maternal (or paternal) education is significantly different on girls relative to boys. In urban Brazil, Thomas (1990) reports that nonlabor income attributed to mothers has a (significantly) bigger effect on the weight for height of daughters, relative to sons, and that nonlabor income in the hands of fathers has a bigger impact on his sons' weight for height. A similar pattern is reported for the impact of parental education on height for age.

10. A child with height h_i in age and gender group, g, will be assigned a z-score of $(h_i - h_{med,g})/\sigma_g$ where $h_{med,g}$ and σ_g are the age and gender specific median and standard deviation, respectively, of heights of well-nourished children.

In 1986, a series of Child Assessment instruments were completed for almost 5,000 children of women in the NLS Youth cohort. These instruments included a set of cognitive, socioemotional, and physiological tests, information from the mother on the child's health, as well as child anthropometric measures. Analysis is restricted to information on 4,704 children less than 12 years of age.[11] These children are not drawn from a random sample of the U.S. population: 38 percent of the children in the sample lived in families with incomes below the poverty line in 1986.[12] Relative to the average U.S. child, those in the sample tend to have younger mothers (with an average age of 25 years) and more minority mothers (slightly less than 50 percent are white, 32 percent are black, and the rest are Hispanic). Their mothers are also less well-educated: 60 percent completed high school and only 18 percent proceeded to further education.

Mean standardized z-scores of child height are reported in Table 1; a z-score of zero implies that the child's height is equal to the median height of a well-nourished child. Girls tend to be slightly taller than boys, relative to the standards, but none of these differences is significant. The average white and Hispanic child is the same height as the median child in the NCHS standards; blacks, however, are significantly taller, reflecting genetic differences. About 3 percent of the sample children are stunted (that is, their heights, given age and sex, are less than 90 percent of the median height of a U.S. child; Waterlow et al. 1977). The distribution of heights of Hispanics is more fat tailed: 13 percent of Hispanic children are stunted.

Many young women have children out of wedlock; in the NLS Child Mother sample, mothers of one-third of all children had never been married by the first survey date after the child's birth. Furthermore, a substantial number of women have changed partners since the birth of the child. The NLS is a panel survey and so it is possible to determine the education of the mother's partner, or husband, in each year of the survey. Among those women who ever report a partner, his level of education changes for 34 percent of all women and 55 percent of black women. This information will be exploited in order to separately study the impact on child height of the education of the *father*,[13] the *current partner* (in 1986) and the average education of all partners or spouses present in the household since the child's birth (weighted by the number of years the person is reported to be present); this variable will be referred to as *partners' mean education*.

The effects of mother's and her partner's education on z-scores of child height are reported for all children in Table 2. Levels of parental education are represented by three dummies (with the excluded category being six years of education or less).[14] Asymptotic t-statistics are reported below the regression coefficients

---

11. This is the same data source used in Desai et al. (1989) who restricted attention to four-year-old children.

12. For details on the sampling frame, attrition, and interviews, see Baker and Mott (1989).

13. Defined as the man reported as the mother's husband or partner in the first year of the survey after the child's birth. For children born prior to the first interview in 1979, the husband or partner in that interview is assigned the status of father.

14. In addition to parental education dummies, the regressions include the mother's height and age at menarche (which affect the health of the child at birth; see Martorell and Habicht 1986), whether a partner or spouse was present during the year of the survey, and dummies for the race, gender and age of the child.

958   The Journal of Human Resources

Table 1
Heights of Male and Female Children: Tests for Differences in z-Scores

	Number of Children	Percent Stunted	Mean Child Height z-Scores		
			Female	Male	Difference
United States					
National Longitudinal Survey: mother and child sample, 1986 (All children < 12 years)					
All children	4,704	3.4	0.127 (0.036)	0.033 (0.041)	0.094 (0.054)
Blacks	1,513	4.2	0.254 (0.070)	0.190 (0.078)	0.064 (0.105)
Hispanics	856	13.1	0.018 (0.088)	−0.102 (0.084)	0.120 (0.122)
Whites	2,335	3.3	0.083 (0.046)	−0.015 (0.058)	0.098 (0.074)
Ghana					
Living Standards Survey, 1987–88 (Children < 12 years)					
Urban	990	15.7	−0.975 (0.086)	−1.209 (0.066)	0.234 (0.108)
Brazil					
Household expenditure survey (ENDEF), 1974–75 (Children < 8 years)					
Northeast urban	9,266	24.8	−1.321 (0.023)	−1.473 (0.024)	0.152 (0.034)
(Children 3–60 months)					
Northeast urban	6,176	22.8	−1.386 (0.027)	−1.538 (0.028)	0.152 (0.039)
Demographic and Health Survey, 1986 (Children 3–60 months)					
Northeast urban	647	11.6	−0.959 (0.076)	−1.203 (0.068)	0.244 (0.102)
Northeast rural	659	22.0	−1.321 (0.023)	−1.473 (0.024)	0.152 (0.034)

Notes: Percent stunted is proportion below 90 percent of median height of well nourished child of same age and sex (based on NCHS standards). z-scores computed with same standards. Standard errors in parentheses.

and χ^2 test statistics for joint significance of covariates are reported at the foot of each panel. Since homoskedasticity of the errors is rejected in the regression models, all estimates of the variance-covariance matrix (and associated test statistics) are based on the jackknife (Efron 1982) which is robust to arbitrary forms of heteroskedasticity.[15]

Maternal education has a bigger effect on child height than her partner's education, presumably because mothers spend more time in child rearing activities. More important for this paper is the fact that independent of the definition of partner's education, mother's education has a bigger effect on the height of her daughter than her son. In all regressions, the education effect on daughter's height is positive and significant, but the effect on son's height is essentially zero. These gender differences are significant (at a 10 percent size of test) in two cases: when partners' mean or father's education are included in the regression. Mothers apparently devote more resources to improving the health of their daughters than to their sons.

In contrast, both the partners' mean education and father's education have a positive effect on son's height but a negative effect on daughter's height, though none of these is significant. The effect of the education of the current partner is much like maternal education and has a bigger impact on girls than boys. This might suggest that current partners, who differ from the father, have preferences regarding child health closer to those of the mother or at least behave as if they do.[16] The effects of the father's and the current partner's education are significant only in the regression that includes both sets of variables in which case the father's education coefficients can be interpreted as measuring the effect of an *absent* father. He has a significant positive effect on his son's height and this effect is significantly larger than the effect on his daughter's height. Absent fathers appear to devote more resources to improving the health of their sons than their daughters. Current partners, on the other hand, have a significantly larger effect on girls relative to boys (with a 10 percent size of test). If the current partner is the father, then there is no significant difference in the impact of his education on sons and daughters.

Stratification by race turns out to be informative (Table 3). The larger impact of maternal education on her daughter's height is significant only for blacks and

---

15. For example, Lagrange Multiplier test statistics for heteroskedasticity (Breusch and Pagan 1980) are about 1,000 for each regression in Table 2. The χ^2 are all over 400 for the regressions in Panel b of Table 3 and for Panel A the test statistics are 182, 458, and 1,245 for blacks, Hispanics, and whites, respectively. The χ^2s have between 30 and 40 degrees of freedom: clearly homoskedasticity is rejected in all these models. The same is true for models estimated with the other three surveys and so heteroskedasticity consistent estimates of the variance-covariance matrix are used for all models. This is a more conservative strategy than simply using the OLS estimates of standard errors which are typically between 10 and 30 percent smaller than the corresponding jackknife estimates. A comparison of the jackknife, White, and ordinary least squares estimators of the variance-covariance matrix is discussed in the appendix; the White estimates perform poorly in the presence of leverage points and in some cases inferences based on these estimates are misleading.

16. This may be because of better matching of preferences. Alternatively, it may reflect that the mother has more power in asserting her preferences over child health in the absence of the biological father.

Table 2
Effect of Education on Child Height: United States (NLS Mother-Child, 1986)

	Females	Males	Difference	Females	Males	Difference
Mother's education						
(1) if 7–12 years	0.739	−0.084	−0.823	0.773	−0.096	−0.870
	(2.05)	(0.26)	(1.70)	(2.04)	(0.28)	(1.71)
13–20 years	0.937	−0.026	−0.963	0.954	−0.088	−1.041
	(2.52)	(0.07)	(1.88)	(2.44)	(0.24)	(1.93)
Partners' mean education						
(1) if 7–12 years	−0.086	0.137	0.223	—	—	—
	(0.63)	(0.87)	(1.07)			
13–20 years	−0.183	0.235	0.418	—	—	—
	(1.11)	(1.17)	(1.61)			
Father's education						
(1) if 7–12 years	—	—	—	−0.242	0.213	0.455
				(0.74)	(0.50)	(0.85)
13–20 years	—	—	—	−0.257	0.467	0.724
				(0.74)	(1.05)	(1.28)
χ^2 for joint significance of						
Mother's education	8.386	0.322	3.621	7.660	0.088	3.966
	(0.01)	(0.43)	(0.08)	(0.01)	(0.48)	(0.07)
Partners' mean education	1.349	1.370	2.623	—	—	—
	(0.26)	(0.25)	(0.14)			
Father's education	—	—	—	0.556	2.993	2.660
				(0.38)	(0.11)	(0.13)
All covariates	209.447	120.217	329.594	202.196	126.460	328.586
	(0.00)	(0.00)	(0.00)	(0.00)	(0.00)	(0.00)

Mother's education						
(1) if 7–12 years	0.682	−0.025	−0.707	0.728	−0.012	−0.740
	(1.75)	(0.07)	(1.31)	(1.86)	(0.03)	(1.37)
13–20 years	0.846	0.019	−0.827	0.899	−0.001	−0.899
	(2.12)	(0.05)	(1.47)	(2.24)	(0.00)	(1.58)
Father's education						
(1) if 7–12 years	—	—	—	−0.608	0.504	1.112
				(1.34)	(1.52)	(1.98)
13–20 years	—	—	—	−0.675	0.875	1.550
				(1.41)	(2.42)	(2.58)
Current partner's education						
(1) if 7–12 years	0.085	−0.143	−0.227	0.509	−0.472	−0.981
	(0.23)	(0.31)	(0.39)	(1.05)	(1.23)	(1.59)
13–20 years	0.100	−0.038	−0.139	0.569	−0.629	−1.198
	(0.26)	(0.08)	(0.23)	(1.14)	(1.52)	(1.85)
χ^2 for joint significance of						
Mother's education	5.971	0.140	2.275	6.521	0.009	2.793
	(0.03)	(0.47)	(0.16)	(0.02)	(0.50)	(0.12)
Father's education	—	—	—	1.324	2.417	7.639
				(0.26)	(0.15)	(0.01)
Current partner's education	0.074	0.628	0.377	1.986	6.938	3.584
	(0.48)	(0.37)	(0.41)	(0.19)	(0.02)	(0.08)
All covariates	207.986	116.616	324.532	209.453	136.309	345.688
	(0.00)	(0.00)	(0.00)	(0.00)	(0.00)	(0.08)

Notes: t-statistics in parentheses below estimated effects; p-values below χ^2 statistics. All statistics based on jackknifed estimates of variance-covariance matrix. Coefficients multiplied by 100. Father's education is education of male spouse or partner reported in first survey after child's birth. Current partner is spouse or partner reported in 1986. Partners' mean education is mean of education of all partners/spouses reported by mother since first survey after birth of child. There are 4,704 children in the sample.

Hispanics[17] and the education of black mothers has an absolutely large and significantly negative impact on her son's height. Partners' mean education has
a significantly bigger impact on sons, relative to daughters, only for whites.[18]
Apparently, black and Hispanic women tend to allocate resources towards their
daughters and white men towards their sons.

Regressions for black children only are reported in the lower panel of Table 3
using alternative indicators of education of the man in the home. Maternal education effects are very robust to the specification of partner's education: in all cases,
she allocates more resources to her daughters. Whether or not current partner's
education is included in the regressions, father's education has a large positive
and significant impact on son's height although this effect is not significantly
larger than it is on daughters.

1. Robustness of Results

Interactions between mother's and her partner's education are small and insignificant. The inclusion of these interactions has no impact on the results described
above. Maternal height is included in each regression to capture both phenotype
and genotype influences on child height; the effect of mother's height is positive
and slightly (but not significantly) larger for girls.

The NLS data also report weight and length at birth for each child. If the
results for child height reflect behavioral differences, then the effect of parental
education on the birthweight and length of a girl should be the same as that on a
boy. In all cases, this turns out to be true. In fact, in a regression of *growth* in
height (current height less birth length), the estimated effects of parental education are almost identical to those described above although the coefficients of
interest are estimated slightly more precisely.

It may be that all the results thus far reflect heterogeneity across households
rather than differences in the impact of parental education on the heights of
brothers and sisters. In the sample of 4,704 children, there are 3,246 mothers, of
whom nearly half have more than one child under twelve. Regression errors, ξ_i,
which incorporate unobserved family specific health heterogeneity, may not be
independent across observations. Random effects estimates exploit the efficiency
gains associated with the structure of the errors.

Corresponding to the results in panel A of Table 3, random effects estimates
are reported in panel A of Table A1. A Lagrange Multiplier test for the absence
of error components (Breusch and Pagan 1980) is significantly different from zero
only for whites in the fully interacted model; a Hausman test for no correlation
between error components and regressors cannot be rejected.[19] In all regressions,
the differences between the ordinary least squares and random effects estimates

---

17. In the case of Hispanics, this is true only for all women relative to those with 0–6 years of education.
Individually, the maternal education dummies are insignificant, but taken together they are jointly significant with a χ^2 of 5.0 and a p-value of 0.04.

18. This is also true if partners' mean education is replaced by father's or current partner's education.

19. For white children, the LM test is 7.9 (with a critical value of 3.84); the Hausman test statistic is
38.4, which is less than the critical value of 53.4 for 38 covariates.

are not only insignificant but also small in magnitude. Since this is true in all the models reported in this paper, we report only least squares estimates of coefficients.

For the subsample of 2,820 children in which there are at least two children in the household, the impact of unobserved heterogeneity across households can be swept out of the estimates. Decomposing the regression error for each child, ξ_i, into two components, a household effect, $\bar{v}_h$, common across siblings, and a child specific effect, v_i, then the inclusion of the household fixed effect, $\bar{v}_h$, in the model (4) controls for *all* (unobserved and observed) household heterogeneity. Since, in this model, the fixed effect, $\bar{v}_h$, subsumes all family and community heterogeneity, $\bar{\mu}_f$ and $\bar{\mu}_c$, I cannot separately identify their effects; I cannot, for example, measure the impact of maternal education on the height of a son. By including interactions between child gender and family (as well as community) characteristics, however, I can estimate the *difference* between the impact of maternal education on a son relative to a daughter and this is exactly what I want. Table 4 presents the results of estimating the regressions

(4') $h_i = h_i(\bar{\mu}_i, I_b^* \bar{\mu}_i, I_b^* \bar{\mu}_f, I_b^* y, I_b^* \bar{\mu}', I_b^* \bar{\mu}_c, \bar{v}_h, v_i),$

where I_b is an indicator function for the gender of the child (and $\bar{\mu}_i$ excludes the gender dummy). The first column of each panel repeats the OLS estimates from Table 3 of the interaction between parental education and the indicator function (set to unity for a son). The second column reports the estimates including all households in which there are at least two siblings in the sample. This sample includes households in which all children are the same gender and so, in the third column, attention is restricted to the 1,702 children in households with at least one son and one daughter.

The upper panel of Table 4 corresponds with panel A in Table 3, stratifying on race and including the average education of the mother's partners. Controlling for all household heterogeneity, among blacks, maternal education has a significantly bigger impact on the height of a daughter relative to a son and amongst whites, the impact of the partner's education is significantly larger on a son, relative to a daughter. These results are true even when comparisons are made between brothers and sisters within the same household; this must be as close to approximating a natural experiment as we are likely to come in this sort of study. Among black children, the partner's education has a significantly bigger effect on a son, relative to a daughter, when controlling for household heterogeneity but this is not significant when brothers and sisters within the same household are compared.

I focus on black children in the lower panel of Table 4 and vary the definition of the partner. In all cases, the impact of maternal education is significantly larger on a daughter relative to a son: this is apparently a robust result. The current partner's education had a bigger effect on a girl's height than on a boy (the OLS coefficient is negative, but not significant); controlling for unobserved household heterogeneity, this result is reversed and the impact of the partner's education is not only bigger on boys but significantly bigger for men with 7 to 12 years of schooling. Similarly without controlling for all household variation, there is no significantly different effect of the father's education on sons and daughters; comparing brothers with sisters, however, father's education has a bigger effect

Table 3
Effect of Education on Child Height: United States (NLS Mother-Child, 1986)

(A) Stratified by race of child
Effect of mother's education and mean of all partners' education

	Blacks			Hispanics			Whites		
	Females	Males	Difference	Females	Males	Difference	Females	Males	Difference
Mother's education									
(1) if 7–12 years	2.281	−2.063	−4.345	0.665	−0.314	−0.979	0.106	1.560	1.455
	(1.34)	(4.33)	(2.46)	(1.29)	(1.56)	(1.77)	(0.30)	(1.05)	(0.96)
13–20 years	2.425	−2.188	−4.612	0.793	0.321	−0.472	0.365	1.599	1.234
	(1.41)	(4.27)	(2.57)	(1.44)	(1.10)	(0.76)	(0.99)	(1.05)	(0.79)
Partners' mean education									
(1) if 7–12 years	0.056	0.060	0.004	−0.009	−0.068	−0.059	−0.293	0.267	0.561
	(0.21)	(0.12)	(0.01)	(0.03)	(0.27)	(0.16)	(1.63)	(1.69)	(2.34)
13–20 years	−0.162	−0.046	0.116	−0.097	0.200	0.297	−0.398	0.333	0.731
	(0.55)	(0.08)	(0.18)	(0.29)	(0.68)	(0.66)	(1.78)	(1.38)	(2.22)
χ^2 for joint significance of									
Mother's education	2.294	19.272	6.907	2.092	7.209	4.997	3.833	1.113	2.085
	(0.16)	(0.00)	(0.02)	(0.18)	(0.01)	(0.04)	(0.07)	(0.29)	(0.18)
Partners' mean education	1.167	0.272	0.149	0.137	1.425	1.145	3.382	3.225	6.426
	(0.28)	(0.44)	(0.46)	(0.47)	(0.25)	(0.28)	(0.09)	(0.10)	(0.02)
All covariates	138.358	108.334	246.885	32.961	20.235	53.258	52.317	38.391	220.080
	(0.00)	(0.06)	(0.00)	(0.00)	(0.05)	(0.01)	(0.00)	(0.00)	(0.00)

(B) Black children
Effect of education of mother, father, and current partner

	Education of Current Partner			Education of Child's Father			Education of Current Partner and Child's Father		
	Females	Males	Difference	Females	Males	Difference	Females	Males	Difference
Mother's education									
(1) if 7–12 years	2.323	−2.034	−4.357	2.297	−2.029	−4.326	2.293	−1.981	−4.274
	(1.37)	(4.10)	(2.46)	(1.36)	(4.43)	(2.47)	(1.36)	(4.34)	(2.44)
13–20 years	2.443	−2.137	−4.580	2.422	−2.197	−4.619	2.422	−2.127	−4.549
	(1.43)	(4.02)	(2.56)	(1.42)	(4.40)	(2.60)	(1.42)	(4.25)	(2.56)
Current partner's education									
(1) if 7–12 years	0.123	−0.447	−0.570	—	—	—	0.083	−0.399	−0.482
	(0.20)	(0.71)	(0.64)				(0.15)	(0.79)	(0.64)
13–20 years	0.023	−0.677	−0.699	—	—	—	0.023	−0.769	−0.792
	(0.03)	(1.04)	(0.75)				(0.04)	(1.28)	(0.92)
Father's education									
(1) if 7–12 years	—	—	—	0.192	1.585	1.393	0.202	1.569	1.367
				(0.02)	(4.36)	(0.42)	(0.02)	(4.12)	(0.01)
13–20 years	—	—	—	0.033	1.562	1.530	0.078	1.812	1.734
				(0.00)	(3.74)	(0.46)	(0.01)	(3.54)	(0.02)
χ^2 for joint significance of									
Mother's education	2.219	17.101	6.682	2.255	20.359	7.165	2.236	19.295	6.837
	(0.17)	(0.00)	(0.02)	(0.16)	(0.00)	(0.01)	(0.16)	(0.00)	(0.02)
Current partner's education	0.223	1.339	0.585	—	—	—	0.069	1.718	0.911
	(0.45)	(0.26)	(0.37)				(0.48)	(0.21)	(0.32)
Father's education	—	—	—	0.428	19.912	0.305	0.198	18.991	0.516
				(0.00)	(0.00)	(0.43)	(0.45)	(0.00)	(0.39)
All covariates	133.092	107.685	240.936	136.877	118.857	255.985	136.334	132.570	269.074
	(0.00)	(0.00)	(0.00)	(0.00)	(0.00)	(0.08)	(0.00)	(0.00)	(0.00)

Notes: See Table 2. The sample consists of 1,513 black, 856 Hispanic and 2,335 white children.

Table 4
Impact of Education on Child Height, Including Household Fixed Effects: United States (NLS Mother-Child, 1986)

(A) Stratified by race of child
Effect of mother's education and mean of all partners' education

Interaction Between Dummy (1) for Son and	Blacks			Hispanics			Whites		
		Fixed Effects			Fixed Effects			Fixed Effects	
	OLS	∃ Sample	If ∃ Boy and Girl	OLS	∃ Sample	If ∃ Boy and Girl	OLS	∃ Sample	If ∃ Boy and Girl
Mother's education									
(1) if 7–12 years	−4.35	−3.11	−2.73	−0.98	−0.30	−0.24	1.46	2.87	2.82
	(2.5)	(6.0)	(4.8)	(1.8)	(1.2)	(0.8)	(1.0)	(1.7)	(1.7)
13–20 years	−4.61	−3.84	−3.57	−0.47	−0.45	−0.50	1.23	2.46	2.40
	(2.6)	(6.7)	(5.5)	(0.8)	(1.3)	(1.3)	(0.8)	(1.5)	(1.5)
Partners' mean education									
(1) if 7–12 years	0.00	1.13	0.84	−0.06	−0.46	−0.41	0.56	0.56	0.65
	(0.0)	(2.1)	(1.4)	(0.2)	(1.3)	(1.0)	(2.3)	(2.2)	(2.3)
13–20 years	0.12	0.42	0.11	0.30	0.53	0.77	0.73	1.45	1.67
	(0.8)	(0.7)	(0.2)	(0.7)	(1.2)	(1.5)	(2.2)	(1.2)	(3.4)
Sample size	1,513	906	564	856	508	296	2,335	1,406	842

(B) Black children
Effect of education of mother, father, and current partner

Interaction Between Dummy (1) for Son and	Education of Current Partner			Education of Child's Father			Education of Current Partner and Child's Father		
		Fixed Effects			Fixed Effects			Fixed Effects	
	OLS	∀ Sample	If ∃ Boy and Girl	OLS	∀ Sample	If ∃ Boy and Girl	OLS	∀ Sample	If ∃ Boy and Girl
Mother's education									
(1) if 7–12 years	−4.36	−3.18	−2.81	−4.33	−3.18	−2.94	−4.27	−3.20	−2.87
	(2.5)	(6.7)	(5.5)	(2.5)	(6.8)	(5.6)	(2.4)	(6.4)	(5.2)
13–20 years	−4.58	−3.84	−3.58	4.62	−3.92	−3.80	−4.55	−3.85	−3.65
	(2.6)	(7.3)	(6.2)	(2.6)	(7.4)	(6.3)	(2.6)	(7.0)	(5.9)
Current partner's education									
(1) if 7–12 years	−0.57	1.12	1.00	—	—	—	−0.48	1.16	1.03
	(0.6)	(4.3)	(3.9)				(0.6)	(4.3)	(3.5)
13–20 years	−0.70	−0.46	−0.53	—	—	—	−0.79	−0.28	−0.50
	(0.8)	(0.9)	(1.0)				(0.9)	(0.5)	(0.8)
Father's education									
(1) if 7–12 years	—	—	—	1.39	2.10	2.24	1.37	2.30	2.36
				(0.4)	(5.6)	(5.8)	(0.0)	(6.2)	(6.1)
13–20 years	—	—	—	1.53	0.67	0.90	1.73	1.71	2.21
				(0.5)	(1.1)	(1.2)	(0.0)	(2.4)	(2.3)

Notes: See Table 2. Regressions include interactions among all covariates in regression model and dummy (1) if child is male. First column in each block (OLS) is estimate reported in third column of each panel in Table 3; second column (all sample) includes all households in which there is more than one child; third column includes only those households in which there is at least a son and a daughter in the household.

on sons and this is significant if the father has 7 to 12 years of schooling. When the characteristics of both the current partner and father are included in the regression, these results persist after controlling for household heterogeneity, and the bigger impact of paternal education is significant for sons of fathers with both 7 to 12 and 13 to 20 years of schooling.

B. Ghana Living Standards Survey, 1987–88

The Ghana Living Standards Survey (GLSS), which was carried out by the Government of Ghana, in collaboration with The World Bank, collected very detailed information on a nationwide random sample of about 3,200 households. The Ghana LSS is part of a program being implemented in several developing countries which, using common instruments, collects extensive socioeconomic information from households on expenditure, income and labor supply, and assets. Demographic data on each individual in the household includes age, sex, education, and anthropometric measures.[20]

The survey is an ongoing effort with a panel dimension since half the households are enumerated for two years; I will focus on urban households enumerated during the first year of the survey, 1987–88. Relative to most other African societies, women are unusually active in the Ghanian economy, especially in trading and extra-domestic activities: they thus wield a good deal of power in the household (Peil 1977, Hill 1975, Bleek 1987). Husbands and wives seldom pool their resources but "prefer to keep their money separate in order to avoid conflicts" (Oppong 1982, see also Guyer 1988). Women are typically responsible for child rearing as well as food production and distribution: they are likely, therefore, to have a large influence on the nutritional status of their children. Fathers, on the other hand, tend to be peripheral figures in the lives of their children (Oppong and Bleek 1982, Nsamenang 1987); this reflects, in part, the fact that Ghana is a matrilineal society, at least in the south.

Fathers are, however, usually responsible for their children's schooling (Bleek 1987, Ghana Teaching Service 1975): investments in the education of women are low (Schultz 1989). Almost half the women in this sample have received no formal education, about 12 percent received some primary education and 40 percent went beyond primary school. Historically, men have received much more education; in this sample, 65 percent have more than primary education and only 30 percent have no education at all.

As in the U.S. sample discussed above, the Ghanian sample is restricted to children aged less than twelve years, of whom there are 990 children living in 412 households. In Ghana, both boys and girls are significantly shorter, on average, than a well nourished United States child of the same age; relative to the U.S. standards, girls are taller than boys, and this difference is also significant (Table 1). About 16.2 percent of children in urban Ghana are stunted (have heights below 90 percent of the U.S. median).

---

20. Data from the survey have been tabulated in Ghana Statistical Service (1989). The anthropometric and health data are described in Alderman (1989).

Regression results are reported in Table 5.[21] Maternal education has a significant positive effect on the height of daughters, which declines with education and this effect is significantly greater than the effect on sons. Paternal education has a significant negative effect on daughters' heights and, for fathers with primary education, also on sons' heights although the latter effect is absolutely smaller and insignificant for fathers with more than primary schooling. Fathers with more than primary education have a significantly greater effect on their sons' height relative to daughters' and, taking both the father education covariates together, the impact is significantly larger on sons (with a *p*-value of 0.08).

Are fathers trying to harm their children? In a matrilineal society, children inherit not from their fathers but their mother's brothers. Fathers may, therefore, divert resources away from their own children to their nephews. Unfortunately, no data are available on members of the extended family to test this hypothesis. Recall that in Ghana women tend to be responsible for food and traditionally fathers pay for children's education. It turns out that in these data, paternal education is positively associated with the grade in which a child is enrolled and that the effect is significantly bigger for sons.[22]

If education is indicative of power in the household allocation process, then women who are better educated than their husbands should be able to assert their preferences and direct more resources towards commodities they care about. In the lower panel of Table 4, a dummy variable is included to identify these women (who account for 8 percent of the sample). Relative to other mothers, the education of a woman who is better educated than her husband has a large and significant (at 10 percent) effect on her daughter's height, no effect on her son's height and this difference *is* significant. This does not simply reflect nonlinearities in maternal education effects since the result is robust to the inclusion of years of education, of more dummies and both years of education and the dummies.[23]

---

21. No education is the excluded category. The restriction that secondary and post-secondary education have the same impact on child height is not rejected; they are therefore grouped together. In addition to parental education, the regressions include maternal and paternal height as well as dummies for the child's age and sex. Since data are available on both parents' height and they are significant determinants of child height, the sample has been restricted to children with both parents present in the household. This restriction also permits an examination of the effect on child height of the differential between the educational attainment of mothers and fathers. If paternal height is excluded (so that female headed households are included) then the estimated education effects are smaller in magnitude. All of this difference can be explained by the change in the sample composition. If the larger sample is used, the substance of the results reported below is unchanged.

22. In a linear regression of the current grade (of all children aged six through 15 years) on polynomials in the child's age, parental education and parental height, girls whose fathers have more than primary schooling are over half a grade ahead of other girls of the same age. Sons of these fathers, however, are over a grade ahead of boys whose fathers have no education (or only primary schooling) and the difference in the effect on sons and daughters (0.62 of a grade) is significant (with a *t*-statistic of 2.0). Whether the mother has more than primary schooling has no impact on the grade of a son but a positive and significant impact on a daughter (who will be 0.80 of a grade ahead of a girl whose mother has only primary schooling or less). The bigger impact of maternal education on daughter's education relative to that of a son is marginally significant (with a *t*-statistic of 1.7).

23. Similar experiments were conducted with the three other surveys used here; none yielded any significant differences in the impact of the education of women better educated than their partners relative to other women. In the United States this is, in part, due to the fact that few women are better

970   The Journal of Human Resources

Table 5
Effect of Parental Education on Child Height:
Ghana Living Standards Survey, 1987–88: Urban Sector

	Females	Males	Difference
Mother's education			
(1) if primary	1.024	−0.181	−1.204
	(1.86)	(0.99)	(2.07)
(1) if more than primary	0.595	0.079	−0.516
	(3.00)	(0.44)	(1.93)
Father's education			
(1) if primary	−0.917	−0.798	0.119
	(2.49)	(2.54)	(0.25)
(1) if more than primary	−0.549	0.034	0.583
	(2.09)	(0.17)	(1.75)
χ^2 for joint significance of			
Mother's education	9.687	1.656	6.059
	(0.00)	(0.22)	(0.02)
Father's education	6.864	8.706	3.675
	(0.02)	(0.01)	(0.08)
All covariates	368.722	511.518	879.355
	(0.00)	(0.00)	(0.00)
Mother's education			
(1) if primary	0.779	−0.074	−0.853
	(1.63)	(0.30)	(1.64)
(1) if more than primary	0.450	0.258	−0.292
	(2.08)	(1.61)	(1.08)
(1) if mother better educated	0.910	−0.234	−1.184
	(1.66)	(0.78)	(1.87)
Father's education			
(1) if primary	−0.943	−0.790	0.153
	(2.53)	(1.94)	(0.31)
(1) if more than primary	−0.368	0.044	0.324
	(1.67)	(0.22)	(1.11)
χ^2 for joint significance of			
Mother's education	14.267	4.560	7.942
	(0.00)	(0.10)	(0.02)
Father's education	7.364	5.856	5.710
	(0.03)	(0.06)	(0.06)
All covariates	340.594	461.549	852.965
	(0.00)	(0.00)	(0.00)

Notes: *t*-statistics in parentheses below estimated effects; *p*-values below χ^2 statistics. All statistics based on jackknifed estimates of variance-covariance matrix. Coefficients multiplied by 100. There are 990 children in the sample.

In the survey, 60 percent of mothers have more than one child under 12; mother-specific random effects estimates are almost identical to those in Table 4.[24] Marriages in Ghana are sometimes polygenous and it turns out that for 12 percent of women in the sample, there are at least two mothers of measured children in the same household. As is the case for the U.S. samples, household-specific random effects are essentially identical to the OLS estimates.[25] Estimates incorporating household fixed effects are reported in Table 6. The significantly bigger impact of maternal education on daughters, relative to sons, is robust to this specification, at least for women with primary education. Furthermore, even when brothers and sisters are compared, there is evidence that the impact of the education of a woman who is better educated than her husband is significantly bigger on daughters.

C. Brazilian Household Surveys 1974–75 and 1986

Two household surveys from Brazil are examined. The first survey, the *Estudo Nacional de Despesa Familiar* (ENDEF), is a random national sample of nearly 55,000 households carried out by the Brazilian statistical agency, IBGE, in 1974–75. It is very comprehensive by large scale expenditure survey standards with data collected on household expenditures and food consumption. In addition to the usual sociodemographic information, each individual reports labor supply and earnings as well as nonlabor income. The height and weight of all members of the household were measured by an anthropometrist.[26] The second survey was collected in 1986 as part of the *Demographic and Health Survey* (DHS) program which has been implemented in about 50 countries worldwide and focuses on fertility, contraception, maternal and child health.

Brazil, like much of Latin America, is a *machista* (male-dominated) society (Neuhouser 1989) although sociologists argue that household allocation decisions are complex and women have a good deal of control over food expenditures and the distribution of food (Goldani 1989, Neuhouser 1989). As in Ghana, women are likely to have a big influence on their children's nutrition. During the twelve years between these two surveys, Brazilian society has seen dramatic changes. Female labor force participation rates have risen by about 20 percent to 37 percent in 1986 (IBGE 1988), while total fertility rates have declined from above 6 in 1974 to about 3.5 in 1986 (National Research Council 1983). The influence of the Catholic church has been eroded with a rise in the popularity of civil marriages, divorce rates and of consensual unions, especially among young adults (Goldani 1989, Henriques 1988). All these changes suggest women have more opportunities outside the home and so their "threat points" will have risen during this period: the

---

educated than their partners. In the Brazilian ENDEF survey (discussed below), education is only reported in groups and so education differences between parents have to be very large in order to be observed in the data.

24. The hypothesis of no group variance is rejected with an LM test statistic of 4.11 but the Hausman specification test statistic (28.67) is less than the critical value.

25. The LM test statistic for no group variance is 5.60 and the Hausman test is 28.60.

26. The data are presented in tabulations by the Brazilian statistical agency, IBGE (1978).

Table 6
Effect of Parental Education on Child Height, Including Household Fixed Effects: Ghana Living Standards Survey, 1987–88: Urban Sector

Interaction Between Dummy (1) for Son and	OLS	Fixed Effects	
		All Households	If ∃ Boy and Girl
Mother's education			
(1) if primary	−1.20	−1.85	−1.85
	(2.1)	(2.6)	(2.4)
(1) if more than primary	−0.52	−0.18	−0.12
	(1.9)	(0.3)	(0.2)
Father's education			
(1) if primary	0.12	0.14	0.11
	(0.3)	(0.2)	(0.1)
(1) if more than primary	0.58	0.50	0.46
	(1.8)	(0.9)	(0.7)
Mother's education			
(1) if primary	−0.85	−1.02	−1.02
	(1.6)	(1.3)	(1.2)
(1) if more than primary	−0.29	0.30	0.37
	(1.1)	(0.5)	(0.5)
(1) if mother better educated	−1.18	−2.21	−2.17
	(1.9)	(2.2)	(1.9)
Father's education			
(1) if primary	0.15	0.21	0.19
	(0.3)	(0.2)	(0.2)
(1) if more than primary	0.32	−0.08	−0.11
	(1.1)	(0.1)	(0.2)
Sample size	990	595	403

Notes: See Tables 4 and 5.

individualistic models of household resource allocations would suggest women will have a bigger influence on outcomes in the later survey.

Anthropometric data in the DHS were recorded for children aged three to 60 months living in the Northeast, the poorest region of Brazil.[27] There are 1,316 children in this sample. To facilitate comparisons, the ENDEF sample will also be restricted to the Northeast; results for both urban and rural children will be

27. Tabulations of these data are presented in BEMFAM-IRD (1988).

discussed although I will focus on urban households. Since the heights of all household members were recorded in ENDEF, the sample will be restricted to 9,266 children less than eight years old, both of whose parents are present in the household.

Although Brazil has invested relatively little in education given its level of income (Schultz 1987) there is no apparent difference in enrollment rates by sex. In the 1974–75 ENDEF sample, almost 30 percent of mothers are illiterate, 16 percent have completed (four years of) elementary school and 9 percent have more education; fathers are very slightly better educated.[28] According to the 1980 Brazilian census, women have recently overtaken men in levels of education and this is reflected in the 1986 DHS: urban women have 4.8 years of education on average, their partners have 4.6 years; in the rural sector, the average woman has spent only 1.9 years at school, her partner 2.1 years.

The average child in the Northeast of Brazil is substantially shorter than a well-nourished child in the United States but slightly taller than a Ghanaian child. There have been dramatic improvements in the nutritional status of Brazilian children over the last fifteen years. The proportion of three- to 60-month-old urban children who were stunted halved between 1974 and 1986 (to 11 percent). Rural children are significantly shorter; 38 percent were stunted in 1974 and 22 percent remained stunted in 1986.

In both Brazilian surveys and in the Ghanaian survey, girls are significantly taller than boys, relative to a well nourished child in the United States. While it may be that there is gender bias in Ghana and Brazil, it seems likely that growth paths there are systematically different from those in the United States. As discussed above, comparisons of levels of standardized anthropometric measures seems to be a very weak basis for drawing conclusions about the presence or absence of gender bias in a society.

1. Estudo Nacional da Despesa Familiar, 1974–75

In the urban ENDEF sample (Table 7), both parents' education have a significant positive effect on child height. The impact of mother's education is bigger on girls although the significance of this difference is marginal; when controls for unobserved household heterogeneity are included, however, the differences are significant among women who have secondary schooling or more (Table 8). Father's education has a bigger effect on boys and this difference is clearly significant (taken jointly) in the OLS estimates; for boys, the effect of paternal education is significantly larger than the impact of maternal education. In the case of paternal education, these differences are no longer significant when household fixed effects are included.

In order to disentangle the role of preferences from technology, each parent's nonlabor income is added to the regression in the lower panel of Table 7: in this sample, 35 percent of fathers and 14 percent of mothers report any nonlabor

---

28. Education in this survey is reported in discrete intervals only; respondents who claimed to be able to read and write but had less than four years of education were deemed "literate."

Table 7
Effect of Parental Education on Child Height: Brazil, ENDEF 1974–75:
Urban Northeast

	Females	Males	Difference
Mother's education			
(1) if literate	0.344	0.217	−0.127
	(6.60)	(3.93)	(1.67)
(1) if completed elementary school	0.445	0.334	−0.111
	(6.17)	(4.09)	(1.01)
(1) if completed secondary school or higher	0.835	0.572	−0.264
	(8.10)	(5.38)	(1.78)
Father's education			
(1) if literate	0.189	0.268	0.079
	(3.54)	(4.80)	(1.02)
(1) if completed elementary school	0.399	0.595	0.196
	(5.39)	(7.24)	(1.78)
(1) if completed secondary school or higher	0.666	1.132	0.466
	(6.96)	(11.12)	(3.34)
χ^2 for joint significance of			
Mother's education	80.117	33.139	4.357
	(0.00)	(0.00)	(0.11)
Father's education	52.984	128.040	11.475
	(0.00)	(0.00)	(0.01)
All covariates	6,242.888	6,791.399	13,032.880
	(0.00)	(0.00)	(0.00)
Mother's nonlabor income	0.232	0.002	−0.231
(Cr$ 000,000)	(2.72)	(0.02)	(1.80)
Father's nonlabor income	0.039	0.029	−0.010
(Cr$ 000,000)	(1.75)	(1.02)	(0.26)
Mother's education			
(1) if literate	0.341	0.216	−0.125
	(6.54)	(3.90)	(1.64)
(1) if completed elementary school	0.434	0.330	−0.104
	(5.99)	(4.03)	(0.95)
(1) if completed secondary school or higher	0.803	0.556	−0.247
	(7.81)	(5.25)	(1.67)
Father's education			
(1) if literate	0.189	0.267	0.079
	(3.53)	(4.80)	(1.02)
(1) if completed elementary school	0.396	0.591	0.195
	(5.36)	(7.20)	(1.76)
(1) if completed secondary school or higher	0.649	1.122	0.473
	(6.77)	(10.85)	(3.36)
χ^2 for joint significance of			
Mother's education	75.744	31.863	4.019
	(0.00)	(0.00)	(0.13)
Father's education	50.579	122.487	11.589
	(0.00)	(0.00)	(0.01)
Mother's = father's nonlabor income	4.82	0.07	2.68
	(0.01)	(0.39)	(0.05)
All covariates	6,275.592	6,800.600	13,074.781
	(0.00)	(0.00)	(0.00)

Notes: *t*-statistics below estimated effects (multiplied by 100); *p*-values below χ^2 statistics. All statistics based on jackknifed estimates of variance-covariance matrix. There are 9,266 children in the sample.

income.[29] Since the health production function, (1), does not depend on income, if it has differential effects on sons and daughters then this must reflect differences in preferences, (2). Because nonlabor income is potentially endogenous, and also likely to be measured with error, regressions with and without income are reported. A comparison of the upper and lower panels of Table 7 demonstrate that its inclusion has a tiny impact on the parental education coefficients.

According to the OLS estimates, father's nonlabor income has no impact on child height. However, with the inclusion of household fixed effects (Table 8), paternal nonlabor income has a significantly bigger effect on a son, relative to a daughter (at least when all multiple child households are included in the sample). Mother's nonlabor income, in contrast, has a positive and significant impact on her daughter's height but no effect on her son's height. This difference is significant (at a 10 percent size of test in Table 7) and is also significant (at 1 percent) when the regressions include controls for unobserved household variation (Table 8). The evidence suggests that women prefer to allocate resources to improving the health of their daughters.

It may be argued that nonlabor income reflects previous labor supply and so is properly treated as endogenous. Since the analysis is restricted to families with young children, most of the parents are early in the life cycle (the average mother is age 32) and thus their nonlabor income is likely to be more than just saved past earnings. But even if endogeneity is not empirically important, the estimated coefficients will be biased if nonlabor income is measured with error.

In general, both concerns provide good reasons for pause. However, it is difficult to explain the *differential* impact of nonlabor income on daughters, relative to sons, invoking either a simultaneity or measurement error argument. The bias in both cases should affect sons and daughters equally, unless women with sons are more (or less) prone to misreporting income than those with daughters or the two groups of women have different tastes for work and savings. Furthermore, the estimates in Table 8 sweep out all household specific fixed effects (including tastes for work and measurement error) and so those estimates should not be contaminated by bias due to unobserved heterogeneity.

I turn next to explicitly testing whether mothers and fathers share the same preferences. As discussed in Section II, if they do, then the distribution of income within the household should have no impact on child height. Put another way, maternal and paternal income effects should be equal. This hypothesis is tested at the bottom of Table 7. It is rejected for daughters but not for sons indicating that preference differences among parents are greater with respect to investments in daughters.

Because these tests may also be biased by simultaneity or measurement error, the third column of Table 7 tests whether differences in the effect of nonlabor income on sons and daughters are different depending on whether the income is attributed to the father or mother. This difference-in-difference is significant (at 5 percent); it is also significant when household fixed effects are controlled (in Table 8). Thus, the evidence is not consistent with the *common preference* model

---

29. Nonlabor income includes income from financial and physical assets, gifts, and income from pensions, social security, and workers compensation. For a fuller description of the data, see Thomas (1990).

Economic Demography I

Table 8
Effect of Parental Education on Child Height, Including Household Fixed Effects: Brazil, ENDEF 1974–75: Urban Northeast

Interaction Between Dummy (1) for Son and	OLS	Fixed Effects All Households	If ∃ Boy and Girl
Mother's education			
(1) if literate	−0.127	0.030	0.030
	(1.67)	(0.41)	(0.41)
(1) if completed elementary school	−0.111	0.055	0.052
	(1.01)	(0.52)	(0.49)
(1) if completed secondary school	−0.264	−0.316	−0.318
or higher	(1.78)	(2.12)	(2.14)
Father's education			
(1) if literate	0.079	−0.074	−0.085
	(1.02)	(1.07)	(1.21)
(1) if completed elementary school	0.196	−0.053	−0.065
	(1.78)	(0.52)	(0.64)
(1) if completed secondary school	0.466	0.174	0.149
or higher	(3.34)	(1.28)	(1.10)
Mother's nonlabor income	−0.231	−0.256	−0.260
(Cr$ 000,000)	(1.80)	(2.32)	(2.28)
Father's nonlabor income	−0.010	0.043	0.035
(Cr$ 000,000)	(0.26)	(1.97)	(1.56)
Mother's education			
(1) if literate	−0.125	0.031	0.032
	(1.64)	(0.43)	(0.44)
(1) if completed elementary school	−0.104	0.055	0.054
	(0.95)	(0.51)	(0.51)
(1) if completed secondary school	−0.247	−0.292	−0.291
or higher	(1.67)	(2.00)	(1.99)
Father's education			
(1) if literate	0.079	−0.076	−0.087
	(1.02)	(1.10)	(1.24)
(1) if completed elementary school	0.195	−0.059	−0.071
	(1.76)	(0.59)	(0.70)
(1) if completed secondary school	0.473	0.152	0.130
or higher	(3.36)	(1.12)	(0.96)
χ^2 for equality of mother's and father's nonlabor income effects	2.68	6.92	6.73
	(0.05)	(0.00)	(0.01)
Sample size	9,266	5,270	3,560

Notes: See Tables 4 and 7.

of the household. The fact that rejection of the model is robust to the inclusion of household fixed effect suggests that it is not due to income being measured poorly or nonlabor income reflecting previous labor supply decisions.

2. Demographic and Health Survey, 1986

Table 9 reports the regression results for the 1986 DHS sample. In the urban sector, maternal education has a significant positive effect on her daughter's height and this is significantly larger than the positive effect on her son's height. A father's education also has a positive effect on his children's heights but the effect is significant only for sons; it is (marginally) significantly bigger for sons than daughters. Removing the restriction that the impact of parental education be linear does not affect any of the results except that the differential effect of father's education on sons and daughters is no longer significant.

In the rural sector, child height is unresponsive to father's education. Maternal education has a significantly positive effect on both sons and daughters, which is larger on sons, but this difference is not significant in the linear model. Permitting quadratics changes the results dramatically. Maternal education effects on both sons and daughters remain significant; for daughters, there are decreasing marginal returns to additional maternal education (with the effect turning negative when education exceeds 7.4 years); for sons, there are increasing marginal returns to education. The difference, however, is significant overall and positive for the vast majority of mothers (namely the 83 percent who have less than 3.6 years of education). It turns out that none of these differences is significant when household fixed effects are included (and so those results are not reported).

The evidence from both Brazilian surveys tell a similar story. Mothers devote more resources to the health of their daughters and fathers prefer to allocate resources to their sons. The differential impact of maternal education on sons and daughters is not only larger in the 1986 survey but also turns from being insignificant in 1974 to significant in 1986. This is consistent with women having more power in 1986 and thus being able to assert their preferences as their opportunities outside of the home improved.

IV. Discussion

The evidence indicates that mothers and fathers invest different amounts of resources in the human capital of their children. Mothers allocate more resources to their daughters and fathers channel resources towards their sons. This is true in the United States, Brazil, and Ghana.

This surely reflects, at least in part, the technology of child rearing which Durkheim (1933) called the sexual division of labor. A good deal of research over the last two decades by psychologists indicates that fathers play a bigger role in the development of their sons than their daughters. Fathers spend more time with their sons and sons show preference for their fathers at an early age (at least from the second year of life) (Lamb 1976; Morgan, Lye, and Condran 1988). Mothers, on the other hand, tend to spend more time with their daughters and

Table 9
Effect of Parental Education on Child Height: Brazilian Demographic Health Survey, 1986: Northeast Region

	Females	Males	Difference	Females	Males	Difference
Urban						
Mother's education (in years)	1.165 (4.08)	0.250 (0.98)	-0.915 (2.39)	2.183 (3.22)	0.776 (1.15)	-1.407 (1.47)
Mother's education squared				-0.079 (1.78)	-0.044 (0.95)	0.034 (0.53)
Partner's education (in years)	0.150 (0.57)	0.797 (2.99)	0.647 (1.73)	0.193 (0.30)	1.222 (1.88)	0.103 (1.12)
Partner's education squared				0.000 (0.01)	-0.033 (0.61)	0.033 (0.49)
χ^2 for joint significance of						
Mother's education				18.169 (0.00)	1.41 (0.25)	6.611 (0.02)
Partner's education				0.561 (0.38)	11.60 (0.00)	2.837 (0.12)
Rural						
Mother's education (in years)	0.987 (2.67)	1.312 (3.28)	0.325 (0.60)	1.901 (2.50)	-0.169 (0.22)	-2.070 (1.91)
Mother's education squared				-0.128 (1.48)	0.159 (1.90)	0.287 (2.38)
Partner's education (in years)	0.095 (0.23)	0.565 (1.45)	0.470 (0.82)	-1.125 (1.26)	0.497 (0.51)	1.623 (1.23)
Partner's education squared				0.169 (1.58)	-0.038 (0.38)	-0.208 (1.41)
χ^2 for joint significance of						
Mother's education				7.485 (0.01)	11.396 (0.00)	5.724 (0.03)
Partner's education				2.541 (0.14)	0.313 (0.43)	2.003 (0.18)

Notes: See Table 4. There are 647 and 659 children in urban and rural samples. respectively.

have a closer relationship with a daughter than a son. For a synthesis of this research, see Lamb (1976, 1987). Longitudinal data on child development indicate that the absence of a father (because of divorce) has a more severe and enduring impact on boys than girls (Hetherington, Cox, and Cox 1978). Similar differences by gender are reported for the impact of divorce on child health (Mauldon 1990).

Do gender specific investments by mothers and fathers reflect only technological differences? In Brazil, women devote nonlabor income towards improving the health of their daughters but not their sons. The difference between the maternal education effects on girls and boys increased between the first and second surveys (in 1974 and 1986, respectively); the difference became significant by the second survey. During the same period, women's opportunities outside of the home improved substantially. In Ghana, if a woman is better educated than her husband, then her daughter benefits more and her son benefits less from her education than if the husband is better educated than his wife. If nonlabor income, opportunities outside the home, and relative educational status are indicative of power in household allocation decisions, then these results suggest that more powerful women are able to assert their own preferences in the allocation of household resources.

Other evidence in the literature suggests I may be picking up differences in preferences of mothers and fathers. Sociologists and demographers have pointed out that the probability of marital dissolution is smaller if a couple has a son (Spanier and Glick 1981). It is argued that this reflects a higher price of marital dissolution to the father with sons (with whom he spends more time) (Morgan, Lye, and Condran 1988). Fertility preferences are also often gender specific. In the United States, the birth interval between first and second born is independent of gender of the first child among white women but, among black women, it is smaller if the first child is a son. Black women apparently want to have a daughter (Teachman and Schollaert 1989). In several developing countries, the data suggest that fathers with sons are more willing to limit their family size than fathers without sons (Caldwell and Caldwell 1978, Mason and Taj 1987).

Different investments in sons and daughters by mothers and fathers might also reflect different returns to these investments. Children participate in work within the house and family business from an early age in Ghana and girls tend to help mothers, boys work with fathers (Kaye 1962). Children in Africa are also frequently a source of old age security for parents (Caldwell 1977); this is likely to be more important for women, who live longer than men. There is, as far as we can tell, no evidence on whether sons or daughters provide more assistance to mothers or fathers though in a matrilineal society like Ghana, where women and daughters retain close ties, it seems plausible that mothers will realize higher returns from investments in daughters than sons. In the United States, Spitze and Logan (1990) report that daughters are more likely to be in contact with and assist their parents (with money, time, or both) in old age and that a single mother is significantly more likely to be in contact with her children if at least one is a daughter. After the father's death, daughters tend to give more attention to their widowed mothers and sons give less (Hess and Waring 1978).

In sum, in a variety of economic, social, and cultural settings, maternal education has a bigger impact on the height of her daughter than son whereas sons benefit more than daughters as paternal education increases. Taken together, all the evidence suggests that this does not only reflect technological differences in child rearing but, rather, it *suggests* that mothers prefer to allocate resources towards daughters and fathers treat their sons preferentially.

Appendix 1

Comparison of Least Squares, Jackknife, and Infinitesimal Jackknife t-Statistics

This appendix compares estimates of quasi-*t*-statistics based on the jackknife, infinitesimal jackknife (Jaeckel 1972, also suggested by White 1980), and the usual formula for the variance-covariance matrix. Estimates are reported both for least squares and for random effects; for the latter, the variance-covariance matrix for the final weighted least squares estimates is computed by the jackknife, infinitesimal jackknife and usual methods. As an example, the estimates using the NLS data on black children (including the education of the father and the mother's current partner) (third column of panel B in Table 3) are repeated in Table A1b.

The difference between least squares and random effects estimates is small. However, differences between the standard *t*-statistics and jackknifed *t*s are in many cases quite large and inference changes in several instances. The jackknife and White estimates are often quite similar but there are three instances in which they differ *dramatically:* the estimate of the effect of father's education interacted with the sex of the child is significant if White *t*-statistics are used (in both the OLS and random effects estimates) but not significant if the jackknife or standard estimates are used.

These differences arise because of a small number of observations which are leverage points and, therefore, have a very large influence on the estimates of the variance-covariance matrix. The primary difference between the jackknife and infinitesimal jackknife lies in the weighting of residuals by a transform of the diagonal element of the hat matrix. This weight has been proposed as a useful indicator of the influence of observations in the regression model (Belsley, Kuh, and Welsch 1980, Handschin et al. 1975). Observations with large values of this weight tend to be outliers in the covariate space and are called leverage points.

Clearly the infinitesimal jackknife or White estimate of standard errors can be *seriously misleading.* This fact has been pointed out by MacKinnon and White (1982), on the basis of a Monte Carlo study and, from my own experience, the problem arises in a variety of empirical models in which there are leverage points. It seems, therefore, that adoption of the jackknife estimator of the variance-covariance matrix is not just a matter of niceties but is good empirical practice. Since the computational burden of estimating White and jackknife estimates is virtually identical, all *t* and χ^2 test statistics in the tables are based on the jackknife.

Appendix Table A1
Random Effects Estimates and Estimates of Quasi-t-statistics

(A) Random effects estimates: NLS (1986) stratified by race of child
Effect of mother's education and mean of all partners' education

	Blacks			Hispanics			Whites		
	Females	Males	Difference	Females	Males	Difference	Females	Males	Difference
Mother's education									
(1) if 7–12 years	2.317	−2.063	−4.227	0.648	−0.314	−1.020	0.147	1.560	1.288
	(1.38)	(4.33)	(2.72)	(1.27)	(1.56)	(2.00)	(0.39)	(1.05)	(0.86)
13–20 years	2.446	−2.188	−4.502	0.776	0.321	−0.499	0.372	1.599	1.092
	(1.45)	(4.27)	(2.86)	(1.43)	(1.10)	(0.87)	(0.94)	(1.05)	(0.71)
Partners' mean education									
(1) if 7–12 years	0.037	0.060	0.066	−0.061	−0.068	−0.016	−0.254	0.267	0.494
	(0.14)	(0.12)	(0.11)	(0.22)	(0.27)	(0.04)	(1.40)	(1.69)	(2.13)
13–20 years	−0.159	−0.046	0.146	−0.182	0.200	0.392	−0.408	0.333	0.702
	(0.51)	(0.08)	(0.23)	(0.52)	(0.68)	(0.86)	(1.82)	(1.38)	(2.21)
χ^2 for joint significance of									
Mother's education	2.294	19.272	8.464	2.092	7.209	5.792	3.833	1.113	1.711
	(0.16)	(0.00)	(0.01)	(0.18)	(0.01)	(0.03)	(0.07)	(0.29)	(0.21)
Partners' mean education	1.167	0.272	0.093	0.137	1.425	1.530	3.382	3.225	5.860
	(0.28)	(0.44)	(0.48)	(0.47)	(0.25)	(0.23)	(0.09)	(0.10)	(0.03)
All covariates	138.358	108.334	237.283	32.961	20.235	53.288	52.317	38.391	199.493
	(0.00)	(0.06)	(0.00)	(0.00)	(0.05)	(0.01)	(0.00)	(0.00)	(0.00)
LM test		1.821			3.023			7.897	
Hausman test		−14.764			−29.338			38.434	

Table A1 (*continued*)

(B) Quasi-*t*-statistics: OLS and random effects estimates: NLS (1986): Black children
Effect of education of mother, father and current partner

| | Coefficient Estimates | | Quasi-*t*-statistics | | | | | |
| | OLS | Random Effects | OLS Estimates | | | Random Effects Estimates | | |
			Standard	White	Jackknife	Standard	White	Jackknife
Education								
(1) if mother's education 7–12 years	2.293	2.377	2.31	1.84	1.36	2.37	1.94	1.43
if mother's education 13–20 years	2.422	2.484	2.41	1.92	1.42	2.45	2.00	1.48
(1) if father's education 7–12 years	0.202	0.156	0.10	1.11	0.00	0.08	0.77	0.00
if father's education 13–20 years	0.078	0.033	0.04	0.25	0.00	0.02	0.10	0.00
(1) if partner's education 7–12 years	0.083	0.069	0.07	0.21	0.15	0.06	0.17	0.12
if partner's education 13–20 years	0.023	0.051	0.02	0.05	0.04	0.04	0.11	0.08
Education * male interaction								
(1) if mother's education 7–12 years * male	−4.274	−4.195	3.04	3.30	2.44	3.14	3.68	2.72
if mother's education 13–20 years * male	−4.549	−4.471	3.20	3.44	2.56	3.32	3.83	2.86
(1) if father's education 7–12 years * male	1.367	1.441	0.56	4.21	0.01	0.63	4.35	0.01
if father's education 13–20 years * male	1.734	1.819	0.70	3.31	0.02	0.78	3.40	0.01
(1) if partner's education 7–12 years * male	−0.482	−0.387	0.30	0.91	0.64	0.25	0.78	0.54
if partner's education 13–20 years * male	−0.792	−0.769	0.47	1.21	0.92	0.48	1.22	0.93
Presence of partner/father								
(1) if current partner exists	−0.053	−0.026	0.05	0.14	0.10	0.02	0.07	0.04
if current partner exists * male	0.347	0.250	0.21	0.68	0.47	0.16	0.53	0.36
(1) if father present after birth	−0.013	0.009	0.01	0.07	0.00	0.01	0.04	0.00
if father present after birth * male	−1.245	−1.303	0.51	3.83	0.01	0.57	3.98	0.01

Mother's characteristics								
Mother's height (cm)	0.109	0.107	4.16	3.71	3.60	3.94	3.51	3.41
Mother's height (cm) * male	−0.044	−0.041	1.19	1.01	0.98	1.12	0.96	0.93
Age of mother at menarche	−0.095	−0.099	2.16	2.42	2.36	2.17	2.43	2.35
Age of mother at menarche * male	0.017	0.019	0.27	0.30	0.29	0.31	0.34	0.33
Child characteristics								
(1) if child is male	7.363	7.173	2.55	2.22	2.06	2.52	2.21	2.06
(1) if child's age is								
6–11 months	−0.639	−0.593	1.32	1.41	1.36	1.23	1.33	1.28
12–17 months	−0.837	−0.855	1.78	1.96	1.86	1.82	2.01	1.91
18–23 months	−0.816	−0.789	1.74	1.69	1.63	1.68	1.66	1.60
24–35 months	−0.054	0.048	0.13	0.14	0.13	0.12	0.13	0.12
36–47 months	0.612	0.612	1.49	1.81	1.74	1.49	1.83	1.77
48–59 months	0.692	0.737	1.64	2.11	2.03	1.75	2.28	2.20
60–107 months	0.737	0.778	1.93	2.47	2.37	2.03	2.66	2.55
108–143 months	0.656	0.728	1.56	2.14	2.05	1.73	2.44	2.34
6–11 months * male	−0.789	−0.891	1.19	0.89	0.86	1.35	1.01	0.98
12–17 months * male	−0.284	−0.291	0.44	0.31	0.30	0.45	0.32	0.31
18–23 months * male	−0.283	−0.387	0.43	0.30	0.29	0.58	0.41	0.39
24–35 months * male	0.080	−0.131	0.14	0.10	0.09	0.23	0.16	0.15
36–47 months * male	−0.913	−1.010	1.60	1.14	1.10	1.76	1.26	1.22
48–59 months * male	−0.949	−1.030	1.63	1.19	1.15	1.77	1.29	1.24
60–107 months * male	−0.689	−0.795	1.32	0.91	0.88	1.52	1.05	1.02
108–143 months * male	−0.273	−0.429	0.48	0.36	0.34	0.75	0.56	0.54
Constant	−8.325	−8.122	4.02	3.51	3.14	3.87	3.39	3.04

References

Alderman, Harold. 1989. "Nutritional Status in Ghana and Its Determinants." Cornell University Food and Nutrition Policy Program. Mimeo.

Alderman, Harold, and Paul Gertler. 1989. "Family Resources and Gender Differences in Human Capital Investments: The Demand for Children's Medical Care in Pakistan." Mimeo.

Ashenfelter, Orley, and James Heckman. 1974. "The Estimation of Income and Substitution Effects in a Model of Family Labor Supply." *Econometrica* 42(1):73–85.

Baker, Paula C., and Frank L. Mott. 1989. *NLSY Child Handbook, 1989: A Guide and Resource Document for the National Longitudinal Survey of Youth 1986 Child Data.* Center for Human Resource Research, Ohio State University.

Barrera, Albino. 1990. "The Role of Maternal Schooling and Its Interactions with Public Health Programs in Child Health Production." *Journal of Development Economics* 32:69–91.

Becker, Gary S. 1964. *Human Capital.* New York: Columbia University Press.

———. 1981. *A Treatise on the Family.* Cambridge: Harvard University Press.

Behrman, Jere R. 1988. "Intrahousehold Allocation of Nutrients in Rural India: Are Boys Favored? Do Parents Exhibit Inequality Aversion?" *Oxford Economic Papers* 40(1):32–54.

———. 1992. "Intrahousehold Allocation of Nutrients and Gender Effects: A Survey of Structural and Reduced Form Estimates." In *Nutrition and Poverty,* ed. S. Osmani. Oxford: Oxford University Press.

———. 1994. "Intrahousehold Distribution and the Family." In *Handbook of Population and Family Economics,* ed. M. R. Rosenzweig and O. Stark. Amsterdam: North Holland. Forthcoming.

Behrman, Jere R., and Anil Deolalikar. 1989. "Seasonal Demands for Nutrient Intakes and Health Status in Rural South India." In *Causes and Implications of Seasonal Variability in Household Food Security,* ed. D. Sahn. Washington: Johns Hopkins.

———. 1990. "The Intrahousehold Demand for Nutrients in Rural South India: Individual Estimates, Fixed Effects, and Permanent Income." *Journal of Human Resources* 25(4):665–96.

Belsley, David A., Edwin Kuh, and Roy E. Welsch. 1980. *Regressions Diagnostics: Identifying Influential Data and Sources of Collinearity.* New York: Wiley.

BEMFAM-IRD. 1988. *Brasil. Pesquisa Sobre Saude Materno-Infantil e Planejamento Familiar.*

Bhuiya, Abbas, Bogdan Yojtniak, Stan D'Souza, and Susan Zimicki. 1986. "Socio-Economic Determinants of Child Nutritional Status: Boys versus Girls." *Food and Nutrition Bulletin* 8.

Bleek, Wolf. 1987. "Family and Family Planning in Southern Ghana." In *Sex Roles, Population and Development in West Africa,* ed. Christine Oppong, 138–53. London: James Currey.

Blumberg, Rae. 1988. "Income Under Female versus Male Control: Hypotheses from a Theory of Gender Stratification and Data from the Third World." *Journal of Family Issues* 9(1):51–84.

Boserup, Esther. 1970. *Women's Role in Economic Development.* New York: St. Martin's Press.

Breusch, Trevor S., and Adrian R. Pagan. 1980. "The Lagrange Multiplier Test and Its Applications to Model Specification in Econometrics." *Review of Economic Studies* 47:225–38.

Browning, Martin, and Pierre-Andre Chiappori. 1993. "Efficient Intra-Household Allocations: A General Characterization." Mimeo.

Browning, Martin, Frances Bourguignon, Pierre-Andre Chiappori, and Valerie Lechene. 1993. "Intrahousehold Allocation of Consumption: Some Evidence on French Data." *Annales d'Economie et de Statistique* 29:137–56.
———. 1994. "Incomes and Outcomes: A Structural Model of Within Household Allocation." *Journal of Political Economy*. Forthcoming.
Caldwell, John C. 1977. "The Economic Rationality of High Fertility: An Investigation Illustrated with Nigerian Data." *Population Studies* 31(1):5–27.
Caldwell, John C., and Pat Caldwell. 1978. "The Achieved Small Family: Early Fertility Transition in an African Society." *Studies in Family Planning* 9(1):2–18.
Chen, Lincoln, Emdadul Huq, and Stan D'Souza. 1981. "Sex Bias in the Family Allocation of Food and Health Care in Rural Bangladesh." *Population and Development Review* 7(1):55–70.
Chernichovsky, Dov. 1985. "Socioeconomic and Demographic Aspects of School Enrollment and Attendance in Rural Botswana." *Economic Development and Cultural Change* 33(2):319–32.
Chiappori, Pierre-Andre. 1988a. "Rational Household Labor Supply." *Econometrica* 56(1):63–89.
———. 1988b. "Nash Bargained Household Decisions." *International Economic Review* 29(4):791–96.
———. 1992. "Collective Labor Supply and Welfare." *Journal of Political Economy* 100(3):437–67.
Cochrane, Susan, Joanne Leslie, and Donald O'Hara. 1982. "Parental Education and Child Health: Intercountry Evidence." *Health Policy and Education* 2:213–50.
D'Souza, Stan, and Lincoln Chen. 1980. "Sex Differentials in Mortality in Rural Bangladesh." *Population and Development Review* 6(2):257–70.
Deaton, Angus. 1989. "Looking for Boy-Girl Discrimination in Household Expenditure Data." *World Bank Economic Review* 3(1):1–16.
Desai, Sonalde, P. Lindsay Chase-Lansdale, and Robert T. Michael. 1989. "Mother or Market? Effects of Maternal Employment on the Intellectual Ability of 4-Year-Old Children." *Demography* 26(4):545–63.
Durkheim, Emile. 1933. *The Division of Labor in Society*, translated by G. Simpson from *De la division du travail social: Etudes sur l'Organisation des Societes Superieures* (1893). London: Macmillan.
Efron, Brad. 1982. *The Jackknife, the Bootstrap and Other Resampling Plans*. SIAM CBMS-NSF Monograph, 38.
Evenson, Robert E., Barry M. Popkin, and Elizabeth K. Quizon. 1980. "Nutrition, Work and Demographic Behavior in Rural Philippine Households." In *Rural Household Studies in Asia*, ed. H. Binswanger et al. Singapore: Singapore University Press.
Fapohunda, Eleanor R., and Michael P. Todaro. 1988. "Family Structure, Implicit Contracts and the Demand for Children in Southern Nigeria." *Population and Development Review* 14(4):571–94.
Folbre, Nancy. 1986. "Cleaning House: New Perspectives on Households and Economic Development." *Journal of Development Economics* 22:5–40.
Gertler, Paul, and Harold Alderman. 1989. "Family Resources and Gender Differences in Human Capital Investments: The Demand for Children's Medical Care in Pakistan." Mimeo, RAND Corporation.
Ghana Statistical Service and World Bank Social Dimensions of Adjustment Project Unit. 1989. *Ghana Living Standards Survey: First Year Report September 1987–August 1988*.
Ghana Teaching Service. 1975. *Report on Population and Family Life Education Survey in Schools and Colleges*. Accra: Ministry of Education.
Goldani, Ana-Marie. 1989. "Women's Transitions: The Intersection of Female Life

Course, Family and Demographic Transition in Twentieth Century Brazil." Ph.D. dissertation. Austin: University of Texas at Austin.

Gronau, Reuben. 1991. "The Intrafamily Allocation of Goods: How to Separate the Adult from the Child." *Journal of Labor Economics* 91(3):207–35.

Guyer, Jane. 1988. "Dynamic Approaches to Domestic Budgeting: Cases and Methods from Africa." In *A Home Divided: Women and Income in the Third World*, ed. Daisy Dwyer and Judith Bruce. Stanford: Stanford University Press.

Handschin, E., F. C. Schweppe, J. Kohlas, and A. Fiechter. 1975. "Bad Data Analysis for Power System State Estimators." *IEEE Trans. Power Appar. Sys., PAS* 94:329–37.

Henriques, Maria-Helena. 1988. "Marriage Systems Changes in Brazil." Fordham University. Mimeo.

Hess, Beth, and Joan Waring. 1978. "Parent and Child in Later Life: Rethinking the Relationships." In *Child Influences on Marital and Family Interactions: A Life-Span Perspective*, ed. Richard Lerner and Graham Spanier, 241–73. New York: Academic Press.

Hetherington, E., M. Cox, and R. Cox. 1978. "The Aftermath of Divorce." In *Mother/Child-Father/Child Relationships*, ed. Joseph Stevens and Marilyn Mathews, 149–76. Washington, D.C.: National Association for the Education of Young Children.

Hill, Polly. 1975. "The West African Farming Household." In *Changing Social Structure in Ghana*, ed. Jack Goody, 119–36. London: International Africa Institute.

Horton, Susan. 1986. "Child Nutrition and Family Size in the Philippines." *Journal of Development Economics* 23:161–76.

IBGE. 1978. *Estudo Nacional da Despesa Familiar: Dados Preliminares*. Rio de Janeiro.

———. 1988. *Anuario Estatistico Brasil*. Rio de Janeiro.

Jaeckel, Louis A. 1972. "Estimating Regression Coefficients by Minimizing the Dispersion of Residuals." *Annals of Mathematical Statistics* 42:1020–34.

Kaye, Barrington. 1962. *Bringing Up Children in Ghana: An Impressionistic Survey*. London: Allen and Unwin.

King, Elizabeth, and Rosemarie Bellew. 1989. "Gains in the Education of Peruvian Women in 1940's–1980's—Patterns and Explanations." PHR, World Bank. Mimeo.

King, Elizabeth, and Lee Lillard. 1987. "Education Policy and Schooling Attainment in Malaysia and the Philippines." *Economics of Education Review* 6(2):167–81.

Lamb, Michael E. 1976. "The Role of the Father: An Overview." In *The Role of the Father in Child Development*, ed. Michael Lamb, 1–36. New York: Wiley.

———. 1987. *The Father's Role: Cross Cultural Perspectives*. London: Lawrence Erlbaum Associates.

Lundberg, Shelley, and Robert A. Pollak. 1993. "Separate Spheres Bargaining and the Marriage Market." *Journal of Political Economy* 101(6):988–1010.

MacKinnon, James G., and Halbert White. 1982. "Some Heteroskedasticity Consistent Covariance Matrix Estimators with Improved Finite Sample Properties." *Journal of Econometrics* 29:305–25.

Manser, Marilyn, and Murray Brown. 1980. "Marriage and Household Decision Making: A Bargaining Analysis." *International Economic Review* 21(1):31–44.

Martorell, Renaldo, and Jean-Pierre Habicht. 1986. "Growth in Early Childhood in Developing Countries." In *Human Growth: A Comprehensive Treatise*, Vol. 3, 2nd edition, ed. F. Falkner and J. Tanner, 241–62. New York: Plenum Press.

Mason, Karen O., and Anju M. Taj. 1987. "Difference Between Women's and Men's Reproductive Goals in Developing Countries." *Population and Development Review* 13(4):611–38.

Mauldon, Jane. 1990. "The Effect of Marital Disruption on Children's Health." *Demography* 27(3):431–47.

McElroy, Marjorie B. 1990. "The Empirical Content of Nash-Bargained Household Behavior." *Journal of Human Resources* 25(4):559–83.

———. 1994. "Altruism, Bargaining and the Comparative Statics of Marriage Market." Mimeo, Duke University.

McElroy, Marjorie B., and Mary Jean Horney. 1981. "Nash Bargained Household Decisions." *International Economic Review* 22(2):333–50.

———. 1988. "Nash Bargained Household Decisions: Reply." *International Economic Review* 31(1):237–42.

Morgan, S. Philip, Diane N. Lye, and Gretchen A. Condran. 1988. "Sons, Daughters and the Risk of Marital Disruption." *American Journal of Sociology* 94(1):110–29.

National Center for Health Statistics. 1976. *Growth Charts*. U.S. Department of Health and Human Services, Public Health Service, Health Resources Administration.

National Research Council. 1983. *Levels and Recent Trends in Fertility and Mortality in Brazil*. Report #21. Washington, D.C.: National Academy Press.

Neuhouser, Kevin. 1989. "Sources of Women's Power and Status Among the Urban Poor in Contemporary Brazil." *Signs* 14(3):685–702.

Nsamenang, A. Bame. 1987. "A West African Perspective." In *The Father's Role: Cross Cultural Perspectives*, ed. Michael Lamb. London: Lawrence Erlbaum.

Oppong, Christine. 1982. *Middle Class African Marriage*. London: George Allen and Unwin.

Oppong, Christine, and Wolf Bleek. 1982. "Economic Models and Having Children: Some Evidence from Kwahu, Ghana." *Africa* 52(3).

Peil, Margaret. 1977. *Consensus and Conflict in African Societies*. London: Longman.

Pitt, Mark, Mark Rosenzweig, and Nazmul Hassan. 1990. "Productivity, Health and Inequality in the Intrahousehold Distribution of Food in Low-Income Countries." *American Economic Review* 80(5):1139–56.

Psacharopolous, George, and Ana-Marie Arriagada. 1989. "The Determinants of Early Age Human Capital Formation: Evidence from Brazil." *Economic Development and Cultural Change* 37:683–708.

Rosenzweig, Mark, and T. Paul Schultz. 1982. "Market Opportunities, Genetic Endowments and the Intrafamily Distribution of Resources." *American Economic Review* 72(4):803–15.

Schoefield, Sue. 1979. *Development and the Problems of Village Nutrition*. London: Croom Heim.

Schultz, T. Paul. 1987. "School Expenditures and Enrollments, 1960–1980: The Effects of Income, Prices and Population." In *Population Growth and Economic Development*, ed. D. G. Johnson and R. Lee, 413–76. Madison: University of Wisconsin Press.

———. 1989. "Women and Development: Objectives, Frameworks and Policy Interventions." WPS 200, PHR. Washington, D.C.: The World Bank.

———. 1990. "Testing the Neoclassical Model of Family Labor Supply and Fertility." *Journal of Human Resources* 25(4):599–634.

Sen, Amartya. 1984. "Family and Food: Sex Bias in Poverty." In *Resources, Value and Development*, ed. A. Sen. London: Blackwell.

Sen, Amartya, and S. Sengupta. 1983. "Malnutrition of Rural Children and the Sex Bias." *Economic and Political Weekly* 18:855–64.

Senauer, Ben, Marito Garcia, and Elizabeth Jacinto. 1988. "Determinants of the Intrahousehold Allocation of Food in the Rural Philippines." *American Journal of Agricultural Economics* 70(1):170–80.

Spanier, Graham B., and Paul C. Glick. 1981. "Marital Instability in the United States: Some Correlates and Recent Changes." *Family Relations* 31:319–38.

Spitze, Graham, and John Logan. 1990. "Sons, Daughters and Intergenerational Social Support." *Journal of Marriage and the Family* 52:420–30.

Strauss, John. 1990. "Households, Communities and Preschool Children's Nutrition Outcomes: Evidence from Rural Côte d'Ivoire." *Economic Development and Cultural ·Change* 38(2):231–62.

Strauss, John, and Duncan Thomas. 1994. "Human Resources: Empirical Modeling of Household and Family Decisions." In *Handbook of Development Economics,* ed. T. N. Srinivasan and Jere Behrman. Amsterdam: North-Holland. Forthcoming.

Subramanian, Shubhar, and Angus Deaton. 1990. "Gender Effects in Indian Consumption Patterns." Research Program in Development Studies Discussion Paper 147, Princeton University.

Svedberg, Peter. 1990. "Undernutrition in Sub-Saharan Africa: Is There a Gender Bias?" *Journal of Development Studies* 26(3):469–86.

Teachman, Jay D., and Paul T. Schollaert. 1989. "Gender of Children and Birth Timing." *Demography* 26(3):411–24.

Thomas, Duncan. 1990. "Intra-Household Resource Allocation: An Inferential Approach." *Journal of Human Resources* 25(4):635–64.

Thomas, Duncan, and Chien-Liang Chen. 1993. "Income Shares and Shares of Income: Empirical Tests of Models of Household Resource Allocations. UCLA. Mimeo.

Thomas, Duncan, John Strauss, and Marie Helene Henriques. 1990. "Survival Rates, Height for Age and Household Characteristics in Brazil." *Journal of Development Economics* 33(2):197–234.

Ulph, David. 1988. "A General Non-Cooperative Nash Model of Household Consumption Behaviour." Mimeo, Bristol University.

Waterlow, J., R. Buzina, W. Keller, J. Lane, M. Nichman, and J. Tanner. 1977. "The Presentation and Use of Height and Weight Data for Comparing the Nutritional Status of Groups of Children Under the Age of Ten Years." *Bulletin of the World Health Organization* 55:489–98.

White, Halbert. 1980. "A Heteroskedasticity-Consistent Covariance Matrix and a Direct Test for Heteroskedasticity." *Econometrica* 48:817–38.

[17]

Income and Outcomes: A Structural Model of Intrahousehold Allocation

Martin Browning

McMaster University

François Bourguignon

Département et Laboratoire d'Économie Théoretique et Appliquée (DELTA) and École des Hautes Études en Sciences Sociales (EHESS)

Pierre-André Chiappori

Département et Laboratoire d'Économie Théoretique et Appliquée (DELTA) and Centre National de la Recherche Scientifique (CRNS)

Valérie Lechene

Institut National de la Recherche Agronomique (INRA)

There is evidence from several sources that one cannot treat many-person households as a single decision maker. If this is the case, then factors such as the relative incomes of the household members may affect the final allocation decisions made by the household. We develop a method of identifying how "incomes affect outcomes" given conventional family expenditure data. The basic assumption we make is that household decision processes lead to efficient outcomes. We apply our method to a sample of Canadian couples with no children. We find that the final allocations of expenditures on each partner depend significantly on their relative incomes and ages and on the level of lifetime wealth.

We thank a referee, Gary Becker, Dwayne Benjamin, James Heckman, Thierry Magnac, Yoram Weiss, Robert Willis, and participants at conferences and seminars for their comments. This research was supported in part by the Canadian Social Sciences and Humanities Research Council.

[*Journal of Political Economy*, 1994, vol. 102, no. 6]

I. Introduction

In microeconomics textbooks, the chapter on consumer theory shows how the preferences of the consumer can be represented by a utility function, which is then maximized subject to a budget constraint. This framework provides an essential support for empirical analyses of behavior, as well as for normative recommendations. Unfortunately, the relevance of these conceptual tools is somewhat hindered by the absence of adequate data. What one generally observes is household consumption or labor supply. But consumer theory does not say much on household behavior if there is more than one person in the household.

The way one invariably deals with this problem is rather simple: one simply ignores it. In most empirical implementation, it is assumed that the tools of consumer theory apply at the household level, without any particular justification. It is thus implicitly assumed that the household systematically behaves "as if" it is a single agent. Casual observation, though, suggests that this may not be a very good assumption. From a more fundamental viewpoint, taking the "unitary" representation of the household as a benchmark is certainly disputable. After all, individualism is supposed to lie at the foundation of micro theory, and individualism obviously requires one to allow that different individuals may have different preferences. Thus the methodologically correct attitude should be to consider first the general, "multiutility" framework. Whether any particular simplification—such as the existence of a household utility function—is acceptable then becomes an open question. The answer depends on both the strength of its theoretical foundations and the adequacy of its predictions for observed behavior.

From a theoretical viewpoint, classical results in aggregation theory strongly suggest that a group does not behave as a single individual except under very strong, specific assumptions. Among the few theoretical attempts to reconcile the single-utility framework with the existence of several individuals within the household, one must cite Samuelson's (1956) household welfare index and Becker's (1981) rotten kid theorem. Both, however, can be shown to rely on restrictive hypotheses. For instance, Samuelson's approach crucially depends on the (very) ad hoc assumption that the members' respective weights in the household index are independent of the environment (wages, prices, and incomes). On the other hand, though the rotten kid theorem has stronger justifications, recent work has stressed that it holds only for transferable utilities (see Bergstrom 1989).

What, then, is the empirical support for the unitary model? Four distinct consequences have been tested in empirical demand systems:

INCOME AND OUTCOMES 1069

"income pooling," symmetry of the Slutsky matrix, negativity of price responses, and the exclusion of income variables from demand equations that condition on total expenditure.

A prediction of the single-criterion model is that only joint (or household) income should matter for allocation decisions and not who receives the income. This is usually referred to as the income pooling hypothesis. The results of Schultz (1990), Thomas (1990), Bourguignon et al. (1993), and Phipps and Burton (1994) suggest quite strongly that the data are not consistent with this hypothesis. As in those studies, the unitary model here is taken in the strict sense of a single objective function that is maximized under the usual constraints of a fixed price budget and nonnegative consumptions. Income pooling might not hold if these constraints are modified or other constraints are added. For example, including conditions ensuring the free participation of the individuals in the household may lead to a dependence of household demands on individual income as well as joint income. We do not consider this type of constraint as consistent with the unitary model since it implicitly introduces the individuality of household members into the picture.

Other disquieting findings can be found in demand studies on (micro) household data (see, e.g., Browning and Meghir 1991; Blundell, Pashardes, and Weber 1993). First, symmetry of the Slutsky matrix is usually rejected. Even though own substitution effects often prove to have the expected sign,[1] the rejection of symmetry suggests that choices cannot be rationalized as the outcome of a constrained maximization problem with a single utility function.

The final disquieting finding concerns the instrumenting of total expenditure in demand models. This is essential on micro data since there are several reasons why total expenditure might be endogenous (see Deaton [1985] or Blundell [1986] for a discussion). The obvious instrument to use is income, but other variables are also used to achieve some overidentification. Unfortunately, the overidentifying restrictions are usually rejected. Although no one has made a systematic investigation of this rejection, it is at least plausible that it is attributable to the invalid exclusion of some income variable.

Clearly the empirical support for the unitary approach is rather weak, to say the least. What recent empirical analysis points toward is that multiperson households cannot be treated as single decision

---

[1] This is true in a wider context than demand studies. For example, Keeley et al. (1978) find positive substitution effects in a labor supply model estimated on data from the Seattle and Denver Income Maintenance Experiment.

makers and that household allocations should probably rather be considered as the outcome of some interaction between household members with different preferences.[2] The goal of the present paper is precisely to develop and estimate a "collective" model of this kind.

The first task, of course, is to derive a formalized model of household behavior that follows the multiutility line of argument. Such a theoretical development, following the initial model of Chiappori (1988, 1992), is provided in a companion paper (Bourguignon, Browning, and Chiappori 1994). Browning and Chiappori (1994) derive (and test) the analogues of the Slutsky integrability conditions for the collective model considered here. The main implications of these results for our present empirical investigation are detailed in Section II.

Having discussed some of the issues that arise in modeling intrahousehold allocation, in Section III we present a parametric model of intrahousehold allocation decision making and show that, given one critical assumption, we can identify almost everything about such decision making using conventional family expenditure data. If a good is consumed by only one person, then we term such a good an exclusive good. Our critical assumption is that we have two such goods, one for each person.

In Section IV, we present some informal empirical analysis using Canadian family expenditure data. Our principal conclusion is that the conventional "single–decision maker" model fails for couples but not for single people. Although complementary to the evidence mentioned above, our finding is more focused in that it specifically identifies the failure of the conventional model with the presence of more than one person in the household.

In Section V, we use the Canadian data on couples with no children to estimate the parameters of our model. The goods we treat as exclusive are men's and women's clothing. Our principal finding is that "who gets what" in the household depends on the relative incomes and ages of the two partners and how wealthy the household is. We also present some estimates of exactly how these factors affect allocation. To our knowledge this is the first time such estimates have been presented in the literature.

---

[2] To be precise, we ought really to refer to multiadult households, possibly with young children. Thus we would not be averse to modeling lone-parent families in which all the children are young using a unitary assumption. In effect, it may reasonably be assumed that, at least until a certain age, children have no decision power in the household. Below we restrict attention to households containing two adults with no children.

II. The Theoretical Framework

A. *Modeling Issues*

To help in discussion of the modeling of intrahousehold allocation decisions, we consider four sets of issues: (i) the partitioning of goods into private and public goods, (ii) the nature of preferences, (iii) the mechanism used to reach decisions, and (iv) what the econometrician can observe.

i) The public/private issue is a familiar one. Although it may be reasonable to treat some goods as private (e.g., alcoholic beverages),[3] there are some goods that clearly have a strong public element (e.g., heating). Where to draw the line between public and private goods is not easy. For example, food is private in the sense that only one person can eat any piece of food, but there is clearly some public element in food preparation. In all that follows we assume that we can unambiguously designate goods to be private or public. To fix ideas, suppose that we are looking at a two-person (A and B) household. We let $\mathbf{q}^A$ and $\mathbf{q}^B$ represent vectors of private goods going to A and B, respectively, and $\mathbf{Q}$ represent a vector of public goods. If we denote total household expenditure on goods by y, then we have the budget constraint

$$\mathbf{p}'(\mathbf{q}^A + \mathbf{q}^B) + \mathbf{P}'\mathbf{Q} = y,$$

where $\mathbf{p}$ and $\mathbf{P}$ are price vectors for the private goods and the public goods, respectively.

ii) We turn now to preferences. The most general preference structure is

$$U^i = f^i(\mathbf{q}^A, \mathbf{q}^B, \mathbf{Q}) \quad \text{for } i = A, B.$$

We refer to this as altruistic preferences. More restrictive forms for preferences have been suggested in the literature. These include the following:

same preferences: $\quad U^i = F(\mathbf{q}^A, \mathbf{q}^B, \mathbf{Q}),$ $\qquad\qquad i = A, B;$

caring or nonpaternalistic: $\quad U^i = F^i(v^A(\mathbf{q}^A, \mathbf{Q}), v^B(\mathbf{q}^B, \mathbf{Q})), \quad i = A, B;$

egotistic: $\quad U^i = v^i(\mathbf{q}^i, \mathbf{Q}),$ $\qquad\qquad\qquad i = A, B.$

Thus with "caring" preferences, each person cares about the other's allocation only insofar as it gives the other person some individualistic welfare. The aggregator functions $F^A(\cdot)$ and $F^B(\cdot)$ are assumed to have $F^i(\cdot)$ strictly increasing in both subutility functions. Note that the subutility functions are the same in both welfare functions even

---

[3] This, of course, ignores any externalities that may be caused.

though the aggregator functions do not have to be the same. Fairly obviously, "egotistic" is a special case of caring in which $F^A(v^A, v^B) = v^A$, and similarly for B.

The issues that arise for the public/private nature of goods and how we model preferences are not independent. For example, if we assume altruistic preferences, then the distinction between private and public goods becomes blurred since both $\mathbf{q}^A$ and $\mathbf{q}^B$ are public in the usual sense. Conversely, if all goods are public, then we cannot distinguish between altruism and egotism.

If we assume caring then, there is also another distinction between goods that we find convenient. If there is a good that only one person in the household cares about, then the distinction between private and public is not very well defined. We thus choose to categorize such a good separately as *exclusive* rather than public or private. For example, cigarettes are private, but if only one person smokes (and, again, there are no externalities!), then it is categorized as exclusive. Conversely, the presence of a telephone is public, but if only one person ever uses it, then it is exclusive. Note that exclusivity depends on the properties of the utility function. The need to distinguish between private, public, and exclusive goods will emerge below. For notational convenience we shall include the exclusive goods in $\mathbf{q}^A$ or $\mathbf{q}^B$ along with private goods; we term such goods nonpublic.

iii) The third set of issues concerns the mechanism the members of the household use to decide what to buy. Many procedures have been proposed in the literature. For example, if each partner has an income and the sum of these incomes is equal to household income, then we could assume that each makes a private decision about what to buy and then look at the Nash equilibria (if any exist) for this "game." More sophisticated versions would take account of the fact that this is a repeated game. Alternatively, we could look at bargaining models following the line initiated by Manser and Brown (1980) and McElroy and Horney (1981).

Chiappori (1988, 1992) has analyzed the case in which we assume only that outcomes are efficient. This is particularly attractive in the context of the household since the "players" have a long-term relationship and are in an environment that does not change much from period to period.

iv) Finally, we have to consider what the econometrician can observe. Typically we observe household purchases of goods only within a certain period. Even if we equate these purchases with consumption (which is what investigators generally do for nondurables), we do not observe the individual consumptions of private goods. Sometimes, however, we may have a private good for which we can observe individual consumptions; we term such a good *assignable*. The distinction between exclusive and assignable when there is no price variation is not always very precise. For example, the individual consumptions of an assignable good can be thought of as two exclusive goods (one for each person). An example here would be clothing. If this is private and the husband consumes only men's clothing and the wife consumes only women's clothing, then we can either think of the total clothing commodity as an assignable good or think of men's and women's clothing as two exclusive goods.

B. *The Sharing Rule*

In all that follows we shall assume that, however allocation decisions are made, they lead to efficient outcomes. We refer to this as the *collective* setting.

We can consider two types of questions about this setting. On the one hand, we may try to test for it; this implies first deriving testable implications. Surprisingly enough, not much is needed for that purpose (see Bourguignon et al. 1994). The only requirement is the presence of variables that may safely be assumed to influence the decision process but not preferences. An example of such variables, used throughout the literature, is different income sources within the household. The presence of such variables gives rise to testable restrictions on demands. For these tests no specific assumption on either the nature of goods (i.e., whether they are public, private, or exclusive) or the form of preferences (altruistic, egotistic, or caring) is necessary (see Bourguignon et al. 1994). Tests of these restrictions are presented in Bourguignon et al. (1993). We find that, though income pooling is strongly rejected, the "collective" restrictions are not.

A more ambitious purpose is to estimate the structural model—that is, individual demands and the decision process—from observed behavior. That is the goal of the present paper. Specifically, we shall be interested in investigating how final outcomes depend on the income each person brings into the household.

Not surprisingly, additional assumptions are needed to achieve identification. Here, we first set out some assumptions: (i) some goods are nonpublic; (ii) preferences are caring; (iii) each member's subutility function is separable with respect to nonpublic consumptions:

$$v^i(\mathbf{q}^i, \mathbf{Q}) = V_i(u^i(\mathbf{q}^i), \mathbf{Q});$$

and (iv) one private good is assignable or we can identify two exclusive goods (one for each person).

Conditions i and ii exclude the most general preference structure in which each member's nonpublic consumption directly influences the spouse's utility (say, through consumption externalities). Condition iii guarantees that each member's marginal rate of substitution between nonpublic goods does not depend on the level of public consumption in the household.[4] Finally, condition iv states that we can observe something about the intrahousehold allocation.

We can now state the two basic results underlying the remainder of the paper. First, let $\hat{\mathbf{q}}^A$, $\hat{\mathbf{q}}^B$, and $x = \mathbf{p}'(\hat{\mathbf{q}}^A + \hat{\mathbf{q}}^B)$ denote, respectively, each member's equilibrium vector of nonpublic consumption and the household's total expenditures on nonpublic goods. Then efficiency has the following consequence.

PROPOSITION 1. *Existence of a sharing rule.*—Under assumptions i–iii and efficiency, there exist scalars x_A and x_B, with $(x_A + x_B) = x$, such that $\hat{\mathbf{q}}^A$ and $\hat{\mathbf{q}}^B$ are solutions of

$$\max u^i(\mathbf{q}^i) \quad \text{subject to } \mathbf{p}'\mathbf{q}^i = x_i \quad \text{for } i = A, B. \tag{P}$$

Proof. Define $x_i = \mathbf{p}'\hat{\mathbf{q}}^i$ and assume that $\hat{\mathbf{q}}^A$ and $\hat{\mathbf{q}}^B$ are not solutions of (P). Then there exist $\tilde{\mathbf{q}}^A$ and $\tilde{\mathbf{q}}^B$ that cost no more but provide a higher private utility for one member without making the other member worse off. Given the strict monotonicity of the aggregator functions $F^i(\cdot)$, the allocation $(\hat{\mathbf{q}}^A, \hat{\mathbf{q}}^B)$ is not a Pareto-efficient bundle since it is dominated by $(\tilde{\mathbf{q}}^A, \tilde{\mathbf{q}}^B)$, a contradiction. Q.E.D.

In words, given assumptions i–iii and efficiency, it is as though allocations in the household are made using a two-stage allocation procedure. At the top stage, total household income is allocated to saving, public goods, and each of the partners for expenditure on nonpublic goods. At the bottom stage each of the partners spends his or her individual total expenditure on nonpublic goods. Given the caring assumption, partner i of course chooses $\hat{\mathbf{q}}^i$. Two things are worth noting. First, at the bottom stage, allocation is independent of the choice of public goods since we have assumed separability. Second, we do not need any assignability for this result (i.e., we do not assume condition iv here).

It is important to emphasize that we are not suggesting that this is the actual procedure followed but simply that the allocation decisions can be seen as though they were generated by such a two-stage procedure if preferences are caring and outcomes are efficient. This as if distinction is familiar: we do not assume that individual agents actually maximize a utility function but rather that they behave as though they do.

Following Becker (1981), we term the division of total expenditure

---

[4] Without condition iii it is still possible to define and identify a sharing rule as below. However, one has to everywhere consider demand functions for private goods that are conditional on the consumption of public goods.

on nonpublic goods between the two partners a "sharing rule." Let z be a vector of exogenous variables that affect the decision process but do not influence preferences, the budget constraint, or the consumption set. Typically, z will contain each member's personal income, plus a range of "extra-environmental parameters" (EEPs in McElroy's [1990, 1992] terminology). They may include sex ratios in marriage markets, laws concerning alimony and child support, changes in tax status associated with different marital states, and, in developing countries, the ability of women to return to their natal homes and prohibitions on women working outside the home. Now let the share of person A in total expenditure on nonpublic goods be given by the function $\rho(z, x)$; we refer to this function as the sharing rule. In proposition 1 we have $x_A = \rho(z, x)x$ and $x_B = [1 - \rho(z, x)]x$.

This idea of a sharing rule is central to all that follows. If preferences are caring and outcomes are efficient, then any allocation of nonpublic expenditures can be rationalized as the outcome of a sharing rule procedure. These are sufficient conditions; it may be that other household decision processes and classes of preferences also give outcomes that could be the result of a sharing rule for expenditures on nonpublic goods (at least locally).

The sharing rule reflects the outcome of the decision process; it can be seen as a "reduced form" of the actual procedure. Additional structure could be introduced with the help of more specific assumptions (e.g., Nash bargaining). We do not follow this path; rather, we only assume efficiency.

C. Estimation

We assume below that we observe at least one factor that affects sharing; that is, z is nonempty. Our goal is to estimate the sharing rule $\rho(z, x)$. This is possible if there is an assignable good or two exclusive goods as stated in the following proposition.

PROPOSITION 2. *Identifying the sharing rule.*—Under the assumptions of proposition 1 and condition iv and

$$\frac{\partial q_1^A/\partial z_k}{\partial q_1^A/\partial x} \neq \frac{\partial q_1^B/\partial z_k}{\partial q_1^B/\partial x} \quad \text{for at least one } k,$$

each member's share ρx and $(1 - \rho)x$ is identified up to a (unique) additive constant.

Proof. We give here the proof if there is an assignable good; the proof for two exclusive goods follows the same lines. Let good 1 be assignable (i.e., we observe the individual demands q_1^A and q_1^B). Let

$q_1^i = f_1^i(x_i)$ be i's Engel curve for good 1. Define $x^A(\mathbf{z}, x) = \rho(\mathbf{z}, x)x$ and $x^B(\mathbf{z}, x) = [1 - \rho(\mathbf{z}, x)]x$. Thus $q_1^i = f_1^i(x^i(\mathbf{z}, x))$. Now define

$$L_k^i = \frac{\partial q_1^i/\partial z_k}{\partial q_1^i/\partial x} = \frac{\partial x^i/\partial z_k}{\partial x^i/\partial x}, \quad i = A, B \text{ and } k = 1, \ldots,$$

where $\partial x^i/\partial z_k$ and $\partial x^i/\partial x$ are the partials of x^i with respect to environmental factors z_k and total expenditure x, respectively. Note that these L_k^i's are observable. Also,

$$\frac{\partial x^A}{\partial x} + \frac{\partial x^B}{\partial x} = 1 \quad \text{and} \quad \frac{\partial x^A}{\partial z_k} + \frac{\partial x^B}{\partial z_k} = 0.$$

Thus

$$\frac{\partial x^A}{\partial x} = \frac{L_k^B}{L_k^B - L_k^A} \quad \text{and} \quad \frac{\partial x^A}{\partial z_k} = L_k^A \frac{\partial x^A}{\partial x}.$$

Note that the first of these expressions is defined for at least one k, by assumption. Hence the partials of the x^A function are all identified, which in turn implies that the partials of $\rho(\mathbf{z}, x)$ are also identified. Q.E.D.

The previous result shows that, for recovering the intrahousehold allocation of nonpublic consumption, we need only to observe how the allocation of one private good (or two exclusive goods) reacts to exogenous changes in the economic environment. This provides the basis for the estimation procedure we present in Section III below.

Two points should be stressed. First, the allocation of private expenditures is identified only up to a constant. It can actually be shown that this is the best we can do unless we can observe the allocation of all nonpublic goods (see Bourguignon et al. 1994). Second, as suggested by the proof, there will be testable restrictions on demand functions. Indeed, once the partials of $\rho(\mathbf{z}, x)$ have been identified, cross-derivative conditions will have to be checked. This will generate partial differential equations on the L_k^i's and second-order conditions on observable consumption behavior; tests based on this are developed in Bourguignon et al. (1994).

What proposition 2 shows is that the existence of an assignable good (or two exclusive goods) is sufficient for identification of the sharing rule (up to a constant). It is not necessary. Given some specific functional form, it may be enough simply to have only one exclusive good. This will be the case for the nonlinear model we derive in the next section. Indeed, under some circumstances we can identify the sharing rule with no information about who gets what of any good (see Bourguignon et al. 1994). This identification, however, relies on estimating second-cross-partials of the (household) demand functions for private goods. The advantage of assuming assignability (or exclusivity) is that the sharing rule is identified from first-order effects, and hence the identification may be more robust. This is conditional, of course, on the validity of the assignability assumption.

We assume that clothing is assignable (or, as discussed at the end of Sec. IIA above, men's clothing and women's clothing are exclusive). It is important to be clear about the implications of this assumption since it is the critical identifying assumption in our work below. Since we are maintaining that preferences are caring, our assumption that each person's consumption of clothing is nonpublic implies that wives care about their husband's clothing only inasmuch as it contributes to the welfare of their husband (and vice versa).[5] Many readers will be thoroughly skeptical of this implication. In particular, it may be that either husbands or wives do care about how their spouses dress; this is a rejection of nonpublicness. An important point to note in this regard is that our assumptions impose testable restrictions on demands. A rejection can be viewed narrowly as evidence that clothing is a public good or more broadly as evidence that the caring version of the collective model is invalid. Of course, if we had other assignable goods, then we could use them to derive the sharing rule. Comparing the sharing rules obtained with different supposedly assignable goods would in fact provide additional tests of the actual nature of these goods and of the general collective framework used throughout this paper.

III. A Parametric Model

To minimize heterogeneity we shall be considering only married[6] couples with no one else in the household. Further, we shall consider only couples in which both partners work full-time. This restriction is necessary to remove any substitution effects between commodity demands and labor supply (see Browning and Meghir 1991). We also assume that the selection into this group is exogenous for all the processes we deal with below.

We denote the wife by A and the husband by B. As above, we let z denote variables that enter the sharing function $\rho(\cdot)$ but do not otherwise affect individual demands. We let y^A (y^B) denote variables that directly enter the demand function for women's (men's) clothing

---

[5] A weaker assumption is that each cares about the other's clothing only up to some minimum and not thereafter. Thus men's (or women's) clothing could be public for low levels of expenditures but exclusive above some threshold.

[6] In the data set we use, "married" includes both legally married and common-law.

but do not enter the sharing function.[7] The vectors $\mathbf{y}^A$ and $\mathbf{y}^B$ may have elements in common (e.g., the region of residence). There may also be variables in $\mathbf{y}^A$ that do not appear in $\mathbf{y}^B$; for example, $\mathbf{y}^A$ might include the age of A but not the age of B.

The vector of sharing factors $\mathbf{z}$ might include differences of variables that appear in one set of $\mathbf{y}^i$ but not the other; for example, if $\mathbf{y}^A$ includes A's age but not B's (and vice versa), then $\mathbf{z}$ might include the difference in ages. However, the most important candidates for inclusion in $\mathbf{z}$ are the incomes of the two partners. They may affect how the partners share expenditures, but they should not affect individual demands once we condition on the total expenditure by each person. This is conditional on taking account of the dependence of demands on labor supply (which is obviously highly correlated with individual income). Since we consider only agents who work full-time in our empirical work, the dependence of demands on labor supply is taken care of automatically.

As discussed in Section II, we assume the existence of a sharing rule. This gives the division of expenditure on nonpublic, nondurable goods conditional on savings and public goods and durables purchases. Formally, let x_A and x_B be the amounts of money for expenditure on nonpublic goods that each partner receives, and let $x = (x_A + x_B)$ be total expenditure on these goods. We do not observe x_A and x_B, but we have

$$x_A = \rho(\mathbf{z}, x)x \tag{1a}$$

and

$$x_B = [1 - \rho(\mathbf{z}, x)]x, \tag{1b}$$

where $\rho \in [0, 1]$.[8]

The household demand for good j is given by

$$
\begin{aligned}
q_j &= \alpha^j(\mathbf{y}^A, x_A) + \beta^j(\mathbf{y}^B, x_B) \\
&= \alpha^j(\mathbf{y}^A, x\rho(\mathbf{z}, x)) + \beta^j(\mathbf{y}^B, x[1 - \rho(\mathbf{z}, x)]),
\end{aligned}
$$

where $\alpha^j(\cdot)$ and $\beta^j(\cdot)$ are the demand functions for good j by A and B, respectively, with either $\alpha^j(\cdot)$ or $\beta^j(\cdot)$ equal to zero for an exclusive good. If good j is not assignable, then we observe only the response of q_j to changes in $(\mathbf{y}^A, \mathbf{y}^B, \mathbf{z}, x)$. As discussed in Section II, we assume that clothing is an assignable good. Since we shall be concerned only with men's and women's clothing, below we drop the j superscript.

---

[7] We could also allow for variables that enter preferences directly and enter the sharing rule. As we shall see below, the parameters associated with such variables are not identified, and so we choose to exclude them a priori.

[8] Formally, the (0, 1) bounds are derived from a model with egotistic preferences. With caring preferences we have $\rho \in [\epsilon, \sigma]$, where $0 \leq \epsilon \leq \sigma \leq 1$.

Note that all the variables on the right-hand side of the demand equations above are observable. We ought, however, to make some allowance for unobservable heterogeneity. There are three potential sources of such heterogeneity: the sharing rule and the two individual preferences. The most satisfactory treatment would be to allow for each of them and then to develop a full stochastic model that would also allow us to take account of the possible endogeneity of the sample selection on married couples in full-time employment. Thus one could then allow that in households in which the sharing rule is highly dependent on relative incomes, there is more incentive for each individual to participate in the labor force. We regard this as a most important area of future research, but here we adopt a much more conventional approach of simply adding error terms to each demand equation and ignoring the possible sample selection bias.

To parameterize our demand functions, we let the log demand for women's clothing ($\ln a$) be

$$\ln a = \alpha_0 + \boldsymbol{\alpha}_A' \mathbf{y}^A + \alpha_x \ln x_A + \alpha_q (\ln x_A)^2, \tag{2a}$$

where we denote $\ln(x)$ as $\ln x$. In the same way, the log demand for men's clothing is given by

$$\ln b = \beta_0 + \boldsymbol{\beta}_B' \mathbf{y}^B + \beta_x \ln x_B + \beta_q (\ln x_B)^2. \tag{2b}$$

Now, let

$$\rho(\mathbf{z}, x) = \frac{e^{\psi(\mathbf{z},x)}}{1 + e^{\psi(\mathbf{z},x)}} \tag{3}$$

to bound ρ between zero and one. Combining (1)–(3) gives the demand equations

$$\ln a = \alpha_0 + \boldsymbol{\alpha}_A' \mathbf{y}^A + \alpha_x \left(\ln \frac{xe^\psi}{1 + e^\psi} \right) + \alpha_q \left(\ln \frac{xe^\psi}{1 + e^\psi} \right)^2 \tag{4a}$$

and

$$\ln b = \beta_0 + \boldsymbol{\beta}_B' \mathbf{y}^B + \beta_x \left(\ln \frac{x}{1 + e^\psi} \right) + \beta_q \left(\ln \frac{x}{1 + e^\psi} \right)^2. \tag{4b}$$

Finally, let

$$\psi(\mathbf{z}, x) = 2(\delta_0 + \boldsymbol{\gamma}' \mathbf{z} + \theta \ln x) \tag{5}$$

(the reason for the scaling by two will become clear below).

The $\psi(\cdot)$ function controls the share of total expenditure each partner receives as we vary the $\mathbf{z}$ variables and total expenditure. The constant δ_0 "centers" the shares; the lower it is, the lower the share of person A. The θ parameter controls how "luxurious" A's purchases are. To see this, note that

$$\frac{\delta \ln x_A}{\delta \ln x} = 1 + 2\theta(1 - \rho).$$

If θ is positive, then A's total expenditure (x_A) is rising proportionately more quickly than total expenditure, with the z variables held constant (since $\rho < 1$). Changes in the z variables affect what each person gets through changes in total expenditure and how much of that each person gets:

$$\frac{\delta \ln x_A}{\delta z_k} = [1 + 2\theta(1 - \rho)]\frac{\delta \ln x}{\delta z_k} + 2\gamma_k(1 - \rho).$$

For example, let z_1 be the wife's income and suppose that γ_1 is positive. Then an increase in the wife's income will (probably) lead to an increase in her total expenditure since it will (probably) increase total expenditure and her share in total expenditure.

As already discussed, we shall only assume efficiency in decision making; this is a relatively weak assumption. One motivation for this assumption would be that the two partners engage in some bargaining with no asymmetric information. Although we do not use such an assumption, we can provide an informal test of whether it is appropriate if we decide a priori how particular factors in the sharing rule affect bargaining positions. The obvious example here is the incomes of the two partners: we may expect that an increase in the relative income of one person increases his or her share of total expenditure on private goods.[9] In any case, if increases in some variable z^A increase A's bargaining strength and some other variable z^B decreases it, then z^A and z^B must have opposite effects on demands. We shall return to this issue in the empirical section below.

An interesting remark is that all the parameters in the sharing rule are formally identified from either of (4a) and (4b) alone. However, this identification is dubious since some of it is achieved simply by the nonlinearity in $\psi(\cdot)$. To check this, we develop a linearized version

[9] Note the "may" here. We do not have any model to this effect and it is not necessarily true in general. This will certainly be the case if there are unobservable (to the econometrician) factors at play in the bargaining, in which case an unobservable increase in bargaining power for one partner may lead to a *decrease* in income since income is not now so important for maintaining a bargaining position. This also abstracts from a consideration of public goods. It is possible that an increase in A's bargaining strength leads to an increase in her welfare, but a decrease in her share of private expenditures if there is a change in public goods purchases that offsets this decrease.

of our model that has a "linear in parameters" unrestricted form. This linearized form serves two purposes. First, we use it to show our concerns regarding the identification of some of the parameters. Second, the linearized model is a good deal easier to estimate than (4); as we shall see, the nonlinear estimation can be quite tedious. Thus we use conventional diagnostics and model selection techniques on our linearized model to help in the selection of a preferred but parsimonious unrestricted nonlinear model.[10]

The details of the derivation of the linearized model are given in Appendix A. For the linearized model we can show that of the parameters in (4a) and (5), only α_A is always identified from the women's clothing equation. Of the other parameters, our interest centers on the parameters of the sharing rule in (5), $(\delta_0, \theta, \gamma)$, and the Engel curve in (4a), $(\alpha_0, \alpha_x, \alpha_q)$. In Appendix A we show that these parameters are identified with two degrees of freedom. That is, we can arbitrarily fix two of them, and then this serves to identify the rest. Of course, when we consider both demands simultaneously—that is, (4b) as well as (4a) and (5)—then we can identify all the parameters except for one. If we take the unidentified parameter to be δ_0, then this is a restatement of proposition 2: we can identify the sharing rule only up to a constant. In our empirical work below we fix the constant δ_0 so that the share of each person at the mean of the data is one-half.

Finally, we know that our assumption of a collective setting implies restrictions on demands. To test them we proceed as follows. First we estimate the parameters of (4a) and (5) from our nonlinear model of women's clothing. Then we estimate the parameters of the following variant of (4b) and (5) for the men's clothing equation:

$$\ln b = \beta_0 + \beta'_B y^B + \beta_x\left(\ln \frac{x}{1 + e^\lambda}\right) + \beta_q\left(\ln \frac{x}{1 + e^\lambda}\right)^2, \qquad (6)$$

where

$$\lambda(\mathbf{z}, x) = 2(\delta_0 + \gamma'_B \mathbf{z} + \theta_B \ln x). \qquad (7)$$

We then test

$$(\gamma, \theta) = (\gamma_B, \theta_B). \qquad (8)$$

We interpret this as a joint test of our assumption that clothing is assignable and that the caring version of the collective model holds.

---

[10] In the empirical section we shall present some results that show that our linearized model is a good approximation to the nonlinear one and that our concerns about identification are well founded.

IV. An Informal Look at the Data

We begin with an informal look at the data. This informal investigation uses data on couples and on singles. It has three goals. First, we wish to highlight some of the principal features of the data. Second, we examine whether our data for couples exhibit some of the same failures of the single-utility model that we discussed in Section I. Finally, we wish to address directly one important objection to the use of clothing to identify "who gets what" in the household.

Our initial interest centers on how clothing expenditures are affected by variables that are not usually included in demand equations. In particular, in the usual demand model the incomes of the husband and wife should not enter the demand equation if we condition on total expenditure. One immediate objection arises to this statement. Suppose that, even within particular occupations, higher-paid jobs require more expensive work clothing.[11] Then the incomes of the husband and wife will enter the demand equations for clothing even if we condition on total expenditure, occupation, and education. To check this we shall use single people as a control: if such an effect is present, then it should show up for singles as well as for couples.

The data we use in this study are drawn from the four Canadian family expenditures (FAMEX) surveys conducted in 1978, 1982, 1984, and 1986. Among other things, these surveys give annual expenditures by households on a comprehensive collection of goods. The fact that expenditures for the whole year are taken means that these data have less of an "infrequency of purchase" problem than, say, the U.K. Family Expenditure Survey or the U.S. Consumer Expenditure Survey. This is important for us since we concentrate on expenditures on men's and women's clothing. Of course, there is still some "lumpiness" in these expenditures even when we take annual expenditures; we shall return to controlling for this below.

We begin with two subsamples: single males in full-time employment and single females in full-time employment. The sample sizes are 1,312 and 1,353, respectively. For each subsample we estimate a clothing demand equation. The dependent variable is the log of clothing expenditures divided by the price of clothing.[12] On the right-hand side we have age variables, the log of the price of clothing, the log of the price of other nondurables, and dummies for region of residence,

---

[11] Below we consider only people who work full-time (see the remarks at the beginning of Sec. III).

[12] In fact, here and for other "log" variables we take the inverse hyperbolic sine. The virtue of this transformation is that it is defined for the whole real line, and it is "log" for high values of the argument and "linear" for values close to zero. Thus we can use this transformation to remove the "left skewness" that taking logs often induces (see Burbidge, Magee, and Robb 1988).

car ownership, city living, home ownership, education (a dummy for more than high school), language spoken (dummies for French and other than English or French), and occupation (a dummy for professional and managerial). We also include total nondurables expenditure variables, where nondurables comprise food, alcohol, tobacco, services, recreation, and clothing. Specifically, we include the log and log squared of this variable deflated by a nondurables price index.

As we have already mentioned, clothing expenditures tend to be lumpy (even when we take annual expenditures). This may induce an endogeneity in the total expenditure variables since the purchase of an expensive coat, say, will lead to abnormally high clothing expenditure and total expenditure. To instrument the two total expenditure variables we use income variables; specifically, we include the log and log squared of deflated income in the instrument set.[13] In the instrument set we also include all the right-hand-side variables listed in the previous paragraph (except for the total expenditure variables, of course), year dummies (to capture intertemporal allocation effects), and (log) prices of durables and cars (to capture within-period substitution effects). Thus we have some overidentification; this is important since we focus mainly on whether (once we condition on total expenditure and other variables such as occupation and education) the income variables enter the demand equation. With some overidentification we can test whether the exclusion restrictions for the income variables are valid.

We estimated the clothing equations for single men and single women separately by instrumental variables. We tested for exogeneity of total expenditure and found that it is decisively rejected in both cases. On the other hand, the overidentifying restrictions are not rejected. This indicates that we do not need income variables in the demand equations once we condition on total expenditure. Thus, for single people, the exclusion restrictions needed to use the income variables as instruments are valid. Another finding that will be used later is that we do need to include the log squared of total expenditure. We also subjected our estimates to a battery of diagnostic tests (discussed in more detail in App. B); we found these qualitative results to be robust.

Turning to couples, in this informal investigation we shall focus on the difference between (log) household demands for men's and

---

[13] The income variable is total gross income. Although it would be desirable to break income into its components, this is not possible for the first two years of the survey (1978 and 1982). It might also be argued that net income is the appropriate concept. Although we do have net income for singles, we do not have such a variable for the husband and wife in the sample we use below. Consequently, we use gross income here to maintain comparability.

women's clothing. This is to allow us to use single-equation methods; clearly if some variable is "significant" in the log difference equation, then it must be "significant" in either the men's or women's clothing demand equation.[14] We have 1,520 couples in our subsample. In figure 1 we plot the difference in log clothing demands against the difference in the (log deflated gross) incomes of the two partners.[15] We also plot the simple ordinary least squares (OLS) line (with no other covariates) and a cubic spline nonparametric fit. Three important features of the data are apparent in this figure. First, the majority of the points are in the northwest quadrant. Thus the husband's income tends to be higher than the wife's, but the expenditure on women's clothing tends to be higher than expenditures on men's clothing. Second, there is a pronounced positive linear association between the two variables (the slope coefficient for the OLS line is .13 with a standard error of .04). Finally, it looks as though the OLS line and the nonparametric curve correspond closely (at least for the bulk of the data).

To allow for the influence of other variables, we ran a regression with the difference in clothing demands on the left-hand side, and on the right-hand side we include the demographic variables given above (with the husband- and wife-specific components for those variables such as education and age that can vary between the partners). We use the same instruments as for singles except that now we include the log and log squared of the wife's gross income and the log and log squared of the ratio of gross incomes. In our first estimated equation we included these four income variables on the right-hand side; thus we are identifying the parameters from the other instruments (year dummies and the prices of nondurables and cars). We find that the four income variables are jointly significant: an $F(4, 1,496)$ statistic of 5.06, which has a 0.05 percent probability under the null. Further investigation indicated that the only one of the four variables that had any real significance was the difference in log gross incomes: the $F(3, 1,496)$ statistic for excluding the other three variables is 1.67. We conclude that the difference in income variable is needed in the difference in clothing demand equation.

To check the robustness of the finding in the last paragraph, we ran a number of checks; they are presented in Appendix B. As before, we conclude that our finding is robust.

It may be worth stressing that the preceding findings are not necessarily inconsistent with the unitary model. But then one must be will-

[14] In the formal analysis in Sec. V below, we model the two demands separately in a simultaneous system.

[15] Here and below differenced variables are always the wife's value minus the husband's value.

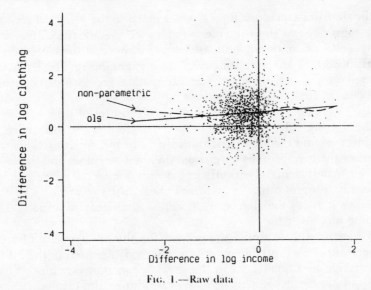

FIG. 1.—Raw data

ing to accept that some of the unobservable variables that explain individual incomes—or wage rates—also affect the common preferences of the household. Our finding is that for a given level of total income, less is spent on women's clothing in households with relatively better off husbands. We believe that this finding is difficult to rationalize in a unitary model.

The principal conclusion we draw from the informal analysis in this section is that incomes matter in demand equations for couples in a way that they do not for singles. There is no obvious way to rationalize the inclusion of income variables in demand equations for couples and not for singles if we assume that these demands are in each case the outcome of the constrained maximization of a single utility function. A very obvious alternative is that husband and wife have differing preferences and that the final allocation decisions made depend on, among other things, who gets the income. All of this leads us to conclude that it is worthwhile to go on and use the structural model of the within-household allocation process developed in Section III. It is to this that we now turn.

V. Empirical Results

We start with the linearized model derived in Appendix A. Even when we do this we are somewhat restricted in how general a model we can begin with since the unrestricted linear form includes quadratics in the candidate variables in the sharing function $\rho(\cdot)$. We include in the demand equations the variables given in the informal section. The most general sharing rule variables we use are the differences in age, education, occupation, and (log) income and the levels of the (log) income of the wife and (log) total expenditure. Note that although own age, education, and occupation are included in each individual's demand, the spouse's age, education, and occupation variables are not. Thus we can include differences of these variables in the sharing rule. Note as well that by including the difference in log incomes and the log of one individual income, we can readily test whether the two incomes have equal (in absolute value) and opposite (in sign) coefficients: the coefficient on the log of the wife's income should be insignificant. As discussed above, the two incomes having opposite signs in the sharing rule will be consistent with many bargaining models.

We begin with a model that allows for the endogeneity of total expenditure. For instruments we use the variables used in the informal section and quadratics in the sharing function variables. When one looks at the exogeneity of total expenditure, the results are very much like those in the informal section. If we include the income variables in the sharing rule, then exogeneity is not rejected. If we exclude the income variables, then the overidentifying restrictions and exogeneity are rejected. We interpret this to mean that we need to include some income variables in the sharing function, but if we do this then total expenditure is exogenous or we have no "good" instruments. We consequently take the total expenditure variable to be exogenous for the sharing process. Formally, this means that we are assuming that the errors on the determination of total expenditure are uncorrelated with the errors on the sharing rule and the clothing equations; that is, we have a recursive set of equations.

Our next tests are designed to reduce the number of variables in the sharing function. In the linearized version we always include total expenditure in the sharing rule and test for the validity of the other variables listed above. To do this we apply a sequence of F-tests on the unrestricted linear model. We found only the differences in age and income to be significant. Consequently, we include only these variables in the sharing function (and total expenditure) when we estimate the nonlinear model.

The estimation of the nonlinear model proceeds in a number of stages. First we estimate each of unrestricted forms (4a)/(5) and (6)/(7) separately. We then estimate them as a seemingly unrelated regression equation (SURE) system (using Telser's SURE estimates[16] to

---

[16] That is, we take the residuals from each equation estimated on its own, put them in the other equation, and reestimate the two equations.

generate starting values). Then we test the constraints (8). In all of this we found that the likelihood function for the SURE system had many local maxima. Since all the equations are linear if we fix the $\psi(\cdot)$ and $\lambda(\cdot)$ parameters in (5) and (7), respectively, we can use grid searches over these parameters to ensure that we have found the global maximum. It is this need to grid search over the parameters of the sharing function that makes it virtually impossible to begin with the nonlinear model with more than a very few variables in the $\psi(\cdot)$ and $\lambda(\cdot)$ functions. Hence the use of the linearized model to cut down on the **z** variables. Note that since we cannot use Wald tests for the significance of particular variables in a nonlinear system (see, e.g., Gregory and Veall 1985), we have to use likelihood ratio tests. Using likelihood ratio tests on systems that have multiple local maxima is also very time consuming, which is yet another reason for doing some of the initial model selection on the linearized model. When estimating the nonlinear model, we also set δ_0 to zero so that each person's share is one-half at the mean of the data (see the discussion toward the end of Sec. III).

In table 1 we present the estimates of the sharing rule parameters from equations (4a) and (6). Columns 1 and 2 refer to women's and men's clothing, respectively; column 3 refers to the system with the equality of the sharing rule parameter estimates set equal (i.e., with [8] imposed). The $\chi^2(3)$ statistic for constraining the parameters equal is 4.11, which has a probability of 25 percent under the null that they are equal. We interpret this to mean that we can treat clothing as assignable in a caring/collective model. If we impose this restriction, then all the parameters are relatively well determined.

As can be seen, the coefficients on the differenced variables are

TABLE 1

SYSTEM ESTIMATES OF SHARING RULE PARAMETERS

| | UNRESTRICTED | | |
| | Women's Clothing (4a) | Men's Clothing (6) | RESTRICTED (8) |
SHARING RULE VARIABLE	(1)	(2)	(3)
Wife's age − husband's age	.170 [49.1%]	.139 [3.80%]	.144 [3.31%]
Wife's log(income) − husband's log(income)	.111 [.95%]	.019 [.29%]	.026 [.005%]
Log(total expenditure)	1.495 [28.6%]	.631 [.32%]	.618 [.28%]

NOTE.—Figures in brackets are probabilities of likelihood ratio statistics under the null that the parameter is zero.

positive so that older and higher-income partners receive more of total expenditure. The coefficient on total expenditure in the sharing rule is also positive. This implies that the wife receives proportionately more as expenditure goes up. Since total expenditure is increasing with lifetime wealth, this implies that women receive more in wealthier households, with relative income shares and age differences held constant.

Figures 2 and 3 give some idea of the magnitudes implied by these estimates. In figure 2 we plot the predicted share of the wife in total expenditure against the wife's share in household (gross) income. We set the ages equal and set total expenditure to the first, second, and third quartiles in our sample. Once again we remind the reader that we have fixed the constant in the sharing function so that the share is one-half when there is no difference in incomes or ages and the household has mean total expenditure. Before discussing the substantive implications of our estimates, we note that all the curves in figures 2 and 3 are close to linear. This gives us some confidence that the initial investigation on the linearized model is not too biased.

Figure 2 shows clearly the two main features of our parameter estimates. First, the share in total expenditure is increasing in the share of income but only modestly. Going from supplying 25 percent of household income to supplying 75 percent (holding total expenditure constant) raises the share in total expenditure by about 2.3 percent. On the other hand, the effect of total expenditure, when the wife's share in income is held constant, is quite substantial. A 60

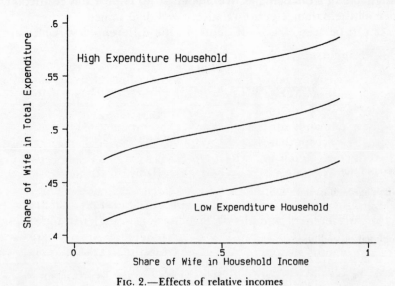

FIG. 2.—Effects of relative incomes

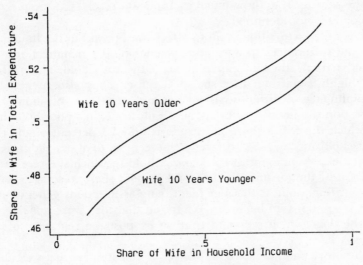

FIG. 3.—Effect of age differences

percent increase in total expenditure (going from the low curve to the high curve) increases the wife's share by about 12 percent. Thus the two effects together can lead to quite sizable changes in the intra-household allocation of expenditure. The share of the wife can range from about 40 percent to about 60 percent. Finally, figure 3 indicates that, while statistically significant, the effect of age differences is small: going from being 10 years younger to 10 years older raises the share by less than 2 percent.

VI. Conclusions

There is clear evidence from many sources that households do not behave as though they are maximizing a single criterion. Section IV of this paper adds to that evidence: individual incomes matter for clothing demands for couples in a way that income does not for singles. If we accept that we need to go beyond the single-utility model, then the next step is to try to sort out what goes on inside the household. This is no mean task given the sort of data we currently have. Indeed many will feel that it is impossible.

In this paper we have invoked a number of assumptions (efficiency, caring preferences, and the assignability of clothing) in order to identify some of what goes on. As we have seen, under these assumptions we can identify everything about how intrahousehold sharing is affected by factors such as relative ages, incomes, and household total expenditure. On the other hand, we have also shown that the location of the sharing rule (how much each person receives at the mean of the data) is not identified.

The only factors that seem to affect sharing within the household are the differences in ages and incomes of the members and the wealth (strictly, the total expenditure) of the household. These effects are highly significant in a statistical sense. They also suggest that the influence of differential incomes and wealth on intrahousehold allocation can be fairly substantial. To illustrate, in a poor household in which the wife's share in income is only 25 percent of the total household income, she receives 42 percent of total expenditure. At the other extreme, in a wealthy household in which she receives 75 percent of the income, she has a 58 percent share in total expenditure. A final point is that our identifying assumptions generate testable restrictions on behavior. We found that they were not rejected by the data, which seems to confirm ex post the relevance of our approach.

Our work should clearly be seen as a first step in what we believe to be a fruitful direction. Household economics (with the obvious exception of Becker [1981]) has not taken individualism seriously enough. We believe that individuals, not households, are the basic decision units and that, as argued in Chiappori et al. (1993), the burden of proof should shift onto those who would claim that the unitary model is the rule and the collective model the exception.

Appendix A

Linearization and Identification

Linearization

Our linearization rests on two familiar approximations. First, for the logistic given in (3), we have

$$\rho \simeq \frac{1 + (\psi/2)}{2}$$

for ψ around zero. The other approximation is the very familiar $\ln(1 + \epsilon) = \epsilon$ for ϵ close to zero. From these approximations and (3) and (5) we have

$$\begin{aligned}
\ln(\rho) &= \ln(0.5) + \ln\left(1 + \frac{\psi}{2}\right) \\
&= \ln(0.5) + \delta_0 + \boldsymbol{\gamma}'\mathbf{z}^d + \theta \ln x \qquad (A1) \\
&= \delta_A + \boldsymbol{\gamma}'\mathbf{z}^d + \theta y
\end{aligned}$$

if ψ is close to zero (i.e., if each partner's share is close to 0.5).

Using this approximation, we can rewrite (4a) as

$$
\begin{aligned}
\ln a = {} & (\alpha_0 + \alpha_x \delta_A + \alpha_q \delta_A^2) + \alpha_A' y^A + (\alpha_x + 2\alpha_q \delta_A)\gamma' z \\
& + (1 + \theta)(\alpha_x + 2\alpha_q \delta_A)\xi + \alpha_q (1 + \theta)^2 \xi^2 \\
& + 2\alpha_q(1 + \theta)\gamma'(\xi^* z) + \alpha_q(\gamma' z)^2,
\end{aligned}
\tag{A2}
$$

where $\xi = \ln x$. Corresponding to this nonlinear equation there is an unrestricted equation linear in quadratics of (ξ, z):

$$
\ln a = \pi_0 + \pi_A' z^A + \pi_d' z + \pi_x \xi + \pi_q \xi^2 + \pi_c'(\xi^* z) + \pi_e'(z)^+,
\tag{A3}
$$

where $(z)^+$ denotes the vectorized outer product of z with redundant components removed. Thus if z is a k vector, then $(z)^+$ is the $k(k - 1)/2$ vector $(z_1^2, z_1 z_2, \ldots, z_1 z_k, z_2^2, \ldots, z_k^2)$.

Using the same approximations, we can also derive linearized forms for the men's clothing equation:

$$
\begin{aligned}
\ln b = {} & (\beta_0 + \beta_x \delta_B + \beta_q \delta_B^2) + \beta_B' z^B - (\beta_x + 2\beta_q \delta_B)\gamma_B' z \\
& + (1 - \theta_B)(\beta_x + 2\beta_q \delta_B)\xi + \beta_q(1 - \theta_B)^2 \xi^2 \\
& - 2\beta_q(1 - \theta_B)\gamma_B'(\xi^* z) + \beta_q(\gamma_B' z)^2
\end{aligned}
\tag{A4}
$$

with unrestricted form

$$
\ln b = \tau_0 + \tau_B' z^B + \tau_d' z^d + \tau_x \xi + \tau_q \xi^2 + \tau_c'(\xi^* z) + \tau_e'(z)^+.
\tag{A5}
$$

Identification

If we use just the women's clothing equation, then we have the following question: Given consistent estimates of the parameters of (A3), can we identify the parameters of (A2)? To look at this, we equate coefficients in (A2) and (A3):

$$
\pi_0 = \alpha_0 + \alpha_x \delta_A + \alpha_q \delta_A^2,
\tag{I1}
$$

$$
\pi_A = \alpha_A,
\tag{I2}
$$

$$
\pi_d = (\alpha_x + 2\alpha_q \delta_A)\gamma,
\tag{I3}
$$

$$
\pi_x = (1 + \theta)(\alpha_x + 2\alpha_q \delta_A),
\tag{I4}
$$

$$
\pi_q = \alpha_q(1 + \theta)^2,
\tag{I5}
$$

$$
\pi_c = 2\alpha_q(1 + \theta)\gamma,
\tag{I6}
$$

$$
\pi_e = \alpha_q(\gamma)^+,
\tag{I7}
$$

where, as before, $(\gamma)^+$ denotes the vectorized outer product of γ with redundant elements ($\gamma_i \gamma_j$ for $i < j$) removed.

As can be seen from (I2), the α_A parameters are just identified; we can ignore (I2) from now on. To look at the identification of the other parameters, denote the number of z variables (i.e., the dimension of the γ vector) by n_d. We consider three cases, depending on whether $n_d = 0$, $n_d = 1$, or $n_d \geq 2$.

Case 1: $n_d = 0$

We have three equations—(I1), (I4), and (I5)—in five unknowns (α_0, α_x, δ_A, α_q, and θ); we cannot identify the latter uniquely.

Case 2: $n_d = 1$

We have six equations—(I1) and (I3)–(I7)— in six unknowns (α_0, α_x, δ_A, α_q, γ, and θ). The Jacobian of the partials of the right-hand sides of these equations with respect to the parameters can be shown to be singular; hence the parameters are not uniquely identified. On the other hand, the conditions (I3)–(I7) do imply some restrictions. For example (note that $n_d = 1$ implies that $\gamma \neq 0$),

$$\frac{\pi_x}{\pi_d} = \frac{2\pi_q}{\pi_e} = \frac{\pi_e}{2\pi_e} = \frac{1 + \theta}{\gamma}.$$

Case 3: $n_d > 1$

We shall consider $n_d = 2$, so that $\gamma = (\gamma_1, \gamma_2)'$ and $(\gamma)^+ = (\gamma_1^2, \gamma_1\gamma_2, \gamma_2^2)$. Rewriting (I7), we have

$$\pi_{e1} = \alpha_q\gamma_1^2, \tag{I7a}$$

$$\pi_{e2} = \alpha_q\gamma_1\gamma_2, \tag{I7b}$$

and

$$\pi_{e3} = \alpha_q\gamma_2^2. \tag{I7c}$$

There are three equations in three unknowns. Since there are overidentifying restrictions ($[\pi_{e2}]^2 = \pi_{e1}\pi_{e3}$), at best we can identify only two parameters. In fact it is trivial to show that the Jacobian of the right-hand side has at most rank 2.

Appendix B

Diagnostics for the Informal Investigation

We present our investigation only for the couples. Similar examinations were made of the single male and single female results.

In figure B1 we plot the residuals from regressing the two variables in figure 1 on the other right-hand-side variables (including the total expenditure variables). This added variable (or partial regression) plot is useful since it gives some idea of the relationship between the two variables to hand, conditioning on the other right-hand-side variables (see Chaterjee and Hadi [1988] for an account of the diagnostics we use here and below). If income is not significant in the demand equations, then there should not be any significant relationship between the two sets of residuals plotted. In fact, though, we see that there is evidence of a positive relationship (the OLS slope coefficient is .16 with a standard error of .04). More important, the

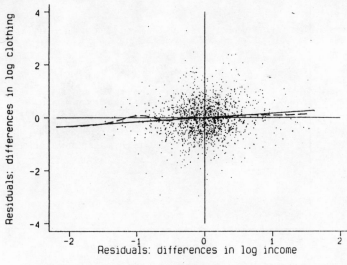

FIG. B1.—Residuals

nonparametric fit is very close to the OLS line. This is consistent with our finding that it is only the difference in log incomes that is important. It also indicates that our positive result is not being driven by outliers.

To investigate the robustness of our findings further, in figures B2 and B3 we present some more diagnostics. The first figure is a leverage-residual plot, that is, a plot of the squared standardized residuals against the "hat" statistic for each observation. Observations with a large residual (e.g., observa-

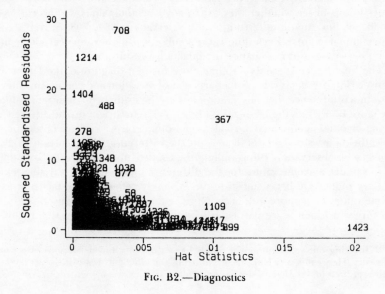

FIG. B2.—Diagnostics

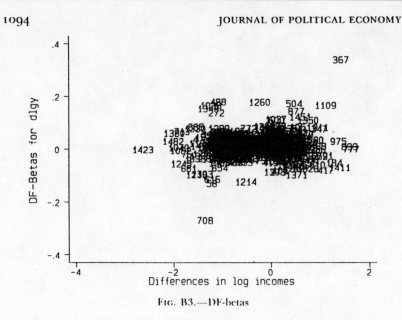

Fig. B3.—DF-betas

tion 708) are ones that are fit badly; those with a large hat statistic (e.g., observation 1,423) are influential observations. Portmanteau diagnostic statistics such as the Cook statistic and the DFFITs statistic can informally be seen as weighted products of these two statistics so that observations that are influential and that fit badly (e.g., observation 367) are likely to give high values for these statistics. The point of identifying outliers is *not* to find points to throw out[17] but rather to identify observations that might be unduly influencing our qualitative inferences so that we can look more closely at these observations to see whether they are in any way anomalous. In this case we could not find anything "wrong" with observations 367, 708, or 1,423 (or other similar points). Excluding various subsets of high-influence/poorly fitted observations did not change the qualitative results.

The final figure presents a rather more focused diagnostic: the DF-betas statistic. The DF-betas value for a particular observation and coefficient shows how much influence that observation has on the estimated coefficient value. In figure B3 we plot the DF-betas statistic for the coefficient on the difference in log incomes against that variable. For example, if we remove observation 367, then the estimated coefficient on the difference in log incomes falls; conversely, observation 708 is pulling the coefficient toward zero. Note that in this figure extreme values for the difference in log incomes variable tend to have higher DF-betas statistics; this is simply reflecting the fact that extreme values have more influence. Once again we use this diagnostic plot to identify which points are particularly influential for our finding that relative

[17] Throwing out valid influential points has an obvious and deleterious effect on efficiency. Hence it is very bad practice to "trim" the sample by removing observations with very high or very low values for particular variables.

incomes seem to matter in the demand equations. Removing the more positive DF-betas observations, of course, reduces the coefficient on the differences in income variable, but we have to remove an implausibly high proportion of the data to reduce this variable to insignificance.

References

Becker, Gary S. *A Treatise on the Family.* Cambridge, Mass.: Harvard Univ. Press, 1981.

Bergstrom, Theodore C. "A Fresh Look at the Rotten Kid Theorem—and Other Household Mysteries." *J.P.E.* 97 (October 1989): 1138–59.

Blundell, Richard. "Econometric Approaches to the Specification of Life-Cycle Labour Supply and Commodity Demand Behaviour." *Econometric Revs.* 5, no. 1 (1986): 89–146.

Blundell, Richard; Pashardes, Panos; and Weber, Guglielmo. "What Do We Learn about Consumer Demand Patterns from Micro Data?" *A.E.R.* 83 (June 1993): 570–97.

Bourguignon, François; Browning, Martin; and Chiappori, Pierre-André. "Identifying Intra-household Decision Processes." Manuscript. Hamilton, Ont.: McMaster Univ., 1994.

Bourguignon, François; Browning, Martin; Chiappori, Pierre-André; and Lechene, Valérie. "Intra Household Allocation of Consumption: A Model and Some Evidence from French Data." *Annales d'Économie et de Statistique,* no. 29 (January/March 1993), pp. 137–56.

Browning, Martin, and Chiappori, Pierre-André. "Efficient Intra-household Allocations: A General Characterisation and Empirical Tests." Manuscript. Hamilton, Ont.: McMaster Univ., 1994.

Browning, Martin, and Meghir, Costas. "The Effects of Male and Female Labor Supply on Commodity Demands." *Econometrica* 59 (July 1991): 925–51.

Burbridge, John B.; Magee, Lonnie; and Robb, A. Leslie. "Alternative Transformations to Handle Extreme Values of the Dependent Variable." *J. American Statis. Assoc.* 83 (March 1988): 123–27.

Chaterjee, Samprit, and Hadi, Ali. *Sensitivity Analysis in Linear Regression.* New York: Wiley, 1988.

Chiappori, Pierre-André. "Rational Household Labor Supply." *Econometrica* 56 (January 1988): 63–90.

———. "Collective Labor Supply and Welfare." *J.P.E.* 100 (June 1992): 437–67.

Chiappori, Pierre-André; Haddad, Lawrence; Hoddinott, John; and Kanbur, Ravi. "Unitary versus Collective Models of the Household: Time to Shift the Burden of Proof." Manuscript. Washington: World Bank, 1993.

Deaton, Angus. "Demand Analysis." In *Handbook of Econometrics,* vol. 3, edited by Zvi Griliches and Michael D. Intriligator. Amsterdam: North-Holland, 1985.

Gregory, Allan W., and Veall, Michael R. "Formulating Wald Tests of Non-linear Restrictions." *Econometrica* 53 (November 1985): 1465–68.

Keeley, Michael C.; Robins, Philip; Spiegelman, Robert; and West, Richard. "The Estimation of Labor Supply Models Using Experimental Data." *A.E.R.* 68 (December 1978): 873–87.

McElroy, Marjorie B. "The Empirical Content of Nash-Bargained Household Behavior." *J. Human Resources* 25 (Fall 1990): 559–83.

————. "The Policy Implications of Family Bargaining and Marriage Markets." Paper presented at the IFPRI–World Bank Conference on Intrahousehold Resource Allocation: Policy Issues and Research Methods, Washington, 1992.

McElroy, Marjorie B., and Horney, Mary Jean. "Nash-Bargained Decisions: Toward a Generalization of the Theory of Demand." *Internat. Econ. Rev.* 22 (June 1981): 333–49.

Manser, Marilyn, and Brown, Murray. "Marriage and Household Decision-Making: A Bargaining Analysis." *Internat. Econ. Rev.* 21 (February 1980): 31–44.

Phipps, S., and Burton, Peter. "What's Mine Is Yours? The Influence of Male and Female Income on Patterns of Household Expenditure." Working paper. Halifax, N.S.: Dalhousie Univ., Dept. Econ., 1994.

Samuelson, Paul A. "Social Indifference Curves." *Q.J.E.* 70 (February 1956): 1–22.

Schultz, T. Paul. "Testing the Neoclassical Model of Family Labor Supply and Fertility." *J. Human Resources* 25 (Fall 1990): 599–634.

Thomas, Duncan. "Intra-household Resource Allocation: An Inferential Approach." *J. Human Resources* 25 (Fall 1990): 635–64.

Name Index

The International Library of Critical Writings in Economics

Input-Output Analysis
Heinz Kurz, Erik Dietzenbacher and Christian Lager

Market Process Theories
Peter Boettke and David Prychitko

The Economics of Local Finance and Fiscal Federalism
Wallace Oates

Price Theory and its Applications
B. Saffran and F.M. Scherer

The Economics of Unemployment
P.N. Junankar

The Economics of Energy
Paul Stevens

Women in the Labor Market
Marianne A. Ferber

The Economics of Science and Innovation
Paula E. Stephan and David B. Audretsch

International Finance
Robert Z. Aliber

Welfare Economics
William J. Baumol and Janusz A. Ordover

The Economics of Inequality and Poverty
A.B. Atkinson

The Economics of Crime
Isaac Ehrlich

The Economics of Integration
Willem Molle

The Rhetoric of Economics
Deirdre McCloskey

The Economics of Defence
Keith Hartley and Nicholas Hooper

Consumer Theory
Kelvin Lancaster

The Economics of Business Policy
John Kay

Microeconomic Theories of Imperfect Competition
Jacques Thisse and Jean Gabszewicz

Alternative Theories of the Firm
Richard Langlois, Paul Robertson and Tony F. Yu

Economic Anthropology
Stephen Gudeman

The Economics of Executive Compensation
Kevin F. Hallock and Kevin J. Murphy

The Economics of Marketing
Martin Carter, Mark Casson and Vivek Suneja

Foreign Exchange Intervention: Theory and Evidence
Sylvester C.W. Eijffinger

The Economics of the Mass Media
Glenn Withers

The Foundations of Long Wave Theory
Francisco Louçã and Jan Reijnders

The Economics of Budget Deficits
Charles Rowley

Economic Forecasting
Terence C. Mills